TREATMENT
OF PATIENTS
IN THE
BORDERLINE
SPECTRUM

TREATMENT
OF PATIENTS
IN THE
BORDERLINE
SPECTRUM

W. W. MEISSNER, S.J., M.D.

Jason Aronson
Northvale, New Jersey
London

Library of Congress Cataloging-in-Publication Data

Meissner, W. W. (William W.), 1931–
　Treatment of patients in the borderline spectrum.

　Bibliography: p.
　Includes index.
　1. Borderline personality disorder—Treatment.
2. Psychotherapy.　　I. Title.
RC569.5.B67M49　　1988　　616.85′82　　88-10526
ISBN 0-87668-917-9

Manufactured in the United States of America. Jason Aronson Inc. offers books and cassettes. For information and catalog write to Jason Aronson Inc., 230 Livingston Street, Northvale, N.J. 07647.

To
Gretchen

with affection,
gratitude, and love

CONTENTS

Preface   xi

I ■ PRETREATMENT ISSUES   1

1 BORDERLINE DIAGNOSIS   3
The Problem ■ Levels of Differentiation ■ Psychological
Testing ■ Differential Diagnosis ■ Adolescence ■
2 PROGNOSIS   62
The Prognosis of Borderline Inpatients ■ Outpatient
Treatment ■ Analyzability of Borderline Syndromes ■
The Assessment of Borderline Patients for Psychoanalysis ■
3 APPROACHES   84
Zetzel ■ Kernberg ■ Masterson-Rinsley ■ The Blancks ■
Gunderson ■ Boyer and Giovacchini ■ Chessick ■ Kris Study
Group ■ Winnicott ■ Fairbairn and Guntrip ■ Modell ■ Adler and
Buie ■ Searles ■ The Kleinians ■ Dimensions ■
4 THE THERAPIST   130

II ▪ THE THERAPEUTIC RELATIONSHIP   135

5 THE THERAPEUTIC ALLIANCE   137
Difficulties ▪ The Nature of the Therapeutic Alliance ▪ Establishing
the Therapeutic Alliance ▪ Deviations in the Therapeutic
Alliance ▪ Maintaining the Therapeutic Alliance ▪

6 TRANSFERENCE   176
Transference Characteristics ▪ Transference Variants ▪ Transference
Mechanisms ▪ Transference Management ▪

7 COUNTERTRANSFERENCE   209
Definition ▪ Countertransference Model ▪ Aspects of Borderline
Countertransference ▪ Countertransference Variation ▪
Recapitulation ▪ Therapeutic Response to Countertransference
Difficulties ▪

III ▪ THE THERAPEUTIC PROCESS   251

8 INTERPRETATION   253
Definition ▪ Nature of Interpretation ▪ Interpretive Strategy ▪
Interpretation within the Borderline Spectrum ▪ Interpretive
Process ▪ Interpretive Schema ▪

9 CONFRONTATION   299
Role in Therapy ▪ Meaning ▪ Reality Testing ▪ Countertransference
Contamination ▪ Regression ▪ Borderline Spectrum ▪ Therapeutic
Alliance ▪ Denial ▪ Antisocial Behavior ▪ Narcissism ▪ Guidelines ▪

10 LIMIT SETTING   316
Need for Setting Limits ▪ Nature of Limit Setting ▪ Forms of Limit
Setting ▪ Specific Contexts ▪

11 REGRESSION   332
Forms of Regression ▪ Borderline Regression ▪ Suicide ▪ Therapeutic
Aspects ▪ Recurrent Regression ▪ Countertransference Issues ▪

IV ▪ ADJUNCTIVE THERAPIES   357

12 GROUP THERAPY   359
Selection ▪ Group Structure ▪

13 *FAMILY THERAPY* 366
Family Patterns ▪
14 *SHORT-TERM THERAPY* 377
Contexts ▪ Selection ▪ Implementation ▪ Termination ▪
15 *HOSPITALIZATION* 390
Borderline Spectrum ▪ Reasons for Hospitalization ▪ Purposes of
Hospitalization ▪ Short-term Hospitalization ▪ Long-term
Hospitalization ▪ Admission to the Hospital ▪ Communication ▪
Therapeutic/Administrative Splits ▪ Limit Setting ▪ Transference–
Countertransference Problems ▪ A Case in
Point ▪ Discharge ▪ Difficulties ▪
16 *DRUGS* 407
Use of Medications ▪ Problems in Prescribing Drugs ▪ Dynamics
of Drug Taking ▪ Medication Selection Based on Target
Symptoms ▪ Medication Selection Based on Diagnoses ▪ Limited
Application ▪

V ▪ THE PATIENTS 417

A ▪ Hysterical Continuum 419

17 *PSEUDOSCHIZOPHRENIA* 420
18 *PRIMITIVE AFFECTIVE PERSONALITY DISORDERS* 435
19 *DYSPHORIC PERSONALITY* 452
20 *PRIMITIVE HYSTERICS* 480

B ▪ Schizoid Continuum 505

21 *SCHIZOID PERSONALITY* 506
22 *FALSE-SELF PERSONALITY* 529
23 *AS-IF PERSONALITY* 557
24 *IDENTITY STASIS* 571

References 584

Index 615

PREFACE

This volume presents a specific and comprehensive approach to the therapy of borderline patients. With rare exception, the literature on the treatment of borderline patients is limited to the lower order of the borderline spectrum and is dominated by the consensus view that the pathology is close to psychosis. The conceptualization of the borderline spectrum is itself a broader view of these conditions and mobilizes a wider array of therapeutic resources. Many approaches that focus on the more primitive levels of the borderline spectrum allow that there may be exceptional borderline persons who are analyzable. I argue that for many higher-order borderlines, classical psychoanalysis may be the treatment of choice. A good case can actually be made that a number of Freud's own patients would fit very nicely within the borderline spectrum.

My intention is to extend the effort begun in my previous work on the borderline spectrum (Meissner 1984a, b). That study surveyed the conceptual and theoretical aspects of borderline psychopathology and, in the process, reached some conclusions that differ from the predominant line of thinking about borderline patients as represented in the categories of the DSM-III. My conclusions were several; they bear repeating as an introduction to the orientation of the present work. They can be listed as follows:

- The term *borderline* does not refer to one diagnostic entity, but rather to a series of discriminable entities of varying degrees of pathological organization. Earlier diagnostic efforts were attempts to draw into a single coherent category a spectrum of heterogeneous, somewhat indistinct forms of psychopathology that represented a continuum of pathological character structures extending from the border of psychosis to the border of neurotic or narcissistic character structures.

- This characterization of borderline pathology as a single entity applies to only a limited segment of the borderline spectrum. It does not apply to many other patients who are also clinically borderline; it has limited application to other borderline patients who measure up to the criteria of borderline functioning only during periods of transient regression.

- This line of thinking leads to a description of the dimensions of the borderline spectrum and delineates forms of pathological integration within it. The implications of this assessment are that the pathological features vary at different levels of the spectrum, with severe degrees of pathology and increasing vulnerability to regression at the lower end, and much less severe and even well-functioning psychic integration at the higher end.

- The therapeutic approach must be tailored to the pathological needs and structural deficits that are in force at the different pathological levels. The therapeutic orientation to patients at the lower end of the spectrum differs from that of patients at the higher end. There is a continuum of shifting modes of understanding and therapeutic orientation that parallels varying pathological characteristics.

The approach in this volume differs both in content and method from the burgeoning research literature on borderline psychopathology. The more clearly and definitely the diagnosis of a single entity is established, the more limited it becomes in applicability and the greater the number of patients it excludes. The strategy I have followed comes out of my ongoing clinical experience in getting to know and trying to help my patients and from the continuous flow of material I hear in supervising other therapists doing psychotherapy or psychoanalysis. I owe a debt of gratitude to these therapists and analysts for sharing their experience with me, thus deepening and broadening my own clinical awareness. If what emerges on these pages cannot claim significant scientific validity in terms of accepted research methodology, it can at least claim heuristic validity that may stimulate further questions and better research. Meanwhile, I hope that it will clarify clinical understanding and help the many clinicians who must face the turmoil and stress of trying to understand and treat the often difficult borderline patient.

Finally, I should call attention to my terminology. Throughout the monograph I use the terms *therapy* and *therapist* generically to refer to psychotherapy and/or psychoanalysis indiscriminately. When I use the terms *psychoanalysis*, *analysis*, *psychoanalyst*, or *analyst*, I am referring specifically to psychoanalysis as such, exclusive of psychotherapy or even of psychoanalytically oriented psychotherapy.

I would like to express my gratitude to my colleagues, Drs. Gerald Adler, Dan H. Buie, James Frosch, and Howard Levine, all from the Boston Psychoanalytic Institute, for their critical reading of portions of the manuscript and for their helpful and clarifying suggestions. My thanks also go to my secretary, Miss Elfriede Banzhaf, for her unrelenting efforts to facilitate this work from its inception to the final product and for her valuable assistance at every stage of the process.

W. W. Meissner, S.J., M.D.

PART I

PRETREATMENT ISSUES

The clinician's approach to the treatment of borderline patients is overlaid with difficult, poorly resolved, and often highly controversial diagnostic considerations. This diagnostic bias leads to further problems relating to evaluation of prognosis and the choice of optimal treatment. My intent here is to provide a context for the subsequent discussion of treatment issues. The chapter on diagnosis advances a view of borderline disorders that departs significantly from prevailing emphases. Throughout I will focus on the borderline spectrum as it is displayed in issues of diagnosis, prognosis, and therapeutic orientation. These considerations are all contingent on the diagnostic calculation of where the patient falls along the borderline spectrum; prognosis and treatment are decidedly different from one level to another. Since patients at the lower end of the spectrum have a more difficult time in therapy and a more guarded prognosis, their pathology calls for different therapeutic approaches and emphases. The approach to and evaluation of higher-order patients are different—for patients at the highest level of psychic integration, often radically different. For some of these patients, psychoanalysis along classical lines may be the treatment of choice.

1

BORDERLINE DIAGNOSIS

THE PROBLEM

The diagnostic problem in dealing with borderline syndromes is the old question of the one vs. the many. Are we dealing with one form of illness that may express itself, behaviorally and symptomatically, in multiple forms? Or are multiple forms of illness sharing certain underlying general characteristics that can nonetheless be analyzed separately, each on its own terms?[1] Two different approaches make the diagnostic picture more complex. Clinicians working mainly in the hospital setting are usually presented with the diagnostic problem of differentiating borderline pathology from the psychotic, whether schizophrenic or affective. Their patients tend to be severely regressed or otherwise close to psychosis. The more primitive borderline characteristics have come to dominate the diagnostic view within this setting. In the private practice setting, largely psychoanalytic in orientation, patients are better organized and more adaptive, and display borderline features much less frequently and intensely, and then only in transient regressive states. The diagnostic problem in this setting is to differentiate borderline pathology from neurotic or higher-level character pathology.

---

[1]The variety of extant systems for defining borderline pathology have been surveyed by Stone (1987).

The concept of the borderline spectrum is an attempt to encompass these difficulties. It implies a continuous series of disordered functions and underlying pathological structures that extends from the border of the psychoses to the border of the more integrated forms of character pathology, particularly the narcissistic personalities. Within the borderline spectrum, levels of functioning and degrees of pathological impairment vary continuously in intensity and extension (Abend et al. 1983). We might be able to carve out of this continuous spectrum a series of more or less describable syndromes that would allow us to discriminate more effectively between levels of pathological impairment and provide a more specific basis for theoretical understanding and therapeutic intervention. In pragmatic terms, the problem is to determine the most advantageous strategy for categorizing the borderline disorders. Does a unified diagnostic approach make more sense? Or does the optimal strategy lie in the direction of greater diversity, heterogeneity, and multiplicity, which would call for a greater degree of specificity and differentiation, both descriptively and theoretically?

Kernberg's (1967) early work followed a unifying strategy. He pulled together the various pathological entities that were thought to range between frank psychosis on the one side and determinable neurosis on the other under a single unified heading, the "borderline personality organization." He lumped these various clinical descriptions under a common heading, and provided a common structural formulation that applied unequivocally to all borderline patients. He emphasized certain structural deficits, including nonspecific ego weaknesses, a tendency toward primary process thinking, primitive defense mechanisms, and a form of pathology of internalized object relations characterized particularly by defensive splitting.

The next significant step toward a unified diagnosis was taken by Gunderson and Singer (1975). Surveying the vast literature on borderline psychopathology, they tried to define those characteristics of this group of patients that would make diagnosis more reliable and thus allow further meaningful research. They came up with six features of the borderline syndrome:

1. the presence of intense affect, usually hostile or depressive;
2. a history of impulsive behavior, usually episodic acts of self-destruction (self-mutilation, drug overdoses, and the like) and more chronic behavior patterns, such as drug dependency or promiscuity;

3. social adaptiveness, reflected in good work or school achievement and generally socially appropriate behavior;

4. brief psychotic experiences, often paranoid and often precipitated by periods of stress or as a result of drugs;

5. psychological testing results in which performance on structured tests is more or less normal, but on unstructured or projective devices reveals bizarre, dereistic, illogical, or primitive responses, reflecting underlying thought disturbances;

6. interpersonal relationships that vacillate between transient, superficial relationships and those that are intense, conflicted, and dependent and reflect varying degrees of manipulation, demandingness, and devaluation.

Gunderson's subsequent work has amplified and extended this approach to borderline pathology. He has devised a semistructured interview—the Diagnostic Interview for Borderlines (Kolb and Gunderson 1980, Gunderson et al. 1981)—and applied it to patients who were given a clinical diagnosis of borderline personality. Gunderson (1977) formulated the characteristics of the borderline sample under five headings: social adaptation, impulse-action patterns, affects, psychotic tendencies, and interpersonal relations. He characterizes borderline patients as generally aware of social conventions, even though their attitude toward them may often be defiant. They tend to lead active social lives and get along reasonably well in social groups. They seem to maintain steady employment, but have a poor capacity to work under stress, or seem to be able to work effectively only in relatively structured situations. More recently the defining characteristics include intense and unstable interpersonal relationships, repetitive self-destructive behaviors, chronic abandonment fears, chronic dysphoric affects, cognitive distortions, impulsivity, and poor social adaptation (Gunderson and Zanarini 1987). These authors also emphasize the overlap between the borderline diagnosis and other psychiatric disorders, most notably schizophrenia and the affective disorders on one hand and other personality disorders (antisocial, narcissistic, histrionic) on the other.

Acting out is a predominant characteristic, usually in the form of destructive acts directed toward oneself or others, and/or in antisocial behavior, including drug and alcohol abuse. Self-destructive behavior is more frequent, usually in the form of overdosing, suicidal threats, self-mutilation (slashing, head banging, burning, and so on). Promiscuity is

frequently reported among females, but deviant sexual habits or preferences seem minimal. The dominant affects seem to be depression,
anger, and anxiety; the depression is usually expressed in chronic
feelings of loneliness or emptiness. Patients within the lower-order
range of the spectrum may often have characteristics of the major
affective or atypical depressive disorders (Soloff et al. 1987).

They do not report continuous or severe psychotic experiences,
although there are some reports of possible hallucinatory ones. The
most common forms of psychotic ideation are either depressive (feeling
worthless or hopeless) or paranoid, with ideas of reference and persecutory delusions (Snyder and Pitts 1986). The fact that patients often
express a feeling of uncertainty or discomfort about such psychotic
experiences suggests that they may not be completely syntonic. Depersonalization is more common than derealization. These patients do not
withdraw from contacts with other people, but rather feel a need to
have people near and feel bothered when alone. They have friends and
keep in touch with them, but are uncomfortable when others try to take
care of them. The most intense relationships are frequently troubled
and disruptive, usually strongly dependent, masochistic, manipulative,
and characteristically devaluing of the object.

The overall effect of Gunderson's work has been to condense and
distill the characteristics originally proposed by Kernberg. Gunderson's approach selects as borderline virtually the same group of patients
as Kernberg's criteria. However, the approach makes the borderline
diagnosis a unified form of personality disorder parallel to other personality disorders (histrionic, narcissistic, schizoid, etc.) (Gunderson
1987). Kernberg's notion of a structural diagnosis has been elided, and
the basis for the diagnosis becomes phenomenological rather than
structural. The result is a greater degree of clarity and definition of
the borderline personality, but at the cost of narrowing the focus and
the defining boundaries of the borderline category to a smaller and
somewhat narrowly defined patient population. This approach finally
culminated in the work of Spitzer and his associates in further developing and articulating the criteria of borderline pathology in the
DSM III.

Regarding the contributions of Spitzer and his group, the schizotypal pattern seems closer to the psychotic border (probably related to
the schizophrenic spectrum), while the borderline personality seems to
function at a somewhat higher level (possibly involving an affective
genetic diathesis). The line of thinking that runs from Kernberg and

Gunderson to Spitzer and his associates focuses on more primitive levels of borderline functioning. In Kernberg's thinking, the borderline personality has been characterized in terms of its most primitive levels of functioning found at best transiently in most borderline personalities, and then only in phases of acute regressive crisis. There is no account of higher-level functioning in patients who may also manifest borderline characteristics and who rarely, if ever, show manifestations of regressed functioning or primitive adjustment.

These diagnostic trends have their purposes and advantages and should not be devalued. A basic research orientation seeks to gain increasing clarity and delineation of the borderline syndrome from other diagnostic categories, but since the result is an inevitable narrowing of the borderline range, the diagnostic label can be applied to a progressively smaller group of better-defined patients (Gunderson 1984, 1987). Correspondingly, the group of patients who are excluded from the diagnosis increases. Such patients may in fact also demonstrate borderline features, but not in the more intense, dramatic, and readily definable form that would satisfy the research demands for clarity of definition. Gunderson (1984, 1987) simply says that patients not fitting into the research criteria are not borderline. Thus, since the optimal path for clinical diagnosis remains uncertain, the inclusion of a narrowed and constricted version of borderline pathology, based on research criteria, in the formal definitions of the official diagnostic manual of American psychiatry may be premature.[2]

Other approaches have pointed in a different direction. The early studies of Grinker and his group (Grinker et al. 1968) defined the borderline syndrome in terms of its predominant characteristics, namely anger as the dominant affect, defective object relations, the failure of self-identity, and the presence of such depressive features as loneliness or emptiness. However, subjecting a large number of variables based on observations of large number of patients to a variety of cluster, discriminate, and factor analyses resulted in four subgroupings. They ranged from the sickest group, closest to the border of psychosis, to a healthier group quite similar to neurotic patients in their general characteristics, whose depression seemed to be primarily anaclitic in character (Grinker 1977). The concept of a spectrum of borderline disorders can be found frequently in the psychiatric lit-

---

[2]I have discussed the diagnostic difficulties and tensions in Meissner (1987).

erature on the subject. Numerous authors have commented on the possibility of thinking about borderline conditions in such terms, and even the later work of Kernberg on a psychoanalytically based classification of character pathology has contributed significantly to this effort.

LEVELS OF DIFFERENTIATION

Use of the Term *Borderline*

Often the term *borderline* is used in a general way to refer to patients who have basically neurotic symptoms but who also convey an impression of more serious psychopathology. Such patients may manifest transient psychotic fragmentation, pathological narcissistic phenomena, character distortions, quasi-addictions and addictions, massive and bizarre as well as multiple symptoms, and a history of behavior disorders and difficult interpersonal relationships. There is also a pattern of atypical reactions early in therapy, including extreme rigidity, the emergence of early archaic material, the manifestation of primitive TR reactions, and often a rapid if not euphoric improvement (Stone 1954).

Zetzel (in Rangell 1955, 1971) drew a strong distinction between borderline states and the borderline personality. The borderline state is a condition of mixed neurotic and psychotic symptoms reflecting a transient regressive condition. When we see a patient in such a regressive state, we cannot yet make a diagnosis of borderline personality, since only the subsequent history, including the patient's response to appropriate therapeutic management, will indicate whether such a diagnosis can be justified. The borderline personality may not always initially present symptoms that would suggest a borderline diagnosis; rather, many apparently normal or neurotic individuals may reveal borderline characteristics only during the course of psychoanalytic or psychotherapeutic treatment or in other regression-inducing circumstances.

The distinction emphasizes an important point in the evaluation of borderline patients (Gunderson and Singer 1975). The evaluation of borderline psychopathology depends on the amount of structure in the observational setting in which patient and clinical observer meet. When patients are evaluated in the more unstructured contexts of psychoanalytic treatment or projective testing, the emphasis falls on ego defects, primitive defenses, and latent thought disorders. Yet when the same patients are observed by competent clinicians in more structured hospital settings or in structured interviews, or in taking more structured objective tests, emphasis is put on more stable personality features and capacities for adaptation.

Levels of Pathology

In the assessment of the spectrum of borderline disorders, the first elements to focus on are those found in varying degrees throughout the borderline spectrum. The spectrum of borderline conditions reveals the following defects in degrees that may vary considerably from entity to entity, or from patient to patient within a given category. The assessment of degrees of impairment is greatly facilitated by Kernberg's (1971) analysis of prognostic factors. The degrees or levels of pathology pertain to levels of consistent characterological functioning of borderline patients. We are not considering the regressive borderline states, which remain a potential in all of these cases. That regressive potential itself is a matter of relative degree, but the essential nature of the character pathology cannot be judged from its transient regressive and seemingly psychotic crisis manifestations.

Object Relations. Perhaps the most critical dimension of borderline pathology is the quality of object relationships. These patients are often described as rapidly developing new object ties that reflect primitive object relationships (Kernberg 1973). Modell (1963), for example, distinguishes between patients who show unstable defenses, fluctuating ego states, and a capacity to suspend or readily abandon object relationships, and a second group whose defenses are more stable, but who seem unable to suspend or abandon their involvement with objects. They are able to retain relationships, but the relationships tend to be distorted. A quick and clinging involvement with objects reflects an intense need to relate to objects on a need-satisfying basis rather than on any mature or reciprocal terms (Brody 1960, Frijling-Schreuder 1969). The intensity of these needs and the clinging to objects as a source of satisfaction can vary considerably in intensity and degree.

All of these patients share a core disturbance in their capacity for object relationships. There is a general feeling of emptiness and hunger along with intense wishes to be nurtured and taken care of that demand immediate satisfaction. If such demands are not satisfactorily met, as may well be the case owing to the patient's excessive expectations or the

inability of the object to respond, feelings of intense rage and destructive impulses toward the object are mobilized, which not only carry
with them fears of retaliation, but also raise the level of vulnerability to
abandonment when and if the object encounters this rage. When the
rage reaches sufficient intensity, it may also trigger a defensive regression to an incorporative level resulting in the fusion of self- and object
representations and psychotic manifestations (Abend et al. 1983).

     This intense hunger and need for satisfaction from objects is also
found in the transference as well. Kernberg (1968) observed that borderline patients often reveal an early activation in the transference of
highly conflictual derivatives of object relationships associated with
relatively dissociated ego states, each one of which seems to represent
an independent transference paradigm. These paradigms more often
than not have a projective quality and reflect the persistence of relatively unmetabolized pathogenic introjects. In acute borderline states,
affective turmoil may reflect an intensification of transference feelings
and may elicit intense countertransference feelings as well (Abend et al.
1983). Such patients often become confused about the nature of the
therapy and the therapist's intentions, and express intense feelings of
urgency, hopelessness, and despair. The outcome is often suicidal desperation or murderous rage that may be expressed in suicidal or destructive behavior (Friedman et al. 1983). The tendency of many such
patients to develop disruptive and turbulent transference reactions in
relatively unstructured therapy situations may serve as a diagnostic
indicator. Often periods of improved functioning and better participation in the therapeutic relationship are followed by disruptions triggered by disappointments in the therapist, or minor failures of empathy, or some disappointing life event. The intensity of the emotional
response and its abruptness point toward a borderline diagnosis (Friedman 1979).

     Transitional Object Relations.   Modell (1963) has emphasized the
role of transitional object relations in the borderline group. There are
intense attempts to maintain an illusion of omnipotence, reliance on
projection, and a denied but nonetheless intense need to depend on the
therapist. Assessment of transitional relatedness on the Rorschach
lends only partial support to this hypothesis (Cooper et al. 1985).
Rather than reliance on past or present transitional objects, borderlines
seem to be characterized by a need to use a variety of experiences and
relationships to objects to seek illusory soothing and thus diminish
separation anxiety. There is an urgent need to see the therapist as

omnipotent and infallibly omniscient (Johansen 1983). While the desperate need for the object may manifest itself in intense clinging and highly emotional involvement with the therapist in some patients, there are others for whom the threat of closeness and the fears of dependency on the object give rise to a defensively motivated distancing and withdrawal. In such patients, a more or less schizoid posture prevents the development of the therapeutic relationship.

The history of transitional object use may have some diagnostic significance. Following the work of Coppolillo and Horton (Coppolillo 1967, Horton et al. 1974), Arkema (1981) found that all of a series of hospitalized borderlines gave evidence of past and present transitional object use. In contrast, Horton and colleagues' (1974) group of nonborderline personality disorders gave no such history. Gunderson and his co-workers (Gunderson et al. 1985, Morris et al. 1986) found only a moderate correlation (0.36 and 0.43) between the childhood use of transitional objects and adult use; about half of child users report use of transitional objects as adults. They conclude that transitional object use may be more common in borderline than in nonborderline patients, but the selection criteria employed in the study focused on more severely disturbed (hospitalized) borderlines. Whether this phenomenon is characteristic only of the lower order of the borderline spectrum remains open to question. The authors observe that there may be a considerable degree of diagnostic crossover, and that application of broader criteria would have included the comparison groups in the borderline category. Examination of transitional indices on the Rorschach supports the prevalence of transitional object phenomenology in lower-order borderline patients as compared to schizophrenic and other character-disorder groups (Greenberg et al. 1987).

Experience of Objects. There is a curious heterogeneity to the borderline individual's experience of objects. The sensitivity of borderline patients to latent and even unconscious impulses and motives has often been remarked. They seem unusually responsive to unconscious fantasies or impulses, as well as more primitive superego elements, in others. Since positive aspects of the ego functioning of the other are held in distrust, there is no integration of the consistent aspects of the ego in the patient's image of objects. The primitive and drive-related aspects of the object are taken as genuine and valid, but the persistent and positive aspects of character, self, and ego are treated as fake or untrustworthy. Consequently, the involvement with objects remains on the level of relatively primitive and undeveloped attachment in which objects are responded to only as need-gratifying and as fluid or inter-changeable, whether idealized or degraded (Krohn 1974).

The borderline's experience of objects seems to bypass the essen-tial qualities of the object's own consistent self-representation, that is, enduring personality traits, character, and other ego attributes. This is often the case in the relationship with the therapist and is reflected in the transference dynamics. The borderline subject maintains only a partial and impoverished contact with important aspects of the object. Keiser (1958) remarked that for these patients such suspect objects can never become part of the patient's ego, but must be retained only as uncertain sources of narcissistic gratification. There is never an accum-ulation of memory residues of objects that might sustain any convic-tions about meaningful identity, empathy, or self-love, no basis for the memories of human kindnesses that might lead to the conclusion that objects may be counted on to be persistently generous and loving, or that, having once given, they might conceivably give again.

This impairment results in the patient's inability to perceive exter-nal objects as realistic and as complete persons. Characteristics of the object not only may be distorted or misrepresented but may be consis-tently omitted, or those characteristics may be included that fit with the predominant feeling toward the object at that time. Thus, the object may be seen as sexually exciting or murderous or despicable without any attempt to include other contradictory qualities in a more compre-hensive picture. The result is that the current image of the object is destroyed and a new picture is created internally which is then taken to be the true representation of the object (DeSaussure 1974). The same discontinuity and shifting of focus takes place within the patient's self-representations, in which there tends to be a series of discontinuous partial self-images, each accepted as reflecting the patient's whole self. These various images seem to have little connection or continuity, and are dealt with in the same way in which contradictory aspects of objects are handled—excluding them from the current image. Consequently, the clinical picture is marked by continuing preoccupation with the self and desperate demands for love from objects, but with an inability to maintain or integrate that love when it is offered.

Object Constancy.   As long as object relations remain on this need-gratifying level, the capacity for object constancy is significantly dimin-ished. Object constancy implies the capacity to maintain a meaningful relationship to a specific object whether one's subjective needs are being satisfied or not, or even when they are being frustrated. In most of the borderline conditions, there is some capacity for object constancy: in varying degrees and at various times patients seem capable of moving beyond the level of mere primitive need-satisfaction, but that object constancy is extremely fragile and can be readily threatened (Frijling-Schreuder 1969, Fintzy 1971). The fragility of object constancy—that is, the diminished capacity for tolerating and integrating the ambivalent aspects of involvement with objects without shifting back and forth between extreme emotional reactions—has been frequently noted (Kernberg 1967, 1970, 1971, Blum 1972, Masterson 1972, Meissner 1978b).

The failure to achieve object constancy implies that the patient is unable to relate to significant objects consistently as whole persons; that the relationship fluctuates in terms of the patient's need state; that the patient has poor tolerance for frustration or ambivalence and poor capacity to endure frustration of needs; that the individual has difficulty in evoking a consistent image of the object when the object is not physically present; and that there is a severe impairment in the individual's capacity to mourn loss of the object, so that separation is extremely difficult. Such patients often avoid the threat of separation by forms of emotional detachment or acting out to provoke reinvolvement with the object or to attract the object's attention (Abend et al. 1983).

Borderline pathology also involves an impaired capacity for internalization related to the inability to establish object constancy. The instability of object-representations and the impaired capacity to maintain the cathexis of objects not only increase the clinging dependence on external objects but also may create a regressive tendency to retreat to other forms of introjection or, on more primitive and psychotic levels, incorporation (Meissner 1971). These impairments are compounded by an intense fear and distrust of those same objects—the *need-fear dilemma* (Burnham et al. 1969). There is a fear of symbiotic fusion along with intense ambivalence, so that while the borderline tends to reach out and cling to objects, he is forced to withdraw when the pain or threat of rejection becomes unbearable (Giovacchini 1973b).

Object Needs. The need for the object may range widely in intensity, just as the fear of abandonment may take various forms: it may mean rejection, or a feeling of isolation and loneliness, or a feeling of inner emptiness, or fear of total annihilation. Fears of abandonment stem from an incomplete internalization of maternal caring. The failure of maternal empathy and the threat of abandonment not only are terrifying but stir primitive savage oral wishes to kill, eat, merge, and the like. These primitive destructive impulses create a primitive guilt that threatens retaliation and loss of love. In addition, the projection of such rage makes the loved object a source of dread, danger, and persecution, serving only to reinforce and increase the pattern of withdrawal (Buie and Adler 1972).

Such intense object needs and fears can also be stimulated in the transference. The fears of abandonment can easily be stirred by any rebuke or failure of comprehension on the part of the therapist, and by a variety of countertransference reactions (Kernberg 1975a,b). These may easily trigger a transient regression, but often there is a return to a level of more integrated secondary process functioning after recovery of a more stable alliance. The therapy may become pervaded by issues of separation and abandonment that often have an either/or quality. Clinging to one object means abandonment by others, and frequently in the childhood history of such patients the therapist hears the same theme: love for one parent seems to imply loss of or abandonment by the other.

Cohesive Self. Establishing object constancy is secondary to the emergence of a cohesive self, which in turn depends on the gradual internalization of equilibrium-maintaining maternal functions (McDevitt 1975, McDevitt and Mahler 1986, Meissner 1986a). The development of the capacity to recognize and tolerate both hostile and loving feelings toward the same object and to value the object for qualities other than need-satisfaction is essential for object constancy and forms a critical step in the direction of more mature and stable object relationships (Horner 1975). In the borderline conditions, the need–fear dilemma remains a pervasive problem expressed in varying degrees of intensity—both the need to cling to objects and the fear of abandonment by objects. The respective forms of borderline pathology can be seen as qualitatively different ways of dealing with, defending against, and resolving this underlying and central dilemma.

A common impairment for these borderline conditions is the inherent fragility and vulnerability of nuclear structures, resulting in impaired self-cohesiveness. The potential breakdown of such nuclear structures poses a continual threat, which must be countered by a variety of defensive and avoidance maneuvers (Kohut 1972, 1977). Kernberg (1970) has pointed out that individuals at the "lower level" of character pathology have poor integration of self-representations so that the inner world is peopled by caricatures of both the good and horrible aspects of important objects without effective integration of these aspects. Such residues of object relations [introjects in a more structural perspective (Meissner 1978b)] create an inner experience of the self composed of a chaotic amalgamation of shameful, threatened, impotent, yet at the same time exalted and omnipotent images.

This defective integration of the inner world of introjects and the failure of a stable self-concept frequently result in a diffusion of identity characteristic of this lower level of character pathology (Kernberg 1970). In fact, acute identity diffusion is typical of the transient regression of borderline states. But even on the characterological level, such patients may jump from one isolated and more or less coherent self-image to the next without any intervening connections to maintain the continuity of self-image. Attempts to assist patients to develop some capacity for synthesis are often resisted, while they continue to rely unconsciously on the fantasied magical powers of the therapist to provide what is missing and to transform them into more integrated persons.

The impairment of narcissistic structures and the corresponding failure of integration of self-structures find a variety of pathological expressions in borderline conditions. Besides the deficits in the sense of identity, there are a variety of states of self-organization in which partial or fragmented self-integration is achieved. The more or less discontinuous shifting from one introjective configuration to another in borderlines has been variously described (Kernberg 1967, Meissner 1978a). In addition, however, other patients may resolve the problem of inner instability by a mimetic imitative-introjective shaping of a transient self-integration that remains dependent on involvement with or attachment to a particular object (Meissner 1974). This is the classic "as-if" pattern described by Deutsch (1942). Other forms may achieve relative stabilization and narcissistic equilibrium by a more persistent inner splitting of fragmentary self-integrations [e.g., Winnicott's false self-organization (1960)].

Self- and object-representations may gain some degree of internal integration, but their cohesion depends on inclusion of qualities derived from external objects of dependence (Abend et al. 1983). Resistance to self-integration is often accompanied by unconscious fantasies of even more frightening dangers resulting from allowing the self to be whole and unified; many patients begin to experience a more severe anxiety only when the capacity for synthesis is in some degree achieved (DeSaussure 1974). Where the dependence on objects is so intense that the distinction between self and object becomes blurred or lost, loss of the object can provoke a severe annihilation anxiety in which any separation from the object precipitates the fear of loss equivalent to annihilation of the self (Frosch 1967a,b).

Less serious disturbances in the sense of self may fall short of the sort of identity diffusion or fragmentation of self-structures that is often found in more primitively organized borderline personalities or in regressive borderline states. In better-integrated borderline pathology, one may find states of diffusion or lack of definition in the sense of self, or a seemingly endless and frustrated search for meaning or purpose to one's existence, or even a holding back or an inability to commit oneself to an adult course of life, to a specific job or occupation or career, or to a single, specific partner and the implications of intimacy, marriage, family, children, and all the burdens and responsibilities such commitment would entail.

Narcissism. Narcissistic problems are a prominent feature throughout the borderline spectrum. This has often lent confusion to the diagnostic picture. Kernberg (1974, 1984) describes a more primitive set of narcissistic personalities who are clearly borderline. In the view developed here, such patients would qualify as borderline not merely by virtue of their narcissistic difficulties but by reason of the developmental failures in ego, superego, and self-structures detailed here and in previous discussions (Meissner 1984). Such patients nonetheless often reveal well-developed forms of narcissistic pathology and bring their narcissistic needs into the transference and the therapeutic interaction (Rothstein 1982). Elements of idealizing and mirroring transferences are not at all uncommon, but these expressions are distinguished from those in narcissistic personalities by their often shifting configurations and by the extent to which they are contaminated by aggressive derivatives (Meissner 1979b, 1984a). Thus, borderline patients manifest all varieties of the vicissitudes of pathological narcissism, including all variations of the dynamics of shame (Fisher 1985, Meissner 1986b). Jacobson (1964) noted years ago that the predominance of shame and inferiority over guilt and the replacement of true guilt conflicts with conflicts of shame and inferiority and paranoid fears of exposure were suggestive of borderline ego and superego defects. As with other dimensions of pathology in the borderline spectrum, these attributes vary in intensity and degree, depending on the patient's level in the borderline spectrum. At more primitive levels, the pathological effects of disturbed narcissism are more severe and more impregnated with aggressive distortions, and contribute the greatest disturbance in the patient's object relations and the maintenance of a cohesive and integrated self-organization.

Regressive Potential. The potential for disintegration of narcissistic structures and the vulnerability of self-cohesiveness, along with the ambivalent, highly conflicted, and precarious cathexis of objects, set the stage for the regressive potential so characteristic of borderline patients. The regressive tendency is often linked with defective ego structure and is associated with the general fluidity of the borderline personality, the regression often being transient and fairly readily reversible, sometimes reaching in a limited way psychotic or near-psychotic levels (Kernberg 1967, Blum 1972, Giovacchini 1973b).

The borderline regression is typically met in the context of a long-term and relatively intense therapeutic relationship. The pace and the depth of the regression exceed that normally expected in the therapeutic context and often precipitously reach a depth that seems nearly psychotic. The regressive pulls seem to exceed the capacity of the ego to control or modulate them. Such regressions can be severely disruptive of the therapeutic work, can have a radical all-or-none quality, and can often be frightening in that they impinge on issues of life and death (Frosch 1967a,b). There is a failure of the differentiation between self and object, between inner and outer reality; there is an emergence of primitive defenses, including splitting, projection, primitive idealization, and denial (Kernberg 1967). There is an intensification of the dilemmas of need and fear in relation to the therapist with periods of apparent fusion and a loss of the distinction between fantasy and reality, between the patient's projections and the real qualities of the therapist. Unresolved feelings of abandonment and neglect are stirred, together with an emergence of primitive rage, with an intensification of destructive clinging and at the same time tendencies to destructive acting-out, suicide, or depressive withdrawal and schizoid isolation (Adler 1974).

The regressive potential is often difficult to evaluate and may require a trial of analysis or intensive analytically oriented therapy to mobilize regressive pressures in the patient. The evaluation of regressive potential depends on the context in which such patients are seen and on the selective factors that brought them there. Friedman (1969), for example, describes the regressive behavior in the inpatient setting, including enraged acting-out and destructiveness, self-destructive behavior, verbal and physical abuse, disruptive and assaultive behavior, generally toward staff and rarely toward other patients, and the reactive involvement of the staff in intense and highly conflictual relationships. In such patients, the regressive potential is more severe and the propensity for destructive acting-out much greater; they cast a broad net to ensnare others in their intensely dependent and destructively ambivalent involvement. These hospitalized patients function at a lower level of the borderline spectrum and should be contrasted with patients whose regression is relatively slow in developing, often only after months or more of intensive therapy or analysis, and whose regression remains more or less confined to the therapeutic setting. In these latter patients, the emergence of a borderline state is usually a function of some breakdown in the therapeutic relationship, a lack of empathic understanding on the part of the therapist, or some other form of countertransference vicissitude. In any case, the transference distortions do not usually generalize to other objects, and do not become a form of self-perpetuating psychosis outside the therapy (Ekstein and Wallerstein 1954, Fintzy 1971).

The borderline ego does not step into psychosis either through simple loss of reality testing or through development of delusional thought systems. Loss of reality testing, for example, is usually relatively limited to one area of the patient's experience and can be fairly readily regained by effective therapeutic intervention (Frijling-Schreuder 1969). The borderline regression can be further contrasted to psychotic regression by being reversible, transient, related to a vicissitude of object relations (implying the persistence of attachment to objects), more frequently involving depersonalization and derealization (Chopra and Beatson 1986), and remaining ego-alien and unsystematized (Gunderson and Singer 1975). A valid and moot question remains whether the transient regressive episodes observed in some borderlines are indeed psychotic or not.

Projection.   A number of authors have noted the propensity for projection in borderline conditions (Rosenfeld and Sprince 1963, Kernberg 1967, 1973, Blum 1972, Buie and Adler 1972, Robbins 1976, Meissner 1984a). Moreover, as Giovacchini (1972) noted, the general tendency of these patients to externalize is consistent with the pattern of acting-out and use of action defenses (Perry and Cooper 1986). They transpose inner problems into external difficulties, so that there is an exclusive preoccupation with reality without consideration of input from the self. The result is a constant tendency to blame forces outside the self for difficulties and problems and to shirk any responsibility. Within therapy, patients distort the relationship with the therapist by projections that prevent them from establishing personal contact with the therapist and even undermine an often tenuous therapeutic alliance.

These projective distortions may include expectations of omniscience and omnipotence in the therapist, while at the same time subjecting him or her to devaluation and attacks reflecting the patients' own inner fears of vulnerability and impotence (Adler 1970). The tendency to assign omnipotence to the therapist is paralleled by the assumption of impotence, need, and dependence in the patient. Such patients set unrealistic and grandiose goals, so that progress in the treatment gives little satisfaction because it does not measure up to the fantasized goal.

Such projective turmoil is found only in more primitive forms of borderline pathology or in borderline regressive states. On a more characterological and less regressed level, however, significant relationships tend to be discolored by projective expectations and interpretations. Projective distortions are found in reasonably healthy and neurotic individuals, but in the borderline they tend to dominate the perception of the object and are also less open to correction by other qualifying or contradictory evidence (Abend et al. 1983). They are usually testable and correctable in the therapy, in contrast to psychotic paranoid distortions, which maintain an intensity and delusional fixity that resists modification.

Ego Defects. The last of the common elements of the borderline spectrum are defects in ego and superego. A number of authors have pointed to ego defects as specifically central to the borderline pathology (Ekstein and Wallerstein 1954, 1956, Rosenfeld and Sprince 1963, 1965, Kernberg 1967, 1973, Frijling-Schreuder 1969, Frosch 1970, Blum 1972, Buie and Adler 1972, Giovacchini 1973b, Atkin 1974, Klein 1975). The extent to which they are relevant for borderline states as opposed to the more stable forms of borderline personality organization is an important issue. Here, too, the evaluation of the severity of ego defects depends critically on the selective and contextual factors under which patients are evaluated.

Ego defects include a variety of primitive defense mechanisms such as projection, denial, splitting, primitive idealization (Rosenfeld and Sprince 1963, Kernberg 1967), defects in reality testing or in the sense of reality (Frosch 1970, Gunderson and Singer 1975), and impairments of the synthetic function (Rosenfeld and Sprince 1963, 1965, Giovacchini 1973a, Atkin 1974). All forms of ego weakness are subject to degrees of intensity, ranging from minor and incidental impairments to severe disorganization and dysfunction characteristic of psychosis. If we look at Kernberg's (1967, 1971) indices of ego weakness, it is clear that they are subject to a wide range of variation and degree of impairment. He lists primitive defensive operations, a lack of impulse control, anxiety tolerance, developed sublimatory channels, a tendency to primary process thinking, and a weakening of reality testing.

The prominence of any or all of these indices suggests borderline pathology, since they point in the direction of psychosis and away from neurosis. But primitive defenses can be found in modified form even in neurotic and classically analyzable patients (Abend et al. 1983). In such patients, projection does not take the form of delusional distortion of reality, but may manifest itself in misinterpretation, suspiciousness, guardedness, misguided convictions, misinterpretations of contexts and meanings, and so on—the "soft signs" of paranoia (Meissner 1978b). Even splitting, which Kernberg makes the touchstone of borderline pathology, can be seen in milder and less pervasive degrees in healthier and better-organized patients. Some borderline patients resort to splitting easily and frequently, others do not; in some borderlines splitting and repression occur side by side (Perry and Cooper 1986). There is some question whether the inner organization of any of these patients is as dominated by the splitting process as Kernberg would indicate. Splitting may be regarded as reflecting the cognitive disposition to categorize in extreme rather than modulated terms (black vs. white), rather than serving as a specific defense mechanism. My argument is not that such primitive defenses cannot be characteristically identified in the borderline pathologies, but that they are subject to degrees of variation and that careful discrimination is required to make the diagnosis. Primitive defenses can be readily identified in lower-order borderline conditions, but would be less apparent and considerably less disturbed in the higher-order borderlines.

Deficits in the control of impulses are also subject to considerable variation. The higher-order borderline regresses only gradually under the influence of a more or less controlled analytic regression, and does not have a serious problem with impulse control; this becomes a problem only when the patient reaches more regressed levels of functioning. Even then, the lack of impulse control is usually related to specific vicissitudes of object relationships—alliance failures or countertransference difficulties within the therapy. This is a far cry from the flamboyant and poorly controlled expression of impulses, frequently in the form of destructive acting-out, seen in lower-order borderline pathology and frequently in the hospital setting (Perlmutter 1982). A similar observation can be made about the lack of anxiety tolerance, in that many treatable patients turn out to be borderline but demonstrate a considerable capacity for the tolerance of anxiety, and even in the face of increasing regression retreat only to a level of separation anxiety, frequently without any need to intensify symptoms or to act out in self-destructive ways.

The capacity for sublimated activity takes the form of enjoyment of work and life, a capacity for creative achievement, and the ability to invest oneself in activities or a profession beyond mere narcissistic needs and to derive a degree of satisfaction from such activity (Kernberg 1971). The evaluation of such sublimatory potential is extremely difficult, since, as Fast (1975) has noted, many borderline personalities achieve considerable degrees of creative expression and accomplishment in areas of creative work such as art, music, poetry, and the like, while their capacity to apply themselves with the same energy and industry to areas of everyday work or the holding down of a job is severely compromised. There is a considerable gradation from the severe constriction of sublimatory potentials and the susceptibility to drive derivatives and narcissistic needs found in more primitive forms of borderline organization and the often highly developed capacity for creative expression found in some higher-order borderline personalities.

The role of reality testing in borderline pathology has been viewed contradictorily, partly because the capacity for reality testing is variable in these patients, and partly because of the inherent ambiguity of the borderline concept. Reality testing is caught in the tension between the need to discriminate between borderline conditions and the neuroses on one hand, and the need to keep the borderline condition clearly discriminated from the psychoses on the other. The former concern emphasizes the vulnerability of borderline reality testing, while the latter emphasizes its preservation as a distinguishing feature from the psychoses. The argument is compounded by the difficulties in assessing ego functions like reality testing in regressive states as opposed to more characteristic personality functioning. In general, reality testing and reality contact are well established and well maintained by borderlines in their general run of functioning, but they are jeopardized under circumstances in which regression takes place, that is, under the influence of emotional stress, alcohol, drugs, or the emergence of a transference psychosis (Kernberg 1967, 1971). Borderlines tend to preserve reality testing under normal circumstances and readily reverse the loss of reality testing in regressive states—features that discriminate them from the psychotics (Kernberg 1967, 1971). As with other parameters of ego functioning, the vulnerability of reality testing is generally correlated with the level of regression, but susceptibility to such regressive influence is more marked in the lower forms of borderline personality integration. Where defects in reality testing are relatively stable and permanent, they have the character of the projective distortions or illusions (Abend et al. 1983).

Superego Defects. Ego and superego integration are interrelated, so that where one finds severe ego defects, one may also expect to find impediments in the structure and functioning of superego. Good superego integration cannot be achieved without good ego integration, but severe superego defects can exist along with reasonably well-integrated ego functioning. Defective superego integration, based on relatively archaic and destructive introjective elements and marked by severity, primitive functioning, and susceptibility to projection, has frequently been described (Kramer 1958, Kernberg 1967, 1973, Blum 1972, Buie and Adler 1972). Tendencies to projection can be seen in the overidealizations and overexpectations as well as the punitive, demanding, rejecting quality of object relations. This gives rise to an alternating pattern of overvaluation and devaluation (Adler 1970), and to intense and highly conflictual relationships with staff members in the hospital setting (Friedman 1969, Adler 1973).

The levels of superego integration have been delineated by Kernberg (1967, 1970, 1971, 1984). He points out that the combination of guilt, remorse, and self-concern suggests greater superego integration, while impotent rage, helplessness, and hopelessness point toward poorer superego integration and a lower level of character pathology. He also cautions against the use of depression as an index of levels of pathology, since both excessive depression or its absence in schizoid withdrawal may indicate lower levels of character organization (Kernberg 1967). Others have emphasized the role of guilt conflicts and the defenses against them (Abend et al. 1983). In general, both the intermediate and the lower levels of character pathology manifest a lack of superego integration, but on the intermediate level this is reflected in superego projections (reflected in a lessened capacity for guilt and a tendency to paranoia), contradictions in value systems, and severe mood swings. At the lower level of character organization, superego integration fails because of the intensity of the pregenital aggression, which prevents adequate synthesis of contradictory self- and object-images. This failure of integration can be cast in terms of the failure of internalization and the maintenance of relatively primitive introjective configurations as derivatives of object relationships (Meissner 1971, 1978b, 1986a). Guilt conflicts and other internalized superego dynamics are more likely to be found in higher-order (especially analyzable) borderlines.

In Kernberg's terms (1970), the split between good and bad images interferes with superego integration and results in an overidealization of self- and object-images, leading to fantasized ideals of power and perfection. The projection of bad self- and object-images, subsequently reintrojected as distorted experiences of the parents as frustrating or punitive, leads to the reinforcement and pathological predominance of sadistic superego precursors and a diminished capacity to integrate these with narcissistically impregnated and idealized components of the ego-ideal. This pathological mechanism is marked in lower levels of character pathology, but can also be detected at the intermediate level. Where there is sufficient integration of good and bad internalized object relationships or images, the central core of the ego is protected by a more stable repressive barrier, thus creating the conditions for the progressive integration of sadistic superego precursors with the ego-ideal.

On the higher level of character organization, sadistic superego precursors may be expressed in a harsh, punitive, or demanding superego. The actual level of functioning may depend not only on the quality of pathological character traits and on the interpersonal environment, but also on the degree of pathological superego pressures on the ego. Thus, a sadistic and relatively well-integrated superego in a depressive-masochistic character may produce a severe depression that is sufficiently disorganizing that nonspecific manifestations of ego weakness appear, making the patient's functioning seem worse than the actual level of the character pathology (Kernberg 1970).

Other indicators of levels of pathological organization can serve as prognostic indicators as well (Kernberg 1971). These include the extent to which pathological introjections are enacted by character traits and the extent to which such introjects are tolerated by the patient's ego; the greater the degree of self-destructiveness expressed in such traits, the lower the level of character functioning and the worse the prognosis. A punitive superego may inhibit ego functions, but the more primitive integration of the aggressor-introject into sadistic character traits defends the ego from superego pressures by a sort of pathological freedom and arrogance through identification with the omnipotent and sadistic superego figure. The more the primitive superego introject dominates the organization of the personality, the more there may be a crude expression of socially inappropriate aggression and the abdication of reality testing by the ego in certain social settings in order to accommodate the demands of this pathological introject.

PSYCHOLOGICAL TESTING

Within the past few years, psychological testing has established a secure position in the evaluation and diagnosis of borderline conditions.
Not only has the diagnosis of a borderline disorder through testing
been shown to be as reliable as diagnosis based either upon structured or unstructured interviews (Carr et al. 1979), but the tests have
also demonstrated their usefulness for determining the prognosis
and course of treatment of borderline patients (Kwawer 1979, Berg
1983).

Although most of these studies have been directed to the diagnosis
of the lower-order borderline conditions (as described in DSM III and
below), there is an emergent consensus that the borderline diagnosis
does not constitute a single entity, but rather involves multiple sub-
groups depending on the diagnostic criteria (Singer 1977), or a range of
disorders clustered under a single conceptual umbrella (Berg 1983), or a
continuum of psychopathological severity, representing differences in
development of the object concept, quality of reality testing, and regressive potential (Lerner and St. Peter 1984). The spectrum view (Meissner
1984a) is reinforced by testing results indicating that borderline inpatients suffer from a more severe degree of psychopathological impairment than outpatients. Borderline inpatients have a higher incidence of
psychoticlike symptoms (Evans et al. 1984) as manifested on the
MMPI. Similarly, outpatient borderlines can be distinguished from
hospitalized borderlines by the quality of their human responses on the
Rorschach (Lerner and St. Peter 1984).

Classic View. The classic view of borderline test performance was
originally proposed by Rapaport and colleagues (1945–1946) and has
become more or less the standard view. The tendency to primary
process thinking is often regarded as a central characteristic of borderline conditions (Kernberg 1967, 1971, Gunderson and Singer 1975), but
borderlines do not generally reveal a formal thought disorder on mental
status examination or in a relatively structured interview. On projective
testing they reveal primitive fantasies, difficulty adjusting to the formal
aspects of the testing situation, peculiar verbalizations, fabulizing, combinatory and confabulated thinking, odd or circumstantial reasoning,
mingling of separate perceptions by temporal or spatial contiguity,
overelaboration of affective meaning of perceptions, and so forth. As
Singer (1977) put it, the core group of borderline disorders

. . . consists of those with flamboyant, peculiarly expressed, elaborate, odd associations to the Rorschach blots. These patients'
Rorschach responses are more bizarre and unusual than those
generally found among openly schizophrenic persons. Yet, these
borderline persons are purported to function adequately on the
WAIS, showing little or none of the ideational deviances there
which they display on the far less structured Rorschach procedure.
[p. 195]

Such global indices of borderline psychopathology may not characterize the total range of conditions. I would also argue that a significant
portion of these personalities need not show such cognitive disorganization on projective tests. I would expect such latent disorganization of
thought processes in the lower levels of borderline pathology, but not in
a significant number of higher-order borderlines.

Structured Tests. Nonetheless, certain structured, pencil-and-paper
tests have been used with some notable success in screening for borderline pathology. Patients who meet the DSM III criteria for the borderline personality disorder, for example, show a significantly higher eleva-
tion on certain MMPI scales (depression, hysteria, psychopathic
deviate, and psychasthenia) as compared to chronic schizophrenics
(Evans et al. 1984). The same sample of borderlines showed a significantly lower score on the L scale and an elevated score on the F scale,
suggesting weakened ego defenses and unconventional thinking. A set
of critical items from the MMPI (Lachar and Wrobel 1979), however,
failed to discriminate borderline inpatients from a mixed group of
personality disorders, except for the substance-abuse scale (Pitts et al.
1985); other subscales reflected greater pathology in borderlines but
were not significant.
    Some evidence suggests that the traditional dichotomy between
structured and projective tests may be overdrawn. On the WAIS, for
example, evidence of disordered thinking can be found, although at a
lesser level than that manifested on the Rorschach. Verbal productions,
even on structured tests, may suggest the intrusion of conflictual elements, thought and language patterns reflecting underlying emotional
concerns. Moreover, borderline patients often produce protocols with
significant subtest scatter on the WAIS, reflecting erratic functioning,
characterized by failing easier items while passing more difficult ones.
Evidently, the patient's incapacity to moderate emotional pressures

leaves cognitive functioning relatively exposed to affective influences and results in erratic functioning. Such variability of performance becomes an important indicator of underlying thought disorder in borderline individuals (Carr et al. 1979, Berg 1983).

As Singer (1977) has noted, as long as the verbal interchange with borderline patients remains structured, the quality of disorganized thinking is not apparent. The primary process qualities of the patients' thinking remain relatively egosyntonic and seem to bother them hardly at all. They can express emotionally tuned and logically idiosyncratic notions without any concern or embarrassment. Even on structured tests, however, there are lapses in logical thinking, especially on tasks requiring the use of language. Patients often manifest magical thinking and arbitrary logic in the face of the stress aroused by dealing with test problems. These lapses in logic in dealing with structured tasks seem to increase in patients whose pathology is closer to the border of psychosis (Berg 1983).

Projective Tests. Researchers have used the terms *fabulizing,* *combinatory,* and *confabulated* to describe borderline thinking in response to the Rorschach, particularly the propensity to overspecify secondary elaborations of associations and to use odd combinations and reasoning. The affective elaboration usually cannot be consensually validated by observers, and the intermingling of separate perceptions may take place simply on the basis of contiguity in time or space. Simple perceptions are attributed excessive and needlessly specific affective qualities; other observers have difficulty in accepting the patient's projected and unsupportable affective implications. The borderline's reasoning is marked by circumstantiality and arbitrariness, making his logic difficult to follow and accept. These illogical and fabulized combinations reflect the less severe form of thought disorder, as opposed to more malignant and severe forms in schizophrenics. The high frequency of fabulized combinations is characteristic of borderline Rorschach performance and distinguishes these patients from schizophrenics (Singer 1977). There is often marked slippage in reasoning, a fluidity of thinking with frequent free-associationlike episodes, and often mild neologisms and more or less idiosyncratic use of language (Berg 1983). On the TAT, disruptions in logic may take the form of contradictions within a given story.

Berg (1983) offers a catalog of other characteristic findings on the Rorschach. Reality testing shows brief distortions, which are short-lived and are marked by minor errors of perception or interpretation in response to emotional arousal. Affective responses tend to be poorly organized and reflect a diminished capacity to regulate emotional arousal. Emotional states fluctuate, and need-states are expressed in labile fashion. In TAT stories the emotional expression and behavior of the characters can change erratically and unpredictably. Discharge patterns tend to be global and diffuse, expressed predominantly in color or shading responses (often depicting fires, explosions, blood, and smoke). There is generally a poor capacity to modulate anger, and the color cards are often seen as amorphous, with little formal structure. The perception of reality is generally organized by the accompanying emotional tone.

Action is used to circumvent the experience of emotion and to discharge tension. This tendency seems to be somewhat stronger when the borderline pathology leans more in the direction of affective disorder than when the pathology is dominated by thought disorder and emotional withdrawal (Stone 1980, Meissner 1984a). Drive representations generally take a primitive form, focusing on unsublimated tension discharge and direct satisfaction with little consideration for moral restraints or social conventions. The defensive organization of the borderline reflects an attempt to deal with stress by regressive faltering, interspersed with higher-level functioning. The more primitive defenses include denial, projection, and splitting. The projection of polarized object representations is seen in extreme characterizations (devils and angels, persecutors and victims) appearing often on the same card. The capacity to tolerate ambiguity and ambivalence is limited, reflecting the patient's insecure capacity to integrate various self-images. On the TAT, stories may show sudden changes in emotional tone, reflecting this compromised capacity to integrate conflicting emotions.

Rorschach images are often powerful, monstrous, devouring, and destructive. Any articulated sense of self tends to be cloaked in these aggressive and destructive trappings. Possible solutions take the form of "as-if" adaptations of both self- and object-images, attempts to provoke confirming reactions from the examiner, and the defensive use of regression to mask any capacity for more mature and assertive functioning (Colson 1982). A typical position of retreat from these aggressive and destructive aspects of self-organization is in the victim-introject (Meissner 1984a).

The representation of objects or descriptions of the human figure often contain fragmented and contradictory perceptions or even combinations of human and animal forms, reflecting the incapacity both to integrate aspects of self-organization and to see others in stable and predictable terms. Such responses reflect difficulties in maintaining boundaries between separate object-representations (Kwawer 1979). The formal characteristics of object-representations may be exaggerated and often give a quality of caricature to descriptions of persons, demonstrating the influence of relatively unmodulated affects and the tendency to see the world in terms of black and white dichotomies and to portray objects as either all-good or all-bad. Human figures are generally depicted as shallow and superficial, gratifying or withholding, deprived or enriched. These polarized perceptions reflect the failure or tenuous achievement of self- and object-constancy.

Lerner and St. Peter (1984) examined Rorschach records for levels of differentiation, articulation, and integration of human responses in borderline patients. Not unexpectedly, schizophrenic subjects produced fewer accurate (F+) responses and portrayed human figures at lower developmental levels than borderline or neurotic subjects. Borderlines portrayed human figures at a more advanced developmental level, but inaccurately. This was seen as a restitutive attempt to reach a level of higher cognitive organization, but at the cost of impaired reality testing and conventional thinking. Unexpectedly, borderline inpatients showed the highest level of developmental indices together with the highest degree of inaccurate responses. These findings distinguished borderline inpatients not only from psychotics but also from borderline outpatients, whose accuracy scores were better. The authors conclude that the borderline diagnosis should be regarded as a continuum of severity involving differences in developmental levels of object perception, reality testing, and regressive potential (Lerner 1986). Extension of this line of research suggests that severely disturbed borderline patients have difficulties in maintaining the boundary between inner and outer reality, as contrasted with the failure to maintain a distinction between self and others in schizophrenics (Lerner et al. 1985, Wilson 1985).

The arrests and impediments in superego development are expressed in a poor adherence to conventional and ethical values, an inconsistent capacity to experience guilt, or inconsistent portrayals of such ethical attitudes on TAT cards: one figure can commit crimes without guilt, but another will commit some minor violation and receive harsh judgment and punishment. On the Rorschach, harsh superego attitudes and attacks of conscience can alternate with guiltless letting-go of superego standards. There are also noteworthy variations in self-esteem regulation, at times depicting qualities of glorification, idealization, and grandiosity, and at other times expressing themes of narcissistic vulnerability, humiliation, and degradation. Similar shifts in narcissistic vulnerability can be detected in portrayals of TAT characters.

There is often relatively severe anxiety over the expression of primitive anger and somewhat violent and destructive motifs on the Rorschach. Relationships among characters on the TAT may be full of tension, opposition, and frustration. Themes of expecting abuse and of helplessness and powerlessness are frequent. Aggressive impulses play a dominant role: the environment is perceived as ominous and potentially destructive. Concerns over survival, imminent danger, and powerlessness are frequent. The individual feels constantly menaced by destructive forces; the extent of malevolence expressed in these projections is thought to correspond to the depth of psychopathology (Blatt et al. 1976, Lerner 1986).

There is considerable anxiety over dependency needs and wishes, reflecting oral themes or references to partially developed organisms and fused animals (Siamese twins) (Kwawer 1979). The wishes for dependent attachment are matched by anxieties concerning abandonment and the unresolved mourning of the loss of significant others. The lack of libidinal phase dominance is reflected in instinctual derivatives from different levels of psychosexual development: oral, anal, and genital derivatives are intermingled on the Rorschach and poorly differentiated from specifically genital aims. Libidinal themes are permeated by aggressive content, often bespeaking a narcissistic and exploitative relationship with others.

Testing Process.   Aside from the test findings themselves, the testing process can also manifest areas of impaired functioning and difficulties in object relations. Difficulties in relating to others are often brought into focus in the interaction between the patient and the examiner. The borderline experience of the self and other is often variable, manifested in sudden shifts of mood and attitude toward the testing process itself and the examiner, who may experience reciprocal feelings involving an often confusing pattern of reactions toward the patient, including concern, anger, and guilt. These feelings are often mirror images of the confusing and unstable ego states in the patient. The intensity of such reactive feelings with borderline patients is often greater than that experienced with neurotic patients. The examiner may begin to experience primitive fantasies of rescue, seduction, abandonment, or retribution, stimulated by the patient's behavior. The borderline patient may turn fears of involvement and rejection into criticism and devaluation of the examiner, who may react with rage and guilt, sometimes with helplessness and despair. The patient's often marked tendency to experience others projectively in a rigid and stereotyped manner may distort the testing experience and the relationship to the examiner. Such patients may feel on trial and perceive the examiner as a prosecutor or judge. Where narcissistic issues are a prominent part of the pathology, the patient may idealize or projectively devalue the examiner. In these cases, the patient may attempt to induce a response in the examiner that fits with his own projective expectations.

Finally, the testing process can be marked by a variety of disruptions, probably because of gaps in the patient's ego functioning. The patient may need vigorous encouragement and support when there is anxiety over failure or other intense feelings stirred by the test material. Work with such patients requires a high degree of flexibility and modification of testing procedures when these recurrent failures exist. The examiner's task is to maintain the integrity of the testing procedure in spite of disruptive distortions.

Role of Testing. Psychological testing has a considerable role in the evaluation of borderline patients, particularly in contexts of acute regression or first admission to a hospital, where rapid evaluation and assessment of the personality structure is an important first step in the organization of the treatment program. Testing is often useful, although not as necessary in the beginning of a course of psychotherapy, particularly if the borderline organization of the patient's inner world is uncertain. The skilled use of projective tests not only can facilitate the evaluation of the presence of borderline pathology, distinguishing it from neurotic or simply narcissistic organization on one hand and from psychotic organization on the other, but also can offer a reasonably good assessment of the level and severity of the borderline disturbance in a given case. As we shall see later, testing also may be useful in evaluating the suitability of various forms of treatment and in estimating prognosis.

The testing approach does not bring to the evaluation of the patient an all-or-nothing, positive vs. negative orientation. Testing results always involve a quantitative factor that measures the patient on a scale of intensity or deviance. The question is never merely whether a particular characteristic is manifested in the testing material, but how much and to what degree. The inherent qualities of the testing perspective that view borderline pathology in terms of levels of differentiation are consistent with the differential diagnosis of borderline conditions in spectrum terms.

DIFFERENTIAL DIAGNOSIS

I turn now to a tentative reassessment of the borderline conditions and a possible diagnostic differentiation. Rather than proposing these groupings as discrete entities, I envision them as descriptive groupings or clusters that have a degree of clinical consistency, even though there may be a degree of overlap in concrete cases, and precise lines of discrimination may be difficult to draw. They should not be regarded as discrete diagnostic categories, such as the schizotypal and borderline personalities in DSM III. They are descriptive groupings derived from clinical observation and experience; their value is clinically heuristic, and they need further empirical verification and validation to qualify as established entities.

The groupings represent differentiable patterns of borderline character structure reflecting an attempt to deal with a variety of developmental and object-related vicissitudes. The borderline conditions can be viewed as a spectrum of pathological character disorders embracing two discriminable groupings—the hysterical and schizoid continua.[3]

Hysterical Continuum

The sequence from the pseudoschizophrenic group through the primitive affective personality disorders and the dysphoric personalities to the primitive hysterics represents a progression in levels of pathological disorganization from greater to lesser severity. The sequence might be envisioned as an extension of basically hysterical features from lower to progressively higher levels of character organization and functioning. The parameters that characterize this sequence are decreasing affective lability, increasing anxiety tolerance, increasing tolerance of frustration, decreasing tendencies to externalization and acting out for the release of tension, decreasing signs of ego weakness, decreasing signs of

---

[3]The diagnostic schema of the borderline spectrum is a somewhat condensed reworking of a diagnostic approach that is presented in greater length and detail in Meissner (1984a). It should be noted that a spectrum view has been advanced by Adler (1980b, 1981) and Rinsley (1985), in which borderline pathology is seen as part of a continuum of personality disorders along with narcissistic disorders—the borderline disorders more severe and the narcissistic less so. The view of the borderline spectrum presented here differs in that the spectrum is located within the borderline disorders in addition to existing among personality disorders generally. The material is presented here for the convenience of the reader and to provide a diagnostic framework for the considerations of treatment that follow.

the instability or fragmentation of introjective configurations and the corresponding failure in self-cohesion, a decreasing titer of primitive pregenital aggression, decreasingly primitive organization of defenses, decreasing susceptibility to regressive pulls and the tendency to regressive states, and, most important, a diminution of clingingly dependent and ambivalent involvement with significant objects constantly attended by the threat of abandonment and loss.

Pseudoschizophrenia.[4]   The first group includes a variety of disorders variously described as pseudoneurotic schizophrenia, borderline schizophrenia, ambulatory schizophrenia, or even latent schizophrenia. Hoch and his associates (Hoch and Polatin 1949, Hoch and Cattell 1959, Hoch et al. 1962) emphasize primary symptoms that these patients share with schizophrenia in less striking and intense form, including thought and association disorders of both process and content, disorders of affective regulation, and even disorders of sensorimotor and autonomic functioning. These patients are similar to the schizotypal personality of DSM III (Stone 1983a, Jacobsberg et al. 1986, Widiger et al. 1986), although the overlap may not be exact. The anxiety is diffuse, chronic, intense, and pervasive. The neurotic symptoms are usually multiple, shifting, and confusing; they include obsessions and compulsions, phobias, hysterical manifestations, hypochondriasis, depression, depersonalization, and a variety of apparently neurotic defense mechanisms occurring simultaneously or successively. The obsessions and phobias may often reach delusional proportions. This pan-neurotic picture may include tendencies to acting out and dramatic or histrionic behavior, or even antisocial and drug-dependent behavior, although there is some evidence to suggest that the tendency to act out self-destructively (including suicide) is present less in this group than in more affectively disturbed groups (Stone 1983a). Sexual organization and functioning is chaotic, both in fact and in fantasy (Hoch and Cattell 1959, Weingarten and Korn 1967).

The thought disorder is a persistent and characteristic feature. Clinically this may be more or less evident, but usually can be found on careful observation and mental testing. These patients tend to reason in all-or-nothing fashion, to have difficulty accepting randomness (everything has a reason), to overemphasize the cognitive in the face of uncertainty, and often to manifest paranoid thought patterns (Stone

_____

[4]Clinical examples of pseudoschizophrenic patients, Alan and Barbara, are presented in Chapter 17.

1983b). Rather than clear-cut delusions or hallucinations, there are overvalued ideas, or unreasonable beliefs maintained with less conviction or consistency than delusions. Primary process and schizophrenic-like thought processes are almost without exception revealed under the influence of sodium amytal and in the use of unstructured projective tests like the Rorschach (Deniker and Quintart 1961, Singer 1977; see the foregoing discussion of psychological testing). Moreover, the thought disorder is relatively ego-syntonic. It persists even though patients may present a reasonably good social facade and appropriate behavior, and may even have considerable academic or occupational achievement. Often, however, the record of achievement is somewhat erratic (Weingarten and Korn 1967).

The pseudoschizophrenics represent the lowest order of character pathology within the borderline spectrum. Essential to the diagnosis are the failures of reality testing, the diffuse, intense, and chronic anxiety, the multiplicity and shifting variety of symptomatology and defense organization, and the chaotic sexual functioning. These patients have a high potential for regression, but primary process and psychoticlike symptoms remain a constant, if often subtle, part of the syndrome. Primary process thinking and failures of reality testing are usually evident on clinical examination.

Primitive Affective Personality Disorder.[5] These patients tend to show more affective than cognitive disturbance, possibly reflecting a more affective than schizophrenic genetic diathesis (Stone 1980, 1983a, Meissner 1984a). They may never actually develop psychotic symptoms, but can experience psychotic decompensation in certain circumstances. Such transient regressions may involve a lessening of reality testing but can usually be readily reversed. The underlying issues remain psychotic, but unlike the pseudoschizophrenic, these patients have a higher capacity for consistent functioning during nonregressed periods, so they remain in reasonably good contact with reality and are relatively more capable of adaptive functioning. The propensity for transient regression, however, even though brief and reversible, remains a marked aspect of this form of character pathology. Moreover, the regression

---

[5]This group was previously designated as "psychotic characters" (Meissner 1984a), an unsatisfactory label because of the confusion with Frosch's (1964, 1970) use of the same term for borderline personalities in general. I am adopting this more descriptive terminology in the hope that it will be more precise and less confusing. Case examples are detailed in Chapter 18.

usually takes the form of affective disruption with affective instability, inappropriate anger, lability, often a tendency to severe and precipitous depression, along with tendencies to acting out in self-damaging ways (including suicide, substance abuse, promiscuity, self-laceration, eating disorders, and the like).

These patients generally have a vulnerable ego but are as a rule better off than the pseudoschizophrenics, who have less capacity to organize any stable pattern of defense or neurotic symptomatology. Even when either of these is achieved, it remains susceptible to regressive pulls. The maintenance of a cohesive sense of self is a constant difficulty because the self is continually threatened with dissolution and disintegration, and is plagued by the need to cling to objects as well as by the fear of fusing with them. The need–fear dilemma is thus pitched at a near-psychotic level, and the implicit threat is psychic death. As a general rule, self-object differentiation is preserved but remains problematic and tenuous, and is frequently blurred or even lost in regressive episodes. Where such ego boundaries become porous and uncertain, there is often a preoccupation with identity problems; this is often the case in analysis, where regressive pulls may increase the dedifferentiation and defusion of ego boundaries. In the analytic situation this may result in tenuous identifications with the analyst that have an "as-if" quality (Giovacchini 1967a, Frosch 1970), as well as attempts to increase the sense of differentiation and separation from the analyst in the form of negativism or paranoid distortion. In regressive phases, the intensity of these fears is buffered by a variety of primitive psychotic defenses, but even at levels of better functioning, object contact involves active use of projective and introjective mechanisms that lend a paranoid discoloration to object relationships and intensify the inner feeling of vulnerability and victimization.

The combination of impaired sense of reality and relatively intact reality testing can result in experiences of depersonalization and derealization (Arlow 1966). Where hallucinations or illusions result from regressive states, the primitive affective personality disorder may maintain a greater distance from the psychotic experience and regard it as ego-alien and may even be aware that the hallucinatory experience is internally derived. Outside of regressive episodes, the basic orientation to the world is based on distrust and tendencies to project and externalize. Patients will use action or antisocial behavior to deal with intolerable and painful affects, and will use projection to reinforce their sense of entitlement to manipulate, exploit, or destroy an environment that does not respond to their intense needs (Adler 1970). Neurotic needs are acted out alloplastically in a search for uninhibited gratification, often with minimal insight (Saul and Warner 1977).

Object relations are generally on an intense need-gratifying basis, often leading to unrealistic demands. Frustration of these demands elicits intense, often paranoid, rage. The relationship with objects is often highly conflictual and intensely ambivalent. Narcissistic concerns put the self's wishes ahead of any empathy, sympathy, or loving relationships with others (Saul and Warner 1977). Moreover, the superego remains poorly integrated; superego components have undergone little depersonification or abstraction. Rather, superego functioning reflects often regressed and archaic superego precursors that remain highly susceptible to externalization and projection. Superego integration is highly irregular with multiple lacunae: impulsive acting-out behavior may exist side by side with hypercritical and harshly punitive superego attitudes. There is a capacity for guilt and depression, but this seems fragmentary and inconsistent.

The primitive affective personality disorder, then, has significantly stronger ego capacities than the pseudoschizophrenic group, since they allow significant stretches of reasonably effective adjustment to the work and social environments. The underlying issues, however, particularly those having to do with object relationships, are pitched at a more or less psychotic level and share in the intensity and life-and-death extremes of psychotic anxiety. The primitive affective personality disorder is distinguished by the relative instability of the organization of the self and the ready regression of narcissistic structures to the level of primitive formations characterized by grandiosity and excessive idealization. It has a fragile and highly vulnerable organization with a ready potential for regression, which undermines ego functioning and precipitates psychotic defenses. The primitive affective personality disorders are similar descriptively to the borderline personalities described in DSM III.[6]

---

[6]Discrimination between primitive affective personality disorders and the pseudoschizophrenics is often difficult and uncertain. Patients may shift in their level of functioning and psychic integration so as to appear more or less disorganized or affectively disturbed from one period to the next. The tendency to cognitive disorganization under stress tilts the diagnosis toward a more primitive pseudoschizophrenic one, whereas affective disturbance leads in the direction of the less primitive affective personality disorder. The clinical picture is often mixed, however, and may contribute to the difficulty encountered in discriminating borderline and schizotypal disorders in the DSM III alignment (George and Soloff 1986, Widiger et al. 1986, Plakun et al. 1987).

Dysphoric Personality.[7]   Dysphoric personalities can be characterized by the quality of lifestyle. They share with the other borderline
conditions the difficulties in carrying on their daily lives and of relating
to other human beings. There is a bizarre and often alienated quality to
their lifestyle (Giovacchini 1965, Blum 1972), and a sense of inner
emptiness and deep loneliness (Collum 1972, Chessick 1974).

The failure to achieve oedipal phase dominance means that in the
pathology of these patients material can be detected from all phases of
libidinal development, leading to an often confused and disturbed
picture. Phallic trends are interfered with, so that there is a faulty
relationship between the operation of the drives and the ego, and the
bulk of the libido remains fixed in the oral and anal phases. The fluidity
and variability may be expressed in shifting levels of ego organization,
which are reflected in a fluctuation between reality orientation and
contact with painful aspects of the environment and preoccupation with
idiosyncratic fantasies. The ability of the therapist to establish and
maintain contact with these patients seems to mitigate the influence of
fantasy; but when the alliance weakens or the therapeutic contact is
lost, inner stimuli seem to play a more prominent role (Pine 1974).

The general fluidity and lack of phase dominance in borderline
conditions is related to the propensity for acting out. The more flamboyant and destructive forms of acting out in borderline states may
represent an attempt to restore a sense of reality by the experience of
intense feeling or pain, which counters the emptiness and unreality in
the acute diffusion of identity of the regressive state (Collum 1972). This
regressive form of acting out is more related to the functioning of the
primitive affective personality disorder than to that of the dysphoric
personality. Acting out in the dysphoric personality is more likely to
take the form of externalization by which the patient transposes his
inner conflict and difficulties to the outer world. Consequently, there is
a constant tendency to blame forces outside the self for one's problems,
and to assume little or no responsibility. This externalization and
blaming often takes the form of subtle projections, particularly in the
therapeutic setting (Giovacchini 1972).

The tendency to regression in the dysphoric personality is neither
so intense nor so marked as in the primitive personality disorder.
Dysphoric personalities do undergo brief psychoticlike experiences that
frequently have a paranoid quality (Gunderson and Singer 1975); while

---

[7]See Chapter 19 for case material.

these regressive episodes may be provoked by drugs or severe developmental or emotional crises, they may also result from progressive developments in the psychotherapeutic relationship. In a regressive crisis, dysphoric personality patients, unlike potentially healthy neurotics, are unable to easily establish a confident relationship with the therapist. Rather, magical expectations, the diminished capacity to distinguish between fantasy and reality, episodes of anger and suspicion, and fears of rejection dominate the therapeutic interaction for an extended period. Gradually they can respond to good therapeutic management and, at least partially, relinquish their unrealistic expectations, as well as their fears and suspicions, and are able to establish a workable therapeutic alliance (Zetzel 1971).

Nonetheless, the dysphoric personality generally retains a relatively good level of functioning and adaptation to reality. The regression is more typically seen either as the result of progressive involvement in the therapeutic relationship with its regressive pressures, usually in analysis but frequently in psychotherapy, or in particularly intense relationships with significant objects outside the therapy. The dysphoric personality may be able to maintain relatively good relationships with a wide spectrum of other people in the environment, but may regress to relatively infantile, destructive, and maladaptive involvements with particular objects. This pattern is not uncommon between husbands and wives. The stress precipitating such regressive states is characteristically related to the vicissitudes of object involvement.

In these regressive states intense affects are often unleashed, usually hostile and destructive or depressed (Kernberg 1967, Gunderson and Singer 1975). The destructive impulses may be turned against the self in forms of self-mutilation or impulsive suicidal gestures. Such regressive manifestations reflect the organization of primitive themes of victimization and aggressive destructiveness, and the inner organization of the victim- and aggressor-introjects (Meissner 1978b). Although Kernberg (1971) relates such self-destructive tendencies to the predominance of pregenital and oral aggression, they can be organized into pathological character traits that reflect a more or less self-destructive etiology.

In these cases, less structured and self-directed aggression is reflected in negative therapeutic reactions or in the patients' tendency to derive pleasure and pride from their self-destructive power, enjoying the defeat of those closest to them, including the therapist. This may be rationalized as a submission to a harsh and demanding value system, often religious but not exclusively so. Kernberg stresses the need to distinguish between unconscious self-defeat as a submission to a sadistic superego and a more conscious affirmation of self-destruction as an ego-ideal calling for the sacrifice of any happiness, success, satisfaction, or rewarding relationships to this ideal. The motif of suffering (victimization) thus plays a prominent role. This may also reflect a need to defeat oneself as the price for defeating and unconsciously hated or envied helper. The self-destruction, therefore, becomes a triumph over the envied object: in the negative therapeutic response, it is a triumph over the therapist. The need to defeat the therapist may also be related to oral envy and the seeking of revengeful destruction of a potential but not fully satisfying source of love and gratification. Even at more adaptive levels of functioning, the dysphoric personality carries out in his daily living the motifs of victimization and destructive aggressiveness (Meissner 1978b). This personality manifests a certain passivity, expressed in passive or masochistic behaviors, a sense of ego helplessness, and difficulty in maintaining a capacity to achieve goals. Such a person often anticipates defeat and may adopt a posture of passivity that plays an often subtle role in characterological adjustment, and becomes marked in regressive borderline states.

Primitive defenses (Rosenfeld and Sprince 1963, Kernberg 1967) are identifiable but cannot be said at this level of organization to be distinguishable from the use of similar defenses in neurotic personalities or the higher-order character disorders. It is only in regressive crises that the full flowering of the primitive defenses, including splitting, primitive idealization, projection, denial, omnipotence, and devaluation, as they have been described, for example, by Kernberg (1967), are in evidence. In general, dysphoric personalities tend to function with fairly high-level defenses during nonregressive periods. The defenses are neurotic or near-neurotic. During regressive states, however, they tend to shift to the level of immature or narcissistic defenses (Meissner 1980b).

Similarly, on the characterological level, ego weakness is relative and results only in a tendency toward more direct expression of impulses and a pattern of nonspecific diminishing of impulse control, reflecting the general variability and tendency toward acting out as reactions to the building-up of psychic tension. Depending on the degree of diminished control, it may be necessary for the therapist to set limits and take a more active structuring approach within the therapy. In general, the impulsivity of relatively nonregressed dysphoric personality patients is easily managed and is readily responsive to effective therapeutic intervention. More severe loss of control, however, may reflect a regressive state. The diminution of ego control in such patients has been compared to an unreliable thermostat, where the control is unpredictable and variable, rather than completely lacking (Ekstein and Wallerstein 1954).

In the same way, reality testing is generally well maintained in the dysphoric personality and is in jeopardy only in a regressive borderline state (Rosenfeld and Sprince 1963, Kernberg 1967, Frijling-Schreuder 1969, Masterson 1972). The maintenance of reality testing in ordinary circumstances distinguishes the borderline conditions from the psychoses (Kernberg 1970, 1971); in the dysphoric personality this weakening of the capacity to test reality is seen only in regressive crises (Gunderson and Singer 1975). In contrast to the primitive affective personality disorder, the dysphoric personality is less subject to regressive pulls and therefore maintains a more solid footing in reality. The primitive affective personality disorder may substitute fantasy for reality with relative ease, even though the capacity to test reality is intact. The dysphoric personality, however, retains a relatively firm sense of relationship with reality and the feeling of reality, along with a capacity to test that reality.

We have previously discussed the relationship between primary process thinking and regressive potential. The indices for primary process organization and cognition reflect the regressive functioning of the borderline state and are intimately connected with reactivation of early pathological introjects and primitive defenses, and the partial refusion of self- and object-images (Kernberg 1967). Consequently, on a general characterological level, the dysphoric personality shows little inclination to primary process organization. Some degree of primary process is found in even the best-functioning and well-adapted personalities. On clinical examination the dysphoric personality may give no greater indication of thought disorganization or formal thought disorder than average neurotic patients. Similarly, on unstructured projective tests, these patients may not provide evidence of disorganization of thinking. Such evidence would suggest that the patient was in a regressive state, or that the diagnosis should be changed to a lower order of character pathology. Subtle indicators of less than totally logical or consistent thinking or combination of percepts may be entirely consistent with a diagnosis of dysphoric personality, but similar findings can be found in the Rorschach protocols, for example, of neurotics or higher-level forms of character pathology. A higher incidence of these more subtle signs, however, may reflect a primary process tendency, but does not suggest a formal thought disorder or psychotic cognitive organization.

The object relations of dysphoric personalities share in the need-gratifying quality of borderline object relationships in general, and also reflect the influence of intense narcissistic needs. In the therapeutic context, however, these needs emerge gradually over time as the relationship develops and as the more regressive aspects of the therapy take effect. The rapid, precipitous, and intensely ambivalent involvement with objects that one might find in the primitive affective personality disorder or the pseudoschizophrenic is not characteristic of the dysphoric personality. If that form of involvement with the therapist occurs in the dysphoric personality, it is usually in the context of a partial regression. It is not uncommon for such patients to be propelled into therapy by the distress and turmoil associated with a regressive borderline state, so that such behavior may occur; but it is not useful diagnostically until the further evolution of the therapeutic relationship provides more adequate data.

In addition, object constancy, although vulnerable, is relatively well maintained (Rosenfeld and Sprince 1963, Frijling-Schreuder 1969, Kernberg 1970, 1971). Generally, the increasing intensity of involvement with a given object makes the dysphoric personality's capacity to tolerate and integrate aspects of intense ambivalent feelings more tenuous. Thus, even at levels of characterological functioning, there is a certain instability in object relations, a diminished capacity for empathy (Kernberg 1970), or a peculiar quality of the experience in which instinctually derived aspects of the object have a greater impact than more enduring and consistent character traits or qualities (Krohn 1974). The need–fear dilemma remains an unexplicit but pervasive concern. When the patient is significantly involved with objects, the relationship is pervaded by a subtle, sometimes even explicit, fear of abandonment.

This dilemma in relation to objects may frequently be solved, particularly in women, by a certain clinging dependency and compliant submissiveness. If borderline aggression and attempts to control it are frequently striking aspects of this syndrome, borderline compliance and victimization are no less important and frequently observed components (Meissner 1978c). This form of object involvement has been described by Reich (1953) as a form of narcissistic object choice in women. It teeters on the brink between object relationship and introjection, and comes close to the descriptions of "as-if" personalities and false-self configurations. While the issues may be closely related among these various expressions of borderline compliance and object need, the patterns are different enough to sustain differentiation. Compliance in the dysphoric personality is primarily an expression of the victim-introject and lacks the plasticity and imitativeness of "as-if" personality or the quality of schizoid protectiveness in the false-self organization. Nonetheless, such compliance can be a source of difficulty that must be consistently and cautiously explored in the therapy of such patients.

The difficulties in object relationships find their way into the transference dynamics. Rapid involvement in intense clinging and demanding attachment to the therapist makes a shambles of the therapeutic alliance and impairs any useful transference interpretations (Little 1958, Adler 1975), but is not, by and large, characteristic of the nonregressed dysphoric personality. The patient may tend to act out the transference, projectively distort the therapeutic relationship, or overvalue and devalue the therapist, but these tendencies may be quite subtle and are not as disruptive, chaotic, or severely disturbed as in more regressed states. Such transference reactions are less frequent, but are not unknown even in relatively healthy and nonregressed neurotic patients. More typically, the transference relationship is increasingly contaminated and distorted by the patient's conviction of certain attitudes, judgments, opinions, feelings, or other states of mind attributed to the therapist. Such distortions tend to undermine the precarious alliance and the patient's capacity to engage productively in the treatment process. Generally, these distortions can be corrected, since the patient's capacity to test reality remains intact.

The dysphoric personality, then, is a form of character disorder in which the borderline issues are no longer substantially psychotic, but the anxiety is pervasive and deals primarily with issues of separation, dependency, and loss, or loss of love. The propensity for regression is limited to special circumstances. The particular vulnerability of the dysphoric personality is in object relations, particularly the characteristic quality of the interplay of projections and introjections, which continually distort the patient's experience of the interpersonal environment. In general, these patients maintain a consistent relationship to reality, an integral sense of reality, and an intact capacity to test reality. These capacities are diminished only during periods of crisis and in regressive states. Object relations and transferences have a characteristic variability, reflecting the internally organized configuration of introjective elements. These patients are able to maintain relatively good ego-functioning and reveal ego weakness only in regressive crises—a characteristic that distinguishes them from lower-order borderline conditions. The pathology in the dysphoric personality seems to reside more in the organization of the self and its correlative introjective configurations than in specifiable ego weaknesses.

Primitive (Oral) Hysteric.[8]   Primitive hysterics manifest basically hysterical symptomatology, but the character organization tends to be somewhat more infantile (Sugarman 1979). Prominent characteristics of the hysterical personality might also be included in a list of characteristics of the borderline personality, particularly emotional lability, strong suggestibility, easy disappointment, alternating idealization and devaluation of objects of dependence, compulsive needs for love and admiration, intense feelings of inadequacy, strong dependence on others' approval for maintenance of self-esteem, a tendency to dramatize or act out feelings, and the like. The differences that distinguish the primitive hysteric from the hysterical personality are the level of pregenital (particularly oral) libidinal elements, the prominence of narcissistic elements in the personality organization, the lesser degree of cohesiveness in the self-organization, the greater degree of regressive potential, and the relatively less mature level of defensive organization.

The hysteroid patients of Easser and Lesser (1965) also fall in this part of the borderline spectrum. They are more deeply disturbed than classically neurotic hysterics. Pregenital (primarily oral) fixations produce a caricature of the hysteric with features of emotional instability, irresponsibility, poor work history, chaotic and transient love relationships, early childhood emotional problems, and markedly disturbed sexuality often involving combinations of promiscuity and frigidity. Many of the "grand hysterics" of the past may also have been included in this group.

Long-lasting or significant involvement with objects frequently shows a progressively more regressed, childlike, oral, demanding, and frustrated aggressive quality. The need to be loved, to be the center of attention and attraction is less specifically sexualized and expresses greater helplessness, inappropriate demands, and more primitive narcissistic needs. The combination of pseudohypersexuality with sexual inhibition results in a sexual provocativeness, often crude and inappropriate, which reflects more orally determined exhibitionism and demandingness than sexualized hysterical dynamics. When this takes the form of promiscuity, it has a drifting quality with little stability of object relationships. Conscious sexual fantasies may have a primitive polymorphous-perverse character. There is often a rapid shifting between positive and negative feelings, between submission and childlike imitation and stubborn resentful negativism. Pregenital and specifically oral

---

[8]See Chapter 20 for case material.

factors predominate, so that there is a reduced capacity for stable object relationships and a weakening of the capacity to maintain object constancy. Tendencies to paranoid, masochistic, or depressive patterns of reaction are common (Sugarman 1979). These patients are particularly adept in recreating the child-parent relation within the transference, transforming any elements of authority, suggestion, reward, or punishment into sexualized collusions with underlying hysterical needs that can be matched by approval-seeking compliance (Lionells 1986). Idealization of the analyst and the interpretive function can provide a form of substitute gratification as a reward for being the symbolically castrated, childlike, and obedient patient. Therapists can be drawn into this subliminal bargain insofar as the idealization and the obedient compliance feed into their own unresolved narcissism and enhance their sense of effectiveness in the therapy (Myerson 1969).

Hysteroid dysphoria seems to show many characteristics that overlap those of the primitive hysterics. It may represent a relatively disruptive form of primitive hysteria or a form of dysphoric personality, or may occupy some intermediate ground between. It seems to qualify as a form of borderline disorder with a specific behavioral component, namely, overeating or oversleeping (Liebowitz and Klein 1981). Depressions are usually of short duration, but may recur frequently and are excessively disruptive. Serious rejection or abandonment by the object of attachment may produce more prolonged or severe depressions. Narcissistic elements also play a significant role. The maintenance of self-esteem seems excessively dependent on a continual flow of external approval; physical appearance and attractiveness are matters of great moment. Personality functioning is decidedly hysterical, showing characteristics that are histrionic, flamboyant, highly emotional, seductive, intrusive, and often self-centered or demanding. Choice of love objects and attachments tends to reflect poor social judgment insofar as they are usually inappropriate and almost always overidealized.

The primitive hysteric, then, manifests basic borderline features along with some distinguishing characteristics. Transient attachments and the alternation between idealization and disparagement resemble the "as-if" personality, but the primitive hysteric maintains a better-integrated and more cohesive sense of self without the characteristics that define the "as-if" personality. The primitive hysteric can look like the dysphoric personality at times, but the dysphoric personality alternates to a greater extent between various introjective configurations. The primitive hysteric articulates itself around the victim-introject,

assuming a more depressive structure. Also the primitive hysteric retains the capacity to mobilize hysterical defenses in the interest of
defending against underlying conflict.

Schizoid Continuum

The variant modalities of personality disturbance composing the schizoid continuum can be regarded as attempts to deal with the same
underlying problem, namely, the incapacity to establish and maintain a
coherent and individualized sense of self in the face of a powerful need
for and dependence on objects, accompanied by a fear of loss or
dissolution of self posed by attachment to that object. The respective
entities—identity stasis, "as-if" personality, schizoid personality, and
the false-self personality—are all struggling with forms of need–fear
dilemma; all suffer from impediments of libidinal object constancy, and
represent variant modalities of the attempt to come to terms with this
underlying set of object-related conflicts.

The schizoid personality resolves the conflict by affective withdrawal and the preservation of self by defensive isolation and avoidance
of object involvement. The false-self personality resolves the conflict by
a protective schizoid withdrawal of the true self and a compliant compromise with reality through the false-self facade. The "as-if" personality adopts a superficial, transient, imitative involvement with objects
that equivalently minimizes real, meaningful, or enduring commitment
to an object relationship. The "as-if" adjustment can be taken as a more
fragmentary, transient, and superficial version of the false-self organization. Finally, the resolution of the conflict in identity stasis is
achieved by the maintenance of inner ambiguity and the avoidance of
self-definition.

The schizoid continuum, therefore, shares certain characteristics
that offer some differentiation from the hysterical continuum, although
considerable overlap—even shifting—within the continuum is clinically
evident. In addition to the sense of withdrawal and isolation, there is
generally a rigidity of defenses and a resistance to regression quite
different from the hysterical continuum. This is even truer of the
schizoid personality and the false-self personality, whose defensive organizations are well maintained in the face of regressive pressures. The
"as-if" personality is more likely to show regressive features, but these
are easily absorbed in a new "as-if" configuration. Regression in cases
of identity stasis may be countered by increased schizoid withdrawal or
by retreat to a negative or pseudoidentity (as, for example, in fanatic

adherence to a "cause"). These patients tend to show a much higher titer of borderline compliance (Meissner 1984a).

Schizoid Personality.[9]   The schizoid dilemma and defense are seen most characteristically in the schizoid personality. The schizoid patient complains of feeling isolated, cut off, shut out, out of touch, apart, or strange, or says that life seems futile and meaningless, empty, leading nowhere and accomplishing nothing. Unable to make or sustain commitments, the schizoid reflects a certain apathy toward life. Relationships are affectively empty and characterized by emotional withdrawal. Vital mental activity has disappeared into a hidden inner world, so that the patient's conscious self is empty of feeling and capacity for action. Genuine social interaction is severely limited to a sterile but stable world of facts and rules (Bromberg 1984). Glimpses of intense activity in this inner world can be captured in fragments of dreams or fantasies, but the patient reports these as if he were a dispassionate and neutral observer uninvolved in the inner drama of which he is but the passive spectator. The attitude to the outer world is one of noninvolvement and mere observation, without any feeling, attachment, or sense of participation. In therapy he wants to be rid of his illness, but not at the cost of surrendering his fragile independence and sense of identity (Guntrip 1969).

The schizoid individual often lives alone, characteristically has few or no friends, has few meaningful interactions in the community, is withdrawn and usually hypersensitive, shy, and often eccentric. Unable to express any feeling or to show any anger, he responds to conflict with relative detachment. These patients may also show paranoid characteristics: extreme sensitivity, suspiciousness, and guardedness. They may complain of depression and diminished interest in events and people around them, feeling that life is futile and meaningless, and often expressing suicidal ideation. This "schizoid depression" lacks the inner sense of anger and guilt usually found in affective depressions.

The schizoid's primary defense against anxiety is to keep emotionally isolated, inaccessible, and remote. The schizoid condition, then, consists of a cancellation of external object relations and an attempt to live in a detached and withdrawn manner. The schizoid dilemma is that of destructive love, in which the anxiety arises from the fear of destroy-

---

[9]Case material is present in Chapter 21.

ing and losing the love object through the intensity of devouring, needy dependency (Appel 1974). The schizoid personality cannot exist in a relationship with another person, nor can it exist out of it without risking the loss of both the object and the self. Love relationships consequently are seen as mutually destructive.

While schizoid withdrawal may be regarded as a regressed posture (Guntrip 1969), it is nonetheless a protective, highly defended position that buffers the ego against further disruptive regression (Giovacchini 1973a). In both children and adults, the affective life is constricted and underdeveloped, with a quality of emotional distance and preoccupation with inner thoughts and fantasy life. Despite this turning inward, the integrity of other functions is maintained without the characteristic shifting self-organization seen in primitive affective personality disorders, or even in the dysphoric personality with its shifting back and forth between dissociated states. Thus, the schizoid personality maintains a position of reasonably good functioning in the real world, even though emotionally aloof. The defenses are so rigidly maintained that the character structure is quite stable, and disruptive regressive states are relatively uncharacteristic of this entity (Pine 1974).

In any case, the quality of emotional withdrawal should not mislead us into a belief that schizoid individuals are in fact uninvolved or withdrawn from object relationships. Indeed, their contact with objects is intense, highly ambivalent, and subject to the torments of the schizoid dilemma we have described. Their commerce with objects is intensely colored and distorted by projections that turn objects of dependence into threatening, persecuting, engulfing, devouring objects. Their sense of identity is afflicted with an ontological insecurity, a feeling of basic inadequacy and inferiority (Guntrip 1969). The schizoid self, then, is organized around an internalized victim-introject that acts as the core of the personality organization. The schizoid withdrawal is intended to protect this vulnerable and victimized core. The basic defect of the schizoid character lies at an early level of the internalization of hostile, destructive introjects. These internalized unconscious elements are locked away within the psyche, where they remain always rejecting, indifferent, or hostile. This negative introject becomes a focus for feelings of inner worthlessness, vileness, inner destructiveness, evil, and malicious power. These are the intrapsychic expressions of the victim- and aggressor-introjects (Meissner 1987b).

False-Self Personality.[10]   The false self is essentially a schizoid condition marked by maintenance of a compliant and protective facade motivated by the need to preserve a sense of inner autonomy and individuation in the face of anxiety from intimate contact with objects. Winnicott (1960) originally described a split between the false self, that part of the personality related to and involved with the external environment and real objects, and the true self, which inhabits the inner core of the personality and is hidden away from the scrutiny of observers. The self equivalently regards itself as the true self and correspondingly regards that part of the personality related to external objects or to the physical body as false. The false self protects and preserves the true self and guards it against losing its sense of subjectivity, vitality, and inner autonomy—providing a zone of safety from all harm (Eigen 1973). The dilemma is essentially schizoid in that the inner autonomy and authenticity of the true self is threatened by engulfment in its relationships to objects. The reality of these objects and the relatedness to them are an impingement (Winnicott 1965, Eigen 1973), similar to the infantile impingement of the "not-good-enough-mother," which may threaten to overwhelm or obliterate the self. The false-self facade masks an inner world of loneliness, schizoid isolation, and existential alienation (Cassimatis 1984).

The false-self personality rides on an underlying narcissistic vulnerability based on the persistence of an infantile, grandiose ego-ideal or grandiose self. "True self" is something of a misnomer for this core of the self, which is both alienated and megalomanic. It adapts to the demands of the environment by self-falsification and self-isolation (Eigen 1973). False-self individuals regard their early caretakers and later significant objects as not appreciating or accepting their grandiose attempts to preserve a sense of inner spontaneity and integrity, and they thus retreat to an inner world to preserve this sense of vitality and autonomy. The retreat is to a kind of grandiose self-sufficiency characteristic of schizoid states (Modell 1975). This illusion of grandiose self-sufficiency often motivates these patients to seek treatment. The goal of the treatment for them is to be able to achieve and maintain their isolation and self-sufficiency without the stigmata of loss or abandonment.

The other important component of the false-self personality is compliance. In any healthy personality there is a compliant aspect to

---

[10]See Chapter 22 for case discussions.

the true self that derives from the ability of the infant to comply without fear or danger or the risk of exposure or vulnerability. The socialization of the child requires compliance and adaptability, but there must also be a capacity to override this compliance at crucial points or periods— for example, adolescence. False-self compliance, however, is a substitute way of relating to objects and dealing with the external environment that is fallacious, unreal, and fragile. The actions of the false self seem false, often empty, and lacking in vitality or significance, and may serve as a source of inner desperation and hopelessness.

To external observation, the false-self personality may appear quite normal and adaptive. It may even provide the individual with at least a partial sense of "identity." The tendency to adhere to causes, groups, leaders, and so forth may provide a sense of pseudo-identity, but trouble arises when authenticity and real object involvement are called for. When the false-self personality cannot measure up to or sustain itself in the face of such pressures or demands, the outcome may be a severe regression into a borderline state. At its pathological worst, the false-self organization may cover an underlying schizophrenic process, so that fragmentation of the false-self facade can uncover the underlying schizophrenic process, often in the form of acute disorganization and decompensation.

The false-self personality, then, represents another form of adaptation to or defense against an underlying schizoid dilemma. Rather than adopting a pattern of "as-if" involvement or schizoid withdrawal, the organization of the personality splits, allowing the true self to retreat to an inner world colored with narcissistic isolation and self-sufficiency, and constructs another self-organization based on compliance and the need to buffer the true self from the impingements of the outside world. The false-self personality may sustain this pattern of adjustment and involvement with reality, but the true self remains hidden and withdrawn. The pathology takes the form of the internal organization of the self, which is permeated by underlying narcissistic and object-related conflicts.

"As-If" Personality.[11]   The original description of the "as-if" personality emphasized the patient's impoverished emotional relationships, and included the lack of normal affective involvements and responses. This was less likely to be perceived by the subjects than by

---

[11]See Chapter 23 for case studies.

others; or it might be first detected in treatment. Sometimes patients may be aware of their emotional defect and be keenly distressed by it. They may then experience such states as transitory and fleeting, or recurring in specific situations, or persisting as an enduring, distressing symptom (Deutsch 1942). The patients' relationships are devoid of warmth; expressions of emotion are formal; the inner experience is excluded. Deutsch compares it to the performance of an actor who is well trained to play a role, but lacks the spark to make it true to life.

The "as-if" personality involves failure of object cathexis rather than repression. The relationship to the world is maintained on a level of childlike imitation, expressing an identification with the environment and resulting in ostensibly good, though passive, adaptation to reality and the highly plastic capacity to mold oneself and one's behavior to external expectations. Attachments to objects can be adhesive, but there is such a lack of real warmth and affection in the relationship that the partner often breaks off the relationship. When the "as-if" person is abandoned, any affective reaction may be totally absent, or there may be a spurious ("as-if") response (Gardner and Wagner 1986). The object is soon replaced with a new one, and the process is repeated. The "as-if" organization covers the underlying schizoid emptiness and acts as a defense against the lack of a cohesive self and identity. A similar pattern has been described by Martin (1984) as constituting a "fictive personality."

Deutsch also comments on the generally weak or absent moral character of these patients. Their moral standards, ideals, and convictions tend to reflect those of the individuals to whom they attach themselves, whether for good or evil, and they are easily influenced by social, ethical, or religious groups. Their adherence to each successive point of view may be at first enthusiastic and then easily shifted, even from one contradictory view to another (Gardner and Wagner 1986). They are also quite suggestible, reflecting their passivity and automatonlike identification. The passivity masks aggressive tendencies, so that their apparent goodness and amiability may easily turn to the opposite. The failure of superego formation derives from the failure to achieve a strong enough oedipal involvement and the resulting impairment of oedipal identifications. Superego precursors are not effectively internalized and remain dependent on external objects. The organization of the internal world in these patients is based primarily on the interplay of imitation and introjection, and fails to reach a higher level of more autonomous identifications (Meissner 1974).

"As-if" states can exist over a wide spectrum, ranging from the apparently normal to the definitely psychotic (Ross 1967, Gediman

1985). There is also debate over the connection between "as-if" pathology and imposture, since they embrace many similiar characteristics. However, imposture seems to suggest a more conscious pattern of imitative and deceptive role-playing, while the "as-if" phenomenon is largely unconscious and is related to issues of self-organization and the transient stabilization of identity (Gediman 1985). In fact, "as-if" qualities may be found in varying degrees and at various times in many borderline patients, presumably as a secondary aspect of the failure to establish and maintain a cohesive self-organization and sense of personal identity. They may also be associated with states of depersonalization.

The "as-if" personality manifests a form of borderline compliance associated with the victim-introject (Meissner 1976, 1978b). The "as-if's" imitative compliance provides a resolution of the problem of aggressive and assertive independence by retreat to passive victimization (the victim-introject). At the same time, it solves the dilemmas of narcissistic peril and object-relation conflicts by transitory and superficial "as-if" involvements and their associated internalizations. The issues of compliance are shared with other borderline conditions, particularly cases of identity stasis, schizoid personality, and false-self personality. The discrimination among them is in the manner in which these conflicts are dealt with—whether by diffusion of identity, by "as-if" imitative attachments, by schizoid withdrawal, or by the organization of the false-self.

Whereas "as-if" states may be found in a variety of pathological conditions, either in conjunction with or as a defense against depersonalization, the "as-if" personality is a distinct clinical pattern within the borderline spectrum. The disturbances in narcissism, the capacity for object relations, and the internal organization of the self in the "as-if" disturbance are found at a number of levels of pathological intensity. The "as-if" personality resolves these underlying conflicts by a transient, often superficial, imitative and idealizing attachment to an object. This attachment is paralleled by a modification of the self in terms of imitative and introjective mechanisms which, because of their defensive vicissitudes, lead to no further or more meaningful internalizations (Meissner 1974). As a result, these patients do not present a significant deficit in ego functioning, but rather the pathology lies in the realm of the organization of the self, which achieves a transient cohesiveness through such "as-if" mechanisms. Deficits in structural organization, not only of the ego but more particularly of the superego, are thus secondary to this basic dynamic.

Identity Stasis.[12]   Identity diffusion arises when developmental experiences, particularly in adolescence, demand a commitment to physical intimacy, occupational choice, or competition of various sorts—in general, to a specific form of psychosocial self-definition. The necessity of choice and commitment gives rise to conflicting identifications, each of which narrows the inventory of further choice; movement in any direction may establish binding precedents for psychosocial self-definition. The result is an avoidance of choice, a lack of inner definition of self, and an external avoidance, isolation, and alienation. While identity diffusion designates a more or less acute reaction or crisis (Erikson 1956), the same issues can be found in the form of a basic characterological stagnation—identity stasis. Engagement carries with it the constant threat of fusion and loss of identity, which may be defended against by social isolation, stereotyped or formalized interpersonal relationships, or even the frantic seeking of intimacy with improbable or inappropriate partners. Such attachments, whether as friendships or affairs, are attempts to delineate an identity by mutual narcissistic mirroring. These patients have a characteristic difficulty in committing themselves to any line of action or career choice. Commitments in the areas of work and love are particularly difficult: they find themselves unwilling or unable to make a definitive choice of life partner, just as they may find it extremely difficult to decide upon and commit themselves to a profession or choice of career. All of the difficulties in work identification that we have noted in other contexts can be found in this group of patients as well (Fast 1975). These difficulties in self-definition and commitment may be found in one area but not in others. The patient may have a well-defined work life or career but be unable to make the defining commitment in an intimate love relationship.

Reactions to this underlying diffusion or stasis of identity may take a variety of forms (Erikson 1956). The patients may use a form of distancing, resulting in a readiness to repudiate or ignore or even destroy forces dangerous to the self. They may resort to intense attachment to a set of ideas or an ideology, a group, a cause, or leader—which, by implication, involves repudiation of other causes, groups, leaders, and so on. This kind of attachment may have an "as-if" characteristic or even evolve into a false-self configuration. The attachment may attain an almost paranoid flavor, involving indentifiable paranoid

---

[12]A case of identity stasis is presented in Chapter 24.

mechanisms, particularly the interplay of projections and primitive introjections (Meissner 1987b). The failure of these devices, however, may lead such individuals to withdrawal, self-questioning, and introspective uncertainty. A need for constant self-testing develops, which can result in an almost paralyzing borderline state in which there is an increasing sense of isolation, a loss of a sense of identity, a deep sense of inner uncertainty and shame, and an inability to derive any sense of accomplishment from external activities. There is a feeling that one is the victim of circumstances and forces beyond one's control, without any sense of initiative or responsibility for the direction of one's own fate.

There may be, in fact, a retreat to an identification with the victim-introject as a convenient escape from the uncertainties and emptiness of identity diffusion. Moreover, the narcissistic aspects of this configuration should not be missed. There are protests of potential greatness, missed opportunities, and expansive possibilities. There is an unwillingness to sacrifice any possibilities or limit any potentialities in the determination of specific choice. There is a fear of engagement, a reluctance to compete or assert oneself as separate and individual, a fear of time and its passage, a constant vacillating, doubt, and uncertainty, and an unwillingness to choose that often looks obsessional but is in fact driven by motivations of a different order.

When questions of choice and self-direction emerge, as they inevitably must, any commitment runs into considerable difficulty, whether it be to write a thesis, to apply for a job, to marry, to father a child, and so on. Identity diffusion reflects an inability to establish a stable self-concept and correlatively a lack of integration of internalized object derivatives (Kernberg 1967, 1970). The emergence, establishment, and consolidation of a consistent and coherent sense of identity is related to the integrity and cohesiveness of the self and depends on the capacity for positive and constructive identifications. To the extent that the sense of identity is vulnerable and lacks cohesion, as in these patients, this reflects the internal organization of introjects that are excessively embedded in issues of conflict and defense, thus preventing meaningful or substantial integration.

Identity diffusion is an aspect of all of the borderline conditions, particularly in regressive borderline states. This is undoubtedly a prominent feature of such regressions and must be regarded as correlative to the acute disorganization and loss of cohesion in the organization of the self. However, the difficulties in establishing and maintaining an identity can take a more characterological form, which represents a more or less persistent personality configuration capable of separate and differential diagnosis. It should also be remembered that under the impetus of developmental pressures, or external pressures stemming from environmental situations or life conditions, the configuration may evolve into other forms of borderline adjustment.

Identity stasis, then, represents a form of character pathology that involves an impairment of meaningful identifications and an incapacity for self-definition. The pathology does not reside in the ego or even the superego as much as in the organization and delineation of the self. There is a complex interplay with object relations conflicts, related to the incapacity to define or commit oneself. On a primitive genetic level, however, the underlying fears have to do with the threat posed by separation and individuation and the surrender of infantile objects and one's dependence on them. Ultimately, commitment to a life, whether of work or of love, means to accept limitations and change, the surrender of infantile omnipotence and narcissistic entitlement, and the ultimate acceptance of the finitude of human existence and death. Maintaining the self in a posture of persistent uncertainty, lack of definition, and lack of commitment is to maintain a condition of continuing possibility and a denial of the necessity to ultimately come to terms with the demands and limitations of reality.

ADOLESCENCE

Borderline Syndromes in Adolescence

The difficulties of diagnosing borderline pathology in adolescence are compounded by the interweaving of development and pathology. The diagnostician must decide whether behavioral difficulties, questions of emotional lability and reactivity, difficulties in achieving and maintaining a stable sense of identity, and the general question of adolescent turmoil are to be regarded as part of a normal developmental pattern or as forms of pathological deviance. Kernberg (1979) has commented on the tendency to confuse normal or neurotic identity crises in adolescence with the more severe and pathological identity diffusion characteristic of borderline organization. Identity diffusion, severe pathology of object relationships, and defects in superego integration (incapacity to assume responsibility, lack of concern, defective investment in values, and failures in basic honesty) are signs of borderline pathology and are not normal characteristics of adolescent development.

Diagnostic Difficulties.   In light of these complications, diagnostic evaluation of adolescent patients encounters a number of difficulties. Symptom formation and other neurotic expressions, such as anxiety or depression, may have a severe impact on the adolescent's capacity to function, suggesting underlying ego weakness and a borderline diagnosis. Also, normal adolescent identity crises, manifested by rapidly shifting identifications and attachments to various ideologies or social groupings, must be distinguished from identity diffusion. By the same token, a relatively severe impairment in the capacity for object relationships may be misinterpreted as involving more neurotic issues of dependency and rebellion, thereby causing underestimation of the degree of pathology involved in conflicts with authorities and other social agencies. In the opposite vein, essentially neurotic conflicts with parents and other authority figures may elicit primitive defensive patterns, so that the adolescent's efforts at omnipotent control, projection, and devaluation may begin to look more borderline (Kernberg 1978). Antisocial behavior may be a form of normal or neurotic adaptation to an antisocial cultural subgrouping, or may reflect a more severe form of character pathology. Similarly, narcissistic reactions may mask more primitive narcissistic features, particularly when there is no openly antisocial behavior to alert the diagnostician. Further, the emergence of relatively perverse sexual trends in adolescence may mimic features that are found more typically in borderline personalities.

There is always the risk that the adolescent with certain borderline features may, in fact, be suffering from an evolving and insidious psychotic condition (Simon 1984). As Kernberg (1978) notes, in such cases insidious delusion formation may be mistaken for hypochondriacal tendencies or excessive preoccupation with physical appearance. Narcissistic character pathology is frequently reinforced by narcissistic features within the family context, so that the diagnostician has the problem of disentangling the patient's pathology from the family pathology. Truly narcissistic pathology should be regarded as reflecting an impairment or deficit in earlier childhood development rather than as a by-product of family dynamics and interactions in the present (Kernberg 1978).

Pathological Features.   Kernberg's (1979) paradigmatic view suggests that identity diffusion, severe pathology of object relations, predominantly part-object transferences, lack of superego integration, and primitive defensive operations characterize borderline pathology in adolescence. Thus late-adolescent borderline patients have not accomplished the normal developmental tasks of adolescence. They have failed to achieve an integrated self-concept or identity; they have not consolidated a normal sexual identity with the proper subordination of pregenital to genital strivings and a capacity for tender and erotic feelings in a stable object relationship; they have not been able to loosen parental ties and adopt adult social roles and relationships; finally, they have failed to replace infantile superego regulations with more abstract and depersonified, yet flexible and adaptive, moral values.

Borderline attitudes toward parents reveal excessive involvement with parents, violent rebelliousness, hostile dependency, and generally chaotic interpersonal relations. In psychotherapy, borderline adolescents tend to overidentify the therapist with parental images, or to react defensively and hostilely, often switching among mutually dissociated or combined parental images and a defensive rejection of the therapist as different from these imposed parental images. In this complex of symptoms, Kernberg (1978) emphasizes the importance of identity diffusion as fundamental to the borderline diagnosis. Others (Aarkrog 1977) have emphasized the presence of transient psychotic states in a personality with intact areas of functioning and varying shifts in patterns and levels of functioning. Such cases may have a manifest history of borderline disorder in earlier childhood,[13] or may have developed less apparent vulnerabilities that emerge as a more frankly borderline condition at the onset of adolescence.

Many cases have characteristic narcissistic features. School performance may show contradictory trends of intense ambition and perfectionism along with a sense of failure and withdrawal from activities. Symptomatic depressions reflect feelings of defeat, inadequacy, and shame at the failure to achieve a narcissistic triumph, as well as tendencies to devalue what does not come easily or is not immediately rewarding. A socially engaging facade, charm, and superficial friendliness, along with multiple talents and good intelligence, may mask the underlying incapacity for commitment to life goals or to personal relationships in any depth. Tendencies to omnipotent control, grandiosity, and devaluation may express themselves in violent rebelliousness against the parents, which must be differentiated from more normal adolescent

[13]Opinions regarding the existence of borderline features in children are divided (Meissner 1984a); Chethik (1986) argues not only for the presence of borderline features in latency-age and early-adolescent children but also that the borderline deficits cover a range or spectrum of pathological levels. See also the discussion in Galatzer-Levy (1987).

turmoil. The normal or neurotic adolescent may have conflicts with parents and may criticize or devalue them but also has a capacity to appreciate them and can engage in other meaningful relationships without such devaluation. He can experience guilt and concern and can maintain enduring and nonexploitative relationships with other important figures (friends, teachers, and the like) without the degree of conflict and alternating devaluation and idealization found in the borderline.

Rosenfeld and Sprince (1963) described analytic material from adolescent borderline boys as confused and latencylike. There were features derived from all phases of libidinal development with a lack of phallic phase development. The puberty spurt prompted a leap to the phallic level, reflected in physical maturity and sexual fantasies. But the material had an "as-if" quality, reflecting unstable phallic primacy that readily regressed to oral or anal levels. These authors regard lack of oedipal development and the failure to achieve phallic phase dominance as essential features of adolescent borderline development.

Borderline adolescents will often manifest a mixture of pathological symptoms, including anxiety, depression, hypomanic behavior, stealing, drug or alcohol abuse, confused and perverse sexuality, and even temporary breaks with reality. These symptoms do not fit the pattern of familiar emotional disorders, but seem to be mixed in a confusing and inconsistent fashion. Usually, in such cases, the combination of anxiety and depression masks an underlying identity diffusion. This is different from the more normal discontent with oneself and the world that may be expressed in cynicism and bitterness but continues nonetheless to be engaged in that world; it should also be distinguished from the more ominous delusional and dissociative reaction of a schizophrenic process. Breaks with reality may suggest a diagnosis of schizophrenia but, like transient psychotic episodes in adult patients, they remain time-limited and relatively readily reversible.

Developmental and other adjustment stresses of adolescence create a need in such patients to withdraw from the reality of the adult world and retreat into a fantasy world where they can still entertain visions of themselves as effective, capable, and strong. Thus, the normal adolescent weakening of the barrier between conscious and unconscious thought systems extends in these cases to a point of retreat into fantasy that impedes the adolescent's capacity to deal with real problems and real challenges. This escape into fantasy may at times assume a chronic form, yet remain sufficiently encapsulated so that the normal course of the individual's life is not significantly disrupted. The patient will maintain such a delusional system alongside conscious everyday experience. The diagnosis of psychosis in an adolescent and the differentiation between a psychotic process and a transient borderline state are particularly difficult, especially when the young patient has experienced a psychoticlike regression for the first time. The degree to which the regressive episode becomes actually disabling may be helpful in some cases: if the impairment in the ability to function is such that the individual's adaptive mechanisms are overwhelmed and totally impaired, a diagnosis of psychosis may be warranted. Recurrent or longer-lasting episodes may reinforce the impression of psychosis. The impairment of reality testing may suggest psychosis, but may also speak to a transient regression. Assessment requires an evaluation of prepsychotic personality, the nature of the precipitating stress, the duration and quality of the lapse in reality testing, and the presence of a persisting thought disorder (Simon 1984).

Acting out is almost always a problem in borderline adolescents. This reflects not only the general adolescent lack of frustration tolerance but also particular factors associated with borderline vulnerability. In many cases, it may indicate the presence of sociopathic tendencies. Chwast (1977) associates this tendency with what he calls the "malevolent transformation" that occurs in someone who has felt rejected and hated throughout his life, and who turns this feeling into rejection and hatred of others. The individual loses a capacity for empathy, making antisocial acting out and its consequences more tolerable. The process is reinforced when the youngster feels alienated from or rejected by his environment. Feelings of anxiety and depression arise in connection with dependency needs and the threat of disapproval from significant others. The depression reflects the sense of lost love from these important others, accompanied by a loss of self-esteem and an increased degree of self-hate. The acting out may become a vehicle for avoiding these difficult and painful feelings. Guilt may also induce acting out behavior, but in borderline adolescents the tendency to act out comes more typically from the failure of inner controls due to the underlying ego weakness and failure to achieve sufficient ego integration at earlier levels of preadolescent development.

In the assessment of antisocial behavior in adolescence, important discriminations must be made: between "antisocial behavior" in merely conventional or legalistic terms and antisocial behavior in strictly clinical terms; between antisocial behavior that is within the range of normal reaction to an abnormal antisocial subgroup, and antisocial behavior that reflects a neurotic reaction, usually in the form of strug-

gles over adolescent dependency and rebelliousness; or antisocial behavior as part of a severe character pathology (particularly narcissistic);
or finally, the diagnosis of antisocial personality itself (Kernberg 1975a,
1978). Where the diagnosis of antisocial personality can be made, the
patient can be considered to have an underlying borderline personality
structure. Most of these cases are characterized by poor impulse control, poor capacity to handle and tolerate frustration and anxiety, a
limited capacity for guilt, inadequate resources for effective sublimation
of drives and impulses, manipulative and exploitative behavior, and
chronic hostility and aggression (Chwast 1977).

The pathology of identity in borderline adolescence may reflect the
relative instability and disorganization of psychic systems and expresses
itself in impaired object relationships. The inherent destabilization
caused by adolescent developmental vicissitudes results in varying degrees of depersonalization that the adolescent attempts to counter by
desperately assuming a negative or pseudo-identity or by attachment to
an ideological group or cult. In such cases there may also be distorted
perceptions of reality, in which patients are overwhelmed by feelings of
strangeness and derealization. There may also be a confusion and
defusion of body boundaries. In other cases, a severe schizoid picture
can evolve with typical schizoid characteristics of isolation, loneliness,
and lack of communication with the outside world. The adolescent
seems withdrawn, cares for nothing or no one, and is easily offended
and suspicious. The schizoid withdrawal is accompanied by a high
degree of narcissistic self-investment with feelings of self-sufficiency,
omnipotence, and a contemptuous devaluation of objects, usually as a
defense against feelings of dependence. The pathology of identity may
occasionally take on the dimensions of a psychopathic character, with
apparent lack of guilt and responsibility and peremptory seeking of
immediate fulfillment of wishes, without any consideration of delay or
consequences. The underlying ego weakness and the incapacity to tolerate frustration leave these adolescents unable to deal effectively with
tension and delay of gratification. Impulsiveness is ego-syntonic and
becomes a desperate attempt to confirm the illusion of omnipotence
and to deny underlying fears of rejection and punishment.

The failure in adolescent identity formation may also express itself
in an "as-if" resolution, similar to that seen in adult cases. These
adolescents appear to have normal intellectual and emotional capacities, but with the same lack of authenticity and imitative compliance
seen in their adult counterparts. They are unable to experience feelings
deeply, or to grasp empathically the experience of others. When they

attach themselves to ideologies, the beliefs are not genuinely internalized but rather are based on imitative attitudes and compliance with the expectations of the group. They generally tend to be passive, easily influenced, often suggestible, and often rapidly and radically variable, depending on the input from significant others to whom they may be attached at any given moment (Grinberg and Grinberg 1974).

More systematic efforts have been made to catalog the variations in adolescent borderline phenomena. Goldstein and Jones (1977), reporting on research on high-risk samples from the UCLA Family Project, defined four groups of disturbed adolescents that would seem to fall within the borderline range. The aggressive-antisocial group manifests poorly controlled, impulsive, acting-out behavior. Any degree of inner tension or subjective distress is subordinate to the aggressive disturbances in many areas of functioning, i.e., family, school, peer relations, the law. The second group is involved in active family conflict, characterized by a defiant, disrespectful stance toward parents and belligerence and antagonism in the family setting. Few manifestations of aggression or rebelliousness appear outside the family. The passive-negative group is negativistic and sullen, and shows indirect forms of hostility or defiance toward parents and other authorities. Overt defiance and temper outbursts are infrequent, and there is a superficial compliance to adults' wishes. School difficulties usually take the form of underachievement with little disruptive behavior. Finally, the withdrawn, socially isolated group is characterized by marked isolation, general uncommunicativeness, few, if any, friends, and excessive dependence on one or both parents. Gross fears or signs of marked anxiety and tension are often present. Much of their unstructured time is spent in solitary pursuits.

Another approach tries to articulate adolescent parallels to the Grinker groups. The first group would include the majority of disturbed nonschizophrenic adolescents who are transiently psychotic, act out destructively, and usually have to be hospitalized. The next group manifests precursors in drug and behavior problems that later evolve in a borderline direction. The third group often escapes diagnosis, since they tend to be passive followers, compliantly adapting rather than disruptively rebelling. The last group may look like affective disorders, often reacting to the loss of a dependent relationship. In all these groups the features of the borderline syndrome are not clearly defined (Simon 1984).

A potential borderline disorder may be suggested by behavioral syndromes frequently associated with borderline personality structure.

The presence of such a behavioral syndrome in an adolescent raises the index of suspicion for one of the borderline diagnoses. Such behavioral syndromes include: suicide (Gunderson and Singer 1975, Meissner 1977a, 1984a, 1986b), addiction and alcoholism (Kernberg 1967, Wurmser 1978, Meissner 1981a, 1984a, 1986b), antisocial personality (Kernberg 1975a, 1978, Meissner 1984a), and homosexuality/transsexuality (Socarides 1968, 1980, Meyer 1982, Meissner 1984a).

Developmental Conclusions.   These observations allow us to draw several conclusions. The onset of puberty imposes a fundamental biological and developmental stress on already existing borderline vulnerabilities. Symptoms in a borderline child will continue into adolescent years. In many cases, however, behavior and adjustment difficulties begin to assert themselves in early adolescence for the first time, suggesting that the young person's borderline psychic structure has not been previously evident, and that the stress induced by adolescent development makes the underlying borderline features apparent. It is not at all clear that in the transition out of childhood, in the early phases of adolescence, sufficient diagnostic discrimination can be made among borderline syndromes. At the early adolescent level, we may have to settle for relatively gross discriminations regarding problems in ego integration and the capacity to handle adaptively the stresses of the adolescent period. Where such capacities have failed to develop or are seriously impeded, borderline dysfunction may be relatively severe. However, the underlying borderline impediments may not manifest themselves directly as disruptions in behavior or adaptive functioning, but may become apparent only in the failure to resolve adolescent developmental crises in late adolescence and even early adulthood. Such individuals may achieve adequate or even high levels of adaptation and social orientation, but ultimately may run aground on the tasks of adult orientation and adjustment, particularly establishment of a definitive sense of identity and commitment to a definite life course of career or work achievement and object involvement. The underlying borderline features in such higher-order borderlines would not become evident in the ordinary run of day-to-day experience, and may become manifest only under the highly specific and specialized regressive conditions of the analytic couch.

     In the early phases of adolescent development, the articulation of borderline syndromes is relatively imprecise and vague, and must remain so, at least for the time being, as a function of the degree of rapid and uncertain change that is taking place. In later phases of adolescent development, however, the evolving configurations of adolescent borderline structures begin to approximate the categories identifiable in more adult patients. Although the adolescent process lends a certain increased lability and fluidity to these formations, this gradually diminishes, so that as adolescents move toward adulthood, they approximate one or another of the more recognizable borderline categories, as previously described. As Rinsley (1980) observed:

> Clinical experience with these adolescent patients attests to the borderline early adolescent's symptomatic similarity to the borderline latency child, hence to the latter's more protean, psychotic-like clinical appearance. As the borderline adolescent traverses middle and late adolescence, the clinical picture in many cases comes increasingly to resemble that of the borderline adult. [p. 160]

However, there are also cases in which the borderline features escape detection and come to light only in the progressive failure of the individual to complete the developmental tasks of adolescence and to enter the world of effective adult participation.

2

PROGNOSIS

The treatment of borderline patients is generally regarded as difficult, regardless of the therapeutic approach. Inevitably the therapist encounters severe transference and countertransference problems, marked by frequent interruptions and premature terminations. While the prognosis is guarded in all cases, a more optimistic appraisal depends on the level of pathological deficits and the availability of ego resources. Thus, an opinion has been developing over the years that at least some borderline patients are potentially analyzable (Blum 1972, Abend et al. 1983, Kernberg 1984).

Based on the diagnostic framework provided by the spectrum view of borderline disorders, both the prognosis and the determination of an optimal treatment approach are functions of where the individual patient falls along the continuum of psychopathological severity. Patients who fall at the lower end of the borderline spectrum can be expected to show a worse prognosis than patients who fall at the higher end (Stone 1987). Since the diagnostic trend in many extant studies focuses at the lower end of the borderline spectrum, an effort will be made here to discriminate prognostic factors in terms of the level of pathological integration. Factors of analyzability and decisions about the form of psychotherapeutic intervention are discussed later in this chapter.

THE PROGNOSIS OF BORDERLINE INPATIENTS

Hospitalization

Severely disturbed borderline patients who require hospitalization are usually prone to frequent suicide attempts, to violent acting out both inside and outside the hospital, and seem to be unable to function adequately in social and occupational settings. In the hospital setting, these patients usually have a high rate of discharges against medical advice, are frequent escapees, and have a high rate of self-mutilative or suicidal attempts (Friedman et al. 1983), which require suicide precautions in the hospital. Where paranoid or manic defenses are identifiable, the prognosis is worsened (Simon 1984); the same can be said for antisocial traits (Kernberg 1984).

For such lower-order patients, hospitalization is frequently required to deal with potential acting-out or self-destructive behavior, and/or as a vehicle for establishing a meaningful therapeutic relation and alliance (Masterson 1972, Simon 1984). Masterson indicates an 80 percent success rate for a selected group of such patients, but even here successful inpatient hospital treatment was often followed by relapse after discharge. A particularly ominous prognostic indicator is addiction to heroin before hospitalization. Of the successful patients, none had been addicted to heroin (Masterson 1972).

Long-Term Outcome

The long-term outcome for lower-order borderline patients seems to be more optimistic than that for comparable psychotic patients. A four-teen-year follow-up of schizotypal and borderline personality disorders (roughly equivalent to the pseudoschizophrenics and primitive affective personality disorders) indicated that when borderline personality disorders did not have an accompanying affective disorder, the long-term outcome was better than that of schizophrenia, but about the same as affect disorder patients. At admission, schizotypal patients, who would presumably have a significant loading of schizophrenic genetic factors, functioned better than schizophrenics but not better than patients with affective disorders. The long-term outcome for such patients seems to lie closer to the picture for schizophrenic patients and is less optimistic than for borderline patients as defined by DSM III (McGlashan 1986). The borderline personalities who also manifested signs of affective disorder had a less benign outcome at follow-up than those patients who did not have affective disorder. Those patients who fulfilled criteria for both the borderline and schizotypal personality disorders according to DSM III criteria were equivalent to schizophrenics at the time of admission, but were functioning at a significantly higher level at the time of follow-up (Plakun et al. 1985). Similar follow-up evaluation of lower-order borderline as compared with schizophrenic subjects suggests that borderlines do much better than schizophrenics on measures such as readmission rates, Global Assessment Scale ratings, death and suicide rates, and level of functioning (Stone 1986, 1987). They also do better on measures of living situation, time out of hospital, current treatment, work involvement, heterosexual activity, and global functioning (McGlashan 1986). But the overall picture is not optimistic.

Testing

Diagnostic testing, particularly the use of the Rorschach, has proved a useful adjunct in the assessment of treatability and prognosis. Assessment of the level of psychosexual organization, the degree of humanness as opposed to the alien character of responses, the degree of conflict and oral aggressive themes, and the vulnerability to separation and loss have all been established as useful prognostic indicators. Assessment of the quality of the patient's object relationships and the intensity of oral aggressive imagery were closely related to the state of the therapeutic alliance. Particularly the number and quality of human movement responses seemed to predict the patient's motivation for treatment and the capacity for alliance (Frieswyk and Colson 1980). These factors were predictive both for outcome at the termination of hospitalization and at the same time of a two-year follow-up after hospital discharge. Particularly useful was the assessment of the patient's capacity to establish an effective and collaborative alliance with the examiner in the course of the testing procedure. As Frieswyk and Colson (1980) note:

> In brief, then, an examination of the patient-examiner relationship in the testing situation helps us to anticipate the patient's readiness to enter into a collaborative exploration of unspoken impediments to the formation of a useful alliance. The question, answered in part in that early test relationship, is whether or not it will be possible to facilitate the completion of a task, whether it be a diagnostic or treatment task, and whether or not in the treatment setting one will, with this patient, be able to pursue and attain therapeutic goals. [pp. 251-252]

OUTPATIENT TREATMENT

Difficulties

The outpatient treatment of lower-order borderline conditions is equally challenging, difficult, and uncertain. These patients are difficult to keep in outpatient psychotherapy and frequently disrupt or prematurely terminate such therapy. The therapy is often marked by episodes of impulsive and self-destructive behavior, intense and provocative anger, transient psychotic episodes, and characteristically difficult patterns of relating to the therapist, which create significant countertransference difficulties and put the therapeutic alliance in constant jeopardy. Such patients tend to have a history of previous psychiatric hospitalization and frequent histories of psychotropic medication (most typically diazepam, chlordiazepoxide, and thioridazine). After evaluation a high percentage were referred out of the clinic for treatment (40 percent versus 17 percent of patients with neurotic disorders). Another 40 percent of these patients dropped out of treatment within the first three months of therapy (Skodol et al. 1983).

The result of this study was that patients diagnosed as borderline received the least treatment of any group of patients, in terms both of the percentage of patients actually starting treatment and of the length of the course of treatment. The authors suggest that this result is the effect of a tendency to refer out the most difficult, provocative, and least desirable patients, and reflects the inherent difficulties of managing the early stages of therapy. They also comment that those patients who were taken into treatment and who showed significant improvement were among the least disturbed and least characteristically borderline of the entire sample (Skodol et al. 1983). This might suggest some differentiation in the effectiveness of treatment for those patients who are decidedly in the lower borderline range as opposed to others who may function at a higher level. Even obsessional patients who also manifest schizotypal features tend to have a high rate of treatment failure (Jenike et al. 1986).

In discussing the treatment of schizotypal patients, Stone (1983b, 1985) notes that the more the patient manifests schizophreniclike symptoms (social avoidance, oddity, suspiciousness, and so on), the less the tendency to show improvement as a result of therapeutic intervention. These patients did not get markedly worse; they simply did not move to any great extent in either direction. Improvement was at best slow and uncertain. Positive prognostic indicators included a capacity for emotional warmth and the ability to relate empathically with others. Patients with a predominance of schizoid, paranoid, or narcissistic traits seemed to make little progress in treatment. Stone (1986) also describes a frequently observed natural course of evolution of borderline conditions. A period of about ten years of impulsivity, chaotic relations, and poor functioning is followed by a turning point leading to a more stable life situation and more adequate adjustment. Evaluation of such patients five years after discharge would not reveal much difference from their schizophrenic counterparts; evaluation after fifteen years, however, would show a considerable difference.

In addition, parameters of personality organization or style may offer some indications of prognosis. Kernberg (1971) has provided some useful discriminations. Where paranoid, schizophrenic, or hypomanic characteristics predominate, prognosis is relatively limited. With paranoid patients, prognosis depends to a large extent on the patient's capacity for entering a trusting therapeutic alliance and on the degree of delusional fixity of the paranoid system. Schizoid patients have difficulties in entering a meaningful therapeutic relationship and often strain the therapist's capacity or willingness to engage with an evasive and withdrawn patient. Prognosis for hypomanic personalities depends to a large extent on their capacity to tolerate depression, but this capacity is relatively limited in lower-order borderline patients, who may at the same time be suffering from some degree of affective disorder.

Kernberg makes a strong argument against the advisability of psychotherapeutic treatment for antisocial personalities. Much depends on the degree of antisocial deviance and the extent to which this reflects superego deficits as opposed to adolescent rebellion or other acting out on the basis of authority or dependency conflicts. Similar considerations apply to the assessment of narcissistic features in borderline patients. All borderline patients have narcissistic difficulties, but of varying degree. In the lower-order borderline spectrum, these difficulties are often severe and reflect the high degree of pathological organization of narcissistic structures. In such patients, particularly when the narcissistic organization is permeated by relatively primitive and intense aggressive issues, prognosis is severely limited (Kernberg 1971, 1984). By the same token, patients who are afflicted with drug addiction or alcoholism also have a limited prognosis; if the pathological symptom can be sufficiently controlled or the patient maintained within a protective environment, prognosis may be somewhat better.

Long-Term Outcome

Studies of long-term outcome of the psychotherapeutic treatment of lower-order borderline patients have provided a variety of findings, but there is a general consensus on some points. The results of the Chestnut Lodge follow-up study (McGlashan 1985) offered the following conclusions:

- The outcome results reflect substantial interpersonal variability.

- Predictive factors related to premorbid functioning are notably absent.

- The strongest predictors of good global outcome were high IQ, a lack of affective lability or instability, and the shorter length of previous hospitalization.

- Other predictive variables included a lack of family history of substance abuse, better premorbid heterosexual functioning, lower levels of stress at periods of regression, the absence of schizotypal traits, the availability of affects without accompanying evidence of affective disorder, a capacity for control of aggression in relation to objects, and lack of evidence of chronicity (shorter period of hospitalization and discharge rather than transfer to another institution).

- The prediction of some outcome measures by premorbid counterparts, e.g., the frequency of hospitalization after discharge with the history of hospitalization prior to the index admission, or the level of symptomatic intensity during the follow-up with the length of index hospitalization. Difficulties with intimacy in the follow-up period seem to be modestly predicted by difficulties in intimacy in the premorbid period.

The Waldinger and Gunderson study (1984, 1987) evaluated the psychotherapeutic experience of a group of relatively seasoned therapists treating a broad spectrum of borderline patients. Only half of these private-practice patients continued the treatment beyond six months, and only one-third actually completed the treatment process. More than half of these patients were treated in psychoanalysis, the rest in intensive psychotherapy. Over half of the patients terminated the treatment gradually, rather than precipitously, and only 40 percent terminated with the therapist's approval. Nearly a quarter terminated because of a therapeutic impasse.

This study indicates that even in the private-practice setting the treatment of borderline patients is at best difficult and uncertain, and that improvement as a result of therapy is the exception rather than the rule. In general, the longer patients are in treatment, the greater the degree of improvement, and the more previously effective therapy the patient has had, the better the outcome (Waldinger and Gunderson 1987). The results also suggest that there is an important place for a psychoanalytic approach to the treatment of at least some borderline patients. Analytic patients generally showed the highest degree of improvement on measures of object relatedness and the degree of integration of a sense of self. However, these same patients showed the least improvement on measures of behavior and ego functioning.

Prognostic Indicators

Starting from Kernberg's (1971) emphasis on type of character pathology, ego weakness, degree of superego integration, and quality of object relationships as prognostic indicators, Woollcott (1985) adds a more detailed list. Negative prognostic indicators include a history of brutalization in the early environment; severe behavioral problems in childhood, including poor schoolwork and early work adjustment; indications of antisocial behavior, e.g., cruelty to animals or other children; a family history suggesting borderline or psychotic parents or the presence of schizophrenic or manic-depressive disorder; addictions including alcoholism; the degree of ego syntonicity of symptoms, the severity of primitive defensive operations; the degree of superego pathology; the presence of abulia and/or anhedonia; superficial or highly disturbed object relationships; the presence of major losses or separations; highly pathological narcissistic features; and in the course of therapy itself, the presence of strong negative reactions of the therapist toward the patient, the tendency for antisocial acting out, the development of a negative therapeutic reaction, and the presence of dreams or fantasies in which the content is mutilative, self-destructive, or catastrophic. Indicators that suggest a more optimistic prognosis and help to promote the therapeutic relationship include nonspecific positive personality traits such as warmth, reliability, likableness, interest in people, and the presence of intact sublimatory capacities and skills. In general, Woollcott feels that borderline patients with infantile features probably have a better prognosis and those with narcissistic features a worse prognosis than is generally recognized. He correctly observes that the quality of object relations, particularly those reflected in the therapist–patient relationship and influencing the development of countertransference reactions, is crucial.

In dealing with the higher-order forms of borderline pathology, in both the hysterical and schizoid continua, the prognostic indicators are generally more favorable, either for psychoanalysis or for psychoanalytic psychotherapy. Thus, the primitive hysterics and dysphoric personalities would generally be considered as potential candidates at least for psychoanalytic psychotherapy, if not psychoanalysis in some cases. A similar point is made by Stone (1979, 1980), who groups patients with character types of a more neurotic quality (hysterical, obsessive, depressive/masochistic, phobic, infantile, passive dependent and narcissistic) as more likely to respond to the psychoanalytic method. The question of the discrimination of analyzability will be treated in a later section. In the schizoid continuum, patients suffering from identity stasis have a reasonably good prognosis, but the outcome depends to a large extent on the length of treatment and the willingness of both the patient and therapist to endure over the long haul. The prognosis of the other schizoid variants depends in large measure on the degree of available ego strength and the patient's capacity to establish and maintain a therapeutic alliance. In some cases the prognosis may be excellent and in others guarded at best, but in large measure this assessment is difficult to make outside of a trial of therapy.

In terms of Kernberg's (1971, 1984) breakdown of forms of character pathology, the hysterical and infantile personalities (roughly corresponding to primitive hysterics) would be regarded as having a better prognosis, although Kernberg would rule out psychoanalysis for infantile personalities. Some of his infantile personalities and the impulse-ridden character disorders (probably corresponding to dysphoric personalities) have a more guarded prognosis depending on the degree of ego weakness and the stability of object relationships. Kernberg's view of narcissistic personalities places them largely within the borderline range, especially those with more primitive and unintegrated narcissistic features. These patients occupy some portion of the higher-order borderline range, with more primitive and pathological forms of narcissistic deviation (malignant narcissism) probably falling within the lower-order spectrum. The more narcissistic disorders are permeated by sadistic-aggressive components, the more likely it is that the pathology is borderline (Meissner 1984a); where the sadistic elements call for enactment rather than fantasy formation, the prognosis worsens (Kohut 1977). Where higher forms of defensive organization are part of the clinical picture, as in the obsessive-compulsive or depressive-masochistic personalities, the prognosis improves. A similar alignment of forms of character pathology and their respective prognoses has been developed by Stone (1979, 1980). Phobic and passive-dependent types of personality would also be regarded as having a generally better outlook.

ANALYZABILITY OF BORDERLINE SYNDROMES

There are certainly significant problems inherent in an attempt to assess the analyzability of borderline patients. The literature on borderline assessment and diagnosis deals primarily with what I have described as lower-order borderline conditions. This is true of both the early literature on borderline psychopathology, which associated borderline states with the psychoses and tended to regard borderline pathology primarily as a modified form of schizophrenia, as well as later formulations that have been so strongly influenced by the views of Kernberg. Kernberg's assessment of borderline personality organization presents something of a caricature of borderline conditions, emphasizing the more regressive or primitive aspects. As long as that assessment holds sway, there is little room for an analytic approach to these conditions.

The approach here contends that the criteria of analyzability as applied to cases within the borderline spectrum must be significantly modified from those developed in traditional psychoanalytic terms. It would also seem to be quite rare that the classical psychoanalytic technique could be carried out with borderline patients of any description without the introduction of significant parameters. Thus, the discussion that follows shares in the basic conundrum common to all current approaches to the widening scope of psychoanalysis, namely, to what extent can the parameters necessary for adapting psychoanalytic technique to more primitive forms of character pathology be consistent with the basic requirements of the psychoanalytic modality and still be regarded as authentically psychoanalytic rather than psychotherapeutic? Does the patient have the resources to utilize and respond to the psychoanalytic modality, however modified by parameters, with the anticipation of a better therapeutic result than might be undertaken in a more explicitly psychotherapeutic approach? Thus, the traditionally problematic questions of what constitutes the essence of psychoanalysis and what separates it from psychotherapeutic modalities continue to plague us.

THE ASSESSMENT OF BORDERLINE PATIENTS
FOR PSYCHOANALYSIS

The presence of borderline features or a borderline diagnosis has, in the traditional view, been considered a major contraindication to psychoanalysis (Knapp et al. 1960, Waldhorn 1960, Appel 1974). However, these assessments of borderline pathology usually connoted serious psychopathology akin to the psychoses—predominantly the lower-order borderline conditions. Given this diagnostic context and its implications, there would be little disagreement that such patients would not be suitable for the analytic situation. This conclusion would fail to consider the entire group of higher-order borderline cases.

Abend and colleagues (1983) argue that assessment techniques for these patients are no different from those for any prospective analysand. The assessment focuses on the capacity to work within the analytic setting and to profit from it, the stability or flexibility of the defensive structure, the use of primitive defenses, the quality of object relations, the level of ego strength, the extent of tendencies to impulsive or destructive behavior, and the nature of the patient's motivation. Conclusions from initial assessments are tentative and often require a trial of analysis. Kohut (1971) has also encouraged a trial of analysis for these more difficult patients.

Certain borderline features, when seen in their more acute and regressive forms, would contraindicate psychoanalysis as the treatment of choice. Primary among these are the ego deficits that have been noted in relatively regressive borderline conditions. Analysis would be contraindicated by the levels of fixation and developmental failure and the demands on the ego to defend against regression (Glover 1955). Lapses in reality testing can give rise to magical expectations and an inability to maintain the discrimination between fantasy and reality in the face of the analytic regression (Waldhorn 1960). Such patients may resort to more primitive defenses including denial, projection, magical thinking, hypomanic defenses, and acting out (Guttman 1960). One of the significant findings of the Menninger study (Kernberg et al. 1972) was that patients with significant ego weakness (equivalent to Kernberg's borderlines) did poorly in psychoanalytic treatment, primarily because of poor tolerance for regression and the susceptibility to transference psychosis. Such vulnerable patients are usually difficult to distinguish without a trial of analysis. Attempts to work through primitive transferences may precipitate psychotic regression, acting out, or disruption of the therapeutic alliance. Certain cases of apparently narcissistic pathology may be defending against an underlying psychosis (Rothstein 1982).

The tendency for unstable transference reactions and the vulnerability to transference psychosis in borderline patients have been frequently noted (Guttman 1960, Waldhorn 1960, Goldberg 1974, Kernberg 1974, 1984). Emergence of a transference psychosis is generally regarded as destructive of the analytic situation and a major contraindication. Similarly, in some borderline patients the incapacity to form an effective therapeutic alliance and the unavailability of a reasonably cooperative ego capable of engaging with the analyst in a collaborative and exploratory undertaking were seen as an essential impediment for analysis. Adler (1979) has even questioned the capacity of these patients to form a therapeutic alliance. This view clearly focuses on the more primitive lower-order forms of borderline pathology, who may lack the capacity to achieve stable, evocative memories. Such individuals would be unable to sustain the memory of an object in the absence of that object. Such a marked cognitive deficit would certainly interfere with the capacity for forming stable object relations, let alone entering into a meaningful therapeutic alliance. Other impediments arise from developmental deficits that may shift the relationship toward a narcissistic alliance or narcissistic misalliance (Meissner 1981b). Such patients may participate in the arrangements for analysis without any commitment or meaningful involvement in the process. Magical expectations take the place of motivations for work and change.

The analytic requirement that the patient be able to tolerate a reasonable degree of frustration and anxiety is also one that tends to eliminate certain borderline patients. The analytic situation places a considerable demand on the patient for delay of gratification and for frustration of a variety of wishes and desires, and tends to stimulate a significant degree of anxiety—all of which must be tolerated and worked through for the analytic process to have effect. Patients whose personalities are organized along infantile and more primitively narcissistic lines have great difficulty in sustaining this degree of frustration and anxiety (Waldhorn 1960).

We have already noted the frequency of paranoid attitudes or persecutory anxieties in borderline patients. Such attitudes may be reflected in an intense degree of persecutory anxiety in relationship to the analyst, or may be manifest more subtly as antisocial or rebellious attitudes toward authority figures, often expressed in indirect and muted fashion (Meissner 1978c).

The quality of anxiety may also serve as a contraindication to analysis, since the anxiety is frequently of a more primitive and destructive form than signal anxiety. In borderline patients, the anxiety is frequently traumatic and overwhelming, and stems from relatively primitive developmental levels, expressing itself as a fear of separation, fear of loss of love or the loved object, and even more primitively at times in psychoticlike fears of annihilation. In addition, because of the relatively infantile and often highly narcissistic quality of the borderline patient's personality structure, the motivation for analytic work is based on the instinctual push for gratification or narcissistic completion that expresses itself in magical expectations for a cure by way of symbiotic attachment to a powerful, sustaining analyst-object (Levine 1979, Rothstein 1982). Such motivations leave something to be desired for the successful outcome of the analytic process.

Despite this catalog of characteristics that would exclude borderline patients from the analytic couch, there have been indications, even in terms of the somewhat slanted view of borderline pathology pervading the earlier literature, that left room for the possibility that some borderline patients could in fact be analyzable. In his comments on the widening scope of psychoanalysis, Stone (1954) questioned whether the presumed inability of such patients to develop an effective transference might have more to do with the intensity and ambivalence of transference reactions than with any underlying incapacity. Reflecting the views of the Kris Study Group on Analyzability, Waldhorn (1960) included some questionable borderline states among cases that might be suitable for psychoanalysis. Similary, Greenson (1967) included certain borderline conditions among those patients whom he saw as questionably analyzable, along with impulse neuroses, perversions, addictions, and delinquencies. Diatkine (1968) even went so far as to say that despite the relative intensity and acuteness of symptomatology, some borderline patients may in fact be easier to analyze than some more rigid and resistant neurotics. Kernberg (1968) has also expressed the view that some borderline patients seem to benefit little from the expressive approach he recommends, and for these patients psychoanalysis may be the treatment of choice. The patients he describes, however, seem to be akin to the narcissistic personality disorders—a group that he regards as borderline but that can be distinguished as a separate, potentially analyzable group (Kohut 1971, Meissner 1984a).

The question remains, then, as to the specific criteria for identifying the analyzable borderline. There is general agreement that such an assessment cannot be made on the basis of the intensity or acuteness of the patient's symptoms. Some patients may show little or no sympto-matic disturbance, yet have an underlying borderline structure. Others may develop severe and disturbing symptoms, even symptoms that may appear for a time psychotic, but prove on further experience to have a sufficient degree of stability of inner psychic structure and capacity to permit them to undertake analytic work with considerable success. For this reason, Kernberg's (1977) emphasis on structural diagnosis has been both illuminating and helpful.

What follows is a discussion of some of the criteria of borderline analyzability in terms of the categories provided by Greenspan and Cullander (1973).

Ego Intactness

The basic perceptual and motor functions in borderline patients are generally intact and functional. Adler (1979, 1985), Adler and Buie (1979), and Buie and Adler (1982–1983) raise a particular question, however, regarding the failure of the capacity for evocative memory as a major developmental impediment in borderline psychopathology. The failure to achieve stable, evocative memory of affective object relationships causes some of these patients to react to stress by regress-ing to the level of merely recognitional memory. Stressful events usually involve the loss of important people in their lives, or even the fantasied loss of love or support from them. This deficit typically takes the form of the incapacity to recover positive images or fantasies of the helpful, loving, sustaining people in the patients' life experience, present and past; rather they remain vulnerable to negative, painful, hurtful, or destructive images. In my view, the disturbed memory functioning in such patients is less likely to be due to developmental ego defects than to selective regressive functioning in the face of particular stresses related to borderline regression. More often than not in such patients, memory capacities remain intact in other nonaffectively involved areas of their functioning.

While the ego apparatus is generally intact in borderline patients, the ego functions remain vulnerable to regression. The evaluation of the level of functioning of various aspects of the patients' ego is a matter of primary importance (Abend et al. 1983). Particularly important is the capacity for testing reality, which generally remains relatively intact in borderline patients. Reality testing is not a matter of presence or absence but is subject to wide variations in degree (Abend et al. 1983, Meissner 1984a, b), and thus calls for careful assessment. Total failure is the hallmark of psychosis (Kernberg 1984), but this capacity is often vulnerable in borderline patients, particularly those closer to the psychotic range.

When the patient's reality testing seems fragile and is frequently subject to regressive crises, analysis would not seem suitable, since the regressive pulls of the analytic situation would put considerable pressure on this function. But in some borderline patients the capacity to test reality shows no such vulnerability, nor has it been lost to any significant degree, even in regressive crises. For these patients, the prognosis would be more optimistic. Other borderline patients may show infrequent weakening of this capacity, or may reveal some vulnerability only in certain selected areas of their experience, usually involving significant object relationships. The disturbance is usually mild, and while it is not the most optimistic indicator for psychoanalytic work, neither is it a forthright contraindication.

The patient's cognitive organization also requires assessment. When the clinical examination reveals a frank thought disorder and a tendency to primary process thinking, it is likely that other severe structural problems are present, so that such patients are probably not suitable for analysis. Frequently, however, borderline patients do not reveal any suggestion of thought disorder clinically, but may manifest varying degrees of thought disturbance on projective testing. An assessment of the extent and degree of such disorganization would be important: if the disturbance is relatively mild in degree and does not otherwise interfere with the ego's functioning, this need not serve as a contraindication to analysis.

Ego Flexibility

To what degree can the ego tolerate internal conflict without significant disruption in functioning? If the ego's neurotic formations and defensive organization tends to be excessively rigid, this does not augur well for analysis. Stress in borderline patients may lead to breakdowns of ego functioning in the form of temporary loss of reality testing, fragmentation of the sense of self, loss of the synthetic capacity to integrate thought and affect, or even severe states of inhibition or alteration of drive gratification. A retreat to severe restriction or relatively primitive defense organization probably reflects underlying structural defects and suggests a primitive borderline organization. The degree of such loss of function and the ease of rapidity of recovery would be of central concern.

Vulnerability to regression is a particularly important question. When the capacity to maintain adequate ego functioning is too easily or too frequently lost, or when the extent of regression is relatively severe, that is, when the regression precipitates a reaction of psychotic or near-psychotic proportions, analysis is contraindicated. More often than not, many borderline patients, particularly those in the higher order of the borderline range, experience only mild and infrequent regressive episodes that are not necessarily a contraindication to analysis. It is also critically important to assess such patients at their general and characterological level of functioning, rather than in relatively infrequent regressive phases.

Autonomous Ego Functions

From the perspective of the borderline spectrum, not all borderline patients show the signs of ego weakness that Kernberg attributes to borderline psychopathology. Through most of their life experience, many borderline patients show little or no signs of ego weakness, or may show them only on rare occasions under conditions of regressive stress. The assessment of autonomous ego functions must evaluate the capacity of the patient to function in a conflict-free manner. The patient may retain this capacity in many areas of life, or may manifest a relative inability to function in a conflict-free manner in certain isolated contexts. When such is the case, it augurs well for the analytic process; but when the degree and extent of conflict-ridden functioning are excessive, successful analytic work becomes less likely.

The patient's ability to regress in the service of the ego is also of considerable importance, since it is essential to the psychoanalytic process. The crucial issue is the extent to which the patient can undergo a therapeutic regression without accompanying structural regression, without the loss or disruption of ego functioning. The more such autonomous functions are interfered with by conflict, the less optimistic is the prognosis.

Superego Functioning

The neurotic suffers from a relatively severe and punitive superego, but the superego is sufficiently integrated so that the conflict remains intrapsychic. At the borderline level, however, the superego tends to be even more highly punitive and destructive, and at the same time less well integrated. This results in often contradictory superego demands that may be sadistic, prohibitive, or self-devaluing on the one hand, while primitive ego-ideal demands for omnipotence, power, and perfection persist on the other hand. This may take the form of contradictions in value systems and severe mood swings (Kernberg 1976a).

The propensity of patients to project superego components, thus externalizing the essential conflict, is of critical importance to the assessment of analyzability and reflects the lack of ego-superego integration. This tendency undermines the patient's capacity for concern for others and for guilt. When this tendency is severe, as it often is in lower-order borderline patients, the patient may manifest a variety of paranoid traits, utilizing relative primitive forms of projection and externalization. The critical variable is the extent to which such projective distortions are transient and remain within reach of the patient's capacity to test reality and to integrate projective distortions with other sources of information. If that capacity is impaired or lacking, analysis would be contraindicated.

Affects

Important elements are the patient's capacity for meaningful affective expression and the extent to which affects can become disruptive or disorganizing. Predominant affects are anxiety and depression. Prognosis hinges on the extent to which affects are meaningfully connected to a suitable context and if the patient can tolerate them without undue regression. When they are essentially related to intrapsychic conflicts and not unduly incapacitating (that is, resulting in regressive loss of ego functioning), the prognosis is relatively optimistic. Developmentally immature affects (severe emotional hunger, fear, rage, jealousy, and envy) are characteristically borderline, but to what degree do they pervade the patient's inner world, and to what extent can they be modified? If they have some degree of flexibility and selectivity, particularly in appropriate stimulus contexts (rage in one context, empathy in another), the prognosis would be more optimistic than if the range of affects were more constricted and were experienced indiscriminately in a variety of situations.

It is important to assess both the depth and the intensity of anxiety and depression. The anxiety should be primarily signal anxiety, and the patient should have the capacity to tolerate a significant degree of anxiety without regression. If the anxiety becomes too quickly traumatic, and the patient resorts to regression or to more primitive defenses, the outlook is less promising. If the anxiety is predominantly related to intrapsychic conflict, this would seem to be a more optimistic indicator than if it were object-related (fears of separation, loss of love, object loss, or even annihilation).

Assessment of the intensity and depth of depression should be made. If the depression is primarily reactive and proportional to the stimulus context, this would be a good prognostic indicator. The patient's capacity to mourn significant losses is an important index of the potential success of the analytic process. If the tendency to depression overrides the capacity for mourning, prognosis would be less optimistic (Goldberg 1974). In addition, if the depression tends to be long in duration and/or relatively severe (to the point of suicidal impulses), this becomes a less optimistic index. However, even suicidal impulses must be put into context and cannot be assessed independently as a separate prognostic indicator. Many borderline patients experience suicidal impulses in regressive states; but such states may be relatively rare in their experience, and at the level of their normal characterological functioning, the suicidal intentions are absent. For such patients, the exceptional suicidal element becomes of less prognostic significance.

Drive Organization

Faulty integration of both pregenital and genital drive components is typical in borderline patients. Even where the drive components have achieved more or less stable genital organization, pregenital elements will characteristically be found to contaminate the drive organization. The predominance of primitive oral aggression to which Kernberg ascribes much of borderline pathology is relatively rare, or is seen more characteristically in primitive lower-order forms of borderline organization (Snyder and Pitts 1985). When such primitive aggressive drives come to dominate the drive organization, this would serve as an important contraindication to psychoanalytic work.

It is also important, however, to assess whether the apparent fixations actually represent points of developmental failure, or whether they represent regressive retreats to such fixation points from a level of higher developmental achievement. The assessment of patients in regressive phases does not offer a sufficient basis for this determination but must wait for the longer-term assessment of the patients' levels of characterological functioning. When the drive organization is predominantly pregenital and reflects either major fixations or arrested development, prognosis suffers. When the pregenital elements are primarily regressive, much depends on the frequency, intensity, and depth of the regression. For many borderline patients, particularly those of the higher-order type, such regressions are not characteristic.

Defensive Organization

Borderline patients tend to use a variety of defensive mechanisms and behaviors, including higher-order and primitive forms (Abend et al. 1983). More primitive forms of defense organization are found at lower levels of the borderline spectrum, but higher and lower forms of defense are identifiable throughout. The extent to which the borderline patient resorts to primitive narcissistic defenses, particularly projection, denial, and distortion, suggests the degree of ego weakness. Severe ego weakness would preclude successful analytic work. Borderline patients generally employ a combination of immature and neurotic defenses (Meissner 1980b). In regressive crises, the drive organization tends to shift toward a more immature and narcissistic level. Adequate assessment of the defense organization in any patient requires an assessment of the patient's defensive functioning at more typically characterological levels as well as the regressive. As with all such assessments of regressive crises, the duration and ready reversibility of the regression are key. In many borderline patients, such regressive shifts in defensive organization are relatively rare and consequently may not contraindicate psychoanalysis. The primitive defenses described by Kernberg, including denial, projection, primitive idealization, omnipotent control, omnipotence, and devaluation, are more frequently manifested in regressive states or in more primitively organized borderline personalities who would not be suitable for analytic work.

Relationship Potential

The patient's capacity for object relationships is a direct index of the transference potential and the capacity for therapeutic alliance. The Menninger Study (Kernberg et al. 1972) concluded that patients with a history of poor object relations tended to do poorly in psychoanalysis and that patients with a more optimistic history of object relationships did better. Poor object relations carried great prognostic weight, especially when combined with a significant degree of ego weakness. The patient's capacity for enduring, meaningful, and intimate relationships with significant figures is central. The lack of such a capacity does not augur well for psychoanalytic undertaking. An important aspect of this assessment is the degree of ambivalence, hostility, or outright sadism in preoedipal object relationships. The more troubled, disruptive, or traumatic such relationships might have been in the patient's history, the less optimistic the prognosis. If the patient has in some degree achieved preoedipal developmental tasks, including the capacity to accept limitations in one-to-one relationships without feeling either rejected or devalued, as well as a capacity to tolerate the separation from important objects of dependence, this would tend to support a more positive prognosis.

Evaluation of the capacity to enter into a meaningful therapeutic alliance is a particularly useful and important aspect in the assessment of the patient's relationship potential. The extent to which the patient can enter into a reasonable and cooperative collaboration with the analyst would go a long way toward contributing to a more optimistic prognosis. The clear lack of such capacity is a strong contraindication to psychoanalytic involvement. Often in the assessment of some patients a trial interpretation is useful as a measure of the extent to which the patient can actually engage in collaborative reflection with the therapist.

Motivation

The nature of the patient's motivation plays a central role in the assessment of borderline patients, as in the assessment of any patient for analysis. The basic issue is the extent to which the patient's motivation for treatment reflects a sincere and honest wish for self-understanding, and a commitment to the prospect of intrapsychic change through engagement in a collaborative effort with the analyst. If the patient's motivation is serious and realistic and reflects the need to explore and understand inner tensions and conflicts, the possibilities for a successful analytic undertaking are considerably enhanced. Such motivation must be contrasted with an infantile, narcissistically tinged expectation on the part of some patients that the analyst will work some powerful and magical cure to alleviate all difficulties in their lives without any serious effort or need for work and understanding on their part. If patients do not really want treatment or do not understand what they are getting into, or actually want something else that would satisfy their needs or alleviate their pain, it is better that they not undertake analysis.

Self-organization

One of the central discriminating factors separating borderline psychopathology from narcissistic personality disorders is the achievement in the latter of cohesive self-organization and the capacity to maintain that sense of self in the face of regressive strain. While this capacity is found in the better-integrated narcissistic personality, it remains more highly vulnerable to regressive pulls in borderline conditions. To a degree, the level of self-integration may reflect the vicissitudes of the therapeutic relation. The capacity of the patient to maintain a degree of cohesiveness may depend on the quality of the relationship with the therapist. Maintaining a stable and empathic relationship is a task involving contributions from both patient and analyst. Where such a relationship obtains, the patient may show improvement; where it fails, the patient may appear more borderline. As Stolorow and colleagues (1983) put it, the stability of the relationship is "codetermined as well by the extent of the therapists' ability to decenter from the structures of their own subjectivity and by their ability to comprehend empathically the nature of each patient's archaic subjective universe as it begins to structure the microcosm of the transference" (p. 122). Such dependence on the object's response plays a greater role in lower-order conditions than in higher-order conditions.

The failures of self-cohesion in borderline patients may be seen as failures of identity formation, or as the incapacity to maintain a firmly delineated sense of identity, or as states of depersonalization, or as intense feelings of emptiness, loneliness, or, particularly in regressive crises, as inner fragmentation and loss of self. Patients who are unable to maintain a relatively stable sense of self or whose self-organization is vulnerable to fragmentation are usually borderlines whose pathology is cast at a near-psychotic level. Such patients should not be taken into psychoanalysis. Patients whose identity crises are acute and severe or who are subject to severe states of identity diffusion or depersonalization also are probably not analyzable. However, patients whose difficulties in establishing a firm sense of identity are more peripheral—that is, have more to do with the integration of significant life roles and commitments rather than in a sense of psychic integrity or self-organization—may be potentially analyzable.

The quality of emptiness in borderline patients needs careful evaluation in terms of the depth and quality of the experience and the developmental level it seems to reflect. This experience, accompanied by feelings of panic and despair, seems to reflect critical early-developmental defects and is found in borderline patients who live close to the edge of psychosis (Adler and Buie 1979). In an effort to alleviate or avoid intense feelings of painful aloneness, such patients develop intense needs to be held, fed, and touched, and ultimately seek to assuage the pain of abandonment by merging with a significant object.

Such feelings are activated intensely in the intimate dyadic relationship of analysis. When these needs are not adequately fulfilled, there is an intense reaction of disillusionment, disappointment, and rage. These patients are frequently unable to maintain positive images or fantasies of sustaining objects, either in past or in present experience. This basic inability would prevent such patients from entering into a consistent and meaningful therapeutic alliance. In better-organized and better-functioning borderlines, the fear of abandonment may take a less malignant form. While these fears reflect early developmental vicissitudes, they do not necessarily imply the depth and severity of the inner emptiness and loss of self seen in more primitive personality structures. These difficulties, nonetheless, may reflect a basic incapacity for meaningful and constructive internalization, which deserves careful consideration in the assessment of analyzability. Such patients may be able to undertake the analytic process—that is, engage in and follow through the course of analytic work—but they may have considerable difficulty in the phase dealing with the inevitable mourning process and the associated internalizations essential to successful termination work.

As already noted, additional hints as to the potential analyzability of borderline patients can be drawn from types of character pathology superimposed on the underlying structure. As Stone (1979, 1980) has suggested, character typology may form another index of accessibility to analytically based treatment. Patients with hysterical or obsessive forms of character structure, or those who are predominantly depressive/masochistic or phobically anxious, would be most amenable to a classically psychoanalytic approach. Such forms of character organization tend to cluster toward the higher end of the borderline continuun, and would typically be found among primitive hysterics or dysphoric personalities. Character forms that have a more infantile, passive-dependent, narcissistic, or schizoid organization tend to be poorly organized and reflect deeper levels of psychic dysfunction and structural liability. Such character forms tend to cluster in the middle range of borderline structural impairment; they would more predominantly characterize the dysphoric personality or schizoid variants. The last group of character types—the paranoid, hypomanic, inadequate, explosive, and antisocial personalities—characterize more primitive levels of borderline organization, predominantly the primitive affective personality disorders and pseudoschizophrenics. There seems to be a rough correspondence between forms of character organization and levels of borderline integration, although obviously this parallel is extremely rough and would have to allow for many variations in degree as well as possible exceptions.

If we summarize our impressions of borderline analyzability, we can draw the following conclusions:

1. Some borderline patients are potentially analyzable, but these cases would seem to be limited to the group of higher-order borderlines.

2. Careful assessment must be made of the extent of ego defect, the capacity for object relations, and the vulnerability to regression. Significant impediments in any of these areas would contraindicate analysis.

3. Areas of particular importance are the capacity to form a meaningful therapeutic alliance and the quality of motivation.

4. Adequate assessment cannot be made on an acute basis or in terms of the nature or intensity of symptoms. The assessment of analyzability requires an adequate time span of observation to evaluate the patient's level of characterological functioning rather than acute regressive phases.

5. Most borderline cases require a lengthy period of preparatory psychoanalytically oriented psychotherapy both as a context of assessment and as propaedeutic to entering the psychoanalytic situation.

6. For many cases, a period of trial analysis is advisable.

3

APPROACHES

This chapter surveys prevailing approaches to the psychotherapy of borderline patients. I will present the core ideas and therapeutic emphases of each and, where appropriate, a brief criticism to suggest where my own differs. This may provide some overall impression of the range and diversity of approaches to the psychotherapy of borderline conditions. Coming out of a psychoanalytic orientation, these approaches share many conceptual and technical elements. Each has its own distinctive merits and can serve as an effective basis for therapeutic intervention with certain groups of patients. All are relatively effective and are subject to the same difficulties and frustrations in the treatment of borderline conditions.

ZETZEL

The work of Elizabeth Zetzel stands at one extreme in the treatment of borderline patients. Following the approach set forth originally by Knight (1954a, b), Zetzel recommends that in the treatment of borderlines less is better, and that therapy should be supportive. She (Zetzel 1971) based her approach on a developmental model, in which the failure in borderline development lies in the early mother–child relationship. The developmental defects included (1) failure to achieve definitive self-object differentiation, (2) failure to develop the capacity to recognize, tolerate, and master the trauma of separation, loss, and narcissistic injury, and (3) failure to acquire positive ego identifications that would serve as a basis for maintenance of self-esteem, genuine autonomy, and the capacity to maintain stable one-to-one relations. The vulnerability of self-object differentiation was reflected in difficulties in maintaining the distinction between fantasy and reality, particularly in regressive states. Regressions were related to the borderline's limited capacity to tolerate painful affects. Most telling of all, however, was the incapacity to internalize sufficiently stable identifications, so that for most borderline patients, definitive termination was impossible.

As for therapy, Zetzel argued for limited (rarely more than once-per-week) but regular contacts between patient and therapist. The primary focus of the treatment, she argued, should be on establishing a stable, realistic doctor-patient relationship, which would serve as a basis for correcting developmental deficiencies in the capacity for one-to-one relating, thereby mobilizing thwarted developmental capacities. The therapeutic relationship can be contaminated by efforts of the patient to gain gratification or to disrupt the treatment because of rage at the therapist's refusal to gratify needs. The combination of low frustration tolerance and excessive narcissistic expectations limits the patient's capacity to enter into and establish a meaningful therapeutic alliance. Because of the vulnerabilities of the capacity for internalization and the limited potential for meaningful termination, therapy with borderline patients may have to continue for an extended period of time, and the therapist may need to remain at least potentially available over an indefinite time span.

To my reading, Zetzel's developmental analysis is more appropriate for lower-order borderline patients, and tends to overdraw the developmental deficits. In the borderline spectrum such deficits are neither so absolute nor so uncompromisingly apodictic as Zetzel indicates. Rather, the deficits are subject to a wide range of variability and susceptibility to therapeutic remedy. Nonetheless, Zetzel's emphasis on the centrality and importance of the therapeutic alliance is a point of major significance, which I would fully endorse.

KERNBERG

Kernberg's contribution has been monumental, since he has almost singlehandedly defined the commonly accepted territory of borderline pathology. Kernberg attributes borderline pathology to the developmental failure to adequately negotiate the separation-individuation process, particularly the rapprochement subphase.

At the root of the pathology is an excess of pregenital (oral) aggression, which prevents the effective integration of internalized object relations. There is a condensation of pregenital and genital libidinal aims, strongly contaminated by aggressive derivatives. The configuration of these instinctual conflicts and the unresolved issues of separation-individuation influence the character of borderline transferences. Kernberg describes the developmental process in terms of the interaction between instinctual vicissitudes and the structuralizing effects from the internalization of object relations. The earliest phase takes place prior to the differentiation of self and object and provides the ego core, as well as the rudiments of basic trust. This is followed by a stage of the consolidation of a relatively undifferentiated self-object image, which is libidinally invested and carries a positive affective charge. At the same time, painful and frustrating experiences come to form a separate representation of an undifferentiated, all-bad self-object representation. The all-good and all-bad images remain separated with little or no separation between self and nonself. Pathological fixation at this level leaves the aggressively cathected images predominant and promotes a defensive refusal of the primitive all-good images in order to protect against excessive frustration and rage.

The next stage of development takes place after the differentiation of self and object and results in the splitting of both self and object images into all-good and all-bad alternatives. In the borderline personality organization, differentiation between self and object images is sufficient to allow for the establishment of integral ego boundaries and a differentiation between self and others. But the predominance of primitive aggression prevents developmental movement to a further stage in which self and object images may be integrated into a concept of self and others, embracing both good and bad characteristics. The contamination of self and object images by aggression motivates the defensive splitting from idealized good self and object images as a means of avoiding intolerable anxiety and guilt. Thus, splitting is the major defensive mechanism in borderline conditions and lies at the root of ego weakness and other primitive defense mechanisms. Ego weakness is reflected in the lack of impulse control, anxiety tolerance, and the capacity to sublimate. Borderline patients are able to preserve reality testing, which distinguishes them from psychotics; but also, because of the splitting, they are unable to use repression as an effective defense, a fact that distinguishes them from neurotics.

In his therapeutic approach, Kernberg emphasizes the necessity for maintaining technical neutrality as a basis for the interpretation of split object relations as they manifest themselves in the transference, particularly in idealizing and negative transference expressions. Empathic understanding and human warmth are seen as preconditions for therapeutic work, but they are without therapeutic impact unless they lead to productive interpretations. Kernberg insists on the importance of working through transference derivatives as they contaminate the therapeutic relationship early in the encounter. The goal is to work through the process of separation-individuation to facilitate the patient's ability to reach a level of object constancy. The analysis of primitive defensive operations is an important part of this process and contributes to the modification of their ego-weakening effects.

The paradigmatic picture of borderline pathology that Kernberg presents envisions an early, urgent, and precipitous effort on the part of the patient to distort the therapeutic situation in order to satisfy unrealistic demands. Confrontation of these distortions and interpretation of the transference expressions are essential in order to establish a therapeutic alliance and to continue the therapeutic effort. Countertransference reactions play an important part in Kernberg's therapeutic approach, since they can serve as important vehicles for understanding the patient's transference and the dynamics underlying it.

Kernberg's theories have been criticized from a number of perspectives. His reliance on the differentiated role of libidinal and aggressive drives at a point early in development, before self-object differentiation has taken place, has been strongly criticized (Robbins 1976). His insistence on the postulated role of primitive oral aggression has a decidedly Kleinian cast. The metapsychological status of internalized object relations (Meissner 1978b) and the adherence to the Mahlerian schema of separation-individuation, particularly the location of the pathological defect in the rapprochement phase [a position previously abandoned by Mahler herself (Mahler 1972, Mahler and Kaplan 1977)], seem narrowly construed (Meissner 1984a). From my perspective, Kernberg often draws lines that seem excessively apodictic and unyielding. His insistence on expressive psychotherapy to the exclusion of supportive approaches, the use of the presence or absence of reality testing to discriminate the border with psychosis, and the use of the differentiation between splitting and repression to delineate the border with neurosis seem to me to yield to clinical experience. An essential orientation in this work is that the borderline spectrum is marked by gradations of such phenomena rather than binary expressions of presence or absence. Other students of the borderline conditions have also found it necessary to question the same points (Abend et al. 1983).

Kernberg's clinical approach has also been criticized (Feinsilver 1983). Authors who come to the therapeutic arena with an insistence on the holding environment and empathic acceptance tend to find Kernberg's emphasis on early confrontation and interpretation of transference distortions disturbing. From a Kohutian perspective, the early systematic interpretation of narcissistic transferences would be regarded as premature and counterproductive, and would be seen as reflecting the analyst's countertransference difficulties in dealing with the patient's transferences as they impinge on the analyst's own unresolved narcissism—as, for example, activation of unresolved grandiosity in the face of idealizing transferences, or envy of the patient's grandiosity aroused by the patient's mirroring transference (Mitchell 1986). Others have charged that the "oral rage" of Kernberg's borderlines may be an iatrogenic result of his intrusive transference interpretations that the narcissistically vulnerable patient experiences as threatening assaults. The resulting narcissistic rage justifies the rationale of Kernberg's approach. He continually creates the monster his approach seeks to slay (Atwood and Stolorow 1984).

Kernberg's position has modified in some respects. In his more recent writings (Kernberg 1984), he has been more sympathetic to a point of view that would recognize gradations and degrees of intensity in the utilization of various pathological mechanisms, a view that would be more consistent with the spectrum approach. He has also found room for the supportive approach to the treatment of some borderline patients, particularly where motivation is lacking, where the reinforcement of the pathology by secondary gain is excessive, or where particular life circumstances would exclude more extensive expressive approaches. He has also acknowledged that for many cases a combination of supportive and expressive techniques may be appropriate, a position that is also more in line with the approach taken in this study.

MASTERSON-RINSLEY

Masterson follows Kernberg in tracing the origin of the borderline pathology to the rapprochement subphase of the separation-individuation process, but in a manner even more narrow and decisive than Kernberg himself. The core of borderline pathology for Masterson and Rinsley is the abandonment depression that results from the failure to resolve the rapprochement crisis. This developmental arrest and the associated failure to achieve object constancy impair the individual's ability to relate to separate objects, subject the vicissitudes of object relationships to the individual's varying need states, create a defect in the capacity of evocative memory, and impede the ability to mourn. Any object loss or separation becomes a catastrophe, which reactivates the intense abandonment depression (Masterson and Rinsley 1975).

In their schema, the splitting of the rapprochement phase results in the splitting of the object-relations unit into two separate part-units, each composed of a part-self representation, a part-object representation, and an affect linking them together. They represent internalizations derived from interaction with a borderline mother, who rewards the child's regressive clinging and dependent behavior by maintaining her libidinal availability and inhibits the child's efforts toward separation-individuation by libidinal withdrawal. The resulting part-units are called the withdrawing object-relations part-unit (WORU) and the rewarding object-relations part-unit (RORU). The WORU is invested with aggressive drive energy and includes a maternal part-object, which is viewed as attacking, critical, hostile, and angry; a part of self-representation as bad, helpless, guilty, and ugly; and an affect of chronic anger, frustration, helplessness, rage, covering a profound underlying abandonment depression. The RORU is invested with libidinal drive derivatives and includes a maternal part-object, which is approving, supporting, and loving, together with a part-self-representation as the good, passive, compliant child. The affect of this part-unit is that of feeling good and fed and gratifying the wish for reunion (Masterson 1987).

Masterson (1976) delineates two forms of psychotherapy: supportive psychotherapy and reconstructive psychotherapy. The decision on which approach is utilized is a function of the patient's ego strength, the level of defensive organization, and the degree of separation trauma. Supportive therapy aims at enabling the patient to gain better conscious control of primitive defense mechanisms and their destructive effects, particularly acting out. In contrast, reconstructive psychotherapy aims at working through the abandonment depression, enabling the patient to achieve a greater degree of ego autonomy and integration. In the initial stage of reconstructive psychotherapy, the therapist serves as a transference object whose function is to alienate the patient's self-RORU from the pathology by confronting and clarifying the destructiveness of this alliance. The ensuing working-through includes dealing with resistances, clarifying the reality, and processing the abandonment feelings, all of which stimulate further resistance and require further clarification and work. Confronting the destructive effects of the alliance between the pathological ego and the RORU not only increases the alienation between them but also diminishes the patient's tendency to act out. At the same time, it activates the WORU, which in turn stimulates increased resistance as a defense against the reactivated abandonment depression.

Either aspect of the split part-units can be projected into the transference. Projection of the WORU gives rise to feelings of abandonment and attempts to deny the benefit of the therapy, as well as activating the RORU as a defense. Alternatively, projection of the RORU allows patients to feel better but draws them under the influence of the pathological ego and its self-destructive behavior. In the face of such transference vicissitudes, the therapist must maintain a position as a real object who supports separation and individuation and who continually confronts the denial of the self-destructiveness of the pathological ego. The successful outcome of this process leads to the development of a new alliance between the therapist's healthy ego and the patient's embattled reality ego (Masterson 1987).

The Masterson-Rinsley approach runs into some of the same difficulties in terms of developmental theory that were encountered in Kernberg's formulations. The linkage between borderline pathology and the difficulties of the rapprochement phase, along with the etiological role of a supposedly borderline mother who fails to support normal separation-individuation, seem to be an excessively narrow base for understanding the nature of borderline pathology and the range of its expression. The analysis of the split part-units parallels Kernberg's description of internalized object-relations with its component self- and object-representations and connecting affect. Despite the conceptually narrow and somewhat overgeneralized base of the theory, the Masterson-Rinsley approach emphasizes the importance of the therapeutic alliance as an essential component of any effective therapy with borderline patients, and delineates a set of internalized pathological configurations which not only enter into the transference but form the essential basis for therapeutic intervention.

THE BLANCKS

The work of Gertrude and Reuben Blanck (1974) proceeds along the lines of an essentially ego-psychological approach. They base their understanding of the genesis of borderline disorders in Mahler's separation-individuation process and particularly in the vicissitudes of the rapprochement phase (following the same line of thinking espoused by Kernberg and Masterson). They recognize a range of borderline disorders from the psychotic to the neurotic, the prognosis depending on the degree of available ego structure. Their view of borderline pathology follows closely Kernberg's analysis of split self- and object-representations. Their approach emphasizes both the vulnerability of ego structures in borderline patients and the necessity for utilizing ego-supportive and ego-building techniques in the therapeutic approach to such patients.

They maintain a sharp division between psychoanalysis and psychotherapy. The goal of psychotherapy is structure building, that is, mobilizing the developmental potentialities of the patient to achieve a level of object constancy and identity formation. The weak ego of the borderline cannot tolerate the regressive pressures of psychoanalysis, but rather calls for an approach that both strengthens the ego and tames unruly and disruptive drives. Only if the self- and object-representations have achieved an adequate level of integration is the psychoanalytic approach possible.

Analogous to Kernberg's approach, they emphasize the relatively undifferentiated, split, and distorted nature of self- and object-representations, along with the destructive influence of aggressive derivatives. They stress the need for interpretation in the early stages of therapy to correct these distortions and allow for the possibility of a more benign experience with the therapist as object. Only in these terms is the establishment of a good, workable therapeutic alliance possible. The establishing and consolidation of the therapeutic alliance provide the basis for the patient's capacity to accept further interpretations, which contribute to the evolving of ego structures. Interpretations in this view should be aimed at the highest developmental level that the patient has attained as a way of supporting ego development and encouraging further progression. While the most developed aspect of the ego assimilates interpretations, it may need help to accomplish this.

The tension between reliance on interpretations and reliance on the therapeutic relationship remains a constant problem, and the therapist must determine from moment to moment where the proper emphasis should fall. In general, the interpretation of the revival of past experiences in the transference should precede analysis of genetic origins. Interpretations are aimed at sustaining the therapeutic alliance and strengthening the ego in its capacity to deal with signal anxiety without excessive regression. Supportive techniques are intended to increase the toleration for anxiety and to facilitate developmental processes. Fostering a relationship to the therapist as a good object provides the opportunity for working out developmental issues. If the therapist is sufficiently reliable, predictable, and benign, these effects will be realized. The emotional availability of the therapist and the titration of gratification and frustration in the therapeutic relationship are important variables. The excessive use of gratification runs the risk of avoiding engagement with the patient's aggression and thus deprives the patient of growth-promoting opportunities to utilize aggression in the service of increasing separation and individuation.

Such corrective experiences, as they emerge in the course of therapy, cannot make up for the lack of phase-specific developmental experiences. But most borderline patients need a reparative experience, which should take place on a verbal level rather than on a merely relational level. The Blancks recommend a flexible technique responsive to the developmental needs and defects of the patient. The goals of therapy include establishing a sense of identity, strengthening and improving the level of ego functioning, bringing object relations to a level of object constancy, and facilitating neutralization of disruptive drives and their derivatives. Such therapy does not aim at the resolution of oedipal conflicts, a goal that is more appropriate to psychoanalysis.

The Blancks' approach suffers both from the same conceptual limitations as Kernberg's analysis of ego weakness and intrapsychic splitting and from the narrow conceptualization of the developmental base of borderline pathology. The therapeutic approach tends to lean in the direction of supportive intervention and ego structuring, rather than in the direction of expressive conflict resolution. To this extent the approach seems to be oriented primarily toward the lower end of the borderline spectrum, where issues of ego weakness, vulnerability to regression, and relatively severe distortions of object relationships are predominant aspects of the pathology. While they acknowledge the existence of higher-order forms of borderline pathology, there is little said about a therapeutic approach to such cases.

GUNDERSON

Gunderson's approach to the treatment of borderline patients is somewhat eclectic, deriving from his extensive empirical research and informed by his basically psychoanalytic orientation. His efforts have been directed primarily to increasing the consistency and reliability of the borderline diagnosis. He maintains the distinction between support-ive and expressive-explorative approaches, but notes that this distinc-tion is either very weak or invalid for distinguishing actual therapeutic practice. In fact, he maintains that since there is a considerable cross-over between techniques, a more continuous model embracing both exploratory and supportive techniques is required. Even the Menninger Study (Kernberg et al. 1972), originally the basis for Kernberg's strong distinction between supportive and expressive therapies, involved mix-tures of the two techniques and found that supportive techniques were much more commonly utilized in expressive therapies than had pre-viously been recognized (see also Wallerstein 1986).

Gunderson would see supportive techniques as probably more suitable for the greater number of borderline patients. They are gener-ally more cost-effective and, even though the goals are limited (decreas-ing the likelihood of suicide, increasing adaptive role performance, improving chaotic interpersonal relationships), can often bring about more desirable structural change. In this approach, the frequency of visits is held to a minimum in order to diminish the intensity of transference distortions. The treatment may last indefinitely with grad-ual tapering of frequency. No formal termination is attempted, and the therapist's availability remains open-ended and indefinite—an ap-proach somewhat reminiscent of Zetzel's.

More exploratory and intensive approaches tend to be more ambi-tious, aiming at the restructuring of the basic personality. The approach must be intensive (three or more times a week) and long-term (lasting usually six to ten years). Gunderson does not feel an exploratory approach is the treatment of choice for borderlines, even with adequate motivation and resources. The effort requires experienced and talented therapists and should not be undertaken by inexperienced therapists without capable and ongoing supervision.

Gunderson describes four phases of intensive psychotherapy. The first emphasizes establishing the therapeutic contract, dealing with ques-tions of fees, payments, extra-therapeutic contacts, scheduling, and the distribution of responsibility. This phase tends to be strongly supportive, even when confrontations with the patient's self-destructive behavior or transference distortions are required. It aims at limiting the extent of the patient's self-destructive acting out and establishing a more solid thera-peutic relationship. Establishing boundaries, both between patient and therapist and within the patient, is an aspect of this process.

The second phase focuses more on the here-and-now interaction with the therapist. The therapeutic relationship is tested by a variety of provocative and resistant behaviors. The therapist's steadfast and non-retaliatory capacity to consistently confront and interpret the motives behind the patient's transference enactments is a central part of the work of this phase. The patient gradually begins to make meaningful use of past memories, which facilitates the work of understanding and integration.

The third phase deals more directly with issues of separation and identity formation. Where reactions to separation anxiety had previously tended to be acted out, particularly in relationship to the therapist, the focus now falls more explicitly on the verbalization and interpretation of such conflicts. The gradual emergence of a sense of identity and its attendant vulnerabilities becomes a significant focus. The relationship to the therapist, which has been experienced as needy and conflictually dependent, is increasingly recognized as important but not essential.

The fourth stage focuses on issues of termination during which the therapist may function as a "good mother of separation" (Masterson and Rinsley 1975). During the termination, earlier pathological characteristics are regressively reactivated, including primitive splitting. These need to be reworked in the context of separation from the therapist. In this exploratory approach, Gunderson favors the setting of a termination date and an abrupt stop to the therapy. Tapering may reflect the therapist's conviction that the patient is unable to complete a termination and may prove self-defeating.

The approach that Gunderson describes is sensible and practical and offers a sufficient range and flexibility of approach. It should be remembered that the patients he has in mind are the borderlines that are defined by his own diagnostic criteria, which seem to select patients closer to the border of psychosis or who might be regarded as lower-order forms of the borderline spectrum (Meissner 1984b). Patients who might profit from more intensive approaches, even psychoanalysis, are regarded as not fitting his diagnosis.

This aspect of Gunderson's work reflects some of the difficulties inherent in the tension between research and clinical orientations. While a narrowing of diagnostic criteria has the advantage of greater clarity of definition and reliability of diagnosis, particularly for research purposes, it tends to focus therapeutic techniques specifically on this narrower population and thus leaves patients who do not fit the constraints of this category out of consideration. The perspective offered by the borderline spectrum would see these patients as occupying some part of the lower order of the spectrum, but would include patients functioning at higher levels of adaptation and structural integration, who also at times and in restrictive circumstances have the potentiality for a borderline regression and who manifest in modified and less severely pathological forms other borderline vulnerabilities. Nonetheless, Gunderson's approach lends itself readily to the kind of more flexible therapeutic rationale that would be consistent with a spectrum orientation.

BOYER AND GIOVACCHINI

The work of Boyer and Giovacchini, working both independently (Giovacchini 1967a,b, 1970, 1972, 1973a,b, 1975a,b, 1979, Boyer 1983) and collaboratively (Boyer and Giovacchini 1967, 1980), involves a consistent approach to the treatment of character disorders distinguished by its insistence on the use of classical psychoanalytic technique as the treatment of choice. Their categorization of character disorders embraces a significant segment of the borderline spectrum, primarily the more severely disturbed borderline conditions. Borderline pathology involves developmental defects of both ego and superego. The failures of the patients' early environment and the consequent lack of early gratifications leave a residue of negative memories and pathogenic introjects that impair their capacity to deal with their environment.

The choice of patients for psychoanalysis in this view depends not on diagnosis but on the capacity of patients to use the therapy constructively. This requires that patients are able to sustain themselves between therapeutic hours, and that the analyst is able to tolerate the patients' disruptive and/or regressive behavior within the therapeutic hours, a requirement that obviously varies considerably from one analyst to another. Both Boyer and Giovacchini demonstrate a remarkable tolerance for primitive and regressive behavior and an ability to meet it on therapeutic terms, which may contribute considerably to their ability to utilize classical psychoanalytic techniques in the treatment of such primitive patients.

Giovacchini (1979) insists on the use of interpretations only within the context of the transference and avoids genetic reconstructions that, at least early in the course of treatment, may serve as a defense against the necessity for dealing with immediate transference vicissitudes. While the patient's difficulties reside in a developmental disturbance, usually in the symbiotic phase, attempts to provide the patient with the gratification that was missed at earlier developmental levels within the therapy are probably misguided. The analyst's interpretations are aimed at facilitating the organization of primary process material; internalization by the patient of the calmness and objectivity of the analytic attitude is an important aspect of successful therapy. To a certain extent, success or failure of the treatment is a by-product of the patient–analyst interaction; a given patient may be treatable by one analyst and not by another. Borderline patients often begin therapy with high hopes or with projections of magical omnipotence onto the therapist. Transference distortions of this order can either become fixed delusional beliefs or lead to inevitable disappointment and disillusionment. In the latter case, the transference becomes a repetition of the original traumatic relationship with the mother, and the patient loses hope that the analyst can be of help. These dynamics stir inevitable countertransference effects in the analyst, especially feelings of frustration, inadequacy, and helplessness.

Boyer (1983) puts somewhat greater emphasis on the importance in the early stages of the therapy of establishing the ground rules and structure of the therapeutic relationship. He sees this process, together with the presentation by the analyst of a calm, patient, objective, optimistic attitude, as important contributing factors to establishing a therapeutic alliance. An alliance is not effectively achieved until the patient's cathexis of maladaptive and pathogenic introjects has been sufficiently modified. Particularly in the treatment of borderline patients, the therapeutic process aims at replacing archaic and sadistic introjections in both ego and superego with more adaptive and mature formations. Successful work with borderline patients involves setting the dimensions of the therapeutic contract as a primary piece of business, along with the assumption that the patient possesses untapped ego strengths and capacities for mature adaptation which are masked by the presenting symptoms. This assumption forms the basis for the therapeutic alliance and the utilization of an analytic model in the treatment. Boyer and Giovacchini emphasize the importance of dealing with pre-oedipal object-relations configurations as they manifest themselves in early transference reactions and note that any attempt to prematurely interpret oedipal dynamics or conflicts has the effect of precluding the emergence of pre-oedipal transference states.

There is much in the approach delineated by Boyer and Giovacchini that I find congruent with my own perspective, particularly the emphasis on early structuring of the therapeutic context and the importance of relational and countertransference issues in the treatment of borderline patients. Some of the technical recommendations seem to me to be overstated, as, for example, the idea that early oedipal-level interpretations preclude the emergence of preoedipal transference dynamics. At times this is certainly the case, but at other times in my experience it has been necessary to work oedipal conflicts through to a certain extent before underlying narcissistic and other preoedipal dynamics become manifest.

My major divergence of opinion, however, has to do with the advisability of using classical psychoanalytic technique on all patients within the borderline range. Despite the fact that one of the purposes of my discussion is to urge that psychoanalytic technique has a much more important role to play in the treatment of borderline disorders, I have tended to see this contribution as focused largely on a segment of better-organized and better-integrated personality structures within the borderline range. I would be somewhat dubious about the indiscriminate effort to subject patients from more primitive levels of the borderline spectrum to the rigors of the psychoanalytic couch. In my experience, for some of these patients the risks of precipitant regression and overwhelming anxiety serve notice that a degree of caution is called for. I would follow a line of thinking closer to the more general consensus regarding the suitability of therapeutic approaches to the treatment of borderline patients. While one can admit that some experienced analysts might have the clinical skills and personal capacities that the analytic approach requires, I suspect that for most analytic practitioners the option of treating more primitively organized borderline patients with the classical psychoanalytic approach would be fraught with insurmountable difficulties.

CHESSICK

Chessick's approach to the borderline patient experience (1971, 1974, 1977, 1979, 1982) emphasizes development of the therapeutic alliance from the beginning of the treatment and the need to set limits and maintain the structure of the therapeutic situation if any effective therapeutic work is to be done. As a constructive alliance develops, the patient becomes interested in working on and understanding his own difficulties, rather than in seeking the gratification of impulses by the therapist. This process may require strong, firm limit-setting on the part of the therapist, particularly in the face of the patient's acting-out and destructive tendencies. Chessick reaffirms that a useful alliance is *not*

constructed on the basis of kind, seductive, giving, or charitable behavior by the therapist. Such efforts on the part of the therapist
are manifestations of gross countertransference. Rather, a meaningful alliance is based on the appeal to the rational adult ego of the patient
to join in a serious effort whose purpose is to enable the patient to
resolve conflicts and resume a thwarted course of psychological development.

Chessick's earlier emphasis on the importance of interpretation
has given way to a stronger emphasis on the holding environment à la
Winnicott. He operationalizes this concept by stressing aspects of the
organization and structure of the therapeutic situation, the maintenance of neutrality, and a consistent therapeutic posture. The therapist's role is to behave as a relatively mature adult and to maintain a
realistic and consistent commitment to the therapy. The quality of this
holding and the overall interpersonal experience between patient and
therapist allow the therapeutic alliance to form and thus undermine the
disruptive effects of transference distortions. The patient's refusal to
observe the terms of the therapeutic contract is a clear signal that the
alliance is in jeopardy and must be repaired before any other therapeutic work can be accomplished.

While Chessick is basically in agreement with Kernberg regarding
the place of interpretation, particularly the need for early interpretation
of negative and disruptive transference reactions, he emphasizes that in
these contexts the patient should be confronted with the discrepancy
between the reality of the therapeutic situation and the patient's distortions. Genetic interpretations should be avoided, since they can trigger
disruptive reactions. However, Chessick diverges from Kernberg on
what should be interpreted early in the treatment. He argues that
primitive defenses such as splitting or projection should not be interpreted, since at this early stage the borderline patient is too vulnerable
and too easily injured narcissistically by such interpretations. The patient is only too likely to feel humiliated and controlled and may react
with shame or rage, fueling further transference distortions.

Despite his view of borderline transferences, Chessick leaves room
for the interpretation of self-object transferences at times. The patient's sense of having complete control over a benign object, as
though it were an extension of the self, can be essential to his sense of
psychological integrity. When this link to the object is threatened,
he may experience a sense of inner fragmentation. An empathic response to this sense of vulnerability and a clarification of what might
have happened to shatter the illusion of control can restore the threat-

ened self-object transference because the therapist thus manifests an understanding of the patient's deepest needs and anxieties (Chessick 1979).

Chessick's approach acknowledges the wide range of variability and pathological severity among borderline patients, a view consistent with the understanding of the borderline spectrum. He emphasizes the regressive-progressive axis characterizing borderline disorders and the tremendous range and flexibility patients can demonstrate along this axis. The therapeutic approach should show a degree of flexibility and adaptivity congruent with the inherent variability of borderline conditions. His emphasis on the importance of the therapeutic alliance and the means for maintaining it is similar to that expressed by Boyer and Giovacchini. Consistent with this view, Chessick finds the use of the analytic couch helpful for some patients but not for others (1971). He emphasizes that the determination of the therapeutic approach, including the use of the couch, must be individualized and decided in terms of the structure and dynamics of the patient and assessment of the regressive potential, particularly manifested in paranoid or depressive reactions or in tendencies for destructive acting out. In addition, the principle of flexibility requires that the analyst be willing and able to modify his therapeutic approach, from couch to sitting up and vice versa, when the clinical situation demands.

I can find little in Chessick's approach to differ with or challenge. His use of Kohut's notion of self-object transferences is not one that I find useful, but I can also recognize it as a way of talking about certain aspects of the relationship between patient and therapist that seem to fall outside our ordinary understanding of transference and involve relatively primitive developmental strata. Since I find the concepts confusing and the theory behind them troublesome, I would prefer to address similar clinical phenomena from a different theoretical perspective.

KRIS STUDY GROUP

The study of borderline conditions by the Kris Study Group (Abend et al. 1983) represents a consensus of psychoanalytic opinion. The study emphasizes the continuity between borderline disorders and higher-level dysfunction as in more classically analyzable cases and defines a range of conditions for which psychoanalysis is a useful and effective, if not optimal, treatment.

Consistent with a spectrum approach, the study emphasizes the gradations of psychological defects, including specific functions such as reality testing, defenses, and object relations. The authors emphasize that in their experience of borderline pathology, the failures in reality testing are often episodic and reflect varying degrees of distortion. The defensive organization is often mixed, including both primitive defense mechanisms as defined, for example, by Kernberg (1967), and higher-order defenses as might be found in healthier, analyzable subjects. More primitive forms of object relations are intermingled with identifiable oedipal conflicts in varying degrees, depending on the level of pathological organization. These patterns manifest internalizations from disturbed parental figures, often reflecting severe sadomasochistic conflicts deriving from every level of development and demonstrating pathological narcissistic features. Reactions to separation and loss are often intensified, and the pathology is usually riddled with severe superego conflicts. The study argues that oedipal conflicts have been neglected in the study of borderline conditions, and that these conflicts are usually permeated by earlier preoedipal problems and deficits.

In their technical descriptions, they place themselves at odds with Kernberg at several points. Their position is that no specific techniques or approaches are indicated for the treatment of borderline disorders, but that the application of standard analytic techniques as governed by good clinical judgment is sufficient. The criteria for analyzability do not differ for borderline patients, and they recommend a trial of analysis before commitment to a definitive process, in order to make a more accurate judgment. They take issue with Kernberg's emphasis on confronting transference contradictions and focusing on the splits in the patient's self- and object-worlds as a way of developing a therapeutic alliance. In their view this early confronting approach does not help to heal the underlying split. Moreover, the emphasis on negative transference interpretations runs the risk of distorting analytic neutrality, interrupts the flow of free association, and puts a restrictive focus on aggressive conflicts that may undermine approaches to other conflictual elements, both narcissistic and libidinal. Against any preconceived order of dealing with underlying conflicts, they recommend an even-handed approach to conflict material, dealing with conflicts when they become evident. Patients for whom reality testing is too weak or fragile, in whom the regressive potential, tendencies to projection, acting out, and drive discharge are excessive, are not suitable for psychoanalysis, but are better treated with supportive psychotherapy.

In sum, then, they argue against a concentration on one or other level of developmental or structural defect as central to the pathology. Rather, the cases they have studied seem to vary enormously in symptomatology and character organization. I find myself in sympathy with the general perspective offered by this study, particularly the questioning of a specific developmental defect. The study brings into focus a group of patients underemphasized in other approaches, namely, patients who are functioning at a level of structural integration and organization sufficient to allow them to tolerate and profit from psychoanalytic technique. While other authors, specifically Giovacchini and Boyer and to a certain extent Chessick, have advocated the use of a more classical psychoanalytic technique in the treatment of these patients, their cases often represent the more primitive end of the borderline spectrum. The Kris group, however, focuses on the higher end of the spectrum, a dimension of borderline pathology quite distinctly different from that emphasized in many other approaches (Meissner 1988).

WINNICOTT

The contribution of Donald Winnicott to the understanding of borderline disorders is his understanding of transitional object phenomena and false-self organization. The transitional object model has become a vehicle for expressing certain aspects of the pathology of borderline object relations. It is as though the borderline patient had become stuck at the level of transitional object relatedness. The history of the use of transitional objects and their persistence into adult life have been noted in many borderline patients (see Chapter 1, section on "Transitional Object Relations"). In addition, Winnicott's discussion of the false-self personality has special relevance to the understanding of aspects of the schizoid continuum. The split between the true and the false self is another variant on the schizoid theme, found in varying degrees throughout the borderline spectrum, but in certain patients it takes on a characteristic configuration—the basis for the description of the false-self personality (see Chapter 1).

Winnicott's clinical approach derives from his developmental model, particularly the notion of the holding environment as a function of "good-enough mothering." The holding technique meets the needs of patients with early developmental defects. He extends the notions of holding and good-enough mothering to considerations of therapeutic technique, such as the capacity to play within the therapeutic context as an essential aspect of the therapeutic interaction and as the basis for the communication and reception of change-inducing interpretations.

Winnicott's contributions are seminal and genial, and in consequence have had a far-reaching influence on subsequent thinking about the borderline spectrum, particularly his orientation toward treatment. His concepts can be applied to a wide range of borderline patients. The concept of holding has particular applicability with more primitively organized patients, where the need for establishing a safe and secure context within which the therapeutic relationship can develop takes priority. However, pertinence of this approach varies along the different segments of the borderline spectrum, and even within any given range of pathology may vary considerably from patient to patient. There is little question that the Winnicott approach places the primary emphasis on the relational characteristics and the patterning of interaction, especially nonverbal interaction, between therapist and patient. In my view, this does not provide an effective model, or at least provides only a partial model, for effective intervention with higher-order borderline conditions. With these patients, an approach closer to that recommended by the Kris Study Group, namely a more standard psychoanalytic model, seems more appropriate and effective.

FAIRBAIRN AND GUNTRIP

These object-relations theorists have focused on schizoid patients who would fall within the schizoid continuum. Fairbairn (1952, 1954) provided a unique brand of object-relations theory that viewed instincts as inherently object seeking rather than serving tension discharge. He postulated an ego that was from the beginning of life whole, integrated, and object related. Out of this undivided ego, other psychic structures evolve by a process of splitting (leading to the separation of good and bad impulses and objects) and introjection (by which derivatives of loved or hated objects were internalized and thus became a quasi-autonomous source of intrapsychic activity). These formulations describe the pathology of schizoid patients, who were generally characterized by the inner splitting of the ego and a concomitant withdrawal from object relations as aspects of their central pathology. Guntrip (1961, 1969, 1973) extended and developed Fairbairn's theory and applied it in detail to the analysis of the schizoid personality.

Their approach to the therapy of the schizoid problem focused primarily on issues of ego weakness, on the phenomenon of splitting and its implications (later elaborated by Kernberg), and on the problems related to withdrawal from object relationships. Guntrip was careful to note the frequent intermingling of oedipal issues with schizoid problems, even noting that at times it was necessary to work through oedipal problems with their associated guilt in order to allow a more regressive emergence of schizoid issues. A successful therapeutically controlled regression opens the way to clarifying states of primitive despair and hopelessness. The mobilization of the patient's capacity for rebirth lies in the development of a trusting and security-giving relationship with the therapist in which the patient is allowed to establish a separate existence as a person. The mobilization of these forces depends in large measure on the kind of understanding and support provided by the human environment of the therapeutic relationship.

Fairbairn's understanding of splitting and its implications for ego development have important clinical reverberations. The clinical approach to the treatment of schizoid problems reflects the influence of Winnicott and the emphasis on relational characteristics and the qualities of a good-enough therapist. While the Fairbairn-Guntrip analysis of personality disorders has vastly overextended the understanding of schizoid mechanisms as the root of psychopathology, it can be fairly said that much of their analysis has useful application to certain aspects of schizoid disorders. However, as is often the case with Winnicott's ideas, the emphasis on the importance of relational factors as determinants of therapeutic success can result in an underemphasis on other aspects of the therapeutic interaction, which in many cases may prove to be more decisive.

MODELL

The work of Arnold Modell (1968, 1984) has touched the understanding of borderline conditions at several salient points. He has described a condition of nonrelatedness or lack of communication of affect that takes place in the early stages of the treatment of severely narcissistic patients. In the borderline spectrum, these patients probably fit into the schizoid continuum, representing a form of schizoid personality. The blocking of affect may be massive, resulting in the failure to communicate affective experience, or it may be masked, so that the patient's failure to communicate becomes only gradually identifiable. The failure to communicate shows that the patient is not relating to the analyst. Often, the analyst can detect this state of affairs only through his own countertransference reaction, usually experiencing boredom or sleepy withdrawal.

This relatively persistent affective nonrelatedness calls for a modification of our understanding of the therapeutic action of psychoanalysis, which usually requires a state of affective relatedness. In the opening phase of the treatment with such patients, there is neither a transference nor a therapeutic alliance and no point of affective contact allowing the possibility of meaningful interpretation. Modell also discusses certain forms of motivation that have particular application to the negative therapeutic reaction. Some patients may unconsciously thwart the progress of the therapy out of a sense of not having a right to life, that is, to a separate existence from objects of attachment or dependence. Separation from the nuclear family involves a form of unconscious guilt, involving a sense of disloyalty in abandoning these important objects. There may also be a feeling that differentiation from the rest of the nuclear family will cause their death. Separation may also involve giving up an attachment to painful affects associated with parental figures. The enjoyment of one's own life might imply an abandonment of a chronically depressed parent. These patients share a common fantasy that having something good means that someone else is to be deprived. Thus, achieving a better life as the consequence of a successful psychoanalysis becomes an unacceptable good.

Some of these patients, particularly the more severely disturbed, suffer from an intense form of greed and envy reflected in a wish to take for themselves everything that others may possess. The negative therapeutic reaction then becomes an attempt to deprive the analyst of his therapeutic good. The guilt is related to the wish to take more than one's share or to the feeling that fate has given one more than one's share.

Modell has also contributed to our understanding of borderline object relations by extending Winnicott's notion of the transitional object to the concept of transitional object relationship, which he finds characteristic of borderline or psychotic character structure. In this relationship, the transitional object becomes a substitute for the real environment that allows the illusion of protection from surrounding dangers of the environment. The transitional object is created to fill the needs of the self. Modell (1968) goes on to say:

> The relationship of the subject to the object is fundamentally ambivalent; the qualities of the object are magical and hence there is an illusion of connectedness between the self and the object. The

relation of the subject to the object is primarily exploitative, the subject feels no concern for the needs of the object and cannot acknowledge that the object possesses his own separateness and individuality. The transitional object relationship is dyadic—it admits no others. [p. 40]

Modell (1984) has also extended Winnicott's notion of the holding environment as an integral aspect of the psychoanalytic therapeutic approach. In Winnicott's model, the mother or caretaking adult plays a role in protecting the child from the actual environment; this holding involves the communication of affect in a way that indicates to the patient that the analyst knows and understands the deepest anxieties. Thus, the holding environment creates an illusion of safety and protection that depends on an affective bond communicated between therapist and patient. Modell regards these caretaking elements as an implicit part of classical analytic technique. Any parameters that would introduce the more active presence of the analyst into the analytic situation would have the paradoxical effect of diminishing the analytic holding environment. While the holding environment in the usual analytic setting may be regarded as implicit or silent, in the face of significant developmental arrests, the role of the analytic setting as a holding environment becomes central to the therapeutic action.

Modell describes the treatment process of narcissistic (schizoid) personalities in three phases. The first phase is given over to dealing with the schizoid cocoon or bubble, constituted by the patient's state of nonrelatedness. The patient's defensive system creates an illusion of self-sufficiency in which the analyst is unnecessary and superfluous. The problem for the analyst is dealing with his own countertransference reactions. The holding environment in this phase sets the analytic work in process. The analyst must play a waiting and holding game. Any attempts at interpretation at this stage are either dismissed, unheard, or resented as an unwarranted intrusion.

The middle period, in contrast, sees the gradual establishment of a therapeutic alliance as the patient grows in the capacity for trust and gradual individuation. Positive or idealizing aspects of the transference give way to a form of narcissistic rage as the regression deepens and the insatiable demands become more obvious. The consistent confronting of these narcissistic needs of the grandiose self gradually involves more systematic interpretation of the cocoon fantasy as well. The affective block and the state of nonrelatedness are gradually replaced by more genuine affects, even though these are generally negative and intense.

These negative affects contribute to the process of individuation. The rage in this phase may be fueled by envy, especially envy of the analyst for what he is and has. The threat of negative therapeutic reactions, based on unconscious envy, greed, and guilt, must be dealt with in the interest of supporting continuing separation and individuation.

The final phase comes closer to the model of classical analytic work, recognizing nonetheless the continued potentiality for regression, particularly in periods of separation. In this phase more specifically oedipal dynamics are encountered; castration issues mingle more perceptibly with persistent separation issues. The patient's extreme dependency often requires that this phase be prolonged. The possibility of effective termination depends on the extent to which the transference, based on the transitional object relationship and the cocoon fantasy, has been effectively resolved by interpretations. Where use of the analyst and the analytic situation as a transitional object persists, there is risk of addiction to the analytic process.

Modell's contributions have added valuable insights to the treatment of borderline patients. The phenomenon of the lack of communication of affect and of nonrelatedness to the analytic object is seen in varying degrees throughout the schizoid continuum. It underlies the almost universal difficulties in establishing and maintaining the therapeutic alliance in this group of patients. These issues have less applicability in the hysterical continuum, in which the problem is often an excess of affective communication rather than a lack of it. Transitional object relationships are typical of borderline cases, but again with varying degrees of intensity and relevance. For some patients, the illusory protective and idealizing quality of the transference involvements is quite obvious and dramatic, while in other cases it remains subtle and hardly detectable over long periods of time. My own clinical experience would suggest that to some degree this form of relationship takes place in all patients in the borderline spectrum.

The notion of the holding environment also must be subjected to qualification, particularly in terms of varying levels of borderline pathology. In cases where the developmental deficits are severe and the capacity of the patient for establishing and maintaining a therapeutic alliance is particularly compromised, the holding environment becomes especially pertinent, as Modell has suggested. However, in the higher-order borderlines, where the deficits are more subtle and muted and where the resources of ego and superego are more available and utilizable in the interests of the establishing of the therapeutic alliance, the holding environment plays a more subtle and muted role. There is also some question about what the holding environment actually means and in what ways it is operationalized in the therapeutic context. Modell does not say much about this, except to connect it with the patient's sense of acceptance, security, and understanding.

ADLER AND BUIE

The collaboration of Adler and Buie has resulted in a series of important contributions to the study of the treatment of borderline patients (Adler 1970, 1979, 1981, 1985, Adler and Buie 1972, 1979, Buie and Adler 1972, 1982–1983). Their approach is based on an understanding of the root of borderline pathology in a developmental failure to form holding-soothing introjects, which provide a secure basis for the development of the self. This developmental failure can be traced to maternal inadequacies that impinge on the child's development during the separation-individuation process. To whatever extent the holding function fails to be introjectively internalized from the maternal holding environment, these introjects remain subject to regressive loss or impairment. Adler and Buie ascribe this failure of internalization to the relative instability of the memory basis involved in the formation of the introjects. There is a failure to achieve a solid level of evocative memory capacity, particularly in the context of object relationships, so that under the force of regressive pressures these patients retreat to a level of mere recognition memory, which is responded to by a sense of helplessness, abandonment, and rage. Thus, the borderline personality is constantly threatened by degrees of separation anxiety, experienced as a sense of aloneness or emptiness. The patient is forced to rely on the holding function of external self-objects (à la Kohut) to provide a sufficient degree of holding-soothing that keeps the threatening separation anxiety at bay. The patient seeks a level of incorporation and fusion with the holding self-object in order to maintain an adequate level of security, but the intensity of these pathological needs carries with them the inherent threat of the incorporative destruction of both the self-object and the self.

Their collaborative effort has evolved a psychotherapeutic approach to the treatment of this primary sector of borderline pathology. They propose three phases. The first deals primarily with regressive issues, focused around the emergence of intense separation anxiety, the transient regressive loss of the holding function related to defective holding introjects and transitional objects, and the emergence of rage associated with the self-object's failure to satisfy pathological needs and fears associated with the destructive aspects of incorporation and fusion. This affective turmoil is similar to the need–fear dilemma described in schizophrenic patients (Burnham et al. 1969, Meissner 1984a,b). Adler and Buie emphasize the need for clarification, interpretation, limit setting, and the actual providing of self-object holding, along with proof of the indestructibility of the object, as the vehicles for enabling the patient to understand and work through the difficulties involved in accepting the therapist as holding self-object. This gradual acceptance carries with it elements of idealization.

The second phase is directed to the modification of this pattern of idealization by means of a series of optimal disillusionments, with the therapist maintaining his position as holder-soother within the self-object transference, but with an intermingling of optimal degrees of frustration and support for the emerging autonomy of the patient. The patient gradually replaces the idealization and the dependence on the holding-soothing function of the object with internal resources for personal security.

The progression through the third phase derives from the continued interaction with the therapist within the self-object transference, providing a series of experiences through which the patient can internalize aspects of the therapist as a good object and thus develop relatively autonomous capacities, not only for internal soothing but also as a start to experiencing the reality of his own personal capacities, self-worth, and self-love. These internalizations are thought of as gradually modifying the structure of the pathological superego and as allowing for developmental progression in the growth of the ego toward autonomy. They appeal in this phase to the therapeutic principle that the patient's capacity to know, esteem, and love himself can develop only out of an adequate experience of being known, esteemed, and loved by a significant object. Throughout the course of treatment, Adler and Buie emphasize the need for maintaining the patient's narcissistic equilibrium. Insofar as the patient's pathological narcissism (usually the grandiose self) serves as a basis for whatever sense of security the patient can maintain, any therapeutic work on this pathological formation should be delayed until the basis of security in a stable, self-object transference and in the organization of holding-soothing introjects is solidly established. Thus, the progression in treatment flows from the characteristic borderline pathology, which is resolved into a more specifically narcissistic pathology. The treatment of this narcissistic organization is then completed along the lines advocated by Kohut (1971, 1977, 1984).

The work of Adler and Buie serves as an extension and elaboration of the line of thinking inaugurated by Winnicott and later developed by Modell. However, there are a number of points at which my approach would diverge from theirs. As is the case with other approaches that tend to ascribe the basis of borderline pathology to some aspect of the separation–individuation process, I would not limit the developmental focus to that specific phase or phases of early development. Undoubtedly, many borderline patients reflect serious developmental defects from this level, but for most, developmental complexities arise at a multiplicity of levels: in more primitive cases closer to the border of psychosis, defects can be traced to a time even before the vicissitudes of separation-individuation, and in many higher-level cases, it is evident that forms of oedipal and post-oedipal developmental difficulties must be taken into account (Meissner 1984a). From the broader perspective of the borderline spectrum, Adler and Buie seem to have the lower-order group in their sights.

From a theoretical perspective, I would not be inclined to utilize the Kohutian schema of self-object relatedness. I find the terminology confusing and the theory behind it inadequate (Meissner 1981c). An additional question might be raised regarding the model of cognitive impairment that Adler and Buie have proposed. The defects in evocative memory that they regard as fundamental to the borderline condition do not seem to hold up as a valid assessment of the functioning of borderline patients across the full range of the borderline spectrum. My own experience suggests that such defects may play a role in the pathology of some borderline patients, primarily those in the lower order of the spectrum, but other patients would show no evidence of such a defect in cognitive processing. I would also question the pattern of therapeutic progression from borderline to narcissistic pathology. This suggests that resolution of borderline issues uncovers a layer of narcissistic pathology that then becomes the focus of therapeutic effort. This pattern may obtain in many patients in whom the narcissistic sector plays a significant role in the organization of their internal world, but for other patients the issues may become more decisively phallic, oedipal, or some combination of oedipal and narcissistic.

A further divergence may arise regarding the operationalizing and implementation of the holding environment. The Adler-Buie approach, particularly in the early phase of treatment, emphasizes the use of extra appointments, the availability of the therapist via telephone calls and other contacts, and the use of transitional objects (giving the patient one's vacation address, sending postcards, small gifts, and so on); these are advocated as a part of the therapist's holding function. The emphasis is placed on the presence and involvement of the therapist with the patient as a caring and available object, thus minimizing the patient's fear of separation and the possibility of hostile projections where the therapist might be seen as uncaring, indifferent, rejecting, or abandoning. While the theoretical issue underlying this technical approach has its validity, my own feeling is that it may not play the same dynamic role with all borderline patients and at all levels of borderline pathology. Certainly, the holding-soothing function does not play as dominant a part in the treatment of higher-level borderline patients. And while the utility of the holding function may have its proper application in lower-order borderlines, there is still a question of how it is in fact to be implemented. My approach would emphasize establishing and maintaining the structure of the therapeutic situation, limit setting, and providing a firm and consistent framework within which the possibility of a therapeutic relationship and meaningful therapeutic work can take place. As I read the contributions of Adler and Buie, together with those of other advocates of the holding environment, I am struck by the differences in accent and emphasis on what the holding environment means and what specific actions or interventions should be undertaken by the therapist.

SEARLES

The unique contributions of Harold Searles stem from his long experience with more primitive levels of psychopathology, particularly his in-depth experience in the treatment of schizophrenic patients (Searles 1960, 1965). Consequently, it is not surprising that his thinking in the borderline realm tends to focus on more primitive aspects of the pathology. Much like Buie and Adler, Searles (1978) emphasizes the failure of the borderline patient's ego integration and the failure to develop a perduring internalized image of the self or of meaningful objects. The identity of the borderline patient is thus split and fragmented, a collection of partial and multiple identities that are poorly harmonized and integrated.

Searles's major contributions to the understanding of borderline pathology emphasizes the importance of countertransference as crucial in the therapy and the role of therapeutic symbiosis as an essential aspect of the treatment process. In Searles's approach, verbal interpretations seem to take a back seat to the analyst's nonverbal participation with the patient (1976). He describes the intensity of countertransference feelings that are mobilized in dealing with severely disturbed borderline patients—feelings of guilt, anxiety, intimidation, frustration, and impotence. Resentment and rage are stirred at the patient's assaults and seemingly endless demands—all, one might add, without being able to express these feelings directly to the patient. Searles sees the patient's symptoms as serving as forms of transitional object for both analyst and patient, characteristically reflecting some underlying pathogenic introject or introjects that represent part-aspects of early significant and mothering objects.

The progression in the therapy requires that these introjects be projected onto the analyst, who then comes to personify some aspect of the mother or other significant figures (Searles 1976). This transference involvement leads to a deepening of the symbiotic relatedness between analyst and patient, to the phase of therapeutic symbiosis. Thus, the bond between patient and analyst deepens and comes to represent the bond of dependency between mother and infant. This mutual immersion in the therapeutic symbiosis allows the patient to utilize the analyst as a model for internalizations that gradually resolve the pathogenic autistic and symbiotic issues. The patient must gradually give up the symbiotic world of infantile dependency for the world represented by the analyst. The role of the therapist is altogether critical in this process. Searles feels that any inability in the analyst to perceive the aspects of his own reality that correspond to the patient's projections render that analyst ineffective in his attempts to work with that particular patient. Effective treatment of borderline patients demands the capacity of the analyst to enter into a therapeutic symbiosis with his patients and to accept at least a part of the burden of the psychopathology that emerges in the relationship. The analyst's capacity, rooted in the security of his own humanity, to endure over lengthy periods of therapeutic stress the projective role described to him by the patient in the transference is essential to therapeutic success.

Searles's view of the developmental basis for borderline pathology carries the defect to the earliest strata of development with its roots in infantile autism and symbiosis. This is a view that is shared by a number of other authors (Horner 1975, 1979, Robbins 1981a,b). While it seems reasonable in the light of clinical experience to say that unresolved issues of symbiotic relatedness play a fundamental role in the pathology of some borderline patients, particularly those at the lower end of the spectrum who live closest to the border of psychosis, at the same time it would seem to be stretching a point to hold that such issues in unresolved symbiotic attachment play a significant role in all borderline cases. At the higher level of the spectrum, symbiotic issues do not always play a significant role in the pathology and do not enter significantly into the therapeutic process. My feeling is that if one were to insist on a role for symbiotic determinants in these cases, their impact would differ little from the impact they might have in higher levels of psychopathology—that is, in the character neuroses and psychoneuroses. It seems also to stretch a valid point to claim that the emergence of a therapeutic symbiosis and the immersion of both patient and therapist in it are necessary for effective therapeutic results.

Searles's contribution is unique and emphasizes a valuable aspect of the transference/countertransference interaction—namely, the role of the therapist in the eliciting and shaping of the transference neurosis and its complementary countertransference neurosis. That there may be something in the therapist that corresponds to or provides an even minimal basis in reality for the patient's projections underlines the relational and interactional quality of the therapeutic experience for both participants. This dimension of the transference/countertransference interaction has been emphasized by other writers, particularly Langs (1976) and Giovacchini (1979).

THE KLEINIANS

The Kleinian literature does not pay much attention to borderline conditions as such but approaches these clinical expressions within the Kleinian theoretical framework. Many of the patients treated and described by Kleinian analysts we would regard as essentially borderline. These patients span the borderline spectrum from the most severe, even psychotic, pole to much higher forms of borderline integration. What we would regard as levels of pathological integration within the borderline spectrum would in the Kleinian perspective be regarded as varying degrees of ego integration encompassing a psychotic core. Thus, borderline regressive states would be regarded as manifestations of underlying psychotic processes. The developmental defect is generally located at an early preoedipal level, usually ascribed to a lack of differentiation in the transition from the paranoid-schizoid position to the depressive position (Brown 1987). The defects related to this developmental failure make the evolution and resolution of the oedipal situation defective.

The Kleinian orientation is rooted in the contributions of Klein and Bion, particularly in regard to Bion's elaboration of the notion of the contained-container and his extension of Klein's idea of projective identification. Grotstein (1980, 1983, 1984, also Grotstein et al. 1987a,b) has attempted to adapt the Kleinian framework to a more contemporary, basically American orientation to borderline and narcissistic conditions. Consistent with the Kleinian usage, his orientation emphasizes the connection of borderline conditions with psychotic disorders. The difference between these lies in the fact that the healthy or neurotic part of the personality remains relatively intact even in the abnormal personality structure, and is better integrated in borderline personalities than in the psychotic. The abnormal personality in borderline states is abnormal whether the psychosis is manifested or not. The patient becomes psychotic when the healthy personality becomes more disintegrated. The stability of borderline organization is related more to the protective support offered in a well-structured and well-functioning sociological environment.

The clinical contributions can be traced in the work of Little and Rosenfeld. Little (1966) attributes the early developmental defects to a failure of "good-enough mothering" at the earliest levels of symbiotic relatedness. In psychotherapy, the relationship with the therapist provides a degree of early nurturing experience in which the therapist functions as a protective shield or auxiliary supportive ego. In those areas in which psychotic anxieties or delusional ideas are at work, the borderline patient is unable to make use of verbal interpretations. Only after the experiences of good-enough mothering have been assimilated does the patient reach a level at which verbal interpretation becomes meaningful. This experience of substitute mothering leads to the establishment of a symbiotic bond, akin to the therapeutic symbiosis described by Searles. The success of the process of subsequent separation depends on the degree to which this fundamental unity or delusion of oneness with the therapist can be established and subsequently analyzed. The analysis of any such psychotic level is achieved solely by regression to complete symbiotic dependency; only gradually as the symbiosis is analyzed and resolved does the patient develop the capacity to assume personal responsibility.

The approach of Rosenfeld (1978) shifts the emphasis somewhat to the libidinal, aggressive, and narcissistic dynamics in the borderline patient. He emphasizes the role of the negative therapeutic reaction as characteristic of the borderline involvement in therapy and attributes it to the patient's basic envy, which motivates the need to devalue and triumph over the analyst. Rosenfeld feels that the patient's need of a sense of superiority and omnipotence should be tolerated and allowed to go unchallenged. Ultimately, analysis of the underlying envy and aggression in terms of their infantile roots is required in order to resolve the negative therapeutic reaction. Countertransference plays an important role, as it does with all Kleinian theorists, as a vehicle for the understanding of the patient's projective identifications.

There are risks in premature interpretations of any aspects of the patient's narcissistic or destructive characteristics, regardless of how obvious they may seem. Any interpretation is heard as an accusation of the patient's behavior. The analyst thus runs the risk of becoming the persecuting object. The analyst's resort to the use of interpretation when the primary need in the therapeutic context is a holding environment in which the therapist is unreservedly receptive, empathic, and accepting can often precipitate a transference psychosis.

The primary differences between the Kleinian orientation and the orientation from the perspective of the borderline spectrum concern the nature of the developmental defect and the view of borderline pathology as connected with underlying psychotic anxieties. In the spectrum view, the developmental defects are seen more generally throughout the course of the developmental process rather than as limited to early infantile states. This view is partly conditioned by the perspective on borderline diagnosis: the Kleinian emphasis falls on the psychoticlike aspects of borderline pathology or is cast in terms of the supposed psychotic core. The spectrum view would see the range of borderline pathology as covering a much broader field, including patients in whom the regressive potential is quite muted and in whom there may well be no hint of psychotic regression. Moreover, in a spectrum view the emergence of psychotic symptomatology of whatever kind is regarded as a transient regressive state rather than as a permanent aspect of the personality organization. In technical terms, the same questions would apply to the Kleinian utilization of ideas pertaining to the holding environment, especially the Bionian application of the container-contained metaphor. Important questions regarding the operationalizing of this concept and its implementation remain unsettled. Despite my own reservations regarding the notion of projective identification,[1] the Klein-

---

[1]In general Kleinian usage, it is never clear whether what is being referred to is a one-person or a two-person phenomenon. In Klein's early usage, projective identification referred to a one-person process which implied the dedifferentiation of self-object boundaries, a phenomenon that would normally be regarded as psychotic. Later usage has elaborated the notion of projective identification as a two-person phenomenon, involving some form of projection on the part of one subject and a matching internalization on the part of another. This latter formulation underlies the Kleinian notions of countertransference (see Meissner 1980a, 1987).

ian analyses of the vicissitudes of countertransference and their application to the patient-therapist interaction and the working-through of transference vicissitudes are often ingenious, illuminating, and clinically useful.

DIMENSIONS

The various treatment approaches differ along a number of dichotomous characteristics. The relevant characteristics would include: the degree to which therapeutic intervention with borderline patients is viewed as supportive rather than expressive; the degree to which the therapeutic effect is a function of interpretation as opposed to qualities of the therapeutic relationship; the degree to which emphasis falls on elements of transference as opposed to countertransference; the degree of therapeutic activity or passivity; the degree to which therapists advocate therapeutic neutrality as opposed to a real relationship; the degree of emphasis on long-term versus short-term therapy; the degree to which scheduling of therapeutic sessions should be intensive.

I will discuss three dichotomous dimensions, namely, the issue of supportive versus expressive therapy, the relative emphasis on interpretation versus the therapeutic relationship as the modality of therapeutic change, and the differential emphasis on transference versus countertransference. In none of the therapeutic approaches is the orientation entirely exclusive, that is, emphasizing one aspect of that dichotomy to the exclusion of the other. Most adopt a more flexible perspective: none, for example, would insist that the therapeutic approach to borderline patients should be merely supportive and not also expressive. The question is rather the degree to which supportive and expressive elements in the therapy can be usefully blended into a meaningful therapeutic approach.

Supportive versus Expressive Psychotherapy

The argument over the relative merits of supportive versus expressive approaches to the psychotherapy of borderline patients has persisted from the beginnings of the concept of borderline psychopathology. For the most part that discussion took place in the context of a view of borderline pathology that saw it in more regressive and primitive terms, that is, having reference to lower-order borderline pathology. With some exceptions, the possibility of psychoanalytic treatment for border-line disorders has been regarded as exceptional and useful only for patients who function at a higher level of integration and defensive organization.

More recently, however, there has been a shift toward the use of more expressive modalities. The report of the Kris Study Group on the treatment of borderline disorders (Abend et al. 1983) has argued for the role of psychoanalysis in the treatment of at least some of these patients. The case material on which that report is based would seem to describe forms of higher-order pathology. However, when we focus on the lower-order end of the borderline spectrum, the consensus would suggest that psychoanalysis for such patients is contraindicated; most therapists would opt for some variety of expressive, exploratory, or interpretive psychotherapy as the medium of choice. The complexities and difficulties involved in such intensive therapy and the pragmatic issues of the availability of time and expense often mean that borderline patients will be seen in more limited supportive forms of psychotherapy (Gunderson 1984). It may often be difficult or even impossible to engage the borderline patient in any more intensive or expressive form of psychotherapy.

The operation of these divergent paradigms has been described in the treatment of inpatients (Gordon and Beresin 1983). The more expressive approaches seek to bring about structural change by way of clarifying the patient's distortion of self and the object world through analysis of the transference. More supportive approaches aim rather at helping the patient to adapt to his environment, arguing that early developmental defects are not affected by transference interpretations, which only induce greater anxiety and regression. The latter approach tends to avoid unconscious conflicts, reinforces the patient's defensive structures, and emphasizes the vicissitudes of the doctor–patient relationship rather than the transference. It advocates less frequent meetings, sets more modest goals, and emphasizes the use of firm limit-setting and the activity of the therapist to resist serious regression.

Supportive Approach

The argument for supportive treatment of borderline patients was advanced by Knight (1954a,b), Zetzel (1971), and Friedman (1969). Knight emphasized the weakness of borderline ego functions and the vulnerability to regression, both of which contraindicated psychoanalytic treatment. On the couch, the borderline ego only regressed, was unable to use interpretation, and became embroiled in unresolvable transference distortions. Knight recommended a more structured face-to-face therapy in which the therapist adopted a more active position and tried to stimulate the patient's adaptive and integrative capacities, strengthen ego controls, and support more adaptive defenses. The use of an exploratory or overly permissive approach only encouraged regressive tendencies and undermined the necessity for firm and consistent setting of limits.

Zetzel (1971) in turn emphasized the developmental failures at the heart of the borderline syndrome. For such patients, intensive and relatively unstructured therapy would present significant dangers and would encourage regressive transference reactions. She recommended a therapeutic approach requiring a minimum rather than a maximum of attention. She felt that frequent appointments would not facilitate the therapeutic relationship, but recommended a schedule of no more than once-a-week meetings, careful structuring of the therapeutic situation, firm limit setting, and an active mobilization of the patient's own resources, leading to the progressive mastery of unfulfilled developmental tasks. The aim was to facilitate development by a realistic use of the doctor–patient relationship, rather than involvement in regressive transference reactions.

Friedman (1975) extended these views, emphasizing the need for a greater degree of activity on the part of the therapist, actively structuring the therapeutic situation to help the patient make better use of the real doctor–patient relationship, and setting realistic limits, particularly on the patient's expectations that the therapist be an omnipotent provider of gratification. The importance of resisting and confining the patient's regressive behavior is stressed. Even in the hospital setting (Friedman 1969), limits must be set on the destructive, self-injuring, violent, or abusive rageful behavior that inevitably makes the patient an object of special attention and concern on the part of the staff. The hospital milieu often intensifies or perpetuates such disruptive behavior and reinforces unrealistic infantile expectations for gratification and care. The hospital stay for such patients should be abbreviated; limited and immediate goals for hospitalization should be clarified; limits should be firmly enforced; and where these efforts are not successful, a disciplinary transfer to a more confining and unresponsive hospital situation should be implemented. In general, the more supportive approach recommends focus on current events and recent sources of stress in the patient's life; tends to focus away from transference elements, particularly where they seem regressive; works toward clarifying feelings and reinforcing a sense of reality; and generally takes a more active stance in supporting and reinforcing the patient's adaptive capacities, supporting useful defenses and generally acting as an auxiliary ego (Blum 1972).

A similar approach has recently been recommended by Gunderson (1984). Along the lines developed by Knight (1954a,b), Grinker and colleagues (1968), and Zetzel (1971), he advocates a nonintensive (once-a-week), supportive approach aimed at reinforcing adaptive defenses and dealing with practical, everyday issues. Such an approach provides a stabilizing relationship, diminishes the tendency to regressive transference involvements, and limits the frequency and severity of regressive crises and suicidal attempts. The course of treatment may last indefinitely and is tapered to a close by decreasing frequency of visits rather than termination. Gunderson argues against Kernberg's view that supportive therapy is toxic to the borderline; rather, for many borderline patients, the results are beneficial and may in some cases achieve structural changes.

Expressive Approach

The primary exponent of an expressive or exploratory approach to borderline psychotherapy is Kernberg. Basing his approach on the results of the Menninger Study (Kernberg et al. 1972), he argues that borderline patients do not do well in supportive psychotherapy and preferably should be treated by an expressive, psychoanalytically oriented approach. Supportive techniques mean

> Active supportive measures used to encourage adaptive combinations of impulse and defense while discouraging the uncovering and interpreting of defenses essential to the equilibrium of the patient. . . . Although suggestion and manipulation are characteristic supportive techniques, other techniques such as abreaction, clarification, and selected interpretations are considered supportive when they are geared to the supportive goals described above. [pp. 206–207]

An expressive approach differs from classical psychoanalysis in that a complete transference neurosis is not allowed to develop and no attempt is made to resolve transferences through interpretation alone. Interpretations focus particularly on the negative transference and pathological defenses (Kernberg 1968). Even in supportive psychotherapy, Kernberg insists on the establishment of a rational basis for treatment as a standard of reality against which transference distortions can be evaluated. At the same time, while transference may not be interpreted, it is not ignored. If transference manifestations are not confronted, a gradual distortion of the therapeutic relationship can result with various forms of collusion, acting out, and a reinforcement of a tendency toward primitive transference. Similarly, avoidance of negative transference can result in a benign idealization of the therapist, which only lays the basis for further distortions and negative reactions to the therapy (Kernberg 1984). In Kernberg's view, then, supportive psychotherapy is not the treatment of choice, but may be the modality of last resort, that is, in cases where the lack of motivation, the consolidation of secondary gains, the impoverishment of object relationships, the weakness of the ego, or extenuating life circumstances will not allow a more expressive, interpretive approach (Kernberg 1984).

Along similar lines, Masterson distinguishes between supportive psychotherapy and reconstructive psychoanalytically oriented psychotherapy (1976). The reconstructive approach aims at working through the patient's abandonment depression derived from the separation-individuation phase, leading to increased ego autonomy and integration. The supportive approach, in contrast, aims only at the control of destructive aspects of defense mechanisms and at providing a supportive relationship for the patient as long as is necessary. The discrimination as to which approach is utilized is based on an assessment of the patient's ego strength, defensive structure, and the degree of developmental separation trauma. While supportive approaches have their place, Masterson would regard them as having only limited effect and as achieving limited therapeutic goals.

At the far extreme of the proponents of expressive/exploratory approaches are the British school of analysts, all following the Kleinian orientation to greater or lesser degree and including such figures as Bion, Heimann, Little, Rosenfeld, Segal, and Winnicott, who prefer to use psychoanalytic methods with these patients. Other proponents of the use of a classic psychoanalytic approach, including the use of the couch, are Boyer and Giovacchini (1967, 1980), Boyer (1983), and Giovacchini (1979).

Integrated Approach

In recent years we have seen the emergence of a view of the relationship between supportive and expressive approaches as continuous rather than dichotomous. This view sees these respective modalities as repre-

senting points along a continuum of variants of psychodynamic psychotherapy. It has been argued that even in the hospital treatment setting,
these paradigms can be seen as complementary approaches that can be
adapted or combined to meet the needs of individual patients (Book
1984). In the treatment of borderline patients, the dichotomy between
supportive and expressive modalities may be a false one, since either
approach taken in its restrictive and exclusive sense would seem to fall
short of therapeutic effectiveness. A purely expressive approach runs
the risk of increasing regression, disorganization, and therapeutic dependence, while a merely supportive approach offers little basis for the
development of adequate insight and emotional growth so necessary to
therapeutic change. It remains possible for therapists to adopt a more
flexible and adaptive approach to the clinical situation, which allows
for greater degrees of exploratory and insight-oriented work during
periods of minimal stress and for the shift to more supportive and limit-
setting techniques in the face of regressive stress (Friedman 1976). Even
among proponents of a more dichotomous approach, there has been a
softening of attitudes. Along with his recognition of the inherent heterogeneity of the borderline group, Kernberg (1984) seems to have
relaxed his dichotomous view of treatment approaches to borderlines
and recognized that some patients may profit more from a supportive
approach and others from an expressive approach.

    Part of the difficulty is establishing the meaning of supportive
psychotherapy and determining whether supportive and expressive modalities are in fact distinct and separable approaches, or whether any
given course of therapy must involve, in practical terms, elements of
both modalities. Approaches to these questions take various forms.
Kernberg (1975a, 1984) clearly distinguishes supportive psychotherapy,
expressive psychotherapy, and psychoanalysis as distinct modalities,
each with different indications and techniques. In his view, these should
be neither confused nor combined since each is appropriate to different
ranges of psychopathology. As he sees it, it is possible to shift from an
expressive to a supportive modality but not in the opposite direction.
This dichotomizing approach differs considerably from that of Luborsky (1984), who views both supportive and expressive approaches as
aspects of psychoanalytic psychotherapy, which vary in emphasis and
degree of combination, not only with different sorts of patients but even
at different points in the treatment of the same patient. In his view,
shifting back and forth between modalities is not only possible but
often necessary. Others, such as Gill (1984) and Kris (1985), with
differing emphases, tend to lump expressive psychotherapy on a con-

tinuum with psychoanalysis and would differentiate these from more purely supportive approaches in terms of aims and techniques.

Writing specifically on supportive psychotherapy, Werman (1984) holds to a distinction between supportive and expressive modalities as distinct and separable entities, even though in practice a given therapy may involve aspects of both. He regards the supportive approach as suitable for patients suffering from ego defects, such as would be found in many borderline patients. The supportive therapist acts as an auxiliary ego, supporting the patient's impaired ego functions by using techniques of suggestion, limit setting, clarification, and confrontation. The aim of removing repression, a primary aim of expressive psychotherapy and psychoanalysis, is not part of the supportive approach. Similarly, the transference is utilized rather than analyzed. Whatever the diagnostic category, some patients will be found to be suitable for a supportive approach and others for a more expressive approach. Even here, where the theoretical distinctions are so clearly made, there is ample room for questioning whether the actual clinical examples do not to a significant degree involve exploratory, interpretive, and insight-oriented elements.

My own view is that, while the theoretical discrimination between supportive and expressive modalities has a certain utility from the point of view of articulating and describing aspects of the psychotherapeutic process, attempts to hold rigidly to a dichotomous view that prescribes a given form of therapeutic modality to specific diagnostic entities is neither theoretically sustainable nor clinically practical. Particularly in the treatment of borderline patients, where considerable variability and instability is so often a feature of the clinical situation, the therapist needs to maintain a position of flexibility and adaptibility, allowing the selection of available techniques from the range of psychotherapeutic interventions to deal with the problems presented.

With the borderline patient, particularly lower-order patients in whom the regressive potential is so high, the affective lability so precipitous, and the vulnerability to regressive distortions and undermining of the therapeutic alliance so imminent, the therapist needs to have readily at hand both supportive and expressive techniques. At certain points with such patients, particularly in regressive crises or in the face of distortions of the alliance, supportive techniques are called into play in order to deal with disruptive elements and to maintain the integrity of the therapeutic situation. At other points in the therapy of all borderline patients, there are moments of great stability, greater mobilization of ego resources, a consolidation and sustenance of a therapeutic alliance, and a greater capacity for expressive and insight-oriented work. During such periods, patients are considerably more receptive to interpretations, even though the constructive effect of such interpretations may be eroded by subsequent periods of instability and repression. Nonetheless, the general balance of supportive or expressive techniques relates in a general sense to the levels of psychic integration and the severity of pathological fixations in any given patient.

Since patients from the lower order of the borderline spectrum are expected to have greater difficulties in these respects, it is likely that supportive techniques would be utilized to a much greater extent than expressive techniques. Borderline patients who would be functioning at a much higher level and in the face of a much lower vulnerability to regression would be capable in general of more consistent expressive effort, even though with many of these patients, whether in the face of regressive crises or not, supportive elements are a necessary and integral part of the therapy. The decision as to when and how to utilize this range of therapeutic techniques—when to be relatively supportive and when to move toward more expressive and interpretative emphases— are matters of clinical judgment and experience.

Interpretation versus the Therapeutic Relationship

The second dimension of varying emphasis is the extent to which effective change in the therapy of borderline patients lies in the technique of interpretation as opposed to the therapeutic relationship itself. The emphases vary across the spectrum of approaches, and again it would be difficult to find anyone who would insist on one dimension to the exclusion of another. Theorists who stress interpretation as the modality of change tend to operate within an ego-psychological frame of reference, while those emphasizing the importance of the therapeutic relationship derive their orientation more from an object-relations framework.

Interpretive Emphasis

The major figure who has emphasized the role of interpretation most persistently is Kernberg (1968, 1975a, 1976b, 1984). His model of borderline pathology dictates that relatively primitive transferences are quickly mobilized in the therapeutic interaction and operate as resistances that impede the establishing of a therapeutic alliance, distort the therapeutic relationship, and put the continuance of the therapeutic process itself at risk. Such distorting transference influences must therefore be focused on and interpreted immediately. As Kernberg insists, the interpretation of such transferences requires maintaining a position of technical neutrality, which provides a firm and consistent basis in reality, against which the transference distortions can be evaluated. In this view any attempt at genetic reconstruction should be postponed to later stages of the treatment (Campbell 1982, Frosch 1983, Kernberg 1984, Goldstein 1985, Schaffer 1986).

Relational Emphasis

Relational approaches, on the other hand, emphasize the importance of the relationship between therapist and patient, but in none of these approaches is the role of interpretation and other techniques eliminated. Nonetheless, the conceptualization of the therapeutic relationship and its role in the treatment process varies considerably from author to author. Masterson (1976), for example, emphasizes the need of the borderline patient for a real object to related to. In the early stages of therapy, the therapist serves as a transference object, allowing the working-through of transference distortions and the establishment of a healthier therapeutic alliance. Working out of an ego-psychological framework, the Blancks (1974, 1979) take the position that a combination of therapist characteristics and appropriate technical interventions brings about a therapeutic relationship that fosters more adaptive organization and development in the borderline patient. The characteristics they emphasize include the therapist's reliability, predictability, a benign attitude toward the patient, and sufficient emotional availability to allow a degree of symbiotic gratification, which enables the patient to move toward greater independence. Gratification and frustration in this relationship need to be balanced in order to facilitate the patient's development and greater independence. The Blancks see the patient's participation in the therapeutic relationship as a form of reparative experience.

In a similar vein, Giovacchini (1972), arguing for the utilization of psychoanalysis in the treatment of all character disorders, emphasizes the importance of the current transference context and its interpretation. The availability of a supportive therapeutic relationship holds a central position, which provides a degree of stability and may promote some internalization of aspects of the analytic attitude. The success or failure of treatment depends on the quality of the patient-analyst inter-action. Even the effect of interpretations may depend on and derive from the quality of the therapeutic relationship (Boyer and Giovacchini 1967).

Chessick (1982), disagreeing with Kernberg, takes a somewhat different position regarding interpretations, namely that early interpre-tation of transference distortions are to be avoided because they serve only to inflict narcissistic injury on the patient and intensify negative transference reactions. Chessick's own approach emphasizes the impor-tance of the therapeutic alliance and the establishment of a meaningful therapeutic relationship. Dealing with the various forms of transfer-ence, he argues that the more primitive transferences, both those that are narcissistic (both idealizing and mirror transferences) and those based on the patient's clinging to the therapist as a transitional object (a source of magical protection and security), cannot be dealt with by interpretation, since they are often literally life-saving for the patient and serve to restore a degree of narcissistic equilibrium. He suggests that these transferences be simply left alone or empathically tolerated (after the manner of Kohut), and that in time they will disappear as a more effective therapeutic relationship is established. The more affec-tively disruptive and intense transferences, involving highly erotized or negative transference elements, should be dealt with as soon as possible by tactful clarification and confrontation (Chessick 1979). It has re-cently been suggested that Chessick's work increasingly shows a ten-dency to shift away from reliance on interpretation toward the creation of a reliable holding environment, which allows the patient to harm-lessly discharge rage and more effectively explore early experiences and primitive fantasies (Schaffer 1986).

The progenitor of the emphasis on the quality of the relationship in the treatment of more primitive patients was Donald Winnicott with his emphasis on the role of the "holding environment" and "good-enough mothering" (Winnicott 1965). He also subordinated the func-tion of interpretation to the nature and quality of the therapeutic relationship, observing that

> Interpretation outside the ripeness of the material is indoctrination and produces compliance. A corollary is that resistance arises out of interpretation given outside the area of the overlap of the pa-tient's and the analyst's playing together. Interpretation when the patient has no capacity to play is simply not useful, or causes confusion. When there is mutual playing, then interpretation ac-

cording to accepted psychoanalytic principles can carry the therapeutic work forward. This playing has to be spontaneous, and not
compliant or acquiescent, if psychotherapy is to be done. [1971,
p. 51]

Winnicott's notions of the holding environment and the role of the
therapist as a good-enough mother have had a considerable influence
on therapists who emphasize the relational component of therapy with
borderline patients. Modell (1978, 1984), Adler (1975, 1985), Adler and
Buie (1979), and Buie and Adler (1982–1983) have emphasized the role
of the holding environment, particularly in early phases of the treatment.

A somewhat different approach is found in the work of Searles
(1976, 1978), who minimizes the role of interpretation while emphasizing
the therapist's nonverbal interaction with the patient. While directing
attention primarily to the emotional atmosphere and the complex role of
countertransference in the continuing unconscious exchange between
patient and therapist, Searles asserts the need for a regressive involvement
with the patient in terms of a symbiotic relatedness as an essential root for
any meaningful change. In this therapeutic symbiosis, the bond of
mother–infant dependency is recreated between patient and therapist.

Emphasis on relational factors is also a common feature of the
approach to the treatment of borderline patients by Kleinian analysts,
largely under the influence of Winnicott and Bion. Bion's (1962) notion
of the relation between the container and the contained comes fairly
close to the understanding of the holding environment. For Kleinian
theorists, the focus falls on the dynamic patterns that take place within
the context of the interactive relationship between patient and therapist, patterns usually of projective identification (projection) and introjective identification (introjection). The working out of these interactive
patterns in the dynamics of the therapeutic relationship serves as the
major vehicle for therapeutic understanding and change. Thus, Little
(1966) emphasizes that the therapeutic relationship with the borderline
patient must provide a degree of early nurturing in which the patient
feels protected and sustained. In areas of the patient's experience in
which psychotic anxieties predominate, it is not possible for the patient
to grasp or assimilate interpretations. The patient needs to experience a
degree of good-enough mothering before the ego reaches a point at
which it can utilize verbal interpretations.

Rosenfeld (1978), like Searles, emphasizes the need for the patient
to develop a normal symbiosis as a vehicle for neutralizing the effects of

destructive impulses. Any attempt to interpret this destructiveness is bound to fail, since the patient hears interpretations of this sort as forms of accusation or indictment. The inappropriate use of such interpretations may in fact lead to the development of a transference psychosis when what the patient requires is a holding environment on the part of the therapist who is receptive, empathic, and unambivalently accepting. A similar emphasis can be found in the work of Balint (1968), who, in discussing the basic fault as a fundamental aspect of the pathology of more primitive personality disorders, regards the level of developmental defect as lying at a preoedipal and preverbal level, so that any attempt to deal with this level of pathological organization by techniques of verbal interpretation not only miss the mark but may be counterproductive. Consequently, the curative effects in therapy with such patients must derive from preverbal, implicit, and often unconscious dimensions of the therapeutic relationship itself.

There is a paradox in my reading of Kleinian theorists, who focus so consistently on the dynamics of the therapeutic relationship, but at the same time are relatively aggressive and forthright in interpreting aspects of the patient's inner world, not only in relatively primitive and regressive terms but also early in the course of the therapy. Such regressive interpretations are calculated to gain some degree of control over primitive anxieties that may be disturbing the therapeutic context. Thus, while an important place is given to relational factors, one has to keep in mind the unique and significant place of in-depth interpretations in the Kleinian orientation.

Overview

The dichotomy of emphasis between interpretive versus relational factors in the therapy of borderline patients parallels to a certain degree the dichotomy between supportive and expressive approaches discussed above. The emphasis on one or other aspect is a matter of theoretical orientation, those authors emphasizing the role of interpretation holding closer to a more classical idea of psychoanalytic technique, and those emphasizing relational factors basing their approach more on an object-relational paradigm. Most therapists would agree that interpretive approaches are more effective with patients functioning on a higher level, or in those phases of the therapy where the patient's resources are better integrated and the patient's capacity to work in the therapy is more effectively mobilized.

Thus, the emphasis of the Kris Group (Abend et al. 1983) seems to reflect the fact that their patients were, in general, better functioning and better able to utilize interpretive input. On the other hand, the emphasis of Kernberg on the early interpretation of transference distortions seems calculated to come to grips with these early transference paradigms and to modify them so as to allow a more solid footing for the therapeutic interaction to emerge. Somewhat the same rationale has been provided for early Kleinian interpretations, although the Kleinian proclivity for deep and regressive interpretations is in no way comparable to Kernberg's here-and-now focus on the disruption of the therapeutic relationship. As a general rule, therapists who emphasize the relational component are dealing with patients of a more primitive order in whom the capacity for a meaningful and collaborative relationship has been severely damaged or has not adequately developed, and in whom the necessity for developing a secure, stable, and trustworthy relationship with the therapist takes precedence over any other therapeutic considerations. The emphasis on therapeutic holding and on the role of a symbiotic relatedness in these contexts may reflect the level of defect in the patient rather than any theoretical commitments (Waldinger 1987, Waldinger and Gunderson 1987).

Transference versus Countertransference

The third dimension of differential emphasis is between those who focus on issues related to transference and those who focus more explicitly on countertransference reactions. Obviously, transference and countertransference are two sides of the same coin and cannot exist exclusively. While all therapists would admit the importance of the role of both aspects, there are differential emphases. Kernberg, for example, emphasizes early and immediate focus on patient transferences that serve as resistances. But he also pays serious attention to countertransference issues. Kernberg (1984) stresses the necessity for early interpretation both of negative transferences and of the more primitive aspects of intensely affective positive transferences. Positive transferences that do not serve as resistances or prove to be disruptive to the therapeutic work can serve as a basis for the development of a therapeutic alliance. A similar focus on transference aspects of the therapeutic interaction can be found in the work of Chessick (1977, 1979, 1982). While Chessick would apparently follow Kernberg's lead up to a point regarding the approach to early disruptive and intense transference, whether

erotic or negative, he would caution against the risks of early interpretation and would clearly diverge from Kernberg in dealing with self-
object and transitional object transferences, which he regards as better
left uninterpreted.

Most students of the therapeutic process with borderline patients
recognize the importance of the therapist's countertransference involvement with the patient. Kernberg, Masterson, Gunderson, Adler and
Buie, and Chessick all allow an important place for countertransference
vicissitudes in their understanding of the therapeutic process. But
among therapists who give a particular emphasis to countertransference
dynamics, the British school of Kleinian analysts and object-relations
theorists take a primary place. The laurels on the American scene
clearly go to Searles, who has written extensively and sensitively on the
role of countertransference dynamics, not only in the treatment of
borderline patients but more particularly schizophrenics (Searles 1965,
1976, 1978). Searles argues that the extent to which the therapist is
unable to perceive in himself the reality basis for the patient's projective
transference onto him would render him relatively ineffective in working with that patient. The therapist must be willing and able to bear a
part of the burden of the pathology that comes to exist within the
relationship.

For Kleinian analysts, the countertransference plays a particularly
important role, since it is the aspect of the analyst's engagement in the
therapeutic relationship that reflects the influence of projective identification, that is, the patient's projection and the therapist's introjection
within the therapeutic interaction. Within the Kleinian approach, then,
countertransference serves primarily as a vehicle for unconscious communication and a signaling system to the therapist as to what may be
happening on the level of the patient's transference, as well as providing
clues to the pathogenic organization of the patient's inner world.
Within this approach, then, the focus of therapeutic interest and the
starting point for meaningful interventions lie on the side of the therapist's countertransference experience.

While the varying emphases on transference or countertransference aspects of the therapeutic interaction are not as clearly drawn as
other dimensions, I suspect that the tendency to focus on countertransference dynamics is a reflection of the therapist's involvement with
more primitively organized patients. This, I think, is clearly the case
with the contributions of Searles and of the Kleinians. In the therapeutic interaction with such patients, the unconscious pressures that underlie and stimulate relatively intense countertransference reactions are a

commonly experienced part of therapeutic work (Meissner 1982–1983). With somewhat better-organized patients, the countertransference vicissitudes tend to be more muted or to operate at a lesser degree of emotional intensity and disruptiveness. I will have more to say about both transference and countertransference in Chapters 5 and 6, but it is clear that there is a fair amount of variation in the application of these important aspects of the therapeutic process.

With this melange of positions and opinions as a background, I will turn in succeeding chapters to my own considerations regarding the treatment of borderline patients. The diversity in approaches can be ascribed in large measure to the prior diagnostic difficulties and the variations in diagnostic orientation. Certain forms of technical intervention and emphasis may apply more tellingly with certain groups of patients, groups that form subgroupings within the borderline spectrum. Further, given the inherent variability and vulnerability to regressive pulls that is part of the borderline condition, it may be that varying therapeutic emphases may come into play in different degrees in the course of treatment of any given borderline patient. The reader should be forewarned that the understanding of the therapeutic approach to the borderline patient involves a delicate balancing of potential risks against potential therapeutic gains.

4

THE THERAPIST

The therapeutic process, in whatever context in takes place, always involves a minimum of two participants—sometimes more. In individual therapy, the participants are the therapist and the patient. The focus in this chapter falls on the therapist. My main emphasis is on the limits and fallibility of our knowledge and technical resources and on the fact that more evolves out of what kind of human beings we are than from however well reasoned our therapeutic rationales and technical ploys.

Without question the most important ingredient in the therapeutic matrix is the therapist himself.[1] The therapist's personality enters into the therapeutic process in a more significant way in the treatment of borderline patients than with any other group of patients. The reasons for this are clear from our previous discussion, especially the unavoidably interactive quality of the therapeutic relation and the activation of projective and introjective mechanisms. These are continually pushing or pulling the therapist into countertransference positions that have the potential for frustrating or impeding therapeutic progress. The therapist's own susceptibility to responding in countertransference terms or to getting enbroiled in a transference/countertransference interaction is in part a function of his own personality structure.

---

[1]Generic usage throughout is followed. The sex of the therapist is not considered.

A factor that is not well studied but may have considerable importance in the treatment of borderline patients is the matter of therapist-
patient fit. The importance of this dimension has been demonstrated
with other types of patients (Whitehorn and Betz 1954, 1957, 1960,
Razin 1971, May 1974, Gunderson et al. 1975) and has even more sway
in the approach to therapy that a given therapist might take. Some
therapists do better in maintaining a therapeutic structure, setting appropriate limits, maintaining the parameters of the therapeutic relation,
keeping the patient at the therapeutic task, avoiding countertransference traps, and reinforcing the patient's responsible involvement in the
treatment. These therapists find greater success with patients who need
that kind of structure in order to gain any benefit from the therapeutic
process. For lower-order borderlines who show a significant degree of
instability, lability, and tendencies to act out, the approach may be
optimal. Other therapists seem to find greater success in maintaining a
nurturant, empathic, holding environment within which patients have
the opportunity to gain important self-enhancing inputs that have been
lacking in their developmental experience.

For most borderline patients, it is safe to say that they need both
structure and empathic support. A given therapist may have a greater
capacity to provide one dimension than another, and this is a function
of his own personality, developmental history, maturity, unresolved
conflicts, and values. This dimension cannot be changed by training;
the most that can be expected is that he gain some degree of awareness
and sensitivity to these limitations in himself and understand the impact
they can have on the therapeutic process. A therapist should not be
disappointed or take it as a sign of incompetence or unsuitability for
therapeutic work if he cannot interact successfully with a given patient
or type of patient. If such factors interfere significantly with his work,
this might indicate the need for some therapeutic work on himself.
Many training programs, especially psychoanalytic ones, presume that
these factors operate in everyone, so that a training analysis is a required part of the program.

An important part of the capacity of the therapist is his flexibility.
In the treatment of patients within the borderline spectrum, no single
approach is possible, not only because of the variety of the range of
pathology but also because of the variability from session to session,
from moment to moment, in the therapeutic work. Effective treatment
of these patients requires that the therapist be able to assess the nature
of the patient's basic pathology and to adapt the therapeutic approach
to the characteristics and needs of that level of pathology.

If adaptability in therapeutic approach can be thought of as a kind of macroadaptation, flexibility may be a form of microadaptation. Depending on the lability and instability in the patient's personality structure, the clinical presentation can vary considerably. In relatively unstable patients, the configuration may shift quickly from an objective, reasonable, thoughtful, ego-based orientation to one that is regressive and reflective of the underlying introjective configuration—whether activating the aggressor or victim introject—or even shift rapidly back and forth between them. Emergence of these configurations can precipitate projections that can rapidly undermine the therapeutic alliance. The patient may suddenly and unexpectedly become paranoid, or depressed, distrustful, or angry. Other patients, whose psychic structure is better knit and stable, may suddenly shift to a more regressive posture—a time-limited, episodic, regressive shift that is often surprising in view of the patient's otherwise consistent and nonregressive functioning. In the face of these variations, the therapist must be ready to shift accordingly and to meet the needs of the patient at that moment, becoming more or less active, setting limits when useful, focusing on the distortions in the therapeutic alliance, providing the necessary degree of holding, and so forth. The good therapist must learn to bob and weave and roll with the punches. The therapist has to modify his technique as a result of his ongoing diagnostic reading of the patient. This reading requires an attentive focusing on the multiple aspects of the therapeutic interaction and on the level of the patient's functioning. This would include an assessment of the level of defensive organization, ego functioning, object relations (especially in the moment-to-moment interaction with the therapist), superego functioning, and particularly the data relevant to the introjective configurations (aggressor, victim, superior, and inferior).

Clearly the ideal therapist does not exist—not for any kind of therapy and especially not for the therapy of borderline patients. All therapists have their relative strengths and weaknesses, their skills and blind spots. The balance of strengths and weaknesses is often brought into stark relief by the work with difficult borderline patients. The most important strength for therapists undertaking this work is the capacity to remain steady on course despite the howling winds and raging seas that can so readily be whipped up in these patients. It is often this quality of the therapist and his interaction with the patient that carry the day. It may also be this quality that provides the essential element in developing a holding environment within which the patient can feel secure. This capacity stems from the therapist's ability to resist countertransference pulls and to maintain a balanced sense of his own personal and professional identity as well as perspective regarding his therapeutic role.

It is also important for the therapist to recognize and accept his own limitations. For none of these patients does any therapist have all the answers. There are inherent limitations to what a given therapist can or is willing to tolerate. Even experienced therapists cannot work with too many of these patients at one time—my own judgment is that no therapist should try to work with more than one or two such patients at a time. This is especially true of the more primitive, affectively labile, acting-out patient in the hysterical continuum. It must be recognized, however, that we all do treat some of these patients, perhaps more than we realize. I am convinced that many find their way to the analytic couch—a fact recognized in the widening scope of psychoanalysis (Stone 1954). The therapist must accept his limited capacity not only for working with numbers of such patients but also for effectiveness with each patient. This requires thoughtful consideration of what is involved in his role as therapist and a capacity to stick to those boundaries. Efforts to draw him out of his therapeutic role are a constant aspect of the therapeutic process with borderline patients, and the therapist must be alert to these pressures and steer his course accordingly.

An important matter is taking care of the therapist. Pacing is important. I do not recommend tight scheduling. The therapist needs time to unwind from often demanding and stressful sessions, time to gear up for other sessions that he knows will be difficult and challenging. He needs to take appropriate breaks, both during the course of the day's work and in the form of vacations. This is often difficult when working with borderline patients because of their marked sensitivity to separation and feelings of abandonment. There is a certain responsibility to meet the patient's need in this regard but it must be limited. The therapist must be able to schedule vacation periods adequate to meet his own needs; the difficulties created for the patient by these separations must be managed in whatever way is appropriate. There is no room for guilt in this matter. Not only is the therapist entitled to vacation breaks, but they are a necessary part of his continuing to work effectively. The therapist needs to pay attention to the quality of his life experience. A balanced and satisfying life is a powerful contributory factor in maintaining the capacity to work with difficult patients.

The last aspect I would stress is the importance of consultation and supervision in learning and doing therapy with borderline patients.

The opportunities for therapeutic impasses and disruptions are many. Even for experienced therapists, consultation regarding troublesome cases is always a good idea. Often an uninvolved and objective look at the therapeutic interaction can pick up elements that the therapist might not have been able to see. Even if the consultation yields no more than confirmation that what can be done is being done or offers only sympathetic support, it can be helpful in moving the therapeutic work forward. For therapists who are still learning the ropes, good supervision is mandatory. There is much to be learned about the treatment process with these patients, if only the degree to which the capacity of the process and of the therapist himself is limited. Even for therapists who have mastered many of the basic techniques of psychotherapy, experience with borderline patients becomes an education in the vicissitudes of countertransference and transference/countertransference interaction, and in the basic understanding of the nature of the therapeutic process. None of us is immune to having a patient push us to the limit of our capacity in these areas, and we can learn something more about the therapeutic enterprise and about ourselves from the experience.

PART II

THE THERAPEUTIC RELATIONSHIP

The therapeutic alliance, transference, and countertransference form the heart of the therapeutic process. It is in these dimensions of the process that the central issues of the treatment of borderline patients take shape. It is not merely that they are central, but that they tend to assume a characteristic quality and form in borderline pathology. These aspects of borderline psychopathology dominate the therapy with patients in the lower order of the borderline spectrum, and often emerge transiently and episodically in the treatment of higher-order patients. I would argue that no effective therapy can take place with these patients without engaging in profoundly meaningful and powerfully affective ways with these central aspects of the therapeutic interaction and process.

5

THE THERAPEUTIC
ALLIANCE

DIFFICULTIES

Many authors (Blanck and Blanck 1974, Adler 1975, 1979, 1985, Masterson 1976, Chessick 1979, 1983a, Boyer 1983, Meissner 1984a) have commented on the impaired or defective capacity of borderline patients to form a therapeutic alliance. Adler (1979, 1985) has even gone so far as to describe it as a "myth." These difficulties persist throughout the borderline spectrum with a considerable range of variation.

The literature generally focuses on the impaired capacity found in the more severely disturbed (lower-order) borderline patients, whether in the hysterical or the schizoid continuum, whose capacities for object relationship are easily overwhelmed by the intensity of their affects and the power of their transference reactions. The impediments to the therapeutic alliance tend to take the form of acute disruptions, expressed in forms of acting-out or self-destructive behavior, often occurring in the context of an acute regression within the therapy, and carrying the stamp of markedly disruptive transference paradigms. The therapeutic alliance is often a compromise between their limited capacity for engagement in the therapeutic work and the need for acceptance and security in order to even participate in the process.

In patients in the healthier (higher-order) range of the borderline spectrum, these acutely disruptive and distorting reactions are found much more rarely and only in muted form. They may occur in connection with periods of regression, but the regressions are usually less severe and the disruptions less intense. The difficulties in the therapeutic alliance in these patients tend to take the form of chronic distortions in the therapeutic relationship, which reflect habitual and characterological ways in which patients deal with significant others in their environment. Such therapeutic misalliances are less often disruptive than they are continually and subtly undermining of the work of the therapy. Consequently, the problems created by the failures in the therapeutic alliance call for much different forms of therapeutic intervention at various levels of the borderline spectrum.

There is also a consensus regarding the importance of the therapeutic alliance for effective treatment (Blanck and Blanck 1974, Dickes 1975, Masterson 1976, Chessick 1979, 1983a,b, Boyer 1983). Most authors focus on the difficulties in establishing the therapeutic situation (Masterson 1976, Chessick 1979, 1983a, Boyer 1983), but even Kernberg (1984), who does not address himself to alliance issues as such, envisions a similar process in terms of transference management. All authors recognize the difficulty in establishing the therapeutic alliance as a particular problem in the treatment of borderline patients and emphasize the need for continuous attention to alliance factors from the beginning of the treatment. Without some degree of effective therapeutic alliance, there is no common basis between therapist and patient for advancing or accepting interpretations. The same issue has been addressed in the therapy of borderline adolescents where failures in the therapeutic alliance or limitations in the capacity to form an alliance were a major contributing factor to the lack of therapeutic success (Simon 1984). A review of the Menninger Study indicates that the failure to establish a meaningful alliance, for whatever reason, contributed significantly to the failure rate (Colson et al. 1982).

THE NATURE OF THE THERAPEUTIC ALLIANCE

Definition

There is considerable confusion over the use of the term "therapeutic alliance," some analysts using it almost as the equivalent of transference (Gutheil and Havens 1979) or even rejecting the terminology as merely expressing an aspect of transference phenonema (Gill 1979, 1982, Brenner 1980, Modell 1986). However, I maintain a strong distinction between the therapeutic alliance and the transference, and will try to make clear the technical differences involved in approaching the patient-therapist relationship from either a therapeutic alliance or a transference perspective. The distinction is viable, although less pressing in healthier neurotic patients, who are the usual subjects of psychoanalytic treatment. But in the borderline spectrum, because of the factors weakening the therapeutic alliance or the frequent disruptions or distortions of it, the focus on and understanding of alliance factors is central to the therapeutic process.

There is also some confusion regarding the use of the terms "therapeutic alliance" and "working alliance" (Greenson 1965). Some analysts use the terms synonymously, others distinguish them. For example, Dickes (1975) sees the therapeutic alliance as the more developed and evolved pattern of relationship between patient and therapist, including all the elements that would favor the patient's participation and the effectiveness of the collaborative therapeutic effort. This would include such elements as the patient's positive motivation for treatment, aspects of the positive transference, and the capacity for rational interaction between the patient and therapist—similar to the rational alliance described by Gutheil and Havens (1979). The working alliance would then be regarded as more limited in scope, involving a basic capacity for patient and therapist to work together, and expressing the extent to which the more mature part of the patient's ego can involve itself in the therapeutic process. The term "working" in this view connotes a limitation in the therapeutic relationship that makes it possible for patient and therapist to work together and allows the therapeutic work to progress in some partial or reduced fashion, suggesting that the alliance is limited or impaired to some degree. While this usage is acceptable, the distinction need not be pressed excessively. I will use the term "working" to express a limited or partial alliance, but references to the therapeutic alliance would not necessarily imply that the alliance was completely or fully established.

Although there is a great deal more to be said about the basic nature of the therapeutic alliance, we can take the description of the rational alliance provided by Gutheil and Havens (1979), following the work of Sterba (1934), Zetzel (1970), and Greenson (1965), as our starting point. The therapeutic alliance involves "the therapeutic split in the ego which allows the analyst to work with the healthier elements in the patient against resistance and pathology" (Gutheil and Havens, p. 479).

Components

While a certain consensus regarding definition is possible, difficulties remain in the manner in which the therapeutic alliance is operational- ized. Elements that contribute to establishing the therapeutic alliance include contractual arrangements between patient and therapist regard- ing the logistics of the therapy (scheduling, fees, payment, confidential- ity, etc.), some agreement as to how the parties will work together and for what purposes, and an understanding and acceptance on both parts of their respective roles and responsibilities. Consequently, the thera- peutic alliance embraces many aspects of the relationship between the patient and the therapist that do not fall within the scope of transfer- ence, nor are they pertinent to the real relationship between the two, even though the development and shaping of the therapeutic alliance is intimately related to aspects of both transference and reality.

Moreover, the therapeutic alliance is not something that is inher- ent only in the patient; rather it involves a process of interaction to which both patient and therapist contribute. Consequently, the thera- pist's attitudes, the way in which he regards, responds to, and deals with the patient are important contributing elements to establishing and maintaining the therapeutic alliance. The therapist's respect, considera- tion, courtesy, tactfulness, and empathy are important contributing factors. Further, the therapist must adopt a firm, consistent, and un- changing position vis-à-vis the patient that holds the patient consis- tently responsible for participation in the therapeutic process. An im- portant aspect of the therapeutic alliance in borderline patients is a consistent attitude that refuses to regard the patient as helpless or inadequate, but maintains an expectation of the patient's meaningful involvement in the therapeutic process and an implicit demand that the patient accept and observe his responsibilities both within and outside of the therapy. Parallel to this is a consistent, secure, firm, and unwav- ering posture of the therapist that conveys (in behavior rather than words) that he will fulfill his role and meet his responsibilities in the therapy in a consistent, mature, and constructive manner.

These issues seem almost to transcend the realm of technique, insofar as they express and reflect qualities of the therapists' own personality and values as they enter into the therapeutic process and engage with the needs of the patient. Thus, the therapeutic alliance has profound implications for the outcome of the therapy, since it is a central component of the arena within which patient and therapist engage with each other in the work of the therapy, and provides a matrix within which important interpersonal experiences and crucial identifications, which may modify the patient's pathogenic inner structure, can take place (Chessick 1974, Meissner 1981b).

Not all therapists are comfortable with these specifications of the aspects of the therapeutic alliance. Giovacchini (1979), for example, offers a strong objection to the contractual aspects of the therapeutic relationship, objecting that it sounds too much like a crass business arrangement and that it is implemented more for the convenience of the therapist than for the advantage of the patient. Regarding payment of the fee, for example, he argues that this is wholly for the benefit of the therapist and not for the benefit of the patient.

I would disagree with these assumptions. The contractual arrangements are the necessary structures that make the therapy possible. Given the complex realities of the culture, social structure, and economics within which we function, payment of a fee for services rendered is a necessary part of the interaction between patient and therapist. It involves a set of culturally derived and reinforced assumptions about the nature of the relationship and the reciprocal responsibilities and commitments that both patient and therapist make to the process. In addition, as is the case with other limits within the structure of the therapy, the payment of a fee brings into focus some of the patient's basic conflicts with reality and its demands, and counters the wish for an all-giving, symbiotic, all-gratifying object.

Therapy is simply not possible without an agreement or a viable arrangement between the parties involved in the process. To regard this aspect as not contributing to the patient's well-being is to ignore the fact that a degree of demand on the patient to accept some responsibility for the therapy encourages a motivation to undertake and successfully accomplish the therapy. These aspects are part of the emerging therapeutic process and work to the continuing benefit of the patient.

Relation to Borderline Spectrum

This view of the therapeutic alliance has certain implications for the understanding of the borderline spectrum. The patient's capacity for the therapeutic alliance and the quality of the therapeutic alliance can be expected to vary considerably from one end of the borderline spectrum to the other. Within the hysterical continuum, the range runs from the intense, affectively disruptive breakdowns of the therapeutic alliance in often dramatic and cataclysmic fashion, usually communicated either in forms of intense affect or as relatively dramatic acting out, all the way to the higher-order manifestations, usually found in the primitive hysterics in the form of subtle erosions of the therapeutic alliance. These rarely take a dramatic or disruptive form but rather express themselves in terms of the gradual erosion of the therapeutic relationship or the often unconscious collusive development of a therapeutic misalliance. Patients at this level of the hysterical continuum may often present themselves in hysterical or narcissistic terms. They usually seem to be involved in the therapeutic or analytic process in reasonable or productive ways, tend to observe the superficial terms of the therapeutic contract, but nonetheless enter the relationship with the therapist and engage in the work of the therapy in ways that are frustrating, distorting, or undermining of therapeutic objectives. Rather than hitting the therapist in the face in a sudden and dramatic fashion, as is often the case in lower-order conditions, the distortions of the therapeutic alliance at this level assert themselves subtly and gradually, and may dawn on the therapist's awareness only over extended periods of time. Rather than a regressive crisis, the therapist is confronted with a therapeutic impasse or stalemate.

In the schizoid continuum, the picture is not exactly parallel. Lower-order difficulties in the schizoid realm express themselves either in the form of schizoid withdrawal or distancing that does not allow a meaningful relationship to emerge, or in the noncommunication of affect that treats the therapist as affectively nonexistent and creates a superficial adjustment that thwarts deeper involvement. Higher-order pathology involves similar processes, but in a more subtle fashion that often gives the impression of meaningful involvement but masks a schizoid avoidance that is appreciated only slowly and gradually as an aspect of subtle difficulties and resistances in the therapeutic process.

Therapeutic Misalliances

An important consideration is that problems or disturbances that arise in the alliance sector are not equivalent to or reducible to transference distortions. Langs (1975a,b) has coined the term "therapeutic misalliance" to describe this phenomenon. A therapeutic misalliance is by no means equivalent to transference, even though the therapeutic alliance and the transference (including the transference neurosis) are basically antithetical.

An example may help to clarify the point. Early in a series of evaluative sessions in which a patient and therapist were working toward a decision to undertake a course of therapy, the patient, a young woman in her late twenties who had had difficulties with an earlier eating disorder, and had recently experienced the abrupt and unexplained termination of a therapeutic relationship that had lasted over six years, described her mother as an alcoholic and her father as an overeater. She tearfully complained that her mother would drink and become unavailable to her and that her father would eat and become similarly unavailable. With some trepidation and hesitation a few minutes later in the discussion, she commented that the therapist seemed to be overweight and that made her afraid that he would not listen to her and would not be able to hear her pain.

This material could easily be heard in transference terms, namely, a negative father transference triggered by the similarity between the father's corpulence and the therapist's. If one were to consider the transference only, one would regard this reductively as transference material and would deal with it in those terms. I would suggest, however, that the situation is more complex. What was also being expressed was the patient's concern that the therapist would be unable to hear her internal distress, that he would be unavailable to her and be unable to stay with her during the experiencing of that pain, and that he would be incapable of responding empathically and understandingly. The patient was clearly suffering from an unresolved mourning of the former therapist and was struggling with issues of trust on the brink of entering another such relationship. I would regard these as basically alliance issues. I would feel it premature and nonproductive to respond to the patient's concerns in transference terms, that is, in terms of the genetic connection between her disappointment in her father and the displacement of these concerns to the therapist as a newly experienced object. That interpretation would not be inaccurate, but it would run the risk of bypassing what is affectively immediate for the patient. By the same token, it would respond to the patient's concerns as though they were injected into the therapeutic situation from outside, rather than arising within the interaction as an aspect of the immediate situation to which both patient and therapist are contributing. It is appropriate and even important to respond in terms that deal more directly with the patient's immediate, even existential, concerns that are carried by the transference elements, but which go beyond the transference since they are concerns that are pertinent and alive within the immediate context of the patient's involvement with the therapist, regardless of transference derivatives. For many borderline patients, particularly in the lower-order group, the issues here are existential and involve questions of security, safety, abandonment, emptiness, loss of self-cohesion, and so on.

That the concerns should arise and be expressed in terms of a transference metaphor is by no means irrelevant and may in the long run be of central importance in the resolution of the issues involved, but at this early juncture in the therapeutic relationship it is secondary. The patient's immediate concerns regarding the therapist's availability, empathy, and capacity take priority and must be addressed before any genetic considerations are appropriate or even possible. To respond to this material in transference terms would run the risk of avoiding the patient's immediate concerns by diverting her to a more distant and historical concern, even one as recent as the loss of the first therapist, rather than dealing with the immediate issues. The risk is that such a maneuver can communicate to the patient or be perceived by the patient as a reflection of the therapist's insecurity, anxiety, uncertainty, or other unwillingness or inability to respond to the patient's pressing need of the moment.

ESTABLISHING THE THERAPEUTIC ALLIANCE

Need

The need to establish the therapeutic alliance from the beginning of the therapy and the difficulties inherent in this process in the therapy of borderline patients has been stressed by a number of authors (Atkins 1967, Chessick 1968, 1978, 1979, Giovacchini 1979, Kernberg 1984, Selzer et al. 1987). The difficulty and importance of this undertaking early in the therapy is clearly stated by Atkins (1967):

> The basic capacity for dependence necessary for the therapeutic alliance is impaired in borderline and psychotic patients. . . . It is a therapeutic dilemma that with such patients we are forced to rely upon their very meager capacity for good relationships to begin an analysis. With these patients the eventual acquisition of the capacity for object relationships as manifested in the therapeutic alliance can be regarded as one of the achievements of a successful piece of analytic work. [p. 587]

There is a tendency for lower-order borderline patients to present in a somewhat chaotic or regressive fashion, but such a presentation may also be found in some higher-order patients in an intense regressive crisis. In either case, there is pressure to establish at least the beginnings of a working alliance. It is essential to limit the destructive acting out that the patient may be involved in or may be threatening, and to deal with and resolve the premature transference distortions that may be contributing to the patient's inability to establish a meaningful working alliance (Selzer et al. 1987). Kernberg (1984) points out that not only might it be necessary to set limits within the therapy itself, but the therapist may also find it necessary to intervene in the patient's outside life, even to the point of hospitalization.

Limit Setting

The therapist at the same time must protect his therapeutic neutrality, so that when external limits are required, the use of auxiliary assistance in the form of social workers, nurses, counselors, and others is preferable to direct intervention by the therapist himself (Kernberg 1984). Such a therapeutic/administrative split can be readily accomplished in the hospital setting, but in the outpatient setting becomes somewhat more difficult to accomplish. Even in psychotherapy or analysis, however, the therapist must at times take a strong and firm limit-setting stand in the face of the patient's destructive acting out or in the face of the prospect of such acting out. The patient's acting out is always destructive of the therapy, but when it becomes self-destructive (in the more serious forms of suicide, drug taking, or self-mutilation, or in milder forms of missing or coming late for appointments, self-defeating behavior, or dealing with external relationships in destructive or counterproductive ways), the therapist has all the more reason to be concerned and to attempt to limit the acting-out behavior (Chessick 1979).

A similar conclusion has been drawn in the treatment of adolescents, where early limit setting of destructive acting out may often be the therapist's unique means of establishing the therapeutic alliance. Taking a firm, strong, limit-setting position is often seen by adolescents (and adults) as a gesture of caring on the part of the therapist, who does not follow the model of the parents in their inability to set limits or to exercise their authority in the face of that part of the patient that is out of control or at the mercy of destructive impulses. We will have more to say about limit setting as a technique in the treatment of borderline patients in Chapter 10.

Early Distortions

Most therapists agree with Kernberg (1984) that the need to deal effectively with premature and especially negative transference distortions early in the therapy is of maximal importance. Although Kernberg does not emphasize alliance factors, he does focus on the need to resolve the primitive and immediately available transferences that come into play early in the treatment process, acting not only as resistances but also as factors undermining the establishment of a therapeutic alliance. Kernberg recommends that these transference distortions be focused on immediately and that they should be interpreted in the here-and-now of the therapeutic interaction. He warns against genetic reconstructions at this early phase of the treatment, recommending that they be attempted only in later stages.

I would prefer to deal with these early distortions of the therapeutic relationship as deviations within the alliance sector rather than as transference distortions. Kernberg's emphasis is clinically useful to the extent that early formed, premature, or precipitous transference paradigms are mobilized at this early stage of the therapeutic interaction and result in an undermining of the therapeutic alliance. To the extent that such transference distortions can be effectively focused and clarified, this helps to clear the way for establishing an initial therapeutic alliance. But I would argue that one cannot presume that dealing with the transference elements of itself guarantees or can be presumed to result in the establishing of a therapeutic alliance. It seems more useful, in my view, to regard these early distortions directly in alliance terms and to deal with them on that level.

For example, in the typical context of the initial therapeutic contact with a relatively regressed lower-order patient within the hysterical continuum (the sort of borderline patient that would fit the Kernberg paradigm), the clinging, dependent, and needy quality of the patient's contact with the therapist and the sense of urgency and dire catastrophe that it often generates is derived from primitive needs to attach to and cling dependently to an omnipotent care-taking object. The effort to clarify and interpret these transference elements usually runs afoul of the patient's basic inability to hear interpretations in any but a negative or persecutory fashion that can easily become excessively threatening, or as coming from a powerful or idealized object to whom the patient compliantly submits.

The question remains whether such interpretations bring about a situation in which a therapeutic alliance is effected, or whether they only contribute to a form of transitional relatedness that responds to the underlying need to recreate the lost sense of relatedness to the mother (Feinsilver 1983). The emphasis on alliance factors would focus on and deal with those factors that interfere with and distort the structure of the therapeutic relationship in the here-and-now. The therapist would concern himself with establishing the parameters of the therapeutic situation, particularly those elements involved in the therapeutic contract and in the engagement with the patient in the collaborative work of the therapy. In the face of the patient's demanding and clinging behavior, the therapist would attend to the management of extratherapeutic contacts and would concern himself with aspects of the patient's involvement in the therapeutic effort, including matters of absences, coming late, or difficulties in payment of fees, and with the ongoing utilization of the therapeutic context. The catalog of elements that enter into the establishing of the therapeutic alliance is somewhat complex and involves a multiplicity of issues and influences. But it is to these aspects of the therapeutic interaction that the therapist would direct his concern in his immediate efforts to deal with the patient's distortions of the therapeutic relationship.

These various aspects can be better discussed in terms of the technical problems involved in establishing the therapeutic alliance. But it is worth noting that the focusing of the issue at this initial stage of the therapy, whether in terms of transference or of therapeutic alliance, gives a quite difference cast to the understanding of the issues involved and can point the therapeutic interventions in dealing with this problem in quite different directions. The pragmatic aspects of this problem can be more specifically discussed in terms of the technical problems involved in establishing the therapeutic alliance with borderline patients. Technical considerations for establishing a therapeutic alliance can be considered under two headings: one emphasizes establishing the structure of the therapeutic situation or framework, the other focuses on issues of establishing and maintaining a holding environment. I would like to discuss the merits and demerits of these respective approaches, and then consider my own modifications.

Structuring

As Langs (1975a) has observed, the therapeutic alliance embraces both conscious and unconscious, explicit and implicit components that express the respective needs and ego capacities of both patient and therapist as they enter into the therapeutic interaction. In structuring the therapeutic situation, the therapist expresses something about the reality of his own personality, his working style, values, and therapeutic stance. Any wish for physical contact or gratification, especially gratification of the patient's neurotic needs and wishes, is denied. Any efforts or needs on the part of the therapist to try to establish the therapeutic alliance by seductive giving, coaxing, persuading, or seducing of patients are regarded as antitherapeutic and damaging to the patient's autonomy, and set the therapy in the direction of seeking gratification rather than effective therapeutic work (Chessick 1979, 1983a). The therapist's effort should be to structure the therapeutic situation so that it is not excessively anxiety-provoking for the patient. He does this by developing a personal relationship with the patient in which he is, and is experienced by the patient as, trustworthy, reliable, responsible, capable, honest, consistent, constant in his own sense of identity and autonomy, and sincerely interested in the patient's well-being. This is not a part to be acted, but requires a convergence between his role as therapist and his existence as fellow human being (Stocking 1973).

Consequently, the therapist's setting of the ground rules and boundaries of the therapeutic interaction makes an appeal to the rational and adult ego in the patient as it conveys a sense of the therapist's own identity and role within the therapy. In so doing, the therapist effectively serves as a model for identification and a screen onto which the patient projects transference derivatives (Langs 1975b, Meissner 1981b). Excessive rigidity or controlling behavior should be avoided in negotiating and maintaining the details of the therapeutic contract so as to provide a model of reasonable flexibility and compromise for patients who have difficulty making such reasonable adaptations (Schulz 1980). The therapist also conveys in a concrete manner aspects of his therapeutic stance, his anonymity, concern for the patient, neutrality, and an attitude of interested understanding and commitment. In addition, he conveys a sense of essential confidentiality. He also communicates, if possible, a sense of the mutual engagement with the patient in a process that has the character of an experiment in which both patient and therapist are committed to exploration and understanding of the patient's inner life and experience. The therapist also conveys a sense of his own security, a clear sense of his own boundaries and integrity, his lack of anxiety in the face of the patient's distress and turmoil, and his intention to join in an alliance with the patient's reasonable ego and against the patient's excessive superego restrictions and instinctual turmoil (Boyer 1983).

There is a developmental aspect of this interchange between therapist and patient that involves mutual cuing and reciprocal relatedness that reaches back to the earliest strata of mother–infant interaction for its foundations. To the extent that positive dimensions of earlier developmental experiences can be recaptured, the potential for constructive alliance building is reinforced. To the extent that such factors are lacking or that negative and destructive aspects of the mother–child interaction are tapped into, the potential for meaningful therapeutic alliance is compromised and the basis is reinforced for disruption of the alliance or for a therapeutic misalliance. More is involved on this level than merely specifiable aspects of the contemporary interchange.

The structuring approach involves setting the ground rules for the therapy. These include deciding on a fee, determining the times and frequency of therapy sessions, their duration, arrangements for billing and payment of fees, including payment for missed appointments (Langs 1975a,b, Boyer 1983). The ground rules also include some stipulation of the respective roles and responsibilities of both patient and therapist. The structuring approach implicitly imposes the responsibility on the patient for observing the terms of the therapeutic contract and engaging meaningfully and productively in the work of the therapy. At all points in the negotiations involved in setting up the therapeutic framework, there is an implicit assumption that the patient is responsible not only for participation in the therapy but also for some part of the effectiveness of the therapeutic effort and its ultimate outcome.

The role and responsibility of the therapist should also be articulated. Boyer (1983) states that his role in the process is to be present for the interviews, to be on time, and to seek to understand what is going on in the patient and to help him understand that, when possible. He also tells the patient that he does not give advice, that he expects at times he will be wrong, and that the patient's responses will indicate when that is so. Chessick (1979, 1983a) has offered a somewhat more detailed description of the therapist's contribution to establishing the therapeutic framework and the therapeutic alliance. His list includes: being present at the agreed-upon sessions; being reliably on time; keeping awake and professionally interested in the patient and nothing else (no distractions, such as telephone calls, etc.); keeping to a firm starting and finishing time for the sessions; paying close attention to payment of fees; attempting sincerely and seriously to understand the patient's material and the patient's situation, and to communicate this understanding by interpretation; approaching the therapy from a stance of objective observation and study and with a sense of physicianly vocation; providing a room that is quiet, comfortable, properly lighted, and consistent; avoiding moral judgments or any temptation to introduce material from the therapist's own life and attitudes; avoiding temper tantrums or other extreme emotional reactions whether hostile, retaliatory, or exploitative toward the patient; and finally, maintaining a consistent, clear distinction between fact and fantasy to facilitate the therapist's capacity to avoid countertransference entanglements and traps. As Chessick (1979) states, citing Winnicott (1958), this amounts to the therapist's behaving in the therapeutic interaction as a relatively mature adult who is realistically and consistently dedicated to the work of therapy.

Confidentiality

A special problem arises around issues of confidentiality (Uchill 1978, Meissner 1979c, 1986b). This is essential for the therapeutic process, but the demand for total confidentiality (Langs 1973, 1975b) can rarely be maintained (Uchill 1978, Meissner 1979c). Issues of confidentiality are often a problem with borderline patients, particularly where there may be some paranoid elements in the clinical picture. There are often a variety of demands, many legitimate, for some information about the patient or the therapeutic process on the part of relatives, employers, insurance companies, government agencies, and other concerned parties. In the ordinary hospital setting, information about the patient is available to a wide variety of personnel. The physician is obliged to write progress notes and case history material in the patient's record, which is open to scrutiny by consulting physicians, resident staff, nursing staff, administrators, and so on. Even when the record goes to the hospital record room, it is open to the examination of anyone who works in medical records. In addition, in any teaching context, it is essential that the necessary information be conveyed between the patient's therapist and supervisors or shared with peers in various forms of clinical discussion and teaching. Even in the isolation of private practice, such intrusions on the confidentiality of the therapeutic situation are frequent and pose a problem for the maintenance of the therapeutic framework.

I will discuss later my own approach to dealing with such matters, but would only note here that they are of concern for establishing and maintaining the therapeutic alliance (Uchill 1978). Expectations on the part of either the therapist or the patient that such total confidentiality can or should be maintained are unrealistic and may reflect either excessive idealization on the part of the patient or a wish to undermine the therapeutic effort out of a sense of basic mistrust or even revenge against the therapist. The need for such absolute confidentiality can reflect an underlying paranoid position and a need to protect "secrets" from potentially threatening objects (Applebaum 1978–1979). Rather than total or absolute confidentiality, I prefer to think of essential confidentiality as that degree of respect and protection for the patient's confidential material that is warranted by the therapeutic situation and the legitimate context of information transmission within which it functions.

Holding Environment

The second approach to establishing the therapeutic alliance emphasizes the need for the therapist to maintain a holding environment, which allows the patient to enter into a relationship with the therapist and undertake the work of the therapy. This approach derives from Winnicott's contributions (see Chapter 3) regarding the holding function of the mother vis-à-vis the infant and the analogy of the role of the therapist as the "good-enough mother." The assumption is that the patient approaches therapy with a developmental defect, which limits, distorts, or destroys his capacity to enter into a collaborative therapeutic relationship, and that the initial phases of the therapy must symbolically recreate the aspects of the early parental involvement, allowing the patient to find good-enough mothering in the therapeutic relationship and be enabled to internalize some aspects of the holding environment to provide a basis for the therapeutic endeavor. As Adler (1985) describes this process, the lack of the borderline patient's capacity for holding-soothing forces him to depend on external objects to fulfill these functions in order to keep anxiety at a manageable level and to maintain psychological equilibrium. Following Kohut's usage (1971, 1977), Adler envisions the therapist as serving as a "selfobject" which provides the maintaining functions lacking in the patient (Adler 1980b). The "selfobject" is required to provide the holding-soothing, without which the borderline patient would be threatened by overwhelming and annihilative anxiety.

The aim of the earliest phase of therapy is to establish the therapeutic relationship in which the therapist becomes such a secure holding "selfobject" for the patient. The concept is similar to Levine's (1979) concept of the borderline need for a "sustaining object," also described in "selfobject" terms. As this relationship is established, the ground is laid for the further internalization of adequate holding introjects. Obstacles to this process, which requires intensive therapeutic attention, include:

1. The holding inevitably falls short of the patient's need and thus fails to mitigate the inner sense of loneliness, so that the enraged patient seeks revenge against the inadequate and offending therapist. Not only does his fantasy include the destruction of the therapist, but he also fears the therapist's rageful response in reaction to the patient's hostile assault and rejection.

2. The holding "selfobject," insofar as it is inadequate, becomes the target for hostile projections from the inner world of the patient's aggressive and destructive introjects. The relationship is thus seen as mutually hostile and destructive, and involves the loss of the holding-soothing object.

3. Insofar as the object is endowed with the good qualities of holding and soothing, it also becomes an object for envy by the needy patient, and this envy is usually accompanied by destructive impulses.

The treatment focuses on these dynamic impediments and tries to work them through by a combination of clarification, confrontation, and interpretation in a supportive therapeutic context. The therapist acts as a holding "selfobject," utilizing transitional objects, giving the patient his vacation address, sending postcards, or providing tokens that enable the patient to keep the object in memory, even allowing extra appointments or telephone calls. The therapist must strike a balance between fostering regression and infantile dependence versus safety and security in the relationship.

In the face of the patient's transference distortions, the therapist may have to clarify, confront, and interpret these distortions, particularly when they concern his role as a caring object and his distinguishing himself from the patient's projections. Dangerous acting-out may also have to be confronted. As Adler (1985) puts it, the outcome of this work is that:

> The patient learns that the therapist is an enduring and reliable holding self-object, that the therapist is indestructable as a "good object" (Winnicott 1969), that holding closeness gained by incorporation and fusion poses no danger, and that the patient himself is not evil. [p. 53]

Thus, the good-enough therapist works in a tenuous area between the patient's sense of being empathically understood on the one side and the sense of deprivation and rage when feeling misunderstood on the other. In this sense, the therapist's activity becomes a matrix of holding and reflects his active presence within the therapeutic interaction, often expressed in the form of questions or clarifications or repeated definitions of the work that patient and therapist are undertaking (Adler 1975). An important issue in such engagements is the need to regulate the psychological distance between patient and therapist. The therapist aims at maintaining a degree of optimal closeness that avoids fears of either engulfment or abandonment. Like Freud's (1921) porcupines, excessive closeness risks the danger of the object's sharp quills, and excessive distance raises the threat of abandonment and isolation.

Certainly, the establishment of such a holding or sustaining relationship is no easy matter. Patients have usually been burned before and they enter any relationship with a sense of suspicious guardedness and distrust. The effort to establish a therapeutic alliance usually has to deal with a certain degree of paranoid distrust or schizoid noninvolvement. Holding therapists tend to be much more open and giving in their utilization of extra appointments and telephone contacts. Such extra contacts have the purpose of reinforcing the therapist's role as a holding and sustaining object and should be carefully distinguished from efforts on the part of the patient to attack or manipulate the therapist. The use of such maneuvers should be explored in terms of their positive contribution to the therapeutic endeavor. There is always the risk of the therapist's masochistic submission to the patient's angry or controlling tactics or the need to counter his sense of helplessness by portraying himself as omnipotent and all-caring.

The holding approach is in many respects similar to the process of containment (Feinsilver 1980, 1983). Rather than following Winnicott's notion of holding, containment evolves from Bion's (1977) idea regarding the relationship of the container and the contained. The idea basically underlines the role of the therapist in containing the patient's projections or projective identifications, a dominant motif in the Kleinian literature. As Feinsilver (1983) describes the process:

> This is seen as the central mechanism by which the therapist of the primitively organized patient, as well as the mother of the developing infant, neutralizes the disorganizing effect of the undifferentiated aggression of part-object projections. . . . When primitive aggressive impulses are projected onto a recipient, he

tends to accept the projections and tends to become involved in a reciprocal projective identification. To the extent that the recipient can accept the projections and integrate them into an empathic view of the originator, he is said to be containing the projections. [p. 541]

The projections are the basis for transference distortions, which destroy the therapeutic alliance. The efforts of the therapist to contain these projections lead to the establishment of a transitional relatedness in which the patient feels comforted and protected by an omnipotent maternal presence, warding off the threat of separation anxieties. I would take this formulation as equivalent to Adler's (1985) holding-soothing introject.

Differentiation

Despite the differential emphases of these two approaches, it is not always clear that they are that far apart in terms of clinical practice. It is not unusual for those using the structuring approach to regard establishing and maintaining the therapeutic framework as a way of operationalizing the concept of "holding." At the same time, those who espouse the holding or containing approach often address themselves to issues of activity, limit setting, and establishing ground rules as aspects of the therapist's holding function. Nevertheless, there is a differentiating set of basic assumptions and an attitude that seems to differ in these respective approaches. The structuring approach seems to assume a capacity for at least minimal responsibility and reliability in the patient and places an implicit demand that the patient respond in those terms. The holding approach, in contrast, makes no such assumptions but regards the patient as suffering from a basic defect in these areas, which the holding function is meant to correct.

Each approach runs certain risks. The structuring approach can be excessively demanding, rigid, controlling, or intrusive. It may place a demand on the patient that exceeds his present capabilities. It may also run the countertransference risks involved in forcing the patient to adopt a compliant or submitting posture in the face of the pressures toward structure and responsibility. The therapist runs the risk of becoming an aggressor to the patient's passively compliant and victimized self, can assume a position of power in relation to the patient's impotence, or can infringe on the patient's autonomy. The holding approach also has its inherent risks. It assumes that the patient is not capable of a responsible or reliable response. The negative side of the image of maternal holding is that it creates an oral environment that can in some contexts reinforce unrealistic expectations and idealizations, and reinforce the patient's passivity and dependence (Applebaum 1978–1979).

My Approach

I will at times choose to be more structuring, at other times I will follow a more holding pattern, depending on my diagnostic impression, on my sense of the patient's developmental level or levels, on the state of the transference, and on my sense of what the patient needs at a given moment or stage of the therapy.

First Contact. Establishing the therapeutic alliance begins with the very first contact with the patient, whether by telephone or by other communication. If I am consulted about a referral by another therapist, for example, I generally request that the patient make direct contact with me. This puts the initiative for engaging in the therapy squarely in the patient's hands, so that he or she becomes the responsible agent for establishing contact, making an appointment, and putting the process in motion. During the evaluation process itself, I am carefully attuned to alliance issues, since part of the evaluation of the patient and the estimation of the potentiality for meaningful therapeutic work lies specifically within the alliance sector. I am also aware that the personal qualities I bring to the interaction with the patient have an immediate bearing on the process of establishing the therapeutic alliance. Particular aspects include my respectfulness, courtesy, and tactfulness in dealing with the patient, my respect for the patient's autonomy, and a firm, nonabrasive enactment of my role in setting the conditions within which the therapy is to take place. This is not done in any authoritarian or dictatorial fashion, but the limits within which I feel I am able to conduct therapy are nonetheless clear during the course of the process. In terms of the patient's autonomy, I make it clear from the beginning that together we are entering into a process during which both of us must make an important decision: on my part, it is the decision whether I feel I am able to help the patient and whether I am willing to engage in the work of therapy with that patient; and on the patient's part it is a decision whether he feels comfortable in working with me and feels that the process he is beginning will be to his benefit and whether I can be of help to him.

Negotiation.   When the patient and I have agreed that we are willing to commit ourselves to a therapeutic process, I generally take up the logistics of the therapy. Together we negotiate a schedule of sessions. This usually involves some statement on my part of what I think an advisable scheduling might be, taking into consideration both the needs of the patient and the space available in my treatment schedule, and some response on the part of the patient in terms of schedule, need to fit the therapy schedule into other commitments in his life, and then any necessary consideration of financial limitations.

I usually negotiate the fee with the patient, aiming at one that is a reasonable compensation for my services and within the patient's capacity to meet comfortably. It is probably unreasonable to expect patients to make excessive sacrifices for the sake of therapy. Patients who find this a difficult issue should be aware of possible options for getting therapy, either from other therapists who might settle for a fee closer to their ability to pay or from other institutional sources where easier arrangements are possible. It is an important aspect of these negotiations that the available options be kept open. I also stipulate conditions for payment for missed appointments and inquire about insurance arrangements. I am perfectly willing to discuss any limitations, constraints, or problems that arise with respect to any of these arrangements. My objective in all of these negotiations is to make the conditions for the therapy reasonable and fair to both parties, the patient and myself.

In the course of this discussion, I also briefly touch upon both the patient's and my own role and responsibilities in the therapeutic work. This usually arises in the discussion of what we will do in the therapy. The patient's responsibilities, as I see them, include coming to the therapy sessions, coming on time, meeting responsibilities for payment in a consistent and reliable manner, and bringing up in the therapy matters that are of concern and importance for discussion. My responsibility is to be there and on time for the sessions, to pay attention to what the patient is saying, to minimize any distractions or interruptions, to try to understand the patient's communications and the difficulties with which the patient is struggling, and to give helpful feedback whenever I think it is useful.

Confidentiality.   Certain aspects of the structure of the therapeutic situation I do not mention in any deliberate or active way. I do not make an issue of confidentiality, but prefer to wait until it is raised as a concern by the patient. When the patient does raise the question, I use the opportunity for a thorough exploration of the person's concerns and anxieties in this regard and an open and careful discussion of what is involved in the preservation of confidentiality, and the ways in which material from the therapeutic sessions may in fact be communicated outside of the therapy. In general, I emphasize two points. The first is that no communications will take place between me and outside parties, whoever they may be, without the patient knowing about it and approving. The second is that there are inevitably many contexts in which I might choose to talk about the patient, as, for example, in teaching activities. But my responsibility to the patient is to communicate that material in a way that protects the anonymity and confidentiality of the patient. The patient must feel confident that I will respect this obligation and trust that I will use solid professional judgment in such situations.

The issue of confidentiality does not usually come up as an explicit concern, except with patients who have a paranoid bent. They will often inquire about circumstances in which the possibility arises for communication to outside persons or agencies and about how I handle that kind of situation. My assurance that I do nothing without their knowledge and approval is often, at least for the time being, reassuring. The real crunch for such patients comes when some inquiry is made about the therapy, typically from an insurance company. My method of handling such requests, which keeps the patient informed and involved in every step of the process, is immensely reassuring and builds a sense of confidence and trust, so that the patient knows in a concrete way that I mean what I say about preserving confidentiality (Meissner 1979c, 1986b).

Extra Sessions.   Similarly, I do not discuss the question of setting limits on emergency contacts or telephone calls. Often, particularly with patients in the hysterical continuum who are caught in the throes of a regressive crisis, a sense of urgency and dependence makes it extremely difficult for them to tolerate the emotional turmoil and prompts them to pressure the therapist for extra therapeutic sessions. In the initial stage of the therapy, there may be certain advantages to extra sessions as a way not only of dealing with the patient's immediate anxiety but also of establishing the therapeutic alliance more firmly. There is also a benefit for many patients in *not* having this urgent need responded to immediately by a therapist who is overly willing to act as soother of the patient's turmoil. A balance must be struck between the need for the therapist's extra availability and support and the possibility of reinforcing the patient's regressive need. The therapist must make a judgment as to what is in the best interest of the patient and the therapeutic process. My own tendency is to test the capacity of the patient to tolerate the anxiety and stress until the next scheduled appointment, but if a patient does not respond to this effort, then I would rather offer an extra session than have the patient resort to desperate telephone calls.

In granting such an extra session to an anxious patient, however, I do not lose the opportunity to explore the potential implications of such a course of action. For example, giving a patient such an extra session almost unavoidably communicates to the patient a sense of weakness and defectiveness. I may be more responsive to this need at the beginning of treatment, but the ground quickly shifts to a concern over what is behind it and the problems it creates for the therapy. Generally, this process of confrontation and clarification diminishes this kind of acting out. My objective in all of this is to bring the therapy into a regular and consistent pattern, limiting the therapeutic contacts to the agreed-upon schedule of hours, and focusing the attention of the therapeutic work on long-standing, chronic issues in the patient's life rather than on crisis situations that are more disruptive of the therapeutic process than contributory. A basic maxim is that the purpose of therapy is to facilitate the patient's psychological growth rather than to alleviate anxiety. At times the latter objective must be attended to, but not at the expense of the former.

The problem of the need for extra sessions usually abates quickly, but occasionally it continues to be a problem. Such patients have particular difficulty in settling comfortably into the therapeutic relationship. This may be due in part to the therapist's failure to meet the patient's needs, to make the right interpretation, or to address the pertinent issue. The result is that the patient continues to feel misunderstood, not empathically attuned, and insecure. With such patients, when I have exhausted all resources for confrontation, clarification, interpretation, and limit setting within the therapeutic context, I set a definitive parameter in the therapy that excludes all but unscheduled therapy hours. I then determine with the patient what immediate resources are available in the face of severe anxiety or regressive turmoil. My emphasis is on the need to establish and maintain the basic structure of the therapeutic situation. If there is an emergency, it is better for the patient to go to an acute facility, such as a hospital emergency room. Then the therapy can later explore what was involved in the emergency.

Telephone Calls. I follow a similar pattern in dealing with telephone calls. In the beginning of therapy, the patient's inability to tolerate anxiety or depression or suicidal impulses leads to urgent telephone calls seeking help and reassurance from the therapist. I respond to such needs in some degree, but with a gradual imposition of increasingly stringent limitations. During the first few telephone calls I try to understand the patient's turmoil and offer reassuring comments. Often, little more is required than a few minutes of sympathetic listening and a reassurance that we will talk about the problem at the next scheduled session. I do not let such calls drag on, however. As the number of calls continue, I diminish the time for such conversation, so that the patient gradually gets the idea that the telephone is not an open channel for communication. If this behavior continues, I do not allow the conversation to continue. I indicate to the patient that the call is inappropriate and that we will have to discuss the matter at our next meeting and then hang up. The question of the telephone calls and the patient's anxiety and the unwillingness or inability to tolerate the anxiety then becomes a focus of concern within the therapeutic work.

My feeling is that beneficial therapy does not take place over the telephone, that the use of the telephone is rather a vehicle for acting out and diverts the work of the therapeutic process from its proper context. A therapist may encounter rare exceptions to this view, but they should be regarded as exceptions. Typically patients will call as a result of acute anxiety precipitated by some loss, disappointment, or conflictual situation. Often it is enough that the patient be able to communicate the anxiety or upset to the therapist, realize that the issues are not necessarily urgent, and know that they can and will be dealt with in the therapy. Since it is the patient's uncertainty about these matters that prompts the call, one can presume that behind the urgent need lies a further level of difficulty in the therapeutic alliance. As the therapeutic alliance consolidates and becomes more effective, such needs diminish. For patients who seem to be unable to communicate otherwise with the therapist, the underlying therapeutic misalliance and associated transference distortions must be brought into focus and worked on. In any case, such misuse of the telephone becomes an occasion for meaningful work on the therapeutic alliance. Consequently, I do not give patients my private telephone number, and on rare occasions when patients have been able to gain access to it and have contacted me in that way, I make it clear that that is not a channel over which I am willing to communicate with

the patient and immediately terminate the conversation. The only
number patients have access to is my office telephone, where the opportunity for telephone access is limited and easily controlled.

Giovacchini (1979) gives an example that illustrates my sense of
the status of telephone contacts. For extrinsic reasons, he was unable to
see a patient while she was in the hospital, but the patient was given
telephone privileges and was allowed to call him during the time of her
ordinary sessions. Giovacchini underlines the profound difference between the modality of communication over the telephone and that in
the face-to-face situation in his office. The patient's presentation on the
telephone was rational and sensible. She discussed in a reasonable and
insightful way what she was experiencing during her hospitalization.
While her behavior was psychotic, she was able to give rather sensitive
and accurate descriptions of her behavior, even sympathizing with the
staff who had to struggle with the difficulty she presented. In contrast,
in his office, the patient became regressed, crawled into a fetal position,
babbling and drooling, presenting the picture of a terrified, confused
patient in the throes of a profound psychotic regression.

Such a picture is extreme and perhaps overly dramatic, but it
reflects a tendency that influences the patterns of communications in all
patients, where the constraints of the telephone communication without
the immediate access to the multiple modes of communication and
response available in the vis-à-vis situation dictate and shape the
manner of communication. Patients who communicate by telephone
are in effect going through the motions of talking to their therapist, but
the telephone itself serves as a masking vehicle that prevents more
profound and meaningful communication. In my opinion, there is no
need for the therapist to collude with this defensive need on the part of
the patient.

Therapeutic Framework.   All of these aspects of establishing the
therapeutic alliance deal with the structuring of the therapeutic framework. They are more fully applicable in the context of individual
therapy and in a private-practice setting. They presume that the patient
brings to the therapeutic involvement sufficient psychic structure to
respond to these structuring initiatives on the part of the therapist and
to thus enter into a meaningful therapeutic alliance. These conditions
are not always available. Patients in the lower order of the borderline
spectrum often present in a more regressed and disorganized condition
and have diminished capacity or resources to respond to such structur-

ing initiatives from the therapist. In the face of such turmoil, the therapist may have little choice but to resort to a holding posture and to wait until the patient sufficiently recompensates before taking more structuring initiatives. With some patients, particularly those whose psychic processes are readily permeated by psychotic elements, the therapist may do little more throughout the entire course of the therapy than function as a holding object. With such patients, the approach is largely or even exclusively supportive (Adler 1982, 1985).

But even in these circumstances, the structural components of the therapeutic situation are not simply ignored. They remain operative principles toward which the inherent drive of the therapeutic situation is consistently directed. If the patient is unable to enter into a meaningful working or therapeutic alliance with the therapist in any direct and personal way, careful attention must be paid to the parameters of the therapeutic framework, to issues of missed sessions, coming late, failures to meet payment obligations, and so on. Failure to continue to maintain such parameters and the neglect of issues pertaining to the patient's manner of engaging in the therapeutic work would be equivalent to a collusion with the patient's need to undermine the therapy and would inevitably reflect certain countertransference dynamics on the part of the therapist.

With borderline patients, the alliance sector of the therapy remains a chronic problem throughout the therapeutic course. Not only is the therapeutic alliance with many patients constructed only slowly and painstakingly, brick by brick, over extended periods of time, but it is frequently subjected to regressive dissolution and disruption. With patients in the borderline spectrum, it is never the case that the therapeutic alliance is effectively constructed and, once constructed, remains unalterably in place. This is true also with higher-order patients, with whom the more subtle forms of therapeutic misalliance need constantly to be corrected and worked through, only to frequently resurface in different contexts or in different forms, which themselves require further therapeutic work. The therapist's approach to establishing the therapeutic alliance is almost always called on to strike a balance between holding and structuring in working with the patient on this aspect of the therapeutic interaction. At times of regressive strain the therapist may lean more toward a holding approach, while at times of better integration and better engagement in the therapeutic work a more structuring approach is more productive. It is almost never one without the other.

DEVIATIONS IN THE THERAPEUTIC ALLIANCE

Disruptions

Deviations from the therapeutic alliance usually take the form of either acute disruptions or more chronic therapeutic misalliances. The disruptions are characteristically found in lower-order patients, but may also occur, usually in milder, less disruptive, and more easily recoverable fashion, even in higher-order patients. It is a rare course of therapy with any borderline patient in which one or more such disruptions does not occur, usually in conjunction with some form of regressive crisis. For the most part, they are accompanied by a lapse in reality testing and by an intensification of transference distortions, usually of a negative and hostile variety (Dickes 1967, Kernberg 1984). Transference interpretations alone are not sufficient in themselves to alleviate the situation, but the alliance issues must also be directly addressed (Dickes 1967).

Such regressive cycles may take the form of suicidal threats, which not only create a crisis in the therapeutic alliance but also mobilize severe countertransference difficulties that are emotionally draining and manipulative of the therapist and serve to disrupt the treatment process (Chessick 1978). The patient's suicidal threats can often stimulate the therapist's need to do something, to rescue the patient and may arouse anxieties and feelings of impotence and guilt in the therapist (Giovacchini 1979), as well as rage and countertransference hate (Maltsberger and Buie 1974).

In the face of these regressive crises and the disruptions of the therapeutic alliance, the therapist is required to take a more active confrontative approach to the situation. This calls for active intervention, with particular focus on the alliance issues and on the problem that has given rise to the current disruption. Particular attention must be paid to the potential for acting out. Such acute disruptions can usually be recovered by appropriate structuring, limit-setting interventions, and clarification of the alliance issues. More chronic regressions may take the form of a transference psychosis in which the therapist becomes a delusional object or is included in the patient's delusional system in some fashion (Little 1958). In these delusional transferences, the "as-if" quality of the transference experience is undermined by the failure of reality testing, so that the analyst becomes in the patient's psychic reality the "idealized and deified, and oppositely, the diabolized parent" (Wallerstein 1967).

At times, disruptions of the therapeutic alliance can sound the death knell of the therapeutic process: it is possible for the alliance not to be reconstituted and the patient unilaterally terminates the process. On occasion, the disruption may lead to a temporary breaking-off of the treatment. While these defensive retreats may be conflictually motivated, there are cases in which interruptions may have an aspect of progressive movement. One young man,[1] whose pathology was in the range of the primitive affective personality disorder, broke off treatment after what seemed to be modest therapeutic gain. He came in one day, announcing that he thought he had made enough progress, had gained some important insights, and had decided that it was time for him to try things on his own. I was highly suspicious of his need to escape from the treatment, and presented what I thought were persuasive arguments for his continuing. He remained firm in his resolve, however, and broke off the treatment. He returned some six months later, having apparently retained his therapeutic gains, and wanted to take up the therapeutic work again and deal with his problems further. It was as though the therapy had not been interrupted at all; we picked up exactly where we had left off six months before and continued with the therapeutic work. This patient interrupted his treatment process several more times in the course of the ensuing years, each time with a significant advance in his overall functioning and in the effectiveness of his involvement in the therapy. It would be my impression, in cases like his, that the interruptions were equivalently bids to establish his own autonomy and a sense of himself as able to function in the world without having to cling to the supportive context provided by the therapeutic relationship. The more he was able to establish this aspect of himself, the more he was able to enter into an effective therapeutic alliance, which contributed to the greater effectiveness of his therapeutic work. Even though technically the therapist might prefer that such bids for autonomy be explored and analyzed within the therapeutic context, this may not at times be possible. With this patient, such analysis had to wait until the process had been largely acted out.

Misalliances

Therapeutic misalliances can take a variety of forms. These may affect the problems in establishing the alliance from the beginning or can

---

[1]This patient is Ed, whose case is discussed at length in Chapter 18.

become persistent distortions that have a pervasive and often undermining effect on the therapeutic work. I will discuss the narcissistic alliances first, and then focus on the range of other therapeutic misalliances that can arise.

Narcissistic Alliance.   Patients come to therapy in order to alleviate distress or anxiety, to find relief from their pain, or to correct some condition that is creating difficulties in their life situation. In order to engage with the therapist as a helping figure, a certain fundamental trust is required, at least to the extent that the helper is seen as someone from whom the needed relief can be obtained. The patient must be willing to submit to the therapeutic situation and accept the therapist's competence and capacity to help. There is both a rational and an irrational side to this submission. The rational component has to do with the recognition of the therapist's training, knowledge, experience, and therapeutic competence. On the irrational side, however, other factors enter in, including magical expectations, superstitious beliefs, symbolic elements, preformed transference elements, wishes, narcissistic defenses, and the capacity for basic trust. In a context of heightened narcissistic vulnerability, the patient must at least be able to include the therapist among the narcissistic elements required to preserve his fragile and threatened sense of self.

The willingness of the patient to include the therapeutic relationship in the narcissistic defensive organization is the basis for a narcissistic alliance, which is the minimal basis on which the therapy can begin. In itself, it is a form of therapeutic misalliance, but has the potentiality for developing into a more meaningful therapeutic alliance. In some patients, particularly patients whose difficulties center in the narcissistic sector, the narcissistic alliance may provide the only basis for the possibility of any therapy at all. In some borderline patients, particularly those in whom the archaic narcissistic components dominate the introjective configuration, the capacity for even a narcissistic alliance may be seriously impaired. The demands of the grandiose self or the need to maintain narcissistic equilibrium by attachment to an idealized object (Kohut 1971) may interfere with the capacity of the self to depend on any helping object or may generate such magical and illusory expectations regarding the idealized object that any semblance of therapeutic alliance is undermined and is subjected to the patient's primitive narcissistic needs (Meissner 1977c, 1986b).

Most borderline patients who come to therapy have at least a minimal capacity for a narcissistic alliance, even though their capacities to progress toward a more solid and effective therapeutic alliance may be severely compromised (Corwin 1973). Some patients do not manifest any psychotic features but avoid deeper involvement in the therapeutic process out of a fear of psychotic decompensation. Such patients may maintain a level of engagement based on a narcissistic alliance that allows them to sustain an illusory pursuit of narcissistic perfection within which the therapy itself must be subsumed (Rothstein 1982). Where the capacity for a narcissistic alliance is compromised, either by archaic narcissistic fixations or by deficits in basic trust, the prospects for any meaningful therapeutic effort are severely limited. Even in some of these cases, the therapist's efforts to engage the patient in minimal or supportive ways may allow a narcissistic alliance to emerge. This is often the experience of therapists, even with more severely disturbed psychotic or schizophrenic patients.

With patients whose capacity for narcissistic alliance is severely compromised, or faltering in whatever degree, the therapist can play a crucial role in his capacity to respond sensitively and empathically to the patient's narcissistic vulnerability, to effectively modify the patient's anxiety, and to support his faltering narcissism. To a degree this may involve the mobilization of narcissistic transferences, whether of a mirroring or an idealizing variety, which allow the patient to take refuge in the presumed magical power of the therapist.[2]

Other Misalliances. Therapeutic misalliances are not based solely on narcissistic dynamics. If the therapeutic alliance involves a collaboration and working together on the part of both patient and therapist to bring about symptom alleviation and structural change through insight, then therapeutic misalliances would encompass those interactions designed, consciously or unconsciously, to undermine such goals or to achieve some degree of symptom modification on some other basis (Langs 1975a). There are inherent tendencies in both therapist and patient to create such therapeutic misalliances in every psychotherapeutic situation. As Langs (1975a) puts it:

---

[2]It may be worth noting that some aspects of the therapeutic alliance reflect aspects of the therapist-patient interaction that Kohut (1977, 1984) ascribes to "selfobject transferences." The need for the therapist to contain the level of the patient's anxiety, to respond sensitively to the degree of the patient's narcissistic vulnerability, to create a context of empathic understanding, and to facilitate the patient's engagement in the therapy by way of surrogate auxiliary functioning, all seem implicit in both concepts. They differ in their theoretical connotations, particularly of the merging of boundaries in the "selfobject" relation. See Friedman's (1986) clarifying discussion.

> Efforts toward therapeutic misalliances arise primarily out of unre-
> solved intrapsychic conflicts—inappropriate instinctual drive
> needs, and superego and ego disturbances—and prior disturbed
> object relations and interactions experienced by the patient and
> analyst, which prompt either one to seek gratifications and defen-
> sive reinforcements in their relationship that are not in keeping with
> the search for insight and inner change. [p. 80]

Such therapeutic misalliances may arise from the need for the patient to
act out primarily transference-based fantasies or from deviations in
therapeutic technique or technical errors that reflect countertransference problems in the therapist. Deviations in technique often have
implicit or latent meanings that have important implications for the
therapeutic alliance. The patient's efforts to bring about a therapeutic
misalliance usually reflect influences from his past history, character,
unresolved intrapsychic conflicts, current real-life situations, and other
ongoing responses to the therapist and the therapeutic situation.

In every therapeutic situation, then, there is a certain balance
struck between efforts toward constructing a therapeutic alliance and
other influences moving in the direction of therapeutic misalliance.
Therapeutic misalliances evolve out of the complex interaction between
patient and therapist and reflect complex attitudes that each brings to
the therapeutic interaction. The result is a dynamic process in which
tension arises between conflicting forces, progressive and constructive
on one side and regressive and destructive on the other. The therapeutic
effort constantly strives to strike a balance between these factors that
will allow the therapeutic process to move forward and the therapeutic
engagement to take place in meaningful and effective terms.

It should be noted that not all influences contributing to a therapeutic misalliance come from either transference or countertransference, but significant factors can also arise from outside of the therapeutic interaction. Such influences can come from third parties, such as
insurance companies, agencies, supervisors, hospital administrations,
family, friends, and so on, or may arise from the circumstances under
which the therapy is undertaken, as, for example, in court-ordered
therapy or as a result of anxieties and demands on the part of employers
or families. Misalliance influences may also stem from the circumstances within which the therapy is undertaken, as, for example, with a
candidate who undertakes analysis as a requirement for analytic training. These and other influences may introduce a distortion into the pattern of interaction between therapist and patient that can inhibit the

effectiveness of therapeutic work and limit the potential outcome. Insurance companies, for example, may structure arrangements for payment of fees, review of claims, or peer review that introduce significant distortions into the therapeutic relationship and undermine the therapeutic alliance.

The underlying motivation that gives rise to therapeutic misalliances can involve the patient's unconscious need either to undermine the therapy (Langs 1975a, Giovacchini 1979) or out of a defensive need in the patient, to control the therapist and the therapeutic situation (Omer 1985). There is also a powerful need, particularly in patients within the borderline spectrum, to recreate a set of infantile relationships or an infantile environment that tends to revive and extend earlier pathogenic and unresolved relationships and traumas (Langs 1975a, Giovacchini 1979).

The presence of a therapeutic misalliance can be suspected on subjective grounds. Langs (1975a) offers a list of subjective clues in the therapist: a sense of lack of progress or depth in the therapy: a holding back of material by the patient; a sense that things are not right, a feeling of not liking the patient; a feeling of being used or manipulated, of being ineffectual as a therapist. He may be aware of seductive or aggressive feelings toward the patient that he can't resolve; he may find himself puzzled at a stalemate or regression in the patient. Langs comments, "Subjectively experienced disturbances in his therapeutic attitudes, or any unusual manner of intervening or behaving, are clues to the presence of countertransference problems, and direct the therapist to search for their expression in the actual interaction with the patient" (p. 91).

Issues. The nonnarcissistic forms of therapeutic misalliance can arise on a variety of bases and involve a number of fundamental issues. Some of the more significant alliance issues that arise in the treatment of borderline patients would include:

1. *Distrust.* The patient is unable to form a trusting relationship with the therapist and tends to maintain a guarded and protective attitude. The distrust may take a subtle and pervasive form, but may also intensify to the point of paranoid suspiciousness and withdrawal.

2. *Power.* The patient may view the relationship with the therapist as based essentially on power, so that the therapist is viewed as a powerful and influential figure and, therefore, as potentially dangerous

or threatening, while the patient maintains a view of himself as weak, powerless, and vulnerable. Acceptance of the therapist's intervention or assimiliation and response to the therapist's attempts at interpretation may be viewed implicitly by the patient as forms of submission, which may in its extreme forms be experienced as humiliation.

3. *Authority.* The patient may view the therapist as an authority figure, characterizing him as authoritarian or dogmatic. This reflects underlying unresolved authority conflicts, which stimulate a rebellious or resistant response in the patient.

4. *Compliance.* The issues here are closely related to those of authority and power but have a somewhat different cast. The patient's characterological response to any forms of authority or power exercised over him is to adopt a compliant facade, which serves to mask an underlying defiance. Such patients are often agreeable and act in a cooperative "good patient" manner in the therapy, while at the same time resisting and countering any beneficial influence of the therapy by secret rebellion and rejection.

5. *Responsibility.* When responsibility is at issue in a therapeutic misalliance, the patient is usually trying to avoid taking responsibility, both for the progress of the therapy and for his own life situation. This is usually accompanied by efforts to draw the therapist into taking unwarranted or excessive responsibility. These efforts can be readily identified; they are reflected not only in the patient's failure to take responsibility for observing the terms of the therapeutic contract (e.g., not paying bills, not coming on time), but also in a more subtle form of failure to take responsibility for meaningful and productive initiatives within the therapy. The patient who tries to get his therapist to provide answers, give advice, or initiate subjects for discussion is passing the buck, attempting to draw the therapist into taking on more of the responsibility for the therapeutic work than is appropriate and thus avoiding his own responsibility and initiative.

6. *Caretaking.* This involves a degree of passivity and wish fulfillment on the part of the patient that seeks to draw others into a caretaking role. This effort would draw the therapist into caretaking efforts that lie beyond the proper limits of the therapeutic effort and would implicitly absolve the patient of the need for caretaking efforts of his or her own. This quality of the therapeutic misalliance can be

regarded as a form of avoidance of responsibility, here specifically in terms of self-care and self-interest.

7. *Autonomy*. Autonomy looms as a central issue for all borderline patients, interwoven as it is with the core issue of dependence. Since autonomy is pervasively a central issue in the development of borderline pathology (Meissner 1984a), borderline autonomy is often easily threatened and tenuous at best, and at worst is highly fragile and vulnerable to regressive pulls. For the borderline patient in general, autonomy is redolent with fears of separation and abandonment, while the opposite dimension of dependence is fraught with perils of engulfment and annihilation. These fears are more profound and overwhelming in the lower-order forms of borderline pathology, but they have their place in higher-order forms as well. The patient's dependent needs and conflicts over autonomy constantly undermine therapeutic efforts, negate any dynamic within the therapy that leads toward a greater degree of autonomy, separation, or individuation, and draw the patient constantly into resistance and avoidance of any such progression within the therapeutic work. This dynamic can contribute to frequently observed negative therapeutic reactions. The issues of working through separation anxieties and resolving conflicts over autonomy are particularly important and telling in the termination phase.

MAINTAINING THE THERAPEUTIC ALLIANCE

The vulnerabilities to disruption or distortion of the therapeutic alliance that are inherent in borderline pathology require constant attention and tending throughout the entire course of the therapy. When and if disruptions occur, the repair of the therapeutic alliance takes precedence over all other matters in the therapy. As long as and to the extent that the therapeutic alliance is disrupted, no effective work will take place in the therapy (Chessick 1979). Disruptions of the therapeutic alliance usually occur in the context of a regressive crisis, and require immediate and specific intervention on the part of the therapist. As we have previously noted, such disruptions and regressive crises are more characteristic of the pathology and the therapeutic experience with lower-order borderline patients, while the more chronic and persistent therapeutic misalliances are the rule in higher-order forms. While the disruptions require immediate and urgent attention and repair, therapeutic misalliances tend to remain a more or less subtle, pervasive, and persistent phenomenon that require a much different approach. Management of regression is a separate subject that deserves discussion in its own right (see Chapter 11). We will focus here only on the issues related to repair of the disrupted therapeutic alliance.

Disruptions

In attempting to manage the disruption, the therapist does well to remind himself that it takes place in the context of a regressive crisis and is often a disruption more of a therapeutic misalliance than of a therapeutic alliance. The disruption may occur in dramatic fashion in the form of destructive acting out (e.g., suicide, drug taking, promiscuity) or in the form of acting out around aspects of the therapeutic contract (e.g., missing sessions, coming late, failing to pay the bill, failing to utilize the therapeutic situation appropriately), or it may express itself in the form of angry, hostile, or negative confrontations and interactions with the therapist. In more disturbed patients, a transference psychosis may also emerge.

The disruption may be triggered by events outside the therapy—for example, failures, disappointments, pressures from family or other authorities, narcissistic injuries, lack of empathy on the part of significant others. It could be anything that upsets the tenuous narcissistic balance of the patient, even experiences of success that bring further challenge or responsibility. The disruptions may also be triggered by events within the therapy, including failures of empathy on the part of the therapist, deviations in therapeutic technique (Langs 1975a,b), or an intensification of transference distortions (Kernberg 1984). They may occur in the context of or as a result of countertransference reactions on the part of the therapist.

It is important both that the therapist maintain empathic contact with the patient, even in the course of the regression (Clifton 1974), and that the therapist endeavor as much as possible to identify the source of the disruption. The sources may occur singly or in combination. Typical situations in the therapy when alliance disruptions may occur are at times of separation (e.g., vacations, or even weekends), or when the therapist commits a deviation or error in technique. Important aspects of the repair process include identification of the source of the difficulty, an exploration of its connotations and its implications, specifying in detail its effects on the patient and the feelings that are aroused by it, and acknowledging when appropriate the therapist's failures or mistakes in contributing to the situation.

In borderline patients who react sensitively to separations, I make it a policy to focus actively on the issue of separation, to explore in as much detail as possible the patient's feelings, and to openly acknowledge and reinforce the reality of the situation against which the patient is reacting. Thus, at times of vacation, I make explicit efforts to discuss the feelings of loss, abandonment, and rage, emphasizing that these are occurring in the context of a reality, namely, our separation, and that they are appropriate. I allow myself to stand indicted, and make no defensive attempt to rationalize my going away and for a period of time abandoning the patient. The patient's feelings are thus validated; he feels understood and accepted in the face of his outrage, and also comes to experience once again the reality of my capacity to tolerate and accept his rage without paying him back for it. The patient realizes the firmness of my own boundaries and my persistent autonomy, which neither yields to his manipulations nor experiences any recrimination, shame, or guilt because of it.

The dimensions of the therapeutic contract and the components of the therapeutic structure serve an important function in these contexts, both as indices for recognizing disruptive patterns and as important constituents of the therapeutic alliance. In the face of an alliance disruption, the parameters of the therapeutic structure need to be evaluated and reinforced. If a patient is missing appointments, for example, this must be taken up as a specific therapeutic issue, its sources and meaning explored, and its implications for the therapeutic alliance and the work of the therapy discussed and worked through. Rather than making allowances for patients and tolerating violations of the therapeutic contract (McWilliams 1979), my tendency is to focus on these parameters, to make the effort to work through the issues in order to bring the patient back into line, and to stand firm in the face of the patient's wishes to escape from the implicit responsibility.

With the patient who is reacting to an empathic failure on the part of the therapist, the first order of business would be the restitution of the structure of the therapy, followed immediately and necessarily by an exploration of what is involved in the patient's difficulty in dealing with disappointment in important figures in his life and with the failures of empathy on the part of those figures. In patients who are reacting to specific deviations in therapeutic technique on the part of the therapist, stabilization of the therapeutic situation must lead inevitably to a discussion of the therapist's failure, an exploration of its impact and meaning for the patient, and an open acknowledgment of the error.

In many instances, the disruption may arise from an intensification of transference dynamics or may be accompanied by an intensification of transference distortions (Kernberg 1984). Where such transference distortions are apparent, some confrontation and clarification are called for, but not necessarily in specific transference terms. If the disruption occurs early in the course of the therapy, my tendency would be not to deal with it in any sense as a transference derivative but to focus specifically on the related alliance issues. If distortions arise later in the course of therapy when a significant amount of transference clarification has been done in the course of the previous work, then the opportunity for dealing with these elements specifically as transference is somewhat greater, although even there I would want to be certain that the therapeutic alliance implications were thoroughly explored concurrently. In the face of an acute disruption, any attempt to interpret such transference distortions is liable to fall upon deaf ears and have little useful impact.

Throughout all of these considerations, an important aspect of the therapeutic interaction is the need on the part of the therapist to avoid acting out his own countertransference. This is a point that has been repeatedly and extensively emphasized by most major contributors to the study of borderline pathology and its treatment. Insofar as the therapeutic alliance disruption rides on an underlying therapeutic misalliance, a working-through of the issues related to the disruption inevitably leads to an opportunity at least to consider the misalliance issues. These issues, as we have described them above, all impinge on important aspects of the transference/countertransference interaction and involve implicit pressures on the therapist to respond in terms of a countertransference. We will have more to say about the important issue of the countertransference and its dynamics in Chapter 7, but the important point here is that the therapist, insofar as he is able, be in touch with countertransference issues and avoid responding in such a way as to contribute to and reinforce the disruption in the therapeutic alliance. I have rarely found it useful to express or discuss my countertransference feelings with the patient, but it is always useful, even mandatory, for the therapist to monitor his own responses and to keep them in appropriate check. Countertransference is often a useful signal to the therapist regarding the affective involvement with the patient and the quality of the transference/countertransference interaction, but it should be brought into the therapeutic interaction only on rare occasions.

Misalliances

In contrast to the acute disruptions of the therapeutic alliance, therapeutic misalliances tend to occur in more chronic, persistent, and subtle ways during the course of the therapy. Such therapeutic misalliances are a matter less of critical intervention than of persistent and continuing awareness, attention, and consistency. Hints regarding the existence of a therapeutic misalliance arise in subtle and casual ways, often in seemingly trivial or tangential comments by the patient or in reaction to some intervention or action on the part of the therapist. Clues may also arise from the therapist's own affective response or from more specifically countertransference reactions, a point that Langs (1975a,b) elaborates at length. When such hints or clues arise from the patient, a corrective effort requires that the therapist be alert to these signals, and that he undertake to focus, clarify, and explore the underlying misalliance issue with the patient. The countertransference signals sometimes are the basis for such an exploration, but more often they alert the therapist to a potential therapeutic misalliance. He can then monitor his own countertransference involvement and the possible implications for his dealing with the patient and be alert to confirming or contributing data in the patient's associations, dreams, fantasies, or other clinical material that may point to the persistence of such a therapeutic misalliance.

When the therapeutic misalliance involves some form of deviation in technique on the part of the therapist, it is useful for the therapist's inappropriate or erroneous contribution to be made part of the exploration and discussion, particularly in terms of the extent to which it reflects the underlying alliance issues. It never hurts for the therapist to be open and honest and undefensively objective about his own failures or mistakes. Such deviations provide ample ground for the therapist to explore his own countertransference issues, apart from his involvement with a particular patient.

Effective correction and adjustment of therapeutic misalliances depend on the therapist's capacity to recognize the danger signals, on the extent to which he can avoid interacting with the patient in terms of the alliance distortion, and on his ability to focus on, explore, and, where possible, clarify and interpret the nature of the misalliance and its contributing factors. Any effort on the part of the therapist to reassure the patient, to deviate in compensatory ways from appropriate technical interventions, or to resort to noninterpretive interventions not only runs the risk of fostering additional misalliance problems but also may indicate the therapist's difficulties or failures in understanding the issues and the patient's underlying concerns. It would also imply a denial of the patient's often valid, if unconscious, perceptions of aspects of the therapist's attitudes or behaviors that may have contributed to the therapeutic misalliance (Langs 1975a).

The careful maintenance and tending of the structure of the therapeutic situation is an important consideration in efforts to maintain a consistent alliance: that structure provides the context or the matrix within which positive and ego-enhancing structural changes become possible through the medium of positive and constructive identifications (Meissner 1981b). The maintenance of such therapeutic boundaries not only resists the efforts of the patient to elicit deviations in the therapeutic work and modifies the therapist's own inappropriate needs to pursue such modifications, but also provides a context in which neurotically driven pathogenic interactions can be avoided or minimized. It further provides a context in which the potentiality for maximal projection of pathological fantasies and transferences, which are central to the therapeutic process, can be effectively mobilized and dealt with in useful terms.

An important aspect of the process in this respect is the maintenance of a distinction between fantasy and reality. As Langs has observed (1975a), deviations in technique tend to elicit intense responses in the patient because of the implicit and unconscious meanings they convey, meanings that are then elaborated in terms of the patient's own needs and fantasies. The alteration of appropriate boundaries and roles between patient and therapist may foster conflictual issues related to separation, individuation, incest barriers, seduction, and so on. They introduce a factor of inappropriate gratification of neurotic needs in both patient and therapist.

An important consideration throughout the entire spectrum of therapeutic alliance difficulties and their management and correction is the matter of consistency between words and actions. It is easy enough for a therapist to explore, understand, and interpret apparent deviations in verbal terms with the patient and then respond in some behavioral way on entirely different terms that express and enact aspects of a therapeutic misalliance. One therapist, for example, became aware of the persistent need and tendency on the part of his patient to comply with any suggestions, interpretations, or interventions that the therapist might make, as well as the degree of eagerness on the part of the patient to seek the therapist's approval for such compliant behavior. At the same time as these issues were of central importance in the work of the therapy and had become a focus for considerable reflection and exploration, the situation arose in which it was necessary for the therapist to change one of the patient's therapy hours. Instead of discussing this with the patient in a way that would encourage the patient's participation as a responsible decision maker in the process of changing the hour, the therapist went about it in a rather authoritarian fashion, imposing his will and decision on the patient and making no attempt to elicit any discussion or other consideration. Clearly, the issues that had become a focus for therapeutic concern had not penetrated a deeper level of the therapist's own unconscious needs and conflicts, so that the unresolved aspects of these conflicts played themselves out in the therapist's adopting and enacting an authoritarian role—a role that clearly contradicted the therapeutic role and served to reinforce the therapeutic misalliance.

The dispositions that contribute to therapeutic misalliances on the part of both patient and therapist are deep-seated, involve aspects of the inherent character structure of both participants, and do not yield easily to modification. Working with such aspects of the therapeutic situation requires constant attention, awareness, and vigilant monitoring of the therapist's own behavior, thought patterns, and feelings and also a constant alertness to the intrusion of such elements into the therapeutic work from the side of the patient. Thus, it is safe to say that the persistent working on and working through of such alliance issues is a central and important aspect of the therapeutic effort with all borderline patients and that these issues persist from the beginning of the therapeutic interaction until the end of the process. Regardless of the success of the therapeutic work in modifying such alliance distortions, work on such alliance factors is a central part of the therapeutic process.

6

TRANSFERENCE

The transferences in borderline patients tend to be protean and complex; they involve the derivatives of multiple levels of developmental experience and reflect the residues of the history of significant object relationships that the patient brings to the therapeutic situation. At the same time, they provide a primary focus for therapeutic effort and the central basis on which the success or failure of the therapeutic process is determined.

In keeping with the overriding perspective of the borderline spectrum, transference manifestations vary in intensity and quality, depending on where the patient fits in the spectrum of borderline pathology. Since so much of the borderline literature tends to focus the pathology in more or less univocal terms, emphasizing certain characteristics as pathognomonic (often in the context of formulating the borderline diagnosis as a single entity), I will emphasize the inherent variability and heterogeneity of borderline transference manifestations. I will also discuss some of the central issues related to transference management in the course of the psychotherapeutic or psychoanalytic treatment of borderline patients.

TRANSFERENCE CHARACTERISTICS

The characteristic transference manifestations described in the literature present a picture of borderline transferences as primitive and chaotic, close to psychotic, with little indication of variability or of any degree of ego regulation in the picture. From the perspective of the borderline spectrum, this fairly consistent portrait not only focuses on transferences as they might appear in the hysterical continuum to the exclusion of the schizoid but also seems more characteristic of lower-order forms of transference reaction to the relative exclusion of higher-order forms. Thus, borderline transferences are generally described as precipitous, stormy, and intense, as prone to acting out, as fluctuating, as relatively fixed and resistent to change, as failing to maintain the distinction between fantasy and reality, as reflecting primitive, even primarily or exclusively symbiotic object relationships. I will discuss each of these characteristics in turn.

The precipitous quality of borderline transferences refers to a tendency for them to appear early in the therapeutic interaction, earlier than would be expected in neurotic pathology, and to have an atypical quality (Kernberg 1968, Morgenstern 1975, Abend et al. 1983). They may in fact be activated immediately within the therapeutic encounter and become a significant source of early resistance to the therapeutic process (Kernberg 1968, 1976b, 1979, 1984). Such precipitousness and early activation are often characteristic of transference expressions in the lower-order forms of borderlines in the hysterical continuum, but this is much less frequently the case in higher-order forms. Primitive hysterics may present in classically neurotic hysterical or narcissistic fashion, and develop the relatively intense and disruptive transference manifestations of borderline pathology only after months or even years of psychoanalytic treatment. Frequently the transference reaction will be precipitous, but at the same time concealed, so that the influence of the transference is kept hidden from the therapist. This may often be the case in patients in the schizoid continuum, where the regressive pull of transference reactions mobilizes a defensive tendency to withdraw and withhold, which serves to mask the underlying transference effects. Modell (1984) has underscored the lack of communication of affect of many patients in this situation, which may involve either withdrawal from relatively intense early transference feelings or may reflect a more schizoid avoidance of such transference involvement. In any case, it is rare that apparent transference manifestations are found to be precipitous or intense in the schizoid continuum. Such a case may reflect a regressive decompensation and the failure of protective schizoid mechanisms.

The turbulence and intensity of transference feelings in borderline patients have frequently been noted (Kernberg 1968, Morgenstern 1975,

Friedman 1979, Abend et al. 1983). The affects are often strong, intense, usually dysphoric and stormy in character, and chaotic in quality (Brody 1960, Kernberg 1968). Friedman (1979) even goes so far as to make such intense and stormy transference reactions the hallmark of borderline diagnosis.

The same restrictions that were pertinent regarding the precipitous onset of transference manifestations apply to the intensity of borderline transference affects. Such intense and chaotic affects may be found in any patients in the borderline spectrum, but they are not always quick to reveal themselves. Often, the intensity of borderline affects must await the effects of therapeutic regression before they become more apparent. As a rule, higher-order borderline patients find the intensity of affective reactions threatening, particularly when they occur in a regressive crisis, which threatens the fragmentation or annihilation of the patient's sense of self. In the face of therapeutic regression, the patient will experience a wave of intense affect, usually in the form of extreme anger or terror, which momentarily overwhelms him and leaves him feeling stunned and frightened. These affective episodes may come suddenly and without warning and leave the patient, and at times even the therapist, bewildered and confused. Usually, they are connected with the intensification of transference dynamics and should be analyzed in those terms. It is not at all uncommon for patients anywhere in the borderline spectrum to experience what I have described as a "paranoid spike" (Meissner 1986b), in which the patient has a sudden upsurge of paranoid feelings and anxieties, usually directed toward the therapist. Such affective experiences are transient and are followed by a ready return to the baseline of affective involvement with the therapist.

Nonetheless, they reflect a disruption in the therapeutic alliance and usually are connected with a regressive crisis of some kind. By and large, however, such periods of intense and stormy affective involvement are relatively rare in most borderline patients. In some patients, they may not occur at all during the course of the treatment. The more frequently, the more intensively, and the more disruptively such emotional storms take place, the greater the degree of pathological impairment and the severity of the patient's structural deficits. Consequently, such stormy, intense, and chaotic emotional involvement with borderline patients tends to be much more characteristic of lower-order patients, primarily those in the hysterical continuum—that is, patients who fall within the pseudoschizophrenic or primitive affective personality disorder range.

Both transference acting out, as an aspect of more general tendencies in borderline pathology to deal with inner tensions through action rather than remembering or feeling, and the expression of developmental or other fixations in interpersonal action are regarded as characteristic (Brody 1960, Kernberg 1968, 1984). Kernberg (1979) even goes so far as to consider such acting out as an essential aspect of transference development in borderline patients, and as a particularly prevalent expression of transference issues in borderline adolescents. Such acting out is again more characteristic of primitive levels of borderline pathology and tends to be more indirect and infrequent in higher-order patients. In the latter, tendencies to acting out are far from marked or frequent, and usually take a less severe or destructive path. Acting out in these patients focuses more on aspects of the therapeutic situation than on expression outside the therapy. There may also be a greater degree of forewarning, which allows for therapeutic exploration and discussion. In more primitive patients, however, acting out often has a precipitous and impulsive quality and more detrimental and destructive effects. Such acting-out episodes may take place in relation to empathic failures or crises within the therapy, or may arise in contexts of severe stress or conflict outside of the therapy. Patients usually have an established pattern for acting out in such regressive crises. Suicidal patients are at risk for suicidal acting out, patients with addictive problems will turn to drugs, alcoholics will drink, and patients whose disturbances lie primarily in areas of interpersonal relationships tend to precipitate arguments, disruptive emotional outbursts, marital difficulties, and so on. The patterns of acting out are protean, and although they do not arise solely on the basis of transference dynamics, the therapist is well advised to consider the influence of such transference issues seriously.

Borderline transferences have also been described as fluctuating, in the sense that the analyst may come to represent a variety of transference figures, usually displaced from parental and other objects, in a rapidly shifting and even chaotic fashion (Abend et al. 1983, Kernberg 1984). These shifting patterns can at times lead to a kind of simultaneous double image of the analyst as, for example, both the object of erotic libidinal longings and the forbidding and punitive parent of the opposite sex (Abend et al. 1983). At the same time, transferences can fluctuate dramatically in levels of intensity, of developmental derivation from object relations, and of functioning. As the Blancks (1974) point out, this pattern of variability may be better described by Greenacre's (1959) description as "active transference-neurotic manifestations" rather than the more classically conceived transference neurosis.

These fluctuating patterns derive not simply from the more classically conceived displacement from earlier object-images but also from the broadening scope and quality of transference involvements. The frequently described rapidity and chaotic quality of transference manifestations are more characteristic of the lower-order borderlines, whereas in higher-order patients there tends to be a greater stability and consistency in patterns of transference expression. Even in higher-order patients, however, the levels of functioning and patterns of transference expression are more variable than in the classically neurotic patient in whom the transference paradigms remain relatively fixed and consistent. Even in higher-order patients, under conditions of greater stress and regressive strain, the transference paradigms can vary considerably and, although they lack the rapidly shifting and chaotic quality of more primitive expressions, may in fact mobilize similarly conflicting transference expressions over more extended time intervals. In such cases, contradictory images are often expressed over the course of the treatment, or even from one period of the treatment to another, so their contradictory quality persists despite the lack of rapid alternation.

Authors have also noted the tenacity or persistence of borderline transference distortions (Bion 1957, Morgenstern 1975). The distortions of the therapeutic relationship and of the image of the analyst remain a persistent feature of the therapeutic interaction and are relatively unaffected by interpretations, in contrast to healthier neurotic patients (Abend et al. 1983). Part of this tenacious quality may have to do with the object hunger and a need for the borderline patient to cling to a sustaining object in the person of the therapist, but it may also have to do with defensive needs. Siegman (1967) explains the fixity of transference images as a defensive elaboration for warding off painful or dangerous id strivings and their derivatives, much in the fashion in which screen images connected with less threatening content may be substituted for more painful memories. Thus, the adherence to certain transference images may serve to deny other more painful or damaging object-images. From the point of view of the approach in the present work, however, an additional component of the persistence of certain transference manifestations may have more to do with the internal economy of the patient's introjective configuration and its inherent connections to the maintenance of the sense of self (Meissner 1984a).

In many cases, the borderline capacity to maintain the differentiation between the realms of fantasy and reality is tenuous if not impaired. The attenuation of the "as-if" quality of transference feelings tends to be a more dominant aspect of transference manifestations. The result is often an insistence on literal gratification from the analyst, or a tendency to view the transference and its emotional involvements as real. The patient may often bend his efforts to induce in the therapist some form of reciprocal reaction that corresponds to the patient's own transference feelings. This is in accord with a general tendency in the borderline's subjective experience of objects to respond in terms of unconscious fantasies or impulses in the object or to more primitive superego aspects, while responding to more conscious aspects of the object's ego functioning as though they were less real or trustworthy. Both the selective attention to unconscious aspects and the tendency to obscure the line between the real nature of the therapeutic relationship and the transference fantasies contribute substantially to the patterns of transference/countertransference interaction that play such an important part in the treatment of borderline patients. I shall return to this subject in greater detail in Chapter 7. Again, it should be noted that these tendencies are considerably more prominent and problematic in lower-order borderline patients and less so in higher-order.

The primitive nature of borderline transferences and their derivation from earlier and more primitive levels of psychic development has frequently been noted (Krohn 1974, Kernberg 1976a, 1979, 1984). Some theorists have emphasized that the basis of these primitive transference elements can be found in the earliest prementational developmental phases (Boyer and Giovacchini 1967) or from symbiotic levels of development and relatedness (Horner 1979, Robbins 1981a,b). Searles (1973a, 1977, 1978, 1984) speaks of an "ambivalent symbiosis" in these patients, which must be transformed into a "therapeutic symbiosis" in the course of therapy. Similarly, McGlashan (1983b) refers to a "transferentially actualized symbiosis" resulting in a "we-self" "selfobject."

From my point of view, the emphasis on symbiotic dimensions of borderline transferences seems overstated. For some patients in the more primitive ranges of the borderline spectrum, symbiotic issues are unquestionably at work, but they tend to be amalgamated with later developmental issues in a more complex fashion than is suggested by an appeal to a single layer of developmental experience. Even in such cases, the symbiotic derivatives express themselves in varying forms and with varying degrees of impact on the therapeutic process. In higher-level patients, however, whatever symbiotic residues there are that may play into the patient's psychopathology tend to be considerably more diluted, are embedded in higher-level conflicts and fixations, and may only transiently or tangentially become the focus of the therapeutic work, usually in the context of a regressive crisis. The emphasis on the primitive character of borderline object relationships and derivatives focuses on the realm of the borderline spectrum closest to the psychotic border and does not accurately reflect the complexity and development of borderline relationships on higher levels. A better awareness of the complexity of this issue can be found in the Kris Study Group monograph (Abend et al. 1983).

TRANSFERENCE VARIANTS

Keeping in mind these characteristics of borderline transferences and their qualifications in terms of the range of expression from higher to lower levels of the borderline spectrum, we can turn now to a consideration of the varieties of transference that find expression in borderline personalities. My approach here is merely descriptive of the forms of transference in terms of libidinal, aggressive, and narcissistic derivatives, and as variations of so-called "selfobject" transferences, transitional object transferences, and finally psychotic transferences. Variations of these transference forms may appear in highly individuated combinations and relative degrees of intensity in any borderline patient, according to the developmental history and pathological organization of the patient's personality structure.

Libidinal Transferences

Libidinal transferences can occur either in milder form as positive transference reactions or in the more intense and pathological erotic forms. Positive transferences can occur in borderline patients as in any other patient and take the form with which we are more familiar in the treatment of neurotic patients (Abend et al. 1983). Such transferences are derivatives of phallic-oedipal, libidinal impulses that may be permeated to varying degrees by pregenital influences. Such positive transference manifestations generally do not cause any particular difficulties and can be dealt with in the usual manner. Kernberg (1984) even suggests that these less primitive and modulated forms of positive transference should not be interpreted, since they often contribute to the gradual development of the therapeutic alliance. Such positive transference manifestations can be found anywhere in the borderline spectrum, but are more often characteristically present in higher-order patients and are usually part of the transference involvement in these patients.

Libidinally derived transferences may take a more extreme form, however, and become a major source of resistance (Blum 1973, Giovacchini 1975a). The development of an erotic transference in borderline patients usually is connected with regression. As Blum (1973) comments:

> The intensity and tenacity of eroticized transference, the resistance to interpretation, and the continuing attempts to seduce the analyst into a joint acting-out, as well as the frequent acting-out of such a transference with a substitute for the analyst, confirm the complicated infantile reactions of these patients. These are not ordinary reactions of transference love, and these patients can resemble intractable love addicts. [pp. 63–64]

This form of transference usually reflects a loss of the discrimination between fantasy and reality and an impairment of reality testing. Such eroticized reaction may be mingled with primitive forms of idealization and form a significant contribution to a transference psychosis.

Aggressive Transferences

Aggressive derivatives are expressed in the transference in the form either of negative transference or of a more pathological paranoid transference. Kernberg (1968, 1976b, 1984) has consistently maintained that negative transference is the chief form of transference expression in borderline patients, particularly reflecting the pathological condensation of pregenital and genital aims under the predominant influence of pregenital, primarily oral, aggression. Not only does the presence of a negative transference interfere with the development of a therapeutic relationship (Kernberg 1984), but also the degree of the patient's propensity for negative transference is a measure of potential unanalyzability (Giovacchini 1975a). Borderline patients bring to the therapeutic context a marked degree of ambivalence in object relationships and often severe sadomasochistic conflicts (Giovacchini 1975a, Abend et al. 1983). There is a tendency to see all relationships, including the therapeutic relationship, in terms of power and victimization. Transference relationships often enact themes of power and helplessness in which patients may see the therapist as omnipotent and powerful and themselves as helpless, weak, and vulnerable (Krohn 1974, McGlashan 1983a). The alignment of powerful and powerless between therapist and patient is often reversible, so that, in the fluctuating pattern of transference expression, the opposite configuration may emerge in which the patient feels powerful and omnipotently destructive and sees the therapist correspondingly in the helpless and powerless role. These configurations and their variants are expressions of the underlying introjective configuration, focused around aggressive derivatives in the form of both the aggressor- and victim-introject (Meissner 1978c, 1984a). Whether the patient is in the aggressor or the victim position, the transference configuration is that of a negative transference that expresses underlying aggressive conflicts and dynamics.

The paranoid transference is an extreme expression or intensification of a negative transference. While in the negative transference the therapist may be seen as powerful and the patient as weak, in a paranoid transference the analyst will be seen as threatening, persecuting, or controlling, or as trying to exercise sadistic control or domination over the patient (Kernberg 1984). A paranoid transference may emerge suddenly, usually in response to some action or intervention on the therapist's part that suggests a lapse in empathy or misunderstanding. Most often, the paranoid distortion remains confined to the therapeutic relationship and does not spill out into the patient's external environment. It may even reflect a pattern of splitting in which the therapist becomes the bad object and other significant figures in the patient's environment become good or idealized objects. This is a frequent occurrence in contexts of dual treatment (individual and group) or in the hospital context, where the splitting can take place between staff members or groups. Patients in analysis may find it difficult to remain on the couch and want to sit up to keep an eye on the now suspected and feared analyst and minimize the threat of attack. Such paranoid episodes, or what I have described elsewhere as "paranoid spikes" (Meissner 1984a), may reflect a transient regression in which the patient functions at a lower-than-usual level. Searles (1985) attributes such paranoid reactions to a fear of fusion or oneness with the therapist, which is based on an unconscious identification with aspects of the therapist's own unconscious personality, particularly unintegrated introjective configurations. The threatening fusion in such cases involves the danger of the loss of the patient's own identity-bearing introjects by being absorbed into the object.

While such paranoid manifestations may reflect underlying regression and primitive fears of symbiotic fusion, it is not clear to me from my own clinical experience that the dimensions of such regressions are necessarily as primitive as such formulations suggest. The propensity for paranoid attitudes and feelings in borderline patients is such a marked dimension of the pathology and so close to the surface in most borderline patients that the emergence of paranoid attitudes is neither surprising nor necessarily severely pathological. In most cases, such paranoid attitudes can be dealt with in the therapeutic context, are relatively easily reversed, and, as in the case of other severe transference distortions, usually reflect an underlying disturbance in the therapeutic alliance, which demands therapeutic attention and correction. At the same time, it should be recognized that paranoid transferences also may become delusional and involve significant regressive failures in reality testing, so that the paranoid attitude becomes in fact part of a transference psychosis. This latter situation is found occasionally in more primitive borderline personality structures but only rarely, if ever, in higher-order patients.

Narcissistic Transferences

The delineation of narcissistic transferences was one of the substantial contributions of Kohut (1971). He saw the narcissistic transferences as variations of the patterns of projection of archaic narcissistic configurations onto the therapist—in the theoretical terms of the present work, these transferences involve projections of the narcissistic introjects, both superior and inferior. Thus, the therapist comes to represent either the grandiose self or the idealized parental imago. Activation in the therapy of the omnipotent and idealized object leads to the formation of an idealizing transference in which all power and strength are attributed to the idealized object, leaving the subject feeling empty and powerless when separated from that object. The transference thus represents an attempt to achieve union with the idealized object in order to regain narcissistic equilibrium.

The patterns of idealization that emerge in such transferences may reflect different levels of developmental attainment. Idealizing transferences may show later developmental disturbances in the idealized parent imago, particularly at the time of the formation of the ego-ideal by way of introjection of the idealized object. In its more archaic expressions, narcissistic idealization may take the form of the expression of global, mystical, or religious concerns, linked with all-inspiring qualities that seem somewhat diffuse and vague and not attached to a single admired figure. In such cases, the revived narcissistic equilibrium can be experienced as a sense of omnipotence and omniscience, combined with feelings of aesthetic and moral perfection. These feelings can be sustained as long as the patient can maintain a sense of union with the idealized therapist. Through this connection with the sustaining and idealized object, symptoms related to the narcissistic disequilibrium are modified, particularly affective disturbances of depression, shame, and inferiority, as well as disturbances in work capacity or hypochondriacal preoccupations. At the same time, the union with the idealized object minimizes the threat of further narcissistic regression to even more archaic precursors (Kohut 1971). The narcissistic dynamics in the case of the Wolf-Man (Freud 1918) seem to have followed this pattern (Meissner 1977c, 1986b).

Although Kohut's description of narcissistic transferences applies primarily to narcissistic personality disorders, there is little argument that narcissistic transferences play a significant role in the pathology and treatment of borderline patients. The existence of such idealizing tendencies in borderline transferences has been well documented (Myerson 1974, Giovacchini 1975b, 1979, Chessick 1979, 1983a); usually the analyst or therapist is seen in an omnipotent or omniscient role (Stone 1954, Giovacchini 1973a,b, 1979, McGlashan 1983a, Searles 1985). Kernberg (1974, 1976b, 1984) speaks of primitive idealization in which the therapist is projectively idealized and desperately clung to as a defense against underlying hostile and negative transference feelings. While the phenomenology of such narcissistic states is similar for both Kernberg and Kohut, the theoretical perspectives and the therapeutic approaches differ radically.

Accompanying this pattern of idealization is the correspondingly opposite pattern of devaluation of the therapist (Adler 1970, 1985, Kernberg 1970, Myerson 1974). Despite feelings of worthlessness, the patient demands satisfaction from the idealized object, but when these demands are not met, the patient may turn to a defensive devaluing of the therapist out of a sense of disappointment and narcissistic frustration (Adler 1970, Myerson 1974). Because of envy for the idealized objects, the patient may try to make the treatment process a meaningless exercise, destroying whatever can be obtained in the therapy or from the therapist (Kernberg 1970). The devaluation may take the form of criticism of the therapist, belittling his skill, intelligence, or understanding; comparing him in pejorative terms to previous therapists; disregarding his comments or interpretations as if they were of little impact or value; ignoring his presence in the treatment room; skipping, coming late, or leaving treatment sessions early; and even breaking off the treatment. Such reactions may be expressions of the patient's narcissistic rage or of disappointment and anger that the therapist is not the nurturant or idealized supportive object that the patient had wished for.

The devaluation may also serve a defensive function against longings for closeness and love that may terrify the patient because of their regressive and engulfing implications. Devaluation may also act as a counterpoise to the patient's envy of the idealized therapist. It may reflect a need to counter projective elements in the transference, as, for example, when the therapist may be seen as dangerous and threatening. Devaluation may turn the therapist into a weak and worthless adversary whose threat to the patient is correspondingly diminished. The patient puts himself in the omnipotent position and thus feels safe and invulnerable from the potential attacks of the powerful object that can now be omnipotently controlled (Tonkin and Fine 1985). Or depressive feelings of inferiority and low self-esteem can be projected onto the therapist as a way of getting rid of such feelings, with a corresponding boost to the patient's sense of self-esteem by placing himself in a relatively superior position (Adler 1970, 1985).

In some individuals the narcissistic fixation leads to the development of the grandiose self. The reactivation in analysis of the grandiose self provides the basis for the formation of mirror transferences. Kohut (1971) has described three forms of these:

> The cohesive therapeutic reactivation of the grandiose self in analysis occurs in three forms: these relate to specific stages of development of this psychological structure to which pathognomonic therapeutic regression has led: (1) the archaic *merger through the extension of the grandiose self*; (2) a less archaic form which will be called *alter-ego transference or twinship*; and (3) a still less archaic form which will be referred to as *mirror transference* in the narrower sense. [p. 114]

In the most primitive merger form of mirror transference, the analyst is experienced only as an extension of the subject's grandiose self. Consequently, he becomes the repository of the grandiosity and exhibitionism of the patient. Kohut uses such terms as *merger* and *symbiosis* to describe this extension but reminds us that what is at issue here is not merger with an idealized object but rather the fact that the merger is achieved by a regressive diffusion of the borders of the self to embrace the analyst, who is then experienced as united to the grandiose self. The analogy to the adult experience of cathexis of one's own body or mind reflects the kind of unquestioned control or dominance that the grandiose self expects to exert over the invested object.

With such patients, the analyst may find himself forced to resist the oppressive tyranny with which the patient seeks to control him (Kohut 1971). The quality of this merging and extension of the grandiose self seems to eliminate the object as such and to make it simply a reflection of the self. Consequently, merging of this nature must be regarded as severely regressive and comes closer to the modalities of incorporation that I have described elsewhere (Meissner 1971, 1979a). To this extent, they may be regarded as psychotic in character, or at least regressively borderline.

At a somewhat less primitive level of organization, the activation of the grandiose self leads to the narcissistic object being experienced as similar to and, to that extent, reflecting the grandiose self. In this variant, the object as such is preserved but is modified by the subject's perception of it to suit the subject's narcissistic needs. This form of transference is referred to as alter-ego or twinship transference. Clinically, dreams or fantasies referring to such an alter-ego or twinship relationship with the analyst may be explicit. As Kohut (1971) notes: "The pathognomonic therapeutic regression is characterized by the fact that the patient assumes that the analyst is either like him or similar to him, or that the analyst's pathological makeup is similar to that of the patient" (p. 115). In this type of transference, then, the reality of the analyst or therapist is preserved, but it is modified after the fashion of a transitional object by a projection of some aspects of the patient's grandiose self onto the object.

The most mature and most developed form of mirror transference experiences the analyst as a separate person, but nonetheless one who becomes important to the patient and is accepted only to the degree that he is responsive to the narcissistic needs of the reactivated grandiose self. Kohut appeals here to the model of the gleam in the mother's eye that responds to and mirrors the child's exhibitionism. In this way, the mother participates in and reinforces the child's narcissistic pleasure in himself. Thus, in this strictest sense of the mirror transference, the analyst's function becomes one of admiring and reflecting the grandiosity and exhibitionism of the patient.

This need on the part of the patient may also take a more subtle form in which the patient seeks such admiration and confirmation from the analyst, but constantly acts in a way that reflects the fear of not getting it. Consequently, the patient becomes extremely resistant out of a continuing fear that the revelation of less than ideal impulses, fantasies, or wishes may deprive him of the analyst's admiring eye. For such patients, the grandiose self is not so much confirmed as maintained intact behind a highly defensive facade. In such cases, the analyst runs the risk of becoming a threat to the vulnerability of the grandiose self and may even be seen in persecutory or paranoid forms of transferential distortion.

"Selfobject" Transferences

The so-called "selfobject" transferences come out of the self-psychology that has been developed by Kohut and his followers. While I do not find it theoretically congruent or clinically useful to follow the Kohutian line of development from the conceptualization of narcissistic disturbances into the realm of "selfobject" phenomena, I am convinced on the basis of my own clinical experience that the states of mind and interrelationship that are described in "selfobject" terms nonetheless have clinical validity. I would like, therefore, to include these phenomena in the present discussion, keeping in mind that I am leaving questions open at this point regarding the nature of the phenomena involved and the extent to which they can be regarded as authentically transference phenomena rather than reflecting some other aspect of the therapeutic interaction.

These phenomena should be considered in the context of Kohut's understanding of the nature of borderline states. The essential idea is that the nuclear self, which is thought of in exclusively narcissistic terms (Kohut 1971), is regarded in borderline conditions as continually at risk of fragmentation, disorganization, enfeeblement, or chaos, but that this inner state of fragility and vulnerability is protected and masked by a complex array of defenses. This state of affairs is the result of developmental vicissitudes in which the child's need to establish an autonomous self was denied or negated by the unempathic intrusions of parental "selfobjects" (Kohut and Wolf 1982). The borderline conditions, therefore, in Kohut's terms, are primary disorders of the self.

The relationship between the patient and the therapist as the empathic "selfobject" plays a specific role in the therapeutic process. In a sense, speaking teleologically, the patient's psyche makes the therapist a functional "selfobject" in order to facilitate the processes of growth and structuring of the self. The "selfobject" then serves to evoke and sustain the patient's self-organization and self-experience. Adler (1980a) describes "selfobject" transferences as "transferences in which the analyst and patient are variably fused along a complex continuum in which the analyst performs certain functions for the patient which are absent in the patient and which require the presence and functioning of the analyst for the patient to feel whole and complete" (p. 547). This conceptualization is less in terms of object relations, that is, in terms of the interpersonal relationship between the self and its object, and more in terms of the intrapsychic experience of the "selfobject" relationship, that is, the relationship between the self and its experienced object imagoes. This way of looking at the "selfobject" transference can be related to the establishment of the holding environment (see Chapter 3). The holding environment allows for the establishment of stable "selfobject" transferences, which diminish the fragility and uncertainty of the patient's self-cohesiveness and allow the patient to enter the therapeutic interaction with a greater sense of comfort and security (Adler 1982). This approach envisions the possibility of effective therapeutic change by reason of the involvement in a "selfobject" transference, exclusive of the implementation or effects of interpretation.

"Selfobject" transferences reflect the underlying need-structure that the patient brings to the therapeutic relationship, based on the predominant pattern of "selfobject" deprivation or frustration and the corresponding seeking for the appropriate form of "selfobject" involvement. In these terms, a number of configurations have been described (Kohut and Wolf 1978, 1982). The understimulated self lacks vitality and is plagued by feelings of emptiness, boredom, and apathy, and thus seeks stimulation and even excitement as a means of warding off the pain of inner deadness. The overstimulated self struggles with intense ambition and fantasies of greatness, which force patients to inhibit their capacity for productive or creative effort, or cause them to draw back from contexts in which they may become the center of attention or admiration. Such individuals thus find little satisfaction in external success. The intensity of their own exhibitionistic and grandiose wishes and fantasies is frightening and inhibiting. The overburdened self sees the world as potentially hostile and dangerous and thus reacts with hypersensitivity and feels easily attacked and vulnerable. At times, this pattern of reaction may even approach paranoia. The fragmenting self, on the other hand, frequently becomes disorganized and loses a sense of coordination in various aspects of behavior and functioning. In the face of often trivial narcissistic deprivation, trauma, or disappointment, the patient loses a sense of internal cohesion and integration. Such states of fragmentation may often manifest themselves in hypochondriacal symptoms and preoccupations.

Some of the descriptions of "selfobject" need represent efforts to translate the patterns of transference interaction based on narcissistic dynamics into the perspective of the relationship between self and "selfobject." Thus, mirror-hungry personalities express their need for mirroring in efforts to evoke attention, recognition, admiration, and approval from the object as a way of countering their inner sense of worthlessness, devaluation, and diminished self-esteem. Similarly, ideal-hungry personalities seek out objects whose power, beauty, prestige, intelligence, or other admirable values correspond to their need to attach themselves to the idealized object. Such patients can feel good about themselves and maintain a sense of inner equilibrium and cohesion only insofar as they are connected to these idealized objects. However satiating of such need the attachment to the object may be, the underlying neediness and emptiness will inevitably reassert themselves and lead to dissatisfaction with the currently idealized object and a renewed search for another such object. Variations on the mirroring theme include the alter-ego-hungry personality, who seeks a relationship with the object who can serve as a twin and whose conforming appearance, opinion, or values confirm and sustain the integrity of the self. At a more pathological level, the merger-hungry personalities attach themselves to the object with such intensity that the boundaries between their own identity and that of the object become confused and lead to states of merger in which the subjects are no longer able to discriminate their own thoughts or wishes or feelings from those of the object. The merger transference reconstitutes the fusion with the "selfobject" of early development, akin to the earliest narcissistic union with the mother in which the putative object shows no initiative or autonomy of its own but exists solely as an extension of the self. Such patients often expect that the therapist will know their most private thoughts and feelings without their saying anything about them. In such circumstances, any separation or autonomy of the object becomes intolerable and even devastating. In a somewhat contrasting configuration, contact-shunning personalities are forced to avoid any significant involvement with objects as a way of defending themselves from the underlying intense need for the object. These individuals are sensitive to rejection, but on a deeper level struggle with the basically schizoid fear of engulfment and destruction in the union with the object.

Taking a step back from the Kohutian emphasis in these formulations, I question the extent to which these patterns can be regarded as transferences in any strict sense. Certainly, as I have argued elsewhere (Meissner 1983), the described configurations overlap to a significant degree with familiar personality organizations and character structures. I also think that a case can be made for these descriptions as authentic forms of transference to the extent that identifiable elements of projection or displacement can be identified as undergirding the phenomenology. It is clear that any one of these configurations has the potentiality for drawing the therapist into a matching counterposition, which will serve to respond to and satisfy the patient's implicit need. One might regard such interactions as forms of transference/countertransference interactions (see Chapter 7). Moreover, even if one were not satisfied or able to demonstrate that transference configurations were in fact operative in these contexts, there seems little doubt that, to the extent that these interactions are generated within the therapy, they represent some form or degree of therapeutic misalliance (see the discussion in Chapter 5). To the extent that the therapist is drawn into efforts to respond to the patient's "selfobject" needs, he would in those terms be collaborating in a therapeutic misalliance. The crucial question, however, is the degree to which such misalliance participation may be necessary as an unavoidable component of the therapeutic interaction without which the therapeutic process would founder or not even be possible (Adler 1980a,b).

Transitional Relatedness

An additional model of transference relatedness is based on the original contribution of Modell (1963), and has subsequently been conceptualized as a form of transitional relatedness frequently identifiable in the therapeutic interaction of borderline patients (Coppolillo 1967, Feinsilver 1983). Basing his analysis on Winnicott's notion of the transitional object, Modell (1963) describes the borderline transference as based on a transitional object relation in which some "selfobject" discrimination is preserved, but only imperfectly. The therapist is perceived as outside the self, but is invested with qualities from the patient's own archaic self-image. The intensity of this experience can vary considerably, ranging from relatively high levels of maintained reality testing to the opposite level of transference psychosis. Such transitional relatedness reflects an inherent need for primitively organized patients to become involved in such transitional relationships not only with people but also with inanimate objects, pets, abstract ideas, fantasies, and so on. Within the transitional relationship, the subject utilizes magical thinking to create a secure sense of being protected by an omnipotent maternal presence (Feinsilver 1983). The form of transitional relatedness seems to have a significant degree of overlap with the previously described "selfobject" transferences and would be subject to some of the same reservations. Nonetheless, the "transitional object" usage seems to me much more theoretically manageable than the "self-object" formulations. The "selfobject" transferences, to the extent that they involve projective elements and enter into a kind of transitional relatedness with the object, seem more readily understood in essentially transitional terms.

Transference Psychosis

I have previously discussed the fragility of the capacity for reality testing in borderline patients, particularly those in the lower order of the borderline spectrum. In transference terms, the failure of reality testing in the interaction with the therapist leads to a loss of self-object differentiation and the diffusion of self and object boundaries (Kernberg 1968). The metaphors of fusion and merger are used to describe this phenomenon (Frosch 1967a). Mirroring that takes an extreme form of a merger transference is probably always a form of regressive and primitive transference expression. Such mirroring may reflect an attempt to re-fuse with an omnipotent object as a defense against underlying fears of vulnerability and powerlessness. The fused dyad has been invested with omnipotent powers (McGlashan 1983a) that serve a positive function in preserving the patient's fragile sense of self, but may also become an expression of negative transference elements in which oneness carries with it the threat of engulfment and loss of self and may precipitate a paranoid transference reaction (Searles 1985). These regressive forms of transference constitute a transference psychosis.

Kernberg (1984) ascribes the confusion between the patient's sense of self and object to interacting projections and internalizations, with the result that "inside" and "outside" become confused and patient and therapist interchange their personalities. Reality testing in the transference fails, so that the line between fantasy and reality is blurred and the differences between transference and the real person of the therapist is obscured (Giovacchini 1987b). The therapist is experienced not as similar to the past object but as identical (Little 1958, Wallerstein 1967). The resulting transference psychosis reflects the emergence of delusional material in the transference. As with other forms of borderline psychotic regression, the transference psychosis is transient, often readily reversed by therapeutic intervention, and is usually transference-limited

(Frosch 1967b). The transference psychosis may serve as the basis for acting-out, but by and large the delusion does not extrapolate outside of the therapeutic situation (Modell 1963, Kernberg 1968). In cases in which the transference psychosis becomes excessively disruptive or cannot be contained within the therapeutic context, hospitalization may be necessary (Kernberg 1984).

TRANSFERENCE MECHANISMS

Understanding of borderline transferences requires some exploration of the underlying mechanisms and their dynamic interactions. I will focus here on three mechanisms that contribute to transference formation, namely displacement, projection, and projective identification.

Displacement

Displacement is the basic mechanism of the classic transference paradigm in which an object representation derived from any level or combination of levels of the subject's developmental experience is displaced to the new object in the therapeutic relationship. The object representation is imposed on the new object, namely, the analyst or therapist, so that he now comes to be invested with the affective burdens and connotations that were inherent in the old object relationship. As far as I can see, displacement is still the basic mechanism for libidinally based transferences, both positive and erotic transferences, as described above. The fact that erotic transferences can become delusional at times does not change the basic character of the mechanism by which the transference itself arises. By and large, displacement transferences play a dominant role in neurotic disorders, and in the borderline spectrum are often a prominent feature of the transference involvement of higher-order patients. Particularly the primitive hysterics develop libidinal transferences, often with considerably affective intensity and at times even erotic delusions. In such cases, the phallic-oedipal dynamics tend to play a dominant role in the transference; as one moves further down the borderline spectrum, however, whatever impact such phallic-oedipal derivatives may have in influencing the shape of the transference, they tend to be absorbed in and overwhelmed by more primitive concerns of separation, abandonment, idealization, dependence, and merger.

Projection

More generally in the borderline spectrum, transferences are developed on a projective basis (Berg 1977). In lower-order cases particularly, projective transferences play the dominant role and displacement transferences a much less significant part. I am not attempting to draw a hard line between these two transference types, since I think they can play a role in most forms of transference expression. My view is not that displacement is exclusively characteristic of higher-order pathology and projective transferences are correspondingly characteristic of lower-order pathology (à la Kernberg's distinction between regression and splitting). Rather, both of these mechanisms play a role in and contribute to transference dynamics, but in varying degrees and with varying levels of intensity. As one moves toward the lower pole of the borderline spectrum, projective transferences seem to occupy an increasingly dominant place in the therapeutic interaction. Nor would I go so far as to say that if a transference involves projective mechanisms it should for that reason be regarded as borderline. Rather, the confluence of displacement and projective elements can be found in any transference configuration in any patient. I have suggested elsewhere (Meissner 1981b) that the emergence of a full-blown transference neurosis even in neurotic patients would probably entail projective elements in addition to the more classically conceived displacement elements (Giovacchini 1975b).

The role of projection in the development of transference is in fact quite complex. As I have noted in previous writings (Meissner 1974, 1976, 1978c, 1986b), projections are derived from the underlying configuration of the introjects, which constitute part of the core internalizations of the patient's self-structure. Consequently, the effect of the projective aspect of transference is to make the therapist represent a part of the patient's own self-organization (Searles 1984). It is also consistent with the projective understanding of transference that the introjective configuration on which the projection is based may reflect internalizations from the relationship between objects outside of himself, rather than an internalization based on a relationship between himself and any single significant object. This is often the case in borderline patients who grow up in a family situation in which the parents were related in a sadomasochistic way, thus providing the basis for the child to internalize both the aggressive-victimizing and masochistic-victimized aspects of the parental relationship (Meissner 1978c, 1986b, Searles 1984).

Other aspects of the projective dimension of borderline transferences have been emphasized. The projective elements can take the form of
the construction of an environmental ambience that reproduces aspects
of the infantile environment. This form of externalization differs from
the typically paranoid form in which classically persecutory and hostile
elements are projected onto specific objects and result in feelings of
threat and persecution. Rather, the environment is reshaped to fit the
needs of the internal introjective configuration and to reinforce it.
Needless to say, such an externalization can take place within the
therapeutic relationship: the therapist or analyst can be incorporated in
the patient's construction and drawn into participating in it, either
willingly or collusively. In that event, the therapist can, at least potentially, become an object of projection (Giovacchini 1979). Whether in
the more specific forms of projection or in more general forms of
externalization, the transference projections may not be based simply
on intrapsychically derived distortions, but may have a reality component insofar as they correspond to aspects of the therapist's or analyst's
actual traits or behaviors, which become exaggerated by the patient's
pathological needs (Langs 1978–1979, Searles 1978–1979). The connection with the actual traits of the therapist may involve countertransference elements, but may also relate to real characteristics, exclusive of
transferential considerations.

The tendency for borderline transferences to undergo alternating
patterns based on introjective-projective interactions has also been
noted (Kernberg 1968, 1984). Kernberg (1968) describes this alternation
as between two states, one in which the self-representation is projected
while the patient remains identified with the corresponding object representation, and the other involving projection of the object-representation while the patient remains identified with the corresponding self-
representation. In Masterson's system, the corresponding elements
involve alternative projections of the rewarding and withdrawing part-
units, and the corresponding internal reaction to these projections
(Masterson and Rinsley 1975, Masterson 1976, Rinsley 1977).

My theoretical orientation is somewhat different, although the
phenomenology is the same. I see these alternating patterns in more
specifically structural terms, involving the projection of alternative
aspects of the introjective configurations (Meissner 1984a). These configurations can be usefully designated in both aggressive and narcissistic
terms: the aggressively determined configurations involve that of the
aggressor-introject, as opposed to the victim-introject; the narcissistic
parameters can be similarly described in terms of narcissistic enhance-

ment in the superior introject and the corresponding states of narcissistic depletion reflected in the inferior introject. Both of these interlocking patterns enter into and determine the structure of borderline transferences. At the lower levels of the borderline spectrum, the aggressive determinants operate more intensely and destructively, and the patterns of alternation tend to be more rapid, intense, and extreme. At the highest levels of borderline adjustment, however, both the alternating patterns and the intensity of aggressive themes are often considerably muted and present relatively softened degrees of intensity and polarization (Meissner 1984a, 1986b).

The projection of elements derived from the aggressive introjects provide the basis for both negative and paranoid transference reactions (Kernberg 1966, 1968, 1984, Giovacchini 1975b). By the same token, the projection of the elements of the victim-introject allows the patient to assume the hostile, sadistic, or aggressive position, in which he becomes the aggressor to the therapist's victim. Borderline patients tend to play out the scenarios with varying degrees of intensity and distortion. The patterns are usually defensively and reciprocally linked, so that the aggressive position usually represents a defense against underlying fears of weakness, powerlessness, and vulnerability. By the same token, the victim position can be considered as a defense against underlying fears of his own destructiveness, hatefulness, and power.

Similar patterns take place around narcissistic issues involving introjective configurations representing the residues of narcissistic superiority and inferiority. When the superior narcissistic elements are projected, the result is a form of idealization of the object, just as when the inferior aspects are projected, the result is a corresponding devaluation. This conceptualization differs somewhat from that provided by Kohut (1971). Idealization in the Kohutian schema would involve projection of the idealized parental imago, but there is no component corresponding to the inferior introject involved in devaluation. Clinically, in most cases of pathological idealization, there is an implicit and often subtle devaluation of the self; it is this form of devaluation that is addressed by the subject's introjection of the inferior narcissistic configuration. At the same time, the grandiose self would seem to express the characteristics of the superior introject, so that the forms of mirror transference would presumably involve different forms and degrees of projection of the superior introject, similar to the projections of the grandiose self described by Kohut (1971).

There is some question, however, as to the projective dynamics involved in these mirroring phenomena. The projection is not straightforward, since the object is not viewed as narcissistically enhanced or valued in itself, as would be the case in idealization, but rather only as a reflection of the grandiosity of the self. The object in itself is thus equivalently devalued insofar as it has no value in itself and achieves its value only as a reflection. Rather than a simple projection of the grandiosity onto the object in forms of mirroring, it may be a more complex form of projection of narcissistic inferiority in which the grandiosity remains inherent in the self-organization and is attributed to the object only secondarily and derivatively.

The projective dynamics in the "selfobject" transferences are more obscure. While projective elements may take place in these forms of transference and may be clinically identifiable at times, the transference expression may also take the form of a drawing or pulling of the object or the environment into a position of meeting the pathological needs of the self. Thus, in the various forms of "selfobject" transference, the therapist can be drawn into the process of responding to the needs of the self without necessarily becoming an object of specific projection on the part of the patient. While the transitional transference enjoys a considerable degree of overlap with these "selfobject" transferences, the projective element is somewhat more explicit in that the projection constitutes the self-contribution to the organization of the transitional phenomenon. While the transitional object and the resulting transitional relationship are not constituted solely by the projection, the object as experienced by the patient nonetheless represents an amalgamation or fusion of the objective attributes of the real object, namely the therapist, and the subjectively derived projective content. This view of transitional relatedness leaves open the question of the degree to which the real attributes of the therapist correspond to or even contribute to the shaping of the transference.

Projective Identification

We are faced here with the difficulties deriving from the confusion between projection and projective identification. I have discussed this question in some detail elsewhere (Meissner 1980a, 1987), but in this context certain conclusions can be relevant. As I read Klein's pronouncements on the subject, projective identification emerged from her linkage between projection and introjection, mechanisms she saw operating in constant interaction in a variety of contexts of development of object-related experience in the infant. She argued that the projection of impulses or feelings into another person brought about an identification with that person, based on the attribution to that other of one's own qualities. This attribution became the basis for a certain form of empathy and connection with the object. Thus, by implication, the notion of projective identification added to the basic concept of projection the notes of diffusion of ego boundaries, a loss or diminishing of self-object differentiation, and inclusion of the object as part of the self. In this sense projective identification would have to be regarded as a psychotic mechanism. It also is cast in terms of a one-body system, that is, the entire process takes place within the intrapsychic realm of a single individual: both the projecting and the identifying take place in the patient's mind.

Later elaborations of the notion of projective identification have translated it from a one-body context into a two-body context. The mechanisms come to apply to an interaction between two subjects, one of whom projects something onto or into the other, whereupon the other introjects or internalizes what has been projected. Instead of the projection and identification taking place in the same subject, the projection takes place in one and the internalization in the other (Segal 1957, Malin and Grotstein 1966, Bion 1967, Grotstein 1981). This latter usage has served as a basis for an extensive extrapolation of the concept of projective identification to apply to object-relations of all sorts, including transference (Segal 1977) and even family relationships (Zinner and Shapiro 1972, Slipp 1973, Greenspan and Mannino 1974). This usage is a dominant motif in the Kleinian literature.

Consequently, in the present study, I will maintain the distinction between projection and projective identification. Projective identification will refer exclusively to a one-body context, to a psychotic mechanism in which self-object differentiation is impaired or lost, in which there is confusion of ego boundaries and some part of the self is projected into the object and experienced as such. In the two-body context, where projections involve corresponding internalizations on the part of the other, as is often the case in various forms of transference/countertransference interactions (see Chapter 7), the process involves projection in one subject and introjection in the other. In my view, all projections that involve another person involve subtle pressures to draw the object into conformity with the demands of the projection; projective identification does not differ in this regard.

A word should be said about Kernberg's usage in this respect. He also distinguishes between projection and projective identification. Projection operates as a mechanism for externalizing the all-bad aggressive self and object images and leads to the development of threatening, dangerous, and retaliatory objects against which the patient must defend himself. This basically paranoid mechanism functions within the context of a more or less adequate differentiation of self and objects, but in areas of affective intensity, where regressive pressures come to bear, ego boundaries can be weakened within the particular area of projection, so that patients begin to feel that they identify themselves with the object of projection. This "empathy" increases the fear of the projected aggression and mandates control of the object to prevent it from counterattack; the object must be attacked and controlled before it can attack and destroy the subject (Kernberg 1967, 1975a, 1976b, 1984, 1987b). Kernberg's usage, however, has been challenged by the Kris Study Group (Abend et al. 1983). They agree that borderline patients project and react in paranoid and defensive ways, particularly toward the therapist or analyst. They question, however, whether the special defensive mechanism operating in this regressive fashion differs in any significant way from ordinary projection. The empathy Kernberg describes is not found as a rule in more severely disturbed psychotics, who also project. If projective identification is a more primitive form of projection, one would expect a similar phenomenon in those patients as well. The Kris Study Group, therefore, attributes the difference between projective identification and projection simply to a greater degree of impaired self-object differentiation in more primitive patients. The mechanism involves more than simply aggressive projections, since all conflicts and defensive needs may produce weakening of ego boundaries and a relative failure of self-object differentiation. My own tendency would be more in tune with this criticism, and would restrict projective identification to a context of severe psychotic regression (Meissner 1980a). This usage is fairly consistent with current views of this mechanism in borderline pathology. Projective identification is connected with failures of reality testing (McGlashan 1983a,b, Kernberg 1984), with efforts to control a potentially threatening therapist in a potentially paranoid transference, with delusional and paranoid components of a transference psychosis, and with significant regressive crises (Kernberg 1966, 1968, 1984).

TRANSFERENCE MANAGEMENT

The understanding of the various forms and processes involved in borderline transferences leads inevitably to the question of transference management. In this section, I would like to discuss a number of issues related to dealing with borderline transferences, largely exclusive of questions related to transference interpretation that will be discussed further in Chapter 8. I will discuss the issues of transference management under four headings:

1. The priority of alliance factors over transference factors in dealing with transference distortions—this includes the focusing of clarifying or interpretive interventions;
2. The relationship of transference expressions to the forming and sustaining of therapeutic misalliances;
3. The implications of the interaction of projections and introjections in transference; and
4. A few comments on the use of interpretations in dealing with transference material.

Relation to Therapeutic Alliance

I have already discussed the reasons for focusing on issues related to the therapeutic alliance and its disruption as a matter of first priority and dealing with transference manifestations as a matter of secondary priority. While the approach to alliance issues is dictated by the necessity for constant and immediate attention, the attitude and expectancy toward transference factors is somewhat different. In general, the therapist would prefer to give ample opportunity for the transference manifestations to develop. Transference manifestations compel some form of intervention from the therapist only at points where they create a significant resistance to the treatment process, or at points at which they become sufficiently disruptive or regressive as to undermine or disrupt the therapeutic alliance.

The basic rule of thumb is that transference and therapeutic alliance stand in opposition and are generally inversely proportional, in the sense that the more prominent and influential the transference elements, the less stable and effective is the therapeutic alliance, and vice versa. Therapists who emphasize the centrality of transference phenomena may see an emphasis on alliance factors as a tendency to avoid or minimize the significance of transference; but it can also be argued that whatever the oppositional context within which they operate, there is also a sense in which therapeutic alliance and transference are linked in a mutually interactive process. In this sense, transference can be clarified, interpreted, and effectively dealt with only in the degree to which a workable therapeutic alliance is in effect. But there are also conditions in which the development of the transference requires some preexisting foundation in the therapeutic alliance in order to occur in any meaningful way.

This issue raises the question of what factors are necessary for the stimulation and development of a full-blown transference or transference neurosis. Borderline patients often enter the therapeutic relationship with a significant distortion in the therapeutic alliance. Underlying transference determinants may contribute to the misalliance in significant ways, but it is only when the alliance has been in some degree consolidated or stabilized, even in inchoative and tentative ways, that the transference determinants are allowed to come into focus. In this sense, some form of preliminary alliance, whether in narcissistic terms (narcissistic alliance) or on other grounds (working/therapeutic alliance), is necessary so that the stage is set for the activation and mobilization of more regressive transference elements. In such cases, the patient may need to feel a sense of security and confidence and trust in the relationship to the therapist in order for transference elements to find expression. The metaphors of holding or containment are in fact expressive of this dimension of the therapeutic alliance in that they imply the implementation of a supportive and sustaining environment within which the therapeutic process evolves.

While alliance factors and transference stand in opposition, this line of demarcation is somewhat obscured in the so-called "selfobject" transferences. There is a sense in which the underlying needs of the self, as expressed in "selfobject" transferences, are at least partly responded to in the therapeutic alliance. To the extent that the neurotic or self-related need expressed in the "selfobject" transference is responded to by the object, there would seem to be a high risk for the development of a transference/countertransference interaction. For example, if the ideal-hungry self finds an object that responds to its need to idealize and serves the function of an idealized object, the transference on the part of the subject would seem to correspond to a countertransference on the part of the object. This would be analogous to the case of a negative transference, for example, in which the victimized and vulnerable self of the patient would be matched by a sadistic, hostile, and destructive image of the therapist. But, while a good therapeutic alliance would not respond to the feeling of victimization in this sort of negative transference, there is a sense in which a good therapeutic alliance would be responsive to the basic need being expressed in the "selfobject" transferences. While the alliance for the idealizing subject would not immediately satisfy his need to idealize, it would at the same time offer a context of understanding, security, acceptance, and confidence that would allow his idealizing need to be accepted and empathically understood, so that whatever factors might underlie the need to idealize would be satisfied by a responsive and understanding object. If we presume on the basis of our previous argument that the underlying sense of narcissistic inferiority contributes to the patient's need to idealize, then the participation in a meaningful therapeutic alliance would provide some restitutive balm to the patient's underlying sense of inferiority. It should be pointed out that this view of the therapeutic interaction comes close to the notion of a corrective emotional experience, but it is far from being simply that; rather, it involves significant dynamic issues and processes that are activated within the interpersonal relationship and involve the patterning of projections and introjections underlying the internalizations that are central to the process of cure (Meissner 1981b).

Relation to Therapeutic Misalliance

Transferences lie at the root of most therapeutic misalliances. Whenever the therapist recognizes a misalliance, he has good reason to search behind it for the transference components that may be giving rise to or contributing to it. As Freud (1912, 1915) observed, a certain degree of benign and positive attachment to the therapist may be necessary in setting the therapeutic process on the right footing and allowing the patient to feel sufficiently comfortable to proceed with the analytic work. This degree of positive transference, which usually is admissible to consciousness and facilitates the patient's involvement with the therapist, can thus be an important element in establishing a therapeutic alliance. It is only when the transference, usually in a negative form, becomes a resistance to the forming of the therapeutic relationship that it becomes a focus for concern and interpretation. This form of relatively conscious, benign, and constructive transference does not necessarily contribute, therefore, to a therapeutic misalliance. In contrast, the negative transferences, whether in the merely negative or in paranoid form, always contribute to the formation of a therapeutic misalliance. In the distortions, based on negative transferences, the therapist may be seen as judgmental, critical, unsympathetic, rigid, harsh, sadistic, hostile, powerful, controlling, threatening, abandoning, and so forth. If these aggressive dynamics are extended to the psychotic level, the transference becomes paranoid and the alliance correspondingly disrupted.

The narcissistic transferences are somewhat similar to the positive transferences in the manner in which they may or may not contribute to the therapeutic misalliance. If the intensity of the narcissistic transference is relatively muted and mild, as is often the case in higher-order borderlines, particularly the primitive hysterics, the degree of distortion introduced into the therapeutic relationship may not distort the potential therapeutic alliance to any significant degree. But even in higher-order patients, the degree of idealization or mirroring must be carefully assessed as to its impact on the therapeutic alliance. At times in such patients the distortion may not be severe, but it may contribute to a subtle narcissistic alliance, which requires specific attention in the hope that it can be directed toward a more meaningful therapeutic alliance. As the narcissistic distortion becomes more severe, however, the risk of narcissistic alliance increases, as well as the tendency to form a narcissistically determined therapeutic misalliance. In such cases, the risk of a transference/countertransference interaction in response to the patient's narcissistic need is high.

The "selfobject" transferences are similar to the transference/countertransference risk. To the extent that the "selfobject" interaction takes place on this level, it always involves some degree of therapeutic misalliance. If the needs expressed in the "selfobject" transference can be approached and responded to in terms of the therapeutic alliance, this is far preferable to the transference/countertransference option. Transitional object transferences and the demand placed on the object to respond in terms of transitional relatedness always involve some degree of therapeutic misalliance and introduce a distortion into the therapeutic situation; this happens often in lower-order borderline patients. The transference psychoses not only represent an acute and regressive disruption and breakdown of the therapeutic alliance, but also can be taken as reflecting an underlying therapeutic misalliance, which is usually of a severe, profound, and long-lasting variety.

Transference Interpretation

According to Freud's suggestion, transferences of a relatively mild, benign, and constructive nature, whether they be positive or narcissistic, do not call for a specific therapeutic response as long as they contribute to an effective therapeutic alliance. To the degree that they interfere with that progression, they must become the objects of therapeutic scrutiny and exploration. All other forms of transference, in view of the fact that they tend to undermine the therapeutic alliance and create identifiable misalliances, call for therapeutic intervention. In all of these cases, alliance takes priority over transference as the object of therapeutic effort. The resulting therapeutic misalliance must first be identified, explored, and understood. Once this is done, more specific and identifiable transference elements can be brought into play. In negative and narcissistic transferences, the line between transference elements and aspects of the misalliance can be more clearly drawn. In the "selfobject" and transitional object transferences, this line is often difficult to identify and maintain. Attention to the alliance aspects consistently takes precedence and becomes a vehicle for the next step in the process, namely focusing, exploring, and coming to understand the underlying transference dynamics.

Remembering that the transference develops through the progressive interaction of projections and introjections provides a useful framework for conceptualizing and ultimately interpreting the transference dynamics and their implications. In these terms, I would emphasize that the transference can be understood as an expression or reflection of the patient's self-organization, specifically conceptualized in terms of the introjective configurations that form the basis for the projective elements. In this sense, displacement transferences offer an expression of the patient's sense of self in relationship with specific objects. As the object-representation from some previous relationship is attributed to the therapist, the subject simultaneously adopts a similar role in relation to that displaced object. The nature of the object-representation and the position of the subject in relation to it conveys important communications about the individual's own sense of self. In contrast, in the projective transferences, it is some aspect of the self as integrated within the introjective structure that is projected onto the therapist as object. In this case, the projection also reflects the characteristics of the self-system.

In either case, a cardinal principle of good therapeutic management is to avoid being caught up in the potential entanglement in a transference/countertransference interaction. The transference is in effect an invitation to join in such an interaction. In the displacement transference, part of the impulse in the subject is to reenact the previous relationship, but the transference creates no significant pressures within the therapeutic relationship for the therapist to step into that object role and play out the part. In contrast, in a projective transference, there is an inherent exigency for the object to fit into the requirements, so that, first, the projection is in some degree validated and reinforced, and second, the corresponding introjective configuration that remains internalized can be confirmed in the ongoing interaction with the projected part. For example, the patient who projects some aspect of his aggressive introjective configuration onto the therapist and consequently sees the therapist as critical or hostile or threatening, does so in some degree to preserve his own sense of himself as weak and victimized. If the projection is not validated, the mechanism falters and prevents the subject's own inner sense of victimization from being effectively sustained.

The principles I suggest for effective transference interpretations are the following:

1. Effective interpretation requires focusing the transference dynamics on the self-related configurations involved in the transference. In both displacement and projective transferences, the subject is making a statement about his self, his sense of self, his attitudes and feelings toward himself. This is particularly important in dealing with projective transferences, where the projective element may be readily identifiable in the transference, but where the corresponding introjective dimension that serves as the source of the projection remains either concealed or repressed. In identifying the projection, therefore, the therapist must remain alert to further data, which will allow him to bring into focus that hidden aspect of the patient's self which must be clarified in order for an effective interpretation to be made. Thus, if the patient projects an idealizing image onto the therapist, an effective interpretation must await the surfacing of aspects of the patient's own narcissistic superiority in order to make the connecting link between the projective content and the underlying introjective configuration.

2. An adequate interpretation of transference derivatives must include both complementary aspects of the introjective configurations. Thus, patients who project their own aggression must be helped to become aware of their own corresponding role as victim. These same patients carry within themselves, as an inherent part of their internalized self-organization, elements of aggressiveness, power, and destructiveness. Both the victimized and the aggressive aspects must be brought into focus and must be acknowledged on a conscious level. The inferior and the superior aspects of the narcissistic configuration must also be brought into conscious awareness in order to serve as the basis for an adequate interpretation. Since in both cases they form a mutually related and reciprocally defensive whole within the psychic economy, any attempt to deal interpretively with one side of the configuration without dealing with equal concern and effect with the other side would be foredoomed to failure.

3. The interpretive strategy differs, depending on the underlying mechanism by which the transference arises. In the case of displacement transferences, following the general rule, the interpretation of alliance factors is given precedence over the interpretation of the transference dynamics themselves. The transference dynamics are brought into focus by the clarification and elucidation of the implications of the interaction between patient and therapist in the here-and-now of the therapeutic situation. The exploration, clarification, and interpretation of the alliance issues open the way to a deeper understanding of the transference factors.

The direct interpretation of the genetic factors contributing to the transference is effective not only in clarifying and diminishing the effects of the transference but also in restoring the disrupted or distorted alliance. This approach is obviously not possible in the early stages of therapy before adequate understanding has been gained of the patient's history and developmental experience. But where such genetic material is available, it can be effectively utilized in this fashion.

4. In contrast to the situation with displacement transferences, projective transferences do not successfully yield to genetic interpretation. The same priorities obtain with regard to dealing with alliance factors in preference to transference factors and dealing with them as a way of gaining access to the underlying transference dynamics. Here, the interpretive emphasis must fall specifically on the dynamic aspects of the transference as it operates in the here-and-now of the therapeutic situation. This implies not only a clarification of the elements involved in the transference itself but also the connection of the transference dynamics specifically to the underlying introjective configuration embracing its dual aspects.

The approach to the interpretation of the mirror transference, for example, would involve (1) clarification of the alliance distortion and the dimensions and implications of the therapeutic misalliance, and (2) addressing the dimensions of the underlying introjective configuration, specifically in this case the narcissism of the patient's grandiose self and the associated need for mirroring as well as the underlying narcissistically inferior configuration to which the grandiosity is related as a defensive organization. The interpretation of these transference components is not complete, as I have already emphasized, until both aspects of the narcissistic configuration have been clarified, explored, and interpreted. The difficulty presented by the demands of this technical approach stems from the fact that for most patients involved in a mirroring form of narcissistic transference, the aspects of inferiority inherent in the inferior narcissistic configuration are well concealed, often repressed, and not easily accessible therapeutically. Nonetheless, interpretation remains inadequate until all of these aspects have been brought into play and adequately interpreted. It is only at this stage of the process that the genetic aspects, whether directly obtained or reconstructed, become useful. They should be brought into the interpretative process only when the patient has become aware of the dimensions of the narcissistic disorder and has achieved a degree of curiosity about the origins, specifically of the respective narcissistic configurations that form such a central and vital part of the self-organization.

7

COUNTERTRANSFERENCE

DEFINITION

Countertransference must take its place, along with therapeutic alliance and transference, as one of the major aspects of the therapeutic interaction and as a primary locus of therapeutic action in the treatment of borderline patients. It may help our consideration to clarify what I mean by countertransference and its implications.

The term *countertransference* has been used with various connotations, sometimes referring to all of the therapist's responses to the patient (Kernberg 1984, Gunderson 1984), and sometimes referring more restrictively to specific unconscious transferencelike reactions. Early usage implied that countertransference would, therefore, always introduce some distortion or interference into the therapeutic interaction, reflecting unconscious reactions deriving from infantile residues in the therapist's own personality. Such countertransference reactions are a form of transference taking place in the therapist. They may come about in response to and/or in conjunction with the eliciting stimulation of the patient's transference (the transference/countertransference interaction) or may be motivated solely by factors within the therapist.

Chediak (1979) distinguishes between counterreactions and countertransference:

When the analyst's state of mind pertains to the dyadic interaction, it would be necessary to differentiate among (1) *intellectual understanding* based on information given by the patient and intellectual knowledge possessed by the analyst; (2) *the general response to the patient as a person*, the counterpart of what Strupp (1960) stresses when talking about the patient's reaction to the analyst's personality; (3) *the analyst's transference* to the patient, i.e., reliving of early part-object relationships as elicited by certain features in the patient; (4) *the analyst's countertransference*, i.e., the reaction in the analyst to the role he is assigned by the patient's transference; (5) *empathic identification* with the patient. [p. 117]

The last four categories are forms of counterreaction, while countertransference is given a more restrictive and specific meaning.

I am including both the third and fourth categories, rather than simply the fourth, as forms of countertransference. The third corresponds to what has been called "subjective countertransference" and the fourth to "objective countertransference" (Spotnitz 1969, Kirman 1980).[1] This does not exclude other emotional and cognitive reactions on the part of the therapist to the patient. Although primarily unconscious in origin, countertransference reactions can give rise to conscious derivatives, as is the case for all unconscious reactions. The therapist has the task of continually monitoring his own behavior and experience, just as he continually monitors the patient's behavior and experience, with a view to detecting the manifestations of unconscious transferential processes. At times these manifestations are dramatic and forceful, at other times subtle and implicit.

Clearly, with this understanding of countertransference, not all reactions of the therapist to the patient are countertransference. These may involve aspects of the real relationship or of the therapeutic alliance, both of which are distinct from countertransference. The therapist experiences a wide range of responses to the patient, many of which may reflect his or her current experience with the patient and the interaction with the patient's personality. The tendency to feel assaulted as the result of a patient's angry attack may not, in fact, involve countertransference elements; it may simply be a normal and immediate defensive response—but it may also stimulate a countertransference reaction. The therapist's self-awareness and reflective self-knowledge

---

[1]This distinction parallels Wile's (1972) distinction between "therapist-related" (subjective) and "patient-induced" (objective) countertransferences.

may help to discriminate. These noncountertransference aspects may be conscious or unconscious or both, but they provide a more realistic and valid basis for the therapist's interaction with the patient. Noncounter-transference aspects of the therapist's involvement with the patient encompass both the factors that contribute to the therapeutic alliance and the real relationship, and may involve reactions to the patient's transference that do not involve countertransference (Greenson and Wexler 1969).

Moreover, as Gunderson (1984) points out, one person's therapeutic alliance may turn out to be another's countertransference. The shift or gradation among possible approaches to the patient's transference or therapeutic misalliance may vary among therapists and may reflect countertransference vicissitudes: active versus passive, supportive versus exploratory, confrontative versus interpretive, and so on. For some self psychologists, Kernberg's approach to narcissistic transferences has been labeled as a form of countertransference acting out, reflecting the therapist's own conflicts about grandiosity and envy and turning interpretation into a narcissistic assault. On the other hand, the Kohutian approach has been charged with serving as an exercise in futility, collusion, and overidentification with the patient's narcissistic needs and illusions (Mitchell 1986). Consequently the degree to which countertransference is involved at any point in the interaction between therapist and patient, as opposed to other operative factors, remains a continuing and unremitting problem for the therapist and his relationship with the patient. Part of the emphasis in the present study is on the continuum of variation within the borderline spectrum; this is paralleled in the forms and degrees of countertransference and transference/countertransference.

Countertransference in relation to borderline conditions is therefore not an univocal phenomenon but rather involves a spectrum of levels and intensities of transference/countertransference interactions that can vary considerably in both quality and quantity. Kernberg (1965, 1976a, 1984) describes a continuum of countertransference reactions corresponding to the range of transferences from neurotic to psychotic. Reactions to borderline transferences would fall somewhere in the middle. The more regressive the transference, the more it reactivates regressive features in the therapist and elicits an emotional response that tends to be more global and congruent with the patient's projections. I am proposing that there is also a continuum of countertransference variation within the borderline spectrum itself, in which the quality of the countertransference experience at the lower end of the borderline spectrum is quite different from that at the higher end, and that there are shades of qualitative differentiation between them. The major point is that the nature of transference/countertransference interactions varies in relation to the kind of borderline condition with which one is dealing, and that this will in turn determine, within limits, the nature of appropriate therapeutic interventions.

COUNTERTRANSFERENCE MODEL

Introjective/Projective Basis

The model of transference/countertransference interactions is based on the operation of the paranoid process and on the interaction between introjective and projective processes (Meissner 1978b). The patient's pathological sense of self is structured around a core set of pathogenic introjects. These introjects are products of the internalization of significant ambivalent and defensively elaborated object relationships that have taken place during the course of development (Meissner 1979b). The potential for countertransference is based on a similar introjective organization—less defensive, less pathogenic, better integrated and differentiated—in the therapist (Grinberg 1962, Racker 1968, Langs 1978–1979, Searles 1978–1979, Finell 1985, Loewald 1986). The dimensions of the introjective configurations in the therapist or analyst are the same as those underlying the expressions of transference in patients (see Chapter 6), and give rise to corresponding forms of countertransference based on erotic, aggressive, and narcissistic dynamics or other aspects of the self-system (Meissner 1978c, 1984a, 1986b). As Loewald (1986) has recently emphasized, transference and countertransference cannot be considered separately but become aspects of a complex therapeutic interaction. With reference to the more primitive and difficult patients we are concerned with here, he observes that the analyst's usually higher level of psychic development creates difficulties for him in his ability to know the patient's more primitive levels of psychic experience that come from earlier developmental levels. The analyst can be easily drawn into powerful and unrecognized countertransference responses to these primitive affective currents. He writes:

> These patients' primitive "narcissistic" transferences, usually intertwined with oedipal transferences (and often covered by them) and deficient in subject-object differentiation, tend to overstrain the

soundness of the analyst's organization as a separate individual. . . .
He either may be drawn into a transference-countertransference
whirlpool in which his own ego boundaries become blurred, or
these narcissistic transferences call forth rigid defenses in the analyst that make significant communication difficult. [pp. 284–285]

Analyst and analysand can thus be enmeshed in a kind of psychic force
field compounded out of intermingled transference and countertransference processes.

Analysis of the introjective organization provides a basis for the
understanding of transference/countertransference interactions. The
introjective organization gives rise to projections that color the experience of objects and modify the quality of object relations. This is the
basic mechanism of so-called projective or "externalizing" transferences
(Berg 1977). The corresponding process in the therapist provides the
basis for countertransference (Money–Kyrle 1956).

The projections are usually specifically based on and derived from
those aspects of the introjective configuration that remain inactive or
repressed at any given point in the patient's experience. The patient who
is functioning in terms of the victim-introject, for example, will tend to
project the polar opposite aggressor-introject, so that in the interaction
with the therapist, the aggressive projection will color and influence the
patient's perception of and interaction with the therapist. The therapist
is then cast in the role of victimizer and aggressive persecutor. Similarly, the patient who is functioning in terms of the narcissistically
inferior configuration will tend to project the narcissistic opposite in a
form of idealization of the therapist. The projective device is not simply
an intrapsychic or subjective phenomenon; it may in fact correspond to
actual qualities or traits of the therapist that are exaggerated to meet
the patient's pathological needs (Langs 1978–1979, Searles 1978). The
projection also creates a pressure in the interpersonal interaction to
draw the other member of that interaction to fulfill the expectations
and the inherent demands of the projection. Not only is the therapist in
such a situation seen by the patient as, for example, an aggressive
persecutor, but the projection has an inherent gradient that tends to
elicit an aggressive response from the therapist in his or her interaction
with the patient. The process is further sustained by the extent to which
the patient's projection meshes with aspects of the therapist's own
unresolved aggressive conflicts and, in the present model, aggressive
introjective components. In this sense, the transference/countertrans-
ference sets up an interaction in which the patient's pathological needs

are reinforced (Giovacchini 1972, Appel 1974, Langs 1975a,b). In terms of the countertransference model, this emphasis can be made more specific: what tends to be reinforced is the patient's pathogenic introjective configuration (Meissner 1984a). In this sense, the countertransference reaction in the therapist is unconsciously sought by the patient (Clifton 1974, Searles 1978).

The coercive pressures generated by the transference seek to draw the therapist into the position of answering to the inherent pathological needs of the patient (Searles 1984). Where mirroring needs enter the picture, the transference needs will seek to find an object that is like or the same as the subject in some fashion, thus facilitating the creation of a symbiotic dyad (McGlashan 1983b). Some schizoid patients tend to induce in the therapist feelings that resemble their own feelings, including boredom, isolation, disengagement, and even rage (Appel 1974).

Transference/Countertransference Interaction

The patient's projections can create a counterresponse and reaction in the therapist. They may elicit an unconscious tendency to introject their content, and, insofar as this response takes place, to begin to function in terms of the inherent demands of those introjections. This may set the stage for a counterprojective response on the part of the therapist that derives from the amalgamation of the introjected content of the patient's projections with the therapist's own introjective configurations, which he carries as part of his own personality organization. The resulting introjective organization and the derivative counterprojections coming from the therapist to the patient form the core of what has been described as countertransference (Feinsilver 1983). In addition, within the transference/countertransference interaction, the reciprocal pattern of influences is at work. Aspects of the therapist's introjective configuration are reciprocally projected onto the patient and become internalized by the patient as "identifications" with the therapist's often unconscious and poorly integrated introjects (Searles 1985).[2]

In more severely disturbed patients, the patient's helplessness, impotence, and envy in relation to the omnipotent therapist require that the object be controlled in order to preserve the patient's fragile fantasy

---

[2]These processes have been described by Grinberg (1962) in terms of projective identifications and projective counteridentifications. This basically Kleinian usage is not followed in this discussion for technical and theoretical reasons that are discussed more fully elsewhere (Meissner 1980a, 1987).

of omnipotence. The therapist may be experienced in paranoid fashion as powerful, threatening, and hostile. This can justify the patient's counteraggression and makes the need to control the therapist a life-and-death matter (Racker 1957, Maltsberger 1982–1983, Kernberg 1984). The feeling of omnipotence can be reclaimed by various strategies: by impulsive or magical action, by seduction, by manipulation, or even by compliance, in which any variations from the omnipotent object are minimized and disavowed (McGlashan 1983a, Smith and Steindler 1983). The manipulations make it particularly difficult for the therapist to maintain his therapeutic role in the face of the patient's need to convert him into a substitute infantile object (Giovacchini 1979, Feinsilver 1983).

The interlocking of introjection and projection on the part of both patient and therapist gives rise to profound transference/countertransference interactions that have the potential to be mutually reinforcing. The patient who, for example, projects the aggressive derivatives onto his therapist sets up an unconscious process in the therapist that tends to introject the aggressive content, which thus becomes amalgamated with and reinforces aspects of his own aggressor-introject configuration. This sets in motion within the therapist the process by which he not only begins to act the aggressor toward the patient but also projects the aspects of victimization and vulnerability back onto his patient. This projective content is then internalized and introjected by the patient as a reinforcement of his own victim stance.[3] These complex transference/countertransference interactions have been described as aspects of an intersubjective process (Stolorow et al. 1981, 1983).

These mechanisms have been described in some detail by Racker (1953, 1957). Racker (1957) distinguishes concordant identifications, which reflect a recognition of the other's experience as similar to one's own, from complementary identifications produced as a result of the patient's projection and the corresponding internalization by the therapist.[4] In concordant identifications, the therapist may identify aspects of his own psychic structure with those of the patient (ego/ego, superego/superego, or other aspects of the patient's psychic organization and

---

[3]This projective process, as part of the therapist's countertransference, has also been described by Grinberg (1979) as "projective counteridentification." My objections to this usage parallel my difficulties with projective identification as an aspect of transference (see Chapter 6).

[4]These distinctions are paralleled by Wile's (1972) distinction between "resonant" (concordant) and "reciprocal" (complementary) countertransference.

functioning: introjective configurations, self-representations or images, affective states, etc.). Such identifications may serve as the basis for empathy but can be drawn into countertransference by overidentification. Complementary identifications always involve countertransference, in which the therapist identifies with the patient's transference object or projection, and they elicit corresponding emotional responses in the therapist (Boyer 1983). Racker also underscores the potential threat from mutually reinforcing transference/countertransference interactions, which he describes as a vicious neurotic circle.

These patterns of transference/countertransference interaction have also been described in representational terms by Stolorow and colleagues (1981, 1983). They conceptualize the transference/countertransference interaction as an intersubjective process marked either by "representational conjunction" or by "representational disjunction." The former describes a situation in which the representational configurations and affective significances that structure the patient's experience are assimilated by the therapist into similar configurations in his own psychic life. In disjunction, by contrast, the therapist misreads the patient's experience and assimilates it into his own configurations and affective connotations that distort its subjective meaning. While this formulation is cast in representational (cognitive) terms in contrast to my own emphasis on introjective (structural) aspects, I would argue that countertransference cannot be adequately understood on the basis of the differential organization of subjective worlds. Some forms of countertransference are, in fact, based on the similarities between the subjective worlds of therapist and patient. The view of Stolorow and colleagues, however, has the advantage of focusing on the interactional and intersubjective nature of the transference/countertransference interaction.

Interactive Process

A useful schema for understanding the progressive emergence of a transference/countertransference interaction has been provided by Burke and Tansey (1985). The process is divided into two phases: reception and internal processing. It can be outlined as follows:

Phase I: Reception

The first phase deals with the therapist's reception and experience of the set of self-representations or experiences that are stimulated by the patient's projections.

Subphase 1: Mental set

The therapist's mental set enables him to attend and listen optimally to the patient's communications. This optimal set can be disrupted by characterological difficulties or conflicts in his own mind: blind spots, sensitivities, insensitivities, prejudices, narcissism, unresolved conflicts (usually aggressive or libidinal), arrogance, authoritarian attitudes) or situational problems (lack of sleep, personal crises, pregnancy, overwork, illness).

Subphase 2: Pressure of the interaction

The therapist begins to experience the pull of the patient's emotional interaction. Disruptions come from unconscious needs in the therapist to shut off or limit the patient's communications and projections, to avoid the emotional interaction and limit any introjective response.

Subphase 3: Identification—signal affect

The interaction progresses to a stage of internalization of the patient's projective elements. The introjection is unconscious but can result in alterations of the therapist's self-experience in the form of signal affects. Disruptions occur in the therapist's reaction to or handling of these affects, either in the form of discomfort, anxiety, or depression or in the form of excessive gratification or self-enhancement (e.g., in response to the patient's idealization). Defenses may be set in motion that block the affect and interfere with its signal function.

Phase II. Internal Processing

This phase leads to the utilization of the therapist's subjective experience as a tool for understanding the patient.

Subphase 4: Containment–separateness

The therapeutic task is twofold: to contain and integrate consciously the internal alterations and inner affective experiences stimulated by the interaction with the patient, particularly in response to the patient's projections; and secondly, to separate sufficiently from the immediate experience and involvement with the patient to observe, analyze, and understand what is being experienced in the interaction.

Subphase 5: Working model

The therapist constructs a "working model" or representation of the patient and of the interaction between himself and the patient, which serves as a basis for empathic attunement for both affective and cognitive understanding of the patient's inner experience and of the meanings inherent in the transference/countertransference interaction. Disruptions at this subphase arise from the therapist's inability to achieve an adequate working model, or from his ability to utilize only one aspect of the model successfully, i.e., he may be able to assess his own experience and interaction with the patient ("therapist-interaction working model") but may have difficulty achieving an understanding of the patient's internal experience and his experience of the therapist and the therapeutic interaction.

Subphase 6: Empathic connection

The working models serve as a basis for the therapist to understand his own affective experience and the extent to which his experience is determined by the patient's projection as opposed to being internally determined; to assess the degree of correspondence between his own internal states and the patient's (the degree of concordant versus complementary identification); and to understand the patterns of projection and introjection as reciprocally involved in the transference/countertransference interaction. Each of these tasks has its corresponding forms of disruption. The therapist's failures may enter into the process at any point. He may not be able to grasp or understand certain aspects of the process or his own experiences. Even if his understanding is adequate at all points, he may lack the capacity or skill to communicate what he has learned in ways that can be assimilated by the patient and are useful to him in dealing with his problems.

Interactions in the Borderline Spectrum

It must be remembered that these unconscious transference/countertransference pressures may be active to some degree in all forms of therapeutic interaction but are particularly poignant and forceful in work with borderline patients. The easy availability of these configurations for projection creates a particular pressure within the therapeutic interaction for such countertransference manifestations to arise. This may be seen with particularly dramatic impact in the lower-order and more poorly integrated borderlines in whom the propensity for projection is relatively strong. It is also true to a lesser degree even in the more highly organized and better-functioning forms of borderline organization in which the polar opposites of these configurations may not be as extreme and readily apparent. In this latter category, considerable therapeutic regression and intensification of the therapeutic relationship often has to take place before these manifestations become operative or apparent.

In borderline conditions there is a strong need for and dependency on objects as a means for stabilizing a sense of inner continuity and self-coherence, similar to the "selfobject" needs described by Kohut (1971, 1977). The object for borderline patients is needed as an external prop or stabilizer for the threatening fragmentation or disruption of the patient's sense of self, yet at the same time this dependency is highly ambivalent and feared. Such patients, typically in the schizoid continuum, react with varying degrees of withdrawal or isolation in an attempt to deny their basic need or dependency.

As Kernberg (1968) points out, insofar as the therapist is drawn into this projective interaction, there is risk of recreating in the external interaction within the therapy the original pathological introjective configuration within the patient. The countertransference carries the risk not only of eliciting in the therapist feelings similar to those the patients experienced in relation to their own parents (Abend et al. 1983) but also of stimulating feelings that the therapist may have experienced in his own pathogenic object relations (Langs 1975b). The inner pathological tension between the introjective polar configurations can thus be displaced to a conflict with the external object, with the correlative gain that the pattern of self-organization can be integrated, for the time being, around the residual configuration. In this manner the projection of aggressive derivatives onto the therapist eases the inner tension required to defend against such impulses and allows for a more consolidated sense of self around the victim configuration. To the extent that the therapist can be drawn into fulfilling the expectations of this projection, the patient gains an inner sense of consistency and self-organization, but at the expense of consolidating a basically pathological situation. The same principle, *mutatis mutandis*, applies with equal force to the therapist.

Although the basic dynamics of transference/countertransference interactions are primarily unconscious, they can have more conscious reverberations and concomitants that can alert the therapist to their operation. Unconscious countertransference reactions, as long as they remain at that level, usually disrupt or distort the therapeutic interaction and interfere with an effective therapeutic alliance (Langs 1975a,b). However, when such dynamics can be identified and consciously processed, they provide an opportunity for recognition and resolution of aspects of the patient's pathology that may otherwise remain hidden

(Joseph 1985). McDougall (1978) refers to these forms of unconscious communication as "primitive communications" that flow from the patient's need to reconstruct in the analytic relationship the traumatic contexts from childhood. In this sense, countertransference can become a useful instrument attuned to a level of otherwise unavailable unconscious communication between patient and therapist (Boyer 1978).

ASPECTS OF BORDERLINE COUNTERTRANSFERENCE

The projection of relatively intense and often primitive affects in the borderline transference can often have a powerful effect on the therapist. These feelings are often disruptive and threatening, and include homicidal anger, intense and clinging dependency, helplessness, incestuous wishes, primitive fears of abandonment, despair, hopelessness, and even suicidal depression. To the extent that they feed into the therapist's unresolved conflicts, his or her own unconscious and unresolved wishes, and the primitive urges and defenses against them, they can often create a difficult impasse or turmoil that tends to frustrate the therapeutic work (Masterson 1972, Maltsberger and Buie 1974). Maltsberger (1982–1983) expresses this desperate quality of the therapeutic interaction:

> To treat a borderline patient is like the enterprise of rescuing a drowning man. The drowner, despairing of his life and in a panic, is likely to seize the lifeguard so aggressively as to imperil both himself and his rescuer. When the lifeguard tries to bring some order to the situation, the drowner may not understand. Not until he has been towed half way to shore by the hair does he fully realize that cooperation, not attack, is the only way out. [p. 125]

COUNTERTRANSFERENCE VARIATION

The quality of borderline transferences can vary over a wide spectrum of intensity and degrees of pathological expression. The nature of the countertransference reaction tends to vary accordingly. At the more primitive level of transference interaction with borderline patients, the therapist is often caught up in intense emotional reactions reflecting the patient's primitive emotional struggles with aloneness, abandonment, the primitive hunger for objects, and devouring rage. This may be particularly the case with aggressive derivatives, evoking counteraggressive feelings in the therapist as though the disavowed aggressive aspect of the patient suddenly emerges within the therapist (Kernberg 1984). He may then begin to feel drawn into this emotional maelstrom and begin to experience similarly intense and relatively primitive emotional turmoil (Searles 1978, Langs 1978–1979). Reactions at this level have more to do with the emotional force generated by the patient's projections and transference than with the therapist's own internally derived countertransference (Boyer 1983, Feinsilver 1983).

Clinical experience has repeatedly demonstrated the sensitivity of borderline patients to countertransference reactions. Borderline hyper-responsiveness to unconscious aspects of the object's psychic functioning and the sensitivity to unconscious fantasies and impulses and their derivatives make these patients considerably more responsive to unresolved conflictual elements in the therapist than other, certainly healthier, patients (Krohn 1974). This puts them in increased contact with the unconscious introjective alignment in the therapist and makes them highly reactive to projective derivatives. While sensitivity to countertransference reactions is characteristic across the borderline spectrum, it remains especially telling and disruptive in the more primitive range. This reflects the tuning of such personalities to a different range of interpersonal exchange than is customary in neurotic or healthier patients. There is often an immediate and intense response to a countertransference reaction, which is experienced as though it were consciously intended or, in the case of the aggressive components, as a deliberately instigated and direct attack (Krohn 1974).

In the schizoid form of borderline pathology, patients often present a facade of affective isolation and cold, grandiose self-sufficiency (Modell 1975). The affective block and failure of communication are due to fear of closeness to the therapist. There is a fundamental object-related conflict, basic to the borderline condition, of both an intense need for and a terrifying fear of objects. Patients cope with this underlying conflict by a posture of isolation and withdrawal, warding off any effective contact with objects and adopting a rejecting and disdainful attitude in a vain attempt to convince others and themselves that the vulnerable and helplessly impotent sense of themselves that pervades their inner world does not exist. The patient behaves almost as though the therapist were not in the room. The therapist experiences this attitude as a narcissistic affront and may respond with impatience, anger, boredom, distraction, even sleepiness.

The schizoid variants form a dramatic contrast to the more intensely involved, conflicted, clinging, and hostilely dependent picture

found in other forms of borderline pathology. The underlying conflicts
in both of these primitive types of patients are similar, but the patterns
of defense and behavior organized to cope with these fundamental
conflicts differ radically. The desperate reaching out for contact and
infantile dependence on a sustaining object in the one contrasts radically with the aloof and isolated withdrawal of the other. Within the
borderline spectrum, however, they can both be taken as expressions of
relatively primitive conflicts over involvement with objects, representing comparable levels of personality organization and functioning.

In contrast to these more primitive interactions, transference/
countertransference interactions toward the more differentiated and
higher-order end of the borderline spectrum tend to be less intense, less
primitive, and less easily mobilized. Frequently in such patients, the
borderline characteristics remain concealed or muted for considerable
time, and only under significant degrees of therapeutic regression does
the borderline quality of the patient's personality organization become
more manifest. The transferences of such patients may be pervaded by a
subtle but nonetheless detectable form of magical expectation that the
therapist's power will somehow solve all of the patient's problems, or a
subtle idealization that is reflected in an all-too-willing compliance. Or
the therapist discovers only gradually over time that the therapeutic
effort has stalemated in the face of a continuing elusiveness and subtle
isolation of the patient's real feelings behind a facade of therapeutic
compliance.

At this level of borderline pathology, the countertransference difficulties are of a quite different order. Not only are the transference/
countertransference interactions more subtle and less dramatic, but
there is also less of the quality of evoked affect in the therapist's relation
to the patient. Since the capacity for differentiating reality from fantasy
and the ability to tolerate affective tension is more highly developed in
these patients, the quality of transference projections and their impingement on the therapist has a different character. The impact of the
patient's projections is neither as intense nor as acute as in lower-order
borderlines. The corresponding countertransference reaction is a more
gradual process that evolves more slowly over time as the regressive
aspects of the therapy evolve and begin to exercise greater influence
over the therapeutic interaction. Such patients may for long periods
look no different from neurotic or narcissistic personalities. The borderline aspects may emerge only gradually, or on rare occasions may
rapidly intrude on the therapeutic effort as a result of a more acute
regressive crisis. At such times, there may occur a "paranoid spike,"

which seems strikingly at variance with the patient's usual posture. Such regressive moments are transitory for the most part and yield readily to subsequent exploration and interpretation, thanks to the patient's capacity for reality testing and for distinguishing reality from fantasy.

Rather than the interactional struggles that characterize more primitive borderline transference/countertransference transactions, the difficulties in these patients are more frequently found in subtle distortions of the therapeutic alliance, which tend to be pervasive and persistent. The therapist does not become aware of countertransference reactions and their derivatives directly but frequently finds himself experiencing stalemate or some faltering in the therapeutic work. This may relate to the therapist's own aggressive or narcissistic conflicts, which lead him to collude with the patient's subtle neurotic stance. Thus, appropriate interpretations may be withheld because the patient's inherently victimized stance elicits aggressive elements in the therapist that obtrude on his ability to be appropriately assertive or confronting in the therapy. Or, similarly, the narcissistic aspects of the interaction may provoke the therapist's narcissistic vulnerability, or conversely draw the therapist into a position of therapeutic omnipotence on the basis of a presumed but unexamined inadequacy in the patient.

In many lower-order borderlines, acute and intense transference/countertransference interactions may be precipitated quite early in the therapy, even in the first few sessions. This intense transference involvement and its related countertransference turmoil are very nearly classic for more primitive borderline conditions, as represented by the primitive affective personality disorders or the pseudoschizophrenics. Such patients often convey a sense of desperate urgency, as though their very survival depended on the relationship with the therapist. Suicide or impulses to act out destructively are imminent possibilities for action, rather than simply fantasies. The result is an intense burdening of the therapist and a pressure for him to take responsibility for the patient's survival and safety. This is not characteristic of higher-order patients, but even here the potential exists for more subtle deviations in the therapeutic alliance that may begin to manifest themselves in early sessions. These deviations or therapeutic misalliances (Langs 1975a) are often slow to develop, at least to the point at which the therapist can recognize them, and lack the peremptory quality of lower-order transference/countertransference influences. Early detection and therapeutic response to initial alliance deviations can help in generating an effective therapeutic relationship.

The difficulties may take the form of persistent resistance that does not seem to yield or modify under the influence of continuing and extensive interpretation and working through. In the analytical situation, for example, such patients can comply with the amenities of analytic work, yet effectively avoid any authentic or meaningful involvement with the analyst over extensive periods of time.

Aggressive Aspects

The aggressive aspects of transference/countertransference interactions express themselves in terms of the interplay between aggressor- and victim-introjects in both therapist and patient. The transference regressions that are seen in more primitively organized borderlines are frequently the result of negative primitive transference reactions as a consequence of aggressive projections onto the therapist (Kernberg 1984). These may be expressed as an intensification of distrust or fear of the therapist, who is seen as hurtful and attacking, and may result in sadistic or destructive defensive efforts on the part of the patient to control the powerful and feared therapist. The borderline patient is caught on the horns of a dilemma created by his strong yearning and need for objects along with his continuing rage and rejection of others as these deeply affecting narcissistic needs fail to be met. The patient's rejection and demeaning of the therapist and the correlative projection can arouse feelings of worthlessness and impotence in the therapist and correspondingly evoke his own restitutive aggression (Maltsberger and Buie 1974).

In the transference/countertransference interaction, the borderline patient may adopt a masochistic-depressive posture, accompanied by the projection of aggressive derivatives onto the therapist. Such a vulnerable and impotent position is intolerable and calls forth the countermeasure of attacking the powerful and threatening therapist; it is far preferable to be powerful and attacking than weak, helpless, and victimized. The therapist may respond with a variety of aggressive countertransference manifestations and may feel that he must rescue or somehow alleviate the helpless patient's pain, but is met with escalated narcissistic demands and intensified regression. This stimulates the therapist's own sense of rage and envy, and may lead to angry or destructive confrontations (Adler and Buie 1972, Maltsberger and Buie 1974). The intensity of the patient's hopelessness and despair, particularly in lower-order borderlines, can reach the proportions of suicidal despair and homicidal rage, accompanied by impulses to act out in a regressive crisis (Friedman 1979). The patient's anger, helplessness, and despairing impotence when these intensified narcissistic demands are not gratified prompts the therapist to respond by giving more time, wishing to support the patient in various pain-alleviating ways, providing reassurance, and so on—adopting a posture of omnipotence corresponding to the patient's helplessness and impotence (McGlashan 1983a). This may provide a kind of temporary corrective emotional experience but may also contribute to the intensification of regressive wishes and precipitate a malignant regression (Green 1977). Langs (1975b) describes this as a form of misalliance cure.

The therapist in these situations feels helpless, frustrated, and depleted, the counterpart of the patient's own depleted and frustrated self (Giovacchini 1979). He may respond with an angry assault on the patient's entitlement that merely reinforces the primitive aggressive projection as well as the correlative victimization in the patient (Kernberg 1965). The therapist avoids his own inner despair and the related narcissistic threat by an implicit devaluation and confrontation of the patient. In general, the intense demands placed on the therapist are not only a constant assault on his or her own self-esteem, but can leave him or her feeling drained, frustrated, depleted, and impotent. The therapist's own retaliatory impulses are stimulated primarily in the interest of self-preservation (Maltsberger and Buie 1974). The result can be a form of counteraggression against the patient that makes it difficult to draw the line between the appropriate uses of positive aggression in the therapy (confrontations, limit setting, etc.) and the expression of hostile and destructive impulses in the countertransference. In any case, the therapist is drawn into abandoning the therapeutic position and provides the patient with the object he seeks, whether an omnipotent rescuer or a persecutor (Giovacchini 1973b, Maltsberger and Buie 1974, Searles 1985).

The therapist's self-esteem is largely tied up with a sense of professional identity and competence, an idealized self-representation (Finell 1985). To the extent that the transference/countertransference dynamics undermine and assault that identity (Kernberg 1968, Langs 1975b, McWilliams 1979), the therapist is subjected to regressive pressures that afflict his sense of self and self-esteem (Giovacchini 1979). The projective dynamics and the corresponding introjections that arise in the transference/countertransference interaction introduce distortion into the therapist's sense of self and identity (Giovacchini 1972, Searles 1973, Smith and Steindler 1983). He is often forced into a position where his capacity to function as therapist is compromised or thwarted, where his capacity for empathy is frustrated and confounded (Nadelson 1976), and where he can no longer function intuitively or insightfully (Boyer and Giovacchini 1980). Out of his own defensive need and the need to control the powerful and influential object, the patient attacks the therapist at his most vulnerable points: his values, his professional commitments and ideology, his caring and therapeutic posture (Giovacchini 1972, Giovacchini and Boyer 1975).

In fact, the acute manipulative demandingness and provocativeness of the flamboyant borderline patient is at times easier to deal with than the chronic oral rage and resentment directed against the therapist because of his failure to gratify the patient's wishes for an idealized parent. Such patients have a genius for intuitively sensing the therapist's narcissistic vulnerabilities and for choosing the right moments to exploit them. This may take the form of belittling the therapist's interventions, negating his or her interpretations, or constantly devaluing the treatment and the therapist, making the therapist feel impotent and helpless. Under the continued erosion of such influences, the therapist's largely therapeutic attitudes can be gradually transformed into subtle and pervasive countertransference manifestations that become increasingly aggressive and even sadistic (Chessick 1978).

Under such countertransference pressures, the therapist may find himself resorting to deviations in technique or failing to maintain an adequate therapeutic framework (Langs 1975b)—deviations that can have a profound effect on the patient and the therapeutic process. He may decide to terminate the therapy prematurely, thus relieving himself of a relationship in which he feels trapped, defeated, helpless—obviously an acting out of the therapist's wishes to be rid of a patient who provokes such uncomfortable feelings (Wile 1972, Nadelson 1976). Or his feelings of impotence and ineffectiveness may cause him to regard the patient as untreatable (Boyer and Giovacchini 1980), a fairly common reaction to cases of compulsive drug abuse (Imhof et al. 1984). The therapist's aggressive impulse may also take the form of excessive activity or of becoming more interactive with the patient, either in the interests of overcoming the sense of frustration and helplessness or as a means of exerting control over an otherwise anxiety-producing situation (Adler and Buie 1972). This process may even influence the decision of when to resort to the use of drugs, either as a way of escaping from the transference and the need to understand it or as a magical potion (Chessick 1978).

The therapist must be cautious of the tendency to sadomasochistic acting out in the therapy; it often serves to mask underlying narcissistic transferences (Oremland and Windholz 1971). This is particularly a problem with therapists whose own sadomasochistic conflicts remain to some degree unresolved. The therapist who believes himself to be invulnerable to such feelings or conflicts may be at significant risk for missing an essential part of the therapy and for falling into counter-transference difficulties (Nadelson 1976). The awareness of counter-transference hate can serve as a signal to the therapist that he is reacting masochistically and absorbing too much of the patient's abuse. The aggressive countertransference stance may also express itself in the therapist's need to reassert his or her authority, defensively insisting to the patient on the therapist's own professional competence and value. The patient may then respond, also defensively, with an increased level of anger or anxiety, or may resort to a more compliant stance in which anger is withheld. The need for the patient to protect and buffer such a therapist becomes part of the therapeutic interaction and contributes further to the undermining of the therapeutic alliance.

Projecting the derivatives of the victim-introject onto the therapist can stimulate the therapist's own conflicts over aggression and defensively reactivate the therapist's own masochism (Racker 1958). The therapist's guilt over counteraggressive impulses may result in a reactive masochistic submission to the patient's aggression by which the therapist begins to doubt his own capacities and competence and begins to assimilate the masochistically tinged victim-introjective elements. The patient's aggressive posture, acting out the aggressor-introject, is accompanied by the projection of the elements of vulnerability and victimization onto the therapist. The masochistic introjection of these elements gradually undermines the therapist's sense of self-esteem and competence, and can erode his sense of professional identity. There is a strong temptation for a masochistic submission to the patient's efforts at control. This expresses itself in a sense of guilt, depression, and shame that the therapist is unable to live up to and gratify the patient's magical expectations (Kernberg 1965, Finell 1985).

Variations on these sadomasochistic themes can be implemented by an illness in either the patient or the therapist. Illness can intensify the sense of vulnerability and victimization and play into underlying pathogenic introjective configurations. This reaction in the therapist can precipitate countertransference reactions of guilt, inadequacy, helplessness, shame, or other regressive patterns that interact with the patient's pathological needs (Abend 1982, Schwartz 1987, van Dam 1987). Other patterns of aggressive-victim interaction can be precipitated by the therapist's pregnancy. The pregnancy can stir powerful

currents of envy and destructive hatred in both male and female patients against the therapist for her good fortune and fulfillment and
against the fetus that deprives the patient of the therapist's care and
investment. In such cases, severely pathological, primitive, and destructive feelings can be mobilized that create a situation of considerable
stress and threat for the therapist, this in otherwise well-functioning and
even presumably analyzable patients.

The patient's failure to respond, accompanied by a continual effort
to frustrate the aims and objectives of the therapy, creates a sense of
helplessness and hopelessness in the therapist (Adler and Buie 1972).
The patient may respond not so much with rage as with a sense of
sadness and disillusionment reflecting the original disappointment in
the incompetent and unresponsive mother. These aspects of the patient's own self-image are projected onto the therapist and produce a
therapeutic stalemate in which the therapist feels impotent and frustrated, and finds himself experiencing the urge to do something, anything, even though he or she may feel it to be ultimately unproductive
or countertherapeutic, to relieve the sense of helpless frustration (Giovacchini and Boyer 1975). At such points the therapist may resort to
transferring the patient, terminating the therapy, or hospitalization.
The countertransference, then, becomes the vehicle for redeeming the
therapist's own injured narcissism and for preserving a sense of competent and effective self and self-esteem, but at the cost of devaluing the
patient (Maltsberger 1982–1983).

Narcissistic Aspects

Narcissistic projection also plays an important role in the transference/
countertransference interactions with borderline patients (Giovacchini
1975a). Projecting the inferior and devalued side of the narcissistic
introjective organization frequently takes the form of devaluing or
demeaning the therapist (Adler 1970). In particular, lower-order patients essentially refuse to accept what the therapist offers, but maintain
the level and the intensity of their demand, often resorting to a form of
narcissistic rage when the therapist is unable or unwilling to respond to
their demands. In virtue of the projection, the therapist may be seen as
angry and rejecting. The therapist may introject the implicit projection
in a way that reinforces and plays into his own narcissistic vulnerability,
or may find himself urged to resort to self-defense in a variety of
aggressive manifestations, or may try to redeem his tottering narcissism
by attempting to prove to the patient that he can be the good, loving,

and giving parent that the patient so insistently demands (Greenacre 1956, Myerson 1974, Adler 1985).

Idealizing Interaction. These patients may project the superior aspects of the narcissistic organization as well. They may approach the therapy with an attitude of submissive compliance to a powerful and all-wise therapist whom they invest with the capacity to fulfill their needs and to transform their lives magically. These expectations of magical rebirth may even become delusional as a manifestation of a transference psychosis (Giovacchini 1973b). The therapist's own unresolved narcissistic needs to assume the omnipotent role and provide for all the patient's needs, or to be able to deal effectively with all of the patient's pathological difficulties, put him in a vulnerable position (Finell 1985). These pressures may be particularly poignant in the opening phases of therapy with patients in an acute transient regression. It is particularly important in such settings that the therapist not present himself as an omnipotent figure with inexhaustible resources or capacities to respond to the patient's needs.

In the face of an idealizing transference, the therapist's own narcissistic need to be admired or to defensively counter his own feelings of inadequacy in dealing with such patients can easily draw him into an implicit magical contract with the patient or into accepting the patient's idealization (Greenacre 1956, Finell 1985). However, such idealizations clearly set up difficult transference/countertransference distortions that undermine any possibility of an effective therapeutic alliance. At the same time, the therapist's reaction can be subtle and disguised, and can give rise to significant countertransference vicissitudes. Such patients may engage the therapist by an attitude of hopefulness and compliance, attributing to him a special power and wisdom. This has the quality of an attempt to reexperience a kind of symbiotic relationship with a powerful object who will bring about some form of magical rebirth in the patient—something that the inadequate and vulnerable mother was unable to accomplish. The patient's helpless impotence is matched by the projective magical power of the therapist and runs the risk of ignoring or minimizing the patient's pathology or of raising the level of therapeutic expectation beyond the patient's inherent limitations. This may lead to an inevitable disappointment and disillusionment in the patient, and a sense of frustration and impotence in the therapist. Such a patient seeks to draw a therapist into the position of an omnipotent rescuer, to play the companion to his or her own helplessness, sense of weakness, and vulnerability (Giovacchini 1973a). Similar reactions can be experienced in connection with "selfobject" transferences: the therapist may be at risk of feeling despair and anger at the patient's needs and at his own failure to meet them. The result is often a repetition of infantile traumata rather their amelioration (Adler 1985). In the face of the devaluation of a grandiose and superior patient, the therapist may find himself reacting defensively with impulses to mock, criticize, poke fun at, and otherwise devalue or deflate the patient's offensive self-inflation and entitlement.

The same narcissistic dynamics can be identified in patients at the higher-order borderline level, but the quality of narcissistic interaction at this level of character organization tends to be more subtle, but more pervasive, and has much less tendency to evoke any specific reaction in the therapist. Clinically, these patients often look like narcissistic characters, and only the gradual emergence of specifiable borderline features justifies diagnostic differentiation (Meissner 1979a, 1984a). Narcissistic transferences are identifiable and tend to shift the therapeutic alliance in the direction of a narcissistic alliance. The narcissistic traumata are not as severe, however, and the degree of narcissistic vulnerability is not as profound as in more disturbed borderlines. The preservation of ego strengths and reality testing makes the narcissism of the higher-order patients much more approachable and amenable to interpretation.

Erotic Aspects

Regarding the role of erotized transferences and their correlative countertransference reactions, the original, erotic libidinal sense of Freud's observations on such transference reactions has been broadened to include a diversity of related phenomena, including demands for physical contact, the more disguised desire for sexual relations manifested as wishes for adult love or as assaultive antagonism, demands for approval and admiration, needs to please, wishes to gain acceptance by compliance, dependent clinging, fears of object loss, and so on (Blum 1973). Erotized transferences in borderline patients are characterized frequently by intensity, tenacity, resistance to interpretation, and tendencies to act out the erotic feelings. The patient tries to seduce the analyst into acting out together, or frequently acts out the transference with a substitute object. The patient is thus caught up in an infantile reaction in which the distinction between transference and reality is obscured if not overriden. As Blum (1973) notes, "Patients developing such erotized transference delusions have been predisposed by early ego impairment. The analyst may be 'loved' as the single most precious object tie and reality representative" (pp. 63–64).

This quality of erotized transference is more attributable to the lower level of the borderline spectrum, but better-organized and better-functioning borderline patients are more likely to emphasize the importance of their tie to the analyst and to magnify the sense of clinging dependence on the analyst, without losing the capacity to distinguish between the reality of the therapeutic relationship and the erotized fantasies. Such patients may freely express and indulge themselves with erotic and even perverse fantasies about the analyst that have a highly seductive quality, but at the same time experience a sense of frustration and disappointment that the real relationship with the analyst offers something quite different. Erotic dreams involving the analyst are also frequent.

Such erotized transferences in borderline patients tend to arise secondarily to the underlying but intimately related narcissistic dynamics. In other words, the erotic dynamics in borderline patients usually relate to and draw their impact from the underlying narcissistic disequilibrium and need. In this respect, the erotized transferences of borderline patients differ markedly from the erotized neurotic transferences of healthier patients. The clinging dependence on the therapist as the single most important sustaining object has a sense of totality and urgency that the neurotic transference does not. Moreover, the intensity of this clinging dependence is more often than not found to have powerful narcissistic determinants. The therapist may be attuned to the more explicitly erotic aspects of the transference and fall victim to subtle narcissistic pulls. This can result in a subtle stalemate of mutual admiration and endearment (Blum 1973), which repeats the parents' use of the child to satisfy their own narcissistic needs. As Chessick (1978) comments:

> . . . countertransference can divert the tensions of transference into shared erotic fantasies or frightened flight. Confronted with the calculated narcissistic rage of the patient, this tension can be diverted by the therapist into "falling in love" with the patient, becoming preoccupied with erotic fantasies about the patient, or taking flight from the patient. [p. 23]

RECAPITULATION

This discussion emphasizes the differential aspects of transference/countertransference interactions that can arise in borderline conditions, particularly between lower-order and higher-order borderline groups. This rather complex discussion is schematized in Table 7-1. The attempt has obvious risks and is far from reaching closure. Tables tend to oversimplify and overclarify otherwise complex relationships. There are patients who can clearly be placed in one or another category, others for whom this may be difficult or problematic. Moreover, distinctions, displayed with straight lines and numbers and regarding phenomena that may be more continuous than discrete and may in addition overlap to some degree, can be misleading. With these cautions, let the table serve those who can use it with discretion—*caveat lector*!

THERAPEUTIC RESPONSE
TO COUNTERTRANSFERENCE DIFFICULTIES

The spectrum of possible countertransference reactions covers a wide-ranging complex of forms and degrees of difficulty. Within this far-reaching arena, the divergent features of countertransference experience and the quality of transference/countertransference interactions have been delineated in terms of the varying aspects of the borderline spectrum, casting the distinguishing characteristics in terms of the rather broad categories of lower- versus higher-order borderline organization. This diagnostic differentiation and the correlative aspects of transference and countertransference provide a basis for differing emphases in therapeutic response and in setting priorities for therapeutic intervention. The purpose here is to introduce this perspective into a discussion that all too frequently views the therapy of borderline patients in relatively univocal terms without sufficient regard for the inherent variability within the borderline spectrum.

Countertransference Enactments

Therapy takes place on more than one level. At a minimum, the influence of the therapist expresses itself not only on the level of verbal exchange but also on the level of behavior and action. What therapists say to patients must be placed alongside how they treat their patients, how they behave with their patients, what the affective quality of their interaction is, and how they react in the various contexts of interaction that arise in any course of therapy. These "countertransference enactments" (Jacobs 1986) all communicate significant messages to the patient about the therapist's thoughts and feelings. Ideally, the therapist's thoughts, verbalizations, and actions should be consistent and directed to therapeutic goals. The potential for countertransference difficulties to influence the therapist's thoughts, feelings, attitudes, and words to the patient is great enough; the potential for these unconscious processes to find expression in the therapist's manner, behavior, and action is even greater. Moreover, while all patients are sensitive to such multiple messages, the borderline patient tends to be extremely sensitive and takes a back seat to none in this regard (Little 1958). There is a pressure in such patients to search out evidence to support their pathogenic introjective organization.

A recent supervisory experience with an advanced resident provides an example. The resident, who prided herself on her ability to be empathic and sensitive to the needs of her patients, was working with a woman whose pathology was at a high borderline level, probably in the primitive hysteric range. The patient was using the therapy as a vehicle to express at great length her tale of misery and woe, presenting herself repeatedly as one who was taken advantage of, particularly at the hands of important others in her environment. The therapist's reaction was to feel sorry for the patient, to sympathize with her victimization, and to ally herself with the patient against the unfeeling, uncaring, and exploitative individuals. She would become the concerned and caring object the patient sought. Comments such as "Oh! you poor thing!" or "What a terrible thing to have happen!" were not infrequent. The therapist's intention was to be empathic and understanding, but the tone of her interventions was pitying, condescending, and to a degree infantilizing. Real understanding and empathy, which would have allowed the therapist to deal with the patient's victimized posture rather than colluding with it and reinforcing it, was lacking.

Interaction versus Interpretation

This pressure is especially intense in the lower-order group. When and to the extent that the pressure affects the transference/countertransference interaction, the priorities fall not on the usual technique of interpretation but on aspects of action and reaction with the patient that have a much more immediate and often pressing quality. It is only when these aspects of the therapeutic interaction have been adjusted and the regressive strain has eased that further associative exploration and interpretation become feasible (Little 1966). Thus, for many schizoid personalities, feelings and impulses are so frightening and the threat of regression is so pressing that any silence or passivity in the therapist is

TABLE 7-1

Differential Aspects of Transference, Countertransference, and Transference/Countertransference Interactions in Borderline Conditions

Borderline Conditions	General Transference Qualities	Transference Aspects	Possible Countertransference Reactions
Lower-order *schizoid personality* *primitive affective personality disorders* *pseudoschizophrenic*	Intense, acute, often rapidly mobilized, especially in regressive states, emotionally labile.	*Aggressive.* A/V split, projection, projection experienced as affectively real, acted out > felt, often paranoid.	Reaction tends to be experienced emotionally, subjectively, often intensely.
	Reflect failure of reality-fantasy discrimination (experienced as real by patient).	*Narcissistic.* S/I split, projection, idealization/devaluation, unrealistic, disillusion—depression/rage.	Tendency for reaction to be acted out in therapy.
	Involve clear projective distortion—projective transference > displacement transference.	*Erotic.* Intense, clinging, dependent, delusional, secondary to narcissistic need.	Pull toward regressive split—A/V, S/I—of therapist's introjective organization.
	At severe levels, may involve delusional distortion (transference psychosis).		Activation of counterprojective dynamism.
	Introjective split unstable, vacillating, extreme.		Require more active therapeutic stance—limit-setting/confrontation/clarification > interpretation.

TABLE 7-1 (continued)

Higher-order	Muted, develops gradually in proportion to therapeutic regression, prolonged.	*Aggressive.* A/V split less apparent, depressive/masochistic tendency, compliance.	Reaction less subjectively emotionally experienced, but tends to be reflected in disturbance of alliance sector.
primitive hysteric	Reality perspective usually not lost, split between cognitive awareness and emotional reaction.	*Narcissistic.* S/I split more subtle, rare grandiosity, idealistic, illusions/expectations.	Reactions generally more subtle, less acute/intense, more pervasive.
dysphoric personality			
as-if personality	Projective mechanisms more muted, subtle, inferential—displacement transference > projective transference.	*Erotic.* Similar to the neurotic; object relation more narcissistic: can be affectively intense, but almost never delusional.	Less regressive dissociation in therapist; polarization more ambiguous.
false-self personality	Rarely becomes delusional: regressive crises severe, less frequent.		Less tendency for counterprojective distortion; liability for implicit misalliance.
identity stasis	Tends to stabilize around one polar introjective organization: split less extreme.		More specifically analytic stance feasible, greater passivity—association/interpretation > limit setting/confrontation/clarification.

experienced as rejection and abandonment. Some sense of the reality and presence of the therapist is essential to maintain the therapeutic relationship. In these cases, the qualities of the relationship take precedence over interpretation in the therapeutic process. This tends to create countertransference responses in the therapist that serve to dissociate him from the ambivalence, conflictual dependence, primitive fears of devouring and being devoured, and intense need-fear perplexity. The therapist's countertransference colludes with the patient's needs for schizoid withdrawal and isolation (Appel 1974).

One patient[5] presented superficially as a classical obsessional personality. The analytic hours were filled with superficial and largely irrelevant material. As the analytic regression started to take effect, hints of the patient's underlying narcissistic vulnerability and intense rage began to appear. These moments of affective turmoil were quickly covered over and denied. Gradually, the hours were increasingly filled with silence. Gentle attempts to ease the patient's retreat behind a wall of silence were futile. Whole hours would pass without a word. The analyst found himself impatient, frustrated, and bored. His mind would wander and get lost in all sorts of distracting reflections, none of which had to do with his patient. He found himself frequently dozing and falling asleep. Even worse, he began to think that the patient was unanalyzable, that the analyst should have had better sense than to have accepted him for analysis, wishing that he would quit the analysis, and so on. Clearly, the analyst's narcissism was on the line and was suffering considerable duress.

The patient expressed a wish to stop the analysis. In discussion, they were able to find out that the patient's magical conviction was that the analyst could alleviate his difficulties if he wanted to. All the patient had to do was come to the hours and be there for the required time; that was enough. The rest was up to the analyst. The patient would exert no effort, undergo no pain, and take no responsibility for the progress of his analysis. He was simply waiting the analyst out. If the analyst refused to perform the magic, the patient would quit. This reflected powerful transference issues having to do with his infantile expectations of his parents, which had been severely disappointed. He was an only child with no history of real friendships or other meaningful human contacts. He looked to his parents for his human involvements. Even though he was an only child, he cherished bitter resentments that his

---

[5]Quentin's case is described in Chapter 21.

parents would not make him the center of their lives and that they had not given him more or done more for him. He felt that his mother had not wanted him and that she was more involved with and committed to her artistic career than to him. He saw his father as inadequate and impotent, a failure in life who had failed to provide him a model of real manhood. He saw the analyst as more concerned with the scientific study of his "case" than with him as a human being. The analyst was also inadequate and impotent as an analyst because he could not deal effectively with the patient's difficulties. Quitting the analysis would confirm both these transferential convictions.

The patient clung to his posture of blaming his parents for his problems. They had made him the way he was, and he would make no effort to change himself. It was up to them to do for him what they had not done. It was up to the analyst to do for him what they had not done. Any notion that he had to take responsibility for his own life and happiness was rejected out of hand. When it became clear to him that the analyst could not or would not meet his demands, he stopped coming. Despite the analyst's conscious efforts to the contrary, the hostile countertransference wish was fulfilled. The patient was able to live out his fantasy of becoming the analyst's victim, and the analyst's countertransference played out the role of victimizer.[6]

The priorities for the higher-order group are different. Although the importance of verbal-actual consistency remains, the capacity to maintain perspective and the somewhat lessened need to assimilate elements of their experience to support the pathogenic configuration (while ignoring contradictory data) allow for a greater availability to reality testing and interpretation. These patients are more capable of accepting the therapist as a person with multiple aspects whose unconscious countertransference expressions need not interfere with or override his basic good will and therapeutic orientation.

Emotional Reactivity

In dealing with lower-order forms of borderline psychopathology or with regressive borderline states, it becomes important to the therapeutic work for the therapist not only to be in touch with his emotional responsiveness to the patient but also to be able to freely acknowledge such reactions to himself and, where appropriate, to the patient. The

---

[6]It is not unlikely that a similar pattern of victimization was played out in the Dora case (Meissner 1984–1985).

capacity for the therapist to become conscious of, identify, and acknowledge his initially unconscious countertransference reactions is primary and essential to effective therapeutic management. This internal acknowledgment may alert the therapist to hidden therapeutic issues or to failures in the therapeutic alliance. Self-analysis and monitoring of his own responses may be adequate and appropriate. Where the therapeutic alliance is severely threatened, some more direct interaction with the patient may be called for. At such times, the therapist's capacity to be open and frank about such reactions can be reassuring to the patient, because it confirms the patient's perceptions of the reality of the therapist and helps to consolidate the discrimination between fantasy and reality. On the other hand, the failure to acknowledge such reactions can be extremely disruptive and may even contribute to a malignant regression in the patient (Giovacchini 1973b). As Langs (1976a,b) notes, such regressions may reflect the failure of the therapeutic alliance. In addition, such therapeutic misalliances and the push toward regression are often caused by unresolved countertransference difficulties.

A clinical example may help to clarify some of these issues. The patient,[7] a primitive borderline woman with many characteristics of a pseudoschizophrenic, would, at points of severe regressive crisis, look psychotic and have a strong propensity for acting out aggressive impulses in suicidal and self-destructive ways, including repeated overdosing and episodes of self-laceration. After I had been seeing this woman for about a year in twice-weekly psychotherapy, a holiday came along and I neglected to remind her that we would not be meeting on that particular day. As it turned out, the patient came to my office door and found it locked.

The patient went away in a rage, but much to her credit was able to call me the following day, still angry, and tearfully reproach me for my oversight. I apologized that she had been inconvenienced and told her that we would talk about it when I next saw her.

When she came to my office, the episode was still obviously on her mind, and a simmering resentment and bitterness was not difficult to discern. I asked about her feelings, and she told me of the fantasies she had had on coming to the locked door. At first, she said, she felt bitterly disappointed and hurt, and then was overwhelmed by a wave of anger in which she imagined herself screaming at me and finally throwing things at me. She was afraid that her anger would destroy me somehow, but was able to acknowledge that she was angry enough at that point to

---

[7]Barbara's case is discussed at length in Chapter 17.

want to kill me. Moreover, consistent with her paranoid disposition, she felt that this oversight had been deliberate and derived from my anger at her and my wish to retaliate because of the angry wishes and feelings she had about me. She felt that my behavior had been the result of my own wish to get rid of her, to lock her out in the hopes that she would leave the treatment.

In the course of the discussion, I told her that I was really not aware of the sorts of feelings that she ascribed to me, but that, in looking at the behavior, both she and I had reason to be suspicious. When she had called me to tell me that she had come to my office on the holiday, I had been truly surprised and somewhat chagrined that I had forgotten to tell her about the holiday. But the fact remained that her perception might in some way be accurate.

The effect of this admission was quite striking. She seemed to be relieved, almost immediately relaxed her tense and worried demeanor, and seemed considerably mollified. In fact, my admission had legitimated and justified her anger. The anger began to look realistic and in some degree reasonable, rather than the product of her distorted thinking. The discussion led to a consideration of the patient's fear of the therapist's anger and of the possibility of my retaliation, and moved from there to an extremely useful discussion of her fear of her father's explosive and somewhat paranoid anger. She recounted several episodes in which she had been terrified of his rages and his seemingly capricious, rejecting anger. She was able to talk about her difficulty in dealing with such feelings in ways that were appropriate and constructive.

It became clear to her that, even though such angry feelings might arise in the context of the therapeutic relationship, they could still be put in perspective and did not necessarily destroy the relationship, nor did it mean that, when such feelings were operating in me, they would eliminate the warm feelings I might have toward her or the wishes on my part to be therapeutically useful and helpful to her. My admission meant that any supposition that I was always right and sane and that she was always wrong and crazy was decisively wrong. This understanding between us made it considerably easier for her to talk about angry feelings, to express them without fear of retaliation from me, and consequently to be able to explore and understand them.

Countertransference Monitoring

Particularly with lower-order patients, in dealing with the projective-introjective interaction, the therapist must carefully discriminate between the patient's projection and the potential countertransference responses. Where such countertransferences are operative, it can be countertherapeutic to ascribe them simply to the patient's projections, since this would fail to acknowledge the reality component in the patient's perception. This can both undermine the patient's hold on reality and jeopardize the therapeutic alliance, thus contributing to further regression (Giovacchini 1973b, Krohn 1974). Such discounting of the patient's perception in the therapeutic interaction and a reduction to projection can be both hostile and demeaning, and may represent a form of countertransference counteraggression (Nadelson 1976). This would certainly have been the case for this patient. On the other hand, the open and honest focusing on countertransference reactions and their further exploration in terms of the meaning for the therapeutic interaction can be extremely helpful (Giovacchini 1972).

This does not mean that the therapist will necessarily communicate to the patient all thoughts and feelings, even those reflecting countertransference difficulties. This is by no means always indicated or always useful (Little 1957). It is extremely important, however, that the therapist be in touch with such feelings and attitudes and be ready and able to communicate them when it becomes therapeutically useful in terms of the need to work through the transference/countertransference interaction, particularly in the interest of reestablishing or maintaining the therapeutic alliance. Often countertransference feelings are a useful signal of the nature of the transference/countertransference interaction and a prelude to interpretation (Atkins 1967, Kernberg 1970). Contrary to the usual situation in the treatment of neurotic patients, the borderline patient has a more intense and primitive need at critical points to be reassured of the therapist's reality. Knowing what the therapist is feeling, knowing details of the therapist's life and personality, or even knowing where the therapist will be when on vacation can often be important in sustaining the patient's sense of inner equilibrium and cohesion. The intensification of such demands may reflect the patient's need to confirm contact with a desperately needed sustaining object, the therapist, who is experienced as excessively remote, unavailable, or frustrating.

The handling of countertransference vicissitudes has a powerful impact on the regressive tendencies within the borderline patient. The therapist must continually monitor countertransference reactions and their impact on the regressive potential of the patient (Krohn 1974). Particularly devastating is the effect of countertransference omnipotence. Balint (1968) notes that such omnipotence in the therapist can determine whether the regression in the patient is benign or malignant. Such omnipotence can be reflected in the therapist's attempts to rescue the patient out of his own need to be the good, all-caring, all-giving, and all-powerful parent who can supply every need and ease every pain (Kernberg 1968). This is particularly a problem in regard to devaluing attacks from the patient (Adler 1985). The countertransference stance thus can reflect the therapist's own needs more than a responsiveness to the patient (subjective rather than objective countertransference), and can presumably reproduce the parental position. This reenacts and reactivates the earlier infantile trauma and can effectively undermine the patient's attempt to gain a therapeutic foothold.

The anxiety posed by the reactivation of such basic inner conflicts often stimulates defensive reactions that play themselves out in inhibiting and interfering ways in the therapeutic interaction. As Atkins (1967) notes, the danger is not in the regression itself but in the therapist's unreadiness or inability to meet the patient's regression and the related infantile dependence and to deal with it therapeutically. The more capable and ready the therapist is to meet, accept, and deal with the patient's regression, the less need there is for the patient to follow the regressive option (Stone 1954).

Degrees of Structure

The necessity for establishing and maintaining a sufficient degree of structure in the therapy of borderline patients has been frequently stressed (Kernberg 1971, Adler 1975; see Chapter 5). The need to maintain structure, to be able to test the reality of the patient's perceptions, to set effective limits, to continually work within the frame of reference set by the therapeutic alliance, and to maintain respect and support for the patient's autonomy are all essential aspects of the therapy with these patients—all the more so in the primitively organized borderlines and in states of transient regression. In many higher-order borderlines, however, there is not the same degree of deficit in ego organization, so they can tolerate a considerably higher degree of regressive strain and do not require the same degree of structure in the therapeutic situation. Such patients may tolerate considerable degrees of therapeutic regression without undue disorganization or disruptive acting-out.

This is, in fact, one of the most difficult aspects of the therapy with borderline patients—again, particularly those in the more primitive range—namely, titrating the degrees of activity and passivity, of structure and lack of structure, of regressive strain and ego support. The failure to maintain adequate structure can lead to excessive regression, acting out, and the predominance of transference/countertransference interactions. The maintenance of an excessively rigid or controlled therapeutic situation can interfere with the development of transference manifestations, particularly with the expression of negative transference reactions. This can lead to a therapeutic stalemate in which effective work is negated and the relationship becomes shallow and unproductive and may be accompanied by acting out outside the therapy. In higher-order patients, there may evolve an attitude of therapeutic compliance that is accompanied by a noticeable lack of progression. The therapist consequently is confronted with a therapeutic dilemma: between the need to maintain structure as an essential ingredient in the therapeutic situation and the need to approach the borders of regression as a means of sustaining and activating the potential for therapeutic change.

Negative Transference

In the interest of maintaining the alliance, the therapist must pay careful attention to negative transference elements. A consistent element is the patient's efforts to defeat the therapist, to make the therapy into a meaningless and ineffectual game, as well as to destroy whatever there is in the experience that may be positive and constructive (Kernberg 1970). Behind this lies the need on the part of the patient to maintain the introjective configuration that provides the core of his or her often fragile and unstable self-organization. As we have already suggested, the projective elaboration that underlies the transference/countertransference interaction has as its motivation the preservation of the pathogenic introjective organization. Thus constant attention to focusing, clarifying, and interpreting the negative transference elements is of particular importance in establishing and maintaining a therapeutic alliance (Kernberg 1970, Friedman 1975).

The therapist must maintain a consistent, tactful, nonretaliatory, therapeutically productive attitude toward the patient's rage. Only by working through these introjective dimensions and their reprocessing can the patient gradually give up the pathogenic introject and become capable of experiencing the therapist as a relatively good object. The patient must learn the difficult if primitive lesson that he can feel a sense of intimacy and helpless vulnerability with the therapist without fear of being engulfed or consumed in the process. Similarly, the patient must learn that anger and rage can be expressed within the therapy without danger of provoking a retaliation, destroying the therapist, or disrupting the relationship. In addition, the patient must learn that it is possible to experience the therapist's anger without being destroyed, abandoned, rejected, or otherwise punished.

These aggressive dynamics can play themselves out, not only in more primitive borderline conditions in which the desperate clinging need for objects is considerably more apparent and available, but also in schizoid conditions in which the same powerful dependency needs are operative but in which the patient mobilizes strong isolating and distancing defenses. The patient's rage at the therapist's disappointing or frustrating of this need can be stimulated particularly in contexts in which, for example, the therapist goes on vacation or is absent for some reason, or even when there is failure in the therapist's empathy, responsiveness, or understanding (Stolorow et al. 1981). The patient's readiness to mobilize feelings of vulnerability and weakness and to project the aggressive and hostile components onto the therapist can easily stimulate countertransference responses that diminish or interfere with the therapist's capacity for empathic understanding. This can often give rise in severely disturbed borderlines for a paranoid transference distortion in which the therapist is seen as hostile or destructive and must be rejected.

Therapeutic confrontation is particularly useful when the patient adopts the victimized position, reflecting the underlying victim-introject. A clear statement of the patient's victimized position, or of the potential victimizing effects of a projected course of acting out, can serve as a useful way of focusing on the underlying dynamics and the motivations related to them and of bringing into focus their effects on the therapeutic work, particularly the therapeutic alliance. Such confrontations with the patient's potential self-destructiveness and the need to assume the victimized position carry with them a reassurance that the patient is not on this account abandoned or rejected. They undercut the pull in the countertransference reaction to playing into the patient's victimization, thus reinforcing it. This is especially pertinent in the confrontational stance required with regressive suicidal impulses or tendencies to suicidal acting out (Maltsberger and Buie 1974, Meissner 1977b, 1984b).

Idealization

When the patient is involved in an idealizing transference, viewing the therapist as the omnipotent and magically powerful rescuer, the task of undoing such idealizations requires that the therapist confront the patient continually with the transference distortion while at the same time acknowledging the patient's positive feelings (Kernberg 1968). This task is particularly difficult, since such idealizations often mask paranoid fears or primitive aggressive and hostile feelings toward the transference object. Idealizations are accompanied by a feeling of worthlessness and shame in the patient. The wish is for the therapist to overcome these painful and self-demeaning feelings. The therapist's failure to respond to these needs may be translated into withholding and rejection—the therapist becomes the idealized figure who refuses to give the patient the good things that he or she so desperately desires and needs—a situation that repeats the original traumatic experience in relationship to parental figures (Myerson 1974). The therapist's failure to respond to and meet such narcissistic expectations may turn him from an idealized figure into a magically powerful persecutor.

Acting out

In more primitive borderline patients, acting out becomes a major vehicle for relieving the tension arising from conflicting object needs in the therapeutic relationship. It may also serve as an important way of testing how much the therapist can take and how able he is to control the situation and protect the patient from the chaotic impulses. Insofar as possible, the therapist's interventions should be approached from the perspective of the therapeutic alliance. The emphasis on alliance factors in this connection is particularly important, since the acting out is almost always a reflection of underlying transference/countertransference difficulties (Langs 1975a, 1975b, 1976). The therapist needs to maintain his autonomy and to accept the responsibility for his interventions and their consequences. This includes hospitalization, which may be essential in gaining control of an otherwise destructive situation where the patient is acting out self-destructively (overdosing, cutting himself, or otherwise disorganized) or when suicidal acting out is in question (Meissner 1977b).

The issues of tolerating regression and of maintaining a therapeutic stance are joined in the management of acting out. In dealing with lower-order borderline pathology, the difficulties related to acting out are always a prominent part of the therapy and are particularly crucial in the initial phases of treatment. In the higher-order range of the borderline spectrum, however, the acting out tendencies are less dramatic, less self-destructive, and more subtle, and often do not appear until significant levels of therapeutic regression have been attained.

Acting out at this higher level of borderline organization frequently takes place outside the therapy, reflecting transference dynamics. Such behavior may be precipitated at times of interruption or separation in the therapy. This contrasts with the often more dramatic, manipulative, and tension-related acting out of more primitive borderline patients. In both cases, countertransference problems can interfere with proper management and effective therapeutic response.

The therapist's task in dealing with tendencies to act out is to maintain a firm, consistent, and assertive stance in setting limits without entering into the transference/countertransference interaction that would recapitulate the patient's victimization and put the analyst in a threatening, prohibiting, accusatory, and chastizing position. The therapist's introduction of limit setting and controlling parameters can be easily translated by the patient's projective distortion into hostile and sadistic images. In more primitive acting out, direct limit setting and an active ...tempt to explore the meaning of such behavior are indicated; unresolved aggressive conflicts or unconscious hostile or destructive wishes toward the patient can inhibit appropriate and effective action. For higher-order forms of acting out, interpretation and the exploration of meaning in terms of the therapeutic relationship are more effective.

Termination

Particular difficulties in the termination phase are due to the classic difficulty of the borderline patient in effectively separating from self-sustaining objects and of accomplishing the task of internalization that would complete the work of separation. In this final phase of the therapy, the therapist's inability to tolerate the patient's infantile dependency may lead to a precipitous termination and a need to see the patient as more resourceful or autonomous than he or she may in fact be. The therapist who has difficulty separating and letting go of the patient runs the risk of reinforcing the patient's need for symbiotic dependency and recreating the kinds of parental interactions that thwarted the striving for autonomy in the first place (Masterson 1972).

These countertransference difficulties are reactivated forcefully in the termination phase. Conflicts over dependency and the therapist's role as helping and sustaining object can provide the basis for a collusive mesh with the patient's own inability to tolerate these aspects. The need to see the patient as needing help can play a role here, buttressed by the therapist's own need to see himself as helping and as important to the patient.

Countertransference difficulties must be counterposed to the actuality of the patient's incapacity to accomplish the work of termination. In the face of the separation from the therapist and the inevitable mourning process associated with it, there is a tendency for a regressive retreat to the prior pathogenic introjective configuration. As these formations are reactivated under separation pressures, the tendency for associated projections and negative transference elements to reemerge is significant, and these dimensions must be reworked in the interest of sustaining and reinforcing a persistent therapeutic alliance that will allow the patient to undergo the necessary pain of the mourning process. However, one frequently finds that the capacity for internalization, which is required to make this process an effective and therapeutically useful one, is lacking—particularly in patients at the lower level of the borderline spectrum. A straightforward termination may not be possible, and the alternative course of attenuating the therapy over time may be a necessity (Zetzel 1971). Patients may ultimately be seen on rare occasions at intervals of years, or may even maintain therapeutic contact by occasional telephone calls or letters. The therapeutic contact may never be severed, and the therapy never terminated. The sustaining function of the therapist as an important object in the maintenance of the economy of psychic equilibrium in the patient cannot be underestimated in this context.

In higher-order borderline conditions, the capacity to separate and internalize may be compromised to some degree, but there is nonetheless sufficient capacity to tolerate the necessary mourning and to effect a meaningful separation. The separation work should be attempted with as little dilution as possible. The issues are basically separation and individuation, and require both tolerance and continuing support from the therapist. The work of separation is more problematic, requires more time, may suffer regression more easily, and often requires occasional reworking and reinforcement, in contrast to the typical separation work with neurotic patients. Since separation work is possible for these patients, whereas for more primitive borderlines it may not be, countertransference difficulties will differ accordingly.

Internalization

A significant component of the therapeutic process in dealing with borderline psychopathology is the role of internalizations as an inherent component of the interaction. The transference/countertransference interaction is based on the interplay of projective and introjective processes. The patient's projection of narcissistic components onto the transitional object created within the context of the relationship with the therapist is the basis for the transference. The therapist's corresponding introjection of that projective content and his internal processing of it provide the basis for the countertransference involvement. The interaction sets up a process of mutually interacting projections and introjections for both patient and therapist. For example, the patient might project idealized elements onto the therapist. If the therapist can comfortably and congenially accept this projection, assimilate it, and integrate it with the ongoing flow of his responsiveness to the patient, he remains unconflicted and comfortable both with the idealization and with his own inherent limitations. To the extent that he avoids the countertransference trap, he can respond to the patient not as an idealized superior or omnipotent object but as an ordinary human being who remains interested, respectful, and appropriately committed to the patient and his welfare. He reflects back to the patient from this idealization a sense of the patient's value in his eyes and a projective content that would call forth a different affective response, namely, one of greater equality, balance, mutual involvement, and collaboration, rather than a sense of devaluation, contempt, or trivializing disregard. Such a response would play out the countertransference paradigm and would reinforce the corresponding feelings in the patient of narcissistic inferiority, unimportance, inadequacy, and even shame.

This process takes place in contexts of immediate transference/countertransference interaction but can also develop over much longer periods of time. The patient's need to idealize the therapist is constantly eroded by the flow of realistic impressions of his failings, human limitations, and inadequacies gathered over long periods of therapeutic interaction. The patient must ultimately integrate this flow of awareness into his ongoing assessment of the stature and narcissistically invested superiority of the therapist. But in a good therapeutic relationship, the idealized object is not at all discomfited, conflicted, troubled, or unsettled by his own obvious weakness, limitation, and shortcomings. He is comfortably and easily able to assimilate and integrate these into his overall functioning and suffers no deficit of self-esteem when these shortcomings come to light. The patient learns that is it possible to be competent and effective and have a meaningful place in the world without having to scale the heights of grandiosity and perfection. He learns that there is such a thing as being good enough, that to be imperfect and limited does not necessarily imply worthlessness and shamefulness. In the ongoing interplay of projections and introjections, these gradual modifications of what is internalized from the therapeutic relationship take on a different quality in which the narcissistic titer is modified and pressure of narcissistic demands is shifted from the extreme basis that underlies the patient's psychopathology to a more moderate middle ground that allows for the emergence and development of meaningful ideals, values, and ambitions. A similar process of projective/introjective interchange and internalized transformation can take place for the aggressively derived introjections as well.

These modifications take place within the transference/countertransference interaction, which provides the matrix for the interplay of introjections and projections. The other dimension of the therapeutic process, which comes to bear on the integration of more autonomous and adaptive internalizations, is the therapeutic alliance (Meissner 1981b). Processes of identification take place in parallel with the introjective elements we have been discussing. The capacity for meaningful and constructive identifications increases as the transference vicissitudes are gradually worked through and resolved. As the pathogenic configurations give way to more moderated and realistic forms of self-integration, the path is open for the emergence of meaningful and selective identifications, which tend to be based in the therapeutic alliance.

As the transference elements are resolved, more and more of the therapeutic interaction is based on meaningfully emergent alliance factors. The therapist emerges more clearly and more decisively as an object for meaningful identification. Without any intent or effort on his part, the therapist does in fact serve as a model for identification. From time to time the patient may wish to be like the therapist or may respond to a variety of situations with attitudes, thoughts, or feelings that he connects with the therapist. These become grist for the therapeutic mill. The therapist's task is neither to encourage or discourage such identifications but to allow them to follow their natural course unimpeded by countertransference interferences. To the extent that this can be achieved, the patient's identifications become selective, differentiated, and autonomous, and reflect a pattern of self-generative creativity and expression that is authentically the patient's own and becomes the basis for the integration of an authentic and purposeful sense of self.

SUMMARY AND CONCLUSION

I have concentrated on presenting a model of the transference/countertransference interaction derived from analysis of the paranoid process (Meissner 1978c, 1984a). The model implies that in borderline personalities the organization of the self-system takes place around core pathogenic introjects that are the derivatives of disturbed, developmentally significant object relationships. The introjective organization takes the form of polar configurations based primarily, but not exclusively, on dimensions of narcissism and aggression. Libidinal dimensions probably remain secondary within this configuration.

In lower-order borderline personalities, these introjective configurations remain close to the surface and, separately or in combination, may readily dominate the inner organization of the self and the patient's experience of it. This introduces an internal instability and lability into the patient's self-organization and functioning and provides the basis for projections that tend to influence and distort the patient's experience of significant others. In higher-order forms of borderline disorder, these introjective configurations tend to be more stable, better integrated, and less prone to projection. These patients stabilize their personalities around one introjective configuration, even though the others remain available for activation under regressive pressure or crisis. The parts of the introjective configuration that are dissociated or repressed tend to be projected.

The operation of these projective derivatives in the therapeutic interaction sets up reciprocal patterns of introjection and counterprojection in the therapist, which serve as the basis for countertransference reactions. These involve a partial introjection of the patient's projection and a counterprojection that derives from the interaction of the therapeutically derived introjections with the therapist's own inner introjective configuration. I have applied this model to the understanding of the therapeutic interaction with borderline patients to clarify the differences in transference manifestations between lower-order and higher-order forms of borderline pathology and their characteristic patterns of transference/countertransference interaction. The spectrum perspective developed here points to the progressive differentiation among transference expressions from the lower extreme of the borderline spectrum to the higher. The corresponding transference/countertransference interactions likewise undergo parallel variation and call for a proportionally differentiated therapeutic response and technique.

PART III

THE THERAPEUTIC PROCESS

The issues addressed in this section have to do with techniques and methods of therapeutic intervention. Part II was concerned with the central patterns of interpersonal interaction that structure the therapeutic situation, set the stage for all aspects of the therapeutic process, and ultimately determine the effectiveness or failure of therapeutic maneuvers. Here we focus on some of the key technical resources at the disposal of the therapist in an effort to deal with the patient's pathology. Interpretation, confrontation, and limit setting are the main tools with which the therapist enters the therapeutic arena. They are endemic to all forms of insight-oriented psychotherapy, but in dealing with the borderline spectrum, there are specific problems that arise. My effort here is to provide a nuanced picture of the role and the scope of these interventions at different ranges of borderline pathology. The chapter on regression deals with a particular clinical problem that is a prominent aspect of the treatment of all borderline patients.

8

INTERPRETATION

DEFINITION

Interpretation is the primary and basic technical tool in the psychother-apy of borderline patients (Kernberg 1984), particularly in a psychoana-lytically oriented approach. As therapy shifts more in the direction of an expressive modality, interpretation comes to play an even more prominent and central role. When the therapy is more supportive, interpretation is by no means ruled out but it assumes a more modest role along with other supportive techniques, including clarification, confrontation, giving support, encouragement, advice, and so on.

Interpretation plays an important part in all forms of analytically based psychotherapy, including psychoanalysis, since it is the essential process leading toward developing increasing insight and the gradual resolution of underlying neurotic conflicts. Interpretation is central in the treatment of borderlines as well, but in this context different aspects of the interpretive process assume a differential and at times weightier role. While content always remains important, with many borderline patients the tone, style, mood, and manner of interpretation may be even more significant than with healthier neurotic patients. It may be useful, therefore, to emphasize certain aspects of psychoanalytic inter-pretation, which reflect not only its nature but also the therapist's role and function as interpreter.

Interpretation aims at gaining understanding, and its object is some meaning, set of meanings, or connection of meanings. It is an effort to make sense out of something, or to understand a connection or a relationship among events, contexts, behaviors, or whatever. It does not render judgment but aims only at translating meaning (Boris 1973). By its very nature, interpretation can be no more than tentative and exploratory, and takes the form of sharing a hypothesis (Adler and Myerson 1974, Kernberg 1979). When the interpretive process is working well, therapist and patient are engaged in the communication and exploration of hypotheses that have been arrived at by a collaborative process, based on the patient's intrapsychic content. Interpretation as a process is not something that the therapist does to the patient; rather it is a process that involves interactive participation and mutual engagement on the part of both therapist and patient. In a well-working therapeutic process, interpretation is as likely to arise from the patient as from the therapist (Stocking 1973).

NATURE OF INTERPRETATION

A degree of consistency in the therapist's attitude toward the patient and in his interpretive effort seems to be a necessary component of effective interpretation. The experience of seeking understanding in an empathic relationship with the therapist provides a new experience for the patient, one that is qualitatively different from many experiences in his development, particularly in his relationships with his parents, and creates an ambience in which the gradual introjection of the analyst as an accepting, understanding, and reasonable figure can take place (Boyer 1983). There is room for openness and honesty in making interpretations. The therapist can often usefully acknowledge his uncertainty or doubts or offer his hypothesis as merely tentative or speculative, as focusing on only one aspect of the problem, or as offering a suggestion that the patient may wish to consider, revise, reject, or accept. There is no need in this process to reinforce the patient's sense of inadequacy or inferiority by an implication of the therapist's deeper understanding, sense of infallibility, or superiority. In view of the tentative and often uncertain nature of interpretations, it can even be useful for the therapist to be wrong and to acknowledge it (Appel 1974).

Interpretations may also take the form of questions, which can offer possible directions of thinking, meanings, or can elucidate relationships and connections that facilitate the inquiry (Olinick 1954).

Questions can place demands on the patient or they may bear an element of confrontation, which may elicit reactions of conformity, resentment, envy, and even rage. While questions have their place, they can introduce compounding difficulties with borderline patients that are better avoided.

INTERPRETIVE STRATEGY

Interpretation is never a simple or easy process, but in the treatment of borderline patients it can run into particular difficulties. One is the extent to which borderline patients are able to understand, assimilate, and integrate interpretations. Kernberg (1984) asks whether these patients respond to interpretations because of their actual meaning or because of some other magical or transference-related meaning. He argues that patients can understand and integrate interpretive comments of the therapist when the distortions in their response can be examined and additionally interpreted. These patients tend to hear the therapist's communications through a filter of primitive defensive operations, which must become the objects of interpretation in order for the process to be successful.

A somewhat different position is taken by Chessick (1982), who warns that early in the treatment process borderline patients have greater difficulty in understanding interpretations because their distortions cause them to experience the interpretations as critical or accusatory, causing narcissistic injuries or intensifying negative transference reactions. As others have noted (Little 1958, Wallerstein 1967), when the patient is in a regressive state, transference interpretations have little utility since the interpretation is overridden by the dynamics of a delusional transference in which the differentiation between fantasy and reality has been eroded, and the analyst is experienced as an idealized or diabolized parent.

The capacity for the patient to engage in the process of interpretation is partly a function of the level of pathology. At the higher end of the borderline spectrum, interpretation becomes the primary therapeutic technique and does not differ greatly from ordinary interpretive processes (Abend et al. 1983). There is a gradation, however, in the borderline spectrum as one moves toward the lower level of the pathology. At these lower levels, the effectiveness of interpretations and the interpretive process is increasingly compromised. The level of pathological organization tends to be generally more primitive and regressed in quality, and the increased acute regressive potential in these patients may lead to the transient intensification of regression and create a transference psychosis. Moreover, the same gradation in severity plays a role in the mobilization of countertransference difficulties that may inhibit or interfere with the interpretive process (see Chapter 7).

With some primitive borderlines, the character of the patient's transference, which may be either chaotic or withdrawn, and its intensity may place the therapist in a relatively impotent position in which he is forced into a nonintuitive and interpretively helpless state, itself a form of assault on his sense of professional identity and ego-ideal (Boyer and Giovacchini 1980). In such circumstances, the therapist simply does not have any interpretive resource and must look elsewhere for a way of treating the difficulty. Opportunities for dealing with such an impasse may be found in exploration of the therapist's own countertransference feelings, attention to the disruption or distortion of the therapeutic alliance, clarification of transference feelings and their meaning, or, if none of these avenues is possible or available, patient tolerance by the therapist of his nonintuitive and noninterpretive position.

An opposite countertransference difficulty may create a pressure for the therapist to be increasingly responsive and to engage in a form of "verbal feeding." While there may be a place for increased activity, especially in the form of verbal productions, on the part of the therapist in the face of a regressive movement in the patient, this transference/countertransference interaction can open the way to increasingly inexact interpretations. The more primitive borderline patients often have a need to test the limits of the therapeutic relationship and to defeat its effectiveness. As a result, pressures may be brought on the therapist to respond in ways that correspond to the patient's pathological needs, for example, getting the therapist to be more active and aggressive in his style, manner, and even the content of the interpretation as a way of dovetailing with the patient's inherent need to feel vulnerable and victimized (Gitelson in Rangell 1955). While the prior difficulty may arise more frequently in the treatment of primitive or regressed patients in the schizoid continuum, the latter difficulty may often emerge in the treatment of more primitive patients in the hysterical continuum.

Kernberg

The treatment strategy proposed by Kernberg has been clearly and forcefully articulated and may provide a template for discussion of some controverted issues regarding the use of interpretation with borderline patients. Kernberg (1978, 1979, 1984) insists on a more or less exclusively expressive form of psychotherapy, along the lines of a psychoanalytic model. Any combination of expressive and supportive techniques is thereby ruled out and is seen as undermining the effectiveness of a more psychoanalytic approach.

The form of borderline pathology that provides the prototype for Kernberg's approach lies more in the primitive range of the hysterical continuum. In the therapeutic encounter these patients quite rapidly generate relatively primitive transferences, which serve as powerful resistances and are the bases for severely pathological distortions of the therapeutic relationship. Kernberg (1979, 1984) insists that these primitive transferences should be focused on and interpreted immediately in the therapeutic interaction. Genetic reconstructions do not have a place in this early phase of the treatment but can be utilized later on when the more primitive transferences, involving part-object relationships, have been transformed into better-developed total-object transferences (Kernberg 1975a, 1976b).

Interpretation of these transferences requires that the therapist maintain a position of technical neutrality and a firm and consistent boundary between the patient's transference fantasies and the reality of the therapeutic situation. The therapist must not be drawn into a reactivation of the more pathological and primitive object relations reflected in the patient's transference. The primary techniques, therefore, are clarification and interpretation; any use of suggestive or manipulative techniques is contraindicated. As opposed to psychoanalysis, therapy with borderline patients involves a higher degree of nonverbal communication that plays a characteristic role in shaping the therapeutic situation. Since these nonverbal aspects most often reflect the influence of primitive transferences, therapy cannot be accomplished without exploring and resolving these transferences.

Kernberg's approach deals with the negative and disruptive transferences from the very beginning of the therapy. The sort of transference urgency that he describes is not characteristic throughout the borderline spectrum but is found more consistently in the more primitive patients within the hysterical continuum, particularly those I have described above as pseudoschizophrenics or primitive affective personality disorders. These patients generally come to therapeutic attention in a state of regressive crisis or when functioning at a more chronically regressive level. Transferences that are more modulated, less primitive, and generally positive are not interpreted insofar as they facilitate the establishing of a working or therapeutic alliance (Kernberg 1984). A similar position is espoused by Boyer (1983), who argues that interpretation should be directed primarily toward aggressive drive derivatives in the early phases of treatment and that more oedipally based libidinal interpretations tend to be either useless or damaging. Boyer's tendency in this phase of the treatment is to be gently confrontative of the patient's misperceptions, inconsistencies, and distortions of what happens in the treatment room and to focus less on external events.

Interpretation and the Therapeutic Alliance

What Kernberg describes as early primitive transference distortions is more effectively conceptualized in alliance terms, particularly in the early phases of treatment where the resources and opportunities for transference interpretation are simply nonexistent. Often, this is less a matter of interpreting than of combining confrontation and clarification. This emphasis becomes somewhat clearer in the light of Kernberg's (1984) descriptions. He writes:

> Interpretation should be so formulated that the patient's distortions
> of the therapist's interventions and of current reality, especially the
> patient's distorted perceptions in the hour, can be clarified system-
> atically. In other words, the patient's magical utilization of the
> therapist's interpretations requires interpreting. [p. 106]

The patient's distortions may have their roots in transference determinants and reactions, but at this early phase of the treatment the therapist has little knowledge of that material. The therapist does have an awareness of the patient's behavior and the manner in which he reacts to the therapist's interventions, and can focus on these as distortions of the therapeutic alliance and the therapeutic relationship. Confronting the patient with the pattern of interaction taking place and exploring its meanings, implications, and consequences are therefore entirely appropriate and useful. In the course of such an exploration, it is not unusual for dynamic, defensive, or even adaptive aspects of the patient's interaction with the therapist to come to light. But the opportunities for any deeper interpretation, whether genetic or otherwise, not only are scanty but may in the early phases of therapy prove to be premature and even damaging. Gentle confrontation about the meaning of the patient's behavior, on the other hand, can often help the therapeutic process and may generate some degree of curiosity (Boyer 1983).

Such early clarifications and confrontations and low-level interpretations are directed toward establishing the therapeutic alliance. Success is often a matter of the accuracy, timeliness, and empathy with which such interventions are made. More is involved in the manner than in the substance. Premature oedipal interpretations may only make it more difficult for preoedipal transferences to emerge and establish themselves (Boyer 1983). The Blancks (1974) have emphasized the importance of supporting the patient's fragile ego structure in the course of making interpretations. They distinguish between ego interpretations that are designed to help the patient understand his deficits in order to facilitate further growth and id interpretations that deal primarily with unconscious derivatives. Focusing on the more primitive range of the borderline spectrum, the Blancks emphasize that interpretations must be made in proportion to the capacity of the ego to assimilate and synthesize them. Since the patient's limited capacity to do this often has to be supported and assisted, they recommend that interpretations be directed to the highest developmental level the patient has attained in order to support the ego, reinforce the defensive and adaptive functioning, or deal with aspects of affective life or even earlier preverbal experiences.

In addition, if aspects of the supportive relation to the therapist would be interrupted by any kind of interpretation, the demands of the relationship take precedence. This is somewhat reminiscent of the emphasis on self-object transferences and the techniques for dealing with them proposed by the self-psychologists. As Kernberg (1979) has commented, while the therapist's interpretive efforts to facilitate the integrative and synthetic functions in the borderline patient may serve the interests of growth, they may also arouse intense hatred and envy, not only because the experience of learning about one's self is itself painful but also because the very encounter with the helpfulness of the therapist stirs the embers of primitive envy and the wish to destroy the therapist and his maternal and nuturant image. Consequently, Kernberg argues that the interpretation of the patient's unconscious needs to frustrate and destroy the therapist's interpreting function may be an important part of the therapeutic work. I would hear these comments more specifically in alliance terms than in terms of the transference paradigms emphasized by Kernberg.

Affirmative Interpretations

In transference and countertransference difficulties, some authors have emphasized the importance of an affirmative attitude in interpretive work with borderline patients. Schaffer (1986) has recently summarized this approach. Interpretations are affirmative when they show empathic understanding of what lies behind the patient's behavior, when the therapist can acknowledge and appreciate the adaptive value of the behavior, and when the therapist can acknowledge and accept the patient's motivation for maintaining his lifestyle despite its difficulties. Affirmative interpretations are experienced as empathic, appreciative, and respectful. The implicit message in the therapist's affirmative attitude is that the patient is in no danger of experiencing trauma similar to those he has experienced in the past and that the prospective relationship with the therapist will be sufficiently safe for him to risk exposure of his unconscious wishes and fantasies.

Interpretations that are not sufficiently affirmative may focus on the maladaptive aspects of the patient's behavior or may point out the ways in which the patient's behavior is unrealistic, contradictory, or infantile. They may pay little attention to the motivating forces that underlie the patient's attachment to self-defeating patterns. The implicit message is that these behaviors and patterns should stop as soon as possible, and that the therapist is unappreciative, relatively disrespectful, and unempathic. For these patients, the consequences of exploring and exposing unconscious fantasies and wishes is threatening and dangerous. An affirmative analytic attitude is of the utmost importance in transference interpretations. Analysis of transference manifestations can fail to be affirmative insofar as it portrays the patient's transference as distorted or destructive. The therapist's failure to confirm the patient's experience of the relationship is likely to be experienced as rejection or humiliation, making the therapist a threatening or dangerous object and undermining the push toward attachment or collaboration. If the therapist can approach the transference as plausible and even adaptive, with appreciation for the underlying motivating forces, the patient's reaction is more likely to be positive, to regard the interaction with the therapist as safe, and to move forward to further exploration of the transference phenomenon (Schafer 1983).

Applying this approach to Kernberg's theory, Schaffer (1986) argues that Kernberg builds in certain affirmative elements, namely, the focus on the adaptive value of the patient's transference and defenses and the exploration of the purposes of the patient's behavior in the here-and-now. These affirmative elements, however, are accompanied by more negative ones, which tend to elicit negative reactions from patients. The emphasis on the therapist's pointing out the patient's distortion of his experience of the therapeutic interaction conveys the message that the patient is wrong, misguided, stupid, and so on. Kernberg's approach places a high priority on dealing with the maladaptive aspects of the patient's resistance and transference, but an overemphasis on these aspects may be experienced by the patient as disapproving and rejecting. Some of these emphases may reinforce the patient's experience of the therapist as rejecting and abandoning, so that he begins to experience the therapist in negative terms. Feeling criticized or attacked, he becomes more defensive and more aggressive and tends to act out. Thus, Schaffer argues, the fact that the therapist may unwittingly support the negative and unmanageable aspects of the transference may explain the overemphasis in Kernberg's approach on aggressive determinants and the urgency with which he approaches and deals with the negative transference.

In fairness to Kernberg, he focuses on salient and clinically significant aspects of the therapeutic situation that need to be dealt with effectively if therapy is to succeed. Much of what is at issue in this sort of discussion has more to do with the therapist's attitudes, feelings, style, and manner of interpretation than with the specific content or phraseology of a given interpretation. This aspect of the interpretive process serves only to underline once more the importance of the role of countertransference factors as they color the interpretive process. Where interpretations have a negative cast, one can suspect the operation of unresolved and unmodulated countertransference factors. There is also plenty of evidence to suggest that Kernberg is quite aware of the importance of empathy in the interpretive process. He (1979) writes:

> Empathy, however, is not only the therapist's intuitive emotional awareness of the patient's central emotional experience at a certain point; it must also include the therapist's capacity to empathize with what the patient cannot tolerate within himself. Therapeutic empathy, therefore, transcends that involved in ordinary human interactions and also includes the therapist's integration, on a cognitive and emotional level, of what is actively dissociated or split off in borderline patients. [p. 300]

Interpretations that evolve from a context of valid and accurate empathy are more likely to be affirmative than negative. Kernberg's (1968) approach emphasizes the importance of the patient's introjection of the therapist's interpretive stance as an essential aspect of the process of modifying the patient's pathogenic superego. To the extent that negative elements, which Schaffer describes, enter into the interpretive process, they would hardly contribute to this important aspect of the therapeutic dynamics.

Kris Group

A diversion somewhat different from Kernberg's view was provided by the results of the work of the Kris Study Group (Abend et al. 1983). They take exception to Kernberg's specific recommendations for interpretive work with borderline patients and argue that the interpretive process with such patients does not differ in any significant way from the ordinary psychoanalytic approach. They conclude that, even when significant change or recovery does occur, there is no certainty about what insights might have developed from any particular interpretations, reconstructions, or recovery of memories or what other interventions involving the understanding of transference emotions and fantasies might have contributed to the beneficial outcome. They argue that interpretive efforts in dealing with their population of borderline patients focused on both dyadic and triangular conflicts, on preoedipal, oral, and anal phase conflicts, as well as phallic-oedipal conflicts and their derivatives. They felt that the analysis of libidinal wishes and fears and of narcissistic needs could not be effectively separated from the analysis of aggressive conflicts. In their patients, every conflict, every object relationship, and every phase of ego development, aggressive and libidinal drive derivatives and their narcissistic components seem to be intertwined and inseparable.

It may be that the basic problem is that both Kernberg and the Kris Group are looking at patients from different ranges of the borderline spectrum. Kernberg's patients tend to be more severely disturbed, manifest greater degrees of ego weakness and instability, have more pathological and disturbed object relationships, and have a higher degree of regressive potential, all of which significantly affect the course of therapeutic experience and dictate certain kinds of therapeutic attitudes and interventions. The patients from the Kris Study Group, in contrast, were all regarded as basically analyzable, had less disturbed developmental histories, had a better history of object relationships, manifested different levels of pathological organization, particularly in the mixture of higher- and lower-order defenses and of pregenital and oedipal conflicts, and generally functioned better. Consequently, while Kernberg would emphasize the differences between his borderline patients and the more classically analyzable patient, the Kris Group tends to see their borderline patients more in terms of continuity along a number of parameters with patients in the neurotic spectrum.

INTERPRETATION WITHIN
THE BORDERLINE SPECTRUM

The controversial points in a discussion of Kernberg's technique lead toward an approach dictated from the perspective of the borderline spectrum. My own emphasis would diverge from Kernberg's along the following dimensions:

- The therapeutic approach is viewed in more flexible terms and includes both exploratory/expressive and supportive techniques. In the higher ranges of the borderline spectrum, the psychotherapy process moves in the direction of a psychoanalytic model; I would insist, in agreement with the findings of the Kris Study Group, that a fair number of borderline patients are indeed analyzable and deserve an opportunity for at least a trial of analysis. Patients in the lower order of the borderline spectrum, however, because of the intrusion of primitive transference dynamics and the higher degree of regressive potential, must often be treated with a mixture of expressive and supportive techniques and may even for significant periods of the therapeutic work require no more than a supportive approach.

- The present approach places more emphasis on aspects of the therapeutic alliance and sees the complex interaction between patient and therapist as compounded of alliance and transference factors. For example, while Kernberg argues for the early confrontation and interpretation of negative transferences, I see such manifestations more in terms of problems in the therapeutic alliance, which may reflect underlying transference difficulties but should be dealt with at the beginning of the therapy in alliance rather than transference terms. The purpose of the therapist's effort in dealing with such alliance distortions is to establish the therapeutic alliance, without which further meaningful therapeutic work is hardly possible. In this phase of the therapy, while Kernberg insists on interpretation as the technique of choice, it may indeed play a minor role, often giving way to confrontation and clarification of the behavioral patterns and their implications. It is only when such patterns have been recognized and to a degree defined and articulated, and some of their ramifications and implications explored, that the way is open to further interpretive illumination.

- Levels of conflict generally correspond to the level of anxiety that dominates the patient's pathogenic world. In general, I have not been impressed with the divergence in levels of conflict that Kernberg describes in his patients. Both dyadic and/or preoedipal conflicts and triangular phallic-oedipal conflicts can be found throughout the borderline spectrum. In the more primitive range, however, pregenital and narcissistic issues tend to hold greater pathogenic sway and exercise a severe distorting effect on oedipal dynamics. In the higher ranges of the borderline spectrum there is ample evidence of phallic-oedipal conflicts, but never without pregenital contamination. These are often difficult to tease apart and must be treated in layers of conflict and defense. Essentially, one works with what the patient makes available, always keeping in mind that what is visible from the perspective of the moment is never the whole story and that whatever work is accomplished on the present level of interpretation must be complemented, revised, reedited, and amplified in terms of other levels of conflict and defense as they become increasingly available.

INTERPRETIVE PROCESS

The interpretive process in the treatment of borderline patients can be delineated as follows:

1. *The dependence of the interpretive process on the therapeutic alliance:* The connection has been emphasized by many authors. The interpretive process assumes that the therapeutic alliance is effective and reflects the level of the patient's ability to integrate the interpretation and to participate in the process. To the extent that the interpretation is a form of hypothesis, it requires validation through the continuing collaborative effort and interaction of both therapist and patient (Stocking 1973). Thus, an effective therapeutic alliance (or at least

working alliance) is mandatory for the effectiveness of interpretation and involves the development of the patient's curiosity about his own motivations and the reasons and influences that contribute to his attitudes and behaviors (Boyer 1983).

The interpretive process requires some degree of therapeutic alliance and should also have the effect of reinforcing and stabilizing the alliance. Focusing frequently on the existential transactions involved in the alliance itself may bring into focus contributing transference dynamics and lead eventually in the direction of dynamic and genetic interpretations.

In work with borderline patients generally, the interpretive process is exquisitely sensitive to alliance factors. When the alliance is identifiably fragile, distorted, or disrupted, interpretations must be used with care since they can easily be distorted by the patient's projective needs. However thoughtfully, carefully, empathically, and gently interpretations may be offered, they may be absorbed into the pathogenic needs of the patient's introjective configuration and be transformed into pathogenic input. If patients have even some slender footing in a working alliance, it can be reassuring and relieving for them to be able to express, explore, and discuss their hostile, competitive, ambivalent, and even murderously destructive impulses toward the therapist. In a sense the alliance serves as a buffer against the toxic influences of these pathological affects. The sense of collaborative consolidation with a strong and resilient object strengthens the patient's own capacity to tolerate and deal with these feelings. But patients who lack a sufficiently strong alliance, or in whom the alliance has been disrupted by a regressive crisis, may find it difficult to maintain any distinction between discussing such hostile and destructive feelings and acting upon them. The sense of alliance with the therapist's ego strengths is essential to allow the patient to experience such affects and to deal with them in a more objective, therapeutic, and nontraumatic fashion (Appel 1974).

The interpretation of important object relations can be usefully undertaken only in the context of a reasonably good working alliance; it may not be useful to try to confront the patient's convictions about important objects, since disruption of such object connections may be more damaging than helpful. Patients can be brought gradually to a point of recognizing and understanding the more realistic aspects of their relationships, but only after solid therapeutic effort. The time may come when it is helpful for the patient to recognize that in some degree the hostility toward a negative object was justified, but this realization can be achieved only insofar as the negative distorting elements in the relationship have been sorted out and understood in dynamic and/or genetic terms (Blanck and Blanck 1974). The purpose of interpretation is to assist the patient in building intrapsychic structure; this process can often be a subtle, prolonged, step-by-step effort with a persistent focus on building and maintaining the therapeutic alliance.

Interpretations that do not contribute to or support the therapeutic alliance are not useful. Interpretations that tend to inflict narcissistic injury on the patient, especially early in the treatment process, would not contribute to the establishing of the therapeutic alliance (Chessick 1979). One of the difficulties with more primitive patients is that, if the therapist makes an observation or an interpretation that the patient did not think of first, the patient is confronted with the basic separateness and individuality of the therapist, a realization that shatters the illusion of merger with a good and protective object (Modell 1978). Borderline patients may react to interpretations with an exacerbation of shame, envy, rage, and depression. The difficulties in this process, particularly the reactions provoked by attempts to prematurely interpret negative or narcissistic transferences, have often proved to be discouraging and at times have led to the conclusion that interpretation should be avoided (Schaffer 1986). This has undoubtedly led some therapists to emphasize the importance of the holding environment and to correspondingly deemphasize the work of interpretation in the therapeutic process.

This set of circumstances presents the therapist with a basic therapeutic dilemma that pervades the therapeutic work with borderline patients. As Atkins (1967) has commented in this regard:

> The basic capacity for dependence necessary for the therapeutic alliance is impaired in borderline and psychotic patients. When this basic capacity for dependence is threatened by the existence of grave fears and distrust of one's self with another, this must be the primary subject for the analytic work and interpretation. . . . With these patients the eventual acquisition of the capacity for object relationships as manifested in the therapeutic alliance can be regarded as one of the achievements of a successful piece of analytic work. [p. 587]

2. *The economy of interpretation:* In general in the treatment of borderline patients, caution is urged in the use of interpretations. The therapist should venture into the area of interpretive activity with one eye on the status of the therapeutic alliance. Where an adequate alliance is not available, attempts at interpretation are more likely not only to

fail but also to be misinterpreted by the patient and contribute even greater difficulties to the therapy. The question of balance in the interpretive process is more acute and central in the treatment of borderline patients than with almost any other form of psychopathology. The therapist must be careful of taking the interpretive play away from the patient and into his own hands. Boyer (1983) comments:

> The patient's capacity to think, remember, and analyze for himself will be encouraged. His defensive uses of confusion, forgetfulness, and dependency on the therapist to analyze for him will be interpreted consistently. The analyst will be as passive and make as few interpretations as is consistent with the patient's anxiety. I have the impression that . . . . unnecessary interpretations increase the patient's dependency and interfere with his self-growth. They also rob him of the exhilaration which coincides with successful bids of self-analysis. [p. 114]

This caution and economy of interpretation become increasingly important at lower levels of borderline pathology. It is a principle that is used occasionally and episodically in the work with higher-order borderlines, even those who seem to manifest the healthiest and generally neurotic personality structures, but when one is dealing with patients in whom the pathology is more primitive, labile, and vulnerable to regression, interpretation has to be used with great care. The therapist's effort must be constantly directed toward maintaining the fragments of healthy ego-functioning in the patient and constantly supporting the patient's sense of self-worth and autonomy. Any effort on the part of the therapist that smacks of feeding the patient's infantile hunger and symbiotic wishes serves only to undermine the patient's autonomy and fails to notice what the patient may have to contribute that is of value in advancing the therapeutic work. Taking the play away from the patient—absolving him in any degree of his responsibility for maintaining and contributing to the therapeutic work—neither reinforces the therapeutic alliance nor provides an adequate framework for meaningful interpretation (Appel 1974).

With more regressed patients, then, the use of interpretive techniques should be sparing and restrained. This deviates from the usual principle that in the face of regressive lack of structure, the therapist tries to increase the amount of structure in the therapeutic situation, if only in the interests of holding. This by no means implies that interpretive efforts on the part of the therapist have no place in the face of regressive manifestations in the patient. The point is that in such circumstances interpretation is undertaken only with increased risk and with diminished hope of effectiveness.

There are times when interpretations may be required to bolster a faltering ego or to maintain the patient's defensive organization in the interest of avoiding further and malignant regression. The therapist is often in the delicate position of trying to maintain a careful balance between what seems to be a useful therapeutic regression and the use of structuring parameters, which would be either unnecessary or noncontributory in work with healthier patients (Clifton 1974). One is always confronted with the difficulty of maintaining an appropriate and useful degree of ego distance in the work of interpretation, neither pressing forward excessively so as to undermine the patient's responsibility and initiative and stimulate wishes for dependence and merger, nor excessively withdrawing or withholding interpretive contributions and running the risk of stirring fears of abandonment, inadequacy, and helplessness in the patient (Rangell 1955).

3. *The interpretive process aims ultimately at maintaining a distinction between fantasy and reality:* This issue, the clarification of the boundaries between the patient's fantasy life and its derivatives and reality, is one that pervades the interpretive process from beginning to end. Even at the earliest stages of interpretive work with many patients, the therapist's effort is directed toward beginning to establish the rudiments of a working alliance, which may require some clarification and at least phenomenological interpretation of the patient's experience in the therapeutic relationship as reflecting more therapeutic misalliance than alliance.

The issues of how the clarification and differentiation between fantasy and reality are achieved at later stages in the therapy are often complex and difficult. Kernberg (1984) has observed that in interpretive work with borderline patients, particularly those in a regressive phase, it is helpful for the therapist to keep in mind the primary objectives of the therapy, namely, maintaining a consistent affirmation of the reality of the treatment situation by interpreting current distortions, and helping the patient to get back to a more meaningful process of self-exploration and free association rather than to be focusing the bulk of his energies on grappling with and controlling the therapist. The valid issue in this approach is that it works to reconstitute the alliance and get the therapy back on a more effective track. Kernberg's recommendation is in all likelihood accurate and useful where the alliance is severely distorted because of the patient's regression. However, in cases where transference-based distortions can be brought into focus and where some degree of available working alliance is intact, drawing the patient's attention to his distortions of the therapeutic reality may not be the most effective tactic.

If at all possible, the patient can be encouraged to develop and explore his transference distortion to bring to light the transferential components and thereby reveal more hidden dimensions of the underlying introjective configuration. With many borderline patients, any sense of the reality of the therapist is achieved only after long periods of engagement and increasing familiarity and after considerable working-through of projective distortions (Olinick 1954). The patient's capacity to accept, realize, and integrate interpretive material that would allow a firmer footing and orientation in reality is in part a function of the therapeutic alliance, which may be fragile, tenuous, and often minimal in quality. The question is not whether the interpretive process is oriented toward the gradual establishing of a clearer and more adaptive sense of reality but in what measure and with what pacing and dosage. The dilemma is similar to that posed by Fairbairn (1958) in distinguishing between the dynamics of a closed system as opposed to an open system. To the extent that the patient's psychic economy is trapped in a closed system, the patient can deal only with the psychic reality of his inner psychic world. When this system becomes open, input from external reality can be brought into relationship with the inner dynamics and clear the way for more realistic and adaptive solutions. The transference in Fairbairn's terms is an example of such a closed system and stands in opposition to the real relationship to an object as a form of open system. To the extent that the closed-system dynamics are operating, the subject can relate to the object only in transferential terms, so that the real qualities of the object enter very little, if at all, into determining the nature of the patient's reaction and interaction with that object. The therapeutic problem is how to change the closed system to a more open one. It may be that open-system considerations must be postponed until the dynamics and patterns of the closed system can be adequately explored, understood, and resolved.

4. *Interpretations as affirmative:* Interpretations to borderline patients at whatever level of their pathological organization should aim always at being positive. This principle has been enunciated by a number of contributors, whether in terms of ego building (Blanck and Blanck 1974), facilitating the therapeutic alliance (Boyer and Giovac-

chini 1980, Boyer 1983), or reinforcing the self-worth autonomy, and adaptive value of the patient and his actions (Schafer 1983, Schaffer 1986). My understanding of this principle is specifically in terms of the therapeutic alliance: interpretations are affirmative to the extent they support, reinforce, and consolidate the therapeutic alliance. In these terms, even when the therapist is focusing on some negative aspects of the patient's behavior, he often takes care to interject a positive and sustaining note. One might say to a patient who is struggling to contain his murderous rage, "Though you have experienced your anger as intense and overwhelming, your behavior seemed relatively appropriate and accomplished something." Even when concern for maintaining the patient's sense of self-worth, autonomy, and capacity is involved, it may not play an immediate role in a given interpretive statement in the therapeutic exchange. But the affirmation must not be lost sight of in whatever patient and therapist are working on, and the therapist, if he is wise, will find a way somewhere in the process to interject a positive note in the mix of interpretive elements.

It should be clear that this interpretive principle assumes even greater importance in the treatment of lower-order borderline patients, in whom the propensity is maximal for distortion and for readily assimilating any negative connotations brought to the interpretive process by the therapist. The same sensitivities may exist in higher-order patients, but they are considerably more muted and subtle, and the therapist has correspondingly greater latitude in dealing directly with negative aspects of the patient's character, again in proportion to the level of functioning alliance.

INTERPRETIVE SCHEMA

My own approach to the interpretive process as applied to the treatment of patients in the borderline spectrum[1] is based on my understanding of the paranoid process that organizes the patient's experience—both cognitive and affective—around three basic components, namely, introjections, correlative projections, and paranoid construction (Meissner 1978b, 1986b). Through these aspects of the paranoid process

---

[1]This approach is based on my previous theoretical understanding of borderline psychopathology (Meissner 1984a); a summary statement of that approach and understanding is contained in the final chapter of that work, entitled "Toward a Theory of Borderline Psychopathology" (pp. 423–459).

the patient organizes his experience, both of himself and of the world. The purpose of the entire process is to confirm, reinforce, sustain, and validate the introjective configuration, which provides the core of the patient's sense of self.

Exploring the Projective System

The first task of the interpretive process is identifying and exploring the patient's projective system. This involves identifying elements of the paranoid construction and eliciting and defining the projective elements within it. Since these projective elements derive from the internal introjective configuration, this allows us to shift the therapeutic endeavor to an internal frame of reference and deal with the organization of the introjects as the central focus. The therapist begins this process by listening to the patient's account of his experience of himself and the world in which he lives. The patient effectively provides a descriptive account of his paranoid construction, within which we can identify the projective elements. The therapist's role is essentially passive, with no need to confront or refute the elements of the projective system. He seeks only to learn about that system, to find out what is in it, and to become as familiar with it as he reasonably can.

The patient tells us about his projective system from the very first. There is little in his behavior, demeanor, verbalizations, and opinions that does not provide us with information about himself and his world. A young man tells me about his intense anxiety when called on in class, how he becomes confused and loses his train of thought in discussions with his teachers, and about his anxiety and impotence with women; he is telling me something about his image of himself and his relationships to the world around him. Other aspects of his history fit the picture: he was the baby of the family; he was anxiously and obsessively hovered over by an insecure mother; he always felt like a messy kid who would never grow up; he suffered from persistent enuresis until about age fifteen. He paints a picture of a helpless child-victim lost in a hostile and threatening world of powerful grownups. His response to me in the therapy as a threatening, intrusive, and powerfully controlling object seems to fit well into this picture.

The patient may present experience as fact, as the way things are. An attractive and intelligent young professional woman consistently maintained that she was inferior and inadequate because she lacked the sort of physical attributes that men found attractive. No amount of questioning or contrary evidence could dent her conviction. She constructed her social environment so as to confirm her own feelings of inadequacy and shame. Little surprise that she saw the therapist as devaluing her in the same way; he was, after all, a man like any other man!

The critical elements in these constructions are the patient's projections, which pertain specifically to object relations (Meissner 1971, 1978b). In both cases, relationships were contaminated by the patients' convictions, based on projection, that others were critical, demeaning, out to do them harm and put them in their place. These projective elements are based on underlying introjective components derived from earlier parental imagos.

Certain defining techniques can facilitate this descriptive account. I try to obtain as much explicit and concrete detail as possible. I want to know about actual events, actions on the part of various individuals, reactions, feelings, and particularly the patient's own perceptions and feelings. The affective impact of events and experiences is embedded in the actions. If I am not hearing about those events, I am not hearing about the meaningful aspects of the patient's experience. Parallel accounts can be useful, both interpersonal and historical accounts. Details are important, since they reveal the specific patterns of the patient's behavior. Historical accounts are helpful since they can reveal similar patterns that may have occurred earlier in the patient's experience.

The patient may also tell us about the organization of his introjects. He tells us in direct and indirect ways how he sees himself, how he feels about himself, how he thinks others may regard him and react to him. Hidden affects of depression, fear, shame, inadequacy, weakness, and vulnerability may emerge as direct expressions of the pathogenic sense of self.

The projective system operates in all spheres of the patient's experience, particularly when it is affectively significant or when the patient has some stake or investment. We can presume that it is evident within the therapeutic relationship, and that as the therapy progresses it comes to a dramatic focus within the transference neurosis. Usually, the neurosis is the most vivid and forceful expression of the patient's projective system and becomes the primary vehicle not only for recognizing and defining the system but for beginning to deal with it therapeutically.

The patient's affects are important as vehicles for expressing these elements. Affective communications carry a significant information load. Some signals come from the expression of the patient's affect— sadness, bitterness, regret, anger, fear—but other signals can come from the therapist's own affective response to the patient. Feelings of boredom, irritation, incompetence, inadequacy, even hatred, can provide important signals for the reading of the patient's projective system (see Chapter 7 on countertransference). Within the transference/counter-transference interaction, the patient not only distorts his perception and representation of the therapist, but frequently works to elicit responses from him that serve to confirm these distortions and misrepresentations.

Testing the Projective System

The definition of the projective system sets the stage for an ensuing phase of testing the projective elements. These elements of the patient's projective system need to be tested against the hard stuff of reality, but the question is how this is to be accomplished. The best approach usually is not to challenge or confront the system as a whole, or even any of its elements. As we shall see in Chapter 8, this does not mean that any of the varieties of confrontation may not have a role to play (Corwin 1973), but in this context they run the risk of playing into the projective system rather than unveiling its meaning. Rather, the process of undermining the projective system begins by a more subtle testing of elements of the system against reality by filling out and expanding the details of the system. As the patient does this, he is both communicating a more specific understanding of what is involved in his projective elaboration and presenting to himself the specifics of the reality.

I have emphasized some specific techniques that call into question elements of the projective system and create a sense of distance between the projective elements and an emerging reality perspective (Meissner 1986b). First is tagging feelings. When the patient expresses a feeling content, the therapist can simply tag the content as expressing a feeling. When the patient says, "I don't feel that I could ever do anything right," the therapist tags not the specific content of the statement but the feeling tone: "That is how you feel." Tagging feelings as feelings may require repeated and persistent efforts taking place over a long time and embracing many concrete circumstances and details of the patient's affective experience. The tagging technique aims at establishing the distinction between feelings (and their intimate connection with fantasies) and reality. Thus it contributes to the reality-testing process and to a gradually amplifying awareness of the patient's feelings as forming a coherent and consistent pattern in his experience of himself. It further seeks to establish the connection between the pattern of feelings and specific underlying (often unconscious) fantasies. Since these feelings and fantasies derive directly from introjective configurations, the tagging approach aims at delineating not only the fantasy aspects in the patient's perception of the world around him but also the fantasies involved in his perception and appreciation of himself as a human being.

The second aspect of testing the reality of the patient's perspective tries to define the specific areas within which his knowledge is lacking. The patient will frequently offer interpretations, explanations, conclusions, hypotheses, attitudes as though they were accepted fact. These expressions often convey a sense of the patient's inadequacy, defectiveness, weakness, vulnerability, powerlessness, powerfulness, specialness, superiority—attributes that express the status of the underlying introjects. Any efforts to challenge or refute the patient's view would only meet with staunch resistance and greater rigidity in the patient's defensive position. The therapist can tactfully point out and question the areas in which the patient's knowledge is uncertain. For example, if the patient says that people at work do not like him, the therapist could try to elicit further details about the situation at work. When he fails to provide such details, as is usually the case, the therapist can point out that even though the patient feels unwanted, he really doesn't know whether people at work want him there or not.

In such inquiries, the therapist maintains a neutral position, neither pro nor con. He is saying no more than that the patient does not really know; further, where the patient does not know, he tends to fill in the blanks, to fill the empty spaces from his own imagination. The material used to fill in the blanks in the patient's experience of his reality derives from the constellation of introjects that form the substance of his inner world.

This process moves toward progressively clearer and more discrete delineation of the realm of the patient's largely unconscious fantasy life—both in its external and internal referents. These introjectively derived fantasy systems and their role in early object relations and current transference relations can be further clarified, helping to specify the introjective configuration and progressively delineate it from reality. The testing of the projective system against reality serves an important function in the therapeutic progression. Detailed examination of the elements of the projective system increasingly diminishes their stability and utility for the patient, thus mobilizing important therapeutic elements. As the therapeutic process engages with the projective system more and more meaningfully, it increasingly undermines the system, with the result that the patient's needs to defend and maintain it are mobilized, often to an intense degree. The therapist then has to work with the patient's defensive responses. The projective system is there not simply as a matter of chance. It is an intensely invested, cognitive, affective, and defensive organization whose purpose is the preservation of the introjects as the core elements in the patient's sense of self.

Delineating the Introjective Configuration

As the projective system is gradually undermined, the therapeutic focus shifts to the introjects. Since the projective system, including the paranoid construction, exists to sustain the pathogenic introjects, undermining it leads to unveiling of the introjects. The focus shifts from the external world to an internal one, and the patient begins to give us a more direct and vivid account of that internal world. With the shift the content in borderline patients is usually more depressive: the patient sees himself more explicitly in terms of overwhelming weakness, inadequacy, helplessness, inferiority, defectiveness, worthlessness, and vulnerability. These aspects of the patient's internal world now become the focus of the therapeutic process.

The therapist seeks to learn the concrete details of the patient's feelings of inadequacy, helplessness, inferiority, and so on. Just as the elements of the patient's projective system were based more on fantasy than on reality, so the elements of the patient's introjective system have more to do with fantasies about himself and what he is than with the reality. At this juncture, the patient does not know his own reality; whatever conclusions, attitudes, and feelings he generates about himself are based on a set of feelings and fantasies that for most of his life he has mistaken for himself.

The patient's introjective organization displays itself, of course, in the therapeutic relationship, particularly in the transference. Within that relationship, the patient tends to play himself off against the therapist in a variety of ways. Quite typically, the borderline patient will see himself as weak and inferior (expressing certain qualities of the victim-introject), while he sees the therapist as powerful, strong, and competent (reflecting projected aspects of the aggressor-introject). To the extent that narcissistic components are at work, he may see himself as inferior, inadequate, worthless, and shameful (inferior introject) and the therapist as valued, important, special, omnipotent, and omniscient (projected superior introject). Kernberg (1979) touches on this aspect of the clarification of the introjects when he comments on the need to evaluate the patient's self- and object-representations and their relation to self- and object-roles in the therapeutic interaction.

It is not unusual for patients to be readily in touch with the inferior and inadequate or the helpless and victimized aspects of their introjects, but clinical experience tells us that there is more to it. If part of the introjective organization relates to the fantasy of the patient's weakness, there is a parallel part at the opposite extreme that bespeaks the patient's sense of destructive power. If there is a part expressing his worthlessness, there is also a part holding out for his specialness and entitlement. The introjects, therefore, have a polarized structure in which introjective elements are split on both sides of the middle ground of reality (Kernberg 1966). In relation to important objects, this has a twofold effect. If the self is seen in narcissistic terms as inferior, the object is seen as superior; conversely, if the self is seen as superior, the object is seen as inferior. Or if the self is seen as helpless victim, the object is seen as powerful aggressor; if the self is seen as powerful and destructive, the object is seen as victimized and helpless. Thus, the polar aspects of the introjects tend to focus on one or other side of the self-object differentiation and often shift back and forth. It is critical to this phase of the therapeutic process that both aspects be seen as deriving from the patient's own introjective configuration. The vacillation between the self as superior and special on the one hand and as inferior and worthless on the other is an intrinsic vacillation, both aspects of which derive from the patient's introjective organization. If one polarity of the introjective economy escapes repression and is available to the patient's awareness, the therapist can presume that the opposite polarity is lurking somewhere under the surface.

Consistent with the general pattern of borderline cognitive functioning, the expressions of introjective derivatives tend to be cast in all-or-nothing terms. As the correlative and polarized aspects of the introjects become more clearly defined, it becomes apparent that they operate very much in all-or-nothing fashion. If the therapist is seen as superior, competent, and intelligent, for example, the patient tends to see himself as totally inferior and abject, without any competence or worth at all. When the therapist begins to hear this unmitigated logic of extremes—the logic of all or nothing, black or white, either/or—he knows that he is closing in on introjective territory.

It is clinically important that these polarized aspects are locked together in a reciprocal defensive organization. This understanding yields a critical insight into the depressive dynamics in some borderline patients. It seems to make little sense for the patient to cling with such intensity to a perception of himself as inferior, inadequate, helpless, vulnerable, and victimized. That intense clinging, so resistant to therapeutic intervention, becomes understandable only when it is seen in relation to the opposite polarity, which says that the patient is special, entitled, exceptional. The point to emphasize is that where one aspect of the introjective organization can be seen, the polar opposite is irrevocably and unquestionably present and operative. The therapist must understand and the patient must come to see that the polarized opposites are irrevocably linked together, that they reinforce each other, that they are bound together by the iron clasps of reciprocal defense, that they cannot be separated. Effective clinical intervention requires that both aspects be dealt with and resolved—one without the other will not do.

As the introjects are gradually defined, the process of testing keeps pace. When the patient's feelings of weakness, inadequacy, and helplessness are repeatedly tagged as feeling elements, the gradual understanding emerges that such elements relate to a fantasy derived from the organization of the underlying introjects. The patient knows only the fantasy: he has taken the fantasy for his real self for so long that he no longer knows or recognizes the actuality of his real self. The therapeutic relationship is the primary testing ground for distinguishing between these introjective fantasy elements and the reality of the patient's self, most specifically, directly, and powerfully in the distinction between transference or transference neurosis and the therapeutic alliance.

Narcissistic Configurations. We have been dealing primarily with the aggressive derivatives as they are realized in the introjective configuration. The introjective configuration is also structured along narcissistic lines. The narcissistic polarities take shape along superior and inferior lines, the superior introject taking a form akin to the grandiose self (Kohut 1971) and the inferior introject serving as its polar opposite.

Early pathogenic experiences of enmeshment with a narcissistic mother and consequent traumatic disappointment leave the infantile exhibitionistic and grandiose fantasies isolated and disavowed, or repressed, and as a result inaccessible to more realistic and adaptive ego functioning. This narcissistic fixation takes the form of the grandiose self, the structural embodiment of the residues of infantile omnipotence and narcissistic enhancement. Persistence of the grandiose self carries with it a damming up of primitive narcissistic-exhibitionistic libido that can be manifested symptomatically in the intensification of hypochrondriacal concerns or self-consciousness to the point of shame and embarrassment.

The persistence of the grandiose self, even when repressed and disavowed, involves a potentiality for undermining self-esteem. This results from linking narcissistic expectations to the unrealistic, though disavowed and unconscious, grandiose fantasies and primitive exhibitionistic wishes of the grandiose self. Such fantasies and impulses remain unavailable to the modulating activity of the realistic ego.

Thus, depression can be seen as the underside of states of narcissistic enhancement, particularly grandiosity. Grandiosity and depression are interconnected (Miller 1979). The grandiose person is in desperate need of admiration: whatever he undertakes must be accomplished brilliantly and must be acknowledged by the admiration of others and reinforced by success and achievement. But if one or other of these supports to his fragile narcissism should fail, he is plunged into catastrophic depression. The need for admiration in such individuals is insatiable and consuming: it is his curse, his tragic flaw, the mark of the tyranny of his narcissism that demands total admiration and leaves no room for admiration to be given to any others. Credit, acknowledgment, or praise given to another is praise taken away from him, and gives rise to intense envy. Caught within this overpowering need, he can even be envious of healthier people around him, who do not have such a need for admiration and do not have to exert themselves constantly to impress others and to gain their acknowledgment. As Miller (1979) notes, the grandiose person can never really be free, not only because he is excessively dependent on others for their approval but also because his own precarious narcissistic equilibrium depends on qualities, capacities, and achievements that are inherently vulnerable and can at any point fail. The threat of depression looms for such personalities whenever grandiosity is impinged on by sickness, injury, or even aging (Meissner 1986b). As the narcissistic supplies and the continual reinforcement of the sense of self-importance and specialness are eroded, depression looms as a desperate alternative.

Grandiose fantasies persist as forms of primitive ego-ideals related to primitive identifications (introjections) (Reich 1960). The degree of pathology depends on the capacity of the ego to function realistically—whether it can transpose fantasy ambitions into realistic attainments. Often, the grandiose fantasy becomes so overcathected by the intensity of inner needs that the distinction between wish and reality becomes obscure. Unsublimated and relatively grandiose fantasies can readily shift to feelings of utter dejection, worthlessness, or hypochondriacal anxieties. The narcissistic affliction may take the form of extreme oscillations of self-esteem. Periods of elation and self-infatuation are followed almost cyclically by feelings of total dejection and worthlessness. The infantile value system knows only absolute perfection and attainment or complete destruction and worthlessness. The shift can be precipitated by the most insignificant disappointment or experience of failure. In the logic of such extremes, there are no degrees or shadings. The situation is all or nothing, black or white, omnipotent or impotent. Any shortcoming or failure to attain absolute perfection is translated into terms of absolute failure.

Narcissistic and exhibitionist urges aim at overcoming feelings of inadequacy by seeking attention and admiration. But the failure to attain this acknowledgment leads to the anticipation that whatever attention they do receive will be negative rather than positive. Narcissistic individuals fear that others will see through the facade and recognize the inferiority and defectiveness within. There is, nonetheless, defensive contempt for those whose admiration is simultaneously sought. Contempt turns to self-contempt that is experienced as shame. These patients feel constantly evaluated or judged by outside observers who in effect play the role of the re-externalized critical superego. The narcissistic defense, therefore, takes the form of projection.

Kernberg (1970) has described borderline personalities in whom pathological narcissism plays a dominant role. He views the grandiose and coldly controlling behavior of such patients as a defense against the projection of the basically oral rage that forms a central component of the psychopathology. This aspect of the narcissistic pathology points to the primitive, destructive, and depressive aspects of the introjective configuration. This is reflected in the clinical dialectic of introjection and projection and in the distortion in object relations that is sometimes difficult to detect. Where introjective elements come to dominate the inner realm of the patient's experience, there are often strong conscious feelings of inadequacy and inferiority. These feelings may alternate with grandiose and omnipotent fantasies. Frequently the omnipotence and narcissistic grandiosity of such self-demeaning patients are slow in coming to the surface.

Such individuals often demonstrate a remarkable capacity for consistent and effective work in some areas of their lives, which provides them with significant narcissistic rewards and gratification. They can be outstanding leaders in areas of professional and academic life or distinguished performers in the arts. However, their insistence in living at the extremes and the depressive impact of the failure to live up to and meet the demands of their narcissistic expectations can become impediments to their professional and artistic attainment. There is a failure to integrate ego-ideal precursors and idealized self-images; as a result, the grandiose self on one hand and the unmodified and primitive aggression of the superego on the other are left relatively intact. These structures remain at a primarily introjective level of integration, with the result that primitive elements of both oral and anal aggression are highly susceptible to paranoid projection.

These individuals may present a facade of authoritarian conformity but nonetheless see themselves as getting away with something. This combination of narcissistic grandiosity and primitive aggressive impulses, along with their projection to the outer world, provides the matrix that gives rise to antisocial tendencies and conflicts with authority. The narcissism in such cases may take the form of demanding recognition and reward without the need to work for it or earn it, together with resentment at the world for failing to respond to this demand. This may evolve further into resentment and resistance against all forms of external control.

Shame. One of the primary, direct affective expressions of the underlying narcissistic deprivation or mortification is shame. Shame carries the burden of sensitivity and guardedness, as though it were a vulnerable pain center the patient needed to keep concealed at all costs. The patient's resistance often seems intense and belabored but finally yields up a relatively trivial fantasy to which the feeling of shame is attached. This terrible secret is shared with the analyst as a privileged communication that is enshrined with special significance in the patient's inner world. The therapist may experience a sense of disappointment, a letdown that the secret does not measure up to the echoes of importance the experience has in the patient's perspective. As Kohut (1971) has pointed out, the patient's shame is related to the discharge of relatively crude and unneutralized narcissistic exhibitionistic libido, which leaves him vulnerable to the fear of ridicule and humiliation.

Following Freud's suggestion that shame, along with disgust, was an important inhibitory force opposing the excessive expression of the sexual instinct, Levin (1967) has suggested that shame can function as a signal affect. It serves an important function of preventing overexposure to trauma—the trauma of rejection as well as narcissistic trauma, which can take the form of ridicule, scorn, abandonment, rejection, and so on (Rochlin 1961, Spiegel 1966). Shame thus stands in opposition to the wished-for acceptance or respect, which is a component of self-esteem.

Shame becomes the signal affect for feelings of humiliation, inferiority, or narcissistic mortification. It can play a role in narcissistic projections, since the self-exposure involved in shame must involve a perception of others viewing the self as a failure or regarding him with devaluation or contempt. In a derivative sense as well, shame serves as a painful affect that can in a secondary way serve to stimulate signal anxiety, which arouses the ego to defend against the shame affect by repression or other defensive maneuvers. Shame-prone individuals maintain a certain distance from others as a means of self-protection and as a way of avoiding the intense shame they experience under conditions of self-exposure. In many borderline patients, any attention from others is experienced as shameful. Even when the response of others is one of admiration or praise, these patients react with feelings of shame, becoming guarded and suspicious, presuming that even more dreadful criticism is being kept concealed. Such patients tend to become secretive, even paranoid, as the same shame reactions, at a slightly greater degree of intensity, can easily turn into paranoid symptoms.

The motif of shame was demonstrated sharply by my experience with a borderline woman of about 30 who came to analysis for a depression involving a severe impairment of self-esteem. Diagnostically she fell in the primitive hysteric range. She expected criticism for whatever she did. These feelings could easily be traced to her hypercritical mother, in whose eyes this girl could do nothing right and who regarded her as basically worthless. These expectations found their way into the transference and expressed themselves in her conviction that I would be critical of her, that I would tell her she was a worthless patient who did not deserve to be analyzed. Her conviction was that I was waiting for the analytic material to build up so I could then turn on her and show her how worthless and evil she was. She even felt at times that I was magically reading the perverse and degenerate thoughts that came into her mind and that I could feel only contempt and disgust at what I must be seeing in her. The whole of this material was underlaid quite extensively and intensively with shameful feelings.

Shame and Guilt. Shame is often associated with guilt, but it is better to keep these two signal affects differentiated:

1. In shame, aspects of the self, such as actions, feelings, thoughts, wishes, and so forth, are compared with an idealized self-image that we would wish to see in ourselves or have others see in us. Guilt sees the same self dimensions in relationship to a code of standards and prohibitions of what one ought to be or what one ought to do or not do. The emphasis in shame falls on qualities of the self, while in guilt it falls on the character of what is done or not done.

2. Shame is global in character, focusing on a wishful self-image that embraces the whole person with its ideal characteristics and thus becomes the measure of self-evaluation. Guilt, in contrast, is restrictive and additive, focusing on specific actions and their consequences.

3. Shame takes the form of self-contempt, guilt of self-hatred. This reflects different vicissitudes of aggression: hatred seeks to hurt and destroy; contempt seeks to eliminate something as dirty or evil.

4. In their signal functions, shame and guilt reflect different sets of instinctual wishes. Shame is a reaction to exhibitionistic and scoptophilic wishes, guilt reacts to wishes to attack, hurt, and destroy. The shame experience follows the sequence of exposure, condemnation, rejection, scorn, and hiding; the guilt experience follows the sequence of attack, retaliation by punishment, atonement by restitution.

5. Suddenness or surprise, or discovery, plays a role in shame; not so in guilt.

6. Both affects protect the separate private self from intrusion and merger: shame in expressive and perceptual experience (touching, looking, exhibiting), guilt in motor activity and aggression (attacking, hurting, castrating, killing) (Wurmser 1978).

Shame and guilt are often associated in the patient's experience. Piers and Singer (1953) refer to such complex reactions as "guilt-shame cycles." Shame is related to the frustration of narcissistic aspirations but depends on the perception of such failure on the part of others. Although the experience of shame can be internalized, it often requires the external exposure. The intense experience of shame, not an uncommon feature in borderline patients, can lead to the disturbance of libidinal economy, resulting in diffusion of libidinal energies and deneutralization of destructive energies that are then channeled through the superego against the self. When this happens, it is experienced by the subject as guilt. In such cases, the narcissistic defense takes the introjective route and gives rise to a depressive outcome. The deneutralized energy can also be directed exteriorly in the form of a projective blaming response. Blaming has the advantage of supporting and restoring narcissistic equilibrium.

Envy. Narcissistic defeats for such individuals are experienced as shameful, but more often than not, the shame is mixed with envy. The combination of shame and envy may be followed by self-destructive impulses and a feeling of guilt. But Kohut understands these not as superego attacks but as attempts by the ego to do away with the disappointment of failure. He views these self-destructive impulses as expression of narcissistic rage. Kohut cautions that attempts to deal with shame-prone patients therapeutically by diminishing the power of the ideal system is frequently a technical error, but that transformation of the narcissistic investment in the grandiose self to the ego-ideal system is more frequently successful. His approach is based on strengthening rather than weakening of the ego-ideal.

Envy also plays an important role in the narcissistic pathology of borderline patients and can be found liberally throughout the borderline spectrum. These patients feel deprived and thus entitled to compensatory recognition or acceptance—considerations and benefits that others who have not suffered such deprivations are not entitled to. They commonly feel that they should not have to earn recognition, but that it should be given to them automatically. They are resentful, for example, that they have to work to support themselves, feeling the world somehow owes them a living without any effort of their own. They have an abiding sense of unfairness at having to face, acknowledge, and submit themselves to the restraints and limitations of forbidding reality (Jacobson 1959).

Such feelings of deprivation and resentful entitlement may at times take the form of penis envy in certain female patients (Freud 1916, Jacobson 1959). But the implications in these patients are not simply genital, and the underlying anxiety is not simply concerned with castration issues; the issues are in large measure pregenital and reflect relatively primitive narcissistic conflicts. These feelings also can play a role in the transference. This was particularly true in one of my female patients whose narcissism was quite strongly fixated at an infantile level.

At the birth of her brother, who was two years younger, she felt herself deprived and cheated; she felt she was no longer the center of her parents' affection and attention and was forced to take a second place to her brother. The narcissistic loss and the resulting envy drove her to focus all her resentment on her brother's penis—the only obvious difference between herself and him. This was the only thing she could find that would explain why he had become more important than herself. Penis envy became a pervasive aspect of her neurotic adjustment and led to highly competitive and narcissistic ambitions, which drove her to seek high academic accomplishments. When her efforts did not measure up to the level of her aspirations, she inevitably felt that she was a failure and became depressed. She was convinced that anyone who did not have a penis was not worth anything and could never achieve anything significant in life.

In the transference, she thought that she could improve her situation only by becoming dependent on me and keeping in my good favor. This reflected her childhood conviction that the only way she could maintain any importance or value in her parents' eyes was by a continual attempt to please her father. Pleasing her mother was less helpful, since mother herself was unimportant; she did not have a penis. Only late in the analysis was this patient able to express and work through some of her intense envious feelings toward me. She saw me as a strong, capable, helping person, and came to feel she could rely on and trust me. But beyond this capacity for trust and her therapeutic compliance, there was the conviction that she had to depend on, please, and comply with my wishes, since it was only by her clinging to a powerful penis-bearing object that she could have any hope of magically gaining strength and self-worth for herself. Embedded in this was a deep and abiding sense of envy. The envy was focused on the issue of penis power, but at a deeper, primitive level it masked a primitive oral rage at having been deprived of the pleasures of mother's breast and the accompanying infantile attention and adulation.

Envy of this sort can often be an impediment to treatment. Modell (1971) points out that, while Freud had originally assumed unconscious guilt feelings were responsible for the negative therapeutic reaction, specifically guilt for incestuous and rivalrous impulses, the guilt associated with negative therapeutic reaction may also be related to the conviction that one does not have a right to the better life that might follow as a consequence of therapeutic success. The essential element here is that of envy. Such individuals seem to suffer from a conviction that they do not have a right to such improvement and therapeutic success. They share a common fantasy that if they were to possess something good, this would imply that someone else was deprived. Thus, they cannot accept therapeutic improvement since it means that they are depriving someone else of it. Modell (1971) comments:

These individuals seemed to suffer from a particularly intense form of envy and greed, i.e., they wished to take away all that others possessed. So that in an additional sense the negative therapeutic reaction could be understood as a wish to deprive the analyst of the "good" that he possessed by virtue of his therapeutic skill. [p. 340]

A similar point based on somewhat different theoretical presumptions has been made by Klein (1957), who makes envy a primary contributing factor to negative therapeutic reactions.

Humiliation. The fear of humiliation takes its place along with shame and envy as an expression of inferior narcissistic introjective dynamics. The loss of narcissistic perfection can be experienced as a humiliation. Rothstein (1984) links the fear of humiliation to narcissism, masochism, and sadism. Certain masochistic patients derive narcissistic pleasure from eliciting their own humiliation at the hands of a sadist. Other narcissistic patients enjoy sadistically humiliating others, just as their own superego humiliates them. While masochistic patients may gain unconscious narcissistic gratification through indirectly controlling the inevitable insult, narcissistic patients may have the added fantasy that they can master the implicit danger by an active identification with the sadistic humiliator, thus demonstrating their inherent superiority. The pathogenic integration of narcissistic and aggressive themes is common in borderline patients; the integration can be more complete and nuanced in higher-order patients, but careful therapeutic work will reveal the same elements in them that appear with greater intensity and delineation in lower-order patients. The intrapsychic organization in such patients often reflects the internalization of humiliating introjects derived from parental models. The resulting introjective configuration contains the sadistic, masochistic, and narcissistic components derived from the object(s) of internalization.

Therapeutic Response. In trying to gain greater clarification of the patient's narcissistic introjects, the therapist listens for derivatives of both the superior and the inferior narcissistic introjects. His task is to amplify this introjective material, so that an increasingly elaborate and precise picture of the manner and style in which these introjective components permeate the individual's life experience gradually emerges. On both sides of the narcissistic polarity, the therapist seeks to explore these motifs in all the multiple contexts in which they play themselves out. When the therapist hears the inferior components, the patient's sense of inferiority and inadequacy, his sense of shamefulness and worthlessness, his fears of humiliation, of envy and vulnerability, the therapist's task is to listen with understanding, empathy, and acceptance. He wants to give as much space as is necessary for the patient to develop and explore this side of his feelings about his impoverished and narcissistically depleted self. When the opposite configuration begins to show itself in the patient's sense of entitlement or perfectionism, his exhibitionistic impulses or wishes, and his wish for admiration, the superior narcissistic configuration is put on display. It is equally important for the therapist to provide ample space for the patient to display and explore these aspects of his inner self-organization.

Most therapists find it easier to empathize and accept the patient's narcissistically inferior feelings and attitudes. Difficulties may arise for certain therapists in tolerating the patient's painful, often self-pitying depression, but generally the capacity to tolerate such affects is within the range of the average therapist's working ego. Kohut (1971) cautions against the tendency to react to the patient's grandiosity and narcissistic superiority, particularly insofar as they may be accompanied by attempts to devalue the analyst. The same tolerance and empathic acceptance that one might extend to the narcissistically inferior side should be extended to the narcissistically superior side, however strong the temptation may be to react to it or to try to do something with it by therapeutic intervention (clarification, interpretation, etc.). The emphasis in the stage of clarification falls on exploration and understanding rather than on therapeutic intervention or change.

Part of the process of clarification of the introjects depends on their display in the transference. The clarifying process tries to link aspects of both superior and inferior narcissistic introjects, as discovered in the other aspects of the therapeutic work, with the patterns that emerge in the transference, as deriving from a common root. Recognizing and acknowledging these patterns in the ongoing interaction with the therapist can often make a powerful impression on the patient and add conviction and vividness to the basic patterns.

There is more to be done than offering the patient acceptance and empathic understanding of his narcissistic needs. As the respective introjective configurations are progressively clarified and defined, the possibilities for meaningful therapeutic intervention enlarge. At first little can be done with the superior narcissistic configuration, except to allow it to expand and emerge and become more adequately delineated. As this process evolves, however, the therapist can carefully note and identify its defensive aspects. The defense in this context, however, may not be directed against underlying oral aggression and envy, a dynamic that is not uncommon in borderline personalities (Kernberg 1974), but rather may be directed against the components of the opposite narcissistic introjective configuration, that is, against the inferior configuration (Meissner 1984a). The grandiosity and other elements of narcissistic superiority are maintained on the basis of defensive need against feelings of shame, worthlessness, depression, envy, and inferiority. The therapist can listen to the patient's material where it expresses such narcissistically superior elements and learn in what manner and to what extent they contribute to defensive and narcissistic needs.

In my experience the narcissistically inferior components are generally more available for interpretive processing, since this aspect of the patient's narcissism is under less defensive pressure. Therapeutic efforts aim at establishing an accepting, understanding, and empathically attuned bond with this aspect of the patient's personality. Processing of the inferior components leads both to an increased understanding of their connection with defensive attitudes and to increased questioning of the origins and reasons behind these narcissistically impoverished feelings and attitudes. The inquiry progresses to the stage of discovering the origins and derivations of the inferior introjects in the patient's life history and experience. Exploring and coming to understand this aspect of the patient's pathology gradually unveil the opposite components of grandiosity and superiority. Any efforts to intrude on, manipulate, or modify the patient's narcissistically defensive stance will only increase the titer of narcissistic embattlement and undermine any opportunity for strengthening the therapeutic alliance. If the therapist can ally himself with the narcissistically inferior side of the patient and can put himself in understanding, accepting, and empathic contact with the patient's sense of shamefulness, enviousness, worthlessness, inferiority, and so on, the chances for meaningful therapeutic work are considerably enhanced.

Shame, for example, is one of the primary signal affects of the inferior introject. The shame-prone individual is often caught in a dilemma between defensive shamelessness or shameful concealment (Kinston 1983). Such patients often go to great lengths to hide their sense of shamefulness and inadequacy from the therapist. They may retreat to the protective confines of an isolated and self-sufficient grandiose self. The therapeutic task is to help them become aware of their underlying feelings of shame (Morrison 1984).

Shame can be allieviated only by acceptance of the self—acceptance of the self not only by others but also by oneself. The process can begin with acceptance by the therapist of the patient's narcissistically inferior sense of self. The therapist, however, does not lose sight of the fact that the patient's shameful posture rides on an underlying failure on the part of the real self to attain the narcissistically invested demands of the ideal self. The result of this failure is that the patient is left with a subjective sense of defectiveness and inadequacy. In other words, the shame experience is defending against underlying narcissistic and exhibitionistic wishes to be admired and praised. Following the dictates of pathological narcissism, for such patients not to receive the expected and demanded degree of acknowledgment, admiration, and praise is equivalent to their being inadequate and shameful. There is no middle ground, to be ordinary or average or "good enough" is not acceptable.

Exposure of this narcissistically vulnerable and inadequate aspect of the patient is a delicate and painful matter and requires considerable tact and care on the part of the therapist. If such exposure is too rapid or intrusive, the patient may respond with an increase of narcissistic demand and rage. Vulnerability to shame involves an exquisite sensitivity to any narcissistic affront or devaluation. It is only when patients achieve a degree of sufficient trust and openness in the therapeutic interaction that they can begin to reveal the underlying sense of narcissistic vulnerability and deficit that they need to protect so vigilantly. The patient will not be able to resolve his envy of others until he has reached a point at which he is able to accept that what he has is good enough, that he can get along very well with that, and that not having something that others may possess is in no way a deprivation or defeat for him.

Narcissistic Transferences. As the components of the narcissistic configuration become increasingly identifiable, the same elements come to express themselves in the transference and transference neurosis. The degree and pace with which this occurs vary considerably from patient to patient, but as these elements manifest themselves, the therapist begins the task of identifying them with the patient. If the transference is idealizing, qualities of narcissistic perfection and superiority are attributed to the therapist and the aspects of narcissistic inferiority to the self. The therapist must be alert to this self-devaluation and its implications. The idealization is at first best accepted and tolerated without comment or attempt at correction. When to move on to the greater clarification of these introjective configurations is a matter of clinical acumen: the therapist would have to wait until the idealizing transference had been relatively securely established and the excessive threat to the patient's narcissistic vulnerability had sufficiently diminished.

In contrast, mirror transferences represent attempts to preserve the original infantile narcissism by its concentration on a grandiose self. To the extent that all power and perfection belong to the grandiose self, all imperfections, particularly the aspects of the inferior narcissistic configuration, must be projected to the outside. In the respective forms of mirror transference (see Chapter 5), the patient enlists the object in the service of sustaining and supporting the grandiose self. As was the case in dealing with the idealizing transference, the reactivation of the grandiose self in the mirror transference must be accepted and tolerated. The task becomes more onerous for the therapist because the emergence of the grandiose self is inevitably accompanied by devaluation of the object. Not only do the elements of the superior configuration carry with them important communications about the patient's inner world, but they also inevitably carry along bits and pieces of the other side of the narcissistic configuration, against which the patient's grandiosity and superiority are defending.

I emphasize again that efforts to engage with and work directly on aspects of the patient's grandiosity are bound to prove unsuccessful. The better therapeutic tack is to try to gain access to the elements of narcissistic inferiority; to the extent that these can be focused, explored, and understood in the complexity of their origins and motivations, the narcissistic defenses will yield and the supporting substructures of the narcissistic superiority and grandiosity will crumble. The narcissistic configurations are in essence pathological and are connected in a reciprocal, defensive relationship. Whatever side of the narcissistic configuration dominates the clinical picture, it maintains itself by reason of defensive pressures against the opposite side. This understanding governs the strategy of clinical intervention in cases where the narcissistic configurations play a significant role in the patient's psychopathology.

The clarification of the pathogenic introjects, including the gradual delineation of the component elements, identification of the polarized aggressive and narcissistic dimensions, awareness of their reciprocal defensive involvement, and the manner in which they form an integral whole within the subject's experience of himself, as well as progressive differentiation between elements of fantasy and reality, all contribute to the gradual delineation and undermining of the embeddedness and investment in the introjects. This much of the process is rarely sufficient for effective therapeutic intervention but leads to the next step: exploring and establishing their derivation.

Since the introjects are internalized derivatives of object relationships, exploration of their derivation requires clarifying the specific ties to past and/or present objects in the patient's experience. How to accomplish this is a matter of clinical judgment and technique. With some patients exploration of this area of their experience can be done fairly actively, but this is not often the case. More frequently, the exploration must be more indirect and subtle, and requires a considerable degree of self-discipline and patience on the part of the therapist. Little by little, the picture of the patient's past relationships, particularly with parental figures, becomes clearer. The pitfalls are known to any experienced therapist. It often takes a considerable amount of time and work before reliable information about the patient's past experiences becomes available. Early reminiscences or even the first or second rendition of the patient's past experience cannot be taken as having unquestionable validity. The picture the patient paints in the first rough sketching of his past will be progressively filled in, resketched, refined, and recast as the therapy progresses. It is not simply a matter of recapturing a past reality. Rather, what is in question is the recapturing of the patient's experience, which may be overladen and permeated with elements of fantasy, wish, desire, and defense (Spence 1982). The task is to retrace the patient's experience, to establish the links between the present organization and structure of the introjects and the patient's past experience of object relationships. The critical objects in this context are, of course, the parents, though not exclusively. Other important figures may enter in, depending on the peculiarities of the patient's life experience. Siblings may play a vital role, or other relatives such as aunts or uncles, or even nonfamily figures.

Aggressive Transferences. In time the therapist finds that the polarized aspects of the introjects derive from ambivalent relationships to significant objects of the patient's experience. Aspects of the primary polarities organized around the dynamics of aggression and narcissism can usually be related to specific objects in the patient's life. For example, in terms of aggression, the victim-introject derives from the patient's relationship with and attachment to a victimized object. In a sadomasochistic relationship between parents, this "identification with the victim" more frequently takes place with the mother, for both male and female children, but not exclusively. In the interaction between the parents, the father may also play the victim role, or father and mother may alternate victimized and victimizing positions.

The aggressive introject, the "identification with the aggressor," derives from attachment to and dependence on a relatively aggressive object, usually the father. But one may encounter aggressive, hostile, and destructive elements in the mother's character that can contribute to the child's emerging identification with the aggressor. Similarly, the narcissistic elements derive from the narcissistic aspects of the same object relationships. The child may introject the depressive and devalued aspects of the parental object but at the same time internalize parallel elements of narcissistic grandiosity, specialness, and entitlement in the parents' own introjective alignment. Since the introjective accumulation within the patient represents a re-creation of elements derived from these important objects, the introjects come to represent a form of dependent, narcissistically motivated clinging to the infantile past, and can be thus understood as preserving a level of infantile fantasy and attachment to these objects.

The pattern of derivation of the introjective configuration was dramatically demonstrated in a young housewife who came into treatment for her chronic depression and dissatisfaction with life. Behind her feelings of worthlessness and inadequacy as wife and mother and as a human being there emerged the opposite feelings of specialness and entitlement, that she was different from other people, set aside by fate to suffer and to go unrecognized and unrewarded for her extraordinary merits. Important determinants of these feelings were her intense penis envy, directed particularly at a much older brother who had been a brilliant student, concert pianist, and the apple of her mother's eye. Even more influential was the relationship with her mother, a woman who saw herself as mistreated by the fates, who held herself apart as being different from and superior to other human beings, who reveled masochistically in her victimization and suffering, and who jealously reviled the world for its failure to appreciate her and to acknowledge her superiority. The introjective configuration in my patient was a mirror image of her mother's. Mother and daughter had formed a special magical bond, a union of narcissistic glorification through suffering, solidified by the constant expectation that true worth and superiority would have their day. The bond was motivated by the intense and continually frustrated yearning of this young woman for closeness, acknowledgment, and acceptance from a narcissistic mother whose own pathology allowed her to acknowledge little merit in her daughter, let alone in herself.

At times the parallels between the organization of the patient's introjects and the source objects are more obscure. Introjection is, after all, a dynamic process. The product of the introjective internalization is compounded not only of elements derived from the pertinent objects but also of dynamic determinants from the patient's subjective inner world. These elements interact to constitute a realm of internalized object derivatives that remain essentially transitional (Modell 1968, Meissner 1971).

The therapeutic relationship becomes an important ground on which the pattern of relating to significant objects manifests itself. A patient's increasing dependence on and involvement with the therapist give rise to regressive pressures that reactivate infantile projections; these become the basis for infantile distortions of the therapeutic relationship that represent the core elements in the transference neurosis. This same patient in the transference saw me as a powerful and all-knowing wizard who would finally bring about a magical change in her life that would bring her the acknowledgment and admiration she so desperately sought.

Derivation of the Introjects

Exploring the derivation of the introjects has the additional benefit of clarifying that the patient's experience of himself and the world around him—particularly his relationships with other important figures—is dependent on experiences and patterns of responding deriving from his own infantile past. The disparity between that past and his own present experience reinforces insight into the fantasy quality generated from the introjects and clarifies the distinction between elements of that experience and the real world of the patient's present life. In the transference neurosis, of course, this understanding and realization are borne in on the patient with particular force, since it allows him to see clearly and vividly how the patterns of infantile relating play themselves out in inappropriate and unrealistic ways.

The progressive clarification and exploration of the derivation of the introjects lead to the next logical question—namely, what is the patient's motivation for retaining these introjects and clinging to them with such tenacity? Dealing with this level of motivation is a critical juncture in the therapeutic progression and often gives rise to the stiffest and most vigorous resistance. Thus far in the therapeutic process, we have been concerned with clarifying the elements involved in the patient's pathology and trying to understand their organization along a number of important parameters. At this point, we begin to explore the patient's motivation for maintaining the pathogenic self-organization. I emphasize that this represents a different order of motivation from that involved in object-related contexts concerned with the usual kinds of libidinal and aggressive derivatives. The motivation here is subjectively oriented, partly narcissistic, and partly self-preservative.

We now begin to approach not merely what is involved in the patient's pathology but also his reasons for clinging to it. The patient clings to his introjects in a variety of ways and resists any attempts to change or modify them. Why are these introjects so intensely invested and so important to the patient? It must be remembered that the introjects provide the essential core around which the experience of the patient's inner world and sense of himself as an individuated and in some degree coherent entity are organized. A threat to the cohesion of the introjective configuration becomes a threat to the organization of the patient's sense of self.

These pathogenic introjects represent an adherence to the now internalized infantile derivatives of the patient's object experience; in internalized form, they prolong the infantile dependence on and attachment to those objects. Narcissism is an important parameter of this dependence. The introjection preserves a residue of infantile narcissism that expresses itself in the often repressed or split-off feelings of omnipotence, superiority, and specialness; they are the "exceptions" (Freud 1916). Working through this level of the patient's narcissism is crucial for the success of the therapy.

It is a paradox of this infantile involvement with internalized objects that the objects are preserved and sustained at the cost of the subject. The internalization of these pathogenic introjects is a source of quasi-distortion and impairment within the patient's own self-organization and inhibits or distorts his capacity to achieve any real sense of autonomous self-identity. The cost to the depressed young housewife described earlier was considerable in terms of her chronic dissatisfaction, depression, and sense of tormented worthlessness and envy. She was willing to pay this exorbitant price for the sake of a golden fleece— a sense of specialness, superiority, moral hauteur, and entitlement. The idealized and aggrandized image of her mother was preserved at the cost of considerable neurotic impairment and unhappiness.

But these dynamics also operate to preserve objects in the patient's external world. For example, one frequently finds in the family involvements of borderline patients hidden loyalties and attachments that operate to reinforce and sustain the patient's introjective alignment; at the same time they have the effect of protecting certain dependent relationships within the family and the individuals involved in them. Often in this context, family myths arise that represent forms of adherence to a family projective system, usually organized in such a way as to preserve the introjective alignment of all the family members and to maintain a delicate balance in the narcissistic equilibrium (Meissner

1978a). The introjective alignment within the patient actually serves as a vehicle for the preservation of elements of threatened parental narcissism. This same young woman's adherence to the narcissistically embedded code of specialness and superiority through suffering was calculated to reinforce and sustain the mother's highly vulnerable and fragile narcissism.

Another example of this sort of family involvement was evident in a young man[2] who had experienced considerable success in his life and had gained a high degree of professional standing. His torment was his sexuality; despite anguished struggle to suppress and deny his sexual urges, he would occasionally visit topless bars and massage parlors, and on rare occasions even flirt with prostitutes. These adventures were accompanied by severe anxiety and followed by profound guilt and remorse. His self-punishment took the form of a delusional conviction that he had contracted some venereal disease and that this would destroy his career and marital life. The most severe of these episodes was a conviction that he had contracted AIDS from a prostitute who had sucked his penis. This delusion persisted for several years and staunchly resisted any efforts at dissuasion.

Underlying this clinical picture were significant issues concerning his family involvement. He was the only child of ne'er-do-well parents who lived at a near-poverty level, largely because of the father's alcoholism. Despite his academic successes the patient had it drummed into him by his chronically depressed and highly masochistic mother that he was basically no good, that he would never amount to anything, and that no one from their family could expect to get anywhere in life. Reacting to her husband's unavailability and to the chronic atmosphere of conflict and antagonism, she tightened the emotional ties to her son, letting him sleep in her bed until he was a teenager while her husband slept elsewhere, making him her dependent love object, guarding against any interest he might have in girls, preventing him from dating and going to dances, constantly warning him about sex and its dangers, making him feel that any interest outside the family was an abandonment of her. The patient's way of dealing with this situation was to conform to his mother's expectations, trying to be a perfect, sexless, impeccably good boy. His relationships to girls were always circumspect, never intimate or sexual. In his adult life he was Mr. Clean, but always guilty because of his success and his sexuality—both violations

---

[2]Tom's case is discussed in Chapter 22.

of his mother's expectations. His delusional self-punishment served the purpose of paying the price for his violation of the family code. What better punishment for violating his mother's demands and turning his back on her through sex than to suffer a painful, disgraceful disease that was sure to end in death?

The work of articulating the introjective configurations involves focusing the intrinsic relatedness and unity of the introjective polarities, understanding that they derive from each other and are locked together in mutual and reciprocal defensive interaction. The patient is faced with a radical choice: either accept both sides of the polarity or surrender both. He cannot have one without the other. He also cannot surrender one without surrendering the other. In addition, the work of articulation brings into increasing focus the fantasy aspect of the introjects and their disparity from the elements of the real world of the patient's experience of himself and his environment.

Surrendering the Introjects

These progressive insights lead inevitably to the issue of surrendering the introjects. This requires confrontation and working through the infantile dependence and the narcissistic investment in the introjects. Not infrequently, as the narcissistic defenses are undermined in borderline patients, intense rage and envy are stimulated. This rage and envy often emerge in the relationship to the therapist and become significant aspects of the therapeutic work. They are manifestations of the narcissistic dynamics that divide the world into haves and have-nots and the distribution of goods in either/or, all-or-nothing terms. The patient's envy of the therapist and what he has—whether worldly goods, social position, intelligence, psychic health, or even a penis—must be worked through in terms of the underlying narcissistic dynamics. This working-through sets in motion a process of mourning in which the attachment to the infantile objects is gradually given up and the loss of those objects is accepted and integrated. As the mourning process continues and the potency and influence of the introjects diminish, one begins to experience with such patients a gradual and increasing emergence of autonomous ego capacities.

Mourning the Transference Object

As the patient's infantile dependence on past objects begins to be modified and gradually to wane, the therapeutic dependence may begin to wax in important and problematic ways. Instead of surrendering and resigning infantile attachments, the patient seeks to replace them with a dependent attachment to the therapist. The motivational basis for this attachment needs to be explored, clarified, and focused in the same terms as the patient's explicit and recognizable narcissistic and self-preservative needs. Dependence on the therapeutic situation and on the therapist requires resolution on its own terms, quite independently of the working-through of infantile attachments to past significant object relationships. In many borderline patients, the therapeutic dependence tends to reinforce the inferior, weak, vulnerable, and victimized aspect of the organization of the introjects—the victim-introject. Keeping in mind the patterns of introjective organization, the therapist must remind himself that the more powerful, superior, special, and entitled dimension of the introjective economy remains latent. These residual elements of the introjective dynamics will express themselves in terms of the patient's feelings of inadequacy, difficulty in dealing with periods of interruption of the therapy or absence of the therapist, fears of abandonment, apprehensions over the apparent therapeutic progression, the looming possibility of termination of therapy and thus of doing without the therapist, and so forth. All of these issues are particularly intense and difficult in borderline patients and must be worked through in terms of the therapeutic relationship and seen specifically in the resolution of the residual aspects of the patient's introjective dynamics—particularly the narcissistic dynamics.

As the pressure of these dependency needs increases in relation to the therapist, there may be a defensive shift toward a denial of such dependence and a retreat to a position of artifactual autonomy and self-sufficiency. This may take the form of a return to a narcissistic self-sufficiency, which defends against the pressure of dependency needs by feelings of not needing the therapist or even belittling or devaluing the therapist and the therapy. This may lead in the direction of the activation of the more powerful, superior, and even grandiose aspects of the introjective economy—leaving the more inferior, inadequate, and needy dimensions of the victim-introject more or less out of the picture.

Underlying this pressure toward narcissistic withdrawal and self-sufficiency or pseudoautonomy there may be residual defenses against the patient's sense of narcissistic affront and feelings of rage and envy toward the therapist. This may be accompanied again by the patient's anxiety and guilt over such rageful and envious feelings, along with a longing for love and caring and acceptance on the part of the therapist. It is not difficult to see that these motivations are restimulations of infantile concerns and serve as important defensive maneuvers against the working through of immature attachments and dependencies.

When the patient's infantile dependence on the therapist has become sufficiently intense, it requires working through and surrender. The mourning process involved in the surrendering of infantile attachments to past significant object relationships now extends to the therapeutic relationship and begins the process of giving up the attachment to the therapist. The patient must be helped to work through a variety of regressive infantile pressures that keep him in a position of dependency and satisfy underlying narcissistic needs. As these elements are gradually dealt with, the therapeutic relationship becomes more autonomous and develops an increasing area for the exercise and expression of the patient's sense of initiative and industry. Finally, there is the clearer and more decisive emergence of the patient's own sense of identity (Meissner 1981b).

The resolution of the transference dependency deals specifically with the loss of the transference object. As this mourning takes place, the therapist is gradually surrendered along with the patient's sense of reliance and dependence on him. The therapeutic relationship, particularly in regard to its transference elements, is gradually replaced with a more real relationship based on the mature and autonomous aspects of the patient's developing personality. Thus, the mourning of the transference object is effected by the gradual enlargement of the therapeutic alliance, which takes place through the increasing absorption, reworking, and reintegrating of the infantile aspects of the therapeutic relationship, most acutely and intensely the elements of the transference neurosis, into the therapeutic alliance.

The working through of the mourning process, the loss of the transference object, and the resolution of the transference elements set the stage for the final phase of the therapeutic process, the termination. As the infantile underpinnings and motivations for the organization of the introjects are gradually eroded, the potentiality for the introjection of aspects of the therapist and elements of the therapeutic alliance becomes available, offering the possibility of a more reasonable, realistic, and adaptive organization of the patient's functioning sense of self, as pathogenic introjections are replaced by therapeutic internalizations. These emerging introjections, derived from the therapeutic relationship and influenced particularly by aspects of the therapeutic alliance, are less susceptible to regressive drive influences and drive distortions. They are correspondingly less involved in defensive needs for projection and sustaining of the patient's sense of narcissistic investment. Increasingly, the patient's capacity for modeling himself on the more realistic and adaptive aspects of the therapist opens the way for emerging identifications, which enhance the autonomy and structural capacity to resist drive derivatives in the patient's ego (Meissner 1981b). The termination work continues and enhances the critical internalizations that form the basis of inner structural changes, specifically changes in the ego and superego, which serve as the basis for longer-lasting and adaptive therapeutic change. There is a shift from defensive to adaptive concerns, a refocusing of the patient's interest and investment from the past to the present and future, and, in general, an unleashing of developmental potential for increasing personality growth.

9

CONFRONTATION

ROLE IN THERAPY

Confrontation as a therapeutic technique has a more prominent place in the treatment of borderline patients than in the treatment of almost any other category of psychopathology. Along with clarification, it is the primary channel for dealing with manifest content in the patient's ongoing behavior. Confrontation is part of the therapy in some degree with all patients, but in borderlines, particularly in regressed patients or in regressive crises, confrontation is often essential.

It also involves inherent risks—mainly, as we shall see, in its potential for becoming a vehicle for countertransference. Therapeutic confrontation must not become a vehicle of irritation, frustration, or sadism but must be offered from a therapeutic perspective and with the therapeutic gain of the patient as an objective. Confrontation is never far from slipping over into a more controlling, determining, advising, or authoritative stance, which easily yields to the influence of countertransference reactions and transference/countertransference interactions. As a cautionary note, therefore, it is important to keep in mind that confrontation always serves a subsidiary function to the overriding focus on exploring, uncovering, and understanding the patient's dynamics and underlying motivations (Chessick 1979, 1983a).

Confrontation carries with it the connotations of activity, energy, forcefulness, challenge, and the overcoming of opposition, all of which reflect in some degree the aggressive derivation of confrontation and its deviation from the more neutral therapeutic techniques. In the ordinary run of therapy, confrontation is employed as a means of overcoming resistances, of promoting further therapeutic progress, and of leading to interpretation of the patient's defenses and their underlying motivations. In the treatment of character disorders, the confrontations with the patient's patterns of characterologic behavior are frequently a necessary step in arriving at the underlying conflicts and their unconscious motivation.

MEANING

Buie and Adler (1973) define confrontation as "a technique designed to gain a patient's attention to inner experiences or perceptions of outer reality of which he is conscious or is about to be made conscious" (p. 127). Its purpose is specifically to overcome the patient's resistance to acknowledging or recognizing a particular content or connection and is not meant to force any change in the patient's conduct, attitudes, or decisions.

The distinction from clarification is often difficult since they are almost always used in conjunction. While clarification has the function of making clear or of bringing about recognition, it does so in a more neutral and dispassionate fashion; confrontation adds the note of activity on the part of the therapist—emphasis, even forcefulness. The confrontative element is often carried in subtle ways by the therapist's tone of voice, unusual use of language, humor, the element of surprise, affective tone, and so on. The therapist can even convey emphasis by way of facial expressions: raising an eyebrow, assuming a quizzical or doubtful look, shaking his head. Even a shrug can convey to a patient a sufficient connotation to make an effective confrontation. Confrontations are not always or necessarily forceful; they may be subtle, gentle, inviting as well.

It is generally agreed that the therapist must exercise caution in the expression of his own feelings since they can readily become the vehicle for countertransference influences and will inevitably have a powerful effect on the patient. Any feelings must be expressed only in terms that are beneficial to the patient and with thoughtful consideration of the countertransference implications. Confrontation is primarily a device for directing the patient's attention in a more effective manner to some aspect of his mental content or behaviors or to aspects of his interpersonal or environmental involvements that otherwise would remain hidden or repressed. Confrontation is useful insofar as it leads toward interpretation or makes the material for interpretation more available (Corwin 1973). Confrontation can be regarded therefore as a routine part of psychoanalytic or psychotherapeutic technique and as necessary for the analysis of resistance (Greenson 1967).

Confrontation versus Interpretation

A number of attempts have been made to distinguish confrontation from interpretation. From one point of view, interpretation involves sharing a hypothesis with the patient along with an invitation to engage in its exploration; confrontation, however, involves presenting a more unilateral view of what the therapist regards as reality (Stocking 1973). Confrontation can also be regarded as a starting point for bringing to light new problems, associations, or understandings, which become the object for further exploration, while interpretation implies more of a closure or resolving of some connection or understanding that had been hitherto obscure or in doubt (Devereux 1951). Thus, interpretation has the purpose of resolving internal conflicts by bringing unconscious elements to the surface and drawing them within the patient's awareness, while confrontation is designed more to create conflict where there had previously been none.

Even more subtle differences may come into play. As Boris (1973) observes, there is a difference between accusing the patient of wasting time and observing that the patient is still reacting as if his work with the therapist were doomed to be unproductive. The former renders a judgment, the latter a translation. I am not sure that the latter statement is not more in the order of clarification than interpretation, but it is certainly interpretation. The difference has to do with the presence of the therapist in the intervention. The patient's assent to the first intervention necessarily involves accepting both the fact and the role of the therapist, while assent to the latter requires only acceptance of the fact. In a sense, then, confrontation involves a certain intrusiveness by the therapist, however gentle, which calls for or creates a pressure toward internalization of the therapist by the patient. The interaction is not simply the product of the patient's projective imagination but involves real activity on the part of the therapist.

Heroic Confrontations

Confrontations are not always of the benign or conflictual sort; they may also be dramatic or heroic in quality (Corwin 1973). Corwin defines a heroic confrontation as "an emotionally charged, parametric, manipulative, technical tool demanded by the development of an actual or potential situation of impasse and designed ultimately to remobilize a workable therapeutic alliance" (p. 73). Examples include Alexander's (1950) telling a patient that it was no wonder that no one liked him if he behaved in such an unpleasant manner whenever anyone tried to help him, or Murray's (1973) confrontation of a somewhat paranoid patient by telling him that his premises were wrong, that he could become paranoid if he wanted to, but that he could also accept the analyst and either they could choose to work together or the patient could continue with his paranoid attitudes and run the risk of further sickness and hospitalization. Or similarly, Greenson's (1967) confrontation of an analysand who was in a prolonged resistance and therapeutic misalliance that Greenson found necessary to interrupt by telling him that he was getting nowhere in the analysis and that he ought to consider some other alternatives besides continuing. Only the threat of the loss of the transference object was able to shake the patient's resistance to the development of the transference neurosis and lead to further analytic progress. Such confrontations have as their purpose the reconstitution of a disrupted or distorted therapeutic alliance.

Heroic confrontations are called for when the therapy has reached an impasse, when the therapeutic alliance is in danger of disruption or has reached a point of such chronic distortion that the therapeutic misalliance has frustrated and subverted the work of the therapy. The success of such heroic confrontations depends in large measure on the capacity of both patient and therapist to regain the ground of some workable therapeutic alliance without which therapy is doomed to disruption, stalemate, and failure. An additional note is that confrontation is usually oriented toward reestablishing the patient's sense either of the reality of the therapist and the therapeutic situation or of some other external reality in the life situation.

REALITY TESTING

Because of the marked propensity in borderline patients for projective distortion of the transference relationship and for the setting up of therapeutic misalliances, the work of tactful clarification and confrontation with the reality of the therapeutic situation is often a central and persistent aspect of the therapeutic work with borderline patients (Chessick 1979, 1983a). As Shapiro (1973) observes,

> In general, these are patients who do not have a stabilized sense of self based on introjections, incorporations, and identifications formed out of solid experience with real, responsive, caring, and important people in their developmental past. For these patients, real characteristics of the therapist may be critical elements in the restructuring of the internal objects necessary for adequate ego functioning; and the confrontation of these characteristics in the therapist-patient interaction may be a major aspect of the treatment process. [p. 209]

In therapy with borderline patients, the use of confrontation implies a shift to a more active, involved, and real interaction with the patient. It implies a more supportive orientation, even within the context of a longer-term exploratory effort. Particularly in a regressive crisis or a more chronic regressive stance, when the patient's capacity for therapeutic alliance is tenuous or when the alliance is disrupted or severely distorted and failures of reality testing become apparent, confrontation may be essential to preserve and continue the therapeutic work. As Adler (1982) comments, "Because of these difficulties, such patients are described as requiring a therapist who is active, 'real,' and willing to place himself in a position to intervene when necessary, give advice when appropriate, and confront and set limits in order to prevent dangerous acting-out or serious regression" (p. 4).

COUNTERTRANSFERENCE CONTAMINATION

While at points of regressive crisis confrontation may be essential, it is also at such points in the therapeutic course that patients are most vulnerable to the misuse of confrontation and the contamination by countertransference. In their discussion of this issue, Adler and Buie (1972) emphasize the tenuousness of the therapeutic alliance and the need to utilize confrontation cautiously with an eye to building the patient's trust in the therapist's good judgment and constructive intentions. They list certain restrictions as an aid to this objective:

1. *Assess the reality stress in the patient's current life situation:* When it is external, particularly when it has the effect of creating a regressive reaction in the patient, it is not helpful to increase the level of stress within the therapy. The therapist's empathy and thoughtful evaluation must serve as a guide to the advisability of confrontation and the need for support at any given point.

2. *Avoid breaking down needed defenses:* Here again the titration of activity versus passivity, support versus challenge, calls for a balancing act that is at times delicate. In regressive states, borderlines may need to maintain even primitive levels of defense and it would be therapeutically inadvisable to confront such defenses when there is danger of precipitating a more severe regression. However, there are also times when confrontation is required to pull a patient out of a regressive slump and to reconstitute the therapeutic alliance and get the therapy back on course.

3. *Avoid overstimulating the patient's wish for closeness:* Greater levels of activity and attempts to be supportive can have a secondary effect of creating a closer and more personal contact between therapist and patient. This can be both overstimulating and seductive and, while it runs the risk of precipitating further defensive retreat or regression, can also have the long-term effect of creating expectations that will make the continued effectiveness of the therapeutic effort more precarious. The patient may have to take flight in defensive rage or acting-out because of the intensity of the precipitated feelings. This can plunge the patient into intense fear of abandonment, loneliness, and fear of his own raging destructive impulses and destructiveness.

4. *Avoid overstimulating the patient's rage:* Confrontation, particularly when it is connected with limit setting, may serve to reestablish the boundaries between patient and therapist and cause the patient to feel deprived and frustrated. The rage brings with it fears of abandonment and annihilation, which only increase the regressive risks.

5. *Avoid confrontation of narcissistic entitlement:* Buie and Adler (1972, 1973) and Adler and Buie (1972) distinguish between this and the more profound and regressive entitlement to survive. Confrontation of the patient's entitlement, while it may have the intention of calling attention to the patient's narcissistic entitlement, easily misses the mark and serves only to threaten the patient on the level of his entitlement to

survive. Certainly, periods of regression are hardly the time to challenge the patient's narcissism at whatever level. The patient's narcissism is better dealt with only at points at which the therapeutic alliance is more stable and positive, and then preferably through gradual and progressive techniques of clarification and interpretation. Confrontations of the patient's narcissism are at best risky, even when the conditions are optimal. There is always risk in such confrontations of precipitating a regressive crisis.

The confrontation that is offered from a position of consistent caring and respect for the patient's autonomy, and that is generated from a basic concern for maintenance and reinforcement of the therapeutic alliance, can have a powerful therapeutic effect (Adler 1975). It must be remembered, however, that confrontation is a vehicle leading in the direction of further therapeutic work and understanding. Confrontation for confrontation's sake inevitably runs the risk of countertransference contamination. As Myerson (1974) cogently notes, it is more valuable to try to understand where the patients are, and why they are where they are, than to confront them where they are not. Consequently, confrontations that lead in the direction of further exploring the basis for resistances or of examining the roots of transference distortions are therapeutically helpful. Where they do not do this, they run the risk of simply reinforcing the transference/countertransference dynamics and may lead in the direction of further patient compliance and counterproductive submissiveness.

REGRESSION

The risks of regression are obviously more at issue in patients in the lower-order borderline spectrum and are correspondingly less of a problem in higher-order patients. In higher-order patients the same issues are alive, but the patient's capacity to enter and maintain an effective therapeutic alliance serves as a buffer both to the underlying regressive potential and to the patient's vulnerability to countertransference influences. Nonetheless, the rules of thumb for utilizing confrontation are relevant even for these patients and are more reflective of general norms of tact and consideration in dealing with any patients than they are specific to the borderline syndrome. An example of the potential differences between the usage of confrontation in lower-order as opposed to higher-order patients may be seen in the criticisms of

Kernberg's technique by the Kris Study Group (Abend et al. 1983). Kernberg recommends the confrontation of contradictory images generated by the patient within the transference from a position of technical neutrality. Effective confrontation in his view leads to a diminishing of the regression and an increased tolerance of ambivalence on the part of the patient. Kernberg makes this a touchstone of his diagnostic method since such confrontation would lead to further regression in psychotic patients in contrast to borderlines. The Kris Group argues to the contrary that such an effect is not confirmed in their experience with borderline patients, that such a specialized technique is not required for optimal treatment of borderline patients, that there is little value in confronting the split, and that it only distracts from dealing with underlying unconscious fantasies that contribute to the more superficial contradictory self- and object-images (Abend et al. 1983).

Confrontation may be also called for in contexts of regression, particularly when some dangerous or self-defeating consequence is involved in the regressive episode (Buie and Adler 1973, Adler 1982). A young man, who presented with a variety of hysterical and phobic anxieties and who probably could be regarded as a primitive hysteric, began his analysis with a fair amount of precipitant anxiety. In short order, he was seized with panic caused by fear that the analyst would attack him from behind and stab him in the chest. This of course created an immediate threat that the analysis would be prematurely and disruptively terminated. Without having the least idea of what was involved in the patient's panic, the analyst took a fairly strong position and pointed out that the patient was experiencing terror for reasons that neither he nor the patient was yet aware of and that, if the patient allowed his fears to dominate, they were in danger of disrupting the analysis. He insisted that the patient control his fear to avoid self-defeating acting out and that he and the patient try to work together to understand what was happening. The patient quieted down, at least to the degree that he was able to remain on the analytic couch, and the ensuing exploration revealed that the patient's panic was highly over-determined. From one side, the fear of being stabbed in the chest derived from an early experience of a heart operation for a congenital defect that took place at the height of his oedipal years and reflected his infantile idealization and terror of the powerful and magical figure of the doctor-surgeon-analyst. From a second side the fear derived from the fact that the analyst's office had previously been used by the patient's uncle, who was also a psychiatrist and had been quite influential in bringing the patient to analysis. This uncle was only a few years the patient's senior and the patient had experienced a number of hostile and somewhat sadistic encounters with him in his growing-up years.

There are a number of regressive contexts in which confrontation plays an essential role, including malignant regressions and the emergence of suicidal impulses. I will defer discussion of these problems to the section on regression (see Chapter 11).

BORDERLINE SPECTRUM

One way of understanding these differences is to remember that the Kris Group is looking more specifically at analyzable borderline patients, who would presumably fall within the higher-order range of the borderline spectrum; Kernberg's patients, in contrast, tend to be of a more primitive order, presumably from the lower order of the spectrum. Confrontations with higher-order patients would be much more within the range of clarifications and routine confrontations and would yield a much greater capacity for preserving a therapeutic alliance or, in less frequent and less severe regressive states, for more readily reconstituting it. In the lower-order patients, however, the disruptions are more precipitous, more severe; they may easily reach psychotic proportions and call for urgent if not heroic efforts to reconstitute some semblance of a working alliance, including confrontations.

Nonetheless, confrontation and clarification may have important roles to play, especially early in the course of the therapy. Interpretation is not possible or useful until the patient has developed some degree of a working alliance. As long as the therapist's interpretations are caught up in the vicissitudes of the patient's projective distortions and negative transference reactions, they will be heard as either threatening or destructive or, if they reflect a more idealized transference situation, as unempathic reinforcements of the patient's views (Feinsilver 1983). Consequently, a relative focus on the patient's daily life experience and a process of gentle and gradual confrontation and clarification not only can lead to the establishing of a better alliance but also can gradually clarify and delineate the pathological patterns of interaction that the patient generates both within the therapeutic interaction with the therapist and with important objects outside of the therapy (Chessick 1979, 1983a). Success with many borderline patients is a function of the accuracy, empathy, and timeliness of the therapist's gentle and understanding clarifications and confrontations, which lay the basis for later interpretations and, to a degree, induce transference (Boyer 1983). Gentle confrontation and clarification of the patient's feelings about the therapist can open the way to clarification of therapeutic alliance issues and further catalyze transference reactions.

THERAPEUTIC ALLIANCE

We have touched on the relationship between confrontation and the therapeutic alliance. Confrontation can be brought into play in the service both of building a therapeutic alliance and of salvaging a disrupted alliance or a more persistent misalliance (Adler and Myerson 1973b). At times, when the therapeutic alliance is intact and operating meaningfully, confrontation has little if any place. When the alliance is failing or has been disrupted, however, confrontation may be essential (Stocking 1973). The degree to which the alliance is effective also contributes to the level of meaningful empathy, which guides the therapist's decision further to confront or not, and also sets the stage for the patient's receptivity and responsiveness to the confronting initiative (Myerson 1974). In a sense, then, confrontation is a technique that operates in the absence of a therapeutic alliance and therefore bypasses the patient's conscious ego to address more repressed and unconscious aspects of behavior. In a sense, the patient's defenses are bypassed in order to get at those anxieties that underlie resistance to the full flowering of the transference or other repressed or conflictual material (Boris 1973).

Specific contexts in which confrontation is often required in work with borderline patients focus on issues of denial, regression, lying, and, more generally, narcissism. Denial, like other defensive mechanisms, can operate at all levels of intensity but can function at a relatively massive level, even to the point where the patient becomes unaware of any inner feelings or impulses. When such denial affects the assessment of potentially threatening or dangerous consequences of a course of action (Adler 1982), or has become sufficiently embedded so that therapeutic progress is stalemated (Buie and Adler 1972), confrontation may be the only resource in the therapist's armamentarium for breaking through the patient's denial. The element of unmasking denial is inherent in all forms of true confrontation, not, as Weisman (1972) cautions, as a relentless attack against the patient's vulnerability but as a process whose target, in whatever fashion confrontation is implemented, whether verbally or nonverbally, directly or indirectly, is nonetheless a point of protected vulnerability.

DENIAL

The confrontation of denial may be spread over a considerable period of time. One young man,[1] who would fit the description of a false-self organization, experienced occasional episodes of total immobilization, as if he were in a trance-like state in which he had great difficulty following what was happening in his immediate environment and was unable to respond or react in any comfortable manner. Gentle questioning on my part, a subtle insistence that his experience must be connected with a mental process that reflected something significant in his life experience, gradually began to shift the ground and enabled him to slowly come in contact with the underlying affect. Sometimes days after the event he would begin to experience a feeling of anger or irritation, or on rare occasions he would be suddenly overwhelmed with a burst of intense rage which he was completely at a loss to connect with any stimulus or context in the immediate situation.

The rage that underlay these experiences was nearly psychotic in proportion and terrified him, presumably because of a psychotic breakdown that he had experienced over a decade before, in which the intensity of his rage had welled up with overwhelming and traumatic effect. Gradually, the patient began to experience rage attacks that he found overwhelming at the time of their occurrence; but in therapy he was able to reflect and explore on what he had been experiencing and gradually to connect his intense feelings with the traumatic experiences of his difficult relationship with his parents and with his own developmental experiences. When it became clear to me that rage was at the root of his disturbing experiences and that the level of his protective denial prevented any easy access to these feelings, I continued to use a confrontational approach. Whenever any of these episodes came into focus, I was not slow to suggest that what underlay the patient's experience was his anger and rage and that our therapeutic task was to find out what his anger was about. The effort I am describing took place over a period of years of intensive psychotherapy. Thus confron-

---

[1]Steven S. is discussed in Chapter 22.

tation is not always limited to a specific here-and-now intervention but may involve a process that extends over continual periods of time.

ANTISOCIAL BEHAVIOR

A problem that arises especially when antisocial behavior is part of the pathological picture is the need to confront the patient's antisocial acting out and attitudes. As Kernberg (1984) points out, any confrontation of the patient's lying or other antisocial behavior will more than likely be experienced by the patient as a sadistic attack. Even though the risk is that the patient will accuse the therapist of being judgmental or moralistic, the opposite risk is that the therapist's empathic understanding and tolerance of such behavior may be misinterpreted as collusion or even approval. Such a stance may reduce the intensity of negative or paranoid transference and minimize the risk of regression, but it also fosters a corruption of the therapeutic alliance that can only lead to further stalemate and frustration of therapeutic aims. The therapist is required to preserve an ethical and professional position as part of his own professional and personal identity. When his value system and the patient's enacted or professed values come into opposition, the question of the role of the therapist's values and their implementation in the therapeutic context is raised.

Some years ago I was treating a young student[2] in his mid-twenties who would qualify as a dysphoric personality. His life was dedicated to an unremitting guerrilla warfare with his harsh, punitive, and judgmental father. The struggle took the form of an intense and inexorable challenging of all authority figures that was carried out in a continual exercise of compliance and defiance. The result was that this young man generated struggles, arguments, and confrontations with almost everyone and lived in a hate-ridden schizoid world largely of his own construction.

On one occasion he had made an arrangement with a fellow student for a casual social outing. When the fellow student failed to show up, he became enraged, went out to the school parking lot, located the other student's car, and smashed in all of the car windows with a brick. When the patient related this activity to me, I confess I was

---

[2]George G. is discussed in Chapter 19.

taken aback. Such behavior was hardly congruent with my own system of values. I responded by commenting that what he had told me seemed to be a rather unusual piece of behavior, and I wondered whether we might be able to step back from it and examine it. I asked what the patient had been experiencing that might have led him to this behavior.

After a while, the patient asked whether I wasn't shocked by his behavior. I said that I found it a little disturbing, but I wondered whether that was the reaction he had been expecting. Did he want me to respond by being shocked and offended? He agreed that he indeed had wanted me to react in this way. This admission opened the way to a discussion of the provocative nature of this behavior and the implications of his telling me about it from the point of view of the father-transference reaction. In this acting-out behavior that he was convinced I would disapprove of and be shocked at, he was replaying a scenario that he had enacted in countless episodes with his own father.

My effort, as I look back on this experience, was not so much to suspend my own values, my own judgments as to what constitutes right or proper behavior, but rather to put them in the background and to respond to my patient in terms of the predominant values inherent in the therapeutic situation. My option was to shift the focus of the inquiry away from issues of my disapproval toward the underlying issue behind the behavior. In addition to bringing to light the transference material, there was an effort to direct the patient's attention to an exploration of the implications, the consequences, and the underlying assumptions of his behavior. In this case, the destructive acting-out was an expression of his own feelings of impotence, lack of worth, and frustrated rage. By implication, the only resource he could muster in the face of disappointment and rage was to act out in an infantile and destructive manner and thus reinforce his own image of himself as worthless and impotent.

NARCISSISM

Another difficult area in which confrontation can play a significant role is dealing with the patient's narcissism. One context occurs when patient and analyst are caught up in an alliance based on the patient's narcissistic expectations, gratifications, and fantasies, which impedes progress toward a more meaningful and effective therapeutic alliance (Corwin 1973). Gentle confrontation with the patient's narcissistic expectations and fantasies within the limits of his narcissistic vulnerability is a possible vehicle for addressing the distortions in the alliance and helping the patient to gain a better foothold for the therapeutic work. As previously noted, the decision whether to confront or not rests in part on an assessment of the degree to which the patient is utilizing the narcissistic alliance for defensive or resistive purposes, and in part on the extent to which the narcissistic alliance may be the best the patient can do at that point and must be tolerated as necessary for maintaining any therapeutic relationship whatever (see the previous discussion of narcissistic alliance). In the latter instance, confrontation may not be the best tactic but might better wait until some degree of therapeutic alliance has evolved or until enough components of the narcissistic transference are available for interpretation.

Dealing with other aspects of the patient's narcissism is largely a matter of engaging with the patient's entitlements and ultimately working through the underlying components of shame and inferiority. I have been at pains to underline these dynamics and their structural components in terms of the superior and inferior introjective configurations (Meissner 1984a; see Chapter 8). Keeping in mind the distinction between narcissistic entitlement and the entitlement to survive drawn by Buie and Adler (1973), we know it is nonetheless at times essential to confront the patient's entitlements. When these are expressed in the form of provocative behavior, it is useful to point out the patient's entitled attitudes and even to focus on their impact on the therapist. The patient may be outraged at this challenge to his self-proclaimed "rights," but such confrontation may be the only path toward further exploration and understanding. The patient may respond by foregoing his provocative behavior and adopting a more compliant facade out of fear of abandonment and loss of the therapist, but confronting these maneuvers can also lead to further exploration and analysis. Whether such confrontations are made with essentially neutral affect or with a tinge of irritation is a matter of clinical judgment. If the therapist's anger is not completely suppressed, it may bear fruit in letting the patient know that his infantile entitlement can evoke hostility from the important others in his life (Levin 1973).

While excessive entitlements are a reflection of the superior introject, the inferior introject may also play out its brand of entitlement in a form of restricted entitlement (Levin 1970) in which the patient plays out his inferiority, fails to stand up for himself, or allows others to take advantage of him. This behavior also requires confrontation, but this can run the risk of inflicting a narcissistic injury in that it calls attention to the patient's inadequacy and failings. This too, however, can open the way to further exploration and meaningful resolution of the under-lying fears and impediments. The art of confronting a patient's narcis-sism lies in dosing and timing. Confrontations tend to inflict narcissistic injuries on patients, and the therapist must keep in mind that these toxic effects must be administered in tolerable doses, so that untoward side effects are not created. The process is a form of gradual desensitiza-tion, which slowly increases the titration of confrontation and its imme-diacy and directness within the limits of the patient's tolerance and the mitigation of his narcissistic vulnerability (Levin 1973).

As I have argued elsewhere (Meissner 1986b), the therapeutic task in the treatment of narcissism lies in making contact with, articulating, and gradually analyzing the inferior side of the patient's narcissism, particularly the sense of inferiority and shame that pervades the inner world of all narcissistic patients (Morrison 1984), whether the inferior aspect of the patient's narcissistic introjects is relatively conscious or not. In borderline patients, the underlying sense of shame often gives rise to projections that take the form of expecting humiliation or criticism, experiencing the benign reaction of others as humiliation or criticism, and suffering other forms of ridicule, scorn, contempt, and rejection, even from the therapist. Analysis of these components of the patient's inner world cannot proceed unless these elements have been drawn into conscious awareness in some degree (Morrison 1984). Con-frontation can often accomplish this objective. Only when the patient is aware of this dimension of his inner life is it possible to seek further for explanation and understanding.

At times the patient's need to protect this inner shameful self can give rise to forms of secondary shame (Levin 1967, 1973), which may result in defensive blocking and intense shame over inadequacy felt on account of this. The therapist can offer some relief by confronting the patient's excessive shame and the projections or expectations of criticism from the therapist. In each of these instances, the goal of the confrontation is to bring into focus aspects of the patient's inner world or of his interaction with the therapist that impinge on the effectiveness of the therapeutic alliance and create a persistent misal-liance, and/or reflect underlying transference dynamics that require further investigation. In all confrontations the aspect of directing the therapeutic effort toward further exploration and understanding is an essential component, and to the degree that it can be effectively im-plemented in the confrontation itself can serve both as a reflection of and as a contribution to the maintenance of a meaningful therapeutic alliance.

GUIDELINES

I can do no better in summarizing this discussion of confrontation than
to recommend the guidelines offered by Weisman (1972) for the use of
confrontation:

- Confrontation draws upon empathy, but empathy does not mean
  that we share an identity or an ideology.

- Countertransference distortions are likely when we find ourselves
  angry, disappointed, exasperated, gratified, especially frustrated,
  jealous, or in some other way imposing our individual imperatives
  upon the confrontations.

- Confrontations can be contaminated by fantasies of being the
  magic healer, rescuer, shaman, sage, or parent, because this may
  not be the level of need and communication on which the other
  person is operating.

- Confrontation consists of mutually self-corrective activities. It
  is not intended to be a directive or a prohibition. We seek fore-
  bearance, not compliance, firmness, not coercion. We cannot
  offer options, we can only help someone to use the options he
  has.

- Efforts to understand too much are suspicious indications of countertransference ambition. We cannot respond to every demand
  and confront along a vast panorama. Denial cannot be eliminated
  completely, because strategic denial may be a requirement of living
  itself.

- A tendency to overemphasize technique or, conversely, to discourage thoughtful reflection as "cerebral" are signs of countertransference distortions of the field.

- Trust means only that we have a common field of acceptance.
  Although it is feasible to have a mutual alliance at the outset, trust
  is always conditional. The term *trust* is often a shibboleth in
  psychotherapy, but it can become a euphemism that conceals an
  impasse.
- Words are not magic, nor must confrontations be followed by
  signs of conspicuous change. Confrontations are only special vehicles of communication that seek an opening at a point of contact
  with protected vulnerability.

- On the whole, confrontations are only statements about the other person's existence, not hypotheses about his status as a scientific object. We respond to his separate reality and cannot, therefore, be too punctilious about the longitudinal truth of what we say.

- We can generalize; we can be precise. But it is essential that we also be contemporaneous (pp. 118–119).

10

LIMIT SETTING

NEED FOR SETTING LIMITS

The setting of limits is a specific instance of the need for establishing and maintaining structure, particularly in the face of acute regressive crises or acting-out (Adler 1975, Friedman 1975). The failure to set such limits may often lead to the undermining of the therapeutic alliance and a consequent stalemating of the therapy. In the more primitive border-lines who suffer from more severe ego defects, this is a particular need. Since such patients frequently do not respond to verbal interpretations in areas of regressive functioning, a new set of experiences is required. The therapist's activity and actual setting of effective limits can supply this primitive, nonverbal need for "good-enough mothering" (Little 1966). The patient thus finds an appropriate degree of protective and caring intervention, which was presumably lacking in the early developmental interaction with the mother.

It is often only after the primitive patient has experienced this kind of caring intervention on the part of the therapist that it is possible to explore and interpret some of the meanings of these interactions. In higher-order patients, however, limit setting need not take an active interventionist form but is more frequently a matter of sharing concern and exploring consequences of projected courses of action, emphasizing the more realistic aspects of options that may be to the patient's advantage rather than ones for discharging tension or expressing unconscious and often self-destructive needs. Higher-order patients do not share the same ego-defects that are found in lower-order patients, particularly the lack of anxiety tolerance, the lack of impulse control, and the poverty of sublimating channels described by Kernberg (1967). These ego-weaknesses are more readily found in lower-order patients and contribute to their acting-out potential. In higher-order patients, then, the emphasis shifts from limit setting as such to confrontation, clarification, and interpretation as preferred modalities of intervention. These interventions play a role in the therapy of all patients, but there should be a differential emphasis in their application to various groupings within the borderline spectrum.

NATURE OF LIMIT SETTING

Limit setting is another technique, along with confrontation, that calls upon the therapist to assume a more active and intervening position in relationship to the patient. To the extent that borderline patients tend to act out their instinctual wishes and tensions impulsively, limit setting enters the therapeutic picture as an essential component.

The quality of limit setting that is called for in different ranges of the borderline spectrum can vary considerably: in higher-order patients, limit setting may take the easier and milder forms of exploring with the patient the consequences of a projected course of action, or more generally of maintaining the specific parameters of the therapeutic situation; in lower-order patients, however, the tendency to act out plays a much more significant part in the therapeutic interaction and calls for stronger forms of limit setting, including at times intervening in the patient's life, interfering with the patient's physical activity, bringing restraining agencies and forces to bear to limit the potential destructiveness of the patient's behavior, and at times hospitalization.

In all of these instances, when the therapist tries to set limits, he moves to a more active stance and intervenes in a more decisive and controlling manner. This increase in activity not only emphasizes the confrontational nature of the limit-setting process but, as was the case with confrontation, makes the limit setting itself a potential vehicle for countertransference. Implicit in the activity of limit setting is a degree of aggression, which may have a therapeutic intention but is also open to instinctual contamination. The therapist's intervention will be governed by his judgment as to what is in the best interest of the patient, but this often involves entering into an oppositional relation with the patient and can create powerful reverberations for the subsequent course of the therapy. Indeed, the limits that must be maintained are those within which the therapy can continue to be conducted, and if there is any threat or danger to the therapist himself, he must be able to determine the limits within which he is willing to continue working with the patient (Adler 1985).

FORMS OF LIMIT SETTING

Limit setting can take a variety of forms, corresponding to the nature of the impulse to act out and the patient's capacities for dealing with it. In better-integrated patients, tendencies to act out can often be effectively mitigated and controlled by some form of anticipatory intervention. Some patients are uncomfortable with their impulses to act out and seek help to control their behavior. These patients are usually the easiest to treat. At the other extreme are those patients whose acting-out behavior serves more as a vehicle for release of tension, creates little concern or anxiety, and is relatively ego-syntonic. In between lies a vast territory in which the willingness of the patient to accept responsibility and to effectively control impulses to act out varies considerably.

In patients in whom the impulse to act out creates anxiety and for whom the impulse is ego-alien, often the therapist's effort to clarify, confront, and even at times interpret the basis of the impulse and the possible consequences is enough to forestall the behavior and enable the patient to reestablish reasonable control. Often, the clarification of the patient's feelings, particularly what the feelings may be about and against whom they are directed, or a confrontation and exploration of the possible consequences of the actions envisioned by the patient, or even the interpretation of the patient's impulse in terms of comparing it to similar impulses in other contexts, whether in the patient's current life situation or in the past life experience, to whatever extent that is available, enables the patient to gain some perspective and objectivity about the projected course of action and allows him to bring his ego resources to bear to forestall a self-destructive or potentially detrimental course of action. At times substitute action can be discussed, which would be in the long run more adaptive and effective for the patient. It is also useful for the therapist to anticipate patterns of acting-out behavior, especially when the previous experience leads the therapist to expect that some parallel pattern of behavior might evolve. The classic example is the exploration of a patient's projected behavior during the therapist's vacation. Exploring these possibilities and the comparison of the anticipated pattern of behavior with similar previous experiences can be extremely helpful.

One young man who was given to impulsive rage attacks became furious during the course of an argument with his girlfriend and put his fist through a wall. Not only did he have to pay for the damage to the wall, but he also broke his fist, which had to be put in a cast. This meant that he could not work and subsequently lost his job. In subsequent therapeutic work with this patient, it was extremely helpful to anticipate situations of conflict and tension in which his impulse to act out in some self-destructive way could be discussed and clarified, the feelings explored and connected with a variety of similar and previous contexts, and some sense of adaptive options developed that might provide more mature and even constructive outlets for his anger.

Such anticipatory efforts are not always successful, and failures not only can provoke feelings of failure and guilt in the therapist but may also have reverberations for his professional reputation. But the good therapist has learned how to tolerate a degree of risk, even in the context of limit setting. If the therapist becomes overly controlling or assumes an inappropriate degree of responsibility for the patient's behavior, not only does the risk of acting out increase but the acting out can become a vehicle for the expression of the patient's hostility and counteraggression toward the therapist. In the face of such failures, the therapist is often left with little recourse but to reexamine the patient's behavior and to try to understand what elements and forces, stimuli and motivations, may have entered into the process that led to the acting out and its destructive consequences. Not only can patient and therapist learn from the experience, but they may come to identify patterns of precipitating events or even to recognize aspects of the patient's inner feelings, anxieties, or mounting tension that can serve as a prodromal warning of potential acting out. The management of such tension may call for extra treatment sessions, or even emergency telephone calls, to support the patient in efforts to control the acting-out impulse. These parameters have implications for the maintaining of the therapeutic alliance and should be utilized only in rare circumstances where the impulsive pattern cannot be managed by any other means.

The patient's acting out sometimes takes place outside the therapy, and the therapist's efforts to set limits are confined to the therapeutic setting. But with borderline patients the acting out frequently takes place within the therapy itself, usually around the parameters of the therapeutic contract and the essential structure of the therapeutic situation. For some patients the need to preserve the sense of victimization (victim-introject) forces them to provoke aggressive or devaluing responses from the therapist; this often takes the form of acting out around the dimensions of the therapeutic structure, forcing the therapist to take remedial limit-setting measures. It is essential for the therapist to set limits in order to maintain the parameters of the therapeutic situation, but the risk of being drawn into a transference/countertransference interaction cannot be ignored.

These experiences have considerable potential value in that they immediately involve both patient and therapist in the process. The therapist does not have to rely on a secondhand account, with all its potential for distortion and obscurity, but is himself engaged in the process with the patient, so that the elements that enter into the patient's need to act out can be more directly and effectively identified and dealt with. In a mild form, for example, the patient may act out around the issue of coming to his appointments on time. Usually, this reflects some distortion in the therapeutic alliance and may or may not reflect underlying transference dynamics. But the contributing factors are ready at hand for examination as a part of the ongoing therapeutic interaction and can be explored and dealt with in those terms. The patient who comes late following the therapist's vacation is usually expressing some degree of resentment or anger at his abandonment by the therapist. Clarification and interpretation of the feelings of abandonment can usually effectively modify the patient's behavior (Monroe 1982).

Such anticipatory interventions or even reconstructive explorations after an episode of acting out require a sufficient footing in the therapeutic alliance for their effectiveness. The therapist must strike a balance between excessive concern on the one hand and a lack of concern on the other. However interested or invested the therapist may be in the welfare of the patient, that investment must remain secondary and minor in comparison to the primary therapeutic investment on the part of the patient. For many borderline patients, this is an extremely difficult issue, since many would prefer to hand over the total responsibility for the therapeutic outcome to the therapist. Many patients with narcissistic pathology make the somewhat grandiose assumption that any significant figure should be highly or even completely invested in achieving the well-being of the patient, and any failure to demonstrate this degree of devotion and commitment is regarded as a narcissistic insult. In any anticipatory negotiations, a delicate balance must be struck between assuming too much responsibility for the patient's behavior and not taking a strong enough stand in intervening in that behavior. With many such acting-out patients, I take the position that the patient is free to choose whatever he wants to do and that ultimately he is responsible for whatever choices and decisions he makes, but that my job as therapist is to help him to understand what is involved in his decision and what the potential consequences are of the behavior he intends. I tend to put responsibility on the patient by comments like "It's a free country," or "It's your life; you can do with it as you like!" or "Who am I to tell you what to do?" At times an appeal to the reinforcing aspects of the therapeutic contract can be extremely effective, as, for example, "It's up to you to decide whether or not you want to come to your hour, or whether you want to come on time, but whatever you decide, I still get paid." This may elicit a wry chuckle from the patient, or an angry response; in either case, the point is not lost.

The therapist may need to devise approaches that will enable the patient to maintain better degrees of control over his behavior, even when any understanding or insight into the sources and meanings of the patient's behavior are wanting. The techniques of such control, whether calling the therapist, going to an emergency room, or any other technique that will help the patient deal with the impulse, particularly when it is self-destructive, can be sorted out and agreed upon.

SPECIFIC CONTEXTS

Self-destructive Acting Out

In the face of self-destructive acting out, the therapist is under considerable pressure to maintain the treatment, even when the dangers are homicidal, suicidal, or in other ways aggressive and destructive. Even in these situations, the therapist must be able to tolerate calculated risks, even when the risk involves potential for serious, even fatal, failure (Monroe 1982). The therapist's trump card in these situations is to interrupt or stop the treatment. As Kernberg (1984) has observed, "There are areas in which the therapist must let patients know that he cannot or will not do for them what they cannot or will not do for themselves" (p. 119). This is particularly the case when the patient's acting out takes the form of aggression toward the therapist. It may be behavior that undermines the effectiveness of the therapeutic work

(coming late, missing sessions, failures to utilize the sessions constructively), or it may be direct attacks against the therapist in the form of
failure to pay bills, slandering him outside of the office, stealing from
him, destroying objects in his office, or even actual hostile behavior
directed against the person of the therapist or persons related to him
(Kernberg 1984). In these situations, the most reasonable course of
behavior for the therapist is to interrupt the session and indicate to the
patient that he seems to be out of control and that it is not possible for
any therapeutic work to be done that day. If the provocation continues
and it becomes clear that the patient has little positive therapeutic
motivation but seems determined to undermine, frustrate, and thus
defeat the therapeutic process, it makes sense simply to stop the treatment. Whether the therapeutic impasse is in some degree a function of
the interaction between the patient and this particular therapist is a
matter for clinical judgment; if so, transferral to another therapist may
be useful. But there may be cases in which such referral is predictably
condemned to the same pattern of hostile acting out and therapeutic
failure. In such cases, therapy should be stopped altogether and no
further treatment offered. Again we see the ghost of countertransference: if patients can provoke a therapist to end the treatment, the
therapist can likewise provoke the patient to act out and bring on a
termination. If a therapist puts down an absolute prohibition (no drugs,
no alcohol, no more lateness, etc.) under pain of termination, the
patient will be strongly tempted to violate the prohibition, confirming
once again that the therapist is an abandoning aggressor and the patient
his victim (Maltsberger 1982–1983).

Suicide

At times the outcome of limit setting can be fatal. Early in my career, I
was struggling to deal with a primitive and flagrantly acting-out borderline woman, whom I would regard now as a primitive affective personality disorder with severe tendencies to act out. The major form of
acting out was in suicidal gestures. The usual pattern began with an
attempt at suicide, usually by overdosing. The only drug ever employed
was Valium. The patient would be found comatose and unresponsive at
home with an empty bottle of Valium. She would be rushed to a
hospital, pumped out, and sent to the psychiatric hospital. She would
be admitted on suicide precautions. Within days, she would be back in
gear and starting to act up on the service. She was disruptive, argumentative, and difficult, and took out her anger at the staff in the form of

breaking windows and furniture, attacking staff members, and generally making herself a nuisance. Fortunately she was physically small and her attacks were generally easily controlled.

She was usually confronted about this behavior without much effect and then discharged from the hospital. On other occasions, she would be transferred to a closed ward populated by chronic psychotic patients, understaffed, and spartan. Within days, she would be in good spirits, on good behavior, and pleading for discharge. This pattern continued in a cycle that repeated itself about every two weeks. In the meanwhile, the therapy was getting nowhere. Payment of the bill became an issue. Her fee was twenty-five cents. She had not paid the hospital in months—the overdue fee was about three dollars. I finally decided that the issue had to be joined and the limit set. She refused payment. I told her that we would have to interrupt treatment, and that when she brought me a receipt stating that she had paid her bill, we could resume therapy. She was furious, raged at me for my stubborn pigheadedness, and stormed out of the office. Word came the next morning that she had overdosed and could not be revived. The usual bottle of Valium was empty on the table.[1]

From the perspective of some years later, the outcome was unfortunate, but it could be argued that the patient was in the habit of testing the suicidal limit and that the time would have come, sooner or later, when she would have crossed that boundary. But the fact that it happened in the context of my limit setting reflected the failure of any therapeutic alliance, the intensity and power of her transference rage, and the power of her need to act out that rage against me, the hospital, and her parents. I would not have chosen to do any differently even had I been able to foresee that the inevitable and predictable suicide gesture would have ended so tragically.

Hospitalization

The final form of limit setting is hospitalization. The decision to hospitalize is usually taken in the context of a disruption of the therapeutic relationship in which the therapist feels he has little or no effective therapeutic alliance, and when either psychotic regression or severe,

---

[1]Unfortunately blood levels were not taken so that a firm conclusion cannot be drawn that Valium was the lethal agent. The history and circumstances would point to that conclusion. Cases of lethal Valium ingestion are rare and almost never reported.

destructive acting out in the form of homicidal or suicidal behavior is in question. I view hospitalization as a powerful intervention in the patient's life, but one that is at times absolutely essential. Hospitalization is only rarely and exceptionally called for in the management of higher-order borderline patients, but in the lower-order spectrum hospitalization not only is expected but is a relatively frequent necessity. Insofar as possible, I try to negotiate the hospitalization with the patient on a voluntary basis. With patients who are resistant to such a move, yet continue to threaten destructive or suicidal action, I take the position that by their behavior they are implicitly requesting me to fulfill my obligations to them as therapist and doctor, and that I understand their threats of destructive behavior as their way of telling me that they need hospitalization in order to maintain some degree of control and avoid the dangerous and destructive consequences of their projected behavior.

Hospitalization is a critical decision, since it has important implications and consequences for the subsequent course of therapy. It is possible to maintain the thread of the therapeutic alliance through a course of hospitalization, but it is not an easy task. For many patients, particularly in the lower-order borderline spectrum, hospitalization becomes necessary only in a context of disruption of the therapeutic alliance and a regressive crisis. The therapist's action in initiating hospitalization, therefore, is often interpreted by the patient as punitive, retaliatory, and hostile. If the alliance is at that point already damaged, hospitalization may further injure it. In other cases, however, the therapist and patient have the opportunity of exploring the possibility of hospitalization as a possible option in the therapy, and can evolve a consensus that sees possible hospitalization as a part of an overall therapeutic process that is therapeutic in intent and may have a positive outcome for the patient.

Within Therapy

Limit setting can take place either within the therapy or outside of the therapy. Within the therapeutic interaction, there are a variety of contexts in which limit setting comes into play. The first is in establishing the therapeutic alliance. The stipulation of the arrangements and terms of the therapeutic contract and the conditions for the therapeutic situation are essentially forms of limit setting—setting the limits within which the therapeutic process can take place. Not only does this provide the structure for the therapeutic interaction, but it also sets some of the key parameters around which acting-out can be expected to take place, for example, around issues related to lateness, payment of fees, missing sessions, and so on.

As a number of authors have emphasized (Masterson 1972, Adler 1985), the therapist's limit-setting activity may be experienced by the patient as an exercise of power but also as a form of interest and caring, a context different from what many of these patients had experienced with their own parents, who were in fact disinterested, neglectful, or abandoning. There is a sense in which many borderline patients need and desperately seek controls and a constant structured context within which they can establish a relationship with a caring object. If the therapist in such cases does not intervene and does not set appropriate limits, the patient may feel that the therapist simply does not care or is not concerned for the patient's well-being. In any case, the setting of limits, particularly in terms of the specific aspects of the therapeutic structure, and the continuing effort on the part of the therapist to maintain and reinforce these limits, carries a measurable impact on the construction of the therapeutic alliance.

Establishing a working alliance and limiting potentially destructive and disruptive acting out from the beginning of the therapy are matters of primary concern in the treatment of many borderline patients (Chessick 1979, 1983a, Kernberg 1984). This situation arises almost exclusively with patients in the lower order of the borderline spectrum or in patients who are in a state of acute regressive crisis. In the face of such a disruptive situation, usually presented early in the course of therapy, the therapist has little basis in a therapeutic alliance and must take whatever strong measures are called for to effectively control the patient's behavior and to limit its destructive consequences. In serious life-threatening situations, immediate hospitalization may be required. Other strong confrontations, prohibitions, or effective intervention on the part of outside agencies may be called for. With suicidal or homicidal patients, the therapist may have to notify family members or even police to intercept the patient and prevent the intended destructive outcome. It was in such contexts that the Tarasoff ruling in California, requiring therapists to warn suspected victims of homicidal patients, was put on the books.

A fairly typical situation with disturbed and somewhat regressed borderline patients, especially in the beginning of therapy, is the desperate and urgent effort to engage the therapist in a variety of nonproductive ways, often by seeking extra appointments, trying to extend the allotted time of therapy hours, unnecessary telephone calls, attempts to engage the therapist by contacting other therapists or other clinics to pull the therapist into unwarranted activity, or even a variety of self-destructive behaviors (including self-lacerations, breaking windows and furniture, taking drugs, promiscuous sexual activity, suicidal threats, etc.). An active limit-setting stance is required in these contexts with the purpose of preventing the destructive effects of the patient's behavior and of limiting the acting out around therapeutic parameters, so that the therapeutic work can be gotten on track and effectively confined to the therapeutic context (see the discussion of establishing the therapeutic alliance in Chapter 5).

Later, as the course of therapy evolves, transference dynamics enter the picture with increasing intensity and become more frequently the basis for acting out and the source of tension and conflict within the therapy. Within the therapeutic context, the risk of transference acting out can be dealt with by a combination of clarification, confrontation, and interpretation. The extent to which interpretation can be usefully employed in such situations depends on the degree to which the therapeutic alliance is effectively intact. Where the alliance is disrupted or significantly distorted, interpretive efforts are likely to yield little fruit. Nonetheless, active confrontation and clarification of the issues, particularly in alliance terms, and a clarification of the possibly harmful consequences for the patient and the role of the patient's intended acting out in undermining the work of the therapy are often sufficient to short-circuit the patient's impulse.

In terms of the therapeutic interaction, the tendency for borderline patients to act out aspects of the transference within the therapeutic context can be actively and usefully focused by the therapist and become the subject for exploration and discussion. Such acting out around the transference may take the form of self-deprecating comments, accusations against the therapist, angry attacks against the therapist for failing to fulfill the patient's magical expectations, periods of sullen withdrawal, isolation or resistance, and so on. A useful way of conceptualizing such patterns of acting out is to think of them in terms of the underlying introjective configurations, that is, the degree to which the patient's behavior or engagement in the therapeutic interaction reflects the influence of the underlying aggressive (victimizing/victimized) or narcissistic (superior/inferior) configurations. The patient who complains about his sense of worthlessness, helplessness, and ineffectualness and then behaves in the therapy as though it were of little value and as though he himself has nothing useful to contribute to the therapeutic process would be acting out such patterns, both of victimization and of narcissistic inferiority. These patterns can be confronted within the therapy and, insofar as they distort the therapeutic effort, can be limited and modified. When such patterns spill over outside of the therapeutic hour and begin to be noticed in the patient's outside life, other forms of limit setting must be considered.

Aggression and the expression of physical violence are problems that must be directly confronted and limited if the therapeutic situation is to remain viable. As Kernberg (1984) has emphasized, the therapist cannot treat patients whose tendencies toward violent acting out are a problem unless he has a treatment setting that assures him of a degree of security and protection, both for himself and for the patient. If the therapist assumes he can handle whatever violence might emerge, he runs a dangerous risk and may have to pay for his omnipotence. Even minor expressions of aggressive action are not to be tolerated. One patient[2] who fell within the range of the dysphoric personality found it necessary to sit up during the course of his analysis. While discussing his rage and resentment at his superiors, whom he blamed for the difficult position he found himself in (regardless of the fact that he largely created the situation by his own recalcitrance), he grabbed the tissue box from the table beside him and flung it violently into the wastepaper basket. The analyst, a young woman of slight build, was frightened by this outburst of impulsive behavior.

She said nothing, but after consultation with her supervisor, she confronted the patient about his acting out of his angry impulse and made it clear that such behavior was not tolerable in the therapeutic setting. The patient took umbrage at this and began complaining about the fact that the analyst had not set limits on the patient's own self-destructive behavior outside of the therapy. He was nonetheless able to acknowledge that no one had ever before in his life called him on his behavior, nor had anyone ever made it clear to him that certain behavior was not acceptable. He was able to see in time how his behavior outside of therapy was also unacceptable, and that the reactions of people around him were clearly saying that they were no longer willing to tolerate it. It was in effect reassuring to the patient that the analyst was able to set limits and prevent him from losing control.

As Adler (1985) points out, the deep-seated rage and envy in many borderline patients, particularly those in the lower-order group, make the need to maintain strong limits an especially important part of the

---

[2]John J. is described in detail in Chapter 19.

treatment process. The threats may be genuine, but they may also reflect to a degree the therapist's own unresolved conflicts over aggression, which can be counterprojected onto the patient. In the example above, the woman analyst may have been subject to this countertransference difficulty in some degree. In any case it would seem entirely appropriate that any form of physical aggression within the therapeutic hour is out of place and should be strongly prohibited, regardless of countertransference influences. The therapist in such situations must be able to set a strong limit on physical behavior, while at the same time tolerating and encouraging the patient's verbal expression of aggressive feelings and/or hostility.

For such patients, the line between fantasy and reality is often highly permeable and may be further contaminated by the violence in the real environments in which they live. As Adler (1985) observes, this is a problem particularly in patients who are involved in criminal activities or who are in prison. Dealing with such aggression requires a good deal of empathy with the patient's inner world, which is structured around the polarities of aggressive destructiveness and helpless victimization and vulnerability. Whenever a therapist, regardless of his own unresolved aggressive conflicts, begins to feel that he is in danger of violence, he is well advised to take whatever measures are necessary to alter the situation. As Gutheil (1985) has noted, the often intense rage of primitive borderline patients creates difficulties in therapists, who feel unjustly attacked and may react with forms of countertransference aggression that serve only to cloud their clinical judgment and lead to bad decisions regarding the patient's care. The mobilization of countertransference hate (Maltsberger and Buie 1974) can result in distancing, abandonment, failures of empathy, or regarding the patient as untreatable. Where such responses become maladaptive and lead to unfortunate outcomes, they may provide grounds for litigation.

Regression

One of the important contexts in which limit setting has a critical function is in dealing with regression. Regression assumes major significance in the treatment of borderline patients in proportion to the degree of regressive potential that is such a marked aspect of borderline psychopathology (see Chapter 11). In general, regressive potential increases as one moves from the higher to the lower order of the borderline spectrum.

A regressive response in the patient is a signal to the therapist that something has gone awry in the therapeutic process and calls for an evaluation of the source of the difficulty, which may be in the intensification of the transference or in some lack of empathy or understanding on the part of the therapist; or it may be some technical error the therapist has committed or a piece of defensive avoidance on the part of the patient to keep from dealing with painful or anxiety-provoking issues. The therapist's task in the face of such regression is twofold, namely, to preserve the therapeutic process insofar as possible and to protect the patient from the dangerous or deleterious consequences of whatever actions or behaviors are involved in the regressive state. In setting limits, the therapist is called on to become more active, to deal more directly with the issues connected with the regressive episode, and to take whatever actions are appropriate for containing the regression and its consequences.

An important factor in the implementation of limits is the degree of the therapist's capacity to tolerate the patient's regression and the need to be in touch with countertransference impulses, particularly those connected with the therapist's own sense of omnipotence. This is often a problem to the extent that the patient may need to idealize the therapist in some degree, and may interact with the therapist in such a way as to draw him into a protective, caring, and nurturing position. As Adler (1975, 1985) has observed, the patient's need to idealize may play into the therapist's wishes for such narcissistic gratification and may extend to a transference/countertransference bind, which retards the patient's therapeutic progress. Similarly, while it may be important to maintain a nurturant maternal transference earlier in the course of treatment, the therapist may later resort to it as a means of protecting himself from the patient's rage or envy, thus impeding the patient's growing autonomy and capacity for separation. At times the therapist's need to be actively giving, protecting, caring, nurturing, or rescuing the patient may satisfy needs in the therapist rather than serve to protect the patient. The therapist must be able to accept his own human limitations without any sense of shame or guilt if he is to find ways to be appropriately helpful to his patients in dealing with episodes of regression.

Beyond Therapy

While these various aspects of limit setting within different therapeutic contexts have an essential role in the treatment of most borderline patients—more urgently and dramatically in the lower-order spectrum—

limit setting may not be confined to the therapeutic process itself but may extend beyond it. While such external limits are almost never necessary with higher-order patients and may have only a limited place in dealing with lower-order patients, the therapist must always weigh the need to limit the patient's outside behavior against the inevitable damage to the therapeutic alliance and to the stimulation of omnipotent fantasies about the therapist or reinforcements of the pathogenic introjects that will have to be dealt with in the subsequent course of therapy.

The extent to which the therapist plays into the patient's pathology by reason of his limit-setting activity can often complicate the subsequent therapeutic work. If the patient can experience the limit-setting intervention as caring and protective, the therapeutic context is not necessarily damaged; by and large, however, the more primitive borderline patient will tend to see the therapist's activity in terms of his own projective needs as related to the underlying introjective configuration. Thus, the patient is more liable to feel controlled, smothered, humiliated, even persecuted.

As Kernberg (1984) is quick to caution, the important aspect of the preservation of the therapy is to protect the neutrality of the therapist. This places major limits on the degree to which the therapist can or should intervene in the patient's outside life. Therapy is therapy, but the patient's life is the patient's life and belongs entirely to him. Thus, to the extent that external limits may be needed, it is better to turn to the aid of auxiliary support systems of whatever kind (social workers, nurses, counselors, police, teachers and principals, employers, personnel officers, family members, other social and governmental agencies, etc.). Even within the context of outpatient therapy, the enlisting of other supportive personnel creates a kind of administrative split that allows the therapist to continue to deal with the business of therapy, parole, and so on. It is also important that the therapist establish meaningful and useful contact with these outside agencies and that he keep informed about procedures and their implementation. Part of the therapeutic task, regardless of the outside procedures and their effects, will be to sort through and explore these events and their consequences and implications with the patient in therapy.

The other context in which limit setting is brought into play in a major way outside the therapeutic interaction is hospitalization. Particularly in the treatment of lower-order patients and occasionally, if rarely, in the treatment of higher-order borderlines, hospitalization is necessary. In the context of psychotic regression or in episodes of suicidal or homicidal acting out, it is probably most advantageous for the therapy if the regression can be contained and the treatment continued on an outpatient basis. But regardless of the therapist's good intentions and efforts, the patient always holds the trump cards in this part of the game, and if he chooses to play them, the therapist may have little recourse but to resort to hospitalization.

As with other forms of dramatic and heroic limit-setting, the decision to hospitalize is in part a function of the therapist's capacity to endure the patient's regressive turmoil and to effectively implement other limit setting or structuring interventions that forestall or minimize the need for resorting to hospitalization. Thus, treatment of patients with high regressive potential or high potentiality for acting out of conflictual impulses is always a high-risk game, one in which the therapist is hovering close to the border of catastrophe much of the time. Therapists who cannot tolerate a reasonable degree of uncertainty and risk may end up playing out dimensions of their countertransference hate and their anxiety and end up hospitalizing patients at relatively minor levels of risk (Maltsberger and Buie 1974). Such interventions are often more helpful in alleviating the therapist's anxiety than they are to the patient (Monroe 1982).

11

REGRESSION

FORMS OF REGRESSION

Regression is one of the most difficult problems the therapist of border-line patients has to face. There is a gradation in vulnerability to regression extending from the more moderate and infrequent regression in the highest level of the borderline spectrum to the often chaotic, frequent, precipitous, and profound regression of patients at the lowest level.[1]

We should be clear about what kinds of regression we are talking about. I will focus on the distinctions between therapeutic and malignant regression and between instinctual or topographic and structural regression. Therapeutic regression is a necessary component of the

---

[1]Gunderson (1987) has recently provided a useful description of levels of regression commonly seen in borderline patients, ranging from forms of disruption of the therapeutic alliance (level I), through forms of regressive transference manifestations, therapeutic-alliance disruptions, and regressive behavior including suicidal behavior (level II), to severe regressions that take a psychotic form including the development of a transference psychosis (level III). Within the borderline spectrum, level I regressions can be seen at any level and may be the only or predominant form in higher-order borderlines. Level II regressions are common coin in lower-order patients and may be occasionally experienced in the higher-order group. Level III are found in lower-order patients and almost never in higher-order patients. The potential remains for all patients in the borderline spectrum to approach this level of regression; while it is no surprise in lower-order patients, it is exceptional and infrequent in higher-order patients.

psychoanalytic process, whether in its classic form or in derivative psychotherapeutic forms. The gradual induction of regression in the therapeutic relationship provides the basis for the emergence of free association and the transference neurosis. There is usually an optimal degree of regression in any therapeutic process that allows for the undoing of therapeutic formations and opens the potentiality for progressive reworking of the personality structure. Such regressions are always partial, usually gradual, always reversible, and induce a degree of manageable signal anxiety that derives from the mobilization of infantile conflicts. The level of anxiety is such as to stimulate a therapeutic response but never reaches the level at which it becomes overwhelming or traumatic (Frosch 1967a).

Therapeutic regressions occur along a continuum of levels of intensity and degree. In the emergence of the transference illusion, for example, there are degrees of blurring of the "as-if" quality of the transference involvement and degrees of weakening of the sense of reality (Wallerstein 1967). In most neurotic patients this occurs to a minor degree and is readily resolved and reversed. The loss of reality perspective tends to be somewhat greater, more severe, and more profound in borderline patients. Higher-order borderlines may experience only minor or episodic failures in this respect, but as one moves further down the spectrum, this becomes increasingly difficult to manage and less easy to resolve by interpretive means. At some point, the regression may cross a line that separates the therapeutic from the nontherapeutic.

Therapists differ in the extent to which they regard profound regressions therapeutically useful and in the depth of such regression that they regard as optimal. Winnicott (1958) would argue that a profound degree of regression may be required for more disturbed patients in order to reach the level of developmental trauma and fixation and to mobilize the forces of developmental healing. Winnicott's model would see the therapeutic effort as a form of substitute mothering that seeks to correct the developmental failures by a positive therapeutic experience. For Balint (1968) the regression opens the possibility for a "new beginning." Other therapists (Little 1960, Balint 1968, Searles 1976) feel that regression to a near-psychotic, symbiotic level is necessary for real change in all patients. The problem persists of determining the degree of regression that will be most useful therapeutically and the extent to which regression can be maintained within the therapy without spilling over into the patient's life with destructive effects (Guntrip 1961, Adler 1985).

Regressions may also have to be titrated in order to gain maximal therapeutic advantage. Regression to a relatively primitive level may be important in the therapy of schizoid patients but may not be helpful until levels of primitive defense have been worked through and a sufficient degree of ego strength established to allow the regressive experience to be adequately mastered and creatively resolved (Khan 1960). An important dimension of this process is the extent to which the therapist himself is comfortable with certain degrees of regression and is able to deal with it constructively. The tolerance for regression relates to a sense of safety that patient and therapist share as a result of the building of an effective therapeutic alliance (Adler 1985).

The risk with more primitive patients is that the regression may become malignant. This happens when it becomes traumatic or overwhelming or when it can no longer be constructively resolved and worked through but leads to increasingly severe degrees of regressive infantile demand and disrupts the work of the therapy. The malignant regression leads to the level of the "basic fault" (Balint 1968), a fundamental developmental flaw that is preverbal and beyond the reach of interpretive modification. Such malignant regressions in therapy may result from a combination of the patient's vulnerability and the therapist's countertransference (Adler 1985). I will return to this point later.

A useful distinction can also be made between instinctual or topographic regression and structural regression (Modell 1968). In a topographic regression the contents of the inner world come to invade or interpenetrate the reality-oriented ego of the subject. In the face of such regression, the structural integrity of the self and the sense of identity are preserved. The regression in analysis and the emergence of the transference neurosis are cases in point. The possibility of topographic regression without any significant degree of structural regression requires a sufficiently developed sense of self and a degree of structural cohesion. The preservation of structure maintains the capacity for reality testing. The boundaries between the inner and outer worlds may be fuzzy or blurred, but the structural integrity of the self and its component parts preserves the capacity to differentiate self and object. Thus, in the transference neurosis, the patient may respond to the analyst in emotional terms as though he were the displacement object, but he does not lose the sense of real identity of the object and the difference between the analyst as object and the original object of emotional involvement.

In contrast, structural regression denotes a condition in which psychic structure loses its organization, differentiation, and cohesion.

The failure of structural integrity can affect any psychic structure: ego, superego, self-organization, and so on. It implies a loss of boundaries and dedifferentiation in object relations; a reactivation of earlier developmental configurations; a weakening or loss of reality testing; emergence of more primitive ego functions and defenses, particularly projective and introjective mechanisms; a loss of differentiation (between ego and id, between self and object, etc.); more global and undifferentiated organization; fragmentation and diffusion of a sense of identity; greater degrees of fusion and merger; and in borderline patients, the reemergence of primitive and primarily aggressive instinctual derivatives. The risk in borderline patients lies in the high level of regressive potential, specifically for structural regression. This risk inheres throughout the borderline spectrum, again with degrees of severity and intensity varying from the lower to the higher levels. The more primitive forms of borderline disorder are prone to structural regression: it is a constant threat and occurs relatively frequently and often precipitously. At the higher level of the spectrum, structural regression is seen less often and usually occurs in more moderate degrees of severity and depth. However, even these patients retain an inherent capacity for severe structural regression, given the proper eliciting conditions or stresses.

BORDERLINE REGRESSION

Regressive Potential

The distinction in degrees of regressive potential in borderline patients has gained little more than implicit recognition in the literature on the treatment of borderline conditions. Frosch (1967a), for example, notes that some regressing patients were recognized as such (Winnicott 1955, Little 1958, 1960, Khan 1960), but other patients may be taken into analysis with optimistic diagnoses and then develop severe psychotic or near-psychotic regressions (Reider 1957, Romm 1957, 1959, Peto 1963, Weinshel 1966). In terms of the present analysis, these different manifestations of regression can be seen as reflecting different levels of borderline organization. The recognizably regressed patients were more likely to come from the lower order of the borderline spectrum and those who regressed only later in the analysis from the higher order.

Regressions are by no means found exclusively in the borderline group, but since the regressive potential is a marked aspect of their pathology (Peto 1967, Kernberg 1984), regressions during analysis or psychotherapy come as no surprise. Because of the nature of the structural pathology, the regression in borderline patients tends to involve a greater degree of structural regression than might be the case for healthier neurotic patients (Giovacchini 1979). Even therapeutic regressions in these healthier patients, which characteristically involve instinctual rather than structural regression, always involve some degree, even if minor, of structural regression as well. For many borderline patients, the inherent regressive pull of the analytic process can bring about the emergence of a severe and chaotic regressive state. The patient's pathogenic personality structure and vulnerability of reality testing can produce a state of regressive helplessness or psychosis without any special effort to elicit it. The analytic objective is to hold the regression within therapeutic limits, usually by interpretation of the underlying conflicts and defenses (Atkins 1967). For the most part, borderline patients more characteristically develop such regressive states within the therapeutic setting and in relation to the transference; overflow of the psychosis outside the therapy is infrequent (Kernberg 1984).

Regressions in the borderline group can emerge gradually and slowly as the therapeutic relationship deepens and the transference intensifies, or can occur suddenly and precipitously, usually in response to excessive tension or stress (Adler 1985). It is often preceded by growing dissatisfaction or disappointment with the therapist, triggered finally by an interruption or separation (weekends, vacations, etc.). In its most typical form, as found in patients in the hysterical continuum, the patient's behavior becomes demanding and desperately clinging; impulse control is compromised as is any capacity to modulate affects; rage at the therapist can be so intense that any sense of the therapist as good or helpful is lost; the patient may experience hypochondriacal fears, depersonalization, a sense of dissolution, and fears of falling apart. Most significantly, the dynamics of the introjective-projective process are intensified, increasing the tendency for self-devaluation and depression, for paranoid distortions of the relationship with the therapist, for feelings of inferiority and shame to become overwhelming, for the intensification of feelings of manic inflation and grandiosity, or for a more profound sense of helplessness, passivity, vulnerability, and weakness.[2]

---

[2]A useful description of this process in an extended course of psychotherapy is provided by Munschauer (1987).

In narcissistic terms, the patient's demandingness can take various forms. He may feel worthless himself and so may idealize the therapist from whom he desperately seeks gratification; or he may devalue the therapist and refuse to accept what he offers even while the patient continues or even escalates his demands (Myerson 1974). Certain forms of brittle narcissistic pathology are more vulnerable to the threat of psychotic regression in the transference. These patients find it necessary to cling to narcissistic investments with little capacity for self-observation or empathy. They frequently resort to a defensive system built around a form of schizoid isolation and self-sufficient grandiosity that makes deeper involvement in the therapeutic process or any sense of dependence on the therapist threatening and raises the specter of psychotic decompensation (Rothstein 1982). In general, the regressive reactivation of these introjective configurations pushes the patient further in the direction of already existing pathological tendencies—the patient tends to become more depressed, more manic, more paranoid, more self-destructive. In these patients the inherent vulnerability of the psychic structure to regressive pulls means that the regression is more likely to be sudden, disruptive, frightening, and all-or-nothing, and can readily immerse the patient in a transference psychosis. Then the patient can no longer separate inner from outer, self from object. The boundaries between the patient and the therapist are dissolved and their identities often merge. In the face of this devouring absorption into the therapist, some patients will follow a path of schizoid withdrawal and isolation.

Regression also takes place in the organization of the patient's thought patterns, which take on a more primary process organization. Representations of the self and objects can become splintered and fragmented. In its more extreme forms this can produce a shifting mosaic of part-object images, affects, a mixing of perceptions and fantasy elements, even hallucinatory experiences. These elements can be subjected to confusing patterns of projection and introjection, producing a loss of self-object differentiation and a confusion of fantasy and reality (Peto 1967). These cognitive shifts can be expressed in cognitive developmental terms. Patients may move from a level of relatively normal, formal operational thinking to more concrete operational or even preoperational levels. At this more regressive level, attributes or parts of objects (part-objects) may be used idiosyncratically to represent the object as a whole, and emotional responses are cast in a more fragmentary and all-or-nothing, either-or mold. Affective experience loses its complexity and sense of differentiation and is cast in more global, undifferentiated, unidimensional terms (Lane and Schwartz 1987).

Dreams

The dreamlike quality of some of these cognitive features has been noted, as well as the regressive permeability of the barrier between dream and real experience in some of these patients (Frosch 1967b). Many borderline dreams have a strikingly real quality and invade the patient's waking thoughts to an extent that makes it difficult for them to know what is dream and what is real. The inability of the patient to maintain this sense of differentiation between dream and reality may provide an index either of the level of borderline pathology or of the level of the patient's regression. My own experience in working with the dreams of borderline patients has impressed me with the extent to which the introjective themes get elaborated and played out in the dream material. The roles of aggressor, victim, superior, and inferior are acted out again and again, in varying styles and with varying emphases, in most of these patients.

Besides having an expressive function, borderline dreams may serve a discharge function more evident than the dream activity of other patients. A useful distinction has been provided by Grinberg (1987) between evacuative and elaborative dreams. Evacuative dreams serve primarily to discharge unbearable affects or fantasies into a containing object; elaborative dreams do not seek discharge primarily but contain depressive and reparatory elements for the purpose of working them through. Dreams can also contain a mixture of these modalities in which the discharge function is important but is accompanied by elements of concern and guilt. In healthier, neurotic patients dreams tend to be more elaborative than evacuative; evacuative dreams can be seen in these patients, for example, in more regressive phases of an analysis. In the borderline spectrum, the tendency for dreams to follow an evacuative function is much greater. These dreams serve an important function in the regulation of instinctual pressures; in patients for whom the repressive and regulatory functions are deficient, the evacuative function, together with similar discharge functions of projection onto external objects, comes to predominate. To the extent that these instinctual pressures are not adequately discharged, pressures for acting out can build up. There is a resulting proportion between the extent to which elaborative dream processes are in effect and the tendency to act out. Grinberg (1987) argues that to the degree to which adequate discharge can be accomplished through evacuative dreaming, acting out becomes less necessary. Thus the more the pattern of dreaming is shifted toward elaborative dreams, the less the patient is at risk for acting out. I would take this conclusion a further step to argue that the degree of evacuative dreaming may serve as a useful index for the regressive level of most borderline patients.

Psychosis

The regression in borderline patients can often be severe and profound, to the level of psychosis. This possibility is rare in patients close to the neurotic/narcissistic border but is unfortunately not so rare in patients closer to the psychotic border. Regressions at this level are marked by failures of reality testing, degrees of self fragmentation, dedifferentiation of the boundaries between self and object, and a recrudescence of primitive- and conflictual-drive-dominated introjections. These serve as the basis for relatively primitive projections, in which the therapist is clothed in fantasied attributes orginally connected with the real, threatening parents. The underlying introjections are the internalized residues from earlier experiences with significant (usually primary) objects. When the experience with these objects has been terrifying, threatening, painful, or even merely intensely ambivalent, the therapist is more likely to be seen as hateful, threatening, and persecuting (Frosch 1967a). The therapist literally becomes in the patient's experience "the idealized and deified, and oppositely, the diabolized, parent" (Wallerstein 1967). The projection of these aggressive and hostile derivatives to the therapist creates a situation of intense fear that comes not merely from fears of retaliation but also from the fear that, because of the sense of fusion with the object, destruction of the object means nothing less than psychic annihilation of the self (Frosch 1967a, Giovacchini 1979). The emergence of such distorted, unrealistic, and delusional material in the transference has been designated a "transference psychosis" (Reider 1957) or a "delusional transference" (Little 1958, 1960). Transference psychoses usually involve an unconscious fantasy of fusion with the therapist as a way of warding off fears of annihilation or abandonment (Frosch 1967a). Such transference psychoses can be regarded as regressive variants of infantile psychoses. They may represent reenactments within the transference of an infantile trauma or identifications (introjections) with a psychotic object from childhood. These elements can be traced in the classic case of the Wolf Man, in whom the paranoid psychosis in later life seems to have been related to an underlying and unresolved infantile psychosis (Frosch 1967a, Blum 1974, Meissner 1977c, 1986b).

Diagnostic Indicators

Some authors have called attention to diagnostic signs that can act as forewarnings of impending regression. Adler (1985) stresses the need in the process of assessment to gain a sense of the solidity of the patient's self and the use the patient makes of the therapist. How good a relationship can the patient develop with the therapist? Is it a relationship of developing trust, of connection between real people? Can the patient use the therapist's contribution for therapeutic purposes, or does he need to reject or devalue the therapist from the start? It should be noted that these and similar questions have to do with the assessment of the patient's potential for forming a therapeutic alliance. Generally the appearance of regressive feelings early in the treatment is a bad prognostic indicator and can prove to have greater destructive and self-destructive impact (Adler 1985). Other suggestive signs may be repeated slips of the tongue in early interviews (Reider 1957), or idiosyncratic speech or behavior observed on first contact (Knight 1953a). To these can be added the patient's history of regressive episodes, with some sense of their frequency and severity, and subtle forms of cognitive dysfunction that may suggest tangentiality, circumstantiality, disconnection of sequential thought sequences, or frequent lapses in logic. All of these are plus-minus indicators that serve little more than to alert the clinician to questions of regressive potential. They do not rise to the level of predictive validity. In the borderline spectrum, there are endless pitfalls and lots of surprises.

SUICIDE

The threat or the enactment of suicide is one of the most frequent and devastating features and complications of the treatment of borderline patients. The threat of suicide is not a frequent aspect of the work with higher-order borderlines for whom regressive and self-destructive behavior more often takes milder and less physically destructive forms. The higher-order borderline is more likely to drink, become sexually promiscuous, get into a fight with a love object, or do something self-defeating in his work. Actual physical assaults on the self (self-laceration, mutilation, suicide) are not the rule. They are more the rule in the lower order of the borderline spectrum, where the emotional disruption is more acute and primitive, where the capacities for regulation and modulation are less available, and where the issues tend to be cast in more dire, extreme, life-and-death terms (Kernberg 1987a).

Management Issues

I will not attempt to present an exhaustive discussion of the problem of suicide since it is an extensive problem in its own right. My views on suicide, its dynamics, and its relation to the paranoid process have been developed elsewhere (Meissner 1977a,b, 1986b). The following set of points seems to me to be central to the management of this problem in borderline patients.

1. Suicide in the borderline patient is a serious problem—the more serious, the more primitive the patient's psychic structure and the lower his place in the borderline spectrum. Any suicidal talk or innuendo should not be disregarded but should be made the focus of some sort of therapeutic intervention. This is a particular problem since many patients have a history of repeated suicidal gestures that can lull the therapist into complaisant disregard or underestimation of the degree of suicidality. The unpleasant lesson of experience with suicidal patients is that patients who keep on gesturing are at risk of that additional gesture that proves to be the last—it succeeds (Maltsberger 1982–1983).

2. The therapist cannot stop the patient from committing suicide. It is an unpleasant, anxious, and humbling realization, but one that is too little acknowledged. If a patient is bent on committing suicide, no matter what precautions we might take, he will do it. Patients can find and often have found ways to kill themselves in the hospital. If we physically prevent a patient from killing himself here and now, he can always kill himself there and then. These implications do not preclude taking preventive and precautionary measures, but we as therapists cannot be responsible for keeping the patient alive if he does not wish to remain alive.

In attempting to deal with a suicidal patient, I regard it as fundamental that every effort be made to force the patient back into the position of taking responsibility for his own continued existence or for putting an end to it. My supposition is that if the patient can be shifted into the position of making a decision about suicide, the probability that he will in fact attempt suicide diminishes. Hospitalization is one of the therapist's trump cards. Even when faced with a patient determined to die, one manifesting a high degree of lethality and suicidality, the therapist will want to negotiate with the patient to help him reach a decision whether to be voluntarily hospitalized or not. If the patient maintains his determination to self-destruct and refuses voluntary hospitalization, he has equivalently reached a decision that the therapist must play the trump card and put him in the hospital involuntarily. If the patient refuses to exercise reasonable responsibility, he forces the therapist to do his job and to exercise that responsibility for him (Kernberg 1984).

What is the point of such an exercise? The therapist does not take responsibility for keeping the patient alive; he negotiates with an eye to getting the patient's ego back in operating position, and even when the patient forces him to the wall, he does not take the patient's responsibility away from him, but in response to the pressure takes the initiative of exercising his own professional responsibility. The therapist fulfills his responsibility by placing the patient in the protective confines of the hospital, realizing full well that the patient can readily frustrate that effort by killing himself in the hospital.

3. The threat of suicide reflects a disruption in the therapeutic alliance. This signals to the therapist where the primary therapeutic focus is to be found. The suicidal threat is in part an attack against the therapist and can be viewed as an acting out of the transference in the actual attempt. The therapeutic effort is directed toward reestablishing the therapeutic alliance. No intervention that the therapist makes is done without having that objective in mind. Even the maneuvers that the therapist makes to protect the patient from his own self-destructive impulses and to forestall the suicidal act are made from the perspective of the therapeutic alliance. Part of the therapeutic alliance is the therapist's taking his appropriate responsibility vis-à-vis the patient: this may include involuntary hospitalization as I have suggested. For the patient it is essential that he take responsibility for the continuation of therapy and for his role in the therapeutic interaction. To the extent that the therapist succeeds in reinstituting the therapeutic alliance, the suicidal dynamics are undercut.

The effort does not always succeed. There is a slippery middle ground between the therapeutic respect for the patient's individuality and autonomy and the need to protect the patient from his own self-destructive urges that is not always easy to determine or maintain. Therapists can easily under- or overestimate the patient's lethality. Patients can play a deadly shell game with the therapist that conceals in whole or in part the severity of their suicidal intent (Kernberg 1987a). The therapist can take the threat too lightly and give the patient too much space to act out his intent; or he can overreact, violate the patient's proper area of responsibility, and inadvertently reinforce the suicidal dynamics. Suicides can easily take place in these cracks.

It is also clear that reasonable therapy cannot take place under the gun of suicidal threats. If the patient continues to threaten the therapist with suicide and this cannot be resolved by reasonable therapeutic effort, the therapist has another trump card—ending the treatment. Therapy under such conditions has no basis in a therapeutic alliance and predictably lacks any sound basis for a successful outcome. In such a situation, the therapy is better terminated before it is allowed to deteriorate into further tragedy. Alternate therapeutic resources can be found for the patient. As Kernberg (1984) observes:

> It is important that the therapist who treats borderline patients with chronic suicide potential in an outpatient setting not accept impossible treatment arrangements that require unusual efforts or heroic measures on his part. In the long run, whenever more is demanded of the therapist than would be reasonable in the average psychotherapeutic treatment, the end result is a reinforcement of the patient's self-destructive potential. [p. 262]

There are also times when the chronic risk of suicide is an integral part of the therapy. Kernberg (1984) makes several points about the treatment of such patients that I would fully endorse. The secondary gain of such threats and the hidden meaning of such sadistic behaviors in relation to family, friends, and the therapist should be clarified, confronted, and if possible interpreted. Often patients dominate or manipulate others by their suicidal behavior. Guilt-inducing behaviors often play a major role. The therapist can make it clear to the patient that his suicide would be an occasion for regret, but that the therapist would not feel responsible or guilty about it. The therapist should communicate to the patient's relatives and family that he is chronically suicidal, that the effort to help him deal with this problem will continue, but that there are no guarantees that the process can prevent his suicide in the long run. The patient's suicidal potential and inclinations must be brought into the focus of therapeutic scrutiny at every turn, particularly when transference or other interactions with the therapist are involved. And finally, the therapist does not allow an impossible therapeutic, or rather nontherapeutic, situation to continue. Kernberg (1984) concludes:

> Any psychotherapeutic relationship that extends over many months under unrealistic conditions, without honest communication and clearly delimited and accepted responsibilities on the part of both participants, may also be playing into the patient's suicidal potential. There are times when a psychotherapist, recognizing the impossibility of the treatment situation, has to have the courage to end it, even if the patient uses the threat of suicide to try to keep a sadomasochistic relationship alive. [p. 263]

4. The suicide dynamics play out the pathology of the introjective configurations. The suicidal impulse is an expression of the regressive reactivation and intensification of the introjects—primarily the aggressive introjects and at times secondarily the narcissistic introjects. I see it as fundamental to the suicidal situation that the suicide assumes the valence of the ultimate victimization, enacted in conjunction with an internal persecutor or executioner. These constituents of the suicidal response can easily be recognized as stand-ins for the victim- and aggressor-introjects. Only by elucidating, analyzing, interpreting, and resolving these pathogenic configurations can the suicidal potential in the patient be adequately laid to rest (Meissner 1977b, 1986b).

5. Suicide is fertile ground for the playing out of countertransference issues and for the emergence of transference/countertransference interactions. A common pattern in lower-order borderline patients is an initial idealization of the therapist, who is elevated to the position of the magical, all-understanding, empathic wizard. Unstated is the supposition that this narcissistically enhanced sorcerer will soon work his magic, transform the patient's life, and banish all his troubles. When the magic falters, the projections are reversed, disappointment ushers in rage, and the admired therapist now finds himself reviled, devalued, hated, accused, and threatened by an acutely suicidal patient (Maltsberger 1982–1983). The countertransference risk is in the therapist's need to protect his narcissism and redress the balance by paying the patient back in kind.

If the reader looks back over the recommendations about dealing with the suicidal patient, it is difficult to escape the impression that at every point the potential for countertransference contamination and for dealing with the subtleties of transference/countertransference looms large. Mistakes in this area are easy to make but can have lethal consequences. I believe it essential to emphasize that, whatever the fallibility and limitations of the therapist and the therapeutic process, the basic responsibility for keeping the patient alive lies with the patient and with no one else. Much can be said about countertransference in dealing with suicidal patients, particularly in regard to dealing with negative transference and in the vicissitudes of aggressive transference/countertransference interactions. I would also refer the reader to the excellent discussion of these issues by Maltsberger and Buie (1974).

THERAPEUTIC ASPECTS

Technical Modifications

Most therapists agree that in the face of regressive episodes modifications of the therapeutic approach are called for; the question is what kinds of modifications are useful. Winnicott (1955) argued that the predominance of preoedipal pathology required modifications of analytic technique, including greater activity on the part of the analyst, who must provide adequate holding and good-enough mothering for the patient. This approach shifts the emphasis away from interpretation to the qualities of the object relationship between patient and therapist. Others would argue that such substitute mothering only fosters regression and can be regarded as a form of acting out (Dickes 1967).

Regressions in the transference may serve to deepen the transference or may only deepen the patient's resistance. In the latter case, efforts to interpret the resistance without interpretation of the content may turn the regression around; the price is that recovery of early traumatic material is sacrificed. If there seems to be some therapeutic gain from the regression, a balance of resistance and content interpretations may keep the regression within manageable limits. Empathy with the patient's regressive position is the guide for the therapist's understanding, but mishaps are frequent. Misunderstanding and miscommunication are unavoidable but can be buffered by the therapist's continuing effort to understand and to reconstitute the therapeutic alliance (Peto 1967). Peto's approach remains classical and allows for little deviation in technique. He emphasizes the role of interpretation and avoids other parameters: he does not sit patients up, rarely offers extra sessions, keeps to time schedule, and discourages telephone calls. Frosch (1967b), on the other hand, in preference to this approach would stress the need to utilize supportive measures (including hospitalization) and to deal with reality issues.

In most cases, the regression has a defensive function, but in some cases the regressive state is where the patient feels most alive. The regression may connote an effort on the part of the patient to engage the therapist with these regressive aspects of himself since this is where he lives. Exploration of the regressed aspects of the patient's inner life is crucial for the success of the therapy. Any supportive measures that ignore or minimize these negative and regressive aspects will be experienced as rejection and will convey a sense of hopelessness to the patient that this alien part of himself can ever be remedied and integrated into a meaningful human existence (Clifton 1974). Regressions may have a progressive dimension, allowing, for example, previously split-off aspects of the patient's personality to reemerge and become available for reintegration. At this level, psychoanalysis may have to yield to psychosynthesis that can facilitate the process of integration and the consolidation of a new sense of identity (Corwin 1973).

Alliance Failure. Regressions are synonymous with the failure of the therapeutic alliance. Opinions differ as to how to deal with the disruption of the therapeutic alliance, but there is little argument on the necessity to regain this ground. I have argued for the priority of the alliance issues over transference aspects. There are times, however, in the face of a severe and precipitous regression, when one does not have many options—the therapist has to deal on the spot with whatever he can find to work with. He should not lose sight of the alliance issues and when the opportunity comes, he can be prepared to join with them. Even if transference issues are in the vanguard, he cannot ignore the related issues of recovery and reconstitution of the therapeutic alliance. Since these elements are obviously intertwined, features of the patient's therapeutic alliance reflect not only transference dynamisms but also other aspects of the patient's actual relationships with early caretaking objects (Atkins 1967). It is important that the therapist try to maintain empathic contact with the patient during these episodes since useful information can be obtained from the patient's regressive reaction insofar as it reflects the activation of primitive intrapsychic configurations (i.e., primitive layers of the pathogenic introjects).[3]

Activity. When the therapist begins to get the first signals of a regressive shift, it makes sense to me to try to buffer the regressive trend by increasing the level of structure and activity in the therapeutic interaction. This is opposite to the technique in dealing with therapeutic regressions. There the therapist, especially the analyst in the psychoanalytic setting, maintains the context of silence and neutrality in the interest of fostering regression. When he is confronted with a malignant or structural regression, however, the presumption is that the regression will be disruptive and will not benefit the therapeutic work. Therapists do not try to bring about or foster such regressions: at times they cannot be avoided and we then bend our efforts to make as much use of them therapeutically as possible. If we can catch one *in statu nascendi,* we try to avert it or at least slow it down and thus minimize its destructive effects. The therapist does this by increasing the level of his activity or by changing the regression-inducing parameters of the therapeutic situation. For analytic patients, this may mean not only a higher level of verbal activity on the part of the analyst—more questions, comments, observations—but also sitting the patient up, decreasing the frequency of visits, introducing more supportive techniques, and so on. None of these modifications would be condoned in the treatment of healthier patients whose regressive potential is much less and whose actual regressions remain within the therapeutic range.

The situation for psychotherapeutic patients is much the same, but the shifts may take a different direction. While the level of activity can be increased, the therapist may choose to increase the frequency of appointments rather than decrease them. In the psychoanalytic context, the presumption would be that the intensity of the schedule was having a regressive effect, producing an excessive regressive pull, an intensification of transference, and so on. This may also occur in the psychotherapy context, especially when the frequency is relatively intense. If the

---

[3]I would differ here with Clifton's (1974) view that the therapist must regress with the patient in order to maintain an empathic therapeutic alliance. Empathic contact yes, regression no. To the extent that the therapist regresses, all basis for a therapeutic alliance is lost. The patient is helped not by the therapist's joining the regression but by his ability to preserve his own boundaries and identity in the face of the patient's wish to fuse. Clifton's argument seems to identify empathic contact with therapeutic alliance; in my view they are related but quite different.

frequency is low (once or twice per week), the patient may need additional time to allow consolidation of the working alliance and attain a
greater sense of security and support from the therapist. The therapist
may opt for more frequent and shorter hours—increasing the measure
of supportive contact and diminishing the regressive pulls of more
intensive sessions. It should be added that increasing the level of structure includes attention to the structural dimensions of the therapeutic
situation—questions of attendance, lateness, payment of bills, and the
other aspects (see Chapter 5). These are closely connected with the
maintenance of the therapeutic alliance and are also important dimensions of the structure that is required to buffer regressive tendencies in
these patients. If the therapist were to try to maintain a better level of
therapeutic structure without attending to these aspects, he would be
working at cross purposes.

   Reality Testing.   Insofar as the regressive movement is away from
reality and deeper into fantasy, efforts to draw the patient back toward
reality are not inappropriate. These efforts involve attempts to reality
test the patient's distortions and increasing the titration of reality in the
therapeutic interaction. Increasing the reality of the therapist's presence
is to my mind a function of his increased level of activity and involvement with the patient in the therapeutic effort. Some therapists recommend that the therapist share his feelings with the patient as a means of
making himself a more real object for the patient. While there are
certain contexts in which such revelations can be productively utilized,
they are more the exception than the rule. By and large, such sharing of
feelings does not serve the buffering of the regression well and only
opens the door to a plethora of countertransference risks. Not only can
this device serve as a vehicle for negative countertransference but it may
also subtly satisfy the therapist's narcissistic needs. At best he runs the
risk of decreasing his objectivity and interest in the patient, and at worst
he can unconsciously draw the patient into fulfilling his narcissistic
needs (Clifton 1974).
   Regressive episodes always involve some degree of impairment in
the patient's reality testing. Efforts to help the patient regain some
degree of reality testing have their place but are usually better handled
in a gradual and piecemeal way. If the patient can be helped to review
the specific details of whatever events may have led to or precipitated
the regressive episode, the reality of these events can be gradually tested
and the residues of the patient's observing ego called into play
(Meissner 1986b). The process requires a gradual reestablishment of

the discrimination between present and past, between reality and fantasy, between self and objects, particularly between the patient's self and the therapist. Part of the recovery from such regressive stages involves the recognition of the separateness of the self and the therapist and a capacity to tolerate and accept this state of affairs (Gudeman 1974). While the therapist's stand in reality must be firm and consistent, the therapeutic focus falls more on the elaboration of the details and the understanding of the source of the distortions. Distortions in the transference are especially to the point: insistence on the reality in the face of such distortions may often serve only to goad the patient to greater rage and resentment and may result in the patient's leaving the session or quitting the therapy (Kernberg 1984). The therapeutic task is first to survive the patient's attacks, second to understand the origins of the projective distortions, and finally to help the patient gain some understanding of his experience by reconstituting some degree of working alliance. The objective with borderline patients is viable since regressive episodes in these patients are by and large transient and the therapist can usually count on a return to a more reasonable level of ego functioning and alliance in a relatively short time frame.

Limit setting.   Limit setting may also be necessary to contain the patient's regression. Where the regression takes the form of acting out, whatever appropriate measures can be taken to prevent any destructive or self-defeating effects of the patient's behavior should be brought to bear. Suicide is the classic situation, as we have already discussed, but there can be others. Behaviors that can have consequences for the patient's well-being or that may have deleterious consequences for important relationships and involvements may call for interventions from appropriate third parties to prevent any course of action by the patient that would have self-defeating or destructive consequences (Kernberg 1984).

Within the therapy limit setting can also have a place. Efforts to shore up the structural aspects of the therapeutic situation have a limit-setting effect. Insisting that the patient come to his hours on time sets a limit on the degree of acting out such tardiness involves. The therapist also sets limits by the degree to which he can explore the consequences of the patient's projected course of action. Simply expressing concern can often have a limit-setting effect. Or he may simply refuse to follow the patient's regressive thinking and refocus the discussion on more realistic or structured issues (Adler 1985).

The therapist has to consider the limit of his own ability to tolerate and deal with regressive behavior. He has to decide the limits of his availability while the patient is in regressive turmoil and the limits to which he can stretch his own resources and the inherent resources of the therapeutic process to deal with the patient's regressive needs. Most therapists would agree with Kernberg (1984) that therapy cannot be useful conducted in an atmosphere of threat of physical assault or of a threat of harm to others. In the face of severe and malignant regression, therapists may find it necessary to interrupt the treatment, to insist on hospitalization, or to resign from the case. No therapist should be expected to sustain the impossible or to undertake the heroic.

RECURRENT REGRESSION

Often the course of treatment of more severely disturbed borderline patients becomes an unending saga of recurrent regressions. I supervised one such case of a patient who was never far from the border of psychosis and at any number of points managed to cross it. This young woman's early history was dominated by the paranoid psychosis of her mother and the subsequent divorce of the parents when she was five. The father went to live with his brother and took the patient and her two older sisters with him. The uncle molested her sexually. The parents then reunited after a few years. The mother frequently beat the patient and was particularly virulent and abusive of the little girl's pubescent sexuality, mocking her budding breasts and joking maliciously about menstruation.

Soon after high school, the patient became pregnant and in desperation married the boy. The delivery of a baby girl was traumatic and resulted in psychotic decompensation—the first of many. This was followed by frequent episodes of running away, overdosing, suicide gestures, and multiple hospital admissions. She finally ran away from her husband, abandoned the baby, and was hospitalized for an extended period. The husband was granted custody of the daughter.

From the beginning of the treatment, she presented herself as fragile and vulnerable. The therapist, a woman, had the image of her as a tiny baby who needed mothering. Only gradually did she become aware of the fact that the patient saw herself in such terms and consciously used it manipulatively to get her own way. She acted in the therapy as though she were a puzzle of many pieces and did not want the pieces to be properly assembled to make an intelligible picture. It was better to have the puzzle unsolved and to be taken care of as a baby than to have to grow up. She treated the therapist as an idealized mother, or as a heaven-sent savior. Anger came quickly to the surface when the therapist did not measure up to the task. The therapist interpreted this disappointment, telling her that she seemed to treat her divine savior like a candy machine that she kicked when it didn't deliver. The patient admitted that at such times she saw the therapist more as a divine slave than as a goddess.

The therapist took a firm, limit-setting approach. She opposed the patient's continuing on welfare, insisted that she was able to work and should, and generally pushed her toward taking greater responsibility for herself and her life. She refused to continue discussions of the patient's childhood fantasies, and firmly encouraged her to face reality and get a job. Within a couple months the patient was off welfare and working, but she continued to make efforts to justify a more regressive posture. When she pleaded, for example, that her mother had damaged her brain by beating her about the head, the therapist offered a neurological referral, which the patient angrily declined on the grounds that it would deprive her of an excuse for her difficulties. When the therapist decided to begin a private practice, it meant that the patient's fee would have to increase. The patient was outraged, complained bitterly that she had been betrayed, that the therapist didn't love her and saw her only for the money. The therapist went on vacation, and when she returned the patient was without job or money. Therapy was interrupted.

The patient soon started to work again and therapy was resumed, but the patient was resentful, grouchy, and resistant. She got into a fight at work, quit, and became disruptive and destructive. She was admitted in the throes of a near-psychotic regression. In the hospital she engaged the male attendants who would listen to her fantasies in long discussions and completely ignored the therapist. She accused the therapist of being mean and sadistic. With firm limit setting she improved and was discharged, only to return in a matter of days. Only when the staff threatened to send her to a state hospital did she become more cooperative, and she was placed in a halfway house.

The patient continued in outpatient therapy for several more years. But the course was rocky and uncertain, with a great deal of lability, attacks on the therapist together with wishes to be held and comforted, frequent absences and lateness, and a persistent stubborn resistance. Threats of suicide were frequent and usually came in rather manipulative ways to gain some advantage in her struggle with the therapist. Feelings for the therapist became more intense, along with fears of

retaliation from the therapist for her constant attacks or even abandonment. At one point they agreed to raise the fee. This was followed by a
series of destructive acting-out behaviors, quitting her job, and threatening suicide. She stayed away from therapy for a week, and when she
returned launched a tirade against the therapist for raising the fee, since
it meant that she would have to take a second job as a waitress—a
position she felt was beneath her dignity. Moreover, the therapist was
exploiting her, taking her money, not helping her; she also agreed to
continue therapy. The work then focused on her dependency conflicts,
her fears of needing the therapist and having to depend on her, her
wishes to be taken care of like a helpless baby, and her intense love and
hate for the therapist. When the therapist made it clear that she had no
intention of mothering her and catering to her regressive wishes, it was
not long before she ran away from the halfway house and disappeared.

After three months, she resurfaced, paid her bill, and wanted to
resume therapy. She arrived at the next session in a rage, screaming at
the therapist and threatening to kill herself. She then began to demand
more support from the therapist. A long struggle ensued in which she
tried to convince the therapist that she was helpless and impotent and
that she needed the therapist to be a good mother for her. During the
course of this the therapist remained firm, and the patient improved
considerably. Evidently it was too much of a good thing. When the
therapist began charging for telephone calls as a limit-setting measure,
the patient was off to the emergency room again. She continued to
abuse the therapist, raging against any limits the therapist might set and
repeatedly trying to manipulate the therapeutic structure by various
forms of acting out. She vacillated between wishes to fuse symbiotically
with the idealized mother–therapist and fear of both engulfment and
abandonment. She alternated between feelings of helplessness and
worthlessness and grandiosity. She saw herself as either a saint or a
devil. Acting out around the therapeutic arrangements continued, so
the therapist had to make dealing with issues of missing appointments,
lateness, and paying the bill an ongoing part of the therapy. The
therapy hovered on the brink of breaking off, especially in the face of
the patient's unwillingness to pay her much-reduced fee. The patient
would rage at the therapist, and began to have paranoid fears that the
therapist was trying to kill her, and at the same time she was frightened
by her fantasies of killing the therapist.

During this interval she began dating an appropriate young man,
and the relationship quickly became emotionally intense and stormy.
After an argument, the boyfriend called off a date; the patient over-

dosed and was admitted to a medical ward. The therapist did not return her calls, and after discharge the patient missed several sessions and finally returned, angry at the therapist's apparent equanimity but also somewhat relieved that the therapist had not responded to her anxiety. This was followed by a more flagrant flaunting of the halfway-house rules that led to suspension. She called the therapist, screaming in a rage and demanding readmission to the hospital. An extra appointment was arranged, and when the patient came she begged the therapist desperately to take her home and let her live with her. They were able to focus on the patient's loneliness and feelings of helplessness, and her fears of "going psychotic." The patient was even able to admit reluctantly that her difficulties started when the housemother had left on vacation.

Admission to the hospital proved excessively gratifying to her regressive wishes to be taken care of. She experienced the hospital as a safe place where she could be "pampered" and "protected from Uncle Joe's penis." Both the therapist and the housemother had failed to protect her from the cruel world and abusive men. Discharge put her back in the soup, facing the same old problems. To gain admission to the house she had to be in twice-weekly therapy, and that required that she get and hold a second job. The same situation emerged at work, where her boss told her to shape up or she would be fired. She commented, "I need tough discipline; then I can do good work." Further efforts to regress in the form of overdosing, trying to get admitted to the hospital, and flirting with the rules at the house were frustrated. The therapist and the admitting physicians stood firm, the housemother remained firm in maintaining the threat of discharge, and her boss made it clear that with one more difficulty she was out. She responded with further efforts to get the housemother fired, then expressed fears of staying in the house because of the housemother's "revenge." Demands for a new therapist were resolved by agreeing to return to a once-weekly schedule. The patient was somewhat relieved since her fears of killing the therapist were extremely troublesome. After the schedule was reduced, she repeatedly asked for extra appointments. Subsequently progress was slow but steady. Once the avenues of regressive acting out had been closed off, the patient was forced to deal with issues in the therapy. From that point on, progress was possible. Only when all interested objects of manipulation were joined in a consensus that her regressive efforts had to be resisted was the therapy set on a positive course. Only then could the patient's inner torment, her disappointments and sadness be brought into the open and worked with. The patient finally left the halfway house, moved into her own apartment, soon after married and settled down. She gradually was able to reduce her therapy hours but still sees the therapist on an ad hoc basis.

This case demonstrates two important points. One is the effect of maintaining structure and setting limits in dealing with borderline regression. Everyone involved in the managing of the patient's case had to come to a realization that responding to the patient's regressive wishes was counterproductive, even though at a certain point or in the face of an immediate threat, giving in to the regressive wish was easier and brought immediate resolution to the turbulent situation. The short-run gain was purchased at the cost of long-term defeat.

COUNTERTRANSFERENCE ISSUES

The second point has to do with the avoidance of countertransference traps in the interest of maintaining the therapeutic alliance. The patient was caught in the throes of a turbulent inner struggle between the aggressor-introject (the devil) and the victim-introject (the saint). Her fear of the murderous destructiveness of the aggressor side was defended against by clinging to a position of helplessness and powerlessness, by seeing herself as a helpless baby who needed to be taken care of and pampered. Any suggestion that she grow up, be an adult, and take responsibility for herself was seen as becoming too independent, individuated, and assertive, and thereby as losing her dependent babyhood and becoming too aggressive and powerful. The therapist had to steer a difficult course between these pathogenic alternatives, especially in finding a therapeutic course through the projective distortions that the patient brought into the therapy—seeing the therapist as powerful and destructive on one hand and as a potential victim of her destructive and murderous wishes on the other.

As any number of authors have pointed out and discussed (Atkins 1967, Clifton 1974, Gudeman 1974, Giovacchini 1979, Boyer 1983, Adler 1985), the regressive phase of the treatment with borderline patients is especially fertile ground for the sprouting of countertransference difficulties. The regressive episode pulls the therapist out of his customary and comfortable role as neutral observer into a position of more active intervention and possible decision making. This opens the door to acting out of countertransference. However the therapist decides to respond to the regression, he must keep an eye on the countertransference issues.

Part of the problem is the need for the therapist to tolerate and be comfortable with the intense and primitive needs that are mobilized in the transference during severely regressive periods (Adler 1985). Taking a firm and limit-setting position can easily involve elements of counter-transference rage and the wish to control or retaliate against the patient. In my own theoretical perspective, the patient's regression reactivates and intensifies the more primitive aspects of the introjects and sets up powerful projective pressures that pull the therapist into corresponding countertransference positions. This "involves the active projection of aspects of the patient onto the analyst who, as the recipient of the projections, often feels himself empathically burdened with affects, impulses, and fantasies which owe their intensity to the patient's internal situation" (Atkins 1967). The therapist can easily find himself responding by playing out a countertransference role before he is even aware of it (Meissner 1982–1983, and Chapter 7): he easily slips into becoming the aggressor to the patient's victim, the victim to the patient's aggressor, the omnipotent rescuer for the patient's worthless self-degradation, or the impotent and incompetent foil for the patient's grandiosity. The difficult line to follow is to become none of the above. As in the case just discussed, the line followed was to become a firm, consistent, and therapeutically meaningful limit setter without crossing the border into acting out some anger or disappointment against the patient.

I close this discussion with a quote from Winnicott (1958):

It is commonly thought that there is some danger in the regression of a patient during psychoanalysis. The danger does not lie in the regression but in the analyst's unreadiness to meet the regression and the dependence which belongs to it. When an analyst has had experience that makes him confident in his management of regression, then it is probably true to say that the more quickly the analyst accepts the regression and meets it fully the less likely is it that the patient will need to enter into an illness with regressive qualities. [p. 261]

PART IV

ADJUNCTIVE THERAPIES

This section deals with alternate therapeutic modalities in the treatment of borderline patients. Without challenging or passing judgment on their relative merits, my orientation here is limited to a consideration of these approaches as adjunctive therapies that can be employed in conjunction with individual psychotherapy or analysis. My supposition throughout is that the patient's primary treatment is long-term, individual, psychoanalytically based and oriented psychotherapy or psychoanalysis. My approach, therefore, is governed by a concern with the contexts and situations in which adjunctive approaches can be used to facilitate and enhance the effectiveness of the core work to be done in the individual setting.

12

GROUP THERAPY

Group psychotherapy has a definite place in the treatment of borderline patients. Most therapists would agree that its appropriate role is as an adjunct to ongoing individual psychotherapy, and not as a substitute for it. I will focus this discussion in terms of a series of questions that confront the individual therapist in considering the advisability of adjunctive group therapy.

SELECTION

When does the therapist who is working with a borderline patient in intensive individual psychotherapy think of adding participation in group therapy to the therapeutic regimen, and for what sorts of patients might he recommend this option? Opinions are divided, but in general it is easier to say which patients will not do well in group treatment than to identify those who will (Horwitz 1977). Negative criteria would include excessive ego vulnerability, inability to tolerate regression, severe deficits in impulse control and reality testing, extreme narcissism, and paranoid traits (Horwitz 1977, Scheidlinger 1984); psychotic conditions, including schizophrenia, psychotic depressions, mania, and paranoia, tend to do poorly (Day and Semrad 1971).

Getting any borderline patient into a group so that he can stay in it long enough to get some benefit from it is no easy matter. The dropout rate is high. Patients do not do well in group therapy when they suffer from excessive narcissism, poorly controlled aggression, or excessive anxiety (Slavson 1964, Yalom 1985). Patients do better if they have developed some capacity for relating well with peers, in contrast with often impaired relationships with parental or authority figures (Grunebaum 1957, Horwitz 1977, Grunebaum and Solomon 1980, 1982, Solomon and Grunebaum 1982). Wong (1980b) points out that each group is unique and can provide a different group experience for the patient. Some patients may do poorly in one group but relatively well in another, depending on the composition of the group and the capacities and style of the leader. The patterns of possible combinations of individual and group therapy are also considerable, so that failure of one or two attempts in this direction should not be taken as a final contraindication.

For what patients should adjunctive group therapy be considered? My own view is that group therapy has a place for patients who have particular difficulties socializing, for whom the therapeutic work has reached an extended impasse, or for whom particular transference or countertransference difficulties have arisen. Horwitz (1977) emphasizes demandingness, egocentrism, social isolation, and socially deviant behavior. The situation may often not have reached a point where interruption of the therapy is advisable; such interruption can be more harmful than helpful. A group can help the patient gain useful support and provide a place for testing and clarifying some of the difficulties. My clinical impression is that group work is more often helpful for patients in the hysterical continuum, whose affective turmoil, transference/countertransference difficulties, and tendencies to act out can be readily modulated in the group context, where the intensity and conflict of transference reactions can be more dilute. These patients tend to become rapidly and intensely involved with their objects, and the group can readily incorporate and take advantage of this characteristic. Patients in the schizoid continuum, in contrast, are either so withdrawn and defended or so adept at hiding behind a false facade or creating a screen of false compliance that they are better able to avoid the impact of the group process. Others would add that patients with psychosomatic symptoms or those with excessive severe superegos are good candidates for group (Scheidlinger 1984).

Patients who suffer from excessive narcissism or who manifest a significant degree of paranoid defensiveness do not do well in group situations. It is often difficult to get them to engage in the group process—the other group members either become threatening aggressors or are incorporated into the patient's narcissistic need for admiration and support. Since these difficulties are fairly generally distributed in the borderline spectrum, the fruitfulness of group therapy for such patients is limited. The more primitive the personality structure and the lower the patient stands in the spectrum, the more difficult. Following Rosenfeld's (1979) lead, Roth (1982) has described a series of narcissistic borderline character types that seems to parallel roughly some aspects of the spectrum as developed here. He describes six types of patients, from latent or recovered psychotics, who represent the most primitive group closest to the border of psychosis, to the healthiest group, who show no signs of borderline pathology until they become involved in the regressive pull of the group process. Intermediate types would include Kernberg-style borderlines, schizoid, "as-if," and false-self-type personalities, patients characterized by infantile anxieties and tendencies to act out, and patients who tend to develop relatively severe forms of narcissistic transference. Roth sees all of these patients as benefiting from the group process, but each requires special handling and techniques that adapt the group to the patient's therapeutic needs.

GROUP STRUCTURE

Individual versus Combined Therapy

What kind of group structure is advisable? Should the patient be treated with group therapy alone or in combination with individual therapy? Most authorities in this field seem to recommend combined treatment, either with the patient beginning in individual therapy and adding the group as indicated or having the group as the primary modality and using individual sessions as they seem to facilitate the group work (Day and Semrad 1971, Horwitz 1977, Slavinska–Holy 1980, 1983, Wong 1980b, Yalom 1985). In any case the indications are not very strong (Scheidlinger 1984). Wong (1980b) argues that group treatment alone is generally unsatisfactory and that individual treatment should be included at some point in the therapeutic course. As the group process takes hold and the patient begins to feel regressive pressures, the patient's pain may require additional individual work (Day and Semrad 1971).

Regarding the treatment program for hospitalized patients, Kernberg (1973, 1984) has argued that unstructured group situations seem to mobilize more regressive aspects of the patient's personality structure, specifically the more primitive derivatives of infantile object relationships, while dyadic contexts are more likely to elicit triadic oedipal dynamics. This would imply that combined treatment at both a dyadic and group level should be included in the treatment regimen in order to tap in on different levels of psychic structure and development. Dividing the therapeutic territory in this fashion may be adding excessive clarity to a basically murky situation. Borderline patients vary considerably in their regressive responsiveness. As our previous discussion suggests, not only are powerful regressive forces set in motion in the individual therapy setting, but this is a major source of difficulty in working with more primitive borderline patients. Also this position seems somewhat at variance with Kernberg's often stated positions about individual therapy with borderline patients.

Open versus Closed Group

Is an open or closed group better for borderline patients? I could find little comment on this question. It may not make much difference, and a high degree of individual variation in how patients react to group situations can be encountered. The closed group, in which all the members start and end therapy together as a group, has the advantage of emphasizing peer relations and focusing more directly on issues of dependence and separation, simply because at some point the group stops and separation cannot be avoided as an issue. The open group, in which members enter and leave at different times, allows a greater degree of flexibility. Patients can enter, work in the group for a time, interrupt, leave, return, and so forth. Such groups can function in a variety of roles—supportive, crisis intervention, and, to the extent that the patient stays with it for a longer period of time, exploratory. An open group works better for patients who are unable to negotiate the difficult waters of termination and separation. The group remains an available reference point from which they never need to separate entirely and to which they can return when necessary.

Homogeneous versus Heterogeneous Group

Should the patient be referred to a homogeneous or heterogeneous group? Opinions differ, some recommending groups composed entirely of borderline patients (Scheidlinger and Pyrke 1961, Scheidlinger and Holden 1966, Slavinska–Holy 1980, 1983, Scheidlinger 1984) and some mixed groups (Slavson 1964, Day and Semrad 1971, Horwitz 1977, Wong 1980a,b). Wong (1980a,b) argues that homogeneous groups are less successful since the intense oral demands, envy, rage, devaluation, and idealization are compounded by the similar level of pathology in all the group members. The outcome is usually rapid turnover, poor treatment results, little or no sense of therapeutic alliance, and little group cohesion. Day and Semrad (1971) recommend groups with a mixture of character types, which allows for greater potential interaction and mutual exploration. Having any more than one or two borderlines or psychotics in a group becomes counterproductive. In contrast, Slavinska–Holy (1980, 1983) argues for the use of homogeneous groups. The advantages she emphasizes are that the group shares common defenses deriving from a similar developmental stratum that facilitate simultaneous interpretation in individuals and in the group, and that primitive projections and patterns of idealization and devaluation emerge more clearly, intensely, and dramatically and can be dealt with more directly and forcefully.

My own experience in this area is somewhat limited, but my sense is that a decision about the type of group appropriate for a given patient is a highly individualized one. The majority view that heterogeneous group settings are more successful is probably sound. Much depends on the capacity of the group leader or leaders to deal with the difficulties involved in more homogeneous groups. My experience suggests that the task becomes more difficult and onerous as the number of primitive patients increases. Within the borderline spectrum, however, there is considerable heterogeneity. One could envision a homogeneous group of patients within the borderline spectrum that would in fact have considerable heterogeneity if the patients were drawn from various levels. My preference in such a group would be to limit the number of patients from the lower order of the spectrum and to limit patients from the schizoid continuum. I would limit the former group because of their limited capacity to participate nondisruptively in the group process, and the latter group because of their inherent difficulties in entering into the group process.

Supportive versus Expressive

Should the Group be supportive or expressive? There is no clear answer to this question since much depends on the purpose of the group and the role it would play vis-à-vis the individual therapy. For some patients the supportive aspects of the group play a more important role, for others the group can facilitate more exploratory and expressive efforts. Much also depends on whether the same therapist serves as individual therapist and group leader. Where this is the case, more exploratory efforts can be attempted. Where the roles are occupied by different individuals, the balance of support versus expression is a matter of working out compatible and mutually supporting therapeutic goals. As in most individual therapies with borderline patients, the issue is not either/or but degree and balance: the therapy is both supportive and expressive, at times more one than the other, but never one without the other.

Same versus Different Therapist

Perhaps the most difficult question is the last: should the group therapist be the same as the individual therapist or should they be different? Obviously the personal inclinations and capacities of the therapists in question enter into the picture in a significant manner. Not all therapists are capable or equipped to handle both modalities. Not all therapists are in a position to sustain the strain and stress of undertaking such a dual role. The individual therapy with borderline patients is complex and difficult enough without adding the additional burden of group treatment. It is a fairly common practice for group therapists to see patients individually on an intermittent and limited basis at points of particular difficulty and stress in the group work. Such input is usually quite helpful and serves to keep the patient's work in the group on track. The individual sessions are intended to maintain and facilitate the group process rather than replace it.

Wong (1980b) argues for the advisability of the same therapist serving in both roles and advances several advantages for such combined therapy. First, having two different therapists working in two different modalities is an open invitation to splitting, which can give rise to countertransference difficulties, not only between the patient and the respective therapists but also between the therapists as well. One therapist becomes the all-good, idealized, and even magical object, and the other the all-bad, malign, and persecutory object. In addition, the limits of confidentiality become fuzzy and are easily violated. Effective handling of the splitting problem requires regular communication between therapists, an effort that is often difficult to achieve and maintain. When the therapist is the same, these avenues of resistance and acting-out can be more readily contained and worked through.

Second, continuity of treatment is better preserved. Patients often have a greater sense of support from the group when they know they will see the same therapist later in the individual session. Use of different therapists is often unavoidable if the patient has to be hospitalized, but this is exceptional in the outpatient setting. Tendencies to project onto the therapist and devalue him are less intense, and the opportunities to confront the patient's distortions individually when they arise in the group, or in the group when they arise individually, are mutually reinforcing.

Third, transferences are usually better handled insofar as the group provides a context in which the transference can be distanced, diluted, and deflected (Yalom 1985). Regressive tendencies are buffered by the capacity of the group to reality-test and support the patient through regressive crises. The easing of transference intensity can moderate the countertransference pressures that often arise with borderline patients (see Chapter 7). The group dynamics can also serve to confront the more primitive, aggressive, and narcissistic aspects of the patient's behavior in the more acceptable context of peer interaction rather than in relation to a single authority figure.

Fourth, the group context provides a greater range of opportunity for internalization and identification. In contrast to the unilinear context of the therapeutic dyad, the group stimulates both positive and pathological interactions with the other group members and with the therapist. The pattern of projections is distributed to the whole group and sets up a complex interactive web of projections and introjections. The projections tend to reflect fragmentary aspects of the patient's self-organization and the therapeutic introjections are based on an amalgamation of elements derived from all of these object involvements. These are often more readily assimilated and internalized insofar as the partial selection of complementary attributes for internalization can occur without the conflict-laden difficulties that can contaminate individual relationships (Meissner 1981b).

Finally, working with the patient both individually and in the group allows the therapist a broader focus and range of experience of the emerging and evolving facets of the patient's identity. The therapist can then function more effectively as a stabilizing and integrating force in the patient's milieu. These findings are generally supported by Slavinska–Holy (1980, 1983) in working with exclusively homogeneous groups.

13

FAMILY THERAPY

The importance of family dynamics and the perspective it brings to the understanding of borderline psychopathology and its etiology and genesis cannot be underestimated. I have devoted considerable attention to these issues in my previous work (Meissner 1984a). Considerations of family dynamics and family interaction patterns are significant in the treatment of all patients, whether in psychoanalysis or in psychotherapy (Meissner 1981a, 1982). Family dynamics also play a significant role in the analytic work with young adult patients, who are not far removed from involvement in the emotional patterns of family interaction (Shapiro 1987). I would go so far as to say that in the treatment of borderline patients, at all levels of the borderline spectrum and at all age levels, the family issues can hardly be avoided. These patients are caught up, in intense and often traumatic ways, in an ongoing pattern of response and interaction to influences stemming from the family context (Zinner and Shapiro 1974, Shapiro et al. 1975).

Despite the broad implications of the family perspective and theory on the understanding and treatment of borderline patients, the actual implementation of family therapy as a therapeutic modality is limited in practical terms. Although some have argued for the utility of family therapy in the treatment of adult patients (Berry and Roath 1982), the more commonly accepted position is that such therapy is useful for children or adolescents, and possibly even young adults—

those patients who may still have some degree of meaningful involvement with their respective families (Mandelbaum 1977a,b, Zinner 1978, Shapiro 1978, 1982).

There is a general consensus that family therapy is best employed as a complement to ongoing individual psychotherapy of the disturbed adolescent. Properly employed, the family approach can provide support for the individual therapy by providing relief from persistent family tensions and emotional entanglements (Shapiro 1978). The approaches are used in varying combinations, depending on the clinical setting. In a research setting, the psychoanalytically oriented psychotherapy sessions for the borderline adolescent may be complemented by weekly meetings of the family conjointly and even further by couples therapy for the parents alone. Some therapists prefer to use only individual and family sessions, but the additional component of couples therapy for the parents often allows more focused work on the parental relationship (Zinner 1978).

In dealing with borderline adolescents, it can be presumed that the pathology in the family system is severe, particularly with regard to dynamic interactions around issues of separation and individuation, so inclusion of the family system in the treatment process is almost unavoidable (Shapiro 1979). As Shapiro (1987) comments:

> We find that in the treatment of adolescents who are severely disturbed, where the nature of current dependence of the adolescents and parents on each other is at the center of the adolescent's pathology, a combined treatment including interpretive conjoint family therapy and individual psychoanalytic therapy for the adolescent allows explicit therapeutic work on the parent-adolescent relationship. [p. 60]

There is some variability in the manner in which these modalities are combined and sequenced. Typically, there may be a number of individual evaluative sessions for the disturbed adolescent and other separate meetings with the parents, with or without combined meetings of the entire family. These initial sessions usually have an evaluative focus and are directed to determining the nature of the problems and at reaching a consensus with the family participants as to an advisable course of treatment. This can allow for an emphasis to be made that all of the family members are involved in the pathological family process, and takes some of the onus off the shoulders of the designated patient (Mandelbaum 1977b, Zinner 1978, Jones 1987).

FAMILY PATTERNS

The McLean Group (Gunderson et al. 1980) distinguishes between two types of families of borderline children. In some families, the pattern of interaction between parents and the child involves a degree of parental unavailability that forces the child into an adaptive posture of precocious responsibility and serene acceptance of parental superficiality. With these families, they recommend that family therapy should not be initiated from the outset of the treatment, but that the parents should be seen as a couple separately from the borderline child. This helps to diminish the level of threat to the bond between the parents, who tend to feel threatened by the child's efforts to separate them. After these issues have been successfully dealt with, family therapy can be introduced. Mixing in the sense of frustrated rage and blaming of the borderline adolescent would not only increase the anxiety of the parents but tends to generate unproductive and mutually accusatory sessions, which usually undermine the work of the therapy and end disastrously.

The McLean Group contrasts this with the pattern in other families that involves a mutually dependent relationship between the borderline patient and the family. With these families, fears of separation and difficulties in establishing a therapeutic alliance may be exacerbated by meeting separately with parents and child. Here, emphasis on the issue of separation–individuation and the problems involved in the parental response to it can serve as a helpful and productive focus. The pattern may develop in other directions as well: as Shapiro (1982) notes, intensive family treatment may evolve toward a greater internalization of conflict among the family members, which leads to a gradual stoppage of family therapy and to individual therapy for family members or couples therapy for the parents. In such contexts, family therapy, even when introduced early or at the beginning in the treatment process, can serve as a preparation for more meaningful individual psychotherapy (Berry and Roath 1982).

Therapeutic Alliance

My experience would indicate that there is a considerable degree of clinical variability in the manner in which these issues can be dealt with, and much depends on the dynamics in a given family system, as well as the degree of skill and comfort that the therapist has in treating family problems. One major issue has to do with the therapeutic alliance. The therapeutic alliance with borderline patients is tenuous and precarious at best, but with borderline adolescents it tends to be a particularly troublesome problem. My own course of action is to work individually with the adolescent for whatever period of time is necessary to consolidate a sufficient degree of alliance and a degree of awareness and understanding on the part of the patient of the significance of the patterns of emotional interaction between himself and his family. Only then is it possible to introduce the family therapy as a complement to the individual therapy, with the clear understanding of how the family therapy can contribute to the adolescent's individual therapy and without jeopardy to the therapeutic alliance. Unless these factors are adequately attended to and in some degree resolved, the beneficial outcome of the family therapy can be placed in jeopardy.

An additional question has to do with whether the individual and family therapy should be conducted by the same therapist. Kernberg (1979) argues strongly in favor of an exclusive psychotherapeutic relationship between the therapist and the borderline adolescent. The family therapy should be conducted by another therapist. If the adolescent is involved in the family therapy, the family therapist must have the permission of the adolescent and the family to communicate his observations to the patient's individual psychotherapist. The effective integration of these therapeutic approaches depends on the effectiveness and purposefulness of the communication between the respective therapists. In the studies at the National Institutes of Health (Zinner 1978, Shapiro 1978, Shapiro 1979), one therapist would work with the index patient and the second therapist would treat the parental couple; then both therapists would work together in conjoint family sessions with the family. In view of the inconvenience of co-therapy in an office practice, they recommend that the parental couple be referred to an outside therapist. They also observe that they found it inadvisable for the same therapist to undertake both the individual therapy of the adolescent and the couples therapy. They found this arrangement created complications of confidentiality and a tendency to involve the therapist in the pathogenic communications between parents and children (Zinner 1978).

These cautions are well taken, but my own view is that despite the risks and the potential difficulties it may create for maintaining a solid therapeutic alliance, there are many advantages for the same therapist to function as the individual therapist for the borderline patient and as the family therapist, with or without a co-therapist. Problems of confidentiality do not arise because the patient is a participant in both contexts. I make it a hard and fast rule that if the patient is not available for a given family therapy meeting, that meeting is canceled. I want nothing to transpire between myself as the patient's therapist and his family to which he is not an immediate participant. To behave otherwise would be to invite transference difficulties, distortions, and misunderstandings, and would pose a direct threat to the therapeutic alliance. By the same token, I would not engage in a combination of individual therapy with the patient and couples therapy with the parents. This would lead to unavoidable difficulties and usually has the unfortunate outcome of undermining the therapeutic alliance with the patient and running the risk of the therapist being seen as colluding with the parents. If the parental couple needs therapy, I refer them to another therapist and try to maintain effective contact and communication with that therapist.

Family Interaction

The family emotional system plays a particularly important role in the genesis of borderline psychopathology, and in the case of children and adolescents continues to exercise a pathogenic influence. The operation of more primitive defenses, particularly the interacting patterns of projection and introjection within the family system, works to induce complementary pathology in the other family members with whom the patient interacts and can have the effect of bringing about self-fulfilling prophecies. Particularly in relationship to the parents, it may be important to assess the degree to which the patient is reacting to pathological pressures coming from the parents and to what extent he effectively induces such pressures from them (Kernberg 1979). In many of these families the onset of the child's adolescence tends to induce a form of group regression, which seems to reactivate repetitious patterns of parent–child interaction that may have arisen earlier in the child's life. These patterns of family interaction may be the source for transference responses that arise in the patient's relationship with the therapist (Shapiro 1982).

The family system can be envisioned as a self-contained matrix for transference interactions on its own terms. The ongoing family system involves a set of interlocking transferences around which the family interaction is articulated. Usually, in the analytic situation, transference enters the analytic interaction from the family matrix in which the patient experienced the original object relationships. *The family situation is the native habitat for these transferences.* The ongoing transference involvement has a different quality, since what is transferred is not something out of the family matrix but reflects earlier vicissitudes of the complex history of object relationships within the family itself. The family emotional process is a natural outgrowth of the earliest dynamic interactions within the family, which have their own inherent continuity and history (Meissner 1978a). This linkage between the traditional focus of the transference in the therapeutic relationship and the pattern of transference involvement within the family is one advantage of both therapeutic processes being carried on by the same therapist. It becomes possible to work back and forth between the transference expressions that emerge within the family system and those that come into focus in the individual therapeutic relationship.

Autonomy

Any number of authors have commented on the difficulties that borderline families have in dealing with issues of separation-individuation. Conflicts arise around issues of both dependency and autonomy. Needs for dependency and nurturing are unacceptable and are poorly tolerated, while at the same time developmental shifts toward autonomy and independence are often frustrated and denied (Mandelbaum 1977b). The family fails in its function of facilitating adolescent development. The specific developmental tasks of adolescence include the process of second individuation (Blos 1967) and the development of a sense of personal autonomy as one of the primary ingredients for adolescent identity formation (Erikson 1956, Jacobson 1964). But the pathogenic influences in borderline families, operating in terms of unconscious assumptions and patterns of pathogenic projection and introjection, tend to undermine this process and impede accomplishment of essential developmental steps. These unconscious assumptions generate states of anxiety and depression, and tend to mobilize regressive defenses in response to efforts on the part of individual members to separate and individuate. The result is the emergence of regressive and symptomatic behavior within the family system, which is often focused in scapegoat fashion on the designated adolescent patient (Shapiro 1979). Thus, on the presumption that the parental response to the adolescent patient's impetus toward autonomy is one of the major etiological factors in the formation of borderline personality (Meissner 1984a), the therapeutic work on these issues in borderline families requires that the conflict between the striving for individuation and autonomy and the fulfillment of oral dependency needs must be addressed (Buie 1977). These issues must be worked on in parallel both in the family therapy sessions and in the individual sessions with the adolescent.

Family Emotional System

The family emotional matrix is constructed out of the projection of repressed or disavowed aspects of the introjective configuration in individual family members onto other family members and by corresponding patterns of introjection in these other members. The patterning and quality of these mutually interacting processes determine the dynamic forces operating within the emotional system and dictate the unconscious fantasies and assumptions that arise within it (Shapiro 1982). In this connection Shapiro's group speaks of a "shared family regression" (Zinner and Shapiro 1974) in which autonomous or dependent needs in the borderline adolescent are responded to by withdrawal, retaliation, or empathic failure (Berkowitz et al. 1974a,b, Shapiro et al. 1975). Using the term "projective identification"[1] to express the complexity of mutually reinforcing projections and introjections, they write:

> We observe a complementary use of projective identification of dystonic aspects of their self-representations by these parents, which blurs their capacity to experience themselves as separate from the particular child in areas of conflict. Through the use of this shared defense, parents fail to perceive accurately the reality of the child, developing defensive stereotyped delineations of him [Shapiro et al. 1977, Shapiro and Zinner 1975]. The adolescent's developmental reliance on parental evaluations . . . interferes with his capacity to react against the constraints imposed by their defense needs and inhibits his identity formation. [p. 212]

The borderline adolescent is caught up in the family system as the receiver of a variety of projections from other family members. These projections can be traced separately to interactions between the borderline patient and each of the family members, from whom he may become the recipient of pathogenic projections in varying degrees.

---

[1]My objections to the term "projective identification" have been detailed elsewhere (Meissner 1980a, 1987b). The usage here in regard to the family emotional system implies no more, in my view, than interlocking projections in some family members and correlated introjections in others.

Usually the most central projective components come from one or other or both of the parents, but they can be reinforced, abetted, or modified by projections coming from other family members as well. These projective patterns, evolving within an ongoing family history and interaction and interweaving themselves with the course of the patient's developmental history, are internalized in some combination and become woven into the fabric of his character structure. The patterning of the family projections may take shape around a central theme or motif that can variously be regarded as a family myth or as a set of shared unconscious assumptions that dominate the unconscious emotional life within the family system. The tendencies to splitting and projection in these families have been variously noted (Masterson 1972, Masterson and Rinsley 1975, Shapiro et al. 1975, Zinner and Shapiro 1975, Gunderson et al. 1980, Meissner 1984a).

These interactions in borderline families often result in a pattern of scapegoating (Mandelbaum 1977b), which makes the designated borderline patient the recipient of elements of hostility and hatred within the family system and which elicits a marked pattern of victimization and aggressive conflict in the borderline adolescent. Not only is the adolescent scapegoated by the dynamics within the family system but his sense of self as victim, as the embodiment of the scapegoat, becomes woven into the fabric of his identity. This aspect of the process makes modification of these patterns particularly difficult, not only insofar as the patient has effectively internalized them but also because they serve highly important and intense dynamic needs to stabilize and maintain at least a semblance of cohesive function within the family unit itself.

It is also useful to maintain a multigenerational or transgenerational perspective in dealing with these dynamics within the family. An important aspect of the understanding of the dynamics within the family emotional system is that these patterns do not arise *de novo*. The marital partners bring to their relationship and to the family that arises from it the residues of their own developmental experience and the patterns of introjective dynamics that have been built into the fabric of their own personality structures. These dynamic interactions within the family system involve displacement of transference residues from earlier levels of experience—i.e., the contemporary pattern of interlocking projections and introjections derives from and reflects internalizations and derivatives of the quality of object relations that obtained between parents and child when the child was much younger. However, the contemporary transference residues also derive from earlier levels of experience within the extended family, from internalizations and derivatives of critical object relations in previous generations, from relationships between the parents and their respective parents (the grandparents) and even beyond. The family transference system must, therefore, be seen as transgenerational (Meissner 1978a).

Combined Therapy

I would like to add a few final comments on the problems that arise in the combined individual and family therapy of the borderline adolescent. The difficulties in maintaining a therapeutic alliance with a disturbed adolescent patient are monumental enough, but when the therapist moves into the realm of family therapy, in addition to his work with the patient, he inevitably creates a more complex and even more difficult situation to manage. There is a kind of cost-benefit analysis involved here—the cost in terms of the jeopardy to the alliance and the individual therapeutic effort versus the gains to be gotten from the work with the family. That analysis is not always negative. Where the therapeutic alliance with the adolescent is sufficiently stabilized, where the therapeutic interaction is such that the potential difficulties in the alliance that may arise from the involvement with the family system can be explored and clarified and understood, and where the therapist is able to maintain a sufficiently balanced position in his dual role as individual and family therapist, the process can often be hearteningly successful. My own priorities fall strongly on maintaining the alliance with the patient; if any problems arise in trying to undertake the work with the family that severely threaten the alliance in a way that it cannot be adequately reconstituted or maintained, then the family involvement does not strike me as a good idea.

In undertaking the work with the family, an alliance must also be established with the family as a separate therapeutic unit. This may often come into conflict with the individual alliance with the patient. The problem often arises: whose side is the therapist on? The ultimate answer is that he is on everybody's side, but this position is difficult to maintain, not only in fact but in the experience of it on the part of individual family members. Consequently, the alliance or alliances must be worked on in both therapeutic contexts. The therapist must be willing and able to explore with the patient the nature of his alliance with the family and the purposes for his maintaining a relatively balanced position in which he is in no way choosing up sides but is invested in the best interest of all parties involved, including the patient. With the family the therapist must be clear about the nature of his relationship to the patient and how that interdigitates with his relationship to the family and what his purpose and role are in each of those related contexts. Ultimately, all parties involved must seek the well-being of the patient as it is connected with the better and healthier functioning of the family system. This clarification and stance must be maintained in the face of continual pressures from all sides, both the individual patient and the family, to undermine this position, to draw the therapist into one or other transferential position, and to elicit from him some form of countertransferential response that will serve to undermine the therapeutic alliance, destroy his therapeutic position and make him ineffectual as a therapist, and thus preserve the underlying fantasies and narcissistic and aggressive distortions that are an integral part of the neurotic family system. The therapist in this sense comes to the family as a threat, as an enemy whose purpose is to undermine and destroy the family system that the family as a unit and the individual participants have created in order to avoid other intrapsychic threats and dangers. Thus, powerful motivation exists within the family system to maintain the status quo and to resist any impulse toward change. With any given family system, the extent to which the family as a whole or the individuals within it have the capacity to modify this state of affairs and to allow change to occur remains a question. In some contexts, the mobilization of forces of change results in a realignment of the dynamic influences within the family that can modify the position of the designated patient and allow therapeutic growth. In other instances, the family system remains relatively rigid and immobile; any therapeutic gains can be realized only insofar as the patient is able to separate and dissociate himself from the pressures of the family and to begin to establish his own sense of separate and individuated identity.

It should also be remembered that the role of the therapist in family therapy is quite different from his role as an individual therapist. Regardless of his stance vis-à-vis the individual patient, regardless of the degree of activity or passivity, of the mix of supportive and expressive elements and so forth, in the interaction with the family, the therapist generally must adopt a more direct, forthright, and active position. He allows the family interactions to emerge to a sufficient degree to allow him to begin to identify patterns of interaction, to begin to focus the underlying assumptions within such patterns, and even to begin to identify the various roles of the family members and the ways in which they engage in the patterns of projection and introjection that form the warp and woof of the family emotional system. This divergence in therapeutic roles creates its own pattern of tensions in which the patient may experience the therapist as a much more real object or may experience different facets of the therapist's personality in the interaction with the family that do not play a very significant role in his own interaction with the therapist. This may create a tension between his wish to have a closer relation to the therapist, to know more about him, and to feel more intimately involved with him, and an envy of other family members who may elicit different reactions from the therapist. The patient may experience a sense of abandonment and rage that the therapist treats them somewhat differently. These factors all contribute to the undermining of the therapeutic alliance and often must be addressed in the individual therapy sessions.

Overall, my experience is that the integration of individual psycho-therapy with family therapy for many borderline adolescents is a challenging, difficult, but often richly rewarding experience, both for the patients and for the therapist. The process has many risks, however, only some of which I have been able to touch on here. The whole area of family therapy is almost a discipline unto itself, and it should not be lightly or too readily undertaken without a serious consideration of the risks and gains involved in any given case. Moreover, it should not be used by therapists who do not have an adequate grounding in the principles and techniques of family therapy. Even for therapists who have this background and experience, the process is not an easy one. Therapists who do not have that background can acquire it in training and afterwards. Experience in and knowledge of family techniques can be learned through various forms of instruction and supervision. Where it is properly utilized with due caution and awareness of the complexities and issues involved, this combined modality offers a powerful instrument for the remedying of pathological distortions, not only within the borderline adolescent himself but within the family system, which still maintains a powerful influence on his psychic life.

14

SHORT-TERM THERAPY

CONTEXTS

Short-term therapy utilized as the sole therapeutic modality has a limited application in the treatment of borderline patients. The limitations arise from constraints in the patient's availability for more extensive therapeutic work or from matters of practical expediency. Short-term therapy must be regarded as a relatively inadequate substitute for more extensive, long-term, intensive psychotherapy or psychoanalysis.

The contexts in which short-term therapy has a meaningful role are:

1. *As a form of crisis intervention*: For patients who are otherwise resistant to or unavailable for longer-term therapy, the necessity of treatment may be forced on them by a particular regressive episode that creates some crisis in their life situation. The objective in this context is to enable the patient to ride through the regressive crisis without unduly destructive acting out, and to enable him to reconstitute to a more usual level of preregressive adaptive functioning. Depending on the severity and depth of the regression, hospitalization may be a transient necessity in such cases, but it can also be accompanied by short-term therapy in which the activity and structuring efforts of the therapist enable the patient to reconstitute an adequate degree of psychic integration and

reestablish his level of normal functioning. Insofar as borderline regressions tend to be time-limited and transient, the regressive episode can be expected to modify and resolve within a reasonably short period of time, so the therapeutic contract need not be extended for a significant period of time. In my judgment, the therapist in such situations owes it to the patient to make him aware of the longer-term issues and risks, but the decision whether to continue therapy on a longer-term basis must be left in the patient's hands.

2. *Limited clinical resources*: This situation arises fairly typically in outpatient clinics where the available resources of the clinical staff have been overwhelmed. There may not be enough psychotherapy time available, and it is not uncommon for such clinics to have extensive waiting lists of patients who are interested in psychotherapy but must wait until time and a therapist become available. This situation can also arise in the private-practice setting, where a therapist may have only limited time available and may be able to see the patient only in a short-term focus or may have only occasional hours to make available to the patient. If the patient in such situations is in any degree of crisis, the choice must be made whether it is to the patient's advantage to be referred elsewhere so that more intensive and immediate therapeutic work can be undertaken to deal with the crisis situation. If it is felt that the patient can tolerate whatever degree of regressive strain he may be experiencing, it may be possible to work out a time-limited course of short-term therapy that will at least enable the patient to avoid further regression and to maintain himself in his life situation. Referral to a therapist who can deal with the problem and provide the patient with the necessary therapeutic time is by far the preferable course.

3. *Limited resources of time and/or money*: It is always more convenient for the resistant patient to find external excuses for not entering into a therapeutic process, but there may well be contexts for specific patients in which they are more realistically unwilling or unable to enter into an extended and intensive treatment process. Time (usually because of job or other significant commitments) and money are the major impediments. If the patient is unable to pay a fee that the therapist feels would be reasonable for undertaking the therapeutic effort, it is frequently possible to make an appropriate referral to low-fee clinics. At times therapists may be in the position to make reasonable compromises about fees and to undertake treatment at lower than usual fees, but this decision is very much an individual one and depends

largely on the nature of the therapist's financial situation, his practice, and his life commitments. Referral to a low-fee clinic, however, may be in the best interests of the patient, and if so should be implemented. For an individual patient to come to the decision to engage in a limited and short-term therapeutic effort with a given therapist should be carefully considered in the contexts of the available options and with clear recognition that the choice is not optimal treatment. Such decisions can easily be influenced by rapidly mobilized transference reactions borderline patients, particularly in the form of erotic or idealizing transferences.

4. *The patient's inability to tolerate stress*: Fortunately, one does not often meet such patients, but they do exist. The commitment to a long-term therapy process may place excessive demands on them that they are unable to meet. I have had a number of experiences with patients who seem to be able to undertake a brief period of therapy, at times lasting for months at a time, but then find it necessary to break off the treatment and to escape from it for a time. These patients have then resurfaced, reestablished the therapeutic contact, and continued for another limited period of therapeutic effort, only to find it necessary to interrupt the treatment again. The therapeutic course can evolve over an extended period into the equivalent of a long-term therapy process. Its formal structure, however, is a series of short-term therapy processes, each of which is time-limited and relatively focused in its efforts, each of which is effectively terminated but then again reopened to advance the therapeutic sequence another step or two.[1]

With such patients, the therapist faces a dilemma, namely, whether the patient's need to interrupt the therapy is a form of resistance, or whether in fact it can over the long haul serve some useful and therapeutic purpose. Unfortunately, there is no easy way to discriminate while in the midst of this series of events; one can only judge in retrospect. Often the therapist has no better resource than to do what he can to interpret the aspects of the patient's resistance and motivations for escaping from the therapy and, where these efforts fall short of the mark, to let the patient do as he will, and hope for the best. Not infrequently, these interruptions take the form of a flight into health that is quite resistant to the therapist's efforts to interpret as resistance.

---

[1]The case of Mr. Baker (discussed later in this chapter) followed a similar pattern.

SELECTION

The selection criteria that most advocates of short-term therapy lay down are not very optimistic regarding borderline psychopathology. By and large, these approaches prefer patients who are better functioning, more rewarding, less demanding, and less burdened with severe degrees of psychopathology. Selection criteria tend to focus on the intactness of ego functions, good motivation, and the capacity for a positive therapeutic alliance. Malan (1975, 1976) would exclude patients on the basis of poor ability to make contact, poor motivation, rigidity of defenses, excessively complex or deep-seated issues, excessive dependence or other forms of unfavorable and intense transference, and the risk of intensification of depressive or other psychotic disturbances. Sifneos (1972) emphasizes the capacity of patients to tolerate anxiety and to have good object relations. This would tend to exclude patients with severe narcissistic difficulties. The patient must also be highly motivated for change rather than mere symptom relief. Patients with difficulties in establishing a therapeutic alliance or with admixtures of preoedipal ambivalence do not do well. These criteria would seem to eliminate most patients within the borderline spectrum, with the possible exception of some well-functioning higher-order borderlines. Mann (1973) and Mann and Goldman (1982) would seem to explicitly rule out borderline personality organization, along with serious depression and acute psychosis—but he has in mind lower-order borderlines. Likewise excluded are schizoid patients, patients with strong dependency needs, more severely narcissistic and depressive patients, and patients having difficulties in forming a therapeutic alliance. Davanloo (1980) looks for a capacity to tolerate anxiety, guilt, and depression, good motivation, basically oedipal pathology, a capacity to utilize interpretations, flexible defenses, and an absence of more primitive defenses of projection, splitting, and denial. To the extent that borderline patients suffer from these stigmata, they would be excluded.

Thus there seems to be a strong consensus regarding the limited applicability of short-term treatment in the therapy of borderline patients. By and large, patients in the schizoid continuum are eliminated, both by reason of the prevailing pattern of isolation and withdrawal that characterizes their pathology and by reason of the fact that they are only rarely and exceptionally subject to disruptive regressive episodes that might require crisis intervention. Within the hysterical continuum, patients with more primitive characteristics in terms of issues of self-cohesion, defensive organization, and levels of ego function-ing would be contraindicated as well. The only patients for whom short-term therapy offers any potential utility are those in the higher order of the borderline spectrum, who may require periodic or time-limited interventions in order to buffer a regressive episode and to reconstitute the patient to a level of preregressive functioning relatively quickly.

IMPLEMENTATION

The aim of short-term therapy with borderline patients is primarily to avert the potentially damaging consequences of regressive episodes. Therapeutic insistence, therefore, must fall on bringing some degree of order and structure to the patient's chaos, setting effective limits to curb acting out, particularly acting out that may have damaging or self-destructive consequences, and helping the patient to reorganize his defensive system and his level of self-integration to avert the looming disorganization and profound anxiety of the regression.

The techniques employed in the short-term treatment of borderline patients are generally the same as those recommended for the short-term treatment of other patients with some special considerations. Leibovich (1981, 1983), one of the few therapists who advocate short-term treatment for some borderline patients, emphasizes the positive relationship between patient and therapist (the therapeutic alliance) as crucial, and generally stresses the importance of structure and activity in the therapeutic interaction. Thus, it is important to set a limited and definite time frame for the therapy, emphasizing the reality of the limits and their frustrations, and dealing almost from the beginning with issues of separation. This implies the necessity for the patient to accept his separateness and aloneness and the limitations and deprivations in his life. The imminence of an eventual separation not only puts a greater pressure on and challenge to the patient to accomplish more within the allotted time but also serves to diminish any expectations of merger and excessive dependency. The therapeutic work requires the focusing of a central issue, which can be kept in the foreground of the therapeutic work throughout. The therapist needs to be more active, to assume a more verbal and structuring role in his interactions with the patient, avoiding painful silences and not allowing the patient to retreat and withdraw from the therapeutic interaction.

A Case of Pathological Jealousy

One context in which short-term therapy has some claim to effectiveness is when the patient, for whatever reasons, finds it necessary to
frequently interrupt the therapeutic work. These cases may stretch out
over a period of years, but the cumulative total of therapeutic time
amounts to the equivalent of a short-term effort. A case of this kind was
reported in considerable detail by Balint and his associates (Balint et al.
1972). The patient, Mr. Baker, was referred to Balint because of his
increasingly serious preoccupations with his wife's involvement with a
man who had courted her some twenty years earlier, before their
marriage, but with whom she had had no subsequent contact. The
paranoid jealousy had become severe and threatened hospitalization,
even though the delusion was relatively well circumscribed. The patient
had begun to resort to intensive questioning of his wife, compulsively
and insistently inquiring about the details of her experience with the
other man and tormenting her with his demands and accusations.

History. The patient was from a well-established and well-to-do
family, who had been printers and stationers for several generations.
After graduating from school, the patient began working in the family
firm, which was owned by his father and run by the three brothers, of
whom he was the middle one. At the time of the referral, the father had
recently retired and had sold the bulk of his shares in the company to
the three brothers, giving them a controlling interest.

During the Second World War, the patient was stationed in Cyprus, where he met his wife, a Turkish woman. She was the first and
only love of his life. There was considerable resistance from her family
because of ethnic and religious differences. He was then reassigned to
the Burma front, where he fell ill and had to be hospitalized. When
letters from his fiancée stopped coming, he became agitated and upset.
Finally, a letter from her arrived informing him that she had met a
young officer with whom she had fallen in love. She expressed her
uncertainty about which of the two men she should choose. He wrote
her pleading letters, and finally she wrote that she had broken off the
relationship with the other man and had decided to commit herself to
him. When he recovered, he returned to Cyprus, and they were married.

The patient's previous psychiatric history contained several episodes of depression, one about six years before his contacting Balint, in
which he had been depressed for several months, feeling tired, sleeping
long hours, and not wanting to get out of bed. Significant circum-

stances involved moving into a newly built house a few months before his breakdown and the death of his father-in-law, with whom he had a fairly close relationship. A second depression occurred around the time of his taking a holiday, with feelings and preoccupations similar to those in the previous depression. This depression came soon after he and his two brothers bought a majority interest in the business from their father.

Therapy. The course of therapy extended over a period of about six years and included a total of twenty-nine sessions. Some initial evaluative sessions were followed by a three-month break, and then by weekly sessions for about ten weeks, which were again interrupted and followed by sporadic sessions over the next year or so, and capped by final sessions a year or two later. The therapeutic work was accomplished, however, in about the first fifteen months of the therapeutic contact.

Diagnosis. My impression is that Mr. Baker's personality organization was essentially borderline. I would base this assumption on the repeated regressive crises that mark his clinical course (and the excessive vulnerability to regression it implies), on the conflicts or confusion of sexual identity (homosexual versus heterosexual conflicts) implicit in much of the material, and on the propensity for paranoid delusion. There also seem to have been islands of significant ego weakness in Mr. Baker's personality structure. These seemed to coexist with areas of ego strength. He was, after all, quite successful in carrying on his difficult and demanding life responsibilities as both a businessman and a family man, and functioned quite successfully in most of his social interactions.

Prognosis. What then of the prognosis of such a patient? If we were to look only at the presenting clinical picture, we would have every right to be somewhat guarded. We would expect that the underlying structural vulnerability in the organization of such a personality would not yield quickly or easily to psychotherapeutic intervention. We would be forced to think that an effective course of therapy would have to be long-lasting and difficult. Yet, Mr. Baker's therapeutic breakthrough was accomplished in a mere twenty-seven sessions, extending over only fifteen months. Moreover, the therapeutic gains seemed to have been well maintained through an approximately four-year follow-up. What might we say about this in terms of the tentative diagnosis and its implicit prognosis?

The fact is that patients often surprise us and fail to fulfill our predictions. Based on what we know about the psychological vulnerability of borderline patients, my guess is that Balint's therapy may not have done a great deal to alleviate that aspect of Mr. Baker's psychological existence. However, the major focus of that vulnerability and the narcissistic issues connected with it may well have been sufficiently dealt with and resolved to allow the other more adaptive and competent parts of Mr. Baker's personality to assert control over his psychic life and thus to account for his improved psychic state. The very fact that Mr. Baker's delusions were relatively encapsulated and narrowly focused, even though they reflected broader themes that played themselves out in various areas of his experience, would have to be counted as an optimistic prognostic indicator.

Consequently, Mr. Baker is not at all unusual among patients seen in clinical practice. Patients may come in a regressive crisis, looking relatively ominous, with rather severe psychopathology. Psychotherapeutic work may quickly bring the focal areas underlying the crisis to some resolution, with the result that the symptomatology diminishes and the patient gains some crucial insight and begins to feel and function more effectively. The therapist may feel that the underlying vulnerabilities have not been effectively dealt with or significantly altered, but the patient has gained sufficient mastery of his inner life and of the conflicts that give rise to his distress and may opt for that as an adequate solution. This new-found equilibrium, despite the underlying structural vulnerabilities, may in fact serve as an adequate basis for a long-term satisfactory adaptation. Our capacity to predict which patients will again regress and find their way back to the therapist's office and which will not is not very well developed. Much in fact depends on the stresses, losses, disappointments, and frustrations in the future course of the patient's life. If these impinge upon the crucial areas of his vulnerability, particularly his narcissistic vulnerability, more trouble can be anticipated. The same might be said about Mr. Baker.

Paranoid Dynamics. The classic stance of the paranoid patient is that he presents himself as a victim, while the aggressive, destructive, and sadistic elements are projected to the outside. A constant theme running through Mr. Baker's material is how vulnerable he is, how easily hurt, particularly by women insofar as they will not love him and will reject him. He reinterprets events and circumstances so that he can feel he is a helpless victim. His relentless questioning and challenging of his wife can be seen as an elaborate attempt on his part to reinforce his conviction and view of himself as a victim even in his relationship with her. He moves in an environment that is generally hostile to him. Fate is against him. If two other people have any relationship with each other, it must mean that they are excluding him. Even Balint's interpretations are twisted so that his sense of victimization can be maintained. Balint's comment, for example, that after all his wife Farah had chosen him over his rival was interpreted to mean that she did not in fact love him but had chosen him for some other reason, perhaps pity. In addition, the sense of victimization is strongly reinforced by the Rorschach test report. Mr. Baker sees women as powerful, phallic, and dangerous, and he feels weak, vulnerable, and threatened.

Pathological Internalizations. The origins of this sense of victimization are not difficult to discern: Mr. Baker clearly felt that he was his father's victim. But his sense of victimization is also reinforced and consolidated by his identification with his mother. He saw his mother as a disappointed and unhappy woman, who was completely dominated by the father.

Mr. Baker is apparently more comfortable with feelings of passive victimization than he is with more aggressive components. The aggressive aspects of his personality organization are clearly highly conflictual and difficult for him. Previous regressive crises had occurred when he had taken some significant steps forward or had gained a greater position of assertive independence. The first took place in the context of buying a new home and the death of his father-in-law. The second took place in the context of buying the majority interest in the family business from his father along with his two brothers. The parallel here with the Schreber case (Freud 1911) is difficult to escape, since Schreber's psychotic decompensations also took place in the contexts of competitive achievement and advancement. The aggression is also quite evident in the sadistic cruelty Mr. Baker directed toward his wife. It also shows up in the Rorschach results, where the aggressive aspects of his personality seem directed at the threatening figure of the woman whom he must attack with violent, sadistic, and ruthless onslaughts. His attacking demeanor becomes a main line of defense against the underlying feelings of weakness, vulnerability, and victimization. He becomes the aggressor in an effort to castrate the threatening phallic woman.

Clearly, the model here is provided by the patient's father. He is described as overbearing and unpleasant, and Mr. Baker recounts how he could seldom stand up to his father and felt continually humiliated and inferior in the father's eyes. The patient lived in terror of his father's unpredictability, his capriciousness and rage. Even after the family business had been settled by legal agreement, Mr. Baker did not feel secure and feared that his father would somehow subvert these arrangements. The father was clearly the sadistic persecutor of Mr. Baker's childhood—a circumstance again reminiscent of the Schreber case.

Several aspects of this identification with the cruelly sadistic and aggressive father should be noted. An important part of the patient's relationship with his father was a current of positive affection, a frustrated and unsatisfied yearning for closeness, acceptance, and approval from a good, strong father. The dependency needs and a longing for supportive contact come through in the Rorschach as well. Father-figures on the Rorschach cards are predominantly good figures, and the patient finds an "anchor" on card four, which is usually regarded as referring to the father-figure. Consequently, his need to attack men defensively is compounded with a yearning and seeking for approval and support from a male figure.

Another minor note is that the patient also felt to some extent victimized by his mother. This adds an important note to our consideration here, in that the critical internalizations do not take place on a one-to-one basis in reference to specific objects. It is more usually the case that aggressive components from a variety of objects may be compounded and assimilated in the patient's introjective configuration and contribute to its aggressive organization. Moreover, it is commonly the case in families of such patients that the patterns of victimization and victimizing are not exclusively in one direction—for example, the father constantly victimizing the mother—but may go back and forth between the parents with varying degrees of intensity and variation. It is more usually a mutual and reciprocal victimizing.

A similar polarization is evident with regard to the narcissistic components, although in Balint's presentation the patient's sense of narcissistic superiority and specialness goes begging. Only at one point does Balint suggest that his patient's attitudes were in fact concealing a sense of superiority to his male rivals. It is particularly in terms of the patient's sense of masculine competence and capacity that the elements of narcissistic inferiority play themselves out. Mr. Baker saw himself as inferior to any and all other men; every other man was better, bigger, or more attractive, and in any competition Mr. Baker was bound to lose out. His commitment to the inferior and victim position comes through clearly in his inability to accept the possibility that he might have won out over his rivals for his wife's affection. I said above that Mr. Baker's superiority had gone begging, but if we remember the rules of the game according to which the paranoid process is played, the introjective configuration is the basis for the pathological projection. Mr. Baker not only projects the hostile and aggressive elements to outside agencies and forces but also the narcissistic superiority, which is required to preserve his sense of inferiority and victimization. His view of other men as somehow superior and as rivals who will inevitably defeat and overcome him is such a projection.

Therapeutic Impact. We can wonder what aspects of this interrupted and abbreviated therapeutic process may have had a significant impact on the organization and functioning of this constellation of introjects. The first obvious element is that Baker and Balint managed to hit it off right from the start. For reasons difficult to define, Mr. Baker accepted Dr. Balint as a benign, supportive, and helpful figure who then could become the recipient of Mr. Baker's benign projections, thus providing him with the caring and protecting father-figure for whom he yearned.

It is interesting to note the rationale that Balint gives for his approach. With regard to his choice of foci, he comments that as therapist

> He considered it a fairly classical instance of a jealousy paranoia, with the three classical sources, anal eroticism, homosexuality, and rigid obsessional tendencies. The therapist thought that in this case the most important factor was the patient's homosexuality, which could not tolerate that there were men who would not love him. The fact that he could not accept was that in the case of his wife he defeated his rival, which was the final proof that his rival will forever remain his enemy and could never love him. [Balint et al. p. 29]

I suggest that in meaningful and substantial ways Balint managed to address and help the patient deal with various of the introjective components. Both the aggressive and the victimized dimensions, for example, were made central subjects for exploration, particularly in terms of the patient's relationship with his father, by whom he felt himself constantly diminished and attacked. The discussion of this relationship and the patient's feelings of hatred for the father and for the treatment he had received from him were critical points in the therapy, as Balint himself noted.

Another important element in dealing with the sense of victimization was the linking of the patient's feelings with his identification with his victimized mother, as well as with the father's own sense of insecurity and vulnerability. But Balint also picked up the aspect of the patient's introjection based on the sadistic cruelty of his father. The same cruelty and sadism became Mr. Baker's own and would later be turned against his wife. Balint was even able to draw these elements into the therapy insofar as the patient attempted to do something similar with him, trying to trip him up, or in a sense victimize him, as well as working to place himself in the position of being Balint's victim. Moreover, Balint was able to connect this pattern of interaction with the father with the patient's frustrated longing and affection for the father, as well as with his sense of victimization at the hands of the mother that provided the basis for his displaced ambivalence toward his wife.

If we turn to the narcissistic components, certainly the central focus Balint placed on his patient's sense of inferiority and his view of himself as the unsuccessful and surely defeated rival in any competition with other males, whom he saw as superior to himself in every regard, had to be an extremely effective aspect of the therapy that impinged directly on the narcissistic elements in the patient's introjective configuration. In this respect, Balint was dealing directly not only with the patient's sense of inferiority but also with the projective distortion involved in his view of all other males as superior to himself. Here again, Balint was successful in getting at the genetic roots of the problem, particularly in the context of the father's making him feel inferior and inadequate.

In short, then, I am suggesting that Balint's interventions were successful with his patient insofar as they impinged on, dealt with, and sufficiently modified the patient's underlying introjective configuration. The one element that goes begging in all of this is the patient's narcissistic superiority, which remains untouched and unattended. If one were to prognosticate further areas of difficulty and potential vulnerability for Mr. Baker, it would have to be in this area. I would conclude that short-term therapy of this sort has a limited application, one in which effective therapeutic goals can be realized but in which the basic structure of the patient's introjective configuration will not be significantly modified. Mr. Baker's case shows that even in short-term therapy of this sort, therapeutic interventions can be brought to bear on the patient's introjective organization and that the therapeutic effects of such efforts are not inconsiderable.

TERMINATION

One of the major difficulties in undertaking any short-term or focused work with borderline patients is termination. Even when the issue of termination and separation is raised from the beginning of the therapy as something to be dealt with in the face of the arbitrary time limitation, it cannot be satisfactorily worked through and resolved with these patients and remains problematic. Depending on the degree of the patient's involvement and the level of dependency needs, termination may not be feasible within the time perspective previously agreed on. For some patients, this time limit will have to be extended, for others the therapy cannot remain on a short-term basis and will inevitably become long-term, and for other patients the therapy will have to be interrupted rather than terminated, leaving open the possibility for continuing therapeutic contact. When a specific limit or time of termination has been set, it may be better to stick to that agreement but to regard the stopping point as an interruption rather than a termination. This leaves open the further option for the patient to reestablish therapeutic contact after a therapy-free interval. Some patients, as I have suggested, can benefit from such intervening intervals and can return to the therapy ready to accomplish a further stage in the therapeutic effort. Such seems to have been the case for Mr. Baker.

Short-term therapy should be a part of the therapeutic repertoire of therapists who treat borderline patients with any regularity. Not only does the short-term approach offer a greater range of therapeutic options in the treatment of a good many patients, but there may be a handful of patients for whom the short-term approach is mandated by circumstances or for whom nothing else is possible. Even though the short-term approach is far from the optimal treatment for these patients, it would seem reasonable for the therapist to make available whatever kinds of therapeutic assistance the patient may be able to tolerate and make use of, even when the help is compromised or limited. In such circumstances, a little therapeutic help can go a surprisingly long way.

15

Hospitalization

BORDERLINE SPECTRUM

At one or more points in the therapeutic course, hospitalization is a necessary part of the treatment of many borderline patients. For those in the upper ranges of the borderline spectrum, hospitalization is exceptional and depends on the regressive vulnerability of a given patient. Regressions are mild, easily managed on an outpatient basis, and transient. For other patients, regressions may prove to be severe enough to warrant hospital admission, but these are rare episodes that occur infrequently and are linked to external crises or traumatic life situations. Admission for these patients is on an ad hoc basis and is usually short-term.

For patients in the lower order of the borderline spectrum, closer to the border of psychosis, the story may be quite different. In this range of borderline psychopathology, since the regressive potential is so much higher, regressive episodes occur more frequently and in response to lesser degrees of stress. Consequently, in the midst of a regressive crisis, the therapist may find that the regression can no longer be contained within the structure of the therapeutic situation and hospitalization may become necessary. For some of these patients, admission to an inpatient facility may be an infrequent prospect, although it would not be at all unusual for many such patients to hover near the threshold of admission on repeated occasions or over significant periods of time. More often than not, the threat of suicide is a recurrent issue, and the decision regarding hospitalization hinges on the estimate of the degree of lethality. For other patients in this pathological range, hospitalization becomes a major component of the therapeutic experience, with frequent and repeated admissions (Lerner 1986). It is no surprise to find an extensive record of hospital admissions in the psychiatric records of these patients. For most of them, short-term hospitalization is preferable, although for a selected subpopulation more extensive long-term inpatient treatment may be necessary.

REASONS FOR HOSPITALIZATION

The reasons for hospitalization are multiple and differ for patients who are already in therapy and those who are not. For patients not in therapy, the reason comes down to some disruptive regressive episode, usually attempted suicide, but not exclusively so. Hospitalization becomes an opportunity for evaluation and for initiating therapy. For patients already in treatment, the move toward hospitalization usually reflects some difficulty in the therapy or some disruption of the therapeutic relationship. This may be reflected in disruptions of the therapeutic alliance, negative therapeutic reactions, suicidal behavior (Marcus 1981), frustration and rage because of the realistic limitations of the therapeutic relation (the therapist's failure to serve as an all-nurturing and gratifying object) (Adler 1977), or other disappointments and losses in their current lives (Adler 1985). Sometimes the disruption is simply a matter of the therapist's sense of helplessness, frustration, and anger at such a difficult and recalcitrant patient (Simon 1984). Therapists may often find themselves caught in a seemingly unresolvable impasse, at times as part of a negative therapeutic response, often in borderlines as a result of a regressive transference distortion (usually in the form of a transference psychosis or a paranoid transference), or even as part of an unconscious collusion between therapist and patient—a therapeutic misalliance (Adler 1977, 1985, Carsky 1985–1986; see Chapter 5).

A fairly frequent precipitant of hospitalization with lower-order borderline patients is the threat of suicide (Adler 1977, 1985, Gunderson 1984, Barley et al. 1986). The purpose of hospitalization in such cases is to gain better control over a deteriorating clinical situation (Marcus 1981). More often than not, the threat of suicide in a borderline patient is more manipulative than efficacious, but the therapist cannot take the risk. There are no guarantees that hospitalization will in fact abort a serious suicidal impulse, but it may help deal with the patient's manipulation and enable the therapy to gain a better footing. The suicidal component may not always take the form of an acute suicidal threat. Severe cases of alcoholism may represent a form of slow but certain suicide; anorexia nervosa, in which weight loss is carried to dangerous extremes, is another case in point (Story 1982). Both alcoholism and anorexia are behavioral syndromes that often involve an underlying primitive borderline character structure. The dynamics in such cases share many points in common with suicidal borderlines. Similar problems arise in dealing with the self-destructive behaviors of disturbed adolescents. Hospitalization becomes necessary when outpatient alternatives have been exhausted and when the pattern of self-destructive behavior can no longer be controlled, whether it takes the form of suicide, destructive actions, drug or alcohol abuse, or sexual promiscuity, (Feinstein and Uribe 1985).

Hospitalization may also serve as an effective means of limit-setting as part of the therapy. As Gunderson (1984) observes, "Even though utilization of a hospital may not be necessary, access to a hospital and a readiness to employ it are essential parts of the armamentarium therapists need to treat borderline patients" (p. 132). The comment has a point in the treatment of relatively primitive, regression-prone, and acting-out borderline patients. The availability of admission to a hospital should be included in the therapeutic alternatives from the beginning. It is one effective limit-setting card that the therapist has in his hand. For patients functioning on a higher level, however, for whom the possibility of hospitalization is remote or minimal, it is considerably less likely to be employed in this manner. For such patients, hospitalization is only rarely indicated for occasionally more severe regressions.

Borderline patients are notoriously difficult to treat, and therapists often have difficulty recognizing the degree of strain they suffer in the process. The sense of frustration and resentment against the patient sometimes grows until the therapist's hostility begins to express itself in subtle and undermining ways, or is defended against by increasing concerns for the patient's safety and well-being (Gunderson 1984). This can open the way to all the varieties of countertransference hate (Maltsberger and Buie 1974; see Chapter 7). In such circumstances, where these countertransference dynamics cannot be adequately worked through and resolved, hospitalization may serve to give the therapist needed distance and perspective, and enable the therapy to continue. This is a form of burnout that is all too familiar in contexts where borderline dynamics tend to be pervasive, as in the treatment of drug addicts (Imhof et al. 1984). The degree to which the patient is victimized in this process often calls forth an aggressive response leading to the all-too-common picture of the angry, demanding, and disruptive patient who makes the staff feel impotent and helpless to ward off his feelings of worthlessness and vulnerability (Maltsberger 1982–1983).

PURPOSES OF HOSPITALIZATION

Hospitalization is always implemented for a specific therapeutic purpose. For patients without previous therapy, hospitalization serves as the setting for evaluation and planning of a further course of treatment (Gunderson 1984). This may also be a function of admission for patients in therapy, providing an opportunity for reevaluation, reassessment, or more comprehensive review to clarify therapeutic goals and approaches (Marcus 1981, Adler 1985). As Kernberg (1976a) points out, the more complex therapeutic matrix of the hospital milieu provides a broader context for observation and evaluation of the patient's behavior and social functioning, drawing on different levels of object relatedness and object involvement—patient interaction, staff interaction, group settings, and so on—each of which may elicit different aspects of the patient's social adjustment. These evaluations can complement the understanding of the patient derived from the more restrictive dyadic context of psychotherapy.

Where the therapeutic relation has become embroiled in intensification of transference, transference/countertransference, or disruption of the therapeutic alliance, hospitalization can serve to modify the intensity of these dynamics, provide some breathing room for both participants, and get the therapy back on course (Marcus 1981, Gunderson 1984, Adler 1985). Thus, the hospital can serve a valuable consultative function, supporting and facilitating the long-term objectives of the individual therapy (Wishnie 1975, Marcus 1981). When the disruption takes the form of self-destructive acting-out or a suicidal threat or attempt, the hospital is a resource for dealing with the problem and at least limiting the patient's opportunity for self-destructive action. As I have already indicated (see Chapter 10), the therapist's handling of this sort of regressive crisis has great implications for the course of the therapy. The extent to which the patient can be enlisted in the decision process leading to hospitalization may determine its success and its meaning for the ultimate outcome. When all such possibilities have been exhausted, the therapist may find his hand forced; he must be ready and able to play his trump card, involuntary hospitalization, regardless of the patient's efforts to avoid it. While there are no guarantees that hospitalization will keep the patient alive, and while there is no room for the therapist to take responsibility for keeping the patient alive, our society and its laws dictate our legal responsibility, which we have an obligation to observe. Whatever the consequences for the therapy, they will have to be dealt with in due course.

SHORT-TERM HOSPITALIZATION

A critical decision in facing the prospect of hospitalization is whether it should be on a long- or short-term basis. For the great majority of borderline patients, short-term hospitalization is preferable, particularly when the patient is already in treatment (Singer 1987). Short-term hospitalization is advisable in contexts of transient regressive crisis or disruption of therapy. Such brief hospitalization can accomplish its goals relatively effectively and at the same time minimize the risks of inducing further regression with an extended stay (Friedman 1969, Wishnie 1975, Adler 1977, 1985, Gunderson 1984). Unfortunately, the length of hospitalization is not always dictated by clinical considerations: if the patient has limited financial resources or inadequate insurance coverage, short-term hospitalization may be a necessity rather than an option (Hartocollis 1980).

Short-term hospitalization puts the emphasis on crisis intervention, establishing appropriate limits, interrupting the pattern of destructive acting out, quieting the emotional turbulence of the ongoing regression, and providing whatever measures of containment and control are required. Evaluation and implementation of useful therapeutic measures are brought quickly into play with emphasis on the time-limited and transient nature of the process. The expectation is that the regressive episode will resolve in a reasonably short period of time (Adler 1977).

Particular contexts of short-term hospital intervention are provided by acute interventions in the hospital emergency room and admission to a day hospital. Perlmutter's (1982) observations of the use of the hospital emergency room by borderline patients suggest the following points: the patients tend to be lower-order borderlines with a high degree of emotional lability, high regressive potential, and impaired ego strengths; multiple visits are the rule, often in the context of seeking relief from tension, manipulating the system to gain gratification, or acting out against a therapist; the most common presentation is either a suicidal gesture or some form of self-mutilation; destructive family interaction, particularly with adolescents, is frequently observed, usually in the form of rewarding regressed, symbiotic behavior and punishing or rejecting autonomous behavior. Effective therapeutic interventions include emphasis on the patient's ultimate responsibility and control over the decision regarding life or death, evaluation of acute precipitants, mobilization of immediately available resources (medication, family, social worker, other support systems), and either referral for follow-up therapy or return to a current therapist. This may involve coordination of treatment strategy with the therapist, especially if patients are frequent repeaters. The most difficult decision is whether to admit the patient to a hospital. As Perlmutter (1982) observes:

> While we are striving for a more reasoned approach than repeated hospitalizations of chronically suicidal people, clinical judgment must prevail. Admission may still be indicated if it is part of a rational therapeutic or diagnostic plan, if the patient is psychotic, if the intent to die is imminent and acute, if the patient can mobilize no resources, if the PED [psychiatric emergency department] approach does not help in control of the impulses. The point is that the clinician must balance the possible gains from admission or other interventions against the easily overlooked risk. [p. 194]

Short-term day hospital care has been recommended by a number of authors, particularly for patients who may need continuing support while maintaining a job or other involvements and with whom there is a reasonably well-established therapeutic alliance (Pildis et al. 1978). For some patients, even longer-term day-care programs may have important therapeutic benefits (Gunderson 1984). This approach may be useful for adolescent patients as well, particularly if they have formed an effective therapeutic alliance and can cooperate with the demands of the program (Simon 1984).

LONG-TERM HOSPITALIZATION

Long-term hospitalization is appropriate for patients in whom the longer-term issues of chronic vulnerability or ego weaknesses prevail or when short-term efforts have failed to deal with the regressive issues

(Singer 1987). The lower and lowest levels of the borderline spectrum provide the candidates for such treatment. Severe character pathology, distortions in reality testing, paranoid tendencies and distortions, failures of self-object differentiation, and a history of multiple hospitalizations are the rule (Brown 1980). These would include patients with poor motivation for treatment, poor anxiety tolerance or impulse control, or impoverishment of object relations (Kernberg 1973, Hartocollis 1980, Adler 1985). Other indices might include a prolonged and malignant pattern of self-destructiveness, disturbed or destructive family situations (especially for children or adolescents) where sexual or physical abuse may be involved or where repeated undermining or disruption of outpatient treatment can be expected (Gunderson 1984). Hartocollis (1980) feels that patients with deeply ingrained sadistic or antisocial characteristics can be treated only in a firm, consistent long-term setting. One of the difficulties is that treatment programs that are designed for the long-term care of such primitive and inherently difficult borderline patients are few and far between. Such specialized programs have been designed and put into operation (Sadavoy et al. 1979, 1981, Brown 1980, Gunderson 1984); where they exist they can serve important therapeutic objectives (Tucker et al. 1987).

ADMISSION TO THE HOSPITAL

When the individual therapist and the patient have reached a decision to admit the patient to a hospital, the hospitalization process itself creates a series of problems that require consideration. The first set of problems centers around the admission process itself. In making the decision, the therapist must determine whether he intends the hospital stay to be long- or short-term. This issue should be discussed with the patient and plays a central role in determining where the patient is to be hospitalized. If there is not an adequately staffed and experienced unit equipped to undertake the long-term inpatient treatment of relatively primitive borderline patients, the purposes and potential gains of the admission are not likely to be fulfilled. Inpatient units that have experience in the treatment of psychotic patients may not fill the bill. Often there are no real options—in which case, long-term admission may be contraindicated or may contribute only negatively to the therapeutic course. In such circumstances, short-term hospitalization may be preferable. Insofar as possible, the reasons for and objectives of the hospitalization should be discussed with the hospital staff. It is also possible that an intended short-term hospitalization may have to be extended for therapeutic reasons.

Then there is the question of the nature of the therapist's continuing contact with the patient during the hospital stay. This is in part determined by the circumstances that precipitated the hospitalization and the reasons for its implementation. Does the therapist see the hospitalization as an ending to his therapeutic involvement with the patient? Or does he see it as part of an ongoing therapeutic effort that he and the patient will continue after the patient's discharge? Does the therapist want to maintain contact with the patient during the period of hospitalization? What is the orientation of the hospital program? Does it call for separation from the outside therapist, does it require the outside therapist to continue to act as the patient's primary therapist, is continued contact with the patient encouraged in one or other degree, depending on the therapist's willingness to continue with individual psychotherapy after discharge, or does the staff presume that it will assume total responsibility for the patient's in-hospital treatment? These are all aspects of the relationship between the therapist and the hospital staff that can and do vary considerably from one unit to another. The therapist should be clear about these arrangements and make his preferences known. Many programs accommodate the recommendations of an outside therapist, others do not. This consideration may enter into the process of deciding where to hospitalize the patient. It is more often the case that the hospital staff will want to assume total responsibility for the patient's care in long-term treatment settings; this is less likely to be the case when short-term hospitalization is in question, particularly when return to the outside therapist in a relatively short time is envisioned.

Admission to a psychiatric hospital is traumatic, especially if it is a first admission. The therapist owes it to the patient, insofar as possible, to prepare the ground so that there are no surprises—or at least as few as possible. The worst-case scenario in my experience is when the patient is brought to the hospital under a deception—for example, that someone else is to be admitted. I have seen this happen with expectably disastrous results. If the admission can be processed therapeutically, the chances for a smooth and reasonable transition to the hospital are improved. Circumstances do not always permit this luxury, and admission may have to be made as an emergency. The therapist may simply have to make the best of a bad situation; anything that can be done to ease the process should be done. The therapist's cooperation and participation in the admission process is desirable. Especially when the patient is in crisis, rapid evaluation and effective intervention are called for (Adler 1985).

COMMUNICATION

I emphasize the usefulness of the therapist's input for the hospital staff, the importance of communicating to the staff the circumstances of the admission and particular issues regarding the patient, clarifying the therapist's role vis-à-vis the patient while in the hospital, and cooperating with the requests and recommendations of the hospital staff. This also includes arrangements for seeing the patient, for continued communication with the hospital staff, for distributing therapeutic and administrative responsibilities for the patient, and for whatever else needs to be done to ensure the patient's continuing therapy. Where the hospital requires or requests that contacts with the outside therapist be minimized, these arrangements should be respected, with a clear understanding about the therapist's availability for continuing to see the patient after discharge. Even when he plans to continue the patient's therapy after the hospital stay, the therapist is well advised to wait for the initiative to come from the patient or the hospital. The hospitalization may well lead to the conclusion that therapy should be continued with the same therapist, or the patient may have used the hospitalization as a way of escaping from the previous therapist. Since one cannot know the direction of these options when the patient is admitted, it seems judicious to respect the possibilities. These issues are particularly important when it is the patient's first admission to a given facility or when the therapist is not known to the staff or vice versa.

An important aspect of the admission process is dealing with the patient's family (Gunderson 1984). This has added valence when it is a question of admitting a disturbed child or adolescent for whom the ties to the family are especially intense and important. The success or failure of efforts to establish a therapeutic alliance with young patients in the hospital may hinge on the cooperation of the parents and on their willingness to enter into family therapy (Simon 1984, Wilson and Soth 1985). It is also an issue for many older patients as well, particularly young adults who may still have quite close ties with their families, especially when they are unmarried, or for married individuals for whom the ties to the family of origin are less important than the ties to their own immediate families—to their wives and children. The therapist can serve as an effective intermediary to the family, helping to communicate to them the reasons for hospitalization and facilitating the process of communication between family and hospital. The family may need help in accepting the admission, in tolerating the stress it induces, and in cooperating in the process in a way that will support the therapeutic objectives rather than undermine them. The same issues must be dealt with from their side by the hospital staff, but to the extent that the therapist may know the family and have dealt with them previously during the care of the patient, he is in a much better position to fill this function.

Gunderson (1984) has pointed out the importance of the fit between therapist and hospital staff. When the therapist and the inpatient staff hold opposing views of what constitutes appropriate treatment of borderline patients, conflicts and misunderstandings may provide a fertile field for the patient's splitting. If the hospital staff stresses structure and limit-setting, therapists who emphasize a holding environment and dealing with regressive issues will not find this approach acceptable. If the unit tends to encourage regression, more structurally and adaptively oriented therapists will see that approach as only increasing the patient's pathology.

THERAPEUTIC/ADMINISTRATIVE SPLITS

Other opportunities for splitting are opened by the use of therapeutic-administrative (T/A) splits. Opinions differ regarding the use of such splits: for some the possibility of splitting the transference is excessive (Kernberg 1976a, Adler 1977, Brown 1980), for others the advantages outweigh the disadvantages (Gunderson 1984). T/A splits do make it possible for the therapist to maintain a more neutral and therapeutically consistent position without getting caught up in the vicissitudes of limit-setting and other administrative decisions that affect the patient's life in the hospital. Also, management decisions can be made more objectively and with less of a countertransference burden from the therapy (Brown 1980). The opposite side of that coin, however, is that negative transference may be diverted into the administrative realm rather than being dealt with in the therapy. The effectiveness of a T/A split depends on the success of the communication between therapist and administrator. The therapist should be included in decisions that affect the patient, especially limit-setting decisions, since they inevitably

have significant therapeutic implications. If the outside therapist continues his therapy with the patient, a T/A split is unavoidable. Where
the therapist fulfills both functions, his role is considerably more complex and difficult. Feinsilver (1983) argues that assuming administrative
responsibility in the hospital would destroy the essential transitional
quality of the therapeutic relation. In the face of the unavoidable real
frustration such administration requires, it becomes impossible to
maintain a therapeutic alliance since the therapist becomes identified as
the persecutory bad object. There is some truth to this view, but it may
be a bit too precious; much depends on the capacity of both patient and
therapist to work through the difficulties and maintain the therapeutic
alliance. On the other side the advantage is that all of the action is
concentrated in the therapeutic relationship. The space for acting out or
for splitting the negative transference is correspondingly diminished.

LIMIT SETTING

There is general consensus that one of the important functions of the
hospital milieu in the treatment of borderline patients is limit setting
(Friedman 1969, Adler 1973, 1977, 1985, Wishnie 1975, Kernberg 1976a,
1984, Hartocollis 1980, Marcus 1981, Crabtree 1982, Gunderson 1984,
Schulz 1984). Here the same principles I have previously discussed (see
Chapter 9) apply with variations as required by the hospital setting and
purposes. From the point of view of the therapist, limit setting is not a
means of controlling the patient's behavior; it is a therapeutic measure.
His contribution to the limit-setting process is to bring the therapeutic
perspective into focus in the decision process leading to a particular
setting of limits. This is important when limit setting tends to come from
the administrative side of a T/A split. Unless the therapeutic objectives
are clear and both therapist and administrator are in agreement about
them, the limit setting is liable to become counterproductive. Only too
readily does the provocative and acting-out quality of the borderline's
behavior create a sense of frustration and impotence in the staff, producing a reaction that wants to assert control and power as part of the staff
countertransference. Such limit setting becomes an acting out of the
staff's aggression and thus is more likely to be antitherapeutic. As Adler
(1985) puts it, "A major aspect of successful limit-setting depends on
whether it is utilized as part of a caring, concerned, protective, and
collaborative intervention with a patient or as a rejecting response and
manifestation of countertransference hate" (p. 199).

This consideration may be especially pertinent in regard to the so-called therapeutic discharge—the ultimate option to discharge a patient who is willfully disruptive, destructive, or not cooperating with the treatment program (Gunderson 1984). This may involve a straightforward discharge from the unit, or it may take the form of transfer to a more restrictive and less open unit.

TRANSFERENCE/COUNTERTRANSFERENCE PROBLEMS

If the therapist continues his work with the patient during hospitalization, he can expect to run afoul of the transference and countertransference difficulties that are an unavoidable and inherent aspect of the treatment of primitive borderline patients. The previous discussions of transference (see Chapter 6) and countertransference (see Chapter 7) are equally applicable in this context. The patterns of transference/countertransference interaction that tend to emerge in the hospital setting are determined largely by the pathogenic introjective configurations; in hospitalized patients the dominant configurations are those rooted primarily in aggression, in the form of destructive aggressiveness or helpless victimization (Lerner 1986). Understanding and dealing with these aggressive derivatives as they are played out in the therapeutic relation and in the hospital milieu are central to the successful hospital treatment of these patients (Colson et al. 1985).

One of the helpful functions of the hospital is the clarification of transference and even countertransference issues in the patient's psychotherapy. Where this can be communicated to the therapist in a helpful and constructive manner, it can often facilitate the work of the therapy immensely (Adler 1977, 1985). The very act of hospitalizing a borderline patient opens the door to a variety of transference and countertransference reactions between the therapist and the hospital staff. The admission may prompt feelings of inadequacy, impotence, shame, or guilt in the therapist, partly as his introjective response to the patient's projections or as a reaction to earlier countertransference feelings of grandiosity or omnipotence. These feelings may interact with the omnipotence and grandiosity in the hospital staff that express themselves in devaluation of the therapist and the wish to rescue the patient. These reactions have to be monitored on both sides. When the patient succeeds in splitting his transference and getting the staff to join him in his view of the bad therapist, the consequences for the therapy can only be destructive (Gunderson 1984).

The therapist must also keep in mind the patient's capacity to denigrate the hospital staff, especially when they are involved in limit setting or in otherwise frustrating the patient's wishes. In his regressive crisis, the patient may turn his wishes for magical relief from omnipotent caregivers on the hospital staff, and when the staff fails to respond adequately to these infantile demands, the patient reacts with rage and despair (Wishnie 1975). The caretakers are then experienced as hostile, sadistic, intrusive on the patient's freedom, violating his rights, hardhearted, uncaring, and repressive. These aggressive projections enable the patient to retreat to a victimized stance in which he lives out the internalized residues of hostile and frightening relationships of the past and elicits countertransference reactions from the staff that confirm his sense of himself as vulnerable and victimized (Brown 1980). In the hospital the staff is composed of many different individuals from different disciplines and different levels of training and experience. Each one can become a potential vehicle for the patient's insatiable demands and wishes, and a repository for different aspects of the patient's projections. The opportunities for pathological interactions, splitting, and projection are rife. An important function of the therapy is to clarify and understand these distortions, to work them through so as to preserve the therapeutic alliance with both the therapist and the staff. It may be important as well to assist the staff in understanding its reactions to the patient (Brown 1980).

The therapist must remain alert to the patterns of countertransference response to the patient, both in himself and in the staff. These are inevitable and unavoidable in the treatment of these patients. The demanding, manipulative, entitled, difficult, and provocative dimensions of these patients' regressive behavior can readily elicit feelings of frustration, failure, and hopelessness in the staff (Colson et al. 1985). As with the individual therapist, the patient often can intuitively tune in on repressed or latent aspects of the staff members' personalities that will resonate with their projections. When these projections are internalized, they provide the basis for transference/countertransference interactions. Common countertransference responses would include: seeing the patient as bad, manipulative, or uncooperative rather than as troubled or frightened (Herschman 1972); a feeling by the staff person that he can do no wrong as part of an idealizing or omnipotent projection from the patient; staff fragmentation and divisiveness resulting from the patient's splitting (Hartocollis 1980); a sense of hopelessness and frustration in the staff (usually as a result of the projection of the patient's sense of hopelessness and abandonment depression); and aggressive-sadistic conflicts over setting of limits (Book et al. 1978). Similar patterns of transference/countertransference interaction can work their way into the supervisory relation. When the resident is treating such a patient, he may pass the projections on from the patient to the supervisor. If the patient idealizes or devalues the resident, the resident may in turn idealize or devalue the supervisor and so distort the supervisory experience (Sadavoy et al. 1981).

A CASE IN POINT

If it is true that splits and divisions can occur within the hospital staff or between staff and therapist, it is also true that these difficulties can be modulated effectively when all parties concerned can understand the broad scope of implication of the patient's behavior. This requires open and consistent communication among staff members and between staff and therapist that leads to empathic understanding and consistent patient management. In these circumstances, the resources of the staff can be mobilized so that they become a powerful supportive and reinforcing influence on the therapy itself. An interesting account of this process has been provided by Carsky (1985–1986), who describes the hospital-treatment process of a severely disturbed borderline adolescent. The patient, a young woman of 17, was hostile, demanding, destructively acting out in the hospital, devaluing the therapist, and precipitating sadomasochistic struggles with the staff. Several impasses in this course were resolved only with the staff's support and emotional reinforcement of the therapist's efforts. The staff effectively gave permission for the therapist to rely on the hospital milieu to protect both herself and the patient, and finally the staff supported the idea of terminating the therapy and discharging the patient (therapeutic discharge).

The first therapeutic impasse involved the patient's effort to turn the tables on her therapist and become the destructive aggressor, making the therapist feel frustrated, angry, useless, and helpless. The therapist was able to focus this process but was unable to avoid the trap. In the face of the patient's inexorable pressure, the therapist found herself losing her grip and slipping into a somewhat vulnerable, helpless, and victimized position. It was only when the staff could be mobilized to a more constructive and supportive position in relation to the therapist that this process could be undercut. The ability of the staff to set more effective limits, particularly in confronting the patient's abusiveness, allowed the therapist to shift to a less victimized and more reasonably effective position; only then was the impasse resolved.

A similar pattern developed around the second impasse in which the patient again became abusive, hostile, and attacking toward the therapist. The therapist was again beaten into a position of victimization, feeling devastated and hurt and having little more than impotent rage as a restitutive resource. Once again, the support and understanding from the staff proved to be an important variable, as it allowed the therapist to gain a better sense of the therapeutic balance and to extricate herself from her victim role. This case provides a graphic illustration of the kinds of difficulty, turmoil, and emotional anguish that can afflict the committed and devoted therapist when treating such difficult patients. It demonstrates the necessity of achieving a secure therapeutic posture, from which the therapist can respond to and deal with the vicissitudes of transference and countertransference that are inevitable components of the therapeutic interaction. The capacity for such patients to split the members of the staff in such a way as to undermine the therapist's position and to inflict even greater degrees of vulnerability and victimization are familiar enough, but effective staff communication, understanding, and support of the therapist's effort to gain a meaningful therapeutic foothold and to maintain a sense of therapeutic balance are of the utmost importance. Such efforts can often go for naught, however, if the therapist himself is unable to gain a reasonable foothold based on his integrity, self-awareness, and capacity to maintain and/or regain a meaningful therapeutic alliance with the patient.

DISCHARGE

If there are significant problems attendant on the process of admission to the hospital, there are more problems connected to discharge. Given the degree of sensitivity in these more primitive lower-order borderlines to issues of separation, abandonment, and rejection, the discharge process is frequently difficult and traumatic, and is often attended by a regressive response on the part of the patient, who seeks to find ways to remain in the hospital or, if actually discharged, to find a way back in. This creates a difficult situation of management for the hospital staff between the need to resist the regressive push of the patient to remain in the hospital and the impulses in the staff to discharge the patient prematurely or, as a result of countertransference feelings, to get rid of the patient (Gunderson 1984). This situation is complicated by the fiscal pressures to discharge patients early or to interrupt the course of hospitalization because insurance or other funding has run out.

From the point of view of the therapist, separation from the hospital must be made a central issue to be addressed and worked on as soon as reasonable in the therapy. If the therapist is part of the staff and will not continue with the patient after discharge, the way must be prepared for transfer of therapeutic responsibility back to the prehospital therapist or to a new one. If the patient has not had therapy before, the transition is to a new outside therapist. In any case, discharge of these patients should never be cold, i.e., without follow-up therapy of some kind, whether individual, group, or family. The preference I advocate is for individual therapy as the primary modality. There should not be any gap between discharge and the initiation of that therapy. It is even preferable in many cases for there to be an overlap so that the patient can get into the therapeutic relation and work to some degree before discharge is actually implemented. This provides the opportunity for the patient to work through some of the feelings about his discharge and to gain some footing in the new therapeutic setting.

The conditions of a therapeutic dismissal provide a special case. Here the patient has sufficiently provoked and tested the limits of the hospital staff so that they have concluded the patient cannot be treated in their facility and have discharged him. If the discharge is truly therapeutic, it cannot be the result simply of staff countertransference but must take place in a context of empathy with the patient's underlying difficulties and of willingness to confront the patient's defenses in the hope of preparing the way for possible benefit from future treatment. Crabtree (1982) describes this process with disturbed sociopathic adolescents. The therapeutic dismissal is traumatic in the sense that it confronts the patient's sense of infantile omnipotence that causes him to be convinced it would never happen to him. When his attempts at threat or manipulation fail, he may break down in tears. Feelings of regret, remorse, and loss can be processed and worked through to an extent, but the temptation to rescue must be resisted or the therapeutic effects of the dismissal will be undone.

DIFFICULTIES

It must be acknowledged that these patients are difficult to treat at best and that the rate of failure, even in the best-run treatment programs, is relatively high (Gunderson 1984, Colson et al. 1985). These patients can readily act out their transference resentments in the hospital against the staff, rendering them impotent and eliciting countertransference responses that are countertherapeutic. The prognosis for these patients is notoriously poor (Colson et al. 1985). Certain patients can be especially difficult and can create extreme problems in any well-run ward—for example, persistent delinquents with sociopathic traits, the so-called "outlaw leader" who seems especially adept at drawing out destructive and hostile countertransference responses from the staff (Crabtree 1982). A case of such treatment failure in a borderline adolescent, a not uncommon experience, has been reported by Tashjian (1979).

The inherent difficulties and risks in the treatment of these patients, even in the hospital setting, opens the way to many medicolegal complications. Calling in the lawyers is one way in which angry and retaliative patients can inflict distress and anxiety on the staff (Gunderson 1984). Particular difficulties arise around the setting of limits in the hospital, the risk of suicide or other self-destructive or self-mutilative behavior, and premature or therapeutic discharge. These latter maneuvers are at high risk when the patient may be threatening suicide manipulatively or may be at high risk of suicide but sufficiently conceals it so that the staff allows his discharge. Problems arise that involve the degree of countertransference hate in the staff and the extent to which such patients are acting out their transference rage (Gutheil 1985). Medicolegal considerations cannot be avoided in our society, but the ultimate responsibility of the clinician is to exercise his best judgment in the interest of the patient and his treatment. If society expects its responsible clinicians to carry out this difficult task to good effect, it must provide the legal safeguards that allow the clinician sufficient latitude to do his job reasonably and efficaciously. To the extent that society sets up obstacles to that effort or makes it more risky, therapists and hospital staffs cannot be expected to do more than the law allows.

16

Drugs

USE OF MEDICATIONS

The common wisdom only a few years back was that medications were of little or no use with borderline patients, but the emerging burden of research has shifted that judgment somewhat. Unfortunately we are still in the position of having to make approximations in our use of drugs with these patients, keeping in mind that the use of drugs in this area of psychopathology is always uncertain and more often than not either abortive or unhelpful. The ground is even shifting from an approach to the use of medications on a time-limited or transient basis to a greater willingness to use long-term regimens in the treatment of certain classes of patients. The possibilities for this form of chronic drug treatment are growing as research findings slowly accumulate. Even so, the caveats regarding the use of long-term drug treatment with borderline patients must be taken seriously because of the potential for misuse and abuse, including the high level of addictive vulnerability (Sarwer-Foner 1977).

In my clinical experience, the opportunities for helpful drug intervention are modest at best. To the extent that drugs can in certain cases facilitate long-term, individual, psychoanalytically oriented psychotherapy or psychoanalysis, they should be used; in cases where they interfere with or complicate the work of the therapy, they are less useful. The use of drugs in any clinical practice has to be selective, a circumstance that does not offer the opportunity for much breadth of experience, given the small number of patients involved. Consequently I must rely on the research literature for the most part. My effort here will be directed to focusing the use of drugs by the individual practitioner in the private-practice setting.

PROBLEMS IN PRESCRIBING DRUGS

Problems in the use of drugs with borderline patients arise from the difficulties in the psychopharmacology itself and from the psychopathology of the patients. The literature on drug treatment of borderline patients is sparse, and does not offer the clinician much by way of firm footing. The strategy proposed by Cole (1980) is about the best we have—to treat the patient with drug therapy in terms of whatever border he seems to approach. If there seems to be a possible overlap with psychotic conditions, neuroleptics would be indicated. If the overlap is with affective disorders, possibly antidepressants can be helpful, or even lithium (Pack 1987). This provides little more than a rule of thumb and must have its inherent limitations, as any good clinician can easily see. Closely allied to this approach is the issue of comorbidity—the presumed coexistence (following the logic of DSM III) of borderline personality disorder with other psychiatric diagnoses, usually one of the primary axis I disorders. The rationale of this approach is that drug treatment of the allied disorder would modify the borderline disorder (Cowdry 1987).

The use of drugs with borderline patients introduces a variety of difficulties—not that the borderline diagnosis has any special claim on these problems, but they seem especially exacerbated by the dynamics of the borderline syndromes. Using drugs with borderline patients opens the way to problems in combining drugs with psychotherapy. Splitting problems can arise, placing the psychotherapeutic and pharmacological approaches in opposition and presenting the opportunity for the patient to play off one against the other (Gunderson 1984). Magical hopes can be focused on the drug to the disparagement of psychotherapy, for example; or the patient may interpret the therapist's suggestion of medication as a sign of failure of the therapy, of the therapist's giving up hope, of potential abandonment and failure of the therapy with loss of the therapist, and so on. The splitting can be especially troublesome in the hospital setting, where an administrator might prescribe the drugs while a therapist does the psychotherapy, or in contexts where the therapist (psychologist, social worker, etc.) might not be able to prescribe drugs. Matters can be considerably complicated if the giver of drugs is committed to a belief in the efficacy of drugs and is disparaging of psychotherapy, or the opposite situation, in which a therapist is committed to the talking cure and has no confidence that drugs can be helpful in any significant way. These gaps offer ample opportunity for the patient to split the transference and manipulate the treatment process.

Other significant problems are drug manipulation and drug compliance. Borderline patients are often quite adept at pressuring or beguiling the physician into prescribing medications to which these patients attach magical qualities. It becomes difficult to hold the line of giving medications only when and to the extent that there is a medical indication for them. This can be a problem with patients having some degree of suicidal potential. Such patients can easily stockpile pills, saving them for a situation when they can overdose in an acute regressive crisis. Management of this problem is difficult at best and requires a solid therapeutic alliance as a basis for dealing with it (Havens 1968, Ellison and Adler 1984). Compliance is a frequent problem (Sarwer-Foner 1977). I cannot say whether the problem is a general one among borderline patients, but in my experience it has been rare that they have adhered to the prescription regimen or have not complained of side effects. Difficulties arise from unreasonable expectations regarding drug effects, attribution of magical properties to them, acting out of resistance to or anger at the therapist, intolerance of any inconvenience or discomfort from side effects regardless of benefits from the drug, wishes to destructively undermine or frustrate the therapy, and so on. Many borderline patients manifest paranoid traits in one or other degree: their suspiciousness and distrust can easily focus on the medication, which becomes symbolically overburdened with negative transference derivatives (Meissner 1986b). The therapist can only take the usual means to ensure drug compliance, but in view of the uncertain outcome of any drug regimen in this area, insistence is neither justified nor productive. More important in the long run is effort directed to stabilization of the therapeutic alliance and respect for the patient's autonomy. Any struggle based on dominance and submission is doomed to failure. Problems may also arise from the borderline tendency to compliance and conformity—patients who too willingly take medication should raise suspicions of excessive compliance (Meissner 1984a).

DYNAMICS OF DRUG TAKING

Medication can easily become the vehicle for pathological dynamics, like anything else in the treatment situation. The medication can readily be invested with all the properties of a transitional object (Meissner 1986b). This can be seen as an aspect of the tendency to transitional relatedness in borderline conditions (Adelman 1985). The tendency to experience reality as colored by his own internal state contributes not only to the borderline's object relations but also to his involvement with and use of inanimate objects. To the extent that pills can be drawn into this form of psychic experience, they become potentially the focus for transference-based distortions. The pill has effects that lie beyond the reach of pharmacology and derive from the patient's relation to the therapist. The pill as transitional object thus becomes the potential vehicle for transference/countertransference interactions that derive from and mirror the dynamics of the therapeutic relationship. The pill becomes a vehicle not only for the unrealistic hopes and expectations of the patient but also for the countertransference reactions of the therapist (Chessick 1983a). Medication can be prescribed out of a sense of frustration or desperation, or out of an internalization of the patient's projected sense of hopelessness, or even out of countertransference hate (see Chapter 7, and especially Maltsberger and Buie 1974).

The overall problem is complicated by the complex etiology of borderline conditions and by the heterogeneity of the borderline spectrum (Meissner 1984a). The usefulness and indications for the use of medications vary considerably from one level of the borderline spectrum to another. Because of the higher contribution of organic etiologies to the lower-order borderline conditions (Meissner 1984a,b), medication of various sorts has a larger role to play in the treatment program of that range of borderline pathology than of the higher-order group. In addition the choice of medication is in large measure a function of the patterns of etiological influence that might play into the pathology in any given case. It is not always easy to discriminate these factors, nor is there any assurance that utilization of specific medications that may have a greater or less degree of specificity for major forms of pathology (schizophrenia, affective disorder, anxiety disorders, etc.) will have anything like a comparable level of efficacy in treating the *formes frustres* that characterize borderline conditions.

MEDICATION SELECTION BASED
ON TARGET SYMPTOMS

One approach to the use of medications is to direct them to the alleviation of specific target symptoms (Ellison and Adler 1984). This approach singles out specific symptoms for treatment and selects a drug whose action may control that symptom (Sarwer-Foner 1977, Gunderson 1984, Cowdry 1987). The drug or drugs may be used over a longer period of time if necessary, but may also be used effectively in transient and time-limited fashion. In many borderline patients, there is little need for chronic drug treatment, but when the patient is in a regressive state, medications can be extremely useful. They can alleviate the regressive symptoms, and when the patient recompensates, they are no longer needed. In longer-term treatment, medications aim at controlling more characterological levels of the pathology—when, for example, the patient tends to be more chronically depressed rather than episodically depressed in regressive crises, or when affective turmoil and thought disorganization are characteristic rather than periodic.

A danger in the target symptom approach is the risk of polypharmacy. The therapist can easily be drawn into prescribing multiple drugs in an attempt to alleviate multiple disturbing symptoms. My own preference is to prescribe drugs for shorter time periods in response to specific regressive symptoms and to limit the medication to one drug at a time. Administration over longer periods, or of more than one drug, is a step taken slowly, reluctantly, and carefully, with full cognizance of the potential risks and difficulties.

One of the best established drug treatments is the use of low-dose neuroleptics for patients manifesting thought disorder or schizophreniclike disorganization (Brinkley et al. 1979, Cole 1980, Berger 1987, Soloff 1987). If the baseline pathology has these characteristics, such medication may be indicated on a long-term basis. Such patients often show improved reality testing, diminished anxiety, improvement in thought disorders, and improved mood. Klein (1975, 1977) recommends about 300 mg thioridazine qhs as an effective dose. If the regression takes the form of an acute psychotic episode, the rationale for these drugs is the same as in psychotic patients and usually requires higher doses. The recent study of Soloff and associates (1986a,b) found that haloperidol (doses 4–16 mg) was more effective than amitriptyline in reducing the symptoms of borderlines defined by the Gunderson criteria (Gunderson and Singer 1975, Gunderson and Kolb 1978; see

Chapter 1). In terms of the borderline spectrum, these would be patients in the lower order of the hysterical continuum. Symptom improvement occurred in depression, anxiety, hostility, paranoid ideation, and psychotic behavior. Some of these lower-order patients may respond better to antidepressants than to neuroleptics. A group of patients similar to the pseudoneurotic schizophrenics of Hoch and Polatin (1949) appear to be more responsive to antidepressants, whether tricyclics or MAO inhibitors, than to antipsychotics, despite the fact that they have an identifiable thought disorder (Hedberg et al. 1971, Klein 1977). This suggests that such cases have a higher component of affective disorder than schizophrenic genetic loading.

Antidepressants can be effective in treating depressive symptoms (Klein 1975, 1977, Cole 1980, Ellison and Adler 1984, Soloff et al. 1986b), although in many cases the depression tends to be atypical, particularly when it occurs as part of a regressive crisis. In such cases, MAO inhibitors may be more effective. Antidepressants have a role where there seems to be an overlap between borderline pathology and affective disorder (Ellison and Adler 1984, Berger 1987, Cowdry 1987, Pack 1987), or in patients who show psychomotor retardation and endogenous symptoms (Sarwer-Foner 1977). Lithium is helpful in the management of severe mood swings, emotional lability, and manic states (Klein 1977). There are also cases in which antidepressants may have a paradoxical effect. Soloff and associates (1986a) report an increase in suicidal threats, paranoid thinking, and both assaultive and demanding behavior in borderline inpatients treated with amitriptyline. Apparently antidepressants can be used selectively for specific depressive symptoms but do not do much for other aspects of the disorder. I have had surprisingly good results in treating episodic depressions with benzodiazepines, a result I found puzzling at first but which may be explainable in view of the symptomatic overlap between anxiety and depression (Feighner 1982, Lehmann 1985).

Anxiety can take a number of forms. Anticipatory anxiety can be treated with benzodiazepines. Chronic anxiety-tension states are often more refractory: antidepressants, lithium, neuroleptics, and benzodiazepines have been used with only modest success (Ellison and Adler 1984). If patients react to tranquilizers with increased hostility or dysphoric complaints, antidepressants may be more helpful. Panic attacks that lead to phobic anxiety can be treated with imipramine or MAO inhibitors. Benzodiazepines are effective for anticipatory anxiety and not for panic attacks; antidepressants are good for panic, not for anticipatory anxiety (Klein 1977). There is some evidence to suggest that alprazolam may affect both. Alprazolam has been found to be effective in improving depression and anxiety, but has been reported as increasing behavioral dyscontrol, including hostile and aggressive behavior, destructive and self-destructive acting out, and suicidal behavior (Gardner and Cowdry 1985).

There also seems to be a useful role for carbamapazine, which is more established as an anticonvulsant, particularly in the treatment of temporal lobe disorders. The drug seems to affect several target symptoms, including dysphoric states and behavioral dyscontrol (Gunderson 1984, Gardner and Cowdry 1986, Berger 1987). It is effective in the treatment of episodic behavioral dyscontrol in conjunction with benzodiazepines. Where diagnosis of a seizure disorder is established or suspected, neuroleptics, which tend to lower the seizure threshold, are contraindicated (Cole 1980, Ellison and Adler 1984).

MEDICATION SELECTION
BASED ON DIAGNOSES

The use of drugs can also be approached from the perspective of diagnosis. Attempts to link a specific diagnosis with a definite class of drug has had modest success. In populations selected for lower-order borderline pathology (following the Gunderson and DSM III criteria), the use of low-dose neuroleptics seems well established (Cole 1980, Ellison and Adler 1984, Soloff 1987). Particular studies have pointed to the use of thioridazine (Klein 1975, 1977), haloperidol (Soloff et al. 1986a,b), and thiothixene (Serban and Siegel 1984). One could make a case for almost any of the neuroleptics within the limits set by the patient's tolerance for side effects. Since long-term administration runs the risk of tardive dyskinesia, I prefer to use these agents in time-limited fashion and in conjunction with regressive episodes. The same effects seem to be operative in both borderline personality disorders and schizotypal disorders (Hymowitz et al. 1986, Soloff et al. 1986b). These lower-order disorders, encompassing the range of pseudoschizophrenic and primitive affective personality disorder within the borderline spectrum (Meissner 1984a; see Chapter 1), tend to have a degree of both schizophrenic and affective disorder genetic loading. It would not be surprising if neuroleptics had a degree of effect, perhaps proportional to the psychotic genetic component.

The emotionally unstable character disorders described by Rifkin and colleagues (1972a,b) would fall somewhere in the middle of the hysterical continuum of the borderline spectrum. These would correspond more or less to the primitive affective personality disorders or dysphoric personalities in whom some degree of affective loading can be suspected (Meissner 1984a). The mood swings in such patients can often be improved by chlorpromazine or lithium carbonate (Rifkin et al. 1972b, Cole 1980, Ellison and Adler 1984). This same group may also respond to thioridazine in preference to nonaliphatic phenothiazines or antidepressants, which can be helpful for some patients but often tend to produce irritability (Klein 1975, 1977, Cole 1980, Ellison and Adler 1984).

The syndrome of hysteroid dysphoria (Klein 1977, Liebowitz and Klein 1981) seems to fall in the higher range of the borderline spectrum, manifesting characteristics of both dysphoric personality and primitive hysteric personalities (Meissner 1984a). Use of antidepressants, MAO inhibitors more so than tricyclics, seems to be helpful for some of these patients (Klein 1977). The effect may be enhanced by the adjunctive use of lithium or nonsedating neuroleptics (Klein 1977, Cole 1980, Ellison and Adler 1984). Another subgrouping of the borderline spectrum seems to have some connection with attention deficit disorder. These patients usually have a history of difficulty in childhood, and in adult life have residual difficulties that express themselves in impulsive disorders, episodic dyscontrol, alcoholism, antisocial tendencies, tendencies to acting out, and other characteristics that contribute to a borderline picture (Milman 1979, Andrulonis et al. 1980, Wender et al. 1981, Meissner 1984a). These patients can be helped by psychostimulants, amphetamines, or methylphenidate (Hooberman and Stern 1984).

As a final note, patients who would fall at the highest level of the borderline spectrum, who are described as histrionic (Klein 1977) or as another form of personality disorder (Pope et al. 1983, Ellison and Adler 1984), seem to be resistant to psychopharmacology, or the use of medication is simply ineffective or counterproductive.

LIMITED APPLICATION

Medications have a limited application in the treatment of borderline disorders. They have a broader and more promising application in the lower-order reaches of the borderline spectrum, primarily in the alleviation of acute regressive symptoms, especially psychotic and depressive symptoms. Longer-term use of medications should be approached cautiously and should be employed only in the lower-order spectrum when stabilization of the patient's lability and regressive potential cannot be achieved psychotherapeutically. Medications have an increasingly limited application as one moves up the borderline spectrum. At the higher levels, medication should be restricted to regressive episodes, and at the highest level is probably contraindicated.

PART V

THE PATIENTS

The therapeutic process, in whatever context it takes place, always involves a minimum of two participants—at times more. My emphasis in this section is on the range and diversity of experience with patients, on the limit and fallibility of our knowledge and technical resources in this area, and on the fact that more good comes from what kind of human beings we are than from however well reasoned our therapeutic rationales and technical devices.

I recount here a series of experiences from the various ranges of the borderline spectrum. Each patient has his or her unique story and highly individualized life space that we must engage, come to know and understand, and help the patient to encompass, put in perspective, and ultimately accept. This task and the difficulties involved in accomplishing it vary throughout the borderline spectrum. These cases exemplify the issues, problems, and therapeutic approaches discussed in the rest of the book. Since I have not dealt with adjunctive therapies, all the cases come from treatment experiences consisting of some form of individual psychotherapy or psychoanalysis.

SECTION A

HYSTERICAL CONTINUUM

The hysterical continuum embraces those borderline cases that are included in the current diagnostic categories of DSM III, the schizotypal and borderline personalities, and a good deal more. The DSM III categories are synonymous with lower-order forms of borderline pathology, roughly equivalent to the pseudoschizophrenics and primitive affective personality disorders in the present breakdown. The descriptions here are not meant to stand for discrete diagnostic entities, as is intended by the DSM III labels. Rather they represent ranges of pathological disturbance that share certain descriptive characteristics but cannot be clearly discriminated from neighboring patterns of disturbance. The higher-order categories embrace an entirely different range of pathology and call for quite different understanding, theoretical formulation, and therapeutic approach. These cases demonstrate the often chaotic and precarious nature of therapy with lower-order patients, as well as the more subtle, slippery, problematic, episodically regressive, and often contorted pattern of therapeutic interaction with higher-order patients. With the former, the borderline issues are almost always in the forefront of therapeutic attention; with the latter, the therapy may follow classic and traditional lines for the most part, and only occasionally confront the therapist with identifiably borderline concerns.

17

PSEUDOSCHIZOPHRENIA

DESCRIPTION

The pseudoschizophrenics occupy the lowest portion of the hysterical continuum of the borderline spectrum. They are probably not significantly different from the schizotypal personality disorders of DSM III, and therapeutic recommendations made for that group are equally applicable here (Stone 1983a,b, 1985). Living on the border of psychosis, they show many features of psychosis in their characteristic level of functioning and as a result are often difficult to distinguish diagnostically from schizophrenic conditions. In their regressive phases they look schizophrenic, but these phases are episodic and are interspersed with a higher level of functioning that looks basically neurotic. They tend to present disorganized, regressive, labile, and destructively acting-out clinical pictures. They come to clinical attention in the hospital setting. They often have a history of repeated hospitalizations, and when they regress, the symptoms tend toward the schizophrenic pole with thought disorders, delusions, often paranoid, magical thinking, even at times first-rank Schneiderian signs. The difference between these patients and true schizophrenics is that the psychotic episodes are fairly readily reversible, do not last very long, and are interrupted by periods of relatively normal functioning. The differential diagnosis of these conditions is tricky (Gunderson 1977, Meissner 1984a,b).

The main difficulty in treating these patients is keeping them in psychotherapy. The best chance is to engage them in the therapeutic process while they are still in the hospital. If the process can be established there, continuation on an outpatient basis is more possible. Unfortunately current policies of rapid discharge and patient turnover mitigate against this opportunity. The therapeutic process at best is chaotic, difficult, and fraught with disruptions and acting out. The therapeutic alliance is tenuous and easily disrupted and constantly needs work. If the patient can be kept in treatment and some semblance of alliance established, good therapeutic work is possible. In the best of circumstances, the therapy tends to be largely supportive and oriented to the here and now of the patient's current life difficulties. At points of greater ego integration, more exploratory work is possible—but the opportunities are not generous. The therapist must bide his time and wait for suitable opportunities to help the patient gain any perspective or insight. Medications are often indicated and often helpful.

ALAN A.

Alan was 30 when he was admitted to the hospital for his suicidal thoughts and fears of going crazy, of losing control. He was also terrified that his soul was leaving his body. He was raised in a staunch Roman Catholic background, but felt little attachment to that faith. Despite poor school performance, he was able to graduate from high school. During high school he drank heavily and experimented with drugs. After high school he played guitar in a rock band. Symptoms of depression and depersonalization had been frequent and recurrent. Sleep was difficult because of his fear of monsters and dread that he would die in his sleep. His dreams were terrifying, filled with rampaging monsters and men with guns trying to kill him.

He attributed his problems to an automobile accident at the end of high school in which his girlfriend was killed. Actually his father died about the same time. His relationship with his father was ambivalent and conflictual, and Alan struggled with guilt over his wishes to see his father dead. It was then that he started taking drugs heavily. He remembered fantasies of moving into his father's room and taking his place. He feared that an evil force would destroy his mind because of his murderous wishes against his father. Other fantasies of mutilation preoccupied him from time to time.

Therapy was started in the hospital and continued on an outpatient basis. Antipsychotic medications were used early in the hospitalization, and later discontinued as he reconstituted and the psychotic symptoms seemed to abate. The therapeutic alliance was troubled and difficult from the beginning. His attachment to the resident was desperate, clinging, needy. He needed to please the doctor, fearing that the doctor would reject him and stop seeing him; in that case he would die. His first resident in the hospital had left the service, and the patient felt abandoned and rejected. He was afraid that the doctor had gotten sick of him and dumped him.

Soon after he started with the new resident, there was a struggle over medications. The resident had cut back his dosage, and the patient began to demand Valium. Valium would save his life, and without it he feared that he would die or go crazy. Valium also stopped the bad dreams, especially dreams in which his father came back to life and tried to kill him. After his discharge, he began to substitute beer for the drug—if the doctor would not give him enough Valium, he could drink beer instead. Discharge was followed by complaints that the doctor did not give him enough time. Urgent telephone calls were frequent, and there were panicked calls to the executive doctor at night. When the resident tried to reduce the Valium, the patient resisted mightily. Without the Valium he was prey to horrible nightmares and suicidal thoughts. He begged for more therapy time and became enraged that the doctor would not increase his sessions to twice a week.

Then began a series of self-destructive acting-out behaviors: missing appointments, drinking heavily, scratching his wrists, talking about the ways he could commit suicide—cutting his carotids would be the easiest and most pleasant way. The struggle over the Valium continued, with angry outbursts at the doctor for not giving him what he wanted. In a somewhat placating and manipulative tone, he professed his appreciation that the doctor tolerated his anger and listened to him, two things his father had never done.

The problems escalated around the therapist's forthcoming vacation. He pressured the doctor with questions about the vacation—where he was going, how long he would be gone, and so on. He was afraid that the doctor would forget about him, want to get rid of him. Why would the doctor be interested in him? He did not deserve the doctor's help. He was afraid he could not survive while the doctor was away—he would surely drink more and get into difficulty. When the therapist came back from vacation, the patient did not return. He had dropped out of treatment.

The difficulties in this therapy are fairly typical. There was little alliance—the patient's efforts in the therapy are devoted to manipulating the therapist to get drugs and other forms of gratification. There is no motivation for therapeutic work. The therapeutic course is little more than a series of manipulations, suicidal threats, and episodes of self-destructive acting out. When it became clear that he could not manipulate the therapist, that he could not get what he wanted, he disappeared. There are glimpses of a sense of getting something of importance from the therapist: attention, empathy, and support; but the emerging attachment and dependence are too overburdened with risk. The patient must escape from the therapist's invitation to do better and so he retreats to his victimized and disadvantaged position—an enactment of his attachment to the dead and demeaning father. In the face of loss of the therapist during the vacation, these conflictual pressures become intolerable and are resolved by breaking off the therapeutic relation.

BARBARA B.

The next case has a more positive outcome. It also shows a remarkable progression from severely impaired functioning to relatively normal adaptation and meaningful interpersonal relationships. The treatment course involved a period of several months' hospitalization during which a reasonably solid therapeutic relation was established, followed by more than two years of outpatient psychotherapy on a once-a-week basis.

The patient was transferred to our hospital from a local general hospital, where she had been treated for a near-fatal ingestion and for multiple lacerations. The precipitant for the suicide attempt had been the drafting of her therapist of several years. This had occurred abruptly, without warning for either the therapist or Barbara, and in the face of this loss she decompensated. She was an attractive young woman in her mid-twenties.

Her life in the few months before admission had been a study in contrasts. She lived in a dirty and rundown apartment with several "hip" friends, who were a few years younger than she. There were two homosexual men and two other girls, one of whom was schizophrenic. Barbara was the only one who earned any money. The rest were involved in pot-smoking, LSD, and narcotics. Barbara resented the fact that they depended on her for support. She felt that she was being taken advantage of but was unable to acknowledge or effectively deal with her anger. They were "creeps, schizophrenics, and weirdos." She gradually and more intensely began to turn her destructive impulses against herself in the form of self-laceration. When she was first seen, there were multiple lacerations over her lower abdomen, groin, thighs, and feet.

Her functioning as a nurse provided a striking contrast in her life pattern. She had a RN degree and was working in a responsible and demanding position in the intensive care unit of a large general hospital. Her work there was outstandingly efficient and effective. She would set out each morning dressed in her crisp white uniform as the intelligent, capable, hardworking nurse. When she returned to the apartment in the evening, she would don dirty and sloppy dungarees and immerse herself in the degraded lifestyle of her friends. She felt as though this represented her real self—the efficient nurse was a facade that she could put on to impress people and to deceive them into thinking she was something she really was not.

Her work in the ICU was of high caliber, but it took its toll. Death was never far away. Many of her patients died. If they didn't die, they got better and were transferred out of the ICU back to the medical or surgical floors. One way or another, people were always leaving. This situation was particularly stressful for Barbara. She could not tolerate the repeated loss of people. She tried to keep her relationships in the ICU impersonal and professional. She kept herself distant from her colleagues. She tried to isolate herself emotionally from the patients. She became increasingly depressed. Also, she began to have disturbing and frightening dreams of people dying and of dead bodies lying beside her in her bed. She would awaken frightened and terribly anxious.

It took a long time in the course of the development of a therapeutic relationship before she was able to tell me about her ideas of reference, her paranoid fears, persecutory anxieties—fears that people wanted to kill her or hurt her. These paranoid fears at times seemed to reach delusional intensity—but most of the time she kept them under control and hidden. However, they formed a central element in her pathology with which she was constantly dealing and which often motivated her behavior. It accounted in a primary way for her style of relating to other people and for her difficulties in establishing meaningful relationships. Her entire demeanor was permeated by a distrustfulness, an abiding suspiciousness, and an expectation of hurt or destruction.

Barbara had severe difficulties in college when she decompensated for a brief period and had to be hospitalized. She had become increasingly isolated and bizarre. She quickly recompensated and graduated. The next episode was in nursing school; after the breakdown of a homosexual liaison, she became acutely psychotic and again had to be hospitalized. The clinical picture at the time seemed ominous, and she carried a diagnosis of undifferentiated schizophrenia. Subsequent psychiatric treatment lasted over several years and seemed to have been helpful. At times of stress and disappointment she repeatedly decompensated and was admitted to the inpatient service with a schizophrenialike syndrome.

After the loss of her therapist, she was transferred to our hospital. She responded well to antipsychotic medication, and within a few weeks seemed to have adequately reconstituted so that she could be discharged. Her hospital course was unremarkable; she had been a cooperative patient, was well liked by the staff and patients, and was able to engage effectively in the therapy. She was soon discharged and was followed in once-weekly psychotherapy.

The subsequent months were rocky ones. She was seen periodically at the emergency ward, usually for lacerations. She would become acutely depressed and cut herself, usually in the context of some disappointment or of her rage at someone on whom she had become dependent and who had let her down. These episodes were marked by a severe tension, anxiety, and experiences of depersonalization that were quite frightening to her. The cutting served as a release mechanism for the pent-up rage and also seemed to reassure her that she was real and alive. Her functioning throughout this period was barely adequate: she was able to work steadily, but her interpersonal relationships were sparse and very poor. Her reality testing remained intact, and the general diagnostic impression of her doctors at this stage was that of a severely disturbed borderline personality.

The story thus far gives us a tragic picture of a young woman of extraordinary gifts and intellectual abilities caught up in a process that led to increasing isolation, withdrawal, and a pattern of self-destructive behavior that could only end in suicide unless reversed.

Barbara was the oldest of four siblings. Her relationships with both parents were fraught with conflict. Her father was a relatively successful but difficult man. He was obsessive, controlling, demanding, and perfectionistic. His rule over the family was tyrannical and at times violent. His word was law, and he brooked no opposition. He laid down arbitrary and rigid rules for the family—and dealt out swift and harsh punishment for any infractions. He would fly off the handle at the least provocation and beat the children at any displeasure. While Barbara admired her father's intellectual interests and proficiency, his efficiency, and his capacity to get things done, at the same time she was terrified of him and was repulsed by much of his behavior.

She saw herself and her older brother as the special targets of her father's hostility and violent attacks. She recalled repeated occasions when he would pump her with questions, and if she did not know the answers or didn't answer to his satisfaction, he would strike her in a rage. She would often run in tears to her room and lock the door, terrified of her father's angry outbursts. One of the scenes that she recalled with particular vividness, one that was frequently repeated, took place at the dinner table. He would demand that the children discuss interesting and intellectual subjects, and that they eat everything that was put before them. These scenes became the arena for intense pitched battles. If Barbara would balk at eating something, she would be sent to her room for fifteen minutes and then told to return to the table and eat all of the then-cold food. If she refused, her father would fly into a rage and beat her. She recalled times when she tried to avoid his blows by crawling under the table; he would then try to kick her in the head. Barbara would relate these episodes to me with a frightening intensity of rage and hatred.

The father's general attitude toward Barbara was critical and devaluing. Anything she did or accomplished was subject to little praise and generous criticism. Nothing she did was ever right. Nothing she said or thought was correct, especially if her father held a different view. He was always right—he had to be right. His continual ridicule and devaluing criticism were particularly difficult for Barbara since her intelligence and perceptiveness were remarkable. It was father's view that women were not worth much and were incapable of intellectual attainment of any worth. His attitude toward Barbara's mother was much the same. Having Barbara for his oldest daughter must have been difficult for him. She was very bright and capable, much more so than any of the other children; we can easily guess that he was not a little threatened by Barbara's obvious intelligence. This may also have been the case in his relation with his wife: Barbara felt that her mother might well have been as intelligent as her father. In any case, the father was pushed to constantly tear down and devalue whatever competence or capacity was manifested by the women in his life.

Barbara's mother had adopted a submissive and nonchallenging role in relation to her husband. She never confronted him, never intervened in his angry tirades or vicious beatings of the children. Barbara's resentment at her mother for not protecting her from her father was deep and intense. The mother was apparently chronically depressed, never very warm or affectionate. She would often withdraw from the family and stay in her room for days on end.

The mother's illness became acute on two occasions. The first took place when Barbara was about eleven years old. The mother became severely depressed and suicidal. She had to be hospitalized and was given shock treatments. The second took place a few years later after the death of the mother's own mother. This event proved to be a critical one for Barbara as well. The grandmother had died of cancer, and had suffered a long time. She became increasingly weak and emaciated and in the final months of her life required constant nursing care. Barbara's mother undertook this responsibility. The strain of caring for her mother in the face of an inevitable but slow death took its toll on Barbara's mother. She had increasing difficulties sleeping, began taking Doriden, and within a few months after the grandmother's death had to be hospitalized. She was suffering from chronic Doriden intoxication, but her behavior became bizarre and psychotic with frank hallucinations.

Barbara was a shy and relatively withdrawn child. She kept to herself, had few friends, and played almost exclusively with her brothers and sisters. Academically her performance was quite superior—at the head of her class in elementary and high school. But she felt awkward and embarrassed about her intelligence. She was stimulated to compete with the bright boys in the school, but her success had a price. She felt ostracized and isolated because of her intelligence. She was afraid that her schoolmates would not like her because she was too bright and won all the prizes.

Barbara's sexual development was central to her pathology. It would be an underestimation to say that it was a conflicted development. It was the most difficult and problematic area of her life, as a child, growing adolescent, and adult. She grew up in a family context that severely devalued females. Her mother provided a prime model of the weak and inadequate female—a woman with intellectual gifts and abilities who was devalued and continually undercut. The model of adult femininity was highly depressive and masochistic. Barbara's emerging sense of feminine identity could not but have suffered severe impairment.

Although talk about sex was prohibited, her mother's attitude toward sex gave the impression that it was a dirty and evil business. The mother did not enjoy sex, and avoided it in whatever way possible. The father's attitude was quite different. In his liberalism and declared independence of any social conventions, he felt that the atmosphere toward sex in the house should be uninhibited and free. This difference of opinion provided the battleground for many of their arguments.

Father acted provocatively, walking around the house stark naked, casually appearing in front of the children in the nude. Barbara, the oldest daughter, found this behavior extremely embarrassing. She remembered seeing her father's penis and feeling frightened of it but at the same time fascinated by it. She particularly remembered his having an erection. She recalled vague dreams of her father approaching her sexually, of feeling fright and panic.

Barbara was extremely self-conscious of her sexuality. She recalled when her mother took her downtown to buy her first bra. When they got home, her father took it out and dangled it in front of her brothers and made a joke of it. She felt hurt, angered, and humiliated; she ran to her room in tears. She could never forgive him for that. As she matured, her breasts developed quite fully. Since she was otherwise slender, her breasts seemed quite prominent. She took elaborate precautions to try to hide them. Her mother forced her to get her hair curled once, and she resisted bitterly, hating the way she looked. She never wanted to wear dresses or other girls' clothing. She wore pants and heavy boy's shirts whenever she could.

When Barbara came to our hospital and I first met her, she was a frightened and confused young woman. She seemed anxious, but tried to present herself with a bland, almost casual, facade, relating the events that brought her to the hospital as though she were telling me about something interesting that had happened to someone else. Her manner was simple, even childlike. She was obviously a bright and verbal person and had a basic willingness to be involved and to communicate about herself. She was remarkably introspective and had a unique ability to describe her feelings and inner processes. These qualities were to stand her in good stead in the years ahead.

After several weeks of talking about her self-destructive tendencies, I asked her why she was making herself a mental patient. Her response was intense anger that she could not handle effectively and could not direct at me. Barbara was obviously struggling with her ambivalence—torn between her anger at me for shaming her and trying to force her to function more maturely and her positive transference feelings. Behind this concern lay the inner drama of her relationship with her father, whom she admired and wanted to emulate but whom she also hated for his cruel treatment of her.

About this time, she was talking about people dying in the ICU where she had worked and referred to "dead doctors." She went on to discuss her anger at me. I was the mean, cruel doctor who stripped away her defenses and left her weak and vulnerable. At the same time, she was able to recognize her positive feelings for me. She didn't know which was the more difficult to deal with. The anger was destructive, but the positive feelings were threatening, too, because they carried with them the threat of loss and abandonment. Her view of me as powerful and sadistic was matched by her sense of herself as weak, powerless, and vulnerable—the picture of her victimized mother that she had internalized.

Alongside this view of herself there was another strikingly contrasting self-portrait. Her perception of herself as hateful, destructive, loathsome, and evil was overwhelming. Her concern was to protect me from this powerful and magically destructive evil within her. Her attraction to me and her feelings for me were a danger, because they raised the possibility that I might begin to care about her and thus be sucked in and destroyed by her evil poison. In this scenario I would become the vulnerable victim of her destructiveness.

She labored to keep me at an emotional distance, vacillating between anger at me and her fear of trusting me. She wanted to make our relationship nothing more than a strictly professional one—no personal interest or caring involved. She tried to maintain an image of me as simply doing my job, as she did with her patients as a nurse—no emotional involvement, just performing a professional function. She paid me to perform that function. The payment of the fee became a sort of magical talisman that protected her from deeper feelings about me and ensured that our relationship was a strictly contractual one. She talked about the anger and disgust she felt when her own patients became dependent on her.

One of the important early issues was the impact on her of her grandmother's death. She was still deeply mourning that loss, but for some time she resisted any reference to this area of her feelings. Finally she was able to share with me her feelings of loneliness and despair—that she had lost the only person in the world who really loved and cared about her. I felt that something important was achieved at this stage of Barbara's treatment. It seemed to establish a bond between us that had not been there before. She had been able to show me her hurt, loneliness, weakness, and vulnerability, and had come away without rejection, or loss, or destruction. I had not been overwhelmed or destroyed by the intensity of her feelings, and I had not run from them or withdrawn from her.

Gradually she was able to express her anger and resentment against her parents. She felt that in her early years she had tried hard to please them but never seemed able to do so. After she got to college, and especially after her grandmother died, her behavior became an attack on and rejection of her parents. She began messing herself up, wearing dirty and weird clothes, hanging around with weird people who were really strange and whom she knew her parents disapproved of. She felt that she really wanted to hurt her parents, to show them how badly they had treated her—she wanted to destroy the "extension of the process B.," her way of identifying herself as deeply influenced by her parents. Her anger at her mother was intense for having permitted her father's sadistic attacks upon her and for not having intervened to protect her.

Increasingly she became aware of the ways in which she was like her parents. She began to realize how she was depressed and withdrawn like her mother, how when she was angry she would withdraw and close off communication with other people, that her mother was a nurse, too—and that her mother had been a mental patient as well. Her cutting had been focused largely in the area of her groin and thighs. She saw this as the feminine part of herself, the part of her that was most like her mother.

As time went on, Barbara was gradually and increasingly able to tolerate and talk about her anger at me. When I had asked why she was making herself a mental patient, she had felt hurt and furious. She was afraid to tell me about these feelings, afraid that I would reject her and turn away from her as her mother used to do. A pivotal event in the development of the therapeutic relation occurred one holiday when I forgot to tell her that we would not meet. Her rage at finding my office door locked later led the way to discussion of my possible countertransference and her fears of rejection. I have discussed this episode with regard to its transference/countertransference implications (see Chapter 7), but the upshot was that her anger was legitimated and working it through served to reinforce and consolidate the therapeutic alliance. She remarked that she had never really been able to get angry at her doctor before. But she was afraid of letting the anger out, not sure how far she could go, or what I would do if she did. She did not know whether I would withdraw from her and reject her like her mother, or whether I would turn on her in anger and attack her like her father.

Little by little, she became more comfortable with her anger and was increasingly able to share it with me. As this capacity increased, her anger seemed to diminish. There was a magical quality to this aspect of her treatment, which persisted for a long time. She saw me graphically as a strong and powerful sponge that could soak up the poison she exuded and neutralize it. When I went on vacation during the first couple of years, she would voice her apprehension about what was going to happen when the powerful external control and neutralizing force was taken away from her. Would her evil power once again assert itself? Would her poison again work its magic on the world and the people around her?

Along with this, she became more aware that her mind, her intelligence, the strong, adequate, capable, and masculine part of herself, was also the part that wanted to undercut, revile, degrade, despise, hurt, maim, and lacerate her feminine body. She saw that this part of herself was cast in the model of her father. She was like her father when she was critical, devaluing, and violating herself. She acted out in her own head the drama that she saw so often between her parents. She turned her father's hostile and destructively devaluing attacks against herself and made them her own—a striking example of identification with the aggressor. She had to struggle with two difficult and opposing identifications. She identified with her mother as the weak, vulnerable, depressed, sensitive, hurt, victimized woman. She also identified with her father as the cruel, evil, destructive, powerful, capable, intellectual, critical, demeaning masculine force. These identifications contended with each other within her.

When something happened to provoke her anger, Barbara had a great deal of difficulty in managing the anger. Along with her paranoid fears of rape and murder, there was a strong tendency to feel herself responsible for the bad feelings. At such times, she thought of herself as evil and powerful. She felt that she possessed a destructive power that could make people around her like her and want to be with her, or make them have angry and destructive thoughts and wishes. She saw herself as emitting poisonous influences that corrupted and poisoned people around her. She felt that the evil thing should be destroyed. She would destroy it herself—or other people would want to destroy it. She tried to destroy it by cutting, by starving it to death, or by killing it. It was an evil, horrible, destructive, and powerful monster that had to be destroyed to protect other people from its evil influence. She could gradually recognize how important and powerful such fantasies made her.

Barbara saw the sexual act as an act of brutality of men against women, and pregnancy as the punishment dealt out to women. She described herself as feeling empty during intercourse, as though she became nothing and completely lost any sense of identity. She felt as though she were being engulfed by the male and that all of the power and force belonged to him. The model for this fantasy was the relationship between her parents, in which her father was the powerful one who forced her mother into submission, and her mother was the weak, helpless, vulnerable, and pathetically passive female who had no recourse but submission.

This, incidentally, was also her view of the therapeutic relationship. It was a view that changed only gradually as time went on, and she came to see that our relationship was one of helpful support and cooperation rather than dominance and submission. As these elements were gradually worked through, she increasingly came to be able to form real relationships with men and to feel herself a valued and significant person in the relationship. The issue for her with me, and with other men, was that she could not show the evil and dreadful aspects of herself. She was afraid of letting her "dirty laundry" show, because people would be revolted and disgusted and turn away from her and abandon her. The "dirty laundry" was the hurt, vulnerable, depressed, and lonely feelings associated with her femininity.

The progression in Barbara's treatment and in our relationship had its rocky moments. One of the most difficult centered around a relationship she developed with another of my patients. She became quite fond of this young man, and their relationship became sexual. I found it necessary to intervene since I felt that it would be destructive to her therapy—a form of acting out of the transference. Barbara's response was hurt and anger; she saw me as cold and calculating—dropping a rock in the pond of her emotions and then sitting back and callously watching the ripples. She accused me of being heartless and manipulative, not really caring about her feelings or wishes. I was a tyrant pulling the strings and trying to control her, just like her father. She felt that she had to choose between me and the relationship—an unfair choice that I had forced on her. The result was that it was harder for her to trust me; she began having paranoid thoughts about me, that I was not really interested in her welfare but just wanted to exercise my power over her and manipulate her. This was a clear reflection of her persistent therapeutic misalliance and showed her hovering on the brink of a transference psychosis.

To complete the clinical picture of this patient and to close the story, her therapy was concluded by mutual agreement. She had done well and for some months had been quite symptom free. She was leading a relatively normal and well-adjusted life. Finally she met a suitable young man and decided to live with him. Since he lived in another city, we decided to terminate, with the understanding that she might find it necessary or advisable to seek treatment in the future. For the moment, her prospects seemed optimistic. She was happy at the turn of events in her life and felt confident of her ability to deal with her feelings, particularly her anger, and seemed hopeful for the future. She saw clearly that the positive turn was within her power to accomplish and to continue.

What made it possible for Barbara's therapy to succeed where the previous case failed? Important ingredients were her own basic intelligence, capacity for psychological insight, and positive motivation. I also have no doubt that her therapy succeeded in large part because of the previous therapeutic effort that had been expended in her behalf before she came to me. She and I were able to build on that foundation. From the beginning of our work together, she had a fairly good working alliance. As the therapy progressed there were inevitable contaminations in the form of projective transference distortions. These reflected the underlying introjective configurations that were cast in extreme aggressive terms, but also involved strong narcissistic elements. The major burden of the therapeutic work fell on the aggressive components—the sense of helpless victimization and powerful destructiveness that pervaded her inner world and colored her relationships to the outer world. To the extent that these could be brought into focus and processed, the therapeutic alliance developed and became more solid and mature, and the therapy made progress.

These difficulties in the transference and alliance required that I be alert to their every nuance. When they came into play in the therapeutic interaction, I had to be prepared to actively focus and process them. Part of the success of the therapeutic work with this patient was her capacity to understand and respond to my initiatives. She was sufficiently psychologically minded and motivated to assimilate my questions, obervations, and interpretations effectively in the interest of understanding her troubled experiences. This required a corresponding capacity in me as therapist to engage with her in a meaningful and affectively telling way. A major technical aspect of this work was the consistent, unremitting, and persistent focusing on her feelings toward me—in whatever fashion they found expression, whether verbalized or not. These affective reactions were usually expressed in subtle forms of behavior and unspoken attitudes. At times, it was necessary to surmise what she was feeling—as, for example, after holidays or vacations when resentment and anger at my abandoning her could be inferred even though they were hardly expressed. At these points the therapist must make certain assumptions, make a self-conscious effort to illumine these feelings, and not rest until he feels satisfied that they have been adequately expressed and explored.

Barbara's termination was neither complete nor final. After she was married and moved, I continued to receive letters from her telling me how her life was progressing. She was happily married and in time had a baby daughter, with whom she was delighted. As time passed, she again felt the need for further therapy; she wrote to request a letter to her new therapist telling him about our experience.

18

PRIMITIVE AFFECTIVE PERSONALITY DISORDERS

The primitive affective personality disorders occupy the next level of pathology within the hysterical continuum. They represent forms of lower-order pathology and differ from the pseudoschizophrenics more in affective than in cognitive impairment. The regressive pull in these patients is more toward affective disorder than toward cognitive disorganization. This may reflect a greater degree of affective loading in contrast to the pseudoschizophrenics, in whom the schizophrenic genetic loading may be greater. They tend to be emotionally labile, frequently act out, are often prone to suicide, and have a strong regressive potential, although perhaps not as marked as in the pseudoschizophrenics.

CLARE C.

Clare came to the outpatient clinic complaining of anxiety attacks that had troubled her for several years. She was also homosexual and chronically depressed. She had seen a private therapist for about four years but had stopped because she could no longer afford it. An attempt at group therapy had been unsuccessful.

She was the older of two daughters from a middle-class family. She described her father as weak, impotent, soft, and mothering. Her major difficulties were with her mother, who was rigid, perfectionistic, demanding, and critical. She was chronically depressed and frequently suicidal. Clare did not get along with her mother and currently the mother did not want to have her living at home. The parents were continually at each others' throats, and the mother had talked about divorce for years. There was a history of psychiatric illness in the family: the mother's father was cyclothymic and the father's sister had had a psychotic breakdown.

Clare began therapy with a barrage of complaints about her family, particularly her mother, about her homosexual lover, and about her phobias and anxieties. It did not take long before the acting out began. Efforts to change appointment times were followed by missed appointments. When the therapist confronted her about these episodes, she made facile excuses and adopted a breast-beating posture proclaiming her inadequacy and guilt feelings. She seemed eager to present herself as knowledgeable about her problems, reciting pseudo-insightful comments that she had seemingly acquired in her previous therapy. What came through in all this was a sense of helplessness, discouragement, and vulnerability.

Her complaints of suicidal thoughts and feelings remained fairly constant but seemed to wax and wane in intensity. There were angry tirades against her parents for what they didn't give her, against her lover, with whom she carried on a vengeful love–hate relationship, and against her therapist, who would not give her what she wanted: more therapy time, more medication (she had been taking Tranxene), more support and reassurance. There were a series of manipulative attempts to get herself admitted to the day hospital—seeking consultations with other psychiatrists, calling other clinics, and so on. Her rage at the doctor escalated, and she began verbally attacking him, devaluing, criticizing, and raging at him. She had fantasies of hitting him, strangling him, and tearing up his office. She again attempted suicide by ingestion of the Tranxene. Withdrawal of the Tranxene precipitated another struggle and rageful attack on the therapist.

In this context, she successfully badgered her mother to take her in. This intensified her complaints and rage at her mother. She made increasing complaints about the therapy and her doctor, particularly because of his efforts to set limits and maintain the therapeutic situation. For a time her mother brought her to the sessions, in an effort to keep her in treatment. If her mother did not force the issue, the patient tended not to come to her appointments.

The mother finally asked her to move out. Missing sessions became more frequent and were a focus for repeated confrontation. Threats of suicide and anger at the therapist continued unabated. At times she would miss an appointment, then call for a substitute hour. When the doctor did not give it to her, she would launch into a vitriolic tirade against him and against all men, who are calloused and indifferent and don't care about women or their feelings. News of the doctor's vacation was met with feigned indifference and a grudging admission that she did not want to say that she cared at all. She was angry at his leaving when she was feeling so depressed and suicidal; this was acted out by slashing her wrists and threats of taking Elavil she had stockpiled during her previous therapy.

Finally, it was necessary to confront her basic motivation for therapy. Did she really want therapy or not? Her basic unwillingness to engage meaningfully in the therapy and her unabated need to manipulate the therapeutic relation made the prospects for continued therapy dim. The decision was finally made to terminate, with the agreement that until she decided she was ready to change, no effective therapy was possible.

In this case there was no effective therapeutic alliance and the prospects for gaining one were limited. The patient was more invested in struggling to manipulate the therapist than in any reasonable therapeutic work and change. There were glimmers of the phenomenology of her depressive self-image, but there was little opportunity to get these configurations into focus. The major difficulties for the therapist in such a case are setting limits and dealing with the countertransference feelings that are inevitably stirred. The constant attacks from this patient and the chronic threat of suicide put the therapist under considerable stress. One is never certain in such circumstances that the effort to set limits is not contaminated by aggressive or hostile countertransference feelings. The limits set in this case seem appropriate, even the final one of terminating the therapy.

DAVID D.

The next patient seemed to live on the edge of suicide but was nonetheless capable of maintaining a relatively high level of functioning. When David first came to the clinic he was in his late twenties and was studying law. His presenting complaint was depression and suicidal thoughts. Depression had been a chronic problem, the first severe episode occurring after his parents' separation.

The family background was unstable. The father had been in the foreign service, so the family had had to move frequently and had lived in several foreign countries. David both admired and hated his father. When he was young, his father was often away for months at a time, leaving David feeling abandoned and unwanted. The father was described as handsome and charming but also short-tempered. The parents constantly fought, and David is quite certain that his father had a number of affairs. David recalled often seeing his father naked when they took showers together; he felt physically inadequate and inferior to his father. In contrast the mother was described as intellectual and disciplined. She taught art history in college; David remembers helping her with her Ph.D. but never felt that she appreciated his help.

Besides the repeated bouts of depression, David had problems with alcoholism and drugs. Heavy drinking and use of mescaline and pot had been problems in his college days. He had also had homosexual affairs, the first during college, and is still involved in a homosexual relation. He described frequent depersonalization experiences that were quite frightening to him. His younger brother has similar problems: he is shy, timid, and withdrawn, has trouble making friends, and is often suicidal.

At the beginning of therapy, David seemed awkward and nervous; he stuttered, maintained poor eye contact, and seemed to have great difficulty talking. He saw the other members of his family as superior and powerful; he saw himself as weak, sick, powerless, and inadequate. He worried about himself—he constantly thought about suicide, had hypochondriacal fears about leukemia, worried that his testicles were too small, was afraid he might go crazy. He felt like a frightened little boy, but he was afraid if he lost control he would hurt people around him. He couldn't break off his homosexual relation for fear of hurting his partner. He was afraid if he lost control in therapy, he would scream, throw a temper tantrum, and hurt the therapist—and the therapist would not be able to stop him. The aggressive and victim introjective configurations were well displayed.

He tried to deal with his depression by keeping busy, but he hated the demands put on him by the law school. He felt inadequate and powerless. He was concerned about his roommates finding out he was gay, especially one of the women. He was afraid his depressive complaints would make the therapist depressed.

When the time came to interview for jobs, he complained about the degrading procedure, about having to present himself to people he considered stupid and inferior who had the power to decide his future. His sense of narcissistic superiority and contempt were striking.

In the midst of this continuing turmoil of despair, hopelessness, and suicidal depression, David gradually became more involved in the therapy and began to form a rather good therapeutic alliance. He and the therapist explored his feelings of inadequacy and helplessness, which contrasted with his sense of himself as powerfully hurtful and intellectually superior. In fact his school work was of high caliber, with a high level of performance. During the latter stages of the therapy, he continued to interview for jobs with good success. He lined up several job opportunities that seemed quite promising, but the interviews stirred underlying conflicts. He was anxious about having to talk to such powerful employers, fearful that they would see his weakness and inferiority. The process confronted him with the prospect of moving into a responsible and powerful position himself. He vacillated between wanting to take a small job in a remote country town or a bigger job in a metropolitan center. There was also the issue of leaving therapy. He felt dependent on the therapy and was afraid that if he left he would collapse into a weak, helpless, abandoned baby. He tried to manipulate the therapist into making the decision for him, but finally committed himself to a quite responsible position in another city. The termination was worked through and arrangements were made for continuing psychotherapy in his new life.

The effective element in this therapy seems to have been the patient's level of motivation, his capacity to enter and develop the therapeutic alliance. Despite his multiple difficulties, he engaged usefully in the therapeutic work, did not act out significantly around the parameters of the therapeutic situation, and continued to use the therapy productively. The outcome was favorable: the depression diminished at least to the point of being manageable and not incapacitating, his drinking stopped, he was able to extricate himself from the homosexual entanglement and felt increasingly alienated from the gay world. An important part of dealing with this aspect of his pathology was getting at his hatred and fear of his mother, his fear of aggressive women, his castration anxieties connected with wishes to counter his feelings of inadequacy by raping his mother. The extent to which this material could be brought out and articulated with the predominant motifs of power and powerlessness, superiority and inferiority, helped to diminish the dominance of these pathogenic configurations in his internal world. Along the same lines, important work in the therapy took place around the establishing of the therapeutic alliance. This was accomplished largely by exploration of the introjective configurations and identifying the ways in which these aspects entered into the therapeutic relation. The patient's therapeutic effort has by no means been completed, but the segment related here carried him a good way down the road.

ED E.

The clinical course of this patient was interesting because of its intermittent pattern, which nonetheless had a fairly beneficial outcome. He was in his mid-twenties when I first saw him—a tall, angular man with long stringy hair and reflecting sunglasses that he wore at all times. He was eager for treatment and engaged readily in the process.

A few years before, he had been hospitalized for a severe depression for about six months. He was bitter about this experience and complained heatedly about his "asshole" doctors and how poorly they had treated him. After discharge he tried living at home for a year but couldn't stand the conflict with his parents, particularly his father. Since then he had lived alone, unable to work because of his continuing symptoms, keeping largely to himself, terrified of leaving his apartment even to buy food, spending his time reading and trying to be a writer. He complained of anxiety and continued depression, often with suicidal thoughts, but he "didn't have the guts to do it." He felt he was hypersensitive, vulnerable, and weak. He wore the dark glasses because he was afraid people could see his weakness in his eyes and would take advantage of him. He drank too much, frequently getting drunk; it eased the pain. He felt paranoid at times, afraid of what people on the street were thinking of him, afraid they would turn on him suddenly and attack him, try to kill him. He felt that his back was against the wall; this was his last chance and he had to go all out to make it work. In the first hour, he wanted to know if I would extend the time if he felt he needed to talk. I took this opportunity to establish a piece of the therapeutic framework. I replied that my schedule did not offer much flexibility, but that if it seemed necessary we could schedule additional appointments; I also explained that our work together was long-term, that our success in dealing with the long-term issues was more important than easing his anxiety at a given moment. I sensed the answer was less important to him than the fact that I had taken the trouble to explore the issue and discuss it with him. The episode offered a moment of contact with his reasonable ego.

His story unfolded over time. His father had worked in the family business established by the grandfather. The grandfather was a man of considerable attainment who had become something of a legend in the family. The father was a nervous, perfectionistic man who held high expectations for his only son and put a good deal of pressure on the boy to achieve. Ed felt that his early years were unremarkable except for his conflicts with his father, who was always pushing him to get better marks in school and never seemed satisfied with what he did accomplish. His mother often interceded to get his father to ease up, but without any great success.

One salient feature of these early years came from the latency period. Ed made himself the leader of a gang of boys. He appointed himself as a "ten-star general" and in this company his word was law. He described one occasion when he ordered one of his followers to hang himself. The boy began stringing up the rope and was about to carry out the command when Ed thought he had gone far enough and rescinded the order.

In prep school Ed began to experience greater difficulties. He went to a well-known boarding school; his expectations were lofty, even grandiose. Since his ambition was to become the greatest writer of the century, he reasoned he would have to master all branches of human knowledge. He drove himself mercilessly, studying and reading for long hours, neglecting sleep and food, taking no time for joining in the activities of the other students. He became an object of ridicule among his peers and felt persecuted. In fact he went over the edge, had a breakdown of some sort, and had to drop out of school. He finally got a high-school diploma, went to college, and quit because he did not like the professors or the courses. After that he had his big breakdown and was hospitalized.

Ed used the therapy hours well. We were able to talk about his feelings about himself, how he had once been out to conquer the world and now felt so inadequate and vulnerable. The introjective patterns came quickly to light. His sense of himself as weak and vulnerable spoke of the victim-introject. We discussed the many contexts in his life in which he felt he was a helpless victim, especially in the face of his father's unreasonable tirades and expectations for him. What he really needed was time to pull himself together rather than more pressure to produce. His father would not listen, couldn't understand, would never change his views. The vulnerability was also apparent in Ed's paranoid reactions. Walking down the street, he would be paralyzed with fear that one of the passersby would turn on him, pull out a gun or knife, and murder him. In the grocery store, he picked out a loaf of bread, but when the clerk reached under the counter to get a bag, Ed turned and ran from the store in a panic, convinced that the clerk was reaching for a gun to shoot him. When he finally got up enough courage to go to a large department store to buy a suit, he walked through the front door and was suddenly overwhelmed by the fear that there were armed guards stationed along the walls preparing to gun him down.

If Ed was the victim in these fantasies, in parallel fantasies he played the destructive aggressor. He fantasied turning the tables on the people on the street, carrying an automatic machine gun, and suddenly opening up and killing them all. As he walked past the IBM office building, his mind was filled with hatred and rage at these heartless corporations that lorded it over the rest of the world and screwed people right and left. He imagined with relish taking a brick and hurling it through the plate-glass window, then throwing a bomb that would blow the building and everyone in it to smithereens. These fantasies played out the destructive themes that reflected the aggressor-introject that was the companion piece to his sense of himself as victim.

The components of his pathology were also to a large degree narcissistic. It would not be difficult to discern the elements of narcissistic grandiosity in his history—especially in the grandiose expectations that powered his efforts in prep school. The paradigm of the ten-star general also proved quite useful; I would often muse what it must be like for a former ten-star general to find himself in this predicament. But there were also clear evidences of Ed's narcissistic pathology in his current life. A deep sense of himself as a worthless failure permeated his existence. He would often complain of this, describing himself in derogatory and demeaning terms—worthless, "a pile of shit," useless, a worm whom no one would love or respect, and so on. This sense of depleted self-esteem was at the heart of his depressions and reflected his vulnerability to narcissistic disequilibrium.

These manifestations of the inferior introject were accompanied by contrasting expressions of his grandiosity and narcissistic superiority. He held on to a firm belief in his own intellectual superiority: he felt strongly that he was more intelligent than most and that he had the capacity to be writer of genius. He was often critical of public figures, usually damning their arrogance and stupidity and feeling himself superior. On one occasion he happened to pass a group of men in business suits in front of a fashionable club. He felt enraged at them, envious of their position and money, contemptuous of what he saw as their inferiority. He considered himself smarter than any one of them, yet here they were in a position of privilege and power, and he was condemned to an inferior and worthless position. This attitude was a source of difficulty for him in his work life. On repeated occasions he would get into a hassle with his employer, arguing about something the boss asked him to do, thinking that he knew better, and resenting the boss for telling him what to do. A series of jobs were lost in this fashion.

All in all, however, Ed made progress. The jobs lasted longer as time went on, and he developed a useful skill that made him increasingly employable. He became easily enraged at anyone who put pressure on him or tried to tell him what to do. He even fulminated against his aunt, who had been paying for his treatment, for pressuring him to get on with it and straighten out his life. Needless to say I tried not to fall into that trap. Somewhat surprisingly, our relationship stayed on a fairly steady and even keel. Ed was faithful about his appointments and conscientious about paying the bill. He made arrangements ahead of time when he had to miss an appointment and utilized the therapy time reasonably well. The projective conflicts that so marked his involvement in the outside world did not seem to enter into the therapeutic relation in any significant way. Overall he continued to make detectable and steady progress.

Then one day Ed announced he had decided to stop treatment. He had come to the realization that he was not so special, that he was no different from anyone else, and that he had to stop trying to be different. As he put it, "Everyone has a shit trip and so do I." He used to think that everyone else had to take shit in life but not him. He was sick of talking about and analyzing himself, and it was time to get out and live. He still wanted to be a great writer, but he couldn't be that without experiencing life and being willing to take what it dished out. It was time to be on his own. Part of me was delighted to hear this crystallization of insights we had been working on for such a long time, but part of me was also apprehensive that this was too abrupt and premature. I stalled for time; the most I could get was one or two more hours. I tried to explore the possibility that he was avoiding something, that part of him might want just to escape the treatment. All to no avail; he stuck to his guns and we terminated.

A year and a half passed, and suddenly he surfaced again. He wanted to continue treatment. Things had gone reasonably well for him in the interval. He had managed to stay in the same job and had acquired a girlfriend, with whom he was living. He still wore the dark glasses and felt that he couldn't function without them. Drinking was still something of a problem but less so. Returning to treatment was a humiliating defeat; he had resolved he would never again submit himself to psychiatric treatment. But he had the same problems as before: rage and hatred of the world around him, feelings of loneliness and worthlessness; he vehemently rehearsed all of the old hurts from the past and reveled in sadistic and destructive and murderous fantasies against all his persecutors and victimizers.

The therapy continued as though there had never been any interruption. Ed continued to deepen his insight, particularly into the narcissistic dynamics that played such a central role in his pathology, as well as into the pattern of aggressive forces that played themselves out in his fantasies of destructiveness and in his phobic and paranoid preoccupations. The pattern of interrupting the therapy repeated itself a few more times, and at each cycle there seemed to be a greater degree of consolidation of the therapeutic gains and a better level of overall functioning. Finally Ed announced that he had located a promising job in another part of the country and that he and his girlfriend planned to get married. He left, having completed a course of therapy that extended over half a dozen years with relatively good results. I continued to hear from him periodically by letter for several years after we terminated.

The key elements in this case were Ed's motivation and perseverance in working on his problems, his capacity for insight, and his basic intelligence. From my perspective essential components centered around the therapeutic alliance. Not only were my efforts directed consistently to maintaining the alliance, but the unscheduled interruptions would seem to have put the therapeutic alliance to the test. My consistent position was that Ed and I were trying to work together to find out what we could about his difficulties and that I was in no way about to impose, insist on, or demand much of anything beyond his observance of the structure of the therapy. When he decided not to come to his hour, as happened on a few occasions, I made no issue of it and focused the inquiry on what had motivated his decision—at all points respecting and preserving his right to make that decision. There were no hidden pressures; everything was on the table. When he decided to interrupt the therapy, this position was challenged.

The question I had to deal with was whether the move toward interrupting was motivated by some resistance to the therapy or whether it represented some health-seeking push toward autonomy that should be respected. The move also brought into focus certain issues related to my own countertransference. Was I trying to inhibit his growth toward independence by my caution? Was I caught in a persuasion that he could not function without my healing input to sustain and guide him—a reflection of my own sense of therapeutic omnipotence? Was my need to explore with him the potential sources of his bad behavior a function of something in me that needed to preserve my sense of superiority and power at his expense? Was I re-acting with him some part of his father's demanding, perfectionistic, never-satisfied role? The other side of the equation involved issues of possible rejection and abandonment if I were to endorse his bid to separate too easily or too quickly. Some of these issues could be discussed in the process of clarifying his decision. The outcome was some degree of success in preserving the therapeutic alliance, supporting his struggling auton-omy, and reinforcing his sense of himself as capable of determining his own course even in the face of my doubts and questions. He could make a decision to do what I might disapprove, knowing that I would respect and support his decision and that if it proved to be a miscalculation or mistake, he could come back and continue the process.

This dynamic may have been as important as anything else in determining the therapeutic progress. It is difficult to weigh this in the balance since other important work was taking place simultaneously, namely the focusing, understanding, and processing of the pathogenic introjective configuration. The interpretive work in this sector, which impinged more directly on the transference, carried significant weight. Ed's capacity to see clearly these configurations, their implica-tions, their origins—especially in his relation to his father—and to take steps to change his orientation to the world, to life, and to him-self, had to have an important therapeutic impact. These disparate elements undoubtedly contributed to a more adaptive and constructive outcome.

FRANCINE F.

The next case covers over a dozen years of psychotherapeutic effort. Francine was referred to me after the disruption of her therapy because of the graduation of the resident she had been seeing. Several subse-quent attempts to engage her in therapy with more senior therapists had floundered; the feeling in the clinic was that she needed a consistent and long-term setting that could not be maintained in a training setting, where personnel were constantly changing. Her course to that point had not been optimistic. It was marked by repeated hospitalizations, usually for severe depressions with suicidal gestures. She had a history of excessive alcohol use and drug abuse. Therapy had been difficult at all points, but she had been able to engage in some useful therapy with the last resident for about a year and a half. She had gotten severely depressed after the loss of that relationship and had rejected, even scorned, efforts to replace him with a new therapist. Consequently, our initial contacts were overshadowed by a cloud of uncertainty.

The first part of the therapy was consumed by struggles over establishing the therapeutic situation. I spelled out the terms on which I was willing to work with her and what I saw as her responsibilities. This was done firmly but with an effort to explore and elicit her input at each step of the process. My focus was on establishing the therapeutic alliance. The response seemed to be positive but led almost immediately to a series of urgent and distressed telephone calls and demands for extra therapy time. I gradually cut back on the telephone calls—to the patient's annoyance. She reacted angrily at my increasing unavailability but gradually accepted the limit. I was willing to give her extra therapy hours when I could, but this meant that she was charged for the time, and that option, too, was quickly foreclosed. My expectation was that she would learn to hold her anxiety until her next therapy hour when we could try to work on it. I was trying to construct a therapeutic context in which long-term therapeutic work would be undertaken rather than short-term relief of anxiety or gratification of regressive needs.

These struggles gradually quieted down and we entered into the long haul. This was not accomplished without protests and outbursts of rage at my controlling and imperious style. She raged at me and called me just about every name in the book. Interestingly, I did not take any of this in a personal way. Her rage was in a way like waves dashing against a rocky cliff: I remained calm, unperturbed, immovable. I *was* concerned that her rage might spill over in some form of acting out that would not do her any good. I told her I agreed with her angry attacks against me—that I was all the things she said and that she would have to decide whether she could do business with a therapist like that. For my part, I was more interested in trying to understand what she was feeling.

As we moved into a more settled mode of operating, she began to tell her story—and a sad and tragic story it was. She was born into a well-to-do family, which included her parents, an older brother, a twin sister, and a younger sister. Her father was an ophthalmologist; she presented him as a stormy, labile, irritable, temper-torn, domineering, tyrannical, sadistic figure who loomed over this young woman's life and cast a long, dark shadow. He was violent and abusive, drove fast cars, drank heavily, loved motorcycles, carried on numerous affairs, and generally drained the dregs of the cup. He was finally killed in a motorcycle accident.

He ruled the family with an iron hand. And his rule was cruel and sadistic. For reasons that are unclear, Fran seemed to have been the special target of his wrath, or so she felt. She told stories of how he would shoot her pets for no apparent reason than that she loved them. On one occasion he shot her dog; on another he killed her pet pig and then had it prepared for the family dinner. When she refused to eat it, he beat her and forced her to eat the pig. He would make her stand in front of his desk while he abused her, calling her names and trying to make her cry. She refused to cry in front of him so that these episodes seemed to go on relentlessly until she broke down. He would frequently have his gun on the desk in front of her, and she recalls fantasies of picking it up and killing him.

Her earliest years had been more benign. At the beginning her father was not on the scene all the time. He was apparently still in training in another city. In those years Fran got along reasonably well with her mother. This preoedipal paradise was lost when the father moved in for good. Paradise became hell. Fran resented her father's intrusion and hated him for the way he treated her and the rest of the family. She was the only one who stood up to him and wouldn't cave in under his tyranny. Her mother was totally useless in this situation. The mother was well educated and cultured but quite passive and ineffectual. She dealt with the problems in the family by retreating to her room and isolating herself. She had long-standing depressive problems and had to be hospitalized and treated with ECT on several occasions. Fran could not look to her for help in her struggles with her father.

There was an interesting quality to Fran's discussions of her father. His abusive and cruelly sadistic behavior was never far from her mind. When she turned to that subject in a therapy hour, even in the depths of a depressive funk, she would begin to spit fire—as if some charged energy had been suddenly tapped into and unleashed. The fact was she had a perverse attraction and attachment to her father. He was the powerful man, the man who dominated everything, who had his way with women and could outdo any man. He was daring, dashing, seductive, powerful—an object of envy and admiration despite his destructiveness and sadism. Those qualities made him an object of attachment for Fran. She envied his masculine prowess and power and despised the image of feminine weakness and helplessness cast by her mother. This attachment to her father was cast not only in terms of the aggressive struggle of victimization between them but also in hints of outright sexual abuse. Since there was never more than the mere suggestion, I could not be sure whether her allusions were to real sexual abuse or fantasied abuse.

The stories about her father took up most of the early work in the therapy. The affect was intense and full of rage and hatred. The other side of her attachment to her father was less reachable, and when I commented on it or tried to focus it, I got nowhere. Gradually Fran's mother came more into the picture, at first with glowing accounts of her intelligence and giftedness. The mother was painted as an angelic paragon of feminine virtue and goodness. At times I tried to point out that for all her goodness, the mother didn't do much for Fran, particularly in protecting her from her father. This tack was also met with considerable resistance—I was told in no uncertain terms that I should keep my dirty hands off her mother, who was at that point above reproach. In her own good time, Fran came to the dirty business herself. Gradually the mother came in for more recrimination and reproach. Mother came more and more to be seen as a pitiful figure, helpless and impotent in the face of the father's brutality, ineffectual as a woman, and hopelessly inadequate as a mother.

This whole subject was cast in the framework of a bitter tirade about the position of women, how they are mistreated, abused, and unappreciated by our male-dominated society—the full panoply of feminist rhetoric. I came in for endless abuse as the archetypal representative of all that was evil in the masculine world. I was not only a man but also a psychoanalyst with all that implied about the Freudian view of women as castrated, inferior, and so on; and not only that, but I was Jesuit, an "official representative" of an order that had no women in it and a Church that refused to ordain women priests. I could not win!

As these tirades continued, I could do little but sit them out. The other motif for raging against me was my total incompetence as a psychiatrist. I was a failure in that department; I could not understand her; my interventions were worse than useless. Most of all, I was a poor substitute for her resident, who was far and away the best doctor she had ever had and whose equal could never be found. He understood her, he talked to her about himself and about his life, he let her call on the telephone whenever she wanted—she even had his home telephone number. My efforts were a poor substitute for this paragon of therapeutic virtue.

There were times when this harsh attitude would soften. She would become more forgiving of my ineptitude and try to reassure me with the consoling thought that while I might not understand anything and I might not be able to do anything helpful, at least I stuck with her and provided a place where she could unburden herself. My narcissism was greatly enhanced by this reinforcement—I speak tongue-in-cheek! There was a serious problem here. I often wondered if I was doing any good in my work with her and whether in fact she was beyond my skills as a therapist. At times I dreaded her appointment hours.

The dynamics became more intense when we went to a twice-weekly schedule. The pace quickened and more material became available. She gradually let me in on her secret—the world of creatures she carried with her and to which she would retreat in stress or conflict. This inner psychotic world was peopled by animal characters derived from her childhood pets, all with names and personalities. These characters would come to her rescue when she was in need, would console her when she was troubled or depressed, would protect her if she were in danger. She would actually walk through dangerous areas of the city at night—a serious risk for anyone—with the professed confidence that nothing bad could happen to her while her friends were on guard. She would enter this fantasy world whenever life in the real world became too difficult—a process she described as "going away." No one could know when she was away; she might go away for minutes, or for hours, or even for weeks at a time. In the meanwhile she could carry on her everyday life with the consolation that she was being helped and protected by her friends. She was slow to reveal this inner world to me for fear that I would try to take it away from her. If that happened, she would be totally helpless and vulnerable.

The therapy was difficult, a tortuous course of ups and downs, twisting turns and reversals reflecting the turmoil of her emotions. Periods of severe depressions and suicidal thoughts were interspersed with episodes of energy and apparent progress. Any given hour might cover the gambit of emotions, from empty depression to rageful outbursts. I often found it difficult to follow the thread of her discourse, since she seemed to jump from context to context without apparent transition or connection. I suspected a thought disorder might be contributing to this confusion and disorganization. Usually I was able to discover some thread that gave me enough orientation to avoid complete perplexity. What was important to her was that I kept on trying to understand her.

The most optimistic indicator was the fact that she stayed out of the hospital. She decided somewhere along the line that she was lesbian—prompted no doubt by her hatred of men and her feminist convictions. She became involved in a homosexual relation and set up housekeeping. Her lover was the prototype of all that Fran admired and sought in a woman. She seemed never to tire of singing her lover's praises—a picture much the same as the idealized one she had painted of her mother earlier. As the months went by, the music changed. More and more I heard notes of dissatisfaction about their relationship and about the way her lover treated her. Gradually the titer of anger and resentment grew, finally reaching a crescendo of rage that culminated in the disruption of the relationship and Fran's moving out. I was never convinced that her homosexual involvement was authentic, and often told her so. She grudgingly admitted that I might have been right.

An additional problem was her alcoholism, which seemed to wax and wane as the months passed into years. At certain points the problem became severe, but my efforts to work on it with her seemed to get nowhere. She seemed reluctant to tell me very much about it and it never interfered with our work together. Her position seemed to be that she did not want my help with this problem, or possibly my interference.

This gives a sense of the difficulty in working with this patient. She seemed to be using the therapy for her own purposes and would let me do only so much. Any effort on my part to do more was simply negated. Most of the hours I spent with her were directed completely by her. She came with an agenda and seemed to try to rush through it as though some magical effect would come of her simply reciting her difficulties in my office. My job was simply to listen—nothing more. At times, she would produce a list of topics she wanted to cover and was annoyed if she did not get to every item. She was particularly annoyed at my trying to engage her in exploring anything more extensively, because then I was the cause of her not getting to the end of the list. At times she would tell me to shut up; in a good many hours I was given marching orders at the top of the hour—to keep my trap shut and just listen. She was not interested in anything I had to say. I had little choice but to comply.

There were times when her position seemed to soften and I could put my two cents' worth in. But these could not be forced; I could only bide my time and wait for the opportune moment. My efforts were directed mostly at clarifying something she was saying or expressing my confusion or uncertainty, occasionally focusing something that concerned the distortions in the therapeutic alliance, and even on rare occasions making an interpretation of the transference. Her attacks against me and her need to keep herself in a carefully defended position reflected the abiding sense of vulnerability that she needed to counter by an attacking defense. For her the best defense was a good offense. This could be connected to her struggles with her father and her fear that any influence I might have over her or any shift in the balance of power in the therapeutic relation would put me in a position equivalent to her father and put her in an equivalent position of powerlessness and helpless dependence. It was thus extremely important for her to keep me in my place.

During the course of all this, things continued to improve outside the therapy. She was able to disengage herself from her lesbian entanglements, get control of her drinking, and graduate from college—something her illness had almost derailed. She was in fact a good student, worked hard at her studies, and had good success, which again prompted tirades against her father, who thought that women were worthless and should not be educated, and against the male-dominated society that denied equal educational opportunities to women. She had a series of menial jobs but gradually began to get better and more responsible positions. She had an opportunity for a high-paying position as executive secretary in a large firm but turned it down because she felt she would have to work for men. She married an older man who had been a faithful friend and confidant over the years. Despite the disparity in age and many other difficulties, this relationship persisted and seemed to grow stronger as time passed.

She felt she had to reduce her therapy time because she was exhausting the family money. We cut back to once a week, then to once every two weeks, then once a month over a period of a year or more. Finally we arranged that she could call me when she needed to talk. For four or five years she continued to call me every few weeks or months for an appointment, sometimes more than one. As the therapy continued in the same vein, I had a growing sense that she needed me less and less and that she was gaining control of her own life. We have never terminated, but I have not seen her for several years.

I learned from this therapy that while I might have my ideas of what should go on in the treatment of a patient, the patient may have other ideas—and to a considerable degree the patient holds the trump cards. I could do with and for this patient only what she allowed me to do. She needed to revile and attack me in the context of a therapeutic relationship that persisted for over a dozen years and in some sense has not come to an end. I could accomplish little more than to try to maintain the therapeutic structure. Fortunately she made that job relatively easy. On her part there was a fierce determination to help herself and do better. Fran was a fighter and perhaps I did at least provide a place where she could carry on the fight.

19

DYSPHORIC PERSONALITY

With this group we enter a different range of psychopathology and a different range of treatment problems. The issues here are still borderline, but they do not take the primitive, labile, acted out, and disruptive path so common in lower-order patients. The drama in this group tends to take place on the inner stage of the patient's psychic world rather than on the wider stage of the outside world. That external stage is always available in periods of stress and regression, but it is not the preferred locus. These patients are capable of long-term, intensive, exploratory analytically oriented psychotherapy and in some cases psychoanalysis—quite a different kettle of fish from the pseudoschizophrenics and primitive affective personality disorders we have been considering. I will present material from two psychotherapy cases and from two analyses.

GEORGE G.

George presented a picture of intense inner turmoil and conflict that had far-reaching effects on his capacity to achieve and function and on his relationships with all individuals in his social environment. The therapy lasted over two years, once weekly, and made little impression on this patient's basic pathology.

George was in his early twenties when I first saw him. He had come to Boston to begin graduate studies. He brought with him an eleven-year history of intensive psychotherapy that had started when he was twelve. He was the oldest of three: his sister was still in college and his younger brother was in high school. His father was a successful businessman; his mother worked part-time as a real estate agent.

George's problems began quite early and despite many years of therapy do not seem to have been resolved to any great degree. He was a tall, well-built young man but obviously overweight. He dressed like a middle-aged businessman rather than a graduate student. He was quite concerned about his appearance, especially his receding hairline. He has always had problems in interpersonal relationships, both within and outside the family. He gets along poorly with his siblings, fighting with his sister and generally ignoring his brother. He usually tries to avoid his parents, giving his father a wide berth and only rarely talking to his mother. With his peers, he is generally antagonistic and argumentative. He has no friends, few male acquaintances with whom he associates, and no girlfriends. He has never dated.

He had graduated from college the year before, but this created a problem. He could not bear living at home. Since the college dorm had been a refuge for him, he continued to take courses at the college after graduation so that he could keep his room. He did some part-time work but was unsuccessful in finding a permanent job. The prospect of having to support himself terrified him. His academic record was good, but he did not present himself well in interviews. He finally decided to solve his dilemma by going on to graduate school. He did not do well on the GRE, but presumed that he would be accepted by a prestigious school anyway. When he was not accepted, he had to settle for a second choice—a narcissistic injury. This was made more difficult because of his demands about living conditions: a single room that had to be modern, comfortable, large, and air-conditioned—not an easy combination on a crowded university campus.

The most problematic and difficult relationship in George's life was with his father. George regards his father with awe and terror. He sees him as a genius, brilliant, skilled, artistic, able to do anything well, successful in business, and respected by everyone. When describing his father in such glowing terms, he particularly emphasizes his father's poise and articulateness. He tries to look poised and confident himself, but he is anything but. He has come to acknowledge that his facade doesn't fool anyone, that his anxiety and tension are apparent to all.

If George's view of his father is idealized and admiring, it is also filled with fear and hate. His father was cruel and domineering. His criticism and ridicule of George were unending—his looks, his speech, his table manners, his posture, his lack of knowledge, his failure to read widely enough, his lack of friends, and on and on. Punishment was frequent and severe, even sadistic. One episode that was seared into his memory took place when George was about eight. The family went to a local airport where his father was taking flying lessons. George was playing around one of the hangars and an airport employee caught him burning some paper behind one of the buildings. When his father was informed, he flew into a rage and beat the boy. The father raged at him all the way home, where he beat him again. Then he ordered George to crawl on his hands and knees around the block to his friend's house, tell the friend what he had done, and then crawl home again. George was humiliated. He crawled around the block but couldn't tell the friend what he had done. After he crawled home again, the father checked on whether he had done as ordered; when he found out that George had disobeyed, he beat him again. For all the father's virtues, apparently control of his temper and his sadistic rages was not one of them.

While this traumatic memory stands out, it was only part of an overriding pattern of abuse. When his father was angry at him, he would not speak to George, at times for weeks on end. He often threatened to throw him out of the house, on several occasions forcing him to sleep outside.

George's relationship with his mother was better. She was more understanding and sympathetic toward him, but she could do little about George's conflicts with his father. If George had any problems, he could never go to his father and had to approach his mother instead. She generally acted as intermediary between father and son—sparing George the agony of confronting his father and reinforcing his view of the father as cruel and uncaring. George's demeanor toward his mother was the opposite of that toward his father. With his father he could do little but cower in fear and humiliating submission. With his mother he became the tyrant. He would yell at her and order her around, abusing her with curses and obscene language. This generated a tremendous conflict with his mother, but in the end she usually relented and he got his way. As a result his relationships with females are conflicted and ambivalent. He despises women, seeing them as worthless and inferior, but secretly entertains fantasies of a superwoman who appears weak and helpless but who could destroy him with ease. His fantasy about intercourse is that the woman robs the man of his penis and potency, and that the penis is devoured in a *vagina dentata* fantasy. He compares the vagina to a clam that can clamp down on its prey and devour it.

George had developed a somewhat paranoid attitude toward other people. He trusted no one, was generally suspicious and guarded, and colored his relationships with projections. He interpreted his interactions with others in terms of these projections and could not allow any other view of their actions or thinking. His own thinking tended to be grandiose and omnipotent, even as he felt inadequate, inferior, vulnerable, helpless, and terrified of the outside world. The thought of fending for himself is terrifying. Although his father and mother encourage him to go out and have friends, George is convinced that any such effort would enrage his father because then the father would lose his tyrannical hold on him. He is convinced that other people will automatically reject him and that there is no recourse but an isolated and lonely life. No woman would find him attractive because he has nothing to offer— no money, no good looks—and is unwilling to spend what money he has on them. He regards any sentiment as a sign of weakness. Dependence on another human being means to lose oneself, one's identity, and to be devoured by that other. One of the things that he admired about his father was that he needed no one and could take care of himself without depending on anybody.

George was obsessed by the small size of his penis and the fear of having erections—something he felt he had no control over. This fear came into graphic focus in what he called his "locker-room problem." He traced this problem to the summer before his Bar Mitzvah, which he spent at a boys' camp. He did not get along well with the other boys, who ridiculed him because of his lack of interest in girls and because he could not join in the give-and-take of the camp activities. His method of dealing with these difficulties was not calculated to win him any friends. He stole from boys he disliked and on one occasion sadistically ridiculed a boy whose father had just died. During this period the boys undressed in the locker room for sports or swimming. On these occasions he went through agonies of shame and anxiety, fearing that other boys would see how small his genitals were and that they would ridicule him. He also feared he would get an erection, which would be even more humiliating because then they would all know that he was homosexual. He went to great lengths to avoid being in a position where other boys could see him naked. He secretly admired and envied the large penises and pubic hair of other boys.

George was preoccupied with the fear that he was homosexual. He was stimulated and aroused by the sight of male genitals. He was intensely preoccupied with his attraction for male "models." He divided the males in the world into those who were models and those who were

not. The models were young, slender, good-looking, people he admired
and wished could be his friends. He worried that as he got older he
would be less and less attractive to the models. He also envied them and
felt enraged that they might have gifts or advantages that he did not.
Poise and independence were primary attributes. They had no difficulty
undressing in front of others. Nonmodels were the opposite of models:
they were the slobs for whom he felt nothing but contempt and in
comparison with whom he felt superior. They were coarse, had disgust-
ing body hair, were dirty, and would even go to the toilet in front of
others. His attraction to the models was ambivalent, wishing for contact with them but at the same time fearing it. He had the fantasy that
he could become one of these models by having bodily contact, which
would allow him to possess their large genitals and thus become powerful. There has never been a homosexual experience, however, since he
seemed unable to develop a close enough relationship with anyone for
that to happen.

George's previous therapy had been difficult and marked by episodes of poor impulse control and acting out. On several occasions he
set fires in the therapist's office building or urinated in the hall outside
the therapist's office. There were several episodes of cheating in school,
shoplifting, and gambling. When a roommate (a model) rejected him,
he was furious and defecated in the roommate's bed. He rationalized
that the roommate was spending too much time in the bathroom, and
he seemed unable to connect his behavior with his anger at the roommate. There were multiple anal preoccupations about cleanliness and
using dirty or coarse language, and about anyone witnessing his anal
performances. But he also reveled in fantasies of swimming up to his
neck in shit, a fantasy that gave him intense pleasure. His relation to the
therapist was guarded and distant. He would at times hint at difficulties—phobias, fetishistic practices, antisocial behavior—but any efforts
by the therapist to explore them were met by staunch resistance and
evasiveness. He would not accept any of his difficulties as problems to
be understood and worked on and so to be overcome. He wanted
sympathy for his difficulties and support for his anger against his
oppressors. There was little evidence of a capacity for empathy or
concern for others, little capacity for guilt or grief.

My own work with him carried on many of the same motifs. His
approach to me was as though I were a hostile antagonist who could
not be trusted and had to be constantly watched. A struggle ensued over
arrangements for the therapy. At first he tried to juggle the appointment times. Then after a few weeks he began to demand more therapy

time. I did not cooperate in these efforts—in the first because I did not have alternate hours, and in the second because I was not sure that additional time was indicated. His response was angry and sullen—if I were not going to give him what he wanted, then he was not going to give me what I wanted, a cooperative patient.

Another struggle emerged around the fee. I had informed him that he would be charged for missed appointments. He had accepted this as a matter of course and I presumed that he was accustomed to this arrangement from his previous therapy. In the course of the struggle over appointment times, he had missed several appointments. When he received the bill for these appointments, he flew into a rage. The argument went on for weeks, and when it became clear that I would not budge, he gave up the struggle with a hang-dog submission and sullen resentfulness. Although we explored the many facets of this problem, it was clear that he had not gotten his way and that he would nurture his resentment.

The therapy focused largely on his current difficulties in getting along at school and on his dealings with fellow students and administrators. Struggles over the housing arrangements, which had to suit his needs exactly, or over schedules and courses leading to arguments and conflicts with administrators and teachers were continual and unending. He was constantly trying to manipulate a situation to gain his own ends and was enraged and filled with destructive fantasies when these aims were frustrated or denied. Hateful vengeance was his leitmotif. On one occasion he had made a date to go to a movie with a fellow student. When the other student failed to show up, George went to the parking lot, found the student's car, and smashed all the windows with a brick. This episode became paradigmatic for the way he dealt with life and its frustrations. I pointed out how his reactions put him in an impotent, rageful, and devalued position—that of an angry and powerless child who could do little more than lash out in helpless and destructive fury when he didn't get what he wanted. His sense of entitlement, his view of himself as an "exception" (Freud 1916, Meissner 1978c) who was continually victimized by fate and by others in his environment, gave him the right to get back at those others and take what he needed or wanted for himself. Anyone who stood in his way was an object for hatred and attack.

The role and interplay of the introjective configurations were not difficult to delineate in this case, but I had little success in helping him to identify these patterns and their conflictual origins in his relations with his parents. Clarifying and interpreting the patterns of interaction he generated in the therapy seemed to make some impression, but the effect was modest. There was little change in his behavior or attitudes outside the therapy. Whatever progress might have been made was aborted by a premature termination when he completed his graduate program and took a job. The expectable difficulties arose quickly in the job situation: it was not long before he got into a confrontation with his new boss and was fired. At that point he decided to leave the city and return home.

No matter how defeating and undermining the difficulties in a patient's life, the risks in changing the pathogenic configurations can be even greater. For George to break loose from his attachment to his parents, to step into life and live it on his own terms, was a paralyzing prospect. I spent a little over two years with him and succeeded only in scratching the surface. A lifetime of therapy had made little impression. If the patient lacks the basic motivation to change, the therapist's hands are tied. Furthermore, the pattern of the therapeutic work is dictated largely by the nature of the patient's pathology. Here the focus of the therapeutic work was consumed by the interactional difficulties that filled the patient's current life experience. There was little room here for genetic exploration or understanding. The patient had no curiosity about his early life and how it shaped his personality. He had only bitter resentment and hatred. What he sought in therapy was self-righteous justification and confirmation of his paranoid outlook and his crippled and isolated existence.

HARVEY H.

The next case ran a somewhat more optimistic course. The actual psychotherapy lasted about the same length of time, but the patient's capacity to engage in it was quite different. Harvey was about the same age as George when he was referred to me. At the time he was doing graduate work in psychology at a local university. He had been seen at irregular intervals by a therapist during his college years for his interpersonal difficulties. These took the form of problems with males—authority figures generally but also peers who were aggressive or dominating—and with females. He seemed to be able to attract women easily but had problems sustaining or deepening the relationship. The acute problem had arisen when he was assigned a laboratory project with a male partner who was assertive and domineering. He became terrified of this fellow and could barely control his panic and impulse to flee. His sexual difficulties came to a head when, after two years of more or less steady dating with his college girlfriend, he found himself withdrawing from the relationship, uncertain of his feelings for her and unwilling to commit himself further to her. In his relationships with women he got quickly involved, but as soon as it became sexual he was filled with doubts, feeling inadequate about his sexual prowess and often unable to sustain an erection. He expressed his wish for a meaningful relationship, but could not escape from feeling threatened by intimate contact.

Academically he had functioned on a superior level in college, but in graduate school he had had more difficulty. He did not do well at first, had flunked his qualifying examination on the first try, but then after a summer of hard study had been able to improve his performance remarkably and had passed with flying colors. He felt his early effort reflected some of his psychological difficulties.

Harvey came from a fairly well-to-do family. His father was a social worker who also had a successful private practice, and his mother worked as a teacher. Harvey was closer to his father, looked up to him, often confided in him, feeling that his father's professional position enabled him to understand Harvey's difficulties better than his mother did. But the father also had his difficult aspects. Despite his professional success, he was socially inept; he had few friends and depended on the social contacts the mother made. Father was a rather rigid and perfectionistic man. He had difficulty controlling his temper and would often fly into rages and become physically destructive and abusive. Fights between father and mother were frequent, and his father would often yell at and hit his mother. These fights were terrifying to Harvey; he was afraid that his father would kill his mother. The mother was affectionate and vivacious, easier to get along with than his father. He felt he could turn to her whenever he got into hot water with his father. But she also tended to be extremely sensitive, reacting defensively and violently to any criticism. Between his father's violent outbursts and his mother's defensiveness the family was in constant turmoil.

While his relation to his father had always been intense, Harvey never really understood his father, never knew when his father would explode in a rage over some trifle, and was terrified of his father's violence. In more recent years when arguments erupted, Harvey stood his ground; when his father punched him, Harvey hit him back. He grinned when he recounted this event.

When he first started treatment, he was bothered by obsessional thoughts, particularly songs he could not get out of his head. He found this symptom frightening. He was afraid he was going crazy. Other phobias bothered him and interfered with his work and enjoyment. He also struggled with paranoid thoughts of reference, suspiciousness, and guardedness in his relationships with both men and women, but especially paranoid fears of strong males, as in his experience with the lab partner.

He seemed to engage readily in the therapy—agreed to the terms of the therapeutic contract and for the most part kept to it. There was some initial juggling of the schedule to accommodate changes in his course schedule, but there was no suggestion of acting out. His concerns about his relationship to his father dominated the early work. He idolized his father, and when his father gave him any advice, he adhered to it closely. He recounted a dream in which his father had given him some advice but Harvey had disregarded it in an offhand manner. The father immediately flew into a rage that so terrified him he ran away in a panic. He put any authority figure in a dominating position and then kowtowed to them in complete submission. This made him worry about homosexual inclinations. He had a dream of his roommate naked, and even though he could not remember any attraction, he worried that the dream might mean he was homosexual. This concerned him particularly in regard to his difficulties with women.

He used various devices to meet women. One trick was to spot some attractive women and then propose some fictitious pretext for interviewing them—for a job or a contest. He had some success with this approach but was disappointed that it never seemed to lead anywhere. In all these contacts he presented himself in some important role, hiding behind an imaginary facade—sure that if he were to present himself as himself no woman would find him interesting. When he did get something going with an attractive girl, he quickly began to criticize her, finding fault with some flaw in her appearance, some lack in her intelligence or wit or her ability to match him in repartee. His view was that it was terribly important for his girlfriend to be as perfect as possible since she was a reflection of himself. If people saw that she was beautiful, intelligent, and charming, they would think better of him. He spoke of wanting complete possession and control over her; when I commented on this way of viewing a relationship, he observed that he could think of it only in terms of power and control—who was on top. If he could not feel on top, he would feel demeaned, devalued, beaten down, humiliated. There was no room for equality in his relationships. Even with his professors, his attitude was childish and submissive. He would ask questions so that they could display their superior knowledge. Impulses to challenge or argue with them would be dangerous and would only incur their wrath. It was safer to stay in a nonthreatening and submissive position. When he discussed these concerns with his father, particularly about a connection with homosexuality, his father told him not to worry, that his feelings were really "pseudohomosexual."

This material displays the configuration of pathogenic introjects that this young man strugged with. The narcissistic components are clearly shown in his feelings of inferiority and inadequacy, as well as in his sense of superiority, not only in his relationships with women but also in his competitive attitudes toward his mentors—and ultimately his father. Behind the wish to challenge his professors was his feeling that he was as smart as or smarter than they, and that he could show them up. This was not unlike his attitude toward his father. His father had wanted to become a psychologist but had failed to gain admission to a psychology program and had settled for social work. This was a severe disappointment and narcissistic blow to the father. His son's success in that area was gratifying but also stirred his envy and competitive urge to put Harvey down and keep him in an inferior position. Harvey's sense of superiority to his father (he was in the process of outstripping him professionally) was threatening because it raised the specter of the father's angry and violent retaliation. While on one hand his father seemed to encourage him to do well and succeed, Harvey also felt there was a second message that he should not become too strong, too successful or competent, because then he would become the object of father's enmity and hatred. The result was his continual glorification of the father and the need to consult him and cling to his advice and opinions. The cost was Harvey's own lack of growth to more autonomous and independent adulthood.

Harvey's internal world was dominated by these narcissistic and aggressive derivatives. The aggressive components of power and powerlessness expressed themselves in his relations with authority figures and also with women. The sexual encounter was overburdened with power themes: in intercourse the woman had power over him, power to control and use his penis, and his only recourse was to submit.

Similarly, when questioned by his mentors, he felt impotent and powerless, as though he had no position, stature, or capacity. It became a master-slave situation, a motif that has dominated his experience. He was terrified of failing his courses and having to go home and tell his father he had flunked out. His fantasy was that his father would be disappointed in him and would never speak to him again, that he would be disowned and rejected, forever humiliated. He would be a failure,

462   The Patients

just like his father. He remembered fears of his father's penis, which had seemed so huge and powerful to him. When he was little, he and father took showers together. His father's penis seemed huge and frightening, and he recalled fantasies of this giant penis being shoved down his throat, choking him to death.

All of these elements came out in the therapy. On countless occasions, Harvey talked about his anxieties and difficulties, trying to elicit some advice from me. When I avoided this trap, he became angry and frustrated, complaining that the time and money spent on his therapy were wasted, that I was not worth my salt as a therapist; certainly I was not as good as his father. He had fantasies of hitting me in the head with a baseball bat—something he wanted to do to his father but could not even dare imagine. Eventually the exploration of these themes led to considerations of his anger at his father, his wishes to kill him, to get back at him for all the times he had made him feel small, impotent, and frightened. He fantasied beating father over the head with a club or hanging him by the neck. He would then eat his father's head. We were able to connect the fantasy of eating his father's head with the wish to devour his penis—by consuming father's huge penis-brain Harvey would become powerful and complete as a man. The other side of these fantasies connected with his identification with his weak, vulnerable, powerless mother, who did not have a penis. This maternal introjection provided the basis for his sense of himself as a powerless victim.

All of these themes came into focus in the therapeutic process, particularly centered around his view of me as powerful and intellectually superior. His repeated efforts to draw me into that position had to be resisted and explored and finally understood—especially in reference to the devalued and diminished position he put himself in and the manner in which this dynamic reflected origins in his relationship with both his father and his mother. Despite the ups and downs of this effort, and the emotional turmoil he suffered in the course of it, including episodes of suicidal depression and severe, almost panicky, anxiety, the difficulties did not spill over into any severely destructive acting-out. His difficulties in the outside world became less frequent and less intense, and he seemed to manage his life and his relationships better.

The borderline quality of Harvey's difficulties was manifest not only in the characteristic alignment of his introjective organization but also in its somewhat regressive features—not flagrantly regressive, as one might find in lower-order borderline pathology, but regressive nonetheless. He would repeatedly act out his view of himself articulated in terms of the pathogenic introjects. In almost every sphere of his life he enacted these roles, putting himself in positions that would play out and reinforce the introjective configurations. At certain points, these could reach an intensity of a paranoid reaction, but this was exceptional. More often it was a chronic situation of inferiority, weakness, vulnerability, or impotence that he generated. A major difficulty was his inability to focus the reality clearly and maintain a firm grip on it. His experience was permeated by his fantasy life, which drew its inspiration from the underlying introjective configuration and prevented him from gaining a clear sense of what the reality was. Much of his therapy was devoted to a long-term working through and refocusing of the reality in the various situations in which he experienced these difficulties. Only slowly, and with many reversals and backslidings, did his footing in reality become more secure.

The most effective aspect of the therapeutic work came in the elucidating, exploring, and final interpreting of the introjective patterns that so dominated his internal world and his relationships with others in the external world. In contrast to the previous patient, George, Harvey had the capacity to appreciate these patterns and gradually, as the therapy moved forward, to modify them in meaningful ways. These patterns could be actively explored and understood in the multiple contexts and forms in which they expressed themselves. As this process deepened, Harvey became increasingly aware of their pathogenic quality and more able to see their roots in his relationships and interactions with his parents. Particularly useful in this regard was the degree to which these same patterns could be focused in the transference. Not only was he able to recognize them when I pointed them out, but he was interested in exploring them rather than escaping or denying them. This reflected the better state of the therapeutic alliance, which was fairly easily maintained. The alliance from the beginning had a workable quality, and as the work progressed and the distortions in the transference clarified and were worked through, the alliance evolved, became stronger and more stable, and provided a firm base for useful therapeutic work. Not only does this aspect of the therapeutic interaction reflect Harvey's capacity for making good use of the therapy, but it also suggests that he would have been potentially a good candidate for analysis—a course that circumstances unfortunately prevented.

ISAAC I.

The next patient, Dr. Isaac I., began psychotherapy on a short-term basis and progressed successfully through psychoanalysis. His original

complaints were his difficulties in handling his professional responsibilities. He was constantly behind on his paper work—billing, reports,
records, letters, and so forth. He procrastinated over these tasks until
the last possible minute, when other responsible agencies (hospital
administrators, insurance companies, other doctors, etc.) had to take
strong measures to force him to do his work. He would then feel angry
and resentful that he was being forced to comply and would often find
some way of undermining or undoing the process. He had also gotten
into rather severe interpersonal difficulties with his partner, with his
office staff, and with his wife. His behavior was often hostile, demanding, domineering, and inconsiderate of the needs or feelings of others in
his life. This ambivalence seemed to invade even his work with patients.
With his wife he felt demanding, resentful of her needs, and particularly
angry about the amount of time she invested in her work and in taking
care of the children. There wasn't much left over for him. His need to
control everything in the family was based on his desire to be the central
and most important figure and on his paranoid, phobic concerns about
potential dangers.

     He started therapy with a short-term focus on these problems, but
it quickly became apparent that his problems were more characterological than situational; the short-term therapy became long-term, and over
the course of several years went from once a week to twice a week, and
then to three times a week of analytically oriented psychotherapy. The
need to get at the core difficulties more effectively led to the further
decision to undertake psychoanalysis with the same therapist.

     Isaac was the older of two boys; his brother was two years younger.
His father was a hard-driving, successful businessman who ran the
family business his own father had started. He was described as stubborn, domineering, controlling, and often given to outbursts of anger.
Isaac's relation to his father was difficult and marked by not much
understanding. He could never remember talking with his father without getting into an argument. Mother was a few years younger than
father, and was described as a nice person but not very effective. She
kept her feelings under wraps most of the time, especially about his
father's hostile and controlling behavior. She had multiple medical
problems (depressive equivalents?), and at the time of his initiating
therapy was suffering from a progressively debilitating and terminal
neurological disease.

     The birth of his younger brother was a severe trauma. He expe-
rienced the intrusion of this younger competitor as a loss, particularly
of his mother's attention and affection. He has always been intensely

competitive with his brother and even in his adult years one of the dominant motifs in his obsessive preoccupations about position and wealth has to do with the fact that his brother works with their father in the family business and it is understood that the business will belong to the brother when the father dies. Since the business is lucrative, Isaac feels that the brother has gotten the lion's share and that he has been left out in the cold. This was a source of considerable resentment and feelings of deprivation.

Soon after the brother's birth, Isaac was hospitalized for several days for removal of a birthmark. The separation from his parents was traumatic. He apparently cried and screamed when he left them and recalled feeling terrified and utterly alone.

When Isaac was about five, the family moved from Boston to a smaller city where father was opening a branch of the family business. A few years later, father began to commute regularly to Boston, where he would stay all week and come home for weekends. These absences had a somewhat disruptive effect on the family but also clearly reduced the level of tension in the house. When Isaac was thirteen, the family moved back to Boston. This was difficult for Isaac, since he lost all his chums and schoolmates and was faced with the need to adapt to a whole new environment. He had been an outstanding student, but in his new environment he was not placed in any of the advanced classes in high school. He experienced these changes as a bitter loss and was enraged at his parents for subjecting him to these difficulties. He did not get on with his new school peers; he remembers feeling hostile and resentful, behaving in an intensely competitive and angry way, getting into fights, and finding it difficult to make friends. He began a pattern of self-defeating behavior in which he deliberately performed poorly or sabotaged his performance whenever he felt people were pushing him to do something he did not want to do. His attitude at such times was defiant and rebellious. His performance in high school and college suffered accordingly, but he was still able to get decent grades and get into medical school.

At the time of beginning therapy, he was married and had a daughter and a son, ages 5 and 2. That his marriage was troubled was due in large measure to his struggles with hostility and aggression on one hand and sexuality and intimacy on the other. He had difficulty engaging in a trustful and equal relationship with his wife and struggled with his need to be in control in every area of their life together. Financially he was reasonably successful: his practice was doing well despite his unconsciously determined efforts to undermine himself.

However, he hated to spend money, resented his wife's expenditures, constantly complained about money spent on anything related to the house, his family, vacations, entertainment—just about everything. He felt impoverished and deprived, as though he were on the brink of financial disaster.

As the analysis progressed, Isaac began to struggle with highly conflictual regressive material. He was obsessively preoccupied with reporting every thought and feeling. He seemed bothered by the loss of face-to-face contact that had helped him to preserve a barrier against the primitive urges and longings. It was not long before the theme of victimization emerged, the analyst being seen as a powerful and threatening object before whom he cowered in fear or whom he would have to attack and defeat. The hours became filled with angry, challenging, and hostile material. Images of rape and violence filled his mind. He developed elaborate fantasies of beating up the analyst, hitting him over the head with a club, smearing feces in his face, and shoving them down his throat. Paranoid thoughts followed close behind: worries about what he could safely reveal, how the material would be used against him, and how he could take steps to defend himself. He wanted to challenge and argue with the analyst and so defeat him. If they were to work together there had to be trouble and somebody was going to get hurt. At times he was the helpless and vulnerable victim who had no defenses, no way to protect himself from the analyst's power, and could only submit in impotent resignation to the analyst. At other times, he was the powerful one, the sadistic and cruel aggressor who could attack, defeat, and humiliate the analyst. Anal material pervaded the early months of the analysis—fantasies of shitting on the couch, smearing shit around the office and in the analyst's face, and so on. These fantasies were readily available, intensely experienced, and apparently relished, particularly when the patient was in the powerful sadistic position. In the role of victim, his fear was equally intense and terrorizing.

An important motif in the first year of analysis was his mother's deteriorating health. He was faced increasingly with the prospect of her death. He struggled with feelings of loss, helplessness, and rage that she was dying; he was angry at her; he suffered guilt over his selfishness and his inability to deal with the painful feelings. Spending time with her was difficult—he could barely tolerate the sadness and pain of watching her die. This led to his fear of loss and his vulnerability to it. He could also lose other important people in his life—his wife, his children, his father, even his analyst. He would be abandoned, desperate, and destitute. As the grief work continued, he brought up childhood memories of being close to his mother, memories of seeing her in degrees of undress, fantasies of sexual activity with her.

The fee emerged as a second central issue early in the analysis and persisted—not surprisingly in view of his obsessions about money. At the transition to analysis he and the analyst agreed to continue the psychotherapy fee, with an understanding that when the patient's significant increase in income materialized the fee would be renegotiated. When that point came the analyst raised the question of increasing the fee. The patient reacted by feeling victimized, helpless to do anything about it. He felt he could not afford the increase and that he would have little or no money to live on. The fact that he could at the same time afford a large and expensive addition to his house and could buy a new Mercedes put the lie to his complaints. He was also receiving significant amounts of money from his father as his share of the family business. He was in fact very well-to-do.

The issue of the fee continued for months without resolution. The analytic work focused on his need to feel vulnerable and victimized rather than to work out a reasonable solution. Much of his reaction had a strongly paranoid flavor, but by dint of repeated confrontations, clarifications, and interpretations he was gradually able to appreciate the degree of his distortion and to agree that he could in fact easily afford the increased fee.

In the midst of this work, his mother died. The analysis entered a period of deep mourning and sadness. He became more deeply involved in the analytic process, more dependent and trusting of the analyst, and able to utilize the analysis effectively in working through his intense grief. His dependency also intensified his fears—fear of losing the analyst, fear of closeness and intimacy, fear of homosexual wishes and impulses. Fantasies of homosexual anal rape excited but also terrified him. He imagined the analyst would attack him from behind, tear off his clothes, and rape him anally with his huge and powerful penis. Isaac's only recourse would be to submit to whatever the analyst wanted to do to him. He would be caught on the horns of a wish–fear dilemma. He reacted by a period of withdrawal and increased resistance. He questioned the value of the analysis and the analyst's competence—whether it was really worth the time and money he was putting into it. Obsessive ruminations and worries about the fee and his fears of impoverishment returned. The analyst's vacation reactivated his sense of loss, particularly of his mother. Complaints about the bill and acting-out around paying it seemed endless. Hardly a billing period passed without some complication, delay, or difficulty. This came to be seen as an attack against the analyst and as a way of denying any sense of dependence or attachment. His relation to the analyst was colored by distrust, fear of criticism, paranoid fantasies of how the analyst would attack, humiliate, and criticize him.

Despite his flooding the analytic hours with primitive material and distorting the therapeutic alliance, and activating primitive transference material, the patient was, nevertheless, deeply involved in the analytic process and committed to working it through. Much of the "action" in the analysis took the form of fantasies of helpless vulnerability or primitive sadistic destructiveness, or expressed itself in acting out and struggling over the fee. Although the affects involved were intense and turbulent, there was a sense of unreality about them, as though the patient were going through the motions, enacting a charade of some sort. His angry tirades and threats against the analyst, for example, never aroused the least anxiety or concern in the analyst. It was as though all of that took place at one level of the patient's personality, while at another level he was engaged in solid and meaningful analytic work, was well motivated, and was profiting from it. While the analytic experience seemed regressive and difficult, the patient's life outside became less chaotic, he began to deal more effectively and responsibly with colleagues and associates, and his relationships with his wife and children became more real and affectively rewarding.

This patient had a successful analytic experience. The analysis was undertaken with caution and with a sense that he might be a high-risk case. The lack of libidinal phase dominance, the difficulties in consolidation of gender identity, the tendency to act out his conflicts in self-defeating ways, and the extent to which personal relationships were chronically distorted and discolored by hostile and sadistic projections served to indicate the underlying borderline structure of his personality. In his favor was the analyst's sense of a solid core to the therapeutic relation and the indications of his motivation for treatment. These proved to be the saving graces. Despite the regressive pulls, the regressive shifts were modest and did not result in any acting out that was severely destructive or troublesome. They more often took the form of arguments with his wife or other family members, or of dealing with business matters in ways that were self-defeating. In other words, the regressive behaviors were easily manageable within the limits of the analytic relationship and required no other limit-setting intervention than the therapeutic exploration itself.

In addition, the analysis is striking for the extent to which the primary therapeutic emphasis focused on alliance factors that remained variously operative throughout the course of the analysis. Work on these factors was focused and facilitated by the acting out around and preoccupation with the fee. This provided a central issue in which many of the pathological factors could be explored and understood. In retrospect, it was more important to clarify and process these alliance factors in the ongoing interaction with the analyst than it was to explore and interpret the same elements insofar as they reflected transference issues and could be understood in genetic terms. The approach to these issues was not exclusive, but there was a natural progression from dealing with and working on distortions and acting out around the therapeutic alliance to gaining further understanding by exploring the transferential origins and by genetic reconstruction. The later effort consolidated and reinforced the exploration of the therapeutic alliance, but probably would have had little impact unless the work on the therapeutic alliance had not proceeded to an adequate degree.

Dr. I.'s pathology seemed to center around his aggressive conflicts and the pathogenic configuration of his aggressor- and victim-introjects. The narcissistic configurations played a less prominent although not inconsiderable role. In the next case, the opposite pattern emerged, in which the narcissistic configurations came to play the central part and the aggressive components a more subordinate role.

JOHN J.

John came to analysis through a preceding course of intensive psychotherapy that lasted about six months. When he started therapy, his concerns focused on his difficulties with depression, which tended to be recurrent and at times fairly severe. He was also preoccupied with his relationship with his father, one that had always been difficult and riddled with frustration for him. He was deeply concerned and conflicted about what he assumed was a powerful identification with his father that he felt caused him considerable difficulty in his life. He did not feel in charge of his life; he felt vulnerable to his shifting moods, particularly his depressive periods; he did not feel strongly motivated in his choice of career; he experienced repeated difficulties in his relationships with women; he felt generally emotionally inhibited and constrained and was unable to feel good about himself and his life. Since he had started a training program in social work and hoped to prepare himself to do psychotherapy, it was imperative for him to explore his own unconscious and come to know himself better.

John was nearly forty when he started therapy. He seemed to have postponed the tasks of achieving maturity and establishing himself as an adult. He was the older of two brothers—his brother was two years younger. The early years were less troubled. His father was a lawyer and for a time relatively successful. The father soon began to have difficulties, problems began to arise in his business, and the family slowly slipped into financially hard times. The father was finally diagnosed as manic-depressive and put under psychiatric treatment. He did not do very well, his business failed, and before long—while still in his forties—he was being supported by SSI. His father was a mystery to John—an object of idolization and wonder, of fear and hatred, and of disgust and disdain. At best his father was difficult to get along with—often cold and distant, unaffectionate, intolerant, demanding, perfectionistic, critical, and punitive. John always felt that his father never thought much of him: he did not pay attention to him, never played with him or showed any interest in what he was doing, never told him that he loved him or thought well of him. There had never been any resolution of this difficult relationship, and by the time John came into therapy the father had deteriorated both physically and mentally. There was little hope of salvaging anything at that point.

John's relation to his mother was closer and more affectionate. She was from a Mediterranean background and was a warm, effusive, somewhat hysterical woman, but also intrusive, controlling, and demanding. She maintained a part-time small-crafts business that kept the family afloat. She apparently taught him many of her skills and he found ways to help in her work. While he seemed to cling more to her, she also became more dependent on him. This pattern seemed to increase over the years as he grew older and more capable and his father became increasingly impaired and unreliable. John had a difficult time with his mother's demands on him and tried to find ways to escape. He would often spend time with his friends' families just to get away. In his adult life, he remains in attendance on his mother, looking after her needs, helping her with tasks around her house, repairing and fixing things for her, and so on. At times these efforts are at considerable cost to himself.

John's relationship with his brother has never been very close or friendly. The two brothers were rivals and competitors from the start. John resented his brother and did not like the fact that his mother paid him so much attention. In many ways the two boys have spent the best part of their lives vying for mother's attention and affection. As they both got on in life, the tension and rivalry between them slackened somewhat, so that they have at least a semblance of a more friendly relationship. John has come to realize that his brother has been having a good deal of difficulty on his own and in the course of his treatment has come to a more sympathetic and understanding position regarding him.

John was intellectually gifted and had done well in school. He had gone to a prestigious college and graduated with honors, but there followed a somewhat checkered career. He was a child of the 1960s and was tormented by all the pressing questions and anxieties of that decade. In college he had dropped out and spent a year traveling, mostly in Europe. He was involved in the student strikes and resisted the draft, escaping to Canada, where he lived and worked for almost a year after graduation.

A series of odd jobs followed. He would not work for any corporation and detested any situation in which he would have to take orders from anybody or be accountable to any superior. He gradually settled into becoming a handyman—something he was good at because of his work for his mother. Gradually he drifted more toward carpentry—repairing, finishing, building furniture. He moved to an isolated town where he lived alone for a while; he was later joined by a like-minded girlfriend. They lived together for several years but finally agreed they could not make a life together. He was so discouraged by this that he gave up his woodworking and sought counseling. In the course of this he decided that he really wanted to work with people and that his true vocation lay in helping people with their emotional difficulties. He moved to Boston, enrolled in a social-work training program, and began psychotherapy.

He engaged readily in the therapy and was able to form a reasonable working alliance with his therapist, a young woman who had recently completed her psychiatric residency. The emerging transference seemed idealizing and he took delight in the therapist's skill and competence. At the same time, he kept in reserve his critical evaluations of her work and his need to devalue her whenever he thought she had not done exactly the right thing in working with him. He even fantasied that he was superior to her as a therapist, though he had barely begun learning something about it. The transference elements remained more or less fragmented: at times he reacted to the therapist's passivity and neutrality, aspects of his father's personality that had given him such trouble. Then he would feel that the therapist was crowding him, pressuring him, not giving him any space—feelings that could be traced to his relation to his intrusive and demanding mother, to whom he had such difficulty saying no.

He threw himself into the work of the therapy, spending hours "analyzing" himself, struggling to understand himself, wishing he could do it on his own, feeling diminished and humiliated that he had to depend on someone else. He prided himself on his self-sufficiency and self-understanding, gained through many years of introspection and meditation. He had made Eastern meditation a sort of avocation, having spent a considerable amount of time studying the techniques, learning from various gurus, and even living in India with a famous guru for two years. To accept that all this self-understanding had not done much for his personal life did not make his commitment to the therapy, or later to analysis, any easier. Much of the therapeutic effort was given over to working through these doubts, hesitations, and resistances.

As the constraints on face-to-face psychotherapy and the depth of John's pathology became clearer, the decision was made to shift to psychoanalysis. The hope was that the psychoanalytic modality would make it possible to reach behind John's rather rigid and highly intellectualized defenses. The analyst felt that he was highly motivated for therapeutic work and change, that his self-defeating behavior patterns were becoming increasingly ego-dystonic, and that there was a reasonably well-established therapeutic alliance. At this juncture, the narcissistic problems, his self-doubt and feelings of inadequacy, his need to be special and exceptional, and his longing to ally himself with a strong and idealized authority figure, were only distant clouds on the horizon.

The analytic couch brought John's pathology into closer view. He continually expected people to do things for him, to help him, to give him what he wanted. But these expectations were constantly being frustrated and disappointed. In turn he became enraged, frequently depressed, not knowing what to do with his disappointment and anger, and more often than not solving the problem by withdrawing in haughty disdain, assuring himself that he was quite self-sufficient, could get along without them or their help, and could take care of himself. This attitude came readily into view around his relations with women. He did not find it difficult to attract women, but these relationships soon began to founder on his neediness, his conflicts over dependence, and his sense of entitlement to special treatment. Much of his self-doubt and sense of inferiority was covered by a veneer of self-congratulatory, smug self-satisfaction. As a rule, when some disappointment or failure

would come up, he would brush by it and start to comment on how well
he had handled some aspect of the situation, often complementing
himself on his skill, talent, breadth of knowledge, intuitive understanding, and so on.

Another aspect of the analytic work that was more clearly etched
was John's use of language. There were times when a clear, straightforward, simple declarative sentence found its way out of his mouth, but
rarely. His sentences were more often convoluted, torturous, complex,
laden with big words, and difficult to follow. The diction was formal,
stilted, at times leading to an awkward construction or expression when
the thought he was struggling to express was quite simple. It was as
though the simple direct expression of his thoughts were somehow
dangerous or threatening. We finally came to understand that the
veneer of intellectual sophistication was covering an impoverished and
highly vulnerable sense of himself; this use of highflown language was
his way of achieving a degree of self-inflation, another vehicle of self-
enhancement for a faltering and deflated self-image.

The initial task was to get him comfortable with the analytic
situation. He was preoccupied with his performance, whether he was
measuring up to the analyst's expectations and doing what was expected of him as a good analytic patient. It was not long before
difficulties began to arise. There was a fair amount of acting out around
scheduling arrangements and fee negotiations. There was a tension
between his commitments to his training program and to the analysis.
He began to miss hours with the excuse that he could not resolve
scheduling difficulties having to do with classes, research work, group
meetings, and so forth. The analyst held to the terms of the therapeutic
contract, namely that he was responsible for making the appointments,
for being on time. His decisions to forego the analytic appointments
and to choose other commitments in preference were repeatedly explored. He saw these conflicts as foisted on him by outside forces,
avoiding any acknowledgment that he may have played a role in setting
up the conflict, either in his scheduling of conflicting class hours or in
his failure to negotiate appropriate times for his analytic appointments.

Issues also arose around the fee. He was being seen as a low-fee
patient, a circumstance that created its own difficulties since it implied
that the analyst was not as competent, that he was getting second-rate
care. He often compared the analyst's skills and performance with
stories he had heard about other analysts, usually something he had
read in the literature or accounts he had heard from other analysands
who were with more established and experienced analysts. It was as

though the analyst's performance were under constant scrutiny. There was a constant, often implicit and occasionally explicit, comparison between the level of the analyst's skills and his own. It was not clear whether he held the analyst's work in esteem or whether she was regarded as not quite measuring up.

There was a considerable degree of countertransference strain in all this for the analyst. Her sense of professional competence was put to the test. She began to resent John's critical comments and self-congratulatory commendations of his own capacity for insight and self-understanding. The undertone was that he was capable of doing the analytic work himself without her participation or assistance. His own need to deny any dependency in the analytic relationship and to defensively retreat to a position of self-sufficient isolation was a constant factor in the shaping of the analytic relationship. At the same time, he struggled with intense wishes for the analyst to step into his life and straighten things out, give him advice, tell him what to do and how to behave so that he could achieve what he wanted, and generally solve his problems and take care of him.

As the analytic work progressed, nothing seemed to go well for him. He moved through a series of unsatisfactory relationships with women. The recurrent scenario was one of initial optimism and high hopes that soon ran into difficulty and before long ended in disaster. He seemed to want these relationships on his terms and resented it when the women would make demands of their own or had expectations he found difficult to meet. He painted himself in the role of the sincere, devoted, giving, helpful partner who was used, taken advantage of, and then abandoned by designing and manipulating women. The prototype for these involvements was his mother, and as time went on he was more and more able to express his resentment and anger against her—especially when her demands interfered with his work and commitments. At a somewhat deeper level he resented her for having had his brother and for thus abandoning him. As this resentment came more clearly into conscious focus, he was able to deal more effectively with his mother, to set limits, and in time to feel less resentful of her demands and manipulations.

More difficult and problematic was his relation with his father. The father had died suddenly before John started his analysis. The mourning process was difficult and painful. There were endless regrets and recriminations. He was torn between his admiration and frustrated yearning for affection and love from his father and his rage, resentment, and bitterness at his father's distance, indifference, neglect, abandonment, and pitiful lack of capacity and strength. His father was in his mind's eye a tragic figure, but a tragic figure who retained his heroic proportions and to whom John looked for a sense of approbation and approval—but never with any sense of satisfaction or fulfillment. John vacillated between the torments of grief, loss, and abandonment by his father on one hand, and rage, resentment, hateful despair, and hopelessness on the other. The longing for connection, approval, and loving endorsement from his father remained unsatisfied and unsatisfiable, doomed to frustrated disappointment and impotent yearning.

In his life outside the analysis, things did not go well. The situation in his training program deteriorated day by day. He seemed to have a knack for alienating and disaffecting his teachers and mentors. Time and again, in one course or training situation after another, there were difficulties from missed assignments, incompletes, conflicts with teachers, difficult competitive situations involving other students, and so on. Again and again when assignments were handed in, he felt that professors did not sufficiently appreciate the quality of his work. His grades were modest at best, but in his view his efforts were deserving of much higher marks. He felt unappreciated and misunderstood. More often than not, he paid little attention to the assignment and handed in something the teacher was not looking for. In some courses, a level of initial success suggested that he at least started from a position of advantage; but then he would assume he was at a more advanced level than his classmates and would not put in much work, feeling he knew the material already. When the exam came, he was at a loss and failed miserably. This failure would precipitate enraged tirades against teachers, faculty, deans, administrators. He would declaim angrily against the school: it was a second-rate institution that he should never have chosen since it was so far beneath his capabilities. The teachers who taught the courses were incapable of understanding him and appreciating his abilities. An important aspect of these angry tirades was that the analyst had on occasion lectured at the same school, was generally well regarded as a teacher there, and was highly sought after as a training supervisor.

One area of difficulty followed hard on another and the incidents of conflict and confrontation with teachers and other students multiplied. At the end of the year he was placed on probation and threatened with being dropped from the program. He was hurt, confused, angry, humiliated, enraged, and felt betrayed and deprived. There was only the slimmest chance for him to see that he had provoked the catastrophe he faced. Time and again, he had set himself up in a position of self-aggrandizing superiority, feeling that he knew more than other students, more than the teachers, and that it was beneath him to submit to the ordinary requirements for writing papers, taking exams, and generally accounting for himself. He succeeded only in eliciting resentment and antagonism in his fellow students and an unsympathetic and judgmental response from his teachers. He flunked nearly every course; he was faced with the option of dropping out of school or of undertaking an arduous program of making up the courses—which would at best cost him a year of hard work. It required considerable effort on the part of the analyst and repeated confrontations with the self-defeating aspect of his behavior to bring home some realization that his own attitudes had played a role in bringing about his demise. In all this he was haunted by the specter of his father, who had made such a failure of his life and career. He was following in his father's footsteps. He was constantly preoccupied with the thought that he, too, was tainted genetically with the stigma of his father's illness—that he lived under a curse he could not escape, that no amount of talking could reverse his fate.

In the analytic work, there was a fair amount of acting out. Coming late to appointments, missing appointments, and taking time out were continual problems. He continued to schedule hours vis-à-vis his classes, even though he knew well in advance what the schedule would be. He skipped hours to study for exams, to catch up on laboratory or research projects, and so on. The analyst's efforts to examine these deviations and explore them led nowhere. He felt justified in having the schedule his way. In the first summer after the beginning of analysis, he took an extended leave to study with a special guru in another part of the country. There was little point in challenging or trying to set limits around these episodes. The analyst tried valiantly to explore and understand these decisions, but it was as though in his mind the die had been cast and there was no turning back. No matter what the analytic exploration turned up, it would not interfere with his decision.

This behavior was provocative and devaluing of the analyst and the analytic process. It was as though the patient would undergo the analysis only on his terms, and was unwilling to explore the implications of his approach to the analytic work and his attitudes toward the process. The analyst felt demeaned, devalued, disregarded, and disdained. The patient seemed to distance himself from the analytic work, submitted himself to it in a perfunctory and superficial manner, and would not allow it to influence his thinking or behavior. He could not allow the analyst or the analysis to be important or influential. He seemed bent on proving to himself and to the analyst that he was quite capable of taking care of himself, that he did not need the input of the analytic process to guide him, that he could sort things out for himself and deal with the problems in his life quite on his own. Any admission of weakness and dependency was anathema.

He would show the analyst not only that he did not need her help but that he was entirely self-sufficient. He felt that he was intellectually gifted and that he should not have to work hard at his courses. The material should come easily, without effort; others had to work at it and study to master the material. He knew it already; he even knew as much as or more than the professors. He maintained a sense of smug superiority in the analysis as well. The analyst was still in analytic training and was therefore lacking in skill and understanding. Her level of development was hardly more than his own.

The course of the analytic work was difficult and disruptive. At times his anxiety level became so intense that he could no longer tolerate the analytic couch. At such times he sat up, frightened of the couch and its regressive pull. He clung to the analyst in these face-to-face situations, needily and desperately. He sought approval and support. After a few sessions of sitting up, he reluctantly and wistfully returned to the couch as if to a bed of torment, resigning himself to a difficult and painful agony.

The analytic task with this patient was formidable. The pathology centered around the narcissistic introjects and was displayed in his feelings of superiority, privilege, and entitlement on one hand, and helplessness, weakness, inferiority, and shame on the other. Wishes and threats to leave the analysis were frequent. It was difficult to get a clear fix on the escapist and defensive quality of these impulses. He had little capacity to appreciate the extent to which he was the prime architect of his difficulties. The analytic work focused largely on efforts to confront and understand his attitudes of superiority and inferiority, to trace their implications and consequences in the many contexts in which they arose, to deal with the episodic acting out, particularly when it impinged on the parameters of the analytic situation, and to come to grips with the defenses and resistances he generated in the analytic interaction. The focus on his use of language was especially telling in this regard. When the defensive nature of his intellectualized vocabulary was broached, it elicited an intense and angry defense and rationalization. The analyst was able to establish that when he used such language it was a signal that he was avoiding some area of conflict, particularly an area that was reflective of painful emotions he could not face.

As the inroads on his rigid defenses were established, the analytic process came closer to the core of his emotional life and the introjective configuration that served as its center. His self-inflating and self-enhancing defenses came increasingly into question, thus diminishing their effectiveness. The result was an increasingly intense depression that was intolerable. With it came the necessity of facing up to his own failures and self-destructive behaviors. His impulse repeatedly was to flee the torment, to escape from the inexorable process of self-confrontation and of stripping away the illusions of grandeur and narcissistic enhancement—in effect to escape the analysis. The difficult challenge was to keep him in the analysis and keep him at the analytic work, which made slow, painful, uncertain, and often reversed progress, teetering on the brink of disruption of the analytic process and never far from the impulse to escape.

My purpose here is to convey a sense of the difficulties involved in the therapy of patients at this level of the borderline spectrum. These tend not to be quiet patients. The therapeutic work is active and often tumultuous. The therapist is confronted with a generally unstable configuration of libidinal levels, shifting defensive organization, episodic regressions, acting out, more or less chronic distortions and occasional disruptions of the therapeutic alliance, and intensely mobilized and rapidly shifting transference paradigms. Preoedipal and oedipal dynamics interplay in often confusing and kaleidoscopic patterns. The therapeutic alliance requires constant attention, adjustment, and repair.

This variability makes the analytic process with these patients considerably more challenging and difficult. Patients at this level are by and large analyzable, but they cannot be analyzed according to strict classical analytic norms. The analytic process always involves parameters of various sorts. The process must be adapted to the needs of the patient, and often will follow a course more like that of analytic psychotherapy than of psychoanalysis—even when the patient remains on the couch. At times of regressive strain, the patient's anxiety may become overwhelming and it is advisable to have him sit up for a period, moving back to the couch when the crisis is resolved. The analyst's effort is directed to keeping the patient on the couch as much as possible, and even then parameters may have to be introduced. The analyst may have to vary the level of his activity—questioning, observing, commenting, generally shifting the balance of structuring activity in order to buffer the regressive pull of the analytic situation, which may have become stronger than the patient can usefully manage at that point.

Parameters are also needed to set limits, confront the patient about destructive or self-destructive behavior, and so on. Obviously these patients are not optimal for beginning analysts, but a fair number of such patients find their way into supervised analyses and do reasonably well. The analytic trainees may have a difficult and agonizing experience, but one that often provides a rich training experience. The borderline quality of the patient's pathology is usually not picked up during the screening and evaluation process—even by experienced and capable analysts. The borderline features do not begin to appear until after some period of analysis: after some months or even years of analytic experience, the regressive factors take effect and the patient begins to look increasingly borderline, to the consternation of the analyst and his or her supervisor. In my view, this is hardly a catastrophe, but it does mean that all concerned—analyst, supervisor, and patient—are in for a tough haul.

An additional point is the extent to which these patients tend to reflect particular difficulties in the relationships with their fathers. In all the cases I have discussed—George, Harvey, Isaac, and John—the patient's relation to the father was difficult, conflictual, and often marked by distance, indifference, or harshness and abusive or devaluing treatment at the hands of the father. These cases of dysphoric personality are all male, but similar issues can be found in female patients, some of them in lower-order pathology—for example, Barbara and Fran presented above. Such difficulties with the father tend to pervade the material of borderline males at all levels, and apparently more disturbed lower-order females; I do not have material that suggests the same order of difficulty obtains to the same extent in higher-order females. Females in the primitive hysteric range seem to experience greater difficulties in their relations with their mothers, usually involving ambivalent conflicts and painful identifications.

20

PRIMITIVE HYSTERICS

The primitive hysterics occupy the highest range of the hysterical continuum of the borderline spectrum. They are for the most part analyzable, considering the difficulties of intensive therapy with any borderline patient. The analysis of these patients does not conform to the classical approach, since there is some need to introduce significant parameters, to deal with occasional regressive crises, and to work consistently on the border of transference difficulties and therapeutic misalliances. Analysis with these patients is subject to all the difficulties I have described in the realms of therapeutic alliance, transference, and countertransference, but the expression of these tends to be muted, more subtle, and insidious. By and large these patients may appear to be indistinguishable from other higher-level character disorders, particularly narcissistic and hysterical character disorders. The diagnosis can be made only when the patient is in a regressive phase, and this is often the reason these patients give an impression of a neurotic level personality disorder and are taken into analysis on that basis.

The analytic regression can subsequently unveil the deeper level of pathology that can catch the analyst off guard. The upshot can be a view of the patient as unanalyzable, but I would argue that this may not be a suitable conclusion—at least in some cases. Regarding the patient as unanalyzable may reflect more of the analyst's anxiety and insecurity than the patient's level of pathology.

There is a residual difficulty in the analytic work with these patients that has to do with the degree of successful termination work. Both analytic cases I am presenting here had a reasonably successful course of psychoanalysis according to the classic model, and for several years after termination, they continued to do well. In both cases, some years after the end of their analyses, precipitating circumstances led to acute regression—one, quite paranoid in quality, responded rapidly to a couple of therapy sessions, and the patient easily returned to her customary level of good function; the other collapsed rapidly into an agitated depression that required brief hospitalization. If there had been any doubt about the diagnostic impression of these cases, it was strikingly reinforced by these relatively dramatic regressive episodes in otherwise high-functioning, successful, and socially well-adapted individuals.

In this section, I will discuss three cases, one of intensive analytically oriented psychotherapy and two psychoanalyses. All are women, a circumstance that says something about diagnostic style. There is a general tendency to diagnose borderline disorders more frequently among women (Stone 1980), similar to the diagnostic tilt in hysteria. By and large these cases would fall within the hysterical continuum of the borderline spectrum. I have not found a case I could describe as primitive hysteric in a man; there may be such, but at least in my experience they are rare. I have certainly analyzed male hysterics, but the cases in my experience have fallen short of borderline characteristics. They are often described as mixed neuroses with hysterical features. Males are much better represented among dysphoric personalities and to a lesser extent in the lower order of the hysterical continuum. On the other hand, males are well represented in the schizoid continuum at all levels.

KAREN K.

Karen came to therapy in the wake of a divorce, complaining about her dissatisfaction with her present job and her chronic inability to make commitments. She had graduated from college with high honors and went on to obtain an advanced degree in physics. During the course of this work, she had a number of affairs, finally marrying her thesis adviser. The marriage lasted for two difficult and tempestuous years and ended in divorce. Since she then thought that her real talents lay in art, she abandoned her work in physics and went back to school to take a degree in art. She was at first successful. She came to be regarded as an outstanding talent, "the darling of the department," and had a series of intense, flamboyant, and tempestuous affairs, none of which lasted more than a few weeks. In each instance, the relationship would start off with rapid and deep involvement, become rapidly sexualized and intensely erotic, but soon falter and turn sour. Erotic attachment would turn to bitter resentment and recriminations, and the relationship would become angry and hostile. At the end of the year she had to drop out of the program because her mother refused to support her any more.

The most important affair, which continued over a period of several years, was with a young artist, Ned. She admired his skill with the brush and his powerful use of emotionally charged colors. She felt that his painting was strong and masculine, qualities she greatly admired and felt lacking in herself. He treated her poorly, made many demands on her, and used her as a sounding board for his anxieties and problems. He drank heavily, used a fair amount of drugs, often insisting that she take the drugs along with him, and continued his promiscuous sexual activity despite his involvement with Karen. She became attached to him in a dependent and needy way, suffered his endless abuse, submitted to his demands, did whatever he wanted. The sex tended to the perverse, including both oral and anal practices. When he penetrated her, she described an ecstatic feeling in which her entire being seemed to dissolve in a blissful union. She felt as though she were taken over by his powerful penis and completely absorbed into his strength. She would lose all sense of herself as separate and become absorbed into his being, without any sense of boundary or separation. She was caught in the web of a powerful attraction in which she felt drawn to him by a force she could not resist; but his behavior was so demeaning, abusive, and sadistic toward her that she felt intense hatred and disgust for him. She could not resolve this ambivalence. The price she paid was depression, even to the point of suicidal feelings, and a sense of helpless frustration. In the grip of these feelings she undertook a first course of psychotherapy that lasted about a year. This therapy was not very helpful, although it enabled her to appreciate not only how self-defeating and masochistic her relation with Ned was but the extent to which she hated her mother. It was in an effort to extricate herself from her destructive relation with Ned and to put distance between herself and her mother that she moved to Boston. She hoped to locate work in an academically stimulating environment and possibly find ways of continuing her interest in art.

The therapy began with a great deal of uncertainty and hesitation. She did not know whether she wanted or needed therapy or whether she would be able to find satisfactory work to be able to afford therapy. She did not know whether she wanted to commit herself to living in this part of the country. She seemed to have a difficult time settling down. She had only recently arrived in the city, but was unable to settle on a place to live. She moved, seemingly precipitously and impulsively, from apartment to apartment. The problems were at times with the apartment itself, at times with neighbors or other tenants she did not like. There was a desperate, urgent quality to this shifting around. The issue more often than not seemed to be that she did not want to live in a place like one her mother might choose or approve of.

A similar situation developed on the work front as well. She was well qualified for good positions in a variety of research or academic settings in her field. She found it difficult to settle on a job that suited her tastes. She tried several jobs in succession, finding each attractive and promising at first but soon expressing doubts, becoming dissatisfied with work conditions and demands, disagreeing with company policy (many of these installations were involved in defense projects—something she found offensive). She felt an increasing dislike for fellow workers and was critical of the quality of their work and the poor standards of performance.

Karen's parents were both of German-Jewish extraction and had escaped from Nazi persecution just before the war broke out. After coming to America, the father had considerable success in business, but not in his personal life. He was immature, demanding, selfish, given to temper tantrums; he drank heavily and gambled. He had countless affairs all through his married life. In the family, he seemed to occupy a weak, irresponsible, and unreliable position. Karen's mother, in contrast, was the central and dominating figure in the family, controlling, intrusive, argumentative, always wanting and usually getting her way. The arguments and even physical fights between the parents grew worse, and they finally got divorced when Karen was 13.

Karen felt closer to her father, with whom she found it easier to get along, but also blamed him for much of the trouble in the family because of his gambling and drinking. She hated her mother and regarded her as a witch and a monster. They had always fought over everything, and her mother was constantly threatening to throw her out of the house or to call the police if Karen would not obey. One of the few pleasant memories she had of her mother was of her singing her to sleep, especially with songs from Puccini. These were sad and poignant memories that made her want to cry. Looking back, she could see that her mother was an unhappy and disappointed woman.

The problem at the outset of the therapy was to help her to establish some sense of commitment to the process and to engage in it in a consistent way. There were initial difficulties related to aspects of the therapeutic contract—coming on time, missing appointments, paying her bill. The therapist dealt with each of these by exploring their meaning and focusing the implications for her commitment to the therapy. These minor tendencies to act out around the terms of the therapy diminished somewhat, occasionally resurfaced, and then seemed to disappear. She became increasingly involved in the therapeutic effort and stayed with it fairly consistently.

Early in the process the pieces of a positive and somewhat idealized transference became evident. She compared the doctor to her previous therapist, whom she saw as weak and whom she had been able to manipulate. But the new doctor was like a rock—solid and unmovable. She admired this but also resented it and felt that she needed to test it. In an early dream he came to pick her up in a jazzy, powerful sports car, but when she made sexual advances to him he rebuffed her. There were other highly erotic dreams in which he overpowered her sexually, did whatever he wanted with her, but then confessed to her that he could not control his impulses. As she settled into the therapy, the acting out diminished but the implications of increased closeness and intimacy with the therapist came more into focus. They agreed to increase the time to twice a week, intensifying the transference pressures and conflicts.

Much of the work in the early stages of therapy was in two areas: her highly conflicted and torturous relationship with Ned, and her hate-filled relationship with her mother. Despite the distance she had put between herself and Ned, he remained constantly on her mind. She talked about her fascination with him, his huge and powerful penis, the fantastic sex, his marvelous artistic prowess, and so on. There was little about the negative aspects of the relationship—his selfishness, demandingness, and sadistic treatment of her. She would call him from time to time to have him tell her how much he missed her and beg her to come back. Finally, one vacation period she decided to visit him. The trip was a disaster. She came away feeling that he was interested in her only as a "good fuck," that sex was good only if he was smoking pot, and that otherwise he was impotent. He also had other women on the string and sadistically flaunted them in her face. She returned disgusted and enraged.

Her hatred for her mother seemed an inexhaustible source of complaint and bitterness. She resented almost everything her mother did or tried to do with, for, or against her. She resented that she had to depend on her mother to pay for part of her treatment. Mother had remarried a wealthy man and had offered to pay for Karen's therapy. Mother could never show any real affection or love; all she could do was buy things. Mother had often been abusive, threatening both Karen and her younger brother with dire punishments if they didn't obey. At times she would threaten to call the police or send them off to an orphanage. Mother was also intrusive and controlling. Worst of all, Karen recalled times when her mother had abused Karen and her brother sexually. She would make them undress and give them enemas for no apparent reason. There had also been times when the mother would push things up her anus or in her vagina. She remembers being stimulated by these experiences, but also quite conflicted about them. Now Karen prefers anal intercourse. Her first husband, whom she had married at 19, gave her *The Story of O.* He would force her to have anal intercourse, and even though she felt helpless and humiliated, she saw no recourse but to submit as she had submitted to her mother. It took longer for her to acknowledge that she enjoyed this sort of masochistic surrender. In any case, she blamed her mother for these perverse fixations.

As the therapy deepened, the themes of masculine power and feminine weakness came to the fore. These issues played a role in many aspects of her life. She could not settle on a career path. She saw mathematics and physics as areas of masculine competence and her own competence in these areas as expressing the masculine aspects of her self. But she did not feel comfortable with this. She had considerable success in her work, and though her contributions were at times singled out for praise, she could never accept this recognition, believing that it was flawed or deceptive and that she did not really deserve it. She was offered several positions of increased authority and responsibility but turned them down because she felt she could not measure up to the expectations and responsibilities they involved. She toyed with the idea of going to law school. She generated an attitude of restless dissatisfaction: wherever she was or whatever she was doing was somehow not good enough, not as fulfilling as something else—but what that something else might be she did not know. For her, law meant power, something she yearned for, yet feared.

Her interest in art was more feminine, but she could not rest easily there either. Her work was talented but weak, without power or impact.

She envied what she saw as masculine attributes of strong color and line and felt that such capacities were beyond her. She was condemned to pitifully meaningless and pallid productions that were not impressive.

These preoccupations of masculine versus feminine, power versus weakness, domination versus submission found their way into the therapeutic interaction as well. She saw the therapist, a man, as powerful and influential and herself as weak, helpless, and vulnerable. She struggled with her wishes to please, to be a good patient, to do as he seemed to wish and make him feel that his efforts to help her were productive and satisfying. The way to accomplish this was to submit, to have no ideas or wishes of her own, to do what was expected, to conform, and not to object or question. She felt that if she conformed to the therapist's expectations and did what he wanted, did not challenge or disagree with anything he might say, then he would exercise his magical power and set things right for her. She began to see him as critical, judgmental, intrusive, as forcing on her his ideas about how she should behave and live. She was afraid to make any greater commitment to the therapy because it would mean submitting to the therapist's power, yet at the same time she feared her own impulses to cut and run, to quit the therapy, to throw herself back into the arms of Ned and the sensuous abandon he represented. That course loomed as purposeless, destructive, hopeless, and desperate.

In the therapeutic relation, Karen seemed continually tossed back and forth by her wishes to be close, intimate, and dependent on the therapist (wishes that rapidly became sexualized and cast in intensely erotic terms), and by her opposite wishes to draw back, to be on her own, to go it alone, to abandon herself to the impulses to live without direction or purpose, to seek only pleasure and orgastic release. Conflicts over career, love relationships, and the sense of her own identity were causes of this turmoil. The pressure she generated to violate the therapeutic situation, to turn it into a context of real gratification, to make her relation to the therapist one of real interpersonal love and mutual satisfaction was constant—at least for a long period of the therapy.

These issues intensified around periods of separation from the therapist—at first vacations and holidays, and later to an increasing degree even weekend interruptions. There was a powerful sense of abandonment and loss in these situations, and a countermovement of desperate and needy clinging. When she was attached to the therapist, she felt comforted, reassured, protected; when she had to separate, she felt abandoned, lost, hopeless, desperate, and needy. The therapeutic work centered around the images of herself and of the therapist that were implicit in these contexts, and increasingly focused on the underlying introjective configurations that gave rise to them. Much of the exploration related to these themes centered on her relations with her parents and on the patterns of identification and internalization that came out of these relationships. An important theme was her sense of disappointment and abandonment by her father, who left her naked and unprotected and vulnerable to intrusions and humiliations at the hands of her mother. The intensity of her hatred and rage at her mother required extensive processing before she was able to come to the point of disengaging her sense of herself as victim—helpless and vulnerable before her mother's sadistic and seductive impingements—and begin to set her course in more autonomous and adaptive paths.

Much of this material could conceivably pass for more or less conflict-based neurotic issues. Why do I insist on calling this patient borderline—higher-order borderline, to be more precise? The diagnostic indices would include the lack of libidinal phase dominance, the tendency to act out (particularly around sexual involvements and areas of commitment and responsibility), the rapid mobilization of transference paradigms, the tenuousness and fragility of the therapeutic alliance, the shifting of transference paradigms among conflicting configurations (along lines of introjective patterning involving both aggressive and narcissistic dimensions) both inside and outside the therapy, and the regressive shifts, which were frequent and resulted in mildly self-defeating and self-compromising behaviors.

The therapeutic task with this patient fell in three parts. The first problem was to get the patient engaged in the therapeutic process. There was a fair amount of initial acting out around aspects of the therapeutic structure; these required a strong stand on the part of the therapist, a need to confront the patient on her wish to undermine and frustrate the therapy, and making an issue of her seeming inability to commit herself to the process and take responsibility for it. The second problem was to gain some degree of control over the patient's acting out. While none of the acting out was intense or self-destructive, it was certainly repeating a pattern in which her life remained in turmoil and was frequently cast in terms that would ensure her victimization. The limit setting took the form of exploring her behavior in these instances with an eye to understanding its motivation and tracing the consequences and implications of both actual and projected courses of action. The last part of the therapeutic problem was the progressive and gradual focusing of the patient's introjective configurations as they played themselves out in her everyday life and in her ongoing interactions with the therapist, in both transference and therapeutic alliance terms.

As these issues were explored, interpreted, and understood, the therapeutic ground shifted, and the therapy became more regular and productive, much more like the therapy of any neurotic, or perhaps narcissistic, patient. The acting out lessened, she became more faithful to and responsible for the therapeutic work, and the shifting pattern of transference manifestations settled more consistently into a narcissistic configuration. The entire latter part of the therapy came to focus on the narcissistic issues and dynamics, with quite telling therapeutic effects. But these shifts proved to be more phasic than progressive. Periods of apparent progress were interspersed with phases of regression and recrudescence of self-defeating acting out, impulsivity, dissatisfaction with work or living situations—often contexts that had been quite satisfactory over extended periods now had to be escaped in urgent and impulsive fashion. These periods of regression were perplexing and troublesome to the therapist, who felt that he was seeing all of his therapeutic efforts going up in smoke before his eyes. The difficult task at such points was to maintain the therapeutic continuity, to avoid the countertransference traps of trying to set excessive limits, and to pay attention to the wavering therapeutic alliance. To my knowledge this therapy continues in its staggering and uncertain course; the basic issue is whether the patient can continue to engage in the therapeutic process, and if so whether she can internalize anything from it that will help her to consolidate a more functional ego capacity and a more stable sense of self.

LORI L.

Miss Lori L. presented a somewhat different picture, including a successful analytic experience. She came into treatment because of her continuing interpersonal difficulties and a nagging depression. She had recently come to Boston to pursue advanced clinical training as a psychiatric social worker. She had been recently divorced and was experiencing problems in her relationship with her current boyfriend. During the period leading to the divorce and after, she had been in psychotherapy with a succession of therapists. With two of these she had become sexually involved, something she felt great shame and guilt about.

When the therapist first met with her, he experienced two over-whelming impressions. The first and most superficial was the aura of intense sensuality she generated without any apparent awareness on her part. Her manner was seductive, flirtatious, sensuous. She was tall, brunette, generously endowed, and attractive without being beautiful. She dressed not provocatively but tastefully, accentuating her physical attributes. The overall impression was highly sexual and stimulating. This demeanor contrasted strikingly with her own inner feelings—the second powerful impression she conveyed. The picture she presented of her inner life was of utter misery—feelings that she was filthy and evil inside, worthless and inadequate. Her sense of herself was permeated by a deep sense of shame. Even her sexuality was devalued and despised: she was not beautiful enough to attract and hold onto a man, her breasts were not big enough, she was disgusted by the smells and secretions of her vagina, she could not understand how any man could be attracted to or love her. Sex was exciting and endlessly fascinating. Her sexual involvement with men was intense, rapid, totally uninhib-ited to the point of being polymorphously perverse—no avenue of sexual exchange was ignored. This same quality of intense and imme-diate involvement characterized her engagement in the therapy as well.

In the first interview, she began by complaining that her chair was too far away from the therapist and pulled it closer so that she was no more than an arm's length away from him. She then leaned forward and looked intently into his eyes and face as if searching for something important. The therapist found this rather disconcerting. She spoke of her prior therapy. She described the seductions, complaining that one of these therapists had treated her in a demeaning and critical manner. She was disappointed that she had had several years of therapy to no avail, that the problems that had brought her to treatment were un-changed despite the effort and expense.

The doctor, no doubt reacting out of his discomfort and his coun-tertransference need to deal with the patient's sexuality, moved to establish a more secure position and to get the therapeutic relationship started on the right footing. He observed that she had not really been in therapy as yet and that she had not had a doctor with whom she could do therapy. She nodded assent, and he then asked whether she could tolerate having a doctor and could commit herself to a course of therapeutic work. She seemed puzzled but agreed that this would be a problem for her. She went on to describe her difficulties in relating to men, especially her husband, how she found herself angry and resentful

toward them, feeling the need to put them down, seeing herself as
hurtful, nasty, castrating. She could even sense a nasty edge in her
questions to the therapist, wanting to test him, challenge his power and
authority, put him down. She felt the need to manipulate, exploit, and
control men, but when she was able to do so, she felt only contempt for
them. When she could not control them, she was fascinated and envious
of their power. The doctor's question made her feel that she could not
control him, that he was big and powerful. In comparison she felt small
and inadequate. She despised her husband because he had been too
short and his penis was too small; since her divorce she had dated tall
men. Her current boyfriend was 6′ 5″. (The doctor was a tall, lean young
man, over six feet tall.) She was aware of a deep rage within herself
directed primarily toward men.

Lori came from a well-do-do family—her father, a successful businessman, her mother, and a brother two years younger. She had been
given all the advantages of money and position, had gone to the best
private schools, and had always done well academically. She saw herself
as a busy, energetic, and interested little girl until about the time of
puberty. She then became shy and somewhat withdrawn, and started to
avoid athletics and sports, especially if they were at all competitive. She
felt physically awkward and was ashamed of her body; she found ways
of avoiding gym classes and sports. She preferred to come home and
spend the time with her mother. If something happened to interfere
with this arrangement, she would feel anxious and guilty, as though she
were abandoning her mother and betraying her.

Lori's mother was an intelligent and socially prominent woman
who was also chronically depressed. She had worked early in life as a
secretary, but after her marriage had settled into the role of wife and
mother. Her relationship with her husband was far from satisfactory.
They seemed to go their separate ways. Lori could not recall any
expressions of affection between them. For as long as she could remember, they had slept in separate bedrooms; she was convinced that
there was no sexual life between them. There was little conflict in the
marriage, but also little affection.

As her children grew, time began to weigh heavily on Lori's mother's hands. She engaged in some community activities, had a few
hobbies—needlework, painting—but never invested much time or interest in them. Much of her day was spent taking care of the house,
reading, or sleeping a great deal of the time. The impression Lori gave
was that her mother did little during the day, and that the focus of her

life was on getting her children off to school in the morning and waiting for them to come home in the afternoon.

Lori felt bound to her mother, but the relationship was not all roses. Mother was demanding and perfectionistic. It seemed that no matter what Lori did, her mother could always find fault with it. There was always something for mother to worry about—Lori's skin, hair, teeth, bowel movements, dress, socks, shoes—the list seemed endless. Lori carried into her adult life a sense that there was something not right about her, some defect; it was as though she spent the best part of her energy trying to find the defect and correct it. This was in fact one of the motivating forces behind her seeking therapy and provided one of the operative suppositions with which she entered it, namely that the therapy would correct her defect so that she could become as perfect as her mother thought she should be. This also implied that she had to find the powerful, omnipotent wizard-therapist who could perform this magic. A continuing problem was that Lori's attachment to her mother persisted into her adult life. Mother and daughter were on the phone daily, literally spending hours commiserating with each other. At times of holiday or vacation, Lori could not take advantage of opportunities to relax but felt constrained to spend the time with her mother.

Lori's father was a quiet, mild-mannered man who was content with his life and apparently little bothered by the sexual desert he lived in. He was successful in business and respected in the community. But at home he was Mr. Milquetoast, never asserted himself, and seemed to comply with everything his wife decided. He never took any initiative himself, never suggested any family activity or stated his wishes or desires. He always talked to Lori in baby talk, a habit that infuriated her, but no amount of complaining seemed to put an end to it. She could remember as a little girl feeling very close to her father, sleeping with him at times even into her teens—cherishing fantasies of lying close to him and feeling his penis against her backside. She especially recalled watching showgirls on TV with him, and feeling insulted and furious when he would admire shapely, long-legged beauties.

Lori's relation to her brother was also far from benign. She recalled his birth as traumatic. She remembered not being able to visit her mother in the hospital because she might infect her mother and the baby. She felt she had lost her primary place with her mother because she was inadequate and somehow defective. When she saw the baby she was filled with rage and envy. She hated him for having ruined her paradise in which she had had her parents, especially her mother, all to herself. She felt displaced by the baby and at one point even tried to get into the baby's clothes—reflecting her wish to return to a more infantile position so that she would have her mother's interest and attention back again. She was particularly affected by the baby's penis, since that was the only thing she could see that made him any different from herself and might explain her banishment. She remained intensely jealous of and competitive with the brother as the years passed. She picked on him, criticized him, tried to make him feel inferior and inadequate. As he grew older, he became increasingly successful in giving it back to her in kind. He grew big enough to pin her to the floor when they got into an argument. She would then scream so that her mother would intervene, usually on her side since she was more successful at playing the offended victim. She could also admit that these episodes were pleasurable, especially when he would lie on top of her and she could feel his penis pressing against her body.

Lori married somewhat impetuously, before she had finished college, to someone she had known for years because she was convinced that no one else would want her and that she did not have what it takes to attract any man who might be stronger and more attractive. She regarded her husband as second-best from the start. She felt contempt for him and rage at herself for having attached herself to such an inferior man. She was critical, demeaning, hostile, and attacking for most of their time together. It appeared that as soon as the vows were pronounced, she was determined to break the marriage up. She succeeded; there were constant fights and arguments. It was soon clear to all concerned that the marriage was a mistake, and within a year and a half a divorce was in the works. In the course of all this turmoil, Lori began therapy.

When she entered the present therapy, the therapist's main problem was in maintaining the therapeutic structure. The problem was not one of acting out in terms of the contract but rather of maintaining an effective therapeutic alliance in the actual work of the therapy. Lori immersed herself in the therapeutic relation with intensity and a feeling of needy dependence that she found disturbing. There was a desperate quality in her attachment to the therapist, as though he were the only one who could save her and without his help she would be lost. The transference components were mobilized almost from the beginning and seemed to grow more intense as the work progressed. There were a series of dreams in which the therapist appeared in various distinguished, important, and powerful roles—judge, powerful leader, savior. In one dream, she was invited to the therapist's house, where his wife was distributing champagne to the guests, who were all patients. She was the only one who did not get any; when she asked why, the wife said it was nothing personal, just that they had run out. Lori was disappointed but still felt positively toward the therapist. She was disappointed that the doctor had not given her what she had hoped for. She drew a contrast with dreams about her first therapist, in which she would appear at his house but always inadequately dressed. She felt shame and distress at the way in which she had prostituted herself to gain his approval and please him. She agreed that this pattern of behavior was a way of expressing how she felt about her self internally.

The therapeutic work moved along well, and as the months passed the sessions were gradually increased, at first to twice weekly, then to three times. Despite Lori's turbulent emotions, her quality of desperate and needy clinging, and her impoverished and devalued view of herself, it became increasingly clear that there was a capacity in her to work at the task and not to be deterred from it. This quality together with her obvious intelligence and perceptiveness proved that she had the resources to undertake analysis. The therapist was in training as an analytic candidate. When he brought the case to me for evaluation as a potential supervisor, I was impressed by the progress Lori had made, by the reasonably good success she and the therapist had had in maintaining a reasonable therapeutic alliance, and by her strengths and motivation. My apprehensions centered on her history of multiple therapeutic seductions, on the immediacy and intensity of the transference mobilization, and on the countertransference pulls that the therapist described as difficult and troublesome for him. We agreed that if we were alert to the difficulties and if he felt that he could maintain his balance in the face of predictably more intense transference pressures, we could go ahead with an analysis.

As soon as she hit the couch, the picture changed dramatically. The affective tone became more intense and powerful. The previous suggestions of erotized transference burst into a full-blown erotic and idealized transference in which the boundaries between the "as-if" quality of the transference relationship and reality had been wiped away. Highly sexualized dreams of intense erotic activity between the analyst and herself were prominent. Her rich fantasy life became preoccupied with the person of the analyst, particularly in the form of erotic imaginings of what it would be like to have sex with him, to suck on his penis, to have him rape her anally as well as vaginally. In the face of this sexual onslaught, the analyst, who was a rather good-looking young man only slightly older than the analysand, and who found her attractive, could do little more than hold on for dear life—like another Ulysses strapped to the mast while the song of the Sirens beckoned. There seemed little doubt that the patient was ready, willing, even eager to strip off her clothes on the spot and go at it.

As the analyst stuck to his analytic position, struggling manfully with his own countertransference urges, it became clear to Lori that the wishes that drove her to this intense sexualization of the analytic relation were not going to be satisfied. The part of her that wanted to do away with the analysis and turn it into a sexual orgy, thereby destroying the analytic process and the threat it posed to her neurosis, was frustrated and stymied. The response was to turn upon the analyst in waves of hostility, anger, furious accusations, devaluing criticisms of how useless and worthless the analysis was and how ineffectual he was as an analyst, and threats to break off the analysis. This attack was disconcerting to the analyst because he saw the analysis blowing up in his face; it was troublesome also because the loss of the case would have created difficulties for him in his analytic training. He was forced to struggle with his own feelings of inadequacy and failure. This situation inevitably stirred feelings in him that Lori was in fact unanalyzable, that if she was analyzable he was not the man for the job, that she was too much for him to handle, and so on. The supervision had to deal with these painful countertransference feelings and gain some understanding of the way in which the patient's pathology was operating to defeat the analytic process. If she could get the analyst to give up the struggle, she would find confirmation of her worst fears of her own defectiveness and hopelessness. Gradually they were able to clarify the way in which she utilized her sexuality to avoid underlying depressive issues that had more to do with the impoverished image of herself that reflected deeper narcissistic issues.

Both analyst and analysand were able to survive passage through these rough waters and the analysis gradually settled into a calmer, progressively deepening and effective process. The analytic work brought the narcissistic issues into clearer focus and made it possible for them to be worked on. One side of the narcissism had been clearly stated from the beginning—Lori's sense of inferiority and inadequacy, that she was defective and needed to be fixed up and made whole. Gradually, however, the other side of the narcissism came more to the fore: her sense of being special and privileged, her entitlement that said she should have what she wanted, when and how she wanted it. She had been her father's favorite, his little girl, and he had given her everything she wanted. She expected that life and the world should follow suit, and if they did not she had a right to be outraged.

In the course of working through these vicissitudes, her life continued apace. She remarried but not well. This occurred during the course of the analysis and had more the quality of an acting out than a good marriage choice. Her husband was a narcissistic man with marked character flaws, but she ignored these in the rush of her idealization and infatuation. There may also have been elements of acting out of the transference in relationship. In any case, the marriage foundered rapidly and she soon found herself back in divorce court. This was a bitter and disappointing experience, but helped to put her on notice that her impulses could lead her into deep waters. In other respects, her life and work took on an increasing adaptive and productive orientation.

The termination brought difficulties. Things were going quite well for her and the analytic work was coming to a useful resolution. She began to entertain good job offers in another part of the country; termination seemed an obvious next step. As soon as the analyst suggested it, however, she reacted with anxiety and some regression. Old issues resurfaced, old doubts about herself reappeared, old accusations against the analyst were dusted off and polished up. He only wanted to get rid of her, he was tired of listening to her complaints, he was bored and disinterested, she was not adequate to hold his interest, and so on. The thought of termination terrified her and she found every reason to resist it and postpone it. The analyst and I felt at the time that the difficulties were largely adolescent in tone, and that Lori was struggling with problems in establishing herself once and for all as an independent adult. We did not want to repeat the experience she had had with her parents in the analysis; she had difficulty enough in separating from their clinging dependency. Termination was reached in the face of Lori's reluctance and complaints that she was not ready and might never be ready to terminate. The subsequent events proved her partly right. She continued to return to see the analyst for periodic visits for months after the termination. It was as though she could not let go of the analysis and the analyst all at once, but had to do it piecemeal. The frequency of visits gradually diminished and finally stopped. When last seen, Lori was well on her way to a satisfying and productive life.

MARILYN M.

The next patient presented in somewhat different fashion. She was referred with her husband for couples' therapy. They had been married about fifteen years and the marriage was in process of breaking up. There were three children, a boy, and two girls. The patient was successful in her work as a nurse; at the time she was the head nurse of an ICU. Her husband was a successful lawyer. The problem in the marriage was not difficult to discern. Marilyn's husband was a rather primitive borderline man whose pathology was obvious in the family interaction. He was abusive, demanding, infantile in many of his behaviors; temper tantrums were common; he was unfriendly and antisocial, even to the point of paranoia. When he lost his temper, he lashed out destructively—throwing food on the floor if he did not like it, breaking furniture, beating his wife, punishing the children severely for little or no offense, and so on. His behavior made life in the family a continual hell—no holiday was unspoiled, having any social life or friends was impossible, and the tension and resentment in the house were monumental. In addition, although he earned a salary in the six-figure range, he was stingy, refusing to buy even essential things for the house or the family. Marilyn also worked and was forced to use her own income to pay for the upkeep of the house, for food and clothing for herself and the children. The couples' therapy did not last long; Mr. M. could not tolerate the idea that he might be a contributor to the family problems in any way, and when it became clear that he would have to examine his own behavior, he refused to come.

In the process, it became clear to Marilyn how impossible and pathological her husband's behavior was—something that she had denied despite her clinical knowledge—and how her own pathology played into his sickness. Over the years she had submitted to his disruptive and infantile behavior without complaint or resistance, and had accepted this as her lot in life. She had tried in a variety of ways to satisfy him, to please him, to gain some sense of favor or acceptance in his eyes, but all in vain. Whatever effort she went to, whatever degree of self-effacement and sacrifice, it was never enough to stem the tide of his precipitous rage and bizarre attitudes. The cost to her was a more or less chronic depression and a collection of obsessional anxieties and symptoms. She saw clearly that she had to continue her own treatment or she was headed down a self-destructive path that could even end in suicide. She continued to see me in weekly psychotherapy that was gradually intensified and finally converted to psychoanalysis.

Her own psychic life was a torment of depression riddled with intense anxieties. Almost everything she did was discolored by obsessional doubting and a sense of impending doom. These symptoms had come to the fore around the birth of each of her children. Over and above the depression, she was thrown into an agony of doubt and anxiety over caring for the infant. She was afraid of hurting the child, of dropping or drowning it. Feeding the baby was a torment; she was obsessed with the feeding ritual: cleanliness, adjusting the schedule to the infant's needs, preparation of the food in just the right way. When breastfeeding, she was afraid of infecting the child, somehow poisoning it with bad milk from her breast, harming it psychologically by her handling or her interaction with the child. If the child became ill, she suffered a paroxysm of anxiety and guilt, fearful she had caused the illness, taking extreme precautions, obsessing over any medications that had to be given or other procedures the doctor might recommend. Visits to the pediatrician were occasions of soul-searching and agonized guilt, fears that she would be found to be inadequate, that she would be charged with being a bad mother who was doing damage to her children. All of these anxieties had to be dealt with by obsessional devices, rituals, endless checking and rechecking to make sure everything was in order, preoccupied cleaning and sterilizing. It was a wonder that she and the children survived at all.

Marilyn came by these traits honestly enough. She was raised in a small town, the oldest daughter in a family of four; she had a younger brother and two younger sisters. Her father ran the local general store and her mother took care of the house and helped out in the store. Neither parent was comfortable or happy. Marilyn's father was a gruff, quiet man who never said much, never entered willingly or interestedly in the life of the family, kept very much to himself, and devoted his efforts to the business. He was an intelligent man who read widely and felt himself to be superior to his neighbors, looking down on them as ordinary, ignorant, and inferior. There was little joy in his life and little capacity to enjoy it. The family took no vacations, never went anywhere to visit relatives or see anything. The father never took a day off; he worked in the store from early in the morning until supper time, many times working late. He kept the store open seven days a week, with little apparent reason other than to escape from his wife and family. When he came home, he retreated behind his newspaper. There were times when he seemed to become even more negative and antagonistic to the world around him, almost paranoid. The result was that he had no friends, the family had no friends and no social life.

Marilyn's mother was a paragon of masochism. Unfortunately it was not a quiet masochism, and she complained noisily every step of the way. She never confronted her husband, crossed him, or complained to his face about the quality of life he imposed on the family. But she clearly suffered mightily from it, hated it, struggled with a murderous rage, and complained about and endlessly bemoaned her horrid fate to her oldest daughter. All through her years of growing up, Marilyn's parents lived a life of emotional separation. They slept in separate beds, sat in separate rooms, rarely spoke to each other—lived separate lives in an emotional divorce. In the face of her mother's unending complaints, Marilyn enlisted as her mother's savior, the one who would bring joy into her mother's tortured existence. The cost was endless agony and anxiety. For example, since her mother was constantly threatening suicide, when Marilyn got on the school bus in the morning, she did not know whether she would find her mother facedown in a pool of blood when she got home in the afternoon. She could remember the anxious worry she carried with her through the day, and the apprehension, almost to the point of panic, that she felt as the bus approached her home. At the same time, the mother's praise and her constant refrain that she would be lost without her little angel were music to Marilyn's ears.

Marilyn was an excellent student but socially awkward, especially when it came to boyfriends. She did not feel very pretty or attractive to boys. She was the class "brain" and felt isolated and unpopular on this account. At the same time she suffered from comparison with her sister, who was an average student but who was very pretty and popular and had all the boyfriends she wanted. This was a mixed blessing since their mother was envious of the sister's good looks and was constantly undercutting and criticizing her. Marilyn was partly the beneficiary of this process, since mother would turn to her and praise her for being a good daughter who was not sexual and who stayed home to look after her mother. Marilyn was caught between her own envy of her sister and the gratifying praise and acknowledgment from her mother; at least in relation to her mother she had the edge.

Marilyn's marriage choice was disastrous. She met her husband soon after graduating from nursing school. He was tall and handsome, on his way to a successful career. She fell in love, idealized him beyond all recognition, and was swept off her feet. She remembered that her father warned her against the marriage, but she brushed his objections aside. She felt that this was her one and only chance, that no one would ever be interested in her again and that she had better grab at the opportunity; otherwise she was doomed to eternal spinsterhood. The marriage was difficult from the first. Ed was demanding, given to temper tantrums, and at times abusive. He resented her efforts to work as a nurse, feeling that she was depriving him of her time and attention. When children came, he was resentful of them as well. They took her time and attention, and cost him more money. He refused to involve himself in any of the childcare or childrearing. They were her responsibility, and as far as he was concerned, her job was to keep them out of his way. He insisted that she pay for their upkeep, and any extra expenses were the subject of endless complaints and at times explosions of temper.

The analysis progressed smoothly. Marilyn came to an increasingly deeper understanding of her parents' pathology and how it affected her life. In her girlhood her father had been an object of admiration for his obvious intelligence and what she saw as his hardworking dedication. Gradually she saw how selfish, isolating, stingy, and rigid he had been. It began to dawn on her how similar he and her husband were. A sidelight to this issue was her difficulty in dealing with her then early-adolescent son. He was failing in school, was recalcitrant and rebellious at home, and seemed headed toward a delinquent outcome. Marilyn felt helpless to deal with this situation. She could not set appropriate limits, and any limits she tried to set were easily abandoned or overridden. She got no help or support from her husband, who seemed always to excuse and even support some of his son's rebellious attitudes—undoubtedly because they reflected attitudes of his own. Marilyn came to see that she was creating another copy of the same piece of pathology in her son. This realization horrified her and brought home the realization that if she did not change, she would be ruining her son's life as well. He was following in his father's footsteps, identifying with the least desirable aspects of his father's disturbed personality. Much of the analytic work centered on her conflicts in dealing with this situation, on her difficulties in setting and reinforcing limits, on the elements that gained some hidden and unconscious gratification from her son's delinquent behavior. These disciplinary problems did not arise with her daughters; somehow Marilyn was better able to deal with them in a reasonable and effective way.

An identification with her father played a strong role in Marilyn's own personality. This became much clearer after the marriage broke up. Her husband finally walked out on her and moved to another part of the country. After the divorce, Marilyn was left with the custody of

the children and was largely saddled with their support—her husband
refused to live up to the divorce settlement and was always causing
difficulty about the alimony and child-support payments. While he was
on the scene, the blame could be laid at his door; but after he was gone,
it became clear that there was a part of Marilyn that could not take time
off, that found reasons to work extra hours and weekends, that could
never find time for a vacation—all too reminiscent of her father.

The more powerful theme that overshadowed all others was Marilyn's relation with her mother and her strong identification with her.
She followed the path of her mother's masochism to a fare-thee-well.
She was the uncomplaining and self-sacrificing victim of a cruel fate.
Suffering was for her an ideal, a noble expression of the human spirit.
The idea of standing up for herself or of becoming assertive or aggressive on her own behalf was quite foreign to her mind-set. Better to be
the patiently suffering martyr than to take control of life and try to
achieve a better outcome. It was not difficult for her to see the pattern
in her mother and how dramatically she carried it out in her own life. It
was only with great difficulty that she could acknowledge some of her
own rage at her mother. This came to light through an obsessional
symptom. She began taking the precaution of washing her hands before
writing a letter to her mother. She was afraid that some germ she might
have contacted in the ICU would be transferred to the paper, would
infect her mother, and cause her death. She knew that this thinking was
totally irrational but could not shake the fear. We referred to these
letters as "poison pen" letters. Recognition of these feelings and the
related dynamics did not bring about any miraculous changes. Shifts in
Marilyn's behavior came only slowly and gradually. The analytic work
focused at first on the aggressive conflicts and the aggressively derived
introjective configurations involved in her depressive and masochistic
stand. She lived around the victim-introject that was derived from the
internalization of the same introjective configuration in her mother. It
was reinforced by her defensive need to escape from the destructive and
murderous wishes that reflected the power of her aggressive impulses
and wishes.

I would not want to leave my readers with the impression that
Marilyn's difficulties were entirely aggressive. The narcissistic derivatives played their own significant role in her proneness to depression.
There is little doubt that she considered herself someone very special.
All during her schooling she had been at the top of her class and
thought of herself as especially intelligent and gifted. Her obvious talent
and intellect struck a special bond with her father, who felt himself to be

smarter and superior to his fellows. She expected that things should come easily to her in life, and that when she set her sights on something she would get it. On these terms, her dream of being the princess who was rescued from her miserable life by a knight in shining armor seemed to come true when she met her husband.

The failure of her marriage was not only a bitter disappointment but also an assault on her narcissism. The narcissistic expectations came to the fore around her children. She expected them to be perfect and accomplished. Her son reacted by joining in an outright battle to resist and overthrow these lofty expectations. The two girls did not make a pitched battle of it, but they were also a disappointment to her since they did not distinguish themselves in any special way. The older girl was a reasonably bright student and popular enough, but the younger one was not. This seemed intolerable to Marilyn, who could not accept that her visions of bright, successful, and highly acclaimed offspring were not to be realized. It was a painful realization that her son would never go to Harvard. It was even doubtful that he would graduate from high school. This was especially painful to her, since many of her neighbors' and friends' children were achieving these goals. She felt that her life was a failure, that she had accomplished nothing, that her dreams were in shambles at her feet, and that life was hopeless and desperate.

As these elements were clarified and worked through, Marilyn began to deal more effectively with her life and responsibilities. After picking her way through the difficulties of the divorce, she began to put together the pieces of her life. Her capacity to deal with the children, especially her son, improved considerably, and led to a striking change in the behavior of the children. The son settled down, completed high school, and was accepted at a good college, even though it wasn't Harvard. This was due partly to the change in the home atmosphere after his father left, but it was also due in large measure to Marilyn's ability to take firm stands and set clear limits. Along the way Marilyn eased out of her depression, and for the first time began to see that she could find happiness and satisfaction. The quality of her work improved, particularly as the result of her gaining control of her tormenting obsessional worries over whether she had done something to her patients that would kill them or that she might have done something inadvertently that would cause her to be sued and her life ruined.

The story thus far does not sound much different from an ordinary analysis of a mixed neurosis—and it was not that different for the most part. What are the features that would lead me to regard her as a primitive hysteric? The first point was the rapid mobilization of relatively intense transference elements when she hit the couch. I have come to anticipate this sort of dramatic shift in analyzable patients in the hysterical continuum when they move from the less intense context of sitting-up psychotherapy to the more intense experience of analysis. The transference experience was more than neurotic: she fell in love with me in an intense and encompassing way. Any sense of an "as-if" quality was completely overridden. Second, the configurations of pathogenic introjects had a dominant role in her psychic economy and played themselves out in relatively shifting patterns as the analysis progressed. Third, there was the quality of her depressive episodes. She would become precipitously and intensely depressed, feeling hopeless and helpless, and often entertaining suicidal thoughts. From time to time during these episodes, her thinking would become almost delusional. If she were worried about a patient, she would become absolutely convinced that she had done something damaging to the patient and would cling stubbornly to her conviction in the face of overwhelming contradictory evidence. At times she could become overcome by jealous and even paranoid thoughts that again seemed to reach a level of delusion. These episodes did not last long, never more than a day or two, and when she returned to a more reasonable level she could see how silly her thinking and behavior had been and could even laugh at it at times. This did not seem to prevent the next episode.

The paranoid elements always remained a subtle and hidden aspect of her mental life, but nonetheless fit with the narcissistic and aggressive dynamics that held sway in her inner world. On only one occasion, the paranoia burst forth in unmistakable fashion in what I have come to regard as a "paranoid spike" (Meissner 1986). This occurred at a point at which I had made an interpretation that cast some of her father's less admirable qualities in a somewhat pejorative light. Marilyn reacted with a sudden burst of rage, and a hostile and vicious counterattack. She got off the couch and launched into a tirade at me, defending her father, furious that I would say anything that seemed to diminish him, and painting me as insensitive, cold, unresponsive to her needs, critical of her and her family, and interested only in putting them down and showing them up as inadequate failures. After tearfully screaming at me for several minutes she stormed out of the office, slamming the door behind her. The elements of the negative transference that had been kept largely out of sight until that point came to a sudden head and burst forth in a defensive counterattack. I had become the attacker who threatened her most vulnerable spots, particularly those in which her narcissistic investments were significant. She returned the next day and sat up. We were able to calmly reexamine what had occurred on the previous day and to sort out what had motivated it. The outburst had frightened her, since it was totally unexpected and more vehement than anything she had experienced before. The episode could be reasonably processed in the context of a reconstituted therapeutic alliance, but its occurrence spoke to the capacity for sudden regression and disruption of the therapeutic alliance—a common occurrence in borderline patients subjected to the regressive pull of the analytic couch and situation.

The last component to persuade me that she fell within the borderline spectrum was the difficulty in terminating. She had made excellent progress in the analysis and was able to work through what seemed to be a reasonably good termination. For a while after the end of the analysis, she remained undepressed and her life followed a happy and productive path. Then the depressive episodes started to recur, at first mildly and then with greater intensity. There were also episodes of obsessional doubting, fears of accidents or harm that recalled the old near-delusional experiences, and phobic anxieties. These symptoms brought her back—each time for a few sessions, after which she would seem to reconstitute and go on her way for another few months. She tried antidepressants with little effect other than to exacerbate her cardiac arrhythmia. The depressive episodes were usually related to some disappointment, and other symptoms often could be connected to some difficult or painful emotional event that she could not face head-on. One variety of these events was the occasional visit from her mother—her father had by this time passed away. Her mother's unending complaining, self-pitying, and fault-finding attitudes would drive Marilyn to the point where she could not deal with her rage at her mother, and the outcome was usually depression. Another variety was occasioned by her difficulty tolerating painful feelings. For example, when her son came to the end of the summer vacation and was preparing to return to college, she became obsessed with the idea that he would have a heart attack and die. This threw her into a paroxysm of anxiety and anguish. We decided that the real problem was that she could not tolerate the pain of the sadness at his leaving and the rage at him for abandoning her. It was easier to shift into an obsessional worry that some harm would come to him. This understanding would somewhat magically absolve her of her worry. Consequently, her analysis is not ended, and probably never will be. She remains vulnerable to these miniregressions, which stir up troublesome symptoms but never reach a psychotic level even though her reality testing seems to sag a bit.

I emphasize that both of these latter patients were quite analyzable, and in fact underwent successful analyses. The difficulties encountered in the course of the analytic work were fairly typical and demonstrate features of the analytic experience of such patients. However, even at this higher level of borderline integration, we need to keep in mind the limited potentiality for full-blown and effective termination and the predictable limitation on the patient's capacity to internalize the fruits of the analytic experience in any thoroughgoing or permanent fashion. Both these analytic patients had difficulty in negotiating the rough waters of termination, and both found it necessary to extend the analytic process beyond the formal termination. In addition, both cases ran into further regressive difficulties some years after they had finally separated from the analyst. More often than not, I would conclude, the analytic process even with these higher-order patients may never really come to a close.

SECTION B

Schizoid Continuum

Patients in the schizoid continuum present a set of therapeutic difficulties different from those presented by patients in the hysterical continuum. The spectrum view of borderline disorders specifically includes the schizoid disorders within the range of borderline psychopathology. In contrast to the affective lability, emotional turmoil, intensity, and often precipitous nature of conflictual transference embroilment in the hysterical continuum (which many authors take as paradigmatic for borderline pathology), the schizoid continuum presents the therapist with the problem of engaging the patient in the therapeutic process. Object hunger is not met by desperate clinging and terror of abandonment so much as by defensive withdrawl to protect the fragility, vulnerability, and tenuous independence and identity of the self. The schizoid dilemma pervades all of these cases in one or other form, in one or other degree—the tension between the desperate need for objects and the utter fear of engulfment and loss of self, between the fear of isolation and the fear of bondage (Guntrip 1961).

I would argue that, while these patients represent various degrees and levels of psychopathology and psychological deficit, their core pathology lies in the organization and integration of the self-system rather than in specific ego or superego deficits. Such deficits unquestionably exist, more so in deeper and more severe levels of their pathology, but the issues in the treatment are more characteristically related to the patient's sense of self and its endangerment. This is reflected particularly in difficulties in object relationships and in the maintenance of a secure and stable sense of identity. The schizoid compromise, therefore, aims at solving these dilemmas and dictates the quality of the patient's involvement in the therapeutic relation. Within the framework of this work, these issues cannot always be clearly seen as transference issues; they can be seen more clearly as alliance issues. Issues related to establishing and maintaining the therapeutic alliance take precedence in the treatment of these patients. Similar emphases have been struck in somewhat different conceptual terms by Modell (1978, 1984, 1986) in addressing the need for security and safety in the analytic relation, and by advocates of responsiveness to self-object needs (Kohut 1977, Stolorow and Lachmann 1981, Stolorow et al. 1983). The diagnostic groupings in the schizoid continuum differ in the patterns of their response to these issues and in their path of resolving them.

21

SCHIZOID PERSONALITY

Schizoid personalities present special problems in the treatment situation because of their defensive retreat and affective withdrawal from meaningful involvement in the therapeutic relation. They are generally difficult to engage and keep in therapy. I present here four accounts of periods of psychotherapy with these patients and an example of a psychoanalysis that was prematurely and unilaterally terminated by the patient.

NED N.

This first case presents a form of paranoid-schizoid pathology that foundered on the patient's incapacity to establish a workable therapeutic alliance and on the patient's narcissistic neediness and demands. The case illustrates the difficulties the therapist faces in dealing with this form of schizoid personality. The challenge and primary difficulty is in getting the patient engaged in the therapy and keeping him in it long enough for some useful effect.

Ned was in his mid-twenties when he first sought consultation for his sexual difficulties, particularly impotence. He was married at the time and recalled that he had had only one sexual relation before marriage. That relationship had been disastrous: the woman had finally dumped him, and as a result he became depressed and morose. At this point he met his wife, felt seduced by her, and before he knew it they were married. He had difficulty early in their relation, but things improved after they were married. Recently his sexual difficulties had become more of a problem.

Other difficulties emerged in the evaluation. His style was obsessional as he presented a detailed and careful history. His attitude seemed guarded and defensive, suspicious to the point of being paranoid. He saw the world as a hostile place in which other people were out to get him in whatever way they could. Hume was right when he said, "Homo homini lupus." Ned had difficulties in his work as well. After obtaining a Ph.D. in history, he took a position as a junior instructor in the university. He felt his position there was precarious. While he had always been academically successful, at the top of his class, and had received his doctorate with honors, he felt that other students throughout his career had been envious of him, resented his accomplishments, and tried to undermine or show him up in whatever way they could. He was afraid similar problems had arisen in his department, where he felt other faculty did not like him, resented his success, and wanted to do him in academically. He also had great difficulty in coming for psychiatric help. He feared the psychiatrist's power to control his mind and felt humiliated at having to beg for help. Coming to a clinic was degrading since he felt so far superior to other patients he saw in the waiting area. He could not reconcile himself to the fact that he would have to see a resident, and a woman at that. His wife was seeing a psychiatrist privately and he felt envious and resentful that he had to settle for second best.

Relationships in his family of origin had been highly conflictual. His father and mother had argued constantly and finally separated when he was eight. Ned did not have much good to say about his father. He described him as tough, insensitive, macho, brutal—and as a pathological liar. The father would disappear for weeks at a time. The same had been true of his father's father years before. When Ned was 15, his father disappeared for over two years. His mother had to file a missing-person's report. The father was never very good about support payments. He was constantly in financial difficulties and even got in trouble with the IRS for nonpayment of taxes. Ned himself was sensitive about his father's behavior and feared that people in his department might find out about his background and hold it against him.

His mother was pictured as the more stable and stronger figure. She was the emotional center of the family. After the divorce she went to work and became a vice president in a small sales firm. She is now remarried happily. The first marriage ended because of the father's affairs. Ned's sister, seven years younger and bright but rebellious, was much closer to and sympathetic with his father, while Ned remained closer to his mother. After the divorce, both children lived with their mother and were angry at the parents for the divorce.

As he began the therapy he worried about whether his wife would be jealous of his seeing a female doctor. Their sexual relationship had been poor. He did not feel sexually interested in her. During intercourse he felt detached and indifferent, like an observer. He felt distant and remote from any feelings and was anxious about how he would perform sexually. He blamed his upbringing for his sexual problems. The family religious orientation was Calvinist but hypocritical. His father was like a Jansenist, rigid and strict in his morality, but he would walk around the house nude. Neither he nor the mother had ever told Ned anything about sex; he had to figure it out for himself.

He was more concerned about what was going on in his department. His general feeling was that other faculty members were out to get him, criticizing and undermining him at every turn. The head of the department berated him for using the copying machine. He felt his colleagues were jealous of his attainments, knowledge, and teaching. He felt that he was superior and that they resented him for this. He saw the head of the department as hypocritical and morally corrupt. If he were to speak his mind or achieve any success, he expected to be shot down for it. Even though he felt vulnerable and helpless, he thought he had to speak out, if only to salvage his self-respect. He feels as though he has to hide his talents and refrain from expressing himself. He saw himself in a martyr role, like his mother sticking it out with father, or like his grandmother who stayed with his alcoholic grandfather. They wanted him to "kiss ass," but he had to preserve his own self-esteem, even at the cost of others. There had been an argument in the faculty meeting over his teaching. He felt trapped, criticized, humiliated, and victimized. One of the professors had called him names, and said that he was rigid, defensive, and inadequate. But he felt that he was doing a more than adequate job, that the students liked him. He felt degraded, dragged into the muck of petty and sordid details rather than dealing with intellectual issues and principles.

The therapist experienced considerable difficulty in developing a therapeutic alliance. Ned was decidedly uncomfortable in the therapeutic relation and resentful that he was not given someone more senior and experienced. Early in the process he began to pressure the therapist for advice, guidance, answers. He wanted her to ask questions, point out connections, help him to know what to do about his problems. He thought he had given her as much material as she needed to solve the problems for him. This somewhat magical expectation represented a distortion of the therapeutic alliance and had to be dealt with. He seemed able to grasp the point but could not accept that he and not the therapist would have to do the work of the therapy. His efforts to make her take a more active and responsible role did not abate.

He described himself as a permanent exile, alienated, as if he had to hide and keep a low profile because others were out to get rid of him. There was nowhere he could feel safe, comfortable, accepted, and loved. He was contemptuous of others, considering himself superior, more intelligent, special, and gifted. Yet he felt like a stranger, isolated, different, separate, and distant. He had no friends, and did not even think of his wife as a friend. He was self-righteous about his attitudes, as though he alone were devoted to the ideals of truth, justice, and goodness. Yet he felt dissatisfied with himself, with what he had accomplished and learned. He saw himself as egotistical, but as possessing great strength that gave him the power to help others and do good. He was fascinated by mystical and occult phenomena, at finding the hidden meaning in things. Although he repeatedly experienced failure in his efforts to have sex with his wife, the astrological signs reassured him that he was fertile. Yet he really did not want to have children; he felt pressured into this by his wife.

His faultfinding with the therapist continued. Her shortcomings were a constant source of dissatisfaction, particularly her failure to find the magical solution to his problems. He began to come late for appointments and occasionally to miss them. His attitude was that if the therapy (i.e., the therapist) was not going to solve his problems for him, why should he go to the bother of being on time? When he missed an appointment, there was usually some excuse.

His relationship to the therapist was a problem. He felt superior to her, certainly more intelligent. He struggled with feelings of dependence and tendencies to idealize her, which he vigorously countered by distancing and devaluing maneuvers. The closest he came to recognizing his difficulty was to say that if he were to admit that the doctor was important, he would feel like a parasite and would lose all sense of his own independence. To be attached to another human being meant the loss of his own self, to be destroyed or devoured. His task in therapy was to answer the therapist's questions as exactly and fully as possible, and in this way he would get better. His expectation was that the doctor would work some magic to make things right. The level of mistrust was high, however; he could not know what the therapist was thinking or feeling about him, and this made the relationship suspicious and dangerous. Neither could he divine what his wife thought or felt—she, too, was an object of mistrust.

All of these difficulties were intensified by the therapist's looming vacation. Ned became depressed and increasingly anxious, and was desperate about the therapy. As the vacation drew nearer, he became more agitated about the "homosexuals" who surrounded him in the department, more dissatisfied and accusatory toward the therapist. He questioned the value of therapy even more insistently. The day before her vacation was scheduled to begin, he called the clinic to say that he had decided he did not need any further therapy.

Ned's problems, despite his high level of performance and intelligence, centered in his interpersonal relationships. There was no glimmer of intimacy, friendship, mutual regard, or affection. He was an isolated, affectively remote, suspicious, and at times paranoid man. He could have easily been diagnosed as a paranoid personality. His relationship with his wife was discolored by these same distancing mechanisms—there was little sense of intimacy, sharing, mutual caring, or love. There was instead mistrust, suspicion, and fear of closeness or more intimate involvement. In the therapy, the same issues came into play. The therapeutic alliance was never established on a solid footing. Ned's engagement in the therapy was based on a narcissistic alliance that carried with it magical expectations of cure without his effort or change. The narcissistic dimensions dominated the transference, particularly his need to devalue the therapist in order to reinforce his own sense of narcissistic superiority (his grandiose self) and defend against idealizing elements in his emerging transference feelings. For the therapist to assume a valued position posed too great a threat to his narcissistic equilibrium. Along with this narcissistic dimension, the schizoid dilemma confronted him with the desperate alternatives of annihilation or isolation and abandonment. These same elements had contaminated all of the important relationships in his life; the therapeutic relation was not to be an exception.

The therapist's vacation brought all of these issues to a head. Ned could not tolerate the idea that he would be so dependent on anyone. To admit that need would constitute a severe narcissistic blow to his sense of grandiosity and self-sufficiency. The very idea of involving himself in a helping relationship in any collaborative and dependent way was totally alien and threatening. Moreover, the idea of becoming dependent on a woman and yielding to the tendency to idealize her and make her important was an assault on his sense of masculine superiority and ran in the face of his fear of and demeaning attitude toward women. This reflected his fear of the powerful phallic woman represented originally by his mother. He had little recourse but to break off the therapy.

OSCAR O.

Oscar presents the picture of a patient whose rather traumatic history provided the basis for a therapeutic misalliance that approached the therapy as though it were meant to cater to his every need. He made little use of the therapy and suffered intense disappointment because the therapist could not or would not gratify his wishes. When Oscar came into treatment, he was also in his mid-twenties, was a premedical student who was living with a woman who had a daughter by a previous marriage. He came seeking help with his depression and an inability to concentrate that was causing difficulty in his studies.

He had begun to suffer from anxiety attacks that manifested themselves by sweating, palpitations, and shortness of breath. His style was obsessional: he thought out what he wanted to say and chose his words carefully, showing little affect. He had been in therapy when he started college because of a phobia of public places, which reached the point where he was not able to leave the house. That therapy lasted two years and ended when the doctor, a psychiatric resident, left. He had been furious when the doctor would not give him medication for his symptoms. He could not express his feelings at the time.

His family history was fairly traumatic. His parents' relationship was unhappy and conflictual. They fought constantly, and the marriage ended in divorce when he was eight. The father soon married another woman, thus beginning the most difficult period of Oscar's life. He and his older sister lived with his father and his new wife. He did not get along with his stepmother and his relation to her became traumatic and painful. She was a rigid, demanding, controlling woman who treated him sadistically, even cruelly. She would make him strip naked and beat him all over his body, including his penis. Part of the problem was that Oscar wanted to live with his mother, and since he would never criticize or vilify her, he became the object of the stepmother's hatred. Oscar felt especially resentful of his treatment because his older sister was favored and well treated by the stepmother and his father never raised a finger to protect him or intercede for him.

The reason he could not live with his mother was that she was unreliable, unstable, and addicted to drugs and alcohol. Both her parents had been alcoholics, and her mother had been addicted to morphine. After the divorce the battles over custody continued unresolved for several years. Living with either parent presented severe problems. He could not tolerate the situation at home and ran away several times. He hated his stepmother and felt that living with them was like being in a prison. His mother wanted him to live with her and made endless broken promises. His hopes were constantly being raised and then dashed.

It was not easy to get him to commit himself to the therapy. He felt pressured by a busy schedule of classes and study and was also involved in a variety of other time-consuming activities. He agreed to help the woman he lived with in teaching a cooking course. They needed the money, but he found he was tired, had little time to study, and was afraid of not performing well on his tests. It was hard for him to say no when someone asked him for help. There was gratification in being asked and a sense of satisfaction when he could be helpful. If he tried to say no, he inevitably felt guilty.

Therapy was one more thing he had to fit into his schedule. He began to come late and miss appointments. At one point he missed several appointments in a row. The therapist wrote a letter asking whether he had decided to terminate his therapy. He returned and explained he had forgotten and had missed the appointments because of his exam schedule. He acknowledged that he should have called to cancel, but was afraid that if he did call the doctor would pressure him into coming.

In the meanwhile his difficulties continued. In many areas of his life he was trapped between his need to be compliant and his contrary impulses to defy and rebel. He had general difficulty in dealing with aggressive impulses. He had dreams in which he was in a hostile or dangerous situation, or in which there was an atmosphere of mistrust and he was the object of hostile intent. For example, he would be in Russia, where it was not safe to be an American. He would be accosted by threatening Russians, followed by the KGB, abused, threatened, mistreated. Other symptomatic problems continued to cause him difficulty. He had a variety of phobic concerns. He was convinced there were ghosts in the basement: he was terrified of going into the basement alone or at night. He associated this fear with a movie about ghosts he had seen when he was 8 that had terrified him and given him frightening dreams for years. He remembers being afraid to walk down the street as a child because he had to pass an old house that the kids said was haunted. His depression seemed to wax and wane, but at times became quite acute. At such times he felt helpless and hopeless. He recalled a severe depression at about age 15 when he didn't want to do anything but stay in bed. His mother was concerned and encouraged him to drop out of school, saying that his mental health was more important. The message she sent—that he was sick and had to take care of himself— was probably not the best reinforcement of his confidence. Whenever he smoked grass, he freaked out, became worried about everything, and experienced intense anxiety and fear.

His relationships were a shambles. He kept to himself and was something of a loner. He had no friends; his only personal contacts were with his girlfriend, and even that relationship was uncertain and difficult. He felt isolated and out of control, afraid he was losing his mind at times. Therapy was not helping; nothing seemed to change. Talking about the past was not much help: it only made him feel worse. He was worn-out, tired, desperate. His hopes for therapy were not being realized, so what was the use? Why continue?

He used the therapy hours mainly to complain about his miserable life. There was little capacity to engage with the therapist in any effective therapeutic processing of the material. His attitude toward therapy seemed diffident at best, and his understanding of the process seemed to hinge on the idea that he could use it without any sense of commitment or motivation for real work and that somehow it would make things better for him. More concretely, his expectation seemed to be that if he poured out his tale of woe to the therapist, the therapist would do something that would make him feel better and make things in his life easier. When this prospect was not realized, his motivation for continuing the therapy sagged.

Then came the incident from which this faltering process stumbled to its end. One day the resident was involved in dealing with an emergency that had arisen in the hospital and was delayed in getting to the appointment. There were only a few minutes left when the doctor arrived; he apologized and explained the situation, and the patient seemed to make nothing of it and spent the remaining minutes complaining how terrible his life was and how his symptoms seemed to be increasing recently, especially in relation to the pressure at school. At the next meeting, the therapist tried to discuss his lateness but without great success. The patient merely said that he thought something had delayed the doctor and he decided to wait. He went on to say that his grandmother had suffered a stroke and had to be put in a nursing home.

This led to a long, angry diatribe against his mother for the way in which she treated the grandmother. The grandmother had been a woman of some attainment, had written and published articles, and had collected interesting objects of native art from various parts of the world. His mother was throwing this material out, even the edition of the encyclopedia with the grandmother's articles in it. He was furious with his mother but felt helpless to do anything. He could not confront her and felt guilty about his hostile and angry feelings. Evidently the grandmother represented an element of successful accomplishment in his family that related to his own narcissistic needs. The mother's belittlement and disregard for her mother's accomplishments was a form of attack against Oscar's own hopes and ambitions.

More and more the therapy hours were filled with his disparagement of therapy and the emerging theme of his disappointment with the therapist. Not only did the therapist not give him anything but he was not there when Oscar needed him. Oscar did not know if he wanted to continue. Therapy did not harm, but it didn't do much good. He came to therapy only because he felt he was losing control and couldn't deal with his problems on his own. Therapy only encouraged him not to rely on his own resources (as his mother had encouraged him to drop out of school!). The doctor has knowledge, position, and power, but he withholds this from Oscar and doesn't use any of it to help him. He wanted something different—he wanted to be able to ask direct questions and get some answers. He hated the therapeutic relation: it was unequal and made him feel weak and inferior. It only reinforced his own sense of himself as inadequate and vulnerable. He disliked being in a position in which he had to ask for help. In the face of another holiday interruption, Oscar decided to stop his treatment.

The evident problem in this case is the patient's ambivalence about therapy and his reluctance to commit himself to the therapeutic process. In other words, the therapy began with a therapeutic misalliance that was never effectively modified. The elements that entered into Oscar's schizoid adjustment to the world also determined his approach to the therapy and to the therapist. He was distrustful, suspicious, guarded, and cautious in his relationships with the important objects in his life. Any relation that smacked of dependence was terribly threatening, stirred fears of engulfment and control, and brought to the fore his weak and vulnerable feelings. Such threatening objects had to be kept at a distance; any feelings of affection, attachment, or dependence made any object of emotional involvement a threat. As long as Oscar could immerse himself in study, work, or other preoccupying activity, he felt relatively safe; but when it came to involvement in any meaningful way with other people, there was trouble. The therapist was drawn into this emotional matrix and became an object of ambivalent attachment, full of hope and expectation as well as fearful suspicion and dread. Attempts to deal with this distortion of the therapeutic alliance were unsuccessful and too little was known of the transference components to deal usefully with them. When the therapist missed the appointment, it brought home to Oscar the degree of his need and dependence on the doctor—a realization that was too filled with pain and potential risk. Better to be on one's own!

PAUL P.

The next patient was in his late thirties when he first came to psychiatric attention. He was then engaged in a program of graduate studies leading to a doctorate. His initial complaint was that he was having difficulty in his relationships with women. He would get involved with a woman but then quickly become bored and disinterested and withdraw from the relation. He felt that he was looking for the ideal wife, and when the woman of the moment came up short of his perfectionistic ideal, he was no longer interested. His style was decidedly obsessional with isolated affect and a good deal of intellectualizing; his lifestyle was largely withdrawn and isolated. He was happiest when he could immerse himself in his work and forget about people.

It turned out that the pattern of involvement with women was more general and affected his work life as well. There, too, his perfectionism had an impact. He had had a position as a successful executive with an important company, but it was not long before he began to be bored in this position, feeling that it was not sufficiently challenging and that he was not using his intellectual abilities as much as he had hoped. He decided to continue his education, took a leave of absence from his job, and began a graduate program. This kept him interested for a time, but he soon found that the same pattern was asserting itself. He was now faced with the prospect of writing a thesis and once again found himself bored, disinterested, restless, and wondering about a change in his life direction. Paul's problem involved not only his difficulties in dealing with any form of intimate human relationship but also his problem of committing himself to any definitive life path in either personal relationships or career. This is the pattern I have described as "identity stasis" (see Chapter 1 and the case description in Chapter 24).

Paul came from an average middle-class family. His father was a middle-level business executive who was an outgoing and active man. Paul had fond memories of the things he and his father used to do together. His mother was more emotional and easily upset. He and his father both worried about getting the mother upset. All in all the family was reasonably happy and well off. Paul had a sister five years his junior, with whom he was never very close. She is now happily married and he sees little of her. The family harmony was disrupted by his father's sudden death from a heart attack when Paul was 18. The family was essentially broken up after that. His mother remarried and that husband committed suicide. She remarried again later.

Paul's closest relationship was with Susan; it lasted for several years in on-and-off fashion. They were engaged more than once, but each time he felt compelled to break it off, feeling uncertain about the relation and frightened by the commitment implicit in marriage. Susan remains a somewhat distant but sympathetic friend, and there is no one else in his life whom he can count as a friend. He was lonely and isolated, and felt alienated from any feelings, a stranger to himself. He felt remote not only from his own feelings but from those in other people as well. He worried about his own temper, which frightened him and which he struggled to keep in control. His rage was particularly aroused by slights or devaluations from others. He was troubled by his relation with Susan; he saw her as too needy and dependent, someone he would have to look out for and take care of, like his mother. She wanted too much and her demands made him feel inadequate and threatened. He was looking for a stronger woman who would have all of the idealized qualities he imagined—brains, beauty, good health, independence, resourcefulness, and so on. He measured all women by this ideal and they all come up wanting. He now felt that he was facing a mid-life crisis; he did not know what he wanted. He felt confused and ambivalent about everything.

His wish at the moment was to live on an island where there were no people. He reminisced nostalgically about the period before his father's death when they had lived near his father's parents on an island. Those were golden years and he fantasied recreating that situation somehow. He worried about an early death. His father had dropped dead of a heart attack at 49, and his father's brother had died of a coronary at 42. He wanted to stave off this threat by vigorous exercise and jogging, so he kept to a strenuous training program to prepare to run in the marathon. When his father died, he did not cry. He did not want to talk about his father or his death in therapy.

The therapy was difficult for him. He found it painful to talk about his feelings. He was afraid of exposing himself. He dealt with problems by avoiding them. He worried about what the doctor might think of him; the doctor might see him as he saw himself, not a reassuring prospect. He did feel better after coming and talking, but nothing substantial was changing in his life. It was impossible to try to go back to when he was a child and dig out the past. There were too many years, too many memories—and, as any good therapist might add, too many painful memories and losses, especially the unmourned loss of his father.

His ambivalent relation with Susan continued. He could not decide about it, not knowing what he really wanted from her. He no longer found her attractive, he felt bored and uncomfortable with her; she wanted to know if he loved her and he could not say. But when he withdrew from her he felt lost, alone, scared that he would be alone for the rest of his life and have no one to love and care for him. He liked her companionship and even the sex was all right. But he wanted to have the relationship on his terms, to see or not see her when he wanted, with no demands or expectations from her. She was not willing to settle for that, and when she escalated her demands he felt he had to get out of the relationship. He was afraid of her fragility and neediness; she was like his mother after his father died and after her second husband's suicide. She had fallen apart; he could not tolerate the grief and tears and had to get away from her as quickly as he could.

His fears and ambivalence made the work of therapy problematic. His commitment to the process was continually in question. He did not know if he really wanted treatment—it was too difficult and frightening. He did not know what to do or say. He was frightened by the silences. He wanted the doctor to be more forthright, to give him advice, ask questions, direct him as to what to talk about. He was able to see that this pattern was similar to his behavior with women: he wanted them to take the initiative, to do things for him, to make life easier for him. As the months passed, there was some perceptible shift in his basic pattern. There were moments when he seemed to come closer to some painful feeling; there was even a suggestion of tearfulness at such times. These momentary miniregressions frightened him and he recoiled from them. There were also deliberate efforts to be more socially involved—he dated some other women and tried to befriend other students in his program. The efforts were self-conscious and forced, as though he were struggling to overcome his natural inclination to remain withdrawn and isolated.

Then it came time for the therapist to leave the residency program. This precipitated much material about Paul's painful losses, especially of his father, although he was never able to come to the point of saying that he would experience the loss of the therapist as such. In the throes of this termination work, he made a final decision to break off the relationship with Susan. He told her that it was over and that he did not want to see her any more. He worried about her fragility, about hurting her, and felt guilty about his decision. He was unable to connect this behavior with the loss of the therapist. Nonetheless it seemed likely that the departure of the therapist reactivated the painful history of losses that provided the nidus of his pathology. To be involved affectively with any other human being raised the specter of loss, a painful prospect that he could not tolerate or endure. His efforts to acknowledge loss and to work it through in some productive way were thwarted by the loss of the therapist. Better to escape the pain and agony of such another loss. Better to retreat from any significant emotional involvement, any attachment that promised to expose him to such another painful and intolerable experience. Conclusion: Susan had to go.

Paul's case provides a striking example of the difficulties created by the schizoid dilemma—the tension between the desperate need for objects and the equally desperate fear of involvement. The same dilemma permeated the therapeutic relation. It was unfortunate that the therapist was a psychiatric resident and that when his training program came to an end he had to leave. This imposed another traumatic loss on the already pathogenic base of traumatic losses this patient had suffered. We can only speculate on the possible outcome of Paul's treatment had he been able to continue in therapy over a longer time frame. He had shown signs of increasing involvement in the therapeutic relation, and although the progress in his engagement in the therapy and in the therapeutic alliance was painfully slow, he might have been able to continue on this course and come to some better therapeutic resolution. As it was, the therapy ended in the unwitting creation of another in Paul's experience of cumulative traumatic losses. It is fears of such magnitude, often traumatically engrained, that the therapist encounters in dealing with schizoid dilemma. It is not difficult to see that this creates extreme problems in establishing a meaningful therapeutic alliance. The difficulties lie in the alliance sector rather than in the transference. Paul's problems were due less to the emergence of transference as such than to his sensitivity and vulnerability to loss that had been traumatically induced.

QUENTIN Q.

This last case of schizoid personality was treated in psychoanalysis over a period of three and a half years. Quentin was referred for psychoanalysis because of a cardiac arrhythmia that was felt to be psychogenic and related to his excessive hypochronidriacal concerns and because of his continuing interpersonal difficulties. He complained particularly of the deterioration in his relationship with his wife. They had been married about five years and had no children. Any feelings of warmth or affection he had once had for her had disappeared; now all he could feel was detachment, anger, and resentment. He fantasied arguments in which he would reduce her to tears, or imagined having an affair or asking for a divorce just to get back at her and make her suffer. Any independent judgment or behavior on her part was threatening to him because it impinged on his freedom of action and independence.

The marriage was in fact little more than a charade. They had separate incomes and he insisted on separate checking accounts. Expenses at home were divided equally even though his income was considerably larger. If they went out to dinner or entertainment, she had to pay her own way. Sexual encounters were infrequent and consisted largely of her masturbating him. The general atmosphere in their relationship was by no means cooperative. In his obsessional style, he had defined their appropriate roles and assigned responsibilities. These were written down in a kind of contract, the spirit of which was that he should not be asked to do anything that was not in the contract. If he did anything that was not on the list, he expected some special reward or commensurate payment. The usual arrangement was that they took separate vacations, had separate friends, and socialized as a couple rather infrequently.

Quentin's lifestyle was both obsessional and schizoid. He was preoccupied with issues of control, having things his way, to the point that he could not tolerate his wife making any independent decisions, buying anything for the house, spending any of their joint money, without his approval. For example, she could not just go to the store and buy groceries; he had to go along and approve every purchase. She could not even buy her own clothes unless she used her own money. He was concerned that she would take advantage of him and spend his money recklessly and foolishly, although there was no indication that she was anything but sensible and conservative. He was stingy and suspicious of the motives of anyone with whom he had dealings.

He was obsessed with details. This was partly adaptive, particularly in his work as a research chemist, where attention to detail was important and necessary. He kept detailed records of all aspects of the house economy—how much was spent on what, how long it lasted, how many times it was used, and so on. He even kept a chart on the inside of his closet door listing every item of clothing he owned. On it he recorded each time a given item was worn and how many times it was washed or cleaned.

The schizoid trait was apparent in the marriage as well. He kept his wife at an emotional distance. There was little love or affection between them. Sex was simply a matter of tension discharge. His feelings for his wife were dead, withered in proportion to the degree to which their relationship had threatened to become more intimate and interdependent. He was terrified of becoming emotionally dependent and kept the relationship emotionally sterile. He had no social life to speak of: he and his wife had few friends together, and he had none of his own. At work he was respected for his ability and accomplishments, but he was an isolated figure. It was customary for the employees to go to lunch together, but he never went along. He regarded his fellow workers with contempt; he accused them of wasting time and goofing off. They were "goldbrickers," a term of utter opprobrium. He refused to participate in company outings—an isolated, lonely, strange figure in an otherwise relaxed and friendly environment.

Quentin presented as a severely obsessional personality. His manner was constricted, his affect isolated, and his engagement in the initial evaluation businesslike, precise, and emotionless. It was as though he entered the process as a job to be done, distasteful but nonetheless to be dutifully performed. We agreed readily on the arrangements for the analysis and began on the appointed day.

Quentin's parents were an odd couple. His father was a school principal who had married rather late. He was apparently an intelligent and competent man, but in the family was portrayed as bumbling, ineffectual, never asserting himself or seeming to have any power base. Quentin saw him as a pathetic figure who was cheap, rigid, a poor excuse for a man and a father. His mother was the dominating figure. She was bright, articulate, flamboyant, and charismatic. She had had a varied career as an actress on Broadway, had had a few bit parts in movies, but envisioned her true calling as an artist. She was devoted to her painting and had enjoyed moderate success. She would involve Quentin in her work, using him as a model or enlisting his help in transporting the canvases for her shows and exhibits. This was a source of bitterness for Quentin, who felt that his mother had little interest in him beyond what he could do to help her with her projects.

Quentin's parents had been married for more than a decade before he was born. His feeling was that his mother did not in fact want any children, that she was too absorbed in her work, and that a child was a complication. He was convinced that his conception was an accident and that neither of his parents had wanted him. His resentment toward his parents was deep-seated. He felt that neither parent ever showed much interest in him or spent any time with him. His father was absorbed in his books and hobbies, and his mother in her painting. He felt his mother was happy to get him out of the house and off to school, so that she could be free to do her painting. As soon as he was old enough, he was packed off to summer camp, where he felt abandoned, rejected, and resentful. When he got to high-school age, he was again shipped off to a private boys' boarding school—exiled from home and out of his parents' hair.

For most of these early years, Quentin was pretty much of a loner. There were not many children his age in the neighborhood. This seemed to be comfortable for him, since when he did play with other kids he felt shy, awkward, and clumsy, constantly afraid of being ridiculed or criticized. It did not help that they were the only Jewish family in the neighborhood. When Quentin went to camp he fared somewhat better. He was able to get over his homesickness, his resentment and anger at his parents, and his feelings of abandonment, and begin to take part in various activities. He learned to play softball passably well, and turned out to be a better than average tennis player. He enjoyed tennis and continued to play as an adult. The story was somewhat the same in boarding school. He learned to busy himself in a variety of school activities: he was manager of the freshman football team and played on the tennis team. He struggled with homosexual feelings in this all-male setting but never had any homosexual experiences. He explained that this was because he never got close enough to anybody for that to be possible. There were no girls around, and when dances were scheduled, as for example with nearby girls' schools, he managed to avoid them. He had never dated until he got to college.

Quentin did well academically and was accepted to an Ivy League college. He was interested in science and became a chemistry major. He felt he could become absorbed in his studies and loved the time working in the chemistry lab. His social life was a shambles. He found it difficult to make friends and was painfully shy and awkward around girls. He dated rarely in his first year, and the few occasions when he did were disastrous.

He felt increasingly depressed and anxious and finally sought help. He started in weekly therapy sessions with the school psychiatrist.

His complaints had to do with his general dissatisfaction with his life and his difficulties in achieving academically as well as he wished. He felt emotionally constrained and inhibited. Psychological testing showed considerable repression, constricted affect, elevated indices of depression, anxiety, social withdrawal and problems in sexual identity, difficulties with overwhelming episodes of intense anxiety, and self-hatred. His efforts to deal with anxiety and depression took the form of flight from feelings and from involvement with other people. Sexual difficulties seemed to be related to strong castration anxiety. He seemed to have strong ego strengths and defenses, and there was no indication of psychosis.

The problems he addressed included his lack of any arousal or feeling when being physically intimate with girls and his general fear of women. He could not date a girl more than once; they usually wanted sexual contact and this was extremely threatening for him. The problem seemed to have more to do with his fear of loss of control of his impulses than actual fear of the girls or what they might do to him. Other problems included his need to be compliant with his parents' wishes, and by extension with the wishes or directives of any authority figures. He was caught between his need to remain emotionally dependent on his parents and his wish to be more independent and self-reliant. His attitudes were pessimistic: he saw no point to life, thought that since everything was predetermined it was hopeless to try to make things better. His attitude toward people was contemptuous and reflected a haughty superiority.

He continued to have difficulties dating and having relationships with girls. He began to wonder whether he was homosexual. His parents took the initiative of arranging for him to spend a night with a prostitute. Quentin could hardly believe that his parents, especially his father, would promote this and that he would agree to it. When the experience was over, he felt it had been gratifying but he had not been particularly aroused emotionally and had no inclination to repeat the experience. He was able to establish a relationship with a girl, with whom he engaged in some foreplay, but he could not bring himself to attempt intercourse. If he came to the point of attempting penetration, he would lose his erection. In the meanwhile he carried on a dalliance with homosexuality, going to homosexual parties, making friends with homosexuals, worrying about his sexual identity, his attraction to homosexual men, and his isolated affective involvement with women.

After graduation, he completed a master's degree in chemistry and settled into a research career. Within a few years he was back in psychotherapy, this time with problems of hypochondriasis, self-doubt (particularly of a sexual nature), continuing depression, and a lack of purpose or direction in his life. He worked conscientiously and productively in twice-weekly psychotherapy for almost four years and was successful in resolving some of his problems, enough so as to get married and to move ahead in his career with a greater sense of commitment. Problems remained in his perfectionism, grandiosity, and sense of narcissistic entitlement. The idea of analysis was explored and a decision reached to terminate the therapy with the purpose of moving on into psychoanalysis. In the evaluation process, he was seen as a narcissistic character and was accepted as a control case. He saw several candidates but was not taken into analysis; he was then referred to me for private analysis at a reduced fee.

In the first hour, Quentin was obviously anxious and was terrified of the couch. He commented on how strange it felt, how weird my voice sounded, how scared his heart pounding made him feel. He associated to patients receiving ECT. He worried about his father's getting older, his passivity, his forgetfulness, the probability of his dying. He then reported a dream of his masturbating in the cellar as his wife comes down the stairs. He is jealous of the time she spends tutoring her students. To get back at her he went to the movies alone, feeling hurt and abandoned. He remembered how his roommate in college "fucked his girlfriend" and how he felt left out and ignored. His parents never had sex; mother was probably frigid and not interested. He always felt awkward and anxious with girls. He worried about venereal disease; his father had warned him about that. He was afraid that I was going to be like his father—weak, passive, coddling. Then he would get angry at me, and then have to feel guilty. Anger was a problem: he couldn't let it out and that, he thought, was why his heart was giving him trouble. He hated his father's passivity; he was furious at his boss for making a recent remark about the forty-hour work week. Quentin had come in late one day; the boss doesn't appreciate that he puts in fifty or more hours some weeks. He felt guilty about his father's dying, regretting that he had not done more for him, especially that he had not supported his father more in the face of the way his mother treated him. She was constantly putting him down, criticizing him, making him feel that he was inadequate and lacking as a man. He was concerned about the low fee and what it meant: could he pay me more? Was he getting away with something? Did it mean that I did not have enough patients and that I was not that good an analyst? Maybe he was just being selfish; he did not want to give up any of his money. He felt nervous when he had to assert himself. When he has to pay for anything he feels taken advantage of, even though he knows the feeling is irrational. He hates to spend money and would rather hoard it. He didn't get his wife an anniversary present because he didn't want to spend the money. She was hurt. At the same time he had spent a considerable amount on clothing for himself. He felt guilty and selfish, but also defensive, as though he were entitled to have something for himself and spending the money on her would be like her taking it away from him. If he had to stick up for himself and defend the low fee, he would have to get angry and resentful. The condition of his heart frightened him and made him worry about dying. He was terrified at the thought of an eternity of nothing. He wished he could find some way to make his life interesting and exciting. There was no excitement in his marriage or in his work. Life was boring and dull.

I have repeated the material from this first hour because it rehearses many of the substantial themes of the analysis. Dominant themes include his narcissism, paranoid outlook, affective isolation, defiant attitude to authority, sexual anxieties, hypochondriacal concerns, and the transference. His attitudes toward his parents come through quite clearly: his view of his father as pathetic and weak, his yearning for greater closeness with his father, and his wish for a better father who could teach him how to be a man, who would support and strengthen him rather than his having to support and worry about his father; his resentment and fear of his mother, who was capable of neglecting, hurting, using, manipulating him and his father for her ends. She becomes the prototype of all women who use men and have the power of reducing them to impotent and castrated wimps. Even in the dream his wife enters the masturbatory scene as a threat, as if to say that his penis is not his own and that she will intrude to take it over and control his use of it.

As the analytic process evolved, it settled into an obsessional pattern. Quentin was always on time, rarely missed an appointment, paid his bill regularly. In the analysis, the content was superficial, devoid of affect, preoccupied with detailing everyday events, and boring. It had the quality of a punctilious recitation of the day's activities—without meaning, affect, or reflection. Efforts on my part to penetrate the barrier, to comment on the lack of affect or on the resistance aspect of the patient's comportment, met with stiff, irritated, and at times haughty defensiveness. He argued that he was doing as I had requested, saying everything that came to his mind, and now I was criticizing him for doing what he was supposed to do. I should make up my mind what I really wanted.

Gradually elements of a transference became more available. The transference was to an extent idealizing and involved homosexual elements. He dreamed of visiting an ENT specialist who examined his throat and wanted to know if he had had his tonsils out. There was something at the back of his throat that needed attention. He associated the doctor with Dr. X, whom he had known as a child and whose daughter he had dated once. He had idealized Dr. X and wondered if he was also doing that with me. The throat examination made him think of fellatio—the thought was stimulating and attractive. He reported that people at work knew my name and he was proud of being my patient, a feeling he could never have about being his father's son.

The analysis dragged on in this vein for a long period. Over time we were able to work our way into more meaningful discussion, usually by way of my focusing the material or asking pertinent questions—never on Quentin's initiative. *Pari passu* the transference continued to deepen: I became increasingly a powerful and influential object, idealized, admired, and feared. He increasingly yearned for a close, accepting, even loving relationship with me that would have provided him with the strength he felt he lacked and with the capacity to be a strong and sexually proficient man, and would have enabled him to achieve the levels of narcissistic enhancement that he craved and envied in me. But this goal could be achieved only at the cost of submission to my wishes and to the demands of the analysis—a prospect that was intensely threatening and humiliating. As my status in his eyes grew, the negative aspects of the transference were likewise magnified in proportion: the threat of some hostile retaliation or even arbitrary exercise of my power. If I was idealized, I became an object of admiration and envy and at the same time an object of terror and fear. Quentin was threatened on the narcissistic side by a sense of depletion and inadequacy in relation to my superior status, and on the aggressive side by the fear that he could be hurt, attacked, and destroyed by my superior power and strength. He was in danger of becoming the helpless and vulnerable victim to my hostile, retaliatory, and destructive aggressor.

These shifts within the transference reflected the progressive influence of the analytic regression. This came to a crisis point. Suddenly one day on the couch, Quentin was overwhelmed by terror. He had the thought that I would attack him from the rear, that he would be utterly

helpless and vulnerable, powerless to defend or protect himself, and
that he would be totally annihilated. He experienced a panic, bolted
from the couch, and rushed out of the office. He could not tolerate the
anxiety and had to escape as best he could. He missed the next day's
appointment, which was the last of the week. At the beginning of the
next week he returned. He was unable to talk about what he had
experienced, despite my gentle urging.

   We then fell into a difficult and painful period in the analysis. It
was as though Quentin had closed and locked a door in his mind and
there was nothing I could do that would pry it open. By this time, we
were several years into the analysis and a good deal of improvement
had taken place in Quentin's life and work. He was more at ease, more
able to connect with his fellow workers; his relationship with his wife
was more relaxed and mutually satisfying. It was as though all of his
pathology had become concentrated within the analysis. From the crisis
point on, he would lie on the couch for long periods without saying a
word. I tried to wait patiently, at times trying to prompt him gently—
wondering what he was thinking, commenting on the silence, occasionally asking a question to try to get something going, all to little avail. If
he answered at all, it was perfunctory, brief, often evasive. Whole hours
would pass without a word being spoken. When I would indicate that
the hour was over, he would get up, say good-bye, and leave.

   I began to dread his hours. I felt bored, sleepy (I am sure there were
times when I dozed off), distracted, and irritated. My mind wandered—
I would find myself writing papers in my head, thinking about some
problem I had been working on, daydreaming, wondering what I would
have for dinner, and so on. The thought crossed my mind that I now
found myself in a transferential position. I had become the passive and
ineffectual father that Quentin despised and regarded as pathetic and
pitiful. I had also become the neglectful mother who regarded him as an
intrusion on her professional interests. If she was more concerned about
her painting than about him, I was now more interested in my own
thoughts and projects than in him. His fantasies of vulnerability and
victimization were in the process of being realized.

   The question was what to do. I decided, wisely or not, on a frontal
attack. Was I acting out the aggressor to his victim? I did not know. I
did not know what else to do. I invaded the silence. I told him that I
thought something important was going on in this protracted silence
and in his resistance, and that we had better find out what it was or his
analysis was in danger of self-destructing—a prospect that as far as I
could see was not in his best interest. His resistance was palpable, but I

pressed on. After a while he began to respond—his tone was defensive and argumentative, but we began to hear what he was feeling and thinking. He was frightened by his own feelings of attachment and dependence on me. He felt inadequate and powerless in relation to me; he envied, feared, and hated me for my position, power, and superior knowledge. He was furious at me for making him have such feelings, and he could think of no other way of dealing with them than by closing himself off defensively, drawing a shield around himself, a wall of silence behind which he could protect himself from the potential dangers he faced. In addition, he deeply resented the fact that I refused to exercise my power and knowledge for his benefit. I knew the answers that would solve his problems, but I selfishly refused to share them with him. He was in rage at me for this withholding. He resolved that he would come to the analysis and lie on the couch, but he would do nothing more; he would wait for me to work my analytic magic so that he would no longer have to feel the pain and humiliation about sex and any human relationships. He was furious at his parents for the way they had treated him—they were neglectful and inadequate and could not or did not give him what he needed to be a brilliant and successful man. He wanted them to make it up to him without his having to do anything to help himself. They had made him this way and it was up to them to change it. The same feelings applied to me in the analysis. It was up to me to make things better for him, particularly to arrange it so that he could begin to fulfill the narcissistic expectations of his ego-ideal. He would wait me out until I relented and did what he wanted—he would not lift a finger to change anything in himself or in his life.

Over the course of several weeks, it became clear that I could not respond to his expectations, that what he desired was unrealistic and impossible, and that if he were going to get anywhere he would have to relinquish his demands and accept responsibility for the course of his analysis. He could not, would not relinquish his position. He felt deprived, victimized, and cheated by his parents, by his wife, by me, by fate. He was out to turn the tables, to have things on his terms. If not, he would have none of it. The analysis was at a stalemate. He was adamant. I was in a quandary as to what to do. The Christmas break intervened; we agreed to resume the analysis after the new year. When I returned to my office, I found a curt note telling me that he had decided to terminate the analysis.

In retrospect, it seems clear that there was never a solid therapeutic alliance in Quentin's analysis. At best it could be viewed as a narcissistic alliance in the sense that the underlying proposition was that Quentin would submit himself to the process but that the onus for improving his life situation, for making reparation for his narcissistic injuries and deprivations, would lie with the analyst and not with Quentin himself. His involvement in the analysis was at root grudging. He resented the process because it represented what he had not gotten from his parents. It meant that he would have to do for himself what they had failed to do—a prospect he rebelled against. As the transference elements came more into force, they played into and reinforced this distortion in the therapeutic alliance. The resulting therapeutic misalliance reflected an amalgam of influences that brought the analysis to an end. The transference enacted within the analysis a repetition of the deprivation and victimization he had experienced at the hands of his parents. He became my victim, once again denied and rejected, deprived and victimized. I could not deny my own countertransference wishes; I wanted him to stop the analysis, I thought he was unanalyzable, I was irritated at the difficulties he was creating, I had feelings of inadequacy about finding a way through the impasse, and I felt threatened in my sense of competence and identity as an analyst. I read his termination note with mixed feelings. The ordeal was over. The outcome was not, I fear, in Quentin's best interest.

22

FALSE-SELF PERSONALITY

The false-self personality tries to survive by erecting a facade of com-pliant adaptation between its self and the impinging environment. This is an adaptive mode in many patients in the borderline spectrum, but in some personality structures it becomes predominant and persistent as a way of resolving the schizoid dilemma. The problem in therapy with such patients is for the therapist to find a way in which he can establish contact with the patient's true self and to help that true self to grow, to establish its autonomous identity and independence. I will discuss three cases in the order of increasing ego capacity or, conversely, decreasing pathological potential for regression.

DR. RICHARD R.

The first case is that of Dr. Richard R., a patient whose premorbid life pattern was not without its pathological features but nonetheless seemed to fall within a relatively normal range of development and adjustment. It was not until he was beyond his thirtieth year that his pathology broke through in a somewhat virulent form. His adaptive and functional personality was structured around a false self which came to grief in the face of crucial narcissistic disappointments and decompensated in a psychotic regression.

Dr. R. was brought to the hospital one quiet Sunday morning in a state of acute disorganization and turmoil. He was intermittently struggling so violently that it required several hefty policemen to restrain him; he was disorganized, raving wildly, acutely psychotic. Within a few days, the psychotic disorganization began to abate, and we began the long process of piecing together what had brought him to this state. His recompensation at this point was remarkable. He seemed to be almost visibly struggling to pull himself together and to reengage himself with reality. In a relatively short time he was able to reconstitute, and all marks of the psychosis had disappeared. He was released from the hospital within a few weeks. At the time he was completing a residency training in surgery; he was able to return to his service, and functioned adequately until the completion of his training.

Richard's years of residency in surgery had not been happy for him. At the beginning of his program, he had been intent on proving he was the best resident ever. He was intensely competitive, took every opportunity to show up his fellow residents, and was generally critical of the shortcomings of the program, of the caliber of teachers, and particularly of the work of his immediate superiors. His attitude won him few friends—he felt himself to be generally disliked and socially excluded by the other residents. At the same time, he wanted desperately to be accepted and liked by them. His ambition and almost grandiose competitiveness also got him into difficulty with members of the teaching staff, whom he would sometimes challenge with a hostility that only engendered defensiveness and antagonism. Several times his competitive attitude was pointed out to him by well-disposed teachers, but he resisted their interest, feeling they were trying to put him down or shut him up.

Richard felt he knew more than the other residents and was a more skillful surgeon. He even thought that in many respects he knew as much as or more than his superiors. There was one senior teacher whom he admired. He believed he could learn a great deal from this particular man, wanted desperately to be acknowledged by him, and complained about his inability to communicate with him. Since he thought he could not let him know how he really felt, much of what did transpire between them was due to misunderstanding. He was hurt, rejected, and undercut by the older man's response. As we shall see, the qualities of this difficult relationship mirror many aspects of Richard's relationship with his own father.

A few months before his breakdown, the new chief resident was announced—and it was not Richard. He was disappointed, intensely critical, and devaluing of the man who got the job. Richard was particularly critical of the new chief's conservatism. He considered his surgical judgment poor because he always took the safest course. In his disappointment, Richard began to think that he had been deprived of this coveted position by his superiors because they did not like him and wanted to get back at him for his critical attitude. They were afraid to acknowledge that he did in fact know more than they did; they had to keep him down because otherwise his real worth—as superior to themselves—would have to be acknowledged. He saw the entire staff, including his fellow residents, as involved in a conspiracy to keep him in an inferior position and to prevent any acknowledgment of his ability.

The immediate setting for the acute decompensation was provided by a conference on hypnosis that was being conducted by an internationally renowned medical hypnotist. Richard had been interested in hypnotism for some time. He had been using it with selected clinical patients in performing surgical procedures, and had even once demonstrated it to his colleagues as a technique for inducing deep anesthesia. His interest in hypnosis was motivated by strong inner needs. He felt himself to be a very suggestible person who could be easily swayed to accept any point of view, and this made him vulnerable and weak. His interest and involvement in hypnosis had a decided counterphobic element—it provided a way in which Richard could suggest rather than be suggested to, influence rather than be influenced, and control rather than be controlled. It enabled him to deny his inner feelings of weakness and inadequacy, and provided a channel for his wishes to be powerful and skillful and to control and influence others.

It was in the context of this intensive weekend conference that Richard began to decompensate. He began to feel confused, not knowing who he was. He described himself at this stage as phasing in and out of reality as the delusional system began to assert itself. Richard began to think that he was the famous Dr. X who was conducting the conference, or that he was having a homosexual affair with Dr. X and that he was his favorite colleague and confidant. Gradually, his delusional beliefs became more elaborate and stable. He thought he was a member of an extraterrestrial race of creatures gifted with godlike powers. They were immortal, would never die, and possessed extraordinary powers of being able to transpose themselves to any part of the universe and to assume any identity just by willing it. Thus, by a simple act of will, Richard could become the chief resident or even the famous psychiatrist Dr. X. He debated whether he should become a psychiatrist or not, and if so whether he should follow the regular course of training or simply will it and become one in an instant. He might have to follow the regular training so no one would suspect his real powers and ability.

Richard was born into a middle-class Jewish family. He was the second of three children—he had a sister four years older and one four years younger. His birth and early development were regarded as unremarkable. The family lived in a blue-collar district in an Eastern industrial city. His father was a self-made man. The family's financial condition improved in later years, after Richard's father achieved a managerial position. At home Richard was clearly his mother's favorite. She was rather plain and obese. Her major investment and interest in life were in her children and her home. She was possessive, domineering, and controlling. She ran the house and did most of the disciplining.

Richard was close to his mother and dependent on her. He was a sensitive and obedient child and rarely needed to be punished or disciplined. Maintaining his mother's affection was of central importance for him. She was apparently affectionate and even seductive with him—even into latency and early adolescent years. He recalls that she was always mothering him, that she would often embrace him. This embarrassed him because he was aware of her heavy and pendulous breasts.

Richard was shy and timid. He often played by himself and did not get along well with children his own age in the neighborhood or in school. He felt that part of the reason for this was that his family was Jewish while the rest of the neighborhood was predominantly Catholic. The other children would often pick on him and call him a "dirty Jew." He was constantly getting into fights, but he would not defend himself. He would usually run away and cry, usually to his mother, who would comfort and protect him. Richard was more comfortable playing with girls, but he was afraid that people would think he was a sissy.

Richard's difficulties were complicated by his relationship with his father. His father was a tough, ruthless, aggressive man, who had been a hard-fisted competitor when he was young. He grew up in the streets and had had to fight his way up. He despised and ridiculed his son's weakness and timidity. Richard always felt that his father was cold and harsh, that he could never communicate with him. He wanted desperately to be able to talk with his father, to be close to him, to be liked by his father, and to have his father proud of him. But he never seemed able to gain his father's approval. He could never measure up to his father's expectations—and could certainly never measure up to his father's accomplishments. He reflected that if he had been in his father's shoes, he could never have done what his father had done—he just wasn't strong or tough enough.

As far back as he could remember, Richard had lived in fear of his father. He recalls that his father was often irritable and short-tempered. His parents did not get along well at all—and he always felt that his inadequacy was the reason for that. His father would be angry at him for not standing up like a man and fighting, while his mother would try to protect him. He always felt the need to be close to someone, particularly his mother. His fantasies in this regard were of himself lying on one of his mother's huge breasts, fondling it, and feeling close and warm. This was the only way he felt he could escape the fear and loneliness.

His parents' attitudes played a role in his illness as well. His mother was pitying and protective; for her he was clearly her poor, wounded, sick child, who needed her help. The father's reaction was quite different. He was irritated at his son's sickness and regarded it as a weakness and defect in Richard. It was as though the father was offended and insulted by the idea that his son would have a mental breakdown and have to be admitted to a mental hospital. He reacted with anger and in various ways tried to attack his son's doctors and undermine the treatment. He repeatedly threatened to take Richard out of the hospital, refused to pay the hospital bills, called various hospital officials and doctors, demanding explanations for why his son had not yet been released from the hospital, accusing the doctors of keeping him there for no good reason, and so on.

Richard's early childhood was filled with phobic concerns and anxieties. He was afraid of werewolves and goblins and had dreams in which they attacked him. This was transparently a displacement of his fear of his aggressive father. On one occasion, Richard was accosted on the bus by a male derelict. He was badly frightened, told the school principal about it, but was afraid to tell his parents, particularly out of fear of his father. These fears stayed with him over the years. His dread of his father was displaced into fearful imaginings and dreams of werewolves and into a fear of "dirty old men," who would accost him, presumably for homosexual purposes. The fears reflected Richard's inner concerns about his own passivity and vulnerability.

Richard's feelings of inadequacy were related to another issue. He was born with a congenital hernia, and one testicle failed to descend. This was a source of concern, particularly to his mother. In her obsessive mothering, this became a focus of considerable anxiety. Richard's defectiveness was equivalently an assault on her own sense of adequacy. There were countless visits to doctors and special precautions to protect him from injury. Richard recalls that when he was playing, the hernia would often swell and become somewhat painful, and he would be afraid of hurting himself. He felt he couldn't play the way the other kids did, and would often cry. This fear of being hurt contributed to his fear of fighting. His mother's obsessive concerns about his vulnerability and susceptibility to injury became a part of his own attitude about himself—an anxiety shared between mother and son that contributed to his feelings of inadequacy and of being unable to measure up to his father's tough standards. The mother's protective concern and the father's contempt for such weakness inevitably clashed. It was a sign of his inferiority that his testicle had to be fixed. Richard's concern over his genitals has extended into his adult life. He is concerned that his penis is too small. He often asks the women he sleeps with whether his penis is big enough, whether it is as big as other men's, and whether it is big enough to satisfy them. He has also stubbornly clung to a belief in his impotence, astonishing in view of his sexual history.

Richard's earliest memories of sexual interests related to his experiences in the family. When he was very young, his mother bathed him with his sisters. He recalls his interest in his sisters' genitals and his embarrassment at showing them his own. He felt it was wrong for him to want to look at them and was afraid his mother would catch him at it. His fear was that she would do something terrible to him if she knew he was curious about his sisters' sexual parts. On frequent occasions, starting when he was about 5 or 6 years old, he would play with the girls in the neighborhood. They would go into the cellar, undress, and play games with each other. He recalls that these games were exciting, and he was always fearful of being caught. As he grew older, he had fantasies of having intercourse with his sister. He knew that these were "bad thoughts" and felt guilty about them, and was also afraid of what his parents would think of him or do to him if they knew that he had such evil ideas.

In his adolescent years, Richard began to experiment sexually with many different girls. It was very important to him to have intercourse with as many of the girls he took out as possible. He had to prove that he could get them into bed and screw them; otherwise he was falling short of the performance expected of a man. As time went on, through his college years and after, this pattern of intense sexual activity persisted. He had a strong need for physical contact and a unique ability to draw women to him. With rare exceptions, he was able to get them to go to bed with him. He describes his feelings of warmth and closeness in the sexual embrace. He felt safe and secure with his penis in the woman's vagina—anything short of that was fraught with anxiety and feelings of uncertainty and precariousness. He described the act of intercourse as "getting inside" a woman, where you could finally feel safe and protected. The fantasy reflected an infantile wish to enter into the woman and find security and protection within her womb, a fantasy of return to the maternal matrix, the safe harbor of symbiosis.

Richard carried on an intense sexual life on multiple fronts. He always had several girlfriends with whom he was sexually involved at any one time. By the time he came into treatment, he had women in nearly all parts of the country. Some of these women were married, and some not; many became pregnant. I say "many" because the exact number was never determined. In the course of therapy, the number kept increasing—Richard would casually mention another woman whom he had got pregnant. The number mounted to about fifteen. Some had abortions. Richard generally urged them to have abortions, but some of the women wanted to have their children, particularly the married women. On one occasion, Richard could not arrange for an abortionist and attempted it himself. The abortion was successful, but the woman became very sick and had to be hospitalized. This event frightened Richard severely—he would often refer to this episode and accuse himself of nearly killing this woman.

This unusual track record did not prevent Richard from persisting in the belief that he was impotent because of his defective testicle—even after his successful surgery and even though he knew better from his own medical knowledge. His denial in the face of such overwhelming evidence is striking. It is also striking that Richard had adequate knowledge of and access to contraceptives, yet he made no effort in all these instances to use contraceptive precautions. In part, this was consistent with his conviction of his own impotence, but at a deeper level it reflects his unconscious sadistic wish to hurt and maim the women. These sadistic impulses found their expression indirectly and in a displaced manner in the impregnation and aborting of these many women. The guilt that Richard felt so deeply in relation to these episodes was related to the underlying unconscious sadistic and destructive impulses.

In the face of his fears of inadequacy and his inner doubts about himself, he had a strong need to prove his superiority and ability at every turn. He found it necessary to gain approval from authority figures. This was also a factor in his relationship to me as his therapist. These relationships were contaminated by aspects of his relationship with his parents, particularly his father. The ambivalence was apparent. He had a strong need to be accepted and approved, and was often compliant and conforming in an effort to gain such approval. At the same time, there was a strong impulse to compete and to prove himself as good as or better than the father substitute.

These elements entered into the transference relationship. The psychiatrist was a powerful and influential figure from whom he had much to learn. The doctor was someone who could convey the secret of how to live in a healthy and successful manner, who could show him how to be the strong and successful man he wished to become. In his acute delusional state he adopted the role of a psychiatrist as a member of the godlike race—a position from which he could exercise control over men's minds and influence the course of human events. He saw his therapist in that light, and his expectations of therapy had a magical cast. He seemed to feel that all he had to do was to submit himself to the prescriptions of the psychiatrist and do what was asked of him, and he would automatically (magically) get better. The early course of treatment focused on this attitude, which reflected his childhood wishes to be accepted by his father and to gain strength and approval by pleasing his father. He would follow instructions, including talking about his history and thoughts and feelings in therapy; he would perform the "procedure" and get the job done.

Richard's increasing ambivalence created a problem for him in therapy. He depended on the therapist but at the same time could not express his anger at him because that would run the risk of rejection by the therapist, and then he would be lost. His father's repeated attempts to interfere with his treatment were severely threatening to Richard from one point of view, but they also played into his ambivalence. They intensified Richard's rage at his father for running his life, something Richard had always resented, even as he complied with his father's wishes out of his need to please him and gain his approval. The process became one of choosing between his father and his therapist. It was difficult to follow the demands of therapy and to resist the pressure from his father. In the measure that he was able to do so and remain in treatment, the threat of confronting the father and of expressing his rage at him drew closer, and as it did Richard became all the more terrified of it.

Richard had been obedient to his parents' wishes but, as his therapy made clear, not without considerable resentment and bitterness toward his parents, especially toward his father. When he went to college, Richard took the premed course. It was not clear that this was really his wish—neither was it clear that it was not. What was clear was that his parents, especially his father, had held this up to him from very early in his life as a goal and ambition. This factor became significant in his later course of treatment. Meeting his father's expectations and setting himself on the course of a medical career meant a submission to his father's wishes, a course that was unavoidably loaded with ambivalence and conflict.

This became an important issue in Richard's treatment. After his acute break, he was able to finish his residency training. Then he was confronted with a decision whether to set up a practice. For a time he worked on a part-time basis in another surgeon's office, just enough to support himself. And he agonized over the decision. He endlessly reviewed the possible alternatives, the difficulties, the locale, the opportunities—attempting to avoid coming to any conclusion. This process went on for months, and he became more and more depressed and withdrawn. Gradually, he developed suicidal ideas, which became sufficiently intense to warrant rehospitalization. He went back into the hospital and remained there for more than a year.

Richard's inability to make this decision was multiply determined. It was, from one point of view, a decision to commit himself to a decisive life course—a career decision. That meant becoming adult, taking responsibility. He felt himself unready, unprepared, incapable of accepting the responsibility of caring for patients. He realized he would have to make decisions and take responsibility for the care and treatment of his patients, and he did not feel himself man enough for that. One of his major excuses was that he didn't know enough. With a sort of obsessional perfectionism he felt that he should know everything, and that if he didn't know everything, he knew nothing. On occasions when he had to ask for a consult in the hospital, he felt inadequate because he didn't know as much about the consultant's specialty as the consultant. When the grandiosity and omnipotence of this extremely narcissistic position were pointed out, he responded that only when he knew everything could he feel adequate and secure about treating patients. Moreover, he clung to his conviction that his inability to learn everything was proof of his inadequacy and of his unsuitability for being a surgeon.

The choice of surgery had been influenced by his father's wishes. Richard's compliance was fraught with ambivalence. Richard saw his life as an endless process of striving to please his father and living up to father's expectations. Establishing himself as a practicing surgeon would be complying with these wishes in a definitive way. Part of him clearly wanted this: he spoke of how much it would please his father and of how his father would introduce him to his friends as "my son, the doctor." The thought of his father's pride pleased him, but not completely so. His father's bragging, as he called it, embarrassed him. He had set out to prove himself in a variety of ways. He struggled to overcome all of his fears and doubts about himself. He overcame his fear of drowning by learning to swim and becoming an experienced scuba diver. He overcame his fear of heights by learning to fly an airplane and finally getting his own pilot's license. All of these efforts were strongly counterphobic and competitive. His efforts to overcome these fears were often marked by a willingness—if not an eagerness—to take chances, to take unnecessary risks, to test the limits of his skill and endurance, to prove that he was a man and could face danger and "take it."

The problem in all of this was that the more successful he became in overcoming and defending himself against his inner fears in these ways, the more he became like his father, whom he hated and feared. Richard's father had multiple affairs, a source of continual conflict between father and mother and of great anguish and pain to Richard's mother. Richard hated his father for this behavior and yet strove to become more like his father. Becoming like father was the best way of gaining father's approval and of being able to get close to him. Thus, the conflict was drawn. Richard was trapped between two conflicting and contrasting parental identifications. To be strong and aggressive meant to become like his father—cruel, sadistic, selfish, using women for one's own pleasure, being a tough "loner" and not being afraid of anything, being willing to do anything or hurt anyone to get what one wanted. But not to be that was to become like mother—weak, dependent, sensitive, vulnerable, "gutless," "no balls," homosexual. Richard's solution was to find a safe middle ground where he could avoid either alternative, where he could withdraw himself from life and the ultimate threat of death, where he could hide from his destructive wishes and inner rage.

The increase of ambivalence in early object relations with the parents tends to shift the balance from positive and structuralizing ego-identifications to more defensive introjections, the pattern of internalization that Anna Freud described as "identification with the aggressor." The internalized aggression thus becomes part of the inner world of the child and becomes available for projection to the world of objects. Thus, Richard reexternalized his fear of his father in a variety of phobic manifestations—fears of werewolves and goblins, frightening fantasies of evil-intentioned old men who would hurt him, fears of the dark, phobic responses to any situation of danger or possible hurt. The effect was to increase the sense of the danger and destructiveness of the outside world and to repress and deny his own inner destructiveness. In terms of his own inner self representations, Richard became more and more the weak and vulnerable victim. He had internalized the father's harsh and commanding attitude, which demands that Richard be tough and strong and despises and condemns him because he is not.

The inner fragmentation and division in Richard's psychic structure reflects the form of impaired psychic integration that was described originally by Winnicott (1960) as the "false-self system." Richard had in the course of his interaction with his parents developed a split-off portion of his personality which consisted primarily in his compliant false self. It was the superficial reflection of defensive structures that allowed him to approximate the idealized image projected by his mother—the "good Jewish boy." The intensity of his defensive needs created a significant split between this superficially functional false self and the inner structure of his personality. His parents—and the rest of the world as well—responded to and interacted with the false self and took it for the whole of Richard's psychic reality.

The compliance of the false self is not based simply on imitation or mimicry but represents a form of compliance with the other person's intentions or expectations. This usually takes the form of being "good," always doing what one is told, never causing trouble, never asserting oneself, especially in opposition to the other. The motive may be the desire for acceptance and approval, but it may also involve a dread of becoming separate and autonomous. As Laing (1965) comments,

> The compliance is partly, therefore, a betrayal of one's own true possibilities, but it is also a technique of concealing and preserving one's own true possibilities, which, however, risk never becoming translated into actualities if they are entirely concentrated in an inner self for whom all things are possible in imagination but nothing is possible in fact. [p. 98]

Richard had functioned primarily in terms of this compliant false-self system through most of his childhood. His compliance was in the service of preserving the symbiotic ties to the maternal matrix. Any other course would have entailed—or so it seemed to him—the threat of abandonment and a loss of those ties to the mother upon which he depended for survival. Richard continued through the course of his career to function in terms of this false self. He dealt with reality in terms of a facade—a defensive organization—that he presented to the world and through which he interacted with the world. Even his defenses, however, were not really his own since they were impersonations of his father, rooted in his need to gain approval from the father and to comply with the father's wishes. It was fascinating during the course of his treatment to watch the fragmentation, reemergence, and then further dissolution of the false self. After his first break, Richard had rapid recourse to the false-self system as a set of behaviors or attitudes that he could take up at will and parade before the eyes of onlookers. As he approached the ultimate compliance—the commitment to a career in surgery which he saw as designated for him by his father—the ambivalence that the false self concealed became more intense and the false self was no longer adequate to carry the load. Through most of the rest of his treatment, the question remained whether he would reassume the false self. We both recognized that he could take that course if he wished. His ambivalence and the intense and murderous hatred that lie behind it stood in the way of a more independent and autonomous outcome.

Richard's relation to his father played an important role in the therapy. In his second hospitalization, the hospital became a safe harbor from the conflicts and painful dilemmas that faced him in the outside world. The therapist tried to maintain that place of security. He remained quietly supportive and made few demands. Richard found this difficult to accept. In his eyes, the doctor was the powerful and all-knowing psychiatrist who could read minds magically, like the powerful hypnotist of his delusion. His fear and admiration for his father were transferred to the therapist. The therapist's wish for him to get better was another expectation or demand to which he had to conform. His response was ambivalent—acting the part of the good patient, telling his story, conforming to staff expectations, keeping the rules, dutifully doing his ward job, but at the same time stubbornly clinging to his isolation, his apathy, and withdrawal.

The psychotherapy took shape around his need to conform to the therapeutic expectations of the powerful psychiatrist-father. His ambivalence, however, impelled him to want to defeat and humiliate the therapist, as he had his father. The therapist felt it was important to separate the goals of the therapy from the father's imperious demands. But Richard's patienthood was all that he could claim as his own, and he stubbornly resisted the efforts of both the therapist and his father, as he saw it, to take that away from him.

When he was able to go home for weekends, this problem came into sharper relief. At home he wanted to do little but sit around, watch television, or sleep. This infuriated his father, who attacked him as a lazy bum who ought to get off his ass and get to work. When Richard recounted this episode, the therapist asked what was wrong about relaxing or sleeping. Richard reacted with shocked disbelief and defended the father's position. Men were supposed to work and not waste time sleeping all day. That sort of behavior was terrible and intolerable. Anybody who wanted to do that must be crazy! To go against his father was bad and crazy, and if the therapist suggested that it might be all right for him to make up his own mind about how he wanted to spend his time, then the therapist must be crazy.

The management difficulties in the hospital centered on the problem of maintaining his "safe haven." Understandably the staff was impatient and disturbed by the fact that a doctor was sitting on the ward in such a passive state and was not making observable progress toward getting better and out of the hospital. Matters were not helped by the frequent inquiries of Richard's colleagues and superiors, some of whom were quite prominent physicians. They, too, were disconcerted by his apparent lack of progress. The perspective of a doctor in the position of being a hospitalized patient was bothersome and difficult for many. But these attitudes and pressures only mirrored and colluded with the attitudes of Richard's father. Much of the staff's discomfort took the form of blaming and attacking the therapist for not doing something more effective and helping the patient to get better more quickly.

These difficulties put considerable pressure on the therapy. The therapist tried to avoid falling into either parental role. He did not want to play out the father's position of generating expectations and pressures for the patient to get better; Richard might readily conform and reconstruct another compliant false self without getting at or resolving the underlying issues. Improvement based on conformity, in this view, would not be therapeutic in the long run. Neither did the therapist want to take the role of the mother, who would cater to the patient and too easily tolerate his wish to regress and be taken care of. The ward staff had difficulty tolerating and accepting Richard's apathy and passivity. It became a challenge to their ability and sense of competence to return him as quickly as possible to normal functioning. They could not understand why he had responded so dramatically in his first admission and was not responding now. In their frustration, they made the therapist an easy scapegoat. He was accused of not understanding the patient, of bungling the therapy, and so on. Nonetheless, he stuck to his guns in the face of continuing inquiries, doubts, and pressures to change the therapeutic approach. The patient's family—father, mother, sisters—continued to create difficulties, trying to get him out of the hospital, getting important figures to intervene in the situation, launching angry attacks against the therapist and the staff, and so on. All of this furor had a hidden benefit, namely that each such episode could be taken up in the therapy and explored. Inevitably important issues regarding the meaning of Richard's behavior and its dynamic implications could be discussed and integrated. In the process, the alliance was strengthened and the therapist's position as a reasonable and helping figure further consolidated. The various sides of Richard's ambivalence could be explored, especially in reference to both his parents. By implication, the same issues came into focus in the therapeutic relation—was the therapist going to take the demanding, performance-oriented, and compliance-reinforcing position of his father, or would he become an infantilizing, regression- and dependency-reinforcing, controlling, and engulfing substitute for his mother? The manner in which these configurations reflected Richard's own internal alignment of introjects became an ongoing focus for therapeutic work.

In the context in which such a variety of external pressures were brought to bear, the therapist found it difficult to maintain an objective and neutral position. It was difficult to avoid the Scylla of the paternal role of pressuring Richard to get better and the Charybdis of excessive maternal permissiveness and tolerance for regression. These tensions and their implications had to be continually processed and reprocessed, and the therapist's essential neutrality reemphasized. Steering a course between these alternative transference paradigms, and at the same time exploring, probing, seeking meaning, and continually emphasizing and reinforcing the need for the patient to make up his own mind, set his own course, and take responsibility for his own life, became a delicate balancing act.

STEVEN S.

The second case represents a lesser degree of pathological disturbance, but one that had a persistent and long-term effect on the patient's life course. Steve came seeking psychotherapeutic help on his own after a lengthy process of looking at and testing different therapists. He had consulted several, all of whom were either too passive or too authoritarian. Whatever it was about my style or approach, he seemed to be more comfortable in my office. He felt that I was respectful of him as a person, that I was not out to pressure him, and that there was a degree of freedom in my office that appealed to him.

Steve's life story, despite the quality of his background, was not a happy one. He was the oldest child and only son of his parents. He had two younger sisters, who seem to have reached maturity in reasonable shape—both reasonably well married and one also pursuing a successful professional career. My impression is that the family pathology has centered on Steve. His family was rich and socially prominent. His father was a diplomat of international stature, his mother a prominent socialite. His father was a dominating, egotistical, and self-centered man, opinionated and brimming with self-confidence, who could not tolerate any opposition or deviant opinions. He would fly into a rage at any confrontation or questioning of his judgment or position on a wide variety of subjects and issues. His interpersonal style was openhanded, good-humored, and jocular, but it masked an attitude of contempt and condescending disparagement of anyone he met or had dealings with, regardless of their social position. Steve could recount endless episodes of his father's hale-and-hearty treatment of business and political associates, only to hear the devastating criticisms and ridicule of these same people behind their backs. Steve regarded his father as devious, malicious, sadistic, and two-faced. He despised and hated this aspect of his father. At the same time he stood in awe of his father's competence, power, knowledge, and capacity to manipulate everyone around him to get whatever he wanted. Steve's father had little time for or interest in his son. Contacts were limited to periodic performances in which he was paraded into his father's library (a sort of inner sanctum) and there was forced to stand and answer questions about his school work and his behavior and to be lectured on what was expected of him.

Steve's mother, apparently a woman of considerable intelligence and social charm, was active in community and social projects, and was caught up in the swirl of parties and affairs that her husband's prominent position called for. Behind the facade, one could catch a sense of a frustrated and chronically depressed woman. Her life was superficiality and show. There was no love in her relationship with her husband—she was an ornament for his public persona. There had been no sexual relationship for years, and they slept in separate rooms. She had little time for her children; they were reared essentially by nannies and maids. She never seemed to have any independent opinions or judgment. Everything done in the household was through his decision, direction, or approval. In the inevitable tensions between Steve and his father, she never stood up for her son or offered him a sympathetic ear. Her husband had to be right; there was no room for criticism or even question.

Steve's sisters seemed to make their way through all this, if not with ease, at least not with severe maiming. Not so Steve! He was a sullen, angry, and resentful child. He hated and feared his father and felt removed from and uncertain of his mother. She was not as destructive an influence as his father, but he could find no way to make contact with her or resolve the ambiguity of his relationship with her. He felt that she would put on a show of interest or affection, but that there was no real substance to it. Her life seemed to be a show even in her closest and most intimate relations.

School was a torment. He was sent to the most prestigious private elementary and prep schools. He was frightened of his teachers. His anxiety made it difficult for him to learn, even though he was gifted with above-average intelligence. If he was called on or asked to recite, he was plunged into a paralyzing panic. The constant refrain in his reports was that he was not working up to his potential. This would lead to episodes of being called up on the library carpet that only contributed to his feeling further humiliated, terrorized, and confounded. His relationships with his peers didn't go much better. He felt alienated, isolated, and different—inferior to them and inadequate to the demands of competition, whether in the classroom or out. The only way he could find to deal with his anxieties was to become the class clown, even though the laughter, for the most part, was at his own expense. If people were laughing at him, at least they weren't attacking or humiliating him.

Steve did manage to graduate from high school, but barely. He had no chance at the Ivy League schools that most of his schoolmates attended. Even his admission to a less prestigious college was accomplished through his father's influence. The story was much the same in college. His academic record was spotty, his attitude toward study and learning rebellious and resentful, his participation in campus life practically nonexistent. He was a loner, had few friends, and dated infrequently. In his senior year he became more deeply involved with a girlfriend who was also a senior. They dated steadily for several months.

After graduation, at which his father gave the commencement address, he was at a loss as to what to do. His father could have easily gotten him a job, but that prospect was revolting to him. He decided to spend a year in South America as a lay worker for a Protestant missionary sect. After he had been there a few months, he received a letter from his girlfriend telling him that she was marrying someone else. Shortly thereafter he suffered a severe psychotic break, returned home, and was hospitalized for several months. There was no follow-up that I know of. Steve left home and moved to the Boston area. There he literally spent the next decade doing little or nothing. He sporadically tried some odd jobs, none of which seemed satisfying or promising. He kept mostly to himself, had few friends and almost no social life. He spent his time reading, walking, going to museums and movies, browsing for endless hours, and occasionally taking a course in the extension divisions of local universities.

Although he was well supplied with money by his parents, Steve became increasingly dissatisfied and frustrated. He had a sense of time slipping by, of the purposelessness and meaninglessness of his life. He decided to seek help. He was in his early thirties when we started therapy. At first he seemed eager and anxious to get the ball rolling. He agreed readily to the arrangements for scheduling and fee. I suggested a once-weekly schedule as a beginning. He was punctual and faithful to his appointments and has not deviated from that consistency in the eight years I have seen him. After several months, he requested that we shift to a twice-weekly schedule. We have met on that basis since.

The usual routine is that he comes in, says hello, sits down, and stares thoughtfully out the window for several minutes. I remain silent waiting for him to begin. As a rule this does not take long. Within five or six minutes he launches into a discussion of some recent experience. Generally I listen, try to be sure that I understand what he is communicating about his difficulty or anxiety, and then interject comments, observations, or interpretations as seems appropriate or helpful. Those are the good hours—by far the majority. There have also been bad hours. Having learned that any initiatives on my part are doomed to be unsuccessful, I wait even when a considerable period has passed.

Early in the course of our work together, Steve would come in in the usual fashion and continue in an immobile and silent posture for the whole hour. Attempts on my part to elicit some response would be met by little more than a fleeting glance. I learned that it was better to wait. At first I would wait with my attention directed toward him, studying his face, his posture for some sign or inkling of his thoughts. I began to feel that this generated an atmosphere of expectancy or subtle demand that itself might be counterproductive. He would speak when he was ready and on his own terms. I let my gaze wander, then my thoughts. I would lose touch with him altogether—thinking about some personal issue. This made it easier to pass the time but did not altogether relieve the tedium. Finally I resorted to reading. I would pull out a book and sit there quietly reading, occasionally glancing at him, as he sat silently staring out the window. At the end of these hours, he would stand up, smile, and leave. I felt that there was something not only comfortable in these silent sessions for him but also comforting.

In time the opportunity arose to explore this phenomenon. When I asked how he experienced these hours, he seemed to think they were wonderful. He felt that they were liberating to a degree that he had never experienced before. He could come to my office and not have to say anything at all if he didn't feel like it. He began to realize that it was quite all right with me if we sat there without saying a word. I was not imposing any demand or expectation on him to talk, to perform, or to do anything he did not want to do. He contrasted this with the situation he had experienced at home and in school, where you were not allowed to sit quietly but had to contribute to the conversation, had to know about what was going on in the world, had to be up on current events, had to have opinions and express them. After several months the silent hours disappeared and have not returned.

There was much discussion about his family and his experience growing up in it. His feelings about his parents became conscious and explicit. Little by little he was able to express his feelings toward his father—at first his hatred and disgust at everything his father stood for, and in time his admiration and even, most difficult of all, his frustrated yearning for love and respect from him. What brought these elements into focus with powerful impact was the strength of his identification with his father. Within minutes of an angry diatribe against his father's values and attitudes, Steve would mouth intensely self-critical and self-devaluing statements against himself. As these became more articulate and detailed, it was evident that they were identical to judgments his father had and would make, and that they bore the power and authority of his father's voice. This enigma of his powerful identification with his father, which came out primarily in superego terms, and his rebellion against and disgust for these same attitudes became a central focus of our work.

The power of these sentiments created a therapeutic problem. There was no doubt that to the extent he clung to these attitudes, they were paralyzing him and making his life a shambles. His constant refrain of accusation was that he did nothing worthwhile, he earned no money, he had no job, his life had no direction or purpose. At the same time the judgmental and critical standards he had internalized from his father dictated that no job, career, or enterprise that would possibly lie open to him would be good enough to satisfy his father's expectations. The problem as I saw it was how to bring him to a position in which he might be able to accept his own worth as a human being regardless of his father's attitudes or values. I adopted a deliberate tactic. When he would assume this self-devaluing attitude about some particular matter, I would feign difficulty in understanding what he found so reprehensible about it. He would criticize himself for not working, not having a regular job. I wondered what he found so bad about that. He appealed to the testimony of society and the attitudes of everyone he met. They all worked for a living, and when they asked what he did for a living, he became flustered and apologetic. We then would discuss the difficulty he found himself in, the extent to which others had to make a virtue of necessity (they had to work to live), whether any of them if given the option would work at all or as much as they did, and so on. My part in these discussions was fairly active, playing the role of the devil's advocate. What was remarkable was Steve's staunch defense of his father's attitudes, particularly that a man was worth anything only if he worked for his living, and his worth was measured by how successfully he did that. It also became clear that Steve himself held a much different set of values but could not bring himself to take a stand on them and to validate them for himself.

An additional refinement on this litany of self-deprecation took the form of his bemoaning the fact that he had many soft feminine interests and qualities. He tended to be soft-spoken and mild-mannered, liked to play with children, was disgusted and repelled by the macho, phallic exhibitionism and competitiveness of many of his male peers, enjoyed walking in the woods, loved to contemplate the setting sun—none of which made it as a topic for masculine bantering. He was much more comfortable in the company of women. He could not accept this quality in himself without disparagement and self-denigration. My efforts to bring some measure of balance and objectivity to the discussion seemed to yield little fruit. As in our discussions of his feelings about not having a job or career, my task was to question what was so bad about a man's capacity for tenderness, love of the beauty of nature, or even "soft" intellectual interests like philosophy, theology, and so on. He complained that the real men he knew were scornful of his willingness to wash the dishes, his passive or receptive position in a variety of contexts, his lack of interest and aggressiveness about making money, about competing, about treating women as sexual objects, and so forth.

At one point he reported an interesting dream. In it he found himself confronted by a huge penis which he was required to lick. He was disgusted and did not want to do it, but felt that he was being forced, that he had no choice. The homosexual implications of the dream were clear enough, but we did not pursue them. This was a good example of interpreting the unconscious dream material at a higher level. After some exploration, I interpreted the dream as reflecting how he felt about his position vis-à-vis his father. The dream had occurred during a visit home, and after an extended session of conversation with his father in the hated library. The dream reflected his sense of himself as insignificant, weak, impotent, helpless, degraded. The huge and powerful phallus was his father's, particularly his father's money, which Steve depended on for his support. In taking the money, Steve felt diminished, degraded, dependent—as though his father had all the power and strength and he had none. He went on to associate to a powerful fantasy he had had after he returned home from the visit to his parents that his penis was shriveling up and that he would never be able to get it erect again. This was associated with the conviction that he was dying—from what he didn't know, but the fear was connected to a series of hypochondriacal anxieties.

I shifted the focus here away from the latent homosexual theme and developed the interpretation in the context of material and issues that the patient was able to deal with in some constructive manner. To have taken up the homosexual content would have only contributed to the patient's already sufficiently undermined sense of himself as worthless and inadequate. He did not need the added burden of thinking that I endorsed his homosexual fears. My sense was that the more existential issue of how he felt about himself and how he conducted his life took priority. To the extent that he could begin to function in more adequate, assertive, independent, and phallic ways—something that terrified him ostensibly because of the fear of retaliation from his powerful and phallic father—the homosexual preoccupation that persisted on a more or less unconscious level would dissipate and disappear.

During the course of the therapy he began to make efforts to break out of his pattern of isolated withdrawal. The primary vehicle for these efforts seemed to be his participation in classes and small groups. His normal pattern would be to sneak in the back of the classroom, never making any effort to make contact with any of the other students. He would never ask questions, never contribute to the discussion, and if a group interchange arose, he would beat a hasty retreat. If a teacher called on him, he would be thrown into a panic, unable to think clearly or even speak coherently. At times he would be thrown into an unexpected and overwhelming rage, wanting to attack the teacher. He had all he could do to control these towering rages and would leave the classroom trembling with fury and terror. These episodes would come on him out of the blue, but he would describe himself as though he were in a depersonalized state. He would not know that he was angry but would come to realize that that was what he was feeling days or even weeks after the event. As we processed such experiences, it became clearer that something had happened to trigger his rage, usually something that reminded him of an earlier traumatic experience with his father or with some teacher from his childhood. As the therapeutic work progressed, he was able to experience these attacks, to tolerate the feelings, and to analyze what they were about.

The difficulty seemed to be that he was sitting on such an explosive reservoir of murderous hatred and infantile rage that his psychic regulatory resources were constantly strained to maintain some degree of control. At times, given the proper eliciting conditions, this rage burst forth in overwhelming fashion. He began to experience more extensive rage attacks as his defensive barriers softened and bent before the pressure. He would experience long crying jags and rages in which he would literally beat his mattress unmercifully. He experienced these episodes as a loss of control that reminded him painfully of his psychotic decompensation. I had to remind him that they occurred in appropriate circumstances—usually in the privacy of his apartment. The positive side of these experiences was that he was getting in touch with his pathogenic rage that was embedded in the pathological aggressive introject that formed part of the core of his distorted sense of himself. Much of his demeanor throughout his life and particularly in the wake of his psychotic experience had been a defense against this inner raging monster. He had tried to close it up in a cage, to cut off any expression of its power and destructiveness. He had succeeded only in cutting himself off from his own feelings, both the rageful, destructive feelings and the affectionate, loving feelings. It also had cost him his capacity for any form of self-assertive, aggressive, productive, or independent behavior.

Little by little these patterns changed. He took up the study of mathematics—an area that had consistently defeated him in his school years and was, incidentally, one of the areas of his father's special skill. He plunged into it with intensity and determination. He bought books, pored over them for hours, hired a tutor, and even attended classes.

In the classes, he gradually began to ask questions and to seek help from the instructors. Their response was positive and gratifying. His questions tended to be provocative and thoughtful. The instructors admitted at times that they could not answer his questions and suggested he look further into the philosophy of mathematics to find the answers. He then began to take courses in philosophy.

This endeavor was clouded by the same doubts that seemed to dog his heels at every turn. Gradually he became more comfortable with the classroom situation, engaged in social interaction with other students, and was even able in a limited way to participate in the classroom interaction. As before, he was troubled by the disparity between himself and other students—he was older, they seemed to get things on the first bounce and he took much longer, he was there in a serious effort to learn and understand and they seemed more interested in getting a good mark and socializing. He complained that there did not seem to be anywhere he could fit in and feel comfortable. Our discussions focused largely on what it meant for him to be different, to have a different perspective, different values, different interests, and how anything different or independent had been consistently squashed and prohibited in his upbringing.

Changes took place on the social front as well. He began to make the acquaintance of and date young women. These were at first uncertain efforts that were not always crowned with success. Some of these women were inappropriate objects. With time his choices became more appropriate and he had several sexually active affairs. He began to think about the prospects of marriage and family, something he had never thought possible for him—what woman would want to marry someone who did not work, had no job or career, and did not have any purpose or goal in life?

A gradual, tentative, uncertain progression took place over years of trial and error, repeated efforts and defeats, punctuated occasionally by modest successes. The process was one in which a small, timid, terrorized, and frightened self began to peek out from behind a facade that it had kept in place for most of a lifetime. The facade was based on the sense of himself as weak, dependent, inadequate, worthless, shameful, and despicable. He had not only maintained this portrait of himself but had gone about his life in such a way as to bring this debilitated picture to life. He came to live out the image of his own inner devaluation.

But why would he create in himself and in his own life something that he totally detested and despised? The closest we could come to a meaningful explanation was that his false facade was predicated on the basis of his father's attitude toward him. It was as though he were saying to his father in destructive defiance, "You always regarded me as though I were insignificant and worthless; well, now I am insignificant and worthless. Are you satisfied?" He had created a false self that brought to life his father's unspoken dictates, the result of a kind of perverse compliance with the implicit judgments of the father-king against whom he rebelled with such conscious vehemence, yet with whose unconsciously held view of him he complied to the last letter.

TOM T.

The last case of false self is that of Tom T. Tom came originally to therapy to deal with the issue of his sterility. He had discovered in the course of a medical workshop for infertility that he was suffering from aspermia. This was a bitter disappointment for him and a source of some friction with his wife. She could not contain her own disappointment and depression and blamed him for the fact that she could never have children. She had little or no sympathy with his distress and pain.

When Tom started in therapy, he was a modestly successful lawyer who was a junior partner in a good law firm. He had been married for six years, and his wife had been trying to get pregnant for about three years. Tom was a competent lawyer, well liked by his colleagues and clients, but did not seem to have the kind of success his abilities suggested. Although he had graduated first in his class from law school, he was somewhat diffident about his work, did not promote himself aggressively, and often seemed uncertain and inhibited in areas where he was clearly competent. He constantly sought advice and support from his colleagues, held back from taking certain kinds of cases in areas he felt he did not know enough about, and seemed more at ease in a limited practice of cases he felt adequate to handle. Despite his obvious intelligence, this approach to his work limited his promotion in the firm; he had been there long enough to have risen higher in the hierarchy, but had not.

Tom was an only child. His father had been a laborer and, for most of the years of Tom's boyhood, an alcoholic. Tom remembers nights when his father had come home drunk, torn up the house, abused his mother, and then fallen into a drunken slumber. At other times, his father was a gentle, kindly man who never raised his voice and took more than his share of verbal abuse from his wife. Tom's mother was a chronically depressed, constantly complaining woman who was satisfied with nothing and happy about nothing. She was relentless in complaining to Tom about her husband; she impressed on Tom an unflattering picture of his father. When he would come home roaring drunk, she would grab Tom and hold him in front of herself to keep her husband from attacking her. Tom was terrified.

Caught in the middle of this conflicted relationship between his parents, Tom had a troubled childhood. He became the substitute object for his mother's affection and attention. She put him literally in the place of his father. She confided in him, complained constantly to him about her sad life, behaved at times seductively, even having him sleep in her bed until he was well into his teens. At the same time she preached the evils of sex. He felt that the worst thing he could ever do in his mother's eyes was to be interested in sex. A significant problem arose when, at about the age of 11, he discovered masturbation. He became a chronic masturbator and has continued this activity in his adult life. His compulsive masturbation would plunge him into paroxysms of guilt, forcing him to run to confession. He would feel relief for a short while, but then quickly yield again to temptation. He had to go to great lengths to conceal this from his mother, constantly worrying that she would discover this heinous crime. As an adult he carries on a similar game with his wife, keeping his masturbation a secret and dreading her finding out.

In these early years, he felt that he had to be a model son to bring some solace to his mother's tormented life. He became obsessed with being a perfect student and never getting into trouble of any kind. As he grew up he was troubled by the attraction he felt to girls. Yet he kept his distance from them, never dated in high school, did not participate in the social activities of teenagers, usually with the excuse that he could not afford them. He was outstanding as a student, active in school activities, and popular. He managed to have an active and successful adolescence, even though any but the most superficial associations with girls were proscribed.

In college the situation was not much different. He continued to be Mr. Clean. His academic work was excellent, but his social life was less successful. He did date some, but usually with a group of other students. He did not go out on dates with girls until his senior year. He was always the gentleman, never physical or sexual. Since he was good-looking, girls were attracted to him and struck up friendships with him. His role in these relationships was to be the confidant, the one to whom they could talk about the problems they were having in their studies or with their boyfriends. He never saw himself as an object of interest or attraction; the idea that they might find him sexually attractive never entered his head. He met his wife when he was in first year at law school; they dated for several years, and finally married after he graduated. She was a teacher. She was the first and only woman with whom Tom had been sexually attracted and involved.

The frustration and shame about his infertility, and his rage at his wife for blaming him and not being sympathetic or supportive, resulted in some sexual acting out. He began to frequent massage parlors and meet prostitutes. He was terrified of contracting a venereal disease so he was careful to avoid intercourse. His guilt after these episodes was immense. He felt dirty and sinful, agonized over his sexual impulses, and condemned himself for his sexual perversion. He was conscious only of the compulsive quality of his sexual interest and the intense feelings of guilt after his escapades. It took considerable time to explore and to unearth the motives behind his behavior.

In the meanwhile, he developed a series of convictions that he had contracted a venereal infection. He went down the list: at first it was gonorrhea, then syphilis. He became hypochondriacally obsessed with any symptom to support his belief that he had contracted the disease. When it became clear that he did not have these diseases, he was convinced he had herpes. Herpes was much in the news at the time and was thought to be untreatable and lifelong—a suitable punishment for his crimes. But then this conviction was knocked out of the box by the initial reports about AIDS. Here was the ultimate punishment—a horrible, life-threatening disease that carried with it a social stigma that would tell the whole world he was a sexually perverse, worthless, hateful, despicable wretch. He would fulfill his mother's view of him as obsessed with sex and therefore despicable and degraded. He would die a horrible death and bring disgrace on his parents and family.

The AIDS obsession took on a force that dominated and controlled his life. He worried about every symptom, rash, sniffle, and cough. He avoided any sexual contact with his wife for fear of contaminating her. He bought additional life insurance, more than he needed, anticipating that he would soon die. He wrote a will, and began to put all his effects in order, preparing for the death that soon awaited him. Efforts to reality-test this iron-clad conviction seemed fruitless.

Gradually we were able to get at some of the underlying motivation, starting with his relationship to his mother. She had implanted in him a deep fear and anxiety about sex. Any inkling of sexual desires or impulses was condemned and judged. There was little about sexuality that he did not feel was sinful and seek desperately to suppress or eliminate from himself. He could not accept the idea that he had sexual drives as a basic part of himself as a human being. He stoutly maintained that masturbation was sinful and that he was the lowest of depraved wretches. This was the dictum that his mother had laid on him on countless occasions. The way to remain in her favor and love was to banish all signs and suggestions of sex. This set the stage for his overwhelming guilt. In addition his mother had preached the gospel of deprivation and the triumph of lowliness. She and her family were not meant to have things, let alone nice things; they were not meant to be successful, to have a nice house, or a good job, to be able to afford the pleasures of life. We came to refer to this harsh code as "the curse of the T's."

Tom would pass casual evaluation as an obsessional personality. Much of his pathology is involved in conflict, particularly between his sexual urges and his overweening and harsh superego. Much of his obsessionality is adaptive and functional; his orderliness, attention to detail, and organization serve him well in his profession. The borderline features are reflected in his weakened reality testing, the degree of delusional conviction, and the tendency to act out his conflicts and obsessions. There were times in the course of his therapy when I was convinced that he was in the throes of a psychosis. I tried thioridazine for a time without much effect beyond a dry mouth. Through it all he was able to keep going, stay on the job, and meet his usual obligations. The core of his pathology involved a pathogenic view of himself as evil, worthless, vile, and despicable. These feelings were attached to his sexuality, but we can question whether the sexuality was in fact the cause of his conflicts as much as it was the convenient vehicle for his pathological sense of self. Was he bad because he masturbated and had sexual impulses, or was the sense of badness primary and the sexual conflict secondary?

I preferred to see the pathology in this case as reflecting a more primary false-self disorder that in a sense underlie and gave dynamic power to the more superficial level of conflict. His mother, on the basis of her own sexual conflicts and concerns about inner evilness, laid the charge on him that he should be different from other men, that he should be without sin—innocent and sexless. He strove mightily to live out that dictate. The straight-arrow, innocent, sexually neutral, Mr. Clean image that he portrayed so well to the world, and even for a time to himself, was a facade, a false self founded on his compliance and adherence to the code of values and expectations dictated by his mother. His symptoms, as I saw them, were a rebellion against this code of behavior and values. He had lived out the demands of a false self in compliance with his mother's dictates and ideals. In the face of his wife's puritanical attitudes, and struggling with the disappointment and anguish of learning about his infertility, he staged a sexual revolution of his own. His masturbation had been a secret and silent revolt, ridden with anxiety and guilt. The fires of rebellion were fanned to a white heat and he began to act out his sexual impulses in a more public and risky fashion with pornographic escapades and prostitutes. The struggle was between the compliant and sexless "good boy" of his false self and the more honest, authentic, and autonomous part that constituted his real self.

This view of the pathology set the therapeutic course. The task was to help him come to accept and integrate his own sexuality—and this meant coming to grips with his hypertrophied superego and modifying it in more realistic and adaptive directions. The task was also to help him establish a sense of self that reflected his own authentic personality—and this meant helping him to free himself from his attachment to his mother and his devotion to the moralistic code she represented. This meant abandoning her to her desperate fate, giving up the illusion that he could somehow salvage her life and bring meaning and joy to her depressive existence by his attainment of sexless perfection—thus fulfilling her wishes and making her life worthwhile. This, in turn, meant changing the meaning of his life and transforming the purpose of his existence.

We decided not to pursue the course of analysis for extraneous reasons—primarily the cost and Tom's otherwise crowded schedule—even though I thought that it would have been a reasonable and even optimal approach to his difficulties. I have no doubt that he would have been analyzable. In the therapy, I opted for an approach that was fairly active, even confrontational, engaging his obvious intelligence and capacity to see and analyze connections. The material we dealt with and the manner of approach were otherwise analytic. Our work together has lasted over twelve years. The results have been satisfying in terms of his life and work. True to the borderline structure of his personality, he remains vulnerable to regressive episodes that are often triggered by his inability to feel and integrate his anger at both his wife and his mother, and he has great difficulty bringing our work together to a close. These regressive episodes usually take the form of some sort of sexual acting out that is often mild and transient but that offers sufficient latitude for his obsessional phobia of AIDS to reassert itself. He plunges once again into the turmoil and distress of his obsessional doubting and delusional conviction.

It is my impression that over time and as a result of continuing psychotherapeutic processing these episodes are increasingly short-lived and that his capacity to limit and even at times to subvert them is slowly developing. This, to my mind, is a measure of the extent to which he has been able to free himself from his adherence to the T. family code and its correlative curse—in other words, from his adherence to his mother's unconscious and destructive value system and his emotional attachment and dependence on her. The sexless, Mr. Clean false self is the vehicle for this attachment. If he can free himself from that compliance, he has a chance for a meaningful life.

23

AS-IF PERSONALITY

DESCRIPTION

The features of the "as-if" personality are difficult to define and to recognize clinically. Cases that can be diagnosed as "as-if" personalities are relatively rare; the usual circumstance is to see "as-if" characteristics as a part of the borderline picture but not sufficiently delineated to justify "as-if" personality as a primary diagnosis. In some cases the "as-if" dynamic extends into the realm of imposture.[1] A central dimension of the pathology in these cases is the plasticity of the individual's sense of identity, either actively exploited, as in the case of the imposter, or passively experienced, as is the case in more straightforward cases of "as-if" personality. The therapeutic issues with these patients focus around problems in exploring the underlying motivations for compliant adaptations and in understanding the obstacles to establishing a solid, autonomous, and consistent identity that is authentically the patient's own.

---

[1] A case can be made for an "as-if" dimension in the enactment of dramatic roles on the stage. The outcome is more acceptably expressive, even adaptive, but may in some cases serve the ends of psychopathological needs and express a form of "as-if" adjustment. See the illuminating discussion by Rule (1973).

DEUTSCH'S PATIENTS

It is worth considering Deutsch's (1942) classic case descriptions since she was the first to describe this phenomenon and her case material has not been surpassed. The first was a woman who had been raised as an only child of a noble European family. It was the custom in such circles to hand over the care and training of the child to nursemaids and tutors. On certain specified days the child would be brought to her parents for a formal evaluation of her progress. These were cool, distant, ceremonious occasions; and when the business was done, she would be returned to the care of her tutors. From her parents she received little or nothing in the way of warmth, tenderness, or even punishment. At the same time, an important part of the training program was a strong emphasis on love, honor, and obedience toward the parents—emotions she never had the opportunity to experience directly.

Under such conditions, one could hardly expect much authentic emotional growth. To make matters worse, she had little opportunity for emotional attachment to her caretakers, who worked under the directives given by the parents and who were also frequently changed. To compensate for these deficiencies, the patient developed an active fantasy life about the parents. She developed an elaborate myth in which the parents possessed divine powers through which the patient was able to gain anything her heart could desire. All the stories and fairybook legends she read were distilled into this myth in which narcissism reigned supreme. There was little room for the frustrated yearning for love that permeated her real existence. The narcissistic regression into fantasy was thus a compensation for the deprivation she felt with her parents and for the absence of any substitute libidinal ties. The patient's early outbreaks of rage and resentment were gradually disciplined and brought under control and replaced by a completely compliant obedience.

When she entered a convent school at the age of 8, the "as-if" condition was already well established. Superficially there was no difference between her and any of the other pupils. She had the usual attachment to one of the nuns and apparently tender friendships with other girls; she went devoutly through the practices of religion, and even was seduced into masturbatory practices with apparent feelings of guilt. All of this was without real feeling, significance, or belief, and even without real guilt. All was carried out as a kind of imitation, so that she could be like her comrades. For this patient, there was never any meaningful attachment or libidinal involvement with real objects.

The second patient was a woman whose father had had a severe mental illness and whose mother suffered from neurosis. She thought of her father only as a "man with a black beard." He was largely absent from her life, and she remembered only the times when he would come home from the sanitorium, yet still have to be nursed in an isolated room. The myth she created about her father replaced him with a fantasied man of mystery with whom she had many different kinds of experiences that served to make her a superhuman being. This child, too, was raised for the most part by nurses, but despite this she was able to establish a relatively strong libidinal attachment to her neurotic mother. Her later object relationships reflected some capacity for object libido, especially in homosexual relationships, but never substantially altered the "as-if" quality. An impediment to her attachment to her mother was created by the birth of a younger brother, which stimulated intense feelings of rivalry and aggressive envy.

One avenue of compensating for these losses was her attempt to imitate her brother, whom she almost completely mirrored not only in fantasy but in actual behavior. Unfortunately, this brother also showed signs of childhood psychosis. The sister thus imitated her brother's bizarre behavior and lived with him in a world of fantasy. These imitative behaviors averted her intense hatred and aggressive feelings toward the brother and transformed them into compliant passivity in the form of submissive imitation. There were no other meaningful object relationships that might have mitigated this pathological picture.

A third patient had been born into a family in which the father was an alcoholic and brutally mistreated her mother. Early on, she sided with her victimized mother and created fantasies of rescuing her so that they could live happily together. When she finally discovered that her mother was not simply a passive victim but took pleasure in such brutalization, her disappointment turned to a severe devaluation of her mother that deprived her of her only love object. Her subsequent efforts were turned to trying to make up for this loss by creating a series of imitative relationships of an "as-if" sort. Her libidinal instincts remained relatively primitive; she vacillated between giving them free reign and strongly inhibiting them. She became promiscuous and indulged in a variety of sexual perversions. She would retreat from such periods of acting out by an imitative relationship with some conventional person to whom she became attached. The result was a frequent shifting of interests and occupations, depending on whom she was connected with. All of this took place with a marked lack of affect.

The stream of interests was extraordinarily superficial and unrealistic. She seemed indefatigably active in following them out, but her engagement in so many concurrent activities gave her behavior a hypomanic quality. In the analysis, the analytic work seemed to be unusually successful. The patient began to understand many things about herself, and as she did so the eccentric behavior seemed to fall away. In part, her hidden agenda had been to become an analyst in imitation of Deutsch. When she realized that this was impossible, she collapsed into a state of total lack of affect and inner emptiness. She gradually became increasingly negativistic and resistant to the analytic process.

ULRICH U.

For the most part the "as-if" personality is not seen as a pure culture. The "as-if" characteristics are mixed in with other personality dimensions and traits but at times can reflect a dominant quality of the patient's interaction with his interpersonal environment. These patients represent different degrees of pathological impairment. There is a quality of adaptiveness and compliance, a need if not to please at least to placate, and a tendency to manipulate. Ulrich U. was in his twenties when he came to the walk-in clinic. He had been seeing a private therapist for about three years but could no longer afford the private fees. He had interrupted the therapy to go to Israel, where he planned to spend a year working on a kibbutz. During this period his father had died of a heart attack. When he returned he got a job as mental health worker by faking his CV. He had no education beyond high school but was now in a position to be doing therapy with patients in the hospital clinic. He complained of depression, suicidal thoughts, fears of losing his mind and going crazy, and a chronic problem with insomnia. He was using Dalmane for the sleep problem.

As the therapy began, there was a question of how Ulrich would engage in the process. He was obviously enraged that he could not have therapy from the private psychiatrist he had been seeing, and he was feeling resentful and humiliated by having to seek help from a mere psychiatric resident. At first a struggle took place over the fee. Ulrich complained at length that he was expected to pay for treatment through the clinic; he thought the clinic scale was too high; he was not sure that he could afford it, and not sure that he wanted to pay for treatment with someone so inexperienced. He wondered whether the resident knew enough to treat him, whether he might know more about psychiatry than the resident, and whether he might also be a better therapist than the doctor. There were also difficulties around the appointment times and keeping to the schedule. He was frequently late for appointments or skipped them altogether with the excuse that his own work at the psychiatric hospital took precedence.

These problems were exacerbated by the therapist's vacation, which had been scheduled before Ulrich began his therapy. They had been working together only a few weeks when the vacation intervened. Ulrich was clearly angered by this, but was unable or unwilling to express his resentment directly. The anger came out indirectly in acting out around the appointment times and paying his bill, and in dreams. In one dream he found himself in a concentration camp; the situation was desperate—he had to break out or he would not survive. Despite this undercurrent of displaced and indirect hostility, he presented a pleasant and compliant facade, presumably in an effort to be a model patient. There was a sense that if he played the ideal-patient role, there would be some payoff, some reward. He seemed to expect that the therapist would somehow not charge him or would be so pleased with his interesting and enlightening case that he would want to continue to treat him regardless of whether or not he paid his bill.

The element of playing a role, adopting a persona, was a striking aspect of this patient's orientation. This came through not only in the therapy but also in the other primary contexts of his life. In his work he played the role of professional and therapist—without background, training, or credentials. Being a patient was a threat to his notion of himself as treater. In the clinic he once ran into someone else who worked at the same hospital and explained that he was visiting our clinic for supervision. Admission of his patient status was too threatening and left him feeling too vulnerable and narcissistically depleted.

The same situation obtained with his girlfriend. With her he played the role of the understanding, supportive, affectionate partner, but this was accompanied by a countercurrent of resentment and hostility. They had been living together and decided to get engaged. When she became pregnant, he began to experience cold feet. They decided to have an abortion, largely at his urging. He blamed her for the pregnancy because she had not used her diaphragm. He was angry at her for putting him in a difficult position. He could not understand her needs and resented the pressure she put on him to get married. Why did it have to be his responsibility? She finally expressed her frustration, anger, and resentment at him. She told him he was selfish. As far as he was concerned she was hysterical and excessively sensitive. He broke off the relationship in a rage.

Things came to a crisis in the therapy as well. The hostile undercurrent intensified after the doctor's vacation and was further inflamed by the doctor's canceling several appointments because of scheduling conflicts. It is possible that this represented some countertransference acting-out on the doctor's part based on his resentment of Ulrich's manipulative and devaluing approach to the therapy. This intensified Ulrich's feelings of being treated like a patient, confronted him with the basic inequality in the therapeutic relation, and mobilized all the latent elements of his immense envy of the doctor. At the same time he deeply resented doctors because they were superior to him in the hospital, could give him orders, and stood in judgment on his work with his patients.

All of this came to a head when the doctor was notified that Ulrich had not paid his bill for several months. When the doctor confronted him about this, Ulrich went into an explosion of denial and rage. He denied that the clinic had sent him the bills; how could he be expected to pay when he had not been sent the bills? (In fact he had been sent several bills.) It was an issue of responsibility, and the doctor was trying to put the responsibility on him. He was also angry that he was wasting valuable therapy time talking about it. He basically felt that therapy with a mere resident was not worth anything anyway, so why should he feel any obligation to pay? He was still angry that he could not afford to see his private psychiatrist and felt entitled to treatment without having to pay for it. The therapy was proving too difficult. His basic position was that he should not have to do anything unless it came easy. His ideal was still his father, who never took responsibility for anything. He wanted to remain true to his father and did not really want to change. With that, the therapy came to an end.

VICTOR V.

Victor V. was still in college when he started therapy for his depression and because of concerns over his homosexuality. He was also furious at his father, who had plenty of money but forced him to work thirty hours a week while he was going to school. His father was a professor in a large university, an authoritarian, a rational, obsessional, distant, and generally emotionally unexpressive man. Victor complained that he never felt comfortable in his father's presence, and that they never spent any time together. All his father did at home was complain about money and how much everything cost. His mother was not very much involved in the family but devoted herself to local politics. When he was small, his father was often away from home, and he was terrified that his mother would abandon the family, too. He was afraid to go to school, but never felt he could tell his mother or assert himself because he feared his mother would get angry and leave.

Victor had a sister two years older who was the *enfant terrible* of the family. She would confront and argue with the father, throw temper tantrums, and generally get more than her share of attention from both parents. Comparing himself to her, Victor felt small and inadequate. She was especially successful in getting money out of the father, something Victor could never manage. (She has also had her difficulties: she started in law school, had to drop out for a year, but then was able to return and earn her law degree.)

Victor's psychic life seemed to center around his father as the central and dominant figure. The father was not only the primary object with whom Victor carried out his conflicts and struggles, but he also figured prominently in his dreams and bore the brunt of Victor's accusations. He felt that in large measure his father had never taught him how to be a man, had never showed any interest in him, and was never there to offer any help when he needed it. The father figured prominently in his homosexual dreams: dreams of homosexual play and intercourse with his father, of sucking on his father's large and powerful penis and thus gaining strength and power from it. Other powerful masculine figures figured in dreams in which he would be the object of their attention and would be "fucked," and this would make him feel strong and secure.

Similar feelings and expectations came into play in the therapy. He hoped that the therapist would give him something that would make him feel like a man. He felt inadequate and inferior because of his homosexuality and thought that the doctor knew the secret of masculine strength if only he would tell him what it was. His behavior in the therapy was totally compliant, dutifully conforming to every aspect— coming on time, paying his bill promptly, and trying very hard to be the "good patient." He wanted to be a special patient, and his conviction was that he could achieve that by his compliance and conformity. This was the approach he employed in all his interpersonal relationships. He got along with his homosexual lovers by complying with their every wish, performing whatever perverse act they desired, and fulfilling their expectations. He thought that the therapist had expectations and wanted him to perform in a certain way. He had always done what his parents expected, cleaning his room, doing chores around the house, and so on. His sister argued and rebelled; he felt that she got more out of it and that he was never shown any appreciation or praise for his efforts. He felt like a martyr, taken advantage of and used by everyone, but powerless to help himself or get what he wanted. He felt that he identified more with his mother, whom he saw as more caring but also as dependent and subject to his father. He saw his father as having the power, and his mother as having to placate and please him. He regretted that he was not the son his father wanted—that he was a disappointment to both his parents.

On a few occasions the doctor was delayed by other duties. Victor felt resentful of these lapses, feeling that he was not important or interesting to the doctor. He was frustrated and angry, not knowing what he could do to gain the special status he wished for. He wanted to yell at the doctor but was afraid of what might happen if he let his feelings out. He would feel out of control, more vulnerable, and more afraid of retaliation by the doctor, who might throw him out, tell him that the therapy was finished. He would feel rejected and abandoned—a frightening prospect he felt he had to avoid at all costs.

These feelings were intensified by the doctor's vacation. Victor's anger and fears of abandonment gave him considerable difficulty. Despite the therapist's encouragement to express his feelings, he was afraid of the consequences. The doctor would have the upper hand, would realize the neediness and dependence he so reviled. If he said that he would miss the doctor, that would make the doctor strong and him weak. His parents could never respond to his needs or problems; they would simply tell him to work it out for himself and not to bother them.

As in the case of Steve, the problem in Victor's therapy was to help him extricate himself from the entanglements with his parents, especially his father. His life seemed patterned around a need to find acceptance, love, attention, appreciation, and approval from the significant objects in his environment. His approach to this problem was to discern each person's expectations of him and to find ways to meet those demands by way of compliance and conformity. This plastic adaptability left him with little sense of himself, and at those points in his life when he had to rely on his own inner resources, he began to experience considerable difficulty. The therapeutic task was to make it possible for him to open some space in which he could begin to stand on his own feet. The place where this effort could be joined was in the therapeutic relation.

The therapeutic course was dictated by the need to work through all of the transference vicissitudes, especially the elements of the victim and inferior introjects that seemed to form the core of his personality structure and provided the basis for his "as-if" adjustments. These issues came into focus within the transference in terms of specific displacements from his relations with both his father and mother in the first instance, and to a certain degree his sister. Other transference elements became available projectively in terms of his interacting with the therapist as a powerful, threatening object and his correlative view of himself as weak, vulnerable, and inferior. The task in the therapy was to help the patient clarify and make explicit these introjective patterns. This involved efforts by the therapist to elicit and develop in greater detail the aspects of Victor's view of the therapist as powerful and threatening and himself as vulnerable and inferior. In the degree to which these projective distortions could be remedied, the pathogenic introjective structure was progressively modified, and the basis of his defensive involvement with objects and his need to protect his fragile sense of self and identity by "as-if" involvements would be undercut. These elements were progressively worked through with an eye to establishing and developing the therapeutic alliance. As these distorting transference elements were worked on, the basis for a more solid and productive therapeutic alliance became available. The therapeutic alliance thereby provided the matrix within which crucial internalizations could be accomplished that provided the building blocks for a mature, independent, and autonomous sense of self.

WILMA W.

I would like to include at least one woman in this group, since they often present "as-if" characteristics clinically, and represent an important form of narcissistic object relationship described by Reich (1953). Wilma W. was in her mid-20s when she first came for therapy. She was involved in a graduate program in philosophy, was currently involved in an extramarital affair, and was having difficulties in her marriage. She and her husband had been through a course of sex therapy together, but their relationship was foundering. She was highly obsessional in style, but dealing with an acute depression and uncertain as to her own path in life. Her husband was passive and dependent, expecting her to take the initiative sexually and in all other aspects of their life together. She had great difficulty with this since her own need was to adapt passively to the demands of her sexual partners. She felt more comfortable with her other lovers, since they took the initiative and she could be adaptive to their demands and expectations. As she described these various relationships, which took a variety of forms as the therapy progressed and as she became involved in relationships with different men, the striking feature was her adaptability to the needs of each of the men in question as she moved from relationship to relationship. She had a chameleon quality that permeated her object relationships and dictated different dimensions of her personality.

Wilma was the oldest of three siblings, having a younger brother and sister. She had always felt that her mother had emasculated her father, and she felt that in many ways she had done the same to her husband. Her father was a relatively distant figure; he was hardworking and never around very much. She felt that he was driven and that she was much the same in her own life. He was a lawyer for various big corporations, and had a history of moving from one to another because he would get into fights with his bosses and would be fired. Her mother was depressed, ineffectual, masochistic, and alcoholic.

Wilma was troubled by her husband's passivity and her fears that she had made him that way. She tended to operate more in terms of her intellect than her emotions. She could acknowledge her own competitive feelings toward her husband and her need to criticize his work on his thesis (he was also a graduate student) and to devalue his therapy and his therapist. She felt contempt for his therapist even though she could recognize that what the therapist was saying was true. She could associate to her contempt for other students in her program and could acknowledge that her competitiveness with her husband was related to male-female issues and to questions of who was superior. She had a vivid picture of her mother, who had painted herself as a martyr and the victim of an abusive man, the patient's father. Her mother had told her countless times that she should never allow herself to become the victim of any man.

As her marriage deteriorated, she became involved in an affair. The conflict between her dissolving marriage and the intrigue of a new relationship was difficult. She wanted her relationship with her boyfriend but did not want to surrender her attachment to her husband. She went through a period of guilt and remorse about the marriage relationship, while at the same time she was caught up in a series of affairs. The chameleon and plastic quality of her involvement in these various relationships was evident. It was as though her own sense of identity was determined by the nature of her involvement in each of these relationships.

Similar issues came to light in the therapy. The problem she faced was how to relate to the therapist. Her impulse was to engage the therapist in terms of the therapist's expectations. This was the pattern she had followed throughout most of her life. What was expected of her? What did the other person want or need? The central problem in the therapeutic work was why she continually defined her own sense of herself in terms of the views and expectations of others, including her therapist. She felt empty, fragmented, as though she had no core sense of herself without someone to relate to and be involved with. She felt she could have a sense of existing only by molding herself to a pattern set by others. She worried about earning enough money after her separation; if she were not able to provide for herself, she would be sucked back into dependence on her parents, and then once again she would be in the position of having to please her father and submit to his wishes.

The therapeutic course for this young woman seems apparent. The therapist explored with her each involvement and relationship in detail in order to discover the elements of her passivity and inability to enter these relationships as an independent agent with an autonomous sense of her self. The task, once again, was to help her establish a self that could stand on its own and did not need to function through a relationship with a sustaining object. The therapeutic inquiry settled on the issue of why the establishing of an independent or autonomous stance was so difficult or threatening for her. The undertaking of this effort provided the ultimate focus of the therapeutic work, but the priority fell on the issues related to establishing a secure and nonthreatening relationship. It took some time before the patient began to feel in any decisive way that the therapist could be trusted with her deeper and more troublesome feelings. Once it had been established that the therapist was an empathic and supportive helper, the exploratory enterprise could then be undertaken without excessive resistance. Gradually the patient was able to join the therapist in examining her behavior, attitudes, and feelings and to begin to put them into perspective. As this process evolved, the sense of the therapist as a constant, reliable, and trustworthy object was slowly established. This made it possible for the patient to explore her feelings and behaviors without a sense of threat or judgment.

XENA X.

I close this chapter with an extended quotation from a young woman who exemplifies many of the "as-if" qualities of this range of borderline pathology. Xena X. was in her early thirties when I first met her. She had recently been through a rather productive psychotherapy experience for a period of six years. The therapy had helped this woman to lift herself out of a severe anorectic phase. Unfortunately, for reasons that were not clear to her, the therapist had precipitously terminated her therapy and moved to another part of the country. When she came to see me, she was in considerable distress, caught in the throes of a profound mourning process, struggling with turbulent and troubling emotions of rage and depression. She did not appear to be suicidal, but was suffering intensely from her feelings of hurt and abandonment.

The picture Xena presented of herself had a decided "as-if" cast to it. She had little sense of herself as a substantial, autonomous entity, but experienced herself only in relation to the others in her environment. She made her way through these relationships by becoming in some measure whatever these others expected her to be. In all of her relationships she would react with hurt, anger, disillusionment, and pained disappointment when her compliance and conformity to the other's wishes did not seem to get her what she felt she desperately needed. The therapist's departure was particularly painful in this regard since she had felt especially dependent on his good will and approval of her. His leaving made her feel small, unimportant, as though she mattered to no one and counted for nothing. He had not even paid her the courtesy of an explanation.

Her demeanor as she engaged in the therapeutic relation with me was one of caution, suspicion, and fear, mixed with a glimmer of optimism and hope. She responded positively to me from the first but was also obviously struggling with her impulse to grab on to me in desperate anguish as a last hope. The predominant issue seemed to be whether, if she were to commit herself to a relationship with me, she could rely on me not to abandon her as her previous therapist had. Clearly the issue of having others there for her as props for her fragile, vulnerable sense of self was central to her pathology.

Her father was a successful businessman, who was remote and unavailable. Her efforts to please him and adapt to his expectations, even to the point of suppressing her own feelings, never yielded much success or made their relationship satisfying or close. Her relationship with her mother was a disaster. The mother was a depressed, alcoholic, borderline woman who was never satisfied with anything in her life, including her children. Especially when she was drinking, she would fly into rages at the least provocation and physically attack my patient, call her obscene names, and tell her that she was worthless and that she wished that she had never borne her. The effect of these attacks on Xena was devastating and left her with the feeling that, try as she might, she could never do enough to gain her mother's love or approval. This remained a lifelong conflict and trauma for her.

Not long after we had begun the therapy, following a long holiday weekend, I received a handwritten letter from her.

> Dear Dr. Meissner,
>
> I am writing because I feel myself sinking into what is a terrifying darkness for me. Over the past weekend I have felt an intense frustration growing. I have been keeping my balance just barely day by day. . . . But this weekend I thought it reached a point where I thought I was going crazy. I need something—my spirit is dying.
>
> It feels like my body has taken on the state of my soul. It was incredibly weary, and thought of going back to work seemed like a sentence to psychological torture, if not death. So I called in sick in the hope that somehow I will be able to get out of bed and do something that will rejuvenate me. At work I can command my body to do what others ask me to do, but there is no spirit in it, no heart. I feel as though I am manipulated and controlled by others' desires and needs, whether evil or good. It is weird to see how I walk around like a zombie, responding only to the wishes and desires of others with nothing of my own.
>
> Even as I write, I am afraid that you will think I am trying to manipulate you, to get you to feel sorry for me or to appreciate my superiority. I don't know whether that is so. I decided to write because I felt like I was falling into an intense despair and would end up in hell. Writing helps me to clear my head and get things into perspective. It helps to think that someone else can hear me, that it isn't just me and God alone. I do not feel safe with God, not because of God, but because I can always twist him into something that I am terrified of and therefore must submit to.

There follows a lengthy section filled with obsessional doubts about how much she should eat, and who wants her to eat or not to eat. She does not know what I expect of her, whether I want her to eat until she gets fat or not. She returns to the theme of how she deals with what I say to her:

> One thing I cannot figure out about the things you say is how you expect me to come to such clear conclusions all by myself

and so not be affected by what anyone else says or thinks about me. So much of my experience says that that is not true. You seem to put forth contradictory statements about that. I have learned that when one is loved by others and has one's love accepted, one grows in confidence and knows what love is; and then, when one grows in confidence, one can go even where love is not. Then one is never abandoned again because one knows love in its true nature, i.e. God, and we know that God is always there even if his love and presence is not felt. I can see my error; it is something you chided me for last week. I still see God as a demanding father I have to please like a good little girl. You would say that is immature, not the way an adult thinks.

I am still stuck in thinking that it is important that you see that all my errors are understandable. Maybe I'm afraid to assume responsibility because I'm afraid it will leave me nothing to stand on. I get the feeling that you are trying to wipe out my past so that suddenly I am supposed to be a big girl. Even that leaves me feeling like a child because I feel like I am supposed to do it to please you. I fear that I have nothing to show for my past and my good intentions.

The letter ends with several pages of ruminations and somewhat obsessional doubting about her eating habits and repeated inquiries as to what I think she should do, what foods she should eat, what doctor she should see for her physical condition, and so on.

This letter shows the intense need felt by many of these patients to fit in with the expectations of anyone who becomes important in their lives, at whatever cost to themselves, and it reveals the despair, uncertainty, and agony they experience when the issue is a question of standing alone on their own feet. This aspect of the "as-if" personality becomes the central issue in the therapeutic management of these patients.

24

IDENTITY STASIS

This group is the last in the schizoid continuum and often displays predominantly neurotic conflicts. The aspect of their pathology that stamps them as borderline is the pervasive difficulty they experience in establishing and maintaining an identity, a definite and decisive orientation and commitment in most all aspects of their personal and work life.

These patients are not common, at least in my experience, as a pure type, but my guess is that the problems they reflect in the area of identity formation are quite frequently seen in borderline patients. I have only one such patient that I can present with sufficient depth to convey the features of the therapy.

ZACHARY Z.

Zachary Z. was in his late twenties when he first came to see me—a tall, athletic, handsome man, dressed in an impeccable three-button suit. The difficulties that brought him included a dissatisfaction with his life, a feeling of not knowing where he belonged or what direction his life should take, problems in establishing a meaningful relation with a woman, and an inability to urinate in public lavatories. He had graduated from college and architectural school, and was presently employed in a large local architectural firm. We negotiated the necessary arrangements for the therapy easily and agreed to start on a once-a-week basis.

Our work together has extended over the following decade—at first psychotherapy, then through more than five years of psychoanalysis, and finally back to psychotherapy.

In the early stages of the therapy the rudiments of his life story came into view. He was the oldest son in his family: he had an older sister, and a younger brother and sister. He described his mother in benign terms. She never worked, but ran the household. She was gentle and patient, and he felt close and comfortable with her. But she occupied an insignificant position on Zack's psychic horizon in contrast to his father. His father was trained as an architect, but was also a successful entrepreneur who started his own construction business and made a considerable success of it, enough to make it worth the while of his brothers and cousins to come into the business and turn it into a real family enterprise. The family was financially secure, but the cost was that Zack's father was rarely home, usually busy working late hours or traveling. When he was there he always seemed to be doing something—fixing broken things, working in the garden, and so on. He never had much time to play with any of the kids, Zack included.

Zack's relation to his father was strained and awkward. He never felt that he could talk with him, never felt that his father approved of him or anything he did. He desperately wanted to please his father and get some sense that his father thought well of him, but could not find a way to do this. He would try to help his father in his work around the house, but when the father gave him something to do, he usually didn't do it right and his father would get impatient and yell at him. His father was a baseball fan, so Zack thought that if he could be a good baseball player his father would acknowledge him. But Zack was only a mediocre player. He especially had difficulty batting as a Little Leaguer. He was afraid to swing at the ball—afraid of striking out; then his father wouldn't think well of him. As the years passed, he developed a fantasy of becoming a baseball star, and then his father would see his ability and admire him. When his father came to the games, he never had any sense that his father thought he had done well. It was as though he hadn't played at all. He could also recall times when his father would approach him and try to talk to him when he was in high school, but Zack felt so resentful and infuriated that he would retreat into sullen silence.

Zack was a good student, and was usually at the top of his class in elementary and high schools even though he never worked very hard. He was accepted at the same prestigious college his father had attended. One might have thought that this would have been an occasion for some sense of satisfaction for both father and son, but none seems to have been forthcoming. During his freshman year in college, Zack's father collapsed and died of a massive coronary.

The effect on the family was devastating. Zack did not react very strongly, at least superficially. He did not cry, but went through the wake and funeral stoically, feeling no strong emotions. His feelings were mixed: there was a sadness that his father was gone but also a sense of relief that he would no longer have to contend with his father. His emotional distance and the negative feelings about his father made him feel guilty. As time passed, however, the father's death loomed as a most significant event for Zack—more so than for anyone else in the family. Zack was left with a deep sense of yearning for his father, a sense of unfinished business: he wished he had had a better relation with his father; he missed him, wanted to talk to him, get his advice; and particularly he felt compelled to do well enough in life so that his father would admire him if he were still alive.

The therapy made clear the extent to which this powerful motif dominated Zack's inner life. It hovered over every undertaking and cast a shadow into every corner of his life. Zack was preoccupied with the need to find out what the magical thing was that would allow him to accomplish those objectives. The problem was that he could never be sure. Whatever course he could imagine seemed ambiguous and uncertain. Whatever he did, it had to be a great success. If it was law, he would have to be a famous and successful trial lawyer. If it was business, he would have to become successful and rich. If he decided to be a writer, he would have to write the great American novel, a classic. He had to be a star, to achieve fame and fortune, or else his father would not notice him and not think he was worth anything. After college, Zack did not know what he wanted to do, and finally, because he could not think of anything better and had no idea of what he himself really wanted, he went to architectural school.

His engagement in his architectural training was diffident at best. He cut a good number of classes, studied only sporadically, dallied with various assignments and projects, procrastinating until he had no choice but to do them or get thrown out. Then he would plunge into the effort and somehow get through by the skin of his teeth. At every step, he was ambivalent, wondering why he was doing this, feeling it was not the right thing for him, spending long hours daydreaming and fantasying about traveling the world, enduring heroic hardships, and plunging into one adventure after another. Despite his daydreams, the thought of such adventures in the real world terrified him. He was too nervous, too unsure of himself, and too easily frightened to even entertain any such possibility.

In this fashion he stumbled along. Stardom, as I was to learn, was always somewhere Zack was not, someplace else, some other profession, some other area of engagement or interest. Somehow he managed to get through and finished the program. He took a promising job with a large and important firm. It was soon after this he came to see me.

A similar picture had evolved in Zack's sex life. He would be attracted to beautiful and talented women, but their intellectual gifts and abilities threatened and intimidated him. His good looks made it relatively easy for him to get to know these women, but it was not long before he would begin to feel awkward, ill at ease. It was difficult to maintain a conversation, and he became increasingly shy and withdrawn, finally more or less backing out of the relationship. As he did this, he would begin to find fault with the girl, criticizing her looks, her attitudes, her behavior, whatever. With some of these relationships things would progress to the point of sexual intimacy, and this would precipitate another crisis. Zack would become preoccupied with his sexual performance, constantly feeling inadequate. This led to somewhat hypochrondriacal preoccupations about his penis. He worried about it and maintained that there was something wrong with it. He felt it was too difficult for him to get an erection, and when he did he was convinced that his penis was bent. He sought reassurance from a urologist and while he seemed somewhat relieved by the negative report, he was unable to accept the urologist's opinion as final and valid.

Therapy with Zack was an interesting process, in which he seemed to engage readily. By and large he was on time, missed occasional appointments for business reasons, and was faithful with his payments. He always wore a dark business suit and looked the part of the young, up-and-coming, successful businessman. The hours were not easy. His speech was halting, rambling, tentative. He seemed incapable of making a direct, declarative sentence. He would start a sentence, and before he got halfway through his mind would be diverted by another thought, which never quite found its way to completion, but would slip off to some other subject. Often in the middle of a sentence he would pause and look out the window, and suddenly all sense of contact with him disappeared. His mind was somewhere else, not on the subject. He called these episodes "daydreams," and when asked about them would describe what he had been thinking about. Almost always it was some entirely unrelated subject that had little or nothing to do with the matter in hand. When I tried to pursue the daydream as if it were like a dream or leading to some associative connection, the same pattern of fragmented and diverted thoughts would take hold again. It was as though even the distractions had to be distracted. In time we were able to examine these daydreaming episodes. They served a defensive function, a kind of escape from any affectively toned or meaningful material. We came to recognize this pattern as an avoidance and as serving some important resistances.

Nonetheless, the work of the therapy gradually deepened and intensified. We progressed over stages to twice-weekly sessions, and then three times a week. This intensification of the schedule did not have the effect of mobilizing more material or opening up more meaningful layers of his experience. While he compliantly went along with the process, he fought against it at the same time. His resistance took the form of the avoidance daydreams but also was reflected in more consciously resentful attitudes—feeling humiliated and weak because he had to be in therapy at all, feeling that if he were worth his salt he should be able to deal with these problems without any outside help, and feeling bad about his own sense of weakness and incompetence in dealing with the course of his life. While he committed himself to the therapeutic process, he also felt resistant and recalcitrant, more or less consciously dragging his heels and finding himself unwilling to endorse or put to any purposeful application what he found out about himself in the process.

Gradually over the course of about two years, the therapy seemed to come to a standstill. It became apparent to me that we were not making much progress, that the issues that really lay at the root of Zack's difficulties were eluding the therapeutic exploration, and that we were caught in a therapeutic misalliance that included Zack's narcissistic wish to be magically transformed and his resistance to the therapeutic process based on an underlying fear of dependence and commitment. Hoping to find a way out of this impasse, I suggested psychoanalysis, and after several months of discussing and questioning, we decided to go ahead with it.

In the meanwhile, things were not going well in Zack's life. His social life consisted largely in spending time in the local bar with his buddies, attending the frequent parties his friends threw, and periodic dalliances with various girlfriends. On the business front, it went from bad to worse. Zack was far from enthusiastic about his work. He did not know whether he really wanted to be an architect, and generally hated the work. He would drag himself into the office each day, sit

staring at the work assignments on his desk for a while, go out for a cup
of coffee, then read the newspaper for a few hours, stare out the window
daydreaming, then force himself to try to do a little something. He
would tarry over lunch, get back to work late, and waste more time
until it was time to go home. There were not many exceptions to this
routine, usually only when he felt pressure to get something finished.
The jobs he had to do were not very inspiring, but were mundane and
ordinary projects that he despised, felt were not worth the time or
effort, and certainly were not leading to fame, glory, and stardom.

His employers could not long tolerate his behavior, and he was
soon asked to leave the firm, a painful disappointment, especially to his
narcissistically enhanced view of himself. He turned his attention to
writing the great American novel, but his efforts met dismal failure. His
approach was much the same as his efforts at work, and the outcome
much the same. In short nothing got written, the paper on his desk
remained blank, and the great American novel continued to elude him.

Zack actually passed almost a year and a half in this unproductive
fashion. As his savings dwindled he was forced to decide what he was
going to do to support himself. He obsessed over possible ways he could
be gainfully employed. One option was to work in his father's firm, now
run as a family business by his uncles. But this would have meant
capitulation and defeat, an admission that he couldn't make it on his
own and had to come crawling back to be taken care of in the protective
confines of his family. But more particularly it would have meant that
he had not measured up to his father's standards, that he had lost in the
competition with his father, and that in his father's eyes he was a failure.
He finally decided to take a job in another architectural firm, smaller
and less prestigious than the one he had left, but still quite respectable.

He determined he would do better this time around, but it quickly
became apparent that he was falling into the same pattern. Within a few
months he was again fired. This time he saw the futility of sitting in his
apartment and immediately started looking for a new job. He found
something within a few weeks in a firm with only a handful of employees that dealt with small architectural projects. The owner was an
old friend of the family who was well disposed toward him. They
reached an agreement that committed Zack to a certain amount of
work for a base salary, with incentives for any additional business he
might bring in. Zack did not considerably change his dilatory style, and
work remained a chore for him, but he seemed to be able to stay with
this situation. Perhaps it was a realization that he was at rock bottom,
perhaps it was the consideration and support of his boss, perhaps it was

some effect of his analysis, but he managed to stay with the job over the course of the next several years. The work he did was apparently of good quality, but it was never done with a sense of enthusiasm or satisfaction. It was always a struggle, and he was usually late with everything. Somehow he managed to keep his head above water.

In the analysis, whatever progress was being made was accomplished at a snail's pace. The couch did not work any magical opening up of the material or deepening of the inquiry. The same drifting and vacuous quality was there, along with a sense of his struggling to hold on in the face of the regressive pull of the couch and the analytic situation. One striking aspect of his resistance was his apparent inability to remember anything from session to session. There were times when some significant progress seemed to have been made, some breakthrough accomplished, some important insight generated, only to have it disappear as though it had been written on water. This represented a form of narcissistic resistance (Boschan 1987)

Little by little, elements of the picture emerged and could be joined to gain some better understanding of his problem. The effort was halting, fragmentary, and disjointed. There was little associative material, and when he did get into talking about something, there was a quality of narrow focusing on the subject of the moment and little inclination to broaden the scope associatively. There was a kind of stubborn insistence on one track at a time and no quick shifts or unanticipated jumps to other connected material were tolerated. Attempts to make even the most obvious connections between different areas of his experience were met with a lack of understanding or denial of any connection. The flow of material, sparse as it was, was frequently interrupted by long silences—periods of daydreaming that would in their characteristic way intrude on his thinking whenever anything heavy was coming into view.

In any case, some important issues agonizingly made their way into the picture. The first issue was Zack's difficult relationship with his father. Although a dozen years had passed since his father's death, Zack was still caught in an unresolved mourning process. Much of the time in the early phase of the analysis was given over to that effort. Zack hardly ever spoke of his father without tears. There was a litany of regrets, recriminations, a bemoaning of lost opportunities, and a sense of deep sadness and loss. The motifs of oedipal engagement and competition with the father were slow to come to the surface. The gradual inroads of the mourning process seemed to open the way, at least partly. Zack was terrified of his father and could attach no ostensible or rational reason to this fear. His father had often been remote but never hostile or punitive. While Zack yearned desperately for some closeness and acceptance from his father, any degree of contact with his father aroused such anxiety and fear that he could not tolerate it. Zack hardly ever dreamed, but one of his few dreams was telling. He was engaged in a medieval tournament of knights in armor. Clad in a heavy suit of armor and mounted on a powerful charger, he was to enter the list and do battle with an opposing champion for the favor of a fair princess. Carrying a shield in one hand and a long lance in the other, he rode into the arena, bowed to the royal box, and turned to enter the combat area to the cheering of the crowd. As his opponent entered the arena, he recognized that it was his father. Zack then lowered his lance, turned his horse around, and with bowed head rode out of the arena in disgrace and shame. At first he could not believe he had had such a dream, but it addressed his competitive feelings toward his father—something that he had never been able to acknowledge consciously. The dream became a touchstone for interpreting this aspect of his oedipal conflict and the fear of what it might mean if he indeed were to surpass his father or gain the great starlike success that he so consistently wished for.

As the analytic process deepened, there were signs that the level of regression had intensified and that transference elements were contaminating the therapeutic relationship. Zack's concerns about the adequacy of his penis came to the fore, and he became increasingly anxious about the possibility of his losing control of his body and its functions. A significant amount of work was done on his urinary symptom, much of the material focusing around issues of urethral narcissism and themes of conflict about performance and competition. These were usually cast in narcissistic rather than aggressive terms. His ability or inability to piss off the stern of a sailboat in open waters was cast in terms of narcissistic vulnerability and inferiority rather than rivalrous motifs. The aggressive and competitive components of these symptoms were deeply buried and remained relatively implicit in the interpretive work.

The regressive dimension found expression outside the analysis as well. He began to experience occasional anxiety attacks, amounting to panic, while walking down the street. He would have fantasies of losing control of his body, having an epileptic attack, or a stroke, or a heart attack, and falling on his face in the street, losing control of his bowels and bladder. Some of this anxiety was highly overdetermined, especially by his identification with his father, who had suffered an unexpected and sudden heart attack and died. A significant issue that I was convinced was operative in Zack's pathology was his fear of death. I felt that one important factor in Zack's persistent inability to put his foot on the path of life was that as soon as he did so, he could look down that path to its inevitable termination in death. He could not start the journey because he was terrified of its end. To immerse himself in the stream of life would mean ultimately for him to meet the same fate as his father. After all, his identification with his father had led him to follow in the father's footsteps, to attend the same college, to take up the same profession, and more. When the opportunities arose to pursue this line of inquiry, however, they led to a blank wall. I could never be sure that this aspect of Zack's problem was any more than speculation on my part.

The analysis dragged on—slowly and uncertainly. Zack remained faithful to the process by and large, but there was a persistent reluctance and overall resentment against the analysis and me for dragging him into it. There was an abiding sense that fate had somehow played him a dirty trick that he should have to endure this sort of process; life should have been easy and successful for him without his having to exert any effort. Thus, clearly the same persuasions and convictions that permeated his approach to life in general found their way into the analysis. The analytic hours were filled with long silences. Any approach to meaningful or emotionally loaded material would be broken off in midflight, silence would prevail, and then Zack would observe that he was daydreaming again. Efforts to interpret this pattern gained some understanding of the phenomenon and some acknowledgment on his part that resistance was involved, but all of that made little impression on the occurrence itself.

This pattern did not improve but worsened. We seemed gradually to slip into a stalemate. Efforts on my part to locate and correct the therapeutic misalliance that was based in large measure on a narcissistic base were unavailing. Months passed during which I felt caught on the horns of a classic dilemma—whether to wait and see whether the impasse would resolve or to take some more active stance that would break through the patient's ambivalence and resistance. I chose the former path, but as the months passed my position shifted. The analysis was becoming more psychotherapeutic in technique. In retrospect, I think I was moving to a position or feeling that the analysis was going nowhere and that prolonging it was not going to be helpful to my patient. I decided to go back to sitting the patient up and playing the process along to see whether the option of returning to the couch would turn out to be viable or not. Zack's feelings about the analysis were running along the same lines, and he readily agreed to sit up. We continued at the same level of intensity—four times a week.

In this phase of Zack's treatment we were doing intensive psychoanalytically oriented psychotherapy. The momentum of the therapeutic process continued. My stance was generally more active—questioning, focusing issues, pointing out connections, generally allowing my own associative and interpretive activity to enter more directly into the process, trying to allow Zack enough space to give the material direction, and then following his lead with greater willingness to put in my own two cents' worth from time to time. The focus of the work in this phase was primarily on the narcissistic issues—Zack's need to be a star, his wishful fantasy that something unexpected and magical would happen that would propel him into stardom without any effort or struggle on his part, his unwillingness to come to terms with the demands of reality in every sector of his life experience, and so on.

The shift to sitting up did not change the basic situation, did not diminish his resistance or resentment about therapy, did not precipitate any breakthroughs. But it kept the process going. Zack remained at his job, despite many complaints, difficulties, and negative feelings. His performance was always ambivalent, halfhearted, never enthusiastic or vigorous. Occasionally he might acknowledge that at times he enjoyed and felt challenged by the work, but his general attitude was that it was boring and unimportant and would never lead to the kind of success and fame he dreamed about. The narcissistic glow of idealized expectations was constantly tarnished by the drabness of reality. The prospect of an ordinary life, of ordinary accomplishments, and of an ordinary career, did not seem adequate or exciting enough. As I often put it to him, there did not seem to be a category "good enough" in his head.

The gains were modest. His work performance, as far as I could gather, was at times excellent, at times lackadaisical and negligent. He seemed to do just enough to keep himself afloat, but little more. Keeping his job was a triumph as far as I was concerned. On the personal front, more progress was made. He developed a deeper relationship with one woman that lasted over a period of several years. The relationship was on again, off again. They were engaged two or three times; on each occasion as the prospect of marriage drew near, Zack would get cold feet and pull out. He could not reconcile himself to a commitment to one woman for life. To him it seemed like a life sentence. As the relationship deepened, he would look at every attractive woman who passed on the street as a lost opportunity: they were all more beautiful, more talented, more exciting, more intelligent than his prospective bride. The operative criterion seemed to be whether the woman in question would enhance his standing and facilitate his search for stardom. If he could attach himself to a strikingly beautiful, intelligent, talented woman, she would bring him closer to his wished-for goal.

At one point, his girlfriend threw him out and said that she never wanted to see him again. He was crestfallen, spent a period of time licking his wounds, but then set out again on his search for the perfect woman. The pickings were apparently slim. There was something wrong with every woman he met. After some months he reestablished contact with his former fiancée, and following a time of remarkably attentive effort on his part they were again engaged and soon after married. Another triumphant step forward, I thought.

At this juncture, Zack requested that we cut back the therapy time, partly for financial concerns and partly because of uncertainty about whether he needed to continue the therapy. We cut back to twice a week. A major issue in this phase was his relationship with his new bride. All of his old complaints resurfaced: she was not the woman of his dreams; she was gaining weight, spent too much time in bed, was depressed, and so on. Having made a significant step forward, he seemed to want to undo it. He could not come to terms with the idea of having a less-than-perfect wife who would not add luster to his idealized image of himself. Stardom seemed even farther away.

The next significant event was his wife's pregnancy. Life was dragging Zack down the path to adulthood and responsibility whether he liked it or not. But he was making the trip, complaining and grumbling at every step, cherishing his dreams of stardom and fame, and relinquishing his lost dreams with the greatest reluctance. Fatherhood loomed both as something thrilling, exciting, and challenging and as something terrifying and threatening. Could he accept the challenge, the responsibility? What did this new burden of having a wife and family mean for him? He no longer had the luxury of dallying and temporizing in the vain hope that some white light of inspiration would burst upon him and transport him to stardom. Could he deal with the prospect of having an ordinary family and ordinary children? How would he deal with the problem of his potential disappointment in the limitations and imperfections of a son or daughter of his own? Would he react in ways he thought his father had reacted to him—with disappointment and a failure to communicate any sense of acceptance and approval to the child?

I leave these questions unanswered because Zack's therapeutic effort still continues at its snail's pace. We deal with the same basic problems with sometimes stultifying repetitiousness. They resurface in every facet of Zack's life. The current trajectory of his therapy, as far as I can envision, is along the lines of an attenuated psychotherapy. My sense at this juncture is that Zack will never fully resolve the issues we have been dealing with, but he will make his uncertain way through life with regret, ambiguity, and ambivalence—unwillingly and tentatively walking a path that fate dictates for him rather than one he might choose. I foresee a slow process of reducing the therapeutic time and commitment, gradually increasing the intervals between sessions, until the therapeutic contact approaches an asymptotic minimum.

Reading this case material, the analytic eye cannot help but be impressed by the presence of powerful oedipal themes, particularly issues having to do with Zack's identification with and highly threatening rivalry with his father. While the oedipal themes play a significant role in this case, one must also be impressed with the narcissistic factors, which are even more significant and central in determining the pattern of Zack's psychopathology. But neither one, however powerful and pervasive it may seem in the clinical material, speaks to the overriding conflictual issue in Zack's life, namely his inability to commit himself to any concrete life trajectory. He could not enter into the process of life with all its uncertainties, limitations, and potentialities. This issue was overdetermined on several levels: phallic-oedipal conflicts raised the threat of retaliation from the possibility of competing successfully against the father and thus killing him; narcissistic issues prevented him from engaging in a path of endeavor or commitment that did not guarantee the stardom he imagined and at the same time meant the surrender of alternate possibilities that might fulfill his dreams.

Commitment to any one path of life and work meant the relinquishment of all other possiblities—the dilemma of lost opportunities. These all played a role in determining the failure in his capacity to establish and maintain a secure, stable, and consistent identity—the central flaw that made his pathology a variant of the basic schizoid dilemma. The exquisite vulnerability of the self is protected, not by isolation and withdrawal from meaningful relationships (schizoid personality), not by erection of a compliant facade (false-self personality), not by shifting imitative adaptations ("as-if" personality), but by a withholding from life commitments and definitive roles in an effort to preserve the self from threat by not having an identity, or at least not having an identity sufficiently anchored to the substratum of human existence so as to run the risks of that alternative. The identity stasis patient solves the schizoid problem by presenting a moving target or, even better, as little target as possible.

This form of pathology, to the extent that it can be substantiated, does not have its deficit in neurotic conflict or pervasive ambivalence alone, or in simple narcissistic vulnerability, in specific ego defects, or in superego deficiencies. All of these may enter the picture in varying proportions and degrees, but the basic pathology is in the self-system of these patients, in the incapacity to establish and maintain a definite, consistent, and enduring self-organization and identity. It is this failure in the self-system, along with the sense of core vulnerability dictated by the dynamics of the underlying victim-introject, and the predominance of issues of dependence that creates the characteristic paralysis in life trajectory (as well as in the analytic process) that place these patients within the borderline spectrum. Patients of this ilk are prime candidates for an interminable and irresolvable analytic process.

REFERENCES

Aakrog, T. (1977). Borderline and psychotic adolescents: borderline symptomatology from childhood—actual therapeutic approach. *Journal of Youth and Adolescence* 6:187–197.

Abend, S. (1982). Serious illness in the analyst: countertransference considerations. *Journal of the American Psychoanalytic Association* 30:365–379.

Abend, S. M., Porder, M. S., and Willick, M. S. (1983). *Borderline Patients: Psychoanalytic Perspectives*. New York: International Universities Press.

Adelman, S. A. (1985). Pills as transitional objects: a dynamic understanding of the use of medication in psychotherapy. *Psychiatry* 48:246–253.

Adler, G. (1970). Valuing and devaluing in the psychotherapeutic process. *Archives of General Psychiatry* 22:454–461.

—— (1973). Hospital treatment of borderline patients. *American Journal of Psychiatry* 130:32–36.

—— (1974). Regression in psychotherapy: disruptive or therapeutic? *International Journal of Psychoanalytic Psychotherapy* 3:252–264.

—— (1975). The usefulness of the "borderline" concept in psychotherapy. In *Borderline States in Psychiatry*, ed. J. E. Mack, pp. 29–40. New York: Grune and Stratton.

—— (1977). Hospital management of borderline patients and its relation to psychotherapy. In *Borderline Personality Disorders: The Concept, the Syndrome, the Patient*, ed. P. Hartocollis, pp. 307–323. New York: International Universities Press.

—— (1979). The myth of the alliance with borderline patients. *American Journal of Psychiatry* 136:642–645.

—— (1980a). Transference, real relationship, and alliance. *International Journal of Psycho-Analysis* 61:547–558.

—— (1980b). A treatment framework for adult patients with borderline and narcissistic personality disorders. *Bulletin of the Menninger Clinic* 44: 171–180.

—— (1981). The borderline-narcissistic personality disorder continuum. *American Journal of Psychiatry* 138:46–50.

—— (1982). Supportive psychotherapy revisited. *Hillside Journal of Clinical Psychiatry* 4:3–13.

—— (1985). *Borderline Psychopathology and Its Treatment.* New York: Jason Aronson.

Adler, G., and Buie, D. H. (1972). The misuses of confrontation with borderline patients. *International Journal of Psychoanalytic Psychotherapy* 1: 109–120.

—— (1979). Aloneness and borderline psychopathology: the possible relevance of child development issues. *International Journal of Psycho-Analysis* 60:83–96.

Adler, G., and Myerson, P. G., eds. (1973a). *Confrontation in Psychotherapy.* New York: Science House.

—— (1973b). Introduction. In *Confrontation in Psychotherapy*, ed. G. Adler and P. G. Myerson, pp. 9–19. New York: Science House.

Alexander, F. (1950). Analysis of the therapeutic factors in psychoanalytic treatment. In *The Scope of Psychoanalysis*, pp. 261–275. New York: Basic Books, 1961.

Andrulonis, P. A., Glueck, B. C., Stroebel, C. F., Vogel, N. G., Shapiro, A. L., and Aldridge, D. M. (1980). Organic brain dysfunction and the borderline syndrome. *Psychiatric Clinics of North America* 4:47–66.

Appel, G. (1974). An approach to the treatment of schizoid phenomena. *Psychoanalytic Review* 61:99–113.

Appelbaum, S. A. (1978–1979). How strictly confidential? *International Journal of Psychoanalytic Psychotherapy* 7:220–224.

Arkema, P. H. (1981). The borderline personality and transitional relatedness. *American Journal of Psychiatry* 138:172–177.

Arlow, J. A. (1966). Depersonalization and derealization. In *Psychoanalysis—A General Psychology*, ed. R. M. Loewenstein, L. Newman, M. Schur, and A. J. Solnit, pp. 456–478. New York: International Universities Press.

Atkin, S. (1974). A borderline case: ego synthesis and cognition. *International Journal of Psycho-Analysis* 55:13–19.

Atkins, N. B. (1967). Comments on severe and psychotic regressions in analysis. *Journal of the American Psychoanalytic Association* 15:584–605.

Atwood, G., and Stolorow, R. (1984). *Structures of Subjectivity: Explorations in Psychoanalytic Phenomenology.* Hillsdale, NJ: Analytic Press.

Balint, M. (1968). *The Basic Fault: Therapeutic Aspects of Regression.* London: Tavistock.

Balint, M., Ornstein, P. H., and Balint, E. (1972). *Focal Psychotherapy.* London: Tavistock.

Barley, W. D., Thorward, S. R., Logue, A., McCready, K. F., Muller, J. P., Plakun, E. M., and Callahan, T. (1986). Characteristics of borderline personality disorder admissions to private psychiatric hospitals. *The Psychiatric Hospital* 17:195–199.

Berg, M. (1982). Psychological testing of the borderline patient: a guide for therapeutic action. *American Journal of Psychotherapy* 36:536–546.

——— (1983). Borderline psychopathology as displayed on psychological tests. *Journal of Personality Assessment* 47:120–133.

Berg, M. D. (1977). The externalizing transference. *International Journal of Psycho-Analysis* 58:235–244.

Berger, P. A. (1987). Pharmacological treatment for borderline personality disorder. *Bulletin of the Menninger Clinic* 51(3):277–284.

Berkowitz, D. A., Shapiro, R. L., Zinner, J., and Shapiro, E. R. (1974a). Concurrent family treatment of narcissistic disorders in adolescence. *International Journal of Psychoanalytic Psychotherapy* 3:371–396.

——— (1974b). Family contributions to narcissistic disturbances in adolescents. *International Review of Psycho-Analysis* 1:353–362.

Berry, S. L., and Roath, M. (1982). Family treatment of a borderline personality. *Clinical Social Work Journal* 10:3–14.

Bion, W. R. (1957). Differentiation of the psychotic from the non-psychotic personalities. *International Journal of Psycho-Analysis* 38:266–273.

——— (1962). Learning from experience. In *Seven Servants*, pp. 1–111. New York: Jason Aronson, 1977.

——— (1967). *Second Thoughts.* London: Heinemann.

——— (1977). *Seven Servants: Four Works by Wilfred R. Bion.* New York: Jason Aronson.

Blanck, G., and Blanck, R. (1974). *Ego Psychology: Theory and Practice.* New York: Columbia University Press.

——— (1979). *Ego Psychology II: Psychoanalytic Developmental Psychology.* New York: Columbia Press.

Blatt, S., Brenneis, B., Schimek, J., and Glick, M. (1976). Normal development and psychopathological impairment of the concept of the object on the Rorschach. *Journal of Abnormal Psychology* 85:364–373.

Blos, P. (1967). The second individuation process of adolescence. *Psychoanalytic Study of the Child* 22:162–186.

Blum, H. P. (1972). Psychoanalytic understanding and psychotherapy of borderline regression. *International Journal of Psychoanalytic Psychotherapy* 1(1):46–60.

——— (1973). The concept of erotized transference. *Journal of the American Psychoanalytic Association* 21:61–76.

——— (1974). The borderline childhood of the Wolf Man. *Journal of the American Psychoanalytic Association* 22:721–742.

Book, H. E. (1984). Treatment models need not conflict (Letter). *American Journal of Psychiatry* 141:1133–1134.

Book, H. E., Sadavoy, J., and Silver, D. (1978). Staff countertransference to borderline patients on an inpatient unit. *American Journal of Psychotherapy* 32(4):521–532.

Boris, H. N. (1973). Confrontation in the analysis of transference resistance. In *Confrontation in Psychotherapy*, ed. G. Adler and P. G. Myerson, pp. 181–206. New York: Science House.

Boschan, P. J. (1987). Dependence and narcissistic resistances in the psychoanalytic process. *International Journal of Psycho–Analysis* 68:109–118.

Boyer, L. B. (1978). Countertransference experiences with severely regressed patients. *Contemporary Psychoanalysis* 14:48–72.

—— (1983). *The Regressed Patient.* New York: Jason Aronson.

Boyer, L. B., and Giovacchini, P. L. (1967). *Psychoanalytic Treatment of Schizophrenic and Characterological Disorders.* New York: Jason Aronson.

—— (1980). *Psychoanalytic Treatment of Schizophrenic, Borderline, and Characterological Disorders.* 2nd ed. New York: Jason Aronson.

Brenner, C. (1980). Working alliance, therapeutic alliance and transference. In *Psychoanalytic Explorations of Technique: Discourse on the Theory of Therapy*, ed. H. P. Blum, pp. 137–157. New York: International Universities Press.

Brinkley, J., Beitman, B., and Freidel, R. (1979). Low-dose neuroleptic regimines in the treatment of borderline patients. *Archives of General Psychiatry* 36:319–326.

Brody, E. B. (1960). Borderline state, character disorder, and psychotic manifestations: some conceptual formulations. *Psychiatry* 23:75–80.

Bromberg, P. M. (1984). Getting into oneself and out of one's self: on schizoid processes. *Contemporary Psychoanalysis* 20:439–448.

Brown, L. J. (1980). Staff countertransference reactions in the hospital treatment of borderline patients. *Psychiatry* 43:333–345.

—— (1987). Borderline personality organization and the transition to the depressive position. In *The Borderline Patient: Emerging Concepts in Diagnosis, Psychodynamics, and Treatment*, vol. 1, ed. J. S. Grotstein, M. F. Solomon, and J. A. Lang, pp. 147–180. Hillside, NJ: The Analytic Press.

Buie, D. H. (1977). Discussion of the paper by E. R. Shapiro, R. L. Shapiro, J. Zinner, and D. A. Berkowitz on "The borderline ego and the working alliance: Indications for family and individual treatment in adolescents." *International Journal of Psycho-Analysis* 58:89–93.

Buie, D. H., and Adler, G. (1972). The uses of confrontation with borderline patients. *International Journal of Psychoanalytic Psychotherapy* 1:90–108.

—— (1973). The uses of confrontation in the psychotherapy of borderline patients. In *Confrontation in Psychotherapy*, ed. G. Adler and P. G. Myerson, pp. 123–146. New York: Science House.

——— (1982–1983). Definitive treatment of the borderline personality. *International Journal of Psychoanalytic Psychotherapy* 9:51–87.

Burke, W. F., and Tansey, M. J. (1985). Projective identification and countertransference turmoil: disruptions in the empathic process. *Contemporary Psychoanalysis* 21:372–402.

Burnham, D. L., Gladstone, A. I., and Gibson, R. W. (1969). *Schizophrenia and the Need-Fear Dilemma.* New York: International Universities Press.

Campbell, K. (1982). The psychotherapy relationship with borderline personality disorder. *Psychotherapy: Theory, Research and Practice* 19:166–193.

Carr, A. C., Goldstein, E. G., Hunt, H. F., and Kernberg, O. (1979). Psychological tests and borderline patients. *Journal of Personality Assessment* 43:582–590.

Carsky, M. (1985–1986). The resolution of impasses in long-term intensive, inpatient psychotherapy. *International Journal of Psychoanalytic Psychotherapy* 11:435–454.

Cassimatis, E. G. (1984). The "false self": existential and therapeutic issues. *International Review of Psycho-Analysis* 11:69–77.

Chediak, C. (1979). Counter-reactions and countertransference. *International Journal of Psycho-Analysis* 60:117–129.

Chessick, R. D. (1968). The "crucial dilemma" of the therapist in the psychotherapy of borderline patients. *American Journal of Psychotherapy* 22:655–666.

——— (1971). The use of the couch in psychotherapy of borderline patients. *Archives of General Psychiatry* 25:306–313.

——— (1974). Defective ego feeling: the quest for being in the borderline patient. *International Journal of Psychoanalytic Psychotherapy* 3:73–89.

——— (1977). *Intensive Psychotherapy of the Borderline Patient.* New York: Jason Aronson.

——— (1978). Countertransference crises with borderline patients. *Current Concepts in Psychiatry* (Jan.–Feb.), 20–24.

——— (1979). A practical approach to the psychotherapy of the borderline patient. *American Journal of Psychotherapy* 33:531–546.

——— (1982). Intensive psychotherapy of a borderline patient. *Archives of General Psychiatry* 39:413–419.

——— (1983a). Problems in the intensive psychotherapy of the borderline patient. *Dynamic Psychotherapy* 1:20–32.

——— (1983b). Marilyn Monroe: psychoanalytic pathography of a preoedipal disorder. *Dynamic Psychotherapy* 1:161–176.

Chethik, M. (1986). Levels of borderline functioning in children: etiological and treatment considerations. *American Journal of Orthopsychiatry* 56:109–119.

Chopra, H. D., and Beatson, J. A. (1986). Psychotic symptom in borderline personality disorder. *American Journal of Psychiatry* 143:1605–1607.

Chwast, J. (1977). Psychotherapy of disadvantaged acting-out adolescents. *American Journal of Psychotherapy* 31:216–226.

Clifton, A. R. (1974). Regression in the search for a self. *International Journal of Psychoanalytic Psychotherapy* 3:273–292.

Cole, J. O. (1980). Drug therapy of borderline patients. *McLean Hospital Journal* 5:110–125.

Collum, J. M. (1972). Identity diffusion and the borderline maneuver. *Comprehensive Psychiatry* 13:179–184.

Colson, D. B. (1982). Protectiveness in borderline states: a neglected object-relations paradigm. *Bulletin of the Menninger Clinic* 46:305–320.

Colson, D. B., Lewis, L., and Horwitz, L. (1982). Negative effects in psychotherapy and psychoanalysis. In *Above All Do Not Harm: Negative Outcome in Psychotherapy*, ed. D. Mays and C. Franks. New York: Jason Aronson.

Colson, D. B., et al. (1985). Patterns of staff perception of difficult patients in a long-term psychiatric hospital. *Hospital and Community Psychiatry* 36(2):168–172.

——— (1986). An anatomy of countertransference: staff reactions to difficult psychiatric hospital patients. *Hospital and Community Psychiatry* 37(9):923–928.

Cooper, S. H., Perry, J. C., Hoke, L., and Richman, N. (1985). Transitional relatedness and borderline personality disorder. *Psychoanalytic Psychology* 2:115–128.

Coppolillo, H. P. (1967). Maturational aspects of the transitional phenomenon. *International Journal of Psycho-Analysis* 48:237–246.

Corwin, H. A. (1973). Therapeutic confrontation from routine to heroic. In *Confrontation in Psychotherapy*, ed. G. Adler and P. G. Myerson, pp. 67–95. New York: Science House.

Cowdry, R. W. (1987). Psychopharmacology of borderline personality disorder: a review. *Journal of Clinical Psychiatry* 48 (Suppl.)8:15–22.

Crabtree, L. H. (1982). Hospitalized adolescents who act out: a treatment approach. *Psychiatry* 45:147–158.

Davanloo, H., ed. (1980). *Short-term Dynamic Psychotherapy*. New York: Jason Aronson.

Day, M., and Semrad, E. (1971). Group therapy with neurotics and psychotics. In *Comprehensive Group Psychotherapy*, ed. H. I. Kaplan and B. J. Sadock, pp. 566–580. Baltimore: Williams and Wilkins.

Deniker, P., and Quintart, J. C. (1961). Les signes pseudo-nevrotiques dans les formes limites de la schizophrenie. *Encephale* 50:307–323.

DeSaussure, J. (1974). Discussion of the paper by Samuel Atkin. *International Journal of Psycho-Analysis* 55:21–23.

Deutsch, H. (1942). Some forms of emotional disturbance and their relationship to schizophrenia. *Psychoanalytic Quarterly* 11:301–321.

Devereux, G. (1951). Some criteria for the timing of confrontations and interpretations. *International Journal of Psycho-Analysis* 32:19–24.

Diatkine, R. (1968). Indications and contraindications for psychoanalytic treatment. *International Journal of Psycho-Analysis* 49:266–270.

Dickes, R. (1967). Severe regressive disruptions of the therapeutic alliance. *Journal of the American Psychoanalytic Association* 15:508–533.

—— (1975). Technical considerations of the therapeutic and working alliances. *International Journal of Psychoanalytic Psychotherapy* 4:1–24.

Easser, R., and Lesser, S. (1965). Hysterical personality: a re-evaluation. *Psychoanalytic Quarterly* 34:390–402.

Eigen, M. (1973). Abstinence and the schizoid ego. *International Journal of Psycho-Analysis* 54:493–498.

Ekstein, R., and Wallerstein, J. (1954). Observations on the psychology of borderline and psychotic children. *Psychoanalytic Study of the Child* 9:344–369.

—— (1956). Observations on the psychotherapy of borderline and psychotic children. *Psychoanalytic Study of the Child* 11:303–311.

Ellison, J. M., and Adler, D. A. (1984). Psychopharmacological approaches to borderline syndromes. *Comprehensive Psychiatry* 25:255–262.

Erikson, E. H. (1956). The problem of ego identity. *Journal of the American Psychoanalytic Association* 4:56–121.

Evans, R. W., Ruff, R. M., Braff, D. L., and Ainsworth, T. L. (1984). MMPI characteristics of borderline personality inpatients. *Journal of Nervous and Mental Disease* 172:742–748.

Fairbairn, W. R. D. (1952). *Psychoanalytic Studies of Personality*. London: Tavistock.

—— (1954). *An Object-Relations Theory of the Personality*. New York: Basic Books.

—— (1958). On the nature and aims of psycho-analytical treatment. *International Journal of Psycho-Analysis* 39:374–385.

Fast, I. (1975). Aspects of work style and work difficulty in borderline personalities. *International Journal of Psycho-Analysis* 56:397–403.

Feighner, J. P. (1982). Benzodiazepines as antidepressants: a triazolobenzodiazepine used to treat depression. In *Modern Problems of Pharmacopsychiatry*, vol. 18, ed. T. A. Bass and colleagues, pp. 196–212. Basel: Karger.

Feinsilver, D. B. (1980). Transitional relatedness and containment in the treatment of a chronic schizophrenic patient. *International Journal of Psycho-Analysis* 7:309–318.

—— (1983). Reality, transitional relatedness, and containment in the borderline. *Contemporary Psychoanalysis* 19:537–569.

Feinstein, S. C., and Uribe, V. (1985). Hospitalization of young people: rationale and criteria. *Psychiatric Annals* 15:602–605.

Finell, J. S. (1985). Narcissistic problems in analysis. *International Journal of Psycho-Analysis* 66:433–445.

Fintzy, R. T. (1971). Vicissitudes of the transitional object in borderline children. *International Journal of Psycho-Analysis* 52:107-114.

Fisher, S. F. (1985). Identity of two: the phenomenology of shame in borderline development and treatment. *Psychotherapy* 22:101-109.

Freud, S. (1911). Psychoanalytic notes on an autobiographical account of a case of paranoia (dementia paranoides). *Standard Edition* 12:1-82.

—— (1912). The dynamics of transference. *Standard Edition* 12:97-108.

—— (1915). Observations on transference-love. *Standard Edition* 12:157-171.

—— (1916). Some character-types met with in psychoanalytic work. *Standard Edition* 14:309-333.

—— (1918). From the history of an infantile neurosis. *Standard Edition* 17:1-123.

—— (1921). Group psychology and the analysis of the ego. *Standard Edition* 18:65-143.

Friedman, H. J. (1969). Some problems of inpatient management with borderline patients. *American Journal of Psychiatry* 126:299-304.

—— (1975). Psychotherapy of borderline patients: the influence of theory on technique. *American Journal of Psychiatry* 132:1048-1052.

—— (1976). Dr. Friedman replies (Letter). *American Journal of Psychiatry* 133:453.

—— (1979). Exaggerated transference conflict as a criterion for the diagnosis of borderline personality. *Hillside Journal of Clinical Psychiatry* 1:123-142.

Friedman, L. (1986). Kohut's testament. *Psychoanalytic Inquiry* 6:321-347.

Friedman, R. C., Aronoff, M. S., Clarkin, J. F., Corn, R., and Hunt, S. W. (1983). History of suicidal behavior in depressed borderline inpatients. *American Journal of Psychiatry* 140:1023-1026.

Frieswyk, S., and Colson, D. (1980). Prognostic considerations in the hospital treatment of borderline states: the perspective of object relations theory and the Rorschach. In *Borderline Phenomena and the Rorschach Test*, ed. J. S. Kwawer, pp. 229-255. New York: International Universities Press.

Frijling-Schreuder, E. C. M. (1969). Borderline states in children. *Psychoanalytic Study of the Child* 24:307-327.

Frosch, J. (1964). The psychotic character: clinical psychiatric considerations. *Psychoanalytic Quarterly* 38:81-96.

—— (1967a). Severe regressive states during analysis: introduction. *Journal of the American Psychoanalytic Association* 15:491-507.

—— (1967b). Severe regressive states during analysis: summary. *Journal of the American Psychoanalytic Association* 15:606-625.

—— (1970). Psychoanalytic considerations of the psychotic character. *Journal of the American Psychoanalytic Association* 18:24-50.

—— (1983). *The Psychotic Process*. New York: International Universities Press.

Galatzer-Levy, R. M. (1987). The borderline and severely neurotic child (panel report). *Journal of the American Psychoanalytic Association* 35:189–201.

Gardner, C. S., and Wagner, S. (1986). Clinical diagnosis of the as-if personality disorder. *Bulletin of the Menninger Clinic* 50:135–147.

Gardner, D. L., and Cowdry, R. W. (1985). Alprazolam-induced dyscontrol in borderline personality disorder. *American Journal of Psychiatry* 142:98–100.

—— (1986). Positive effects of carbamazepine on behavioral dyscontrol in borderline personality disorder. *American Journal of Psychiatry* 143:519–522.

Gediman, H. K. (1985). Imposture, inauthenticity, and feeling fraudulent. *Journal of the American Psychoanalytic Association* 33:911–935.

George, A., and Soloff, P. H. (1986). Schizotypal symptoms in patients with borderline personality disorders. *American Journal of Psychiatry* 143:212–215.

Gill, M. M. (1979). The analysis of the transference. *Journal of the American Psychoanalytic Association* 27 (Suppl.):263–288.

—— (1982). *Analysis of Transference*. New York: International Universities Press.

—— (1984). Psychoanalysis and psychoanalytic psychotherapy: a proposed revision. *International Review of Psycho-Analysis* 11:161–179.

Giovacchini, P. L. (1965). Transference, incorporation and synthesis. *International Journal of Psycho-Analysis* 46:287–296.

—— (1967a). The frozen introject. *International Journal of Psycho-Analysis* 48:61–67.

—— (1967b). Frustration and externalization. *Psychoanalytic Quarterly* 36:571–584.

—— (1970). Characterological problems: the need to be helped. *Archives of General Psychiatry* 22:245–251.

—— (1972). Technical difficulties in treating some characterological disorders: countertransference problems. *International Journal of Psychoanalytic Psychotherapy* 1:112–128.

—— (1973a). Character disorders: form and structure. *International Journal of Psycho-Analysis* 54:153–161.

—— (1973b). Character disorders: with special reference to the borderline state. *International Journal of Psychoanalytic Psychotherapy* 2:7–36.

—— (1975a). *Psychoanalysis of Character Disorders*. New York: Jason Aronson.

—— (1975b). Self-projections in the narcissistic transference. *International Journal of Psychoanalytic Psychotherapy* 4:142–167.

—— (1979). *Treatment of Primitive Mental States*. New York: Jason Aronson.

—— (1987a). The borderline state, the transitional object, and the psychoanalytic paradox. In *The Borderline Patient: Emerging Concepts in Diagno-*

sis, Psychodynamics, and Treatment, vol. 2, ed. J. S. Grotstein, M. F. Solomon, and J. A. Lang, pp. 181–204. Hillsdale, NJ: Analytic Press.

—— (1987b). The "unreasonable" patient and the psychotic transference. In *The Borderline Patient: Emerging Concepts in Diagnosis, Psychodynamics, and Treatment*, vol. 2, ed. J. S. Grotstein, M. F. Solomon, and J. A. Lang, pp. 59–68. Hillsdale, NJ: Analytic Press.

Giovacchini, P. L., and Boyer, L. B. (1975). The psychoanalytic impasse. *International Journal of Psychoanalytic Psychotherapy* 4:25–47.

Glover, E. (1955). *The Technique of Psychoanalysis.* New York: International Universities Press.

Goldberg, A. I. (1974). On the prognosis and treatment of narcissism. *Journal of the American Psychoanalytic Association* 22:243–254.

Goldstein, M. J., and Jones, J. E. (1977). Adolescent and family precursors of borderline and schizophrenic conditions. In *Borderline Personality Disorders: The Concept, the Syndrome, the Patient*, ed. P. Hartocollis, pp. 213–229. New York: International Universities Press.

Goldstein, W. (1985). *An Introduction to the Borderline Conditions.* New York: Jason Aronson.

Gordon, C., and Beresin, E. (1983). Conflicting treatment models for the inpatient management of borderline patients. *American Journal of Psychiatry* 140:979–983.

Green, A. (1977). The borderline concept. In *Borderline Personality Disorders: The Concept, the Syndrome, the Patient*, ed. P. Hartocollis, pp. 15–44. New York: International Universities Press.

Greenacre, P. (1956). Problems of overidealization of the analyst and of analysis. *Psychoanalytic Study of the Child* 21:193–212.

—— (1959). Certain technical problems in the transference relationship. *Journal of the American Psychoanalytic Association* 7:484–502.

Greenberg, R., Craig, S., Seidman, L. J., Cooper, S., and Teele, A. (1987). Transitional phenomena and the Rorschach: a test of clinical theory of borderline personality organization. In *The Borderline Patient: Emerging Concepts in Diagnosis, Psychodynamics, and Treatment*, vol. 2, ed. J. S. Grotstein, M. F. Solomon, and J. A. Lang, pp. 83–94. Hillsdale, NJ: Analytic Press.

Greenson, R. R. (1965). The working alliance and the transference neurosis. In *Explorations in Psychoanalysis*, pp. 199–224. New York: International Universities Press, 1978.

—— (1967). *The Technique and Practice of Psychoanalysis.* New York: International Universities Press.

Greenson, R. R., and Wexler, M. (1969). The non-transference relationship in the psychoanalytic situation. *International Journal of Psycho-Analysis* 50:27–39.

Greenspan, S. I., and Cullander, C. C. H. (1973). A systematic metapsychological assessment of the personality: its application to the problem of analyzability. *Journal of the American Psychoanalytic Association* 21:303–327.

Greenspan, S. I., and Mannino, F. V. (1974). A model for brief intervention with couples based on projective identification. *American Journal of Psychiatry* 131:1103–1106.

Grinberg, L. (1962). On a specific aspect of countertransference due to the patient's projective identification. *International Journal of Psycho-Analysis* 43:436–440.

———— (1979). Countertransference and projective counteridentification. *Contemporary Psychoanalysis* 15:226–247.

———— (1987). Dreams and acting out. *Psychoanalytic Quarterly* 56:155–176.

Grinberg, L., and Grinberg, R. (1974). Pathological aspects of identity in adolescence. *Contemporary Psychoanalysis* 10:27–40.

Grinker, R. R. (1977). The borderline syndrome: a phenomenological view. In *Borderline Personality Disorders: The Concept, the Syndrome, the Patient*, ed. P. Hartocollis, pp. 159–172. New York: International Universities Press.

Grinker, R. R., Werble, B., and Drye, R. C. (1968). *The Borderline Syndrome: A Behavioral Study of Ego Functions*. New York: Basic Books.

Grotstein, J. S. (1980). A proposed revision of the psychoanalytic concept of primitive mental states, Part I. Introduction to a newer psychoanalytic metapsychology. *Contemporary Psychoanalysis* 16:479–546.

———— (1981). *Splitting and Projective Identification*. New York: Jason Aronson.

———— (1983). A proposed revision of the psychoanalytic concept of primitive mental states, Part II. The borderline syndrome. Section 1: Disorders of autistic safety and symbiotic relatedness. *Contemporary Psychoanalysis* 19:570–604.

———— (1984). A proposed revision of the psychoanalytic concept of primitive mental states, Part II. The borderline syndrome. Section 2: The phenomenology of the borderline syndrome. *Contemporary Psychoanalysis* 20:77–119.

Grotstein, J. S., Lang, J. A., and Solomon, M. F. (1987a). Convergence and controversy: II. Treatment of the borderline. In *The Borderline Patient: Emerging Concepts in Diagnosis, Psychodynamics, and Treatment*, vol. 2, ed. J. S. Grotstein, M. F. Solomon, and J. A. Lang, pp. 261–310. Hillsdale, NJ: Analytic Press.

———— (1987b). Toward a new understanding of the borderline: reflections. In *The Borderline Patient: Emerging Concepts in Diagnosis, Psychodynamics, and Treatment*, vol. 2, ed. J. S. Grotstein, M. F. Solomon, and J. A. Lang, pp. 311–318. Hillsdale, NJ: Analytic Press.

Grotstein, J. S., Solomon, M. F., and Lang, J. A., eds. (1987). *The Borderline Patient: Emerging Concepts in Diagnosis, Psychodynamics, and Treatment*. 2 volumes. Hillsdale, NJ: Analytic Press.

Grunebaum, H. (1957). Combined psychoanalytic therapy with negative therapeutic reactions. In *Schizophrenia in Psychoanalytic Office Practice*, ed. A. H. Rifkin, pp. 56–65. New York: Grune and Stratton.

Grunebaum, H., and Solomon, L. (1980). Toward a peer theory of group psychotherapy. I. On the developmental significance of peers and play. *International Journal of Group Psychotherapy* 30:23–49.

—— (1982). Toward a theory of peer relationships. II. On the stages of social development and their relationship to group psychotherapy. *International Journal of Group Psychotherapy* 32:283–307.

Gudeman, J. E. (1974). Uncontrolled regression in therapy and analysis. *International Journal of Psychoanalytic Psychotherapy* 3:325–338.

Gunderson, J. G. (1977). Characteristics of borderlines. In *Borderline Personality Disorders: The Concept, the Syndrome, the Patient*, ed. P. Hartocollis, pp. 173–192. New York: International Universities Press.

—— (1984). *Borderline Personality Disorganization*. Washington: American Psychiatric Press.

—— (1987). Interfaces between psychoanalysis and empirical studies of borderline personality. In *The Borderline Patient: Emerging Concepts in Diagnosis, Psychodynamics, and Treatment*, vol. 1, ed. J. S. Grotstein, M. F. Solomon, and J. A. Lang, pp. 37–59. Hillsdale, NJ: Analytic Press.

Gunderson, J. G., Kerr, J., and Eglund, D. W. (1980). The families of borderlines: a comparative study. *Archives of General Psychiatry* 37:27–33.

Gunderson, J. G., and Kolb, J. E. (1978). Discriminating features of borderline patients. *American Journal of Psychiatry* 135:792–796.

Gunderson, J. G., Kolb, J. E., and Austin, V. (1981). The diagnostic interview for borderline patients. *American Journal of Psychiatry* 138:896–903.

Gunderson, J. G., Morris, H., and Zanarini, M. C. (1985). Transitional objects and borderline patients. In *The Borderline: Current Empirical Research*, ed. T. H. McGlashan, pp. 43–60. Washington, D.C.: American Psychiatric Press.

Gunderson, J. G., Schulz, C. G., and Feinsilver, D. B. (1975). Matching therapists with schizophrenic patients. In *Psychotherapy of Schizophrenia*, ed. J. S. Gunderson and L. R. Mosher, pp. 343–359. New York: Jason Aronson.

Gunderson, J. G., and Singer, M. J. (1975). Defining borderline patients: an overview. *American Journal of Psychiatry* 132:1–10.

Gunderson, J. G., and Zanarini, M. C. (1987). Current overview of the borderline diagnosis. *Journal of Clinical Psychiatry* 48 (Suppl.)8:5–11.

Guntrip, H. (1961). *Personality Structure and Human Interaction*. New York: International Universities Press.

—— (1969). *Schizoid Phenomena, Object Relations, and the Self*. New York: International Universities Press.

—— (1973). *Psychoanalytic Theory, Therapy, and the Self*. New York: Basic Books.

Gutheil, T. G. (1985). Medicolegal pitfalls in the treatment of borderline patients. *American Journal of Psychiatry* 142(1):9–14.

Gutheil, T. G., and Havens, L. L. (1979). The transference alliance: contemporary meanings and confusions. *International Review of Psycho-Analysis* 6:467–481.

Guttman, S. A. (1960). Criteria for analyzability (panel report). *Journal of the American Psychoanalytic Association* 8:141–151.

Hartocollis, P., ed. (1977). *Borderline Personality Disorders: The Concept, the Syndrome, the Patient.* New York: International Universities Press.

———— (1980). Long-term hospital treatment for adult patients with borderline and narcissistic disorders. *Bulletin of the Menninger Clinic* 44:212–226.

Havens, L. L. (1968). Some difficulties in giving schizophrenic and borderline patients medication. *Psychiatry* 31:44–50.

Hedberg, D. L., Houck, J. H., and Glueck, B. C. (1971). Tranylcypromine-trifluoperazine combination in the treatment of schizophrenia. *American Journal of Psychiatry* 127:1141–1146.

Herschman, P. L. (1972). Team transference and resistance in the treatment of patients who act out. *Psychiatric Quarterly* 46:220–234.

Hoch, P. H., and Cattell, J. P. (1959). The diagnosis of pseudoneurotic schizophrenia. *Psychiatric Quarterly* 33:17–43.

Hoch, P. H., Cattell, J. P., Strahl, M. O., and Pennes, H. (1962). The course and outcome of pseudoneurotic schizophrenia. *American Journal of Psychiatry* 119:106–115.

Hoch, P., and Polatin, P. (1949). Pseudoneurotic forms of schizophrenia. *Psychoanalytic Quarterly* 23:248–276.

Hooberman, D., and Stern, T. A. (1984). Treatment of attention deficit and borderline personality disorders with psychostimulants: case report. *Journal of Clinical Psychiatry* 45:441–442.

Horner, A. J. (1975). Stages and processes in the development of early object relations and their associated pathologies. *International Review of Psycho-Analysis* 2:95–105.

———— (1979). *Object Relations and the Developing Ego in Therapy.* New York: Jason Aronson.

Horton, P. C., Louy, J. W., and Coppolillo, H. P. (1974). Personality disorder and transitional relatedness. *Archives of General Psychiatry* 30:618–622.

Horwitz, L. (1977). Group psychotherapy of the borderline patient. In *Borderline Personality Disorders: The Concept, the Syndrome, the Patient,* ed. P. Hartocollis, pp. 399–422. New York: International Universities Press.

———— (1987). Indications for group psychotherapy with borderline and narcissistic patients. *Bulletin of the Menninger Clinic* 51(3):248–260.

Hymowitz, P., Frances, A., Jacobsberg, L. B., Sickles, M., and Hoyt, R. (1986). Neuroleptic treatment of schizotypal personality disorders. *Comprehensive Psychiatry* 27:267–271.

Imhof, J., Hirsch, R., and Terenzi, R. E. (1984). Countertransferential and attitudinal considerations in the treatment of drug abuse and addiction. *Journal of Substance Abuse Treatment* 1:21–30.

Jacobs, T. J. (1986). On countertransference enactments. *Journal of the American Psychoanalytic Association* 34:289–307.

Jacobsberg, L. B., Hymowitz, P., Barasch, A., and Frances, A. J. (1986). Symptoms of schizotypal personality disorder. *American Journal of Psychiatry* 143:1222–1227.

Jacobson, E. (1959). The "exceptions": an elaboration of Freud's character study. *Psychoanalytic Study of the Child* 14:135–154.

—— (1964). *The Self and the Object World.* New York: International Universities Press.

Jenike, M. S., Baer, L., Minichiello, W. E., Schwartz, C. E., and Carey, R. J. (1986). Concomitant obsessive-compulsive disorder and schizotypal personality disorder. *American Journal of Psychiatry* 143:530–532.

Johansen, K. H. (1983). Transitional experience of a borderline patient. *Journal of Nervous and Mental Disease* 171:126–128.

Jones, S. A. (1987). Family therapy with borderline and narcissistic patients. *Bulletin of the Menninger Clinic* 51(3):285–295.

Joseph, B. (1985). Transference: the total situation. *International Journal of Psycho-Analysis* 66:447–454.

Keiser, S. (1958). Disturbances in abstract thinking and body-image formation. *Journal of the American Psychoanalytic Association* 6:628–652.

Kernberg, O. F. (1965). Notes on countertransference. *Journal of the American Psychoanalytic Association* 13:38–56.

—— (1966). Structural derivatives of object relations. *International Journal of Psycho-Analysis* 47:236–253.

—— (1967). Borderline personality organization. *Journal of the American Psychoanalytic Association* 15:641–685.

—— (1968). The treatment of patients with borderline personality organization. *International Journal of Psycho-Analysis* 49:600–619.

—— (1970). Factors in the psychoanalytic treatment of narcissistic personalities. *Journal of the American Psychoanalytic Association* 18:51–85.

—— (1971). Prognostic considerations regarding borderline personality organization. *Journal of the American Psychoanalytic Association* 19:595–635.

—— (1973). Psychoanalytic object-relations theory, group processes, and administration: toward an integrative theory of hospital treatment. *Annual of Psychoanalysis* 1:363–388.

—— (1974). Contrasting viewpoints regarding the nature and psychoanalytic treatment of narcissistic personalities: a preliminary communication. *Journal of the American Psychoanalytic Association* 22:255–267.

—— (1975a). *Borderline Conditions and Pathological Narcissism.* New York: Jason Aronson.

—— (1975b). Transference and countertransference in the treatment of borderline patients. *Strecker Monograph Series*, XII.

—— (1976a). *Object-Relations Theory and Clinical Psychoanalysis*. New York: Jason Aronson.

—— (1976b). Technical considerations in the treatment of borderline personality organization. *Journal of the American Psychoanalytic Association* 24:795–829.

—— (1977). The structural diagnosis of borderline personality organization. In *Borderline Personality Disorders: The Concept, the Syndrome, the Patient*, ed. P. Hartocollis, pp. 87–121. New York: International Universities Press.

—— (1978). The diagnosis of borderline conditions in adolescence. *Adolescent Psychiatry* 6:298–320.

—— (1979). Psychoanalytic psychotherapy with borderline adolescents. *Adolescent Psychiatry* 7:294–321.

—— (1984). *Severe Personality Disorders: Psychotherapeutic Strategies*. New Haven: Yale University Press.

—— (1987a). Diagnosis and clinical management of suicidal potential in borderline patients. In *The Borderline Patient: Emerging Concepts in Diagnosis, Psychodynamics, and Treatment*, vol. 2, ed. J. S. Grotstein, M. F. Solomon, and J. A. Lang, pp. 69–80. Hillsdale, NJ: Analytic Press.

—— (1987b). Projection and projective identification: developmental and clinical aspects. *Journal of the American Psychoanalytic Association* 35:795–819.

Kernberg, O. F., Burstein, E. D., Coyne, L., Appelbaum, A., Horwitz, L., and Voth, H. (1972). Psychotherapy and psychoanalysis: final report of the Menninger Foundation's Psychotherapeutic Research Project. *Bulletin of the Menninger Clinic* 36:i–277.

Khan, M. M. R. (1960). Regression and integration in the analytic setting. *International Journal of Psycho-Analysis* 41:130–146.

Kinston, W. (1983). A theoretical context for shame. *International Journal of Psycho-Analysis* 64:213–226.

Kirman, W. J. (1980). Countertransference in facilitating intimacy and communication. *Modern Psychoanalysis* 5:131–145.

Klein, D. F. (1975). Psychopharmacology and the borderline patient. In *Borderline States in Psychiatry*, ed. J. E. Mack, pp. 75–91. New York: Grune & Stratton, 1975.

—— (1977). Psychopharmacological treatment and delineation of borderline disorders. In *Borderline Personality Disorders: The Concept, the Syndrome, the Patient*, ed. P. Hartocollis, pp. 365–383. New York: International Universities Press.

Klein, M. (1946). Notes on some schizoid mechanisms. In *Envy and Gratitude and Other Works, 1946–1963*, pp. 1–24. New York: Delacorte, 1975.

—— (1952). The mutual influences in the development of ego and id. In

Envy and Gratitude and Other Works, 1946–1963, pp. 57–60. New York: Delacorte, 1975.

—— (1957). Envy and gratitude. In *Envy and Gratitude and Other Works, 1946–1963*, pp. 176–235. New York: Delacorte, 1975.

—— (1959). Our adult world and its roots in infancy. In *Envy and Grati-tude and Other Works, 1946–1963*, pp. 247–263. New York: Delacorte, 1975.

—— (1963). On the sense of loneliness. In *Envy and Gratitude and Other Works, 1946–1963*, pp. 300–313. New York: Delacorte, 1975.

Knapp, P. H., Levin, S., McCarter, R. H., Werner, H., and Zetzel, E. R. (1960). Suitability for psychoanalysis: a review of one hundred supervised analytic cases. *Psychoanalytic Quarterly* 29:459–477.

Knight, R. P. (1954a). Borderline states. In *Psychoanalytic Psychiatry and Psychology*, ed. R. P. Knight, pp. 97–109. New York: International Universities Press.

—— (1954b). Management and psychotherapy of the borderline schizo-phrenic patient. In *Psychoanalytic Psychiatry and Psychology*, ed. R. P. Knight, pp. 110–122. New York: International Universities Press.

Kohut, H. S. (1971). *The Analysis of the Self.* New York: International Universities Press.

—— (1972). Thoughts on narcissism and narcissistic rage. *Psychoanalytic Study of the Child* 27:360–400.

—— (1977). *The Restoration of the Self.* New York: International Universities Press.

—— (1984). *How Does Analysis Cure?* Chicago: University of Chicago Press.

Kohut, H. S., and Wolf, E. S. (1978). The disorders of the self and their treatment. *International Journal of Psycho-Analysis* 59:413–425.

—— (1982). The disorders of the self and their treatment. In *Curative Factors in Dynamic Psychotherapy*, ed. S. Slipp, pp. 44–59. New York: McGraw-Hill.

Kolb, J. E., and Gunderson, J. G. (1980). Diagnosing borderlines with a semistructural interview. *Archives of General Psychiatry* 37:37–41.

Kramer, P. (1958). Note on one of the preoedipal roots of the superego. *Journal of the American Psychoanalytic Association* 6:38–46.

Kris, A. O. (1985). Psychoanalysis and psychoanalytic psychotherapy. In *Psychiatry*, vol. 1, chapter 8, ed. R. Michels, pp. 1–13. Philadelphia: Lippincott, 1986.

Krohn, A. (1974). Borderline "empathy" and differentiation of object relation-ships: a contribution to the psychology of object relations. *International Journal of Psychoanalytic Psychotherapy* 3:142–165.

Kwawer, J. S. (1979). Borderline phenomena, interpersonal relations, and the Rorschach test. *Bulletin of the Menninger Clinic* 43:515–524.

Lachar, D., and Wrobel, T. A. (1979). Validating clinicians' hunches: construc-tion of a new MMPI critical item set. *Journal of Consulting and Clinical Psychology* 47:277–284.

Laing, R. D. (1965). *The Divided Self.* Middlesex, England: Penguin Books.

Lane, R. D., and Schwartz, G. E. (1987). Levels of emotional awareness: a cognitive-developmental theory and its application to psychopathology. *American Journal of Psychiatry* 144:133–143.

Langs, R. J. (1973). *The Technique of Psychoanalytic Psychotherapy.* Vol. 1. New York: Jason Aronson.

—— (1975a). Therapeutic misalliances. *International Journal of Psychoanalytic Psychotherapy* 4:77–105.

—— (1975b). The therapeutic relationship and deviations in technique. *International Journal of Psychoanalytic Psychotherapy* 4:106–141.

—— (1976). *The Therapeutic Interaction.* 2 vols. New York: Jason Aronson.

—— (1978–1979). Responses to creativity in psychoanalysts. *International Journal of Psychoanalytic Psychotherapy* 7:189–207.

Lehmann, A. E. (1985). Affective disorders: clinical features. In *Comprehensive Textbook of Psychiatry/IV,* ed. H. I. Kaplan and B. J. Sadock, pp. 786–811. Baltimore: Williams and Wilkins.

Leibovich, M. A. (1981). Short-term psychotherapy for borderline personality disorder. *Psychotherapy and Psychosomatics* 35:257–264.

—— (1983). Why short-term psychotherapy for borderlines? *Psychotherapy and Psychosomatics* 39:1–9.

Lerner, H. (1986). Research perspectives on psychotherapy with borderline patients. *Psychotherapy* 23:57–69.

Lerner, H., Sugarman, A., and Barbour, C. G. (1985). Patterns of ego boundary disturbance in neurotic, borderline, and schizophrenic patients. *Psychoanalytic Psychology* 2:47–66.

Lerner, H. D., and St. Peter, S. (1984). Patterns of object relations in neurotic, borderline and schizoid patients. *Psychiatry* 47:77–92.

Levin, S. (1967). Some metapsychological considerations on the differentiation between shame and guilt. *International Journal of Psycho-Analysis* 48:267–276.

—— (1970). On the psychoanalysis of attitudes of entitlement. *Bulletin of the Philadelphia Association for Psychoanalysis* 20:1–10.

—— (1973). Confrontation as a demand for change. In *Confrontation in Psychotherapy,* ed. G. Adler and P. G. Myerson, pp. 303–317. New York: Science House.

Levine, H. B. (1979). The sustaining object relationship. *Annual of Psychoanalysis* 7:203–231.

—— The treatment of borderline personalities. Unpublished manuscript.

Liebowitz, M. R., and Klein, D. F. (1981). Interrelationship of hysterical dysphoria and borderline personality disorder. *Psychiatric Clinics of North America* 4:67–87.

Lionells, M. (1986). A reevaluation of hysterical relatedness. *Contemporary Psychoanalysis* 22:570–597.

Little, M. (1957). "R"—the analyst's total response to his patient's needs. *International Journal of Psycho-Analysis* 38:240–254.

—— (1958). On delusional transference (transference psychosis). *International Journal of Psycho-Analysis* 39:134–138.

—— (1960). On basic unity. *International Journal of Psycho-Analysis* 41:377–384.

—— (1966). Transference and borderline states. *International Journal of Psycho-Analysis* 47:476–485.

Loewald, H. W. (1986). Transference-countertransference. *Journal of the American Psychoanalytic Association* 34:275–287.

Luborsky, L. L. (1984). *Principles of Psychoanalytic Psychotherapy.* New York: Basic Books.

Mack, J. E., ed. (1975). *Borderline States in Psychiatry.* New York: Grune & Stratton.

Mahler, M. S. (1972). The rapprochement subphase of the separation/individuation process. *Psychoanalytic Quarterly* 41:487–506.

Mahler, M. S., and Kaplan, L. (1977). Developmental aspects in the assessment of narcissistic and so-called borderline personalities. In *Borderline Personality Disorders: The Concept, the Syndrome, the Patient,* ed. P. Hartocollis, pp. 71–85. New York: International Universities Press.

Malan, D. H. (1975). *A Study of Brief Psychotherapy.* New York: Plenum.

—— (1976). *The Frontier of Brief Psychotherapy.* New York: Plenum.

Malin, A., and Grotstein, J. S. (1966). Projective identification in the therapeutic process. *International Journal of Psycho-Analysis* 47:26–31.

Maltsberger, J. T. (1982–1983). Countertransference in borderline conditions: some further notes. *International Journal of Psychoanalytic Psychotherapy* 9:125–134.

Maltsberger, J. T., and Buie, D. H. (1974). Countertransference hate in the treatment of suicidal patients. *Archives of General Psychiatry* 30:625–633.

Mandelbaum, A. (1977a). A family-centered approach to residential treatment. *Bulletin of the Menninger Clinic* 41:27–39.

—— (1977b). The family treatment of the borderline patient. In *Borderline Personality Disorders: The Concept, the Syndrome, the Patient,* ed. P. Hartocollis, pp. 423–438. New York: International Universities Press.

Mann, J. (1973). *Time-Limited Psychotherapy.* Cambridge: Harvard University Press.

Mann, J., and Goldman, R. (1982). *A Casebook in Time-Limited Psychotherapy.* New York: McGraw-Hill.

Marcus, E. (1981). Use of the acute hospital unit in the early phase of long-term treatment of borderline psychotic patients. *Psychiatric Clinics of North America* 4:133–144.

Martin, J. (1984). Infant development: fictive personality and creative capacity. In *Frontiers of Infant Psychiatry,* vol. 2, ed. J. D. Call, E. Galenson, and R. L. Tyson, pp. 111–120. New York: Basic Books.

Masterson, J. F. (1972). *Treatment of the Borderline Adolescent: A Developmental Approach.* New York: John Wiley.

—— (1976). *Psychotherapy of the Borderline Adult.* New York: Brunner/Mazel.

—— ed. (1978). *New Perspectives on Psychotherapy of the Borderline Adult.* New York: Brunner/Mazel.

—— (1987). Borderline and narcissistic disorders: an integrated developmental object-relations approach. In *The Borderline Patient: Emerging Concepts in Diagnosis, Psychodynamics, and Treatment,* vol. 2, ed. J. S. Grotstein, M. F. Solomon, and J. A. Lang, pp. 205-217. Hillsdale, NJ: Analytic Press.

Masterson, J. F., and Rinsley, D. B. (1975). The borderline syndrome: the role of the mother in the genesis and psychic structure of the borderline personality. *International Journal of Psycho-Analysis* 56:163-177.

May, P. R. A. (1974). A brave new world revisited: alphas betas, and treatment outcome. *Comprehensive Psychiatry* 15(1):1-17.

Mays, D., and Franks, C., eds. (1982). *Above All Do Not Harm: Negative Outcome in Psychotherapy.* New York: Jason Aronson.

McDevitt, J. B. (1975). Separation-individuation and object constancy. *Journal of the American Psychoanalytic Association* 23:713-742.

McDevitt, J. B., and Mahler, M. S. (1986). Object constancy, individuality, and internalization. In *Self and Object Constancy: Clinical and Theoretical Perspectives,* ed. R. F. Lax, S. Bach, and J. A. Burland, pp. 11-28. New York: The Guilford Press.

McDougall, J. (1978). Primitive communication and the use of countertransference. *Contemporary Psychoanalysis* 14:173-209.

McGlashan, T. H. (1983a). Omnipotence, helplessness, and control with the borderline patient. *American Journal of Psychiatry* 37:49-61.

—— (1983b). The "we-self" in borderline patients: manifestations of the symbiotic self-object in psychotherapy. *Psychiatry* 46:351-361.

—— (1985). The prediction of outcome in borderline personality disorder: Part V of the Chestnut Lodge follow-up study. In *The Borderline: Current Empirical Research,* ed. T. H. McGlashan, pp. 61-98. Washington, DC: American Psychiatric Press.

—— (1986a). The Chestnut Lodge follow-up study, III. Long-term outcome of borderline personalities. *Archives of General Psychiatry* 43:20-30.

—— (1986b). Schizotypal personality disorder. Chestnut Lodge follow-up study, VI. Long-term follow-up perspectives. *Archives of General Psychiatry* 43:329-334.

McWilliams, N. (1979). Treatment of the young borderline patient: fostering individuation against the odds. *Psychoanalytic Review* 66:339-357.

Meissner, S.J., W. W. (1971). Notes on identification. II. Clarification of related concepts. *Psychoanalytic Quarterly* 40:277-302.

—— (1974). Correlative aspects of introjective and projective mechanisms. *American Journal of Psychiatry* 131:176-180.

—— (1976). Psychotherapeutic schema based on the paranoid process. *International Journal of Psychoanalytic Psychotherapy* 5:87–114.

—— (1977a). The individual: suicide. In Part VII, Problems of dying: the taking of life. In *Human Life: Problems of Birth, of Living, and of Dying*, ed. W. C. Bier, pp. 229–251. New York: Fordham University Press.

—— (1977b). Psychoanalytic notes on suicide. *International Journal of Psychoanalytic Psychotherapy* 6:415–447.

—— (1977c). The Wolf Man and the paranoid process. *Annual of Psychoanalysis* 5:23–74.

—— (1978a). The conceptualization of marriage and family dynamics from a psychoanalytic perspective. In *Marriage and Marital Therapy: Psychoanalytic Behavioral and Systems Theory Perspectives*, ed. T. J. Paolino and B. S. McCrady, pp. 25–88. New York: Brunner/Mazel.

—— (1978b). Notes on some conceptual aspects of the borderline personality. *International Review of Psycho-Analysis* 5:297–311.

—— (1978c). *The Paranoid Process.* New York: Jason Aronson.

—— (1979a). Internalization and object relations. *Journal of the American Psychoanalytic Association* 27:345–360.

—— (1979b). Narcissistic personalities and borderline conditions: a differential diagnosis. *Annual of Psychoanalysis* 7:171–202.

—— (1979c). Threats to confidentiality. *Psychiatric Annals* 9:54–71.

—— (1980a). A note on projective identification. *Journal of the American Psychoanalytic Association* 28:43–67.

—— (1980b). Theories of personality and psychopathology: classical psychoanalysis. In *Comprehensive Textbook Psychiatry/III*, ed. H. I. Kaplan, A. M. Freedman, and B. J. Sadock, pp. 631–728. Baltimore/London: Williams & Wilkins.

—— (1981a). Family relations in the psychoanalytic process. *Contemporary Psychoanalysis* 17(2):209–231.

—— (1981b). *Internalization in Psychoanalysis.* (Psychological Issues, Monograph 50.) New York: International Universities Press.

—— (1981c). A note on narcissism. *Psychoanalytic Quarterly* 50:77–89.

—— (1982). Notes toward a psychoanalytic theory of marital and family dynamics. *International Journal of Family Psychiatry* 3(2):189–207.

—— (1982–1983). Notes on countertransference in borderline conditions. *International Journal of Psychoanalytic Psychotherapy* 9:89–124.

—— (1983). Phenomenology of the self. In *The Future of Psychoanalysis*, ed. A. Goldberg, pp. 65–96. New York: International Universities Press.

—— (1984a). *The Borderline Spectrum: Differential Diagnosis and Developmental Issues.* New York: Jason Aronson.

—— (1984b). Clinical differentiation of borderline syndromes from the psychoses. *Psychoanalytic Review* 71:185–210.

—— (1984–1985). Studies on hysteria: Dora. *International Journal of Psychoanalytic Psychotherapy* 10:567–598.

—— (1986a). The earliest internalizations. In *Self and Object Constancy: Clinical and Theoretical Perspectives*, ed. R. F. Lax, S. Bach, and J. A. Burland, pp. 29–72. New York: The Guilford Press.

—— (1986b). *Psychotherapy and the Paranoid Process*. Northvale, NJ: Jason Aronson.

—— (1987a). A contribution to the issues of borderline diagnosis. In *The Borderline Patient: Emerging Concepts in Diagnosis, Psychodynamics, and Treatment*, vol. 2, ed. J. S. Grotstein, M. F. Solomon, and J. A. Lang, pp. 73–81. Hillsdale, NJ: Analytic Press.

—— (1987b). Projection and projective identification. In *Projection, Identification, Projective Identification*, ed. J. Sandler, pp. 27–49. Madison, CN: International Universities Press.

—— (1988). The borderline spectrum and psychoanalytic perspectives. *Psychoanalytic Inquiry* 8:305–332.

Meloy, J. R. (1988). *The Psychopathic Process*. Northvale, NJ: Jason Aronson.

Meyer, J. K. (1982). The theory of gender identity disorders. *Journal of the American Psychoanalytic Association* 30:381–418.

Miller, A. (1979). Depression and grandiosity as related forms of narcissistic disturbances. *International Review of Psycho-Analysis* 6:61–76.

Milman, D. H. (1979). Minimal brain dysfunction in childhood: outcome in late adolescence and early years. *Journal of Clinical Psychiatry* 40:371–380.

Mitchell, S. A. (1986). The wings of Icarus: illusion and the problem of narcissism. *Contemporary Psychoanalysis* 22:107–132.

Modell, A. H. (1963). Primitive object relationships and the predisposition to schizophrenia. *International Journal of Psycho-Analysis* 44:282–292.

—— (1968). *Object Love and Reality*. New York: International Universities Press.

—— (1971). The origins of certain forms of preoedipal guilt and the implications for a psychoanalytic theory of affects. *International Journal of Psycho-Analysis* 52:337–346.

—— (1975). A narcissistic defense against affects and the illusion of self-sufficiency. *International Journal of Psycho-Analysis* 56:275–282.

—— (1978). The conceptualization of the therapeutic action of psychoanalysis: the action of the holding environment. *Bulletin of the Menninger Clinic* 42:493–504.

—— (1984). *Psychoanalysis in a New Context*. New York: International Universities Press.

—— (1986). The missing elements in Kohut's cure. *Psychoanalytic Inquiry* 6:367–385.

Money-Kyrle, R. E. (1956). Normal countertransference and some of its deviations. *International Journal of Psycho-Analysis* 37:360–366.

Monroe, R. R. (1982). The psychotherapy of the impulsive and acting out patient. *Journal of the American Academy of Psychoanalysis* 10:1–26.

Morgenstern, A. (1975). Experiences within a borderline syndrome. *International Journal of Psychoanalytic Psychotherapy* 4:476–494.

Morris, H., Gunderson, J. G., and Zanarini, M. C. (1986). Transitional object use and borderline psychopathology. *American Journal of Psychiatry* 143:1534–1538.

Morrison, A. P. (1984). Working with shame in psychoanalytic treatment. *Journal of the American Psychoanalytic Association* 32:479–505.

Munschauer, C. A. (1987). The patient chase: a bridge between the theories of Kernberg and Kohut. *Psychoanalytic Inquiry* 7:99–120.

Murray, J. M. (1973). The purpose of confrontation. In *Confrontation in Psychotherapy*, ed. G. Adler and P. G. Myerson, pp. 49–65. New York: Science House.

Myerson, P. G. (1969). The hysteric's experience in psychoanalysis. *International Journal of Psycho-Analysis* 50:373–384.

——— (1974). Two types of demanding regression: discussion of paper by Dr. Adler. *International Journal of Psychoanalytic Psychotherapy* 3:265–272.

Nadelson, T. (1976). Victim, victimizer: interaction in the psychotherapy of borderline patients. *International Journal of Psychoanalytic Psychotherapy* 5:115–129.

Olinick, S. L. (1954). Some considerations of the use of questioning as a psychoanalytic technique. *Journal of the American Psychoanalytic Association* 2:57–66.

Omer, H. (1985). Fulfillment of therapeutic tasks as a precondition for acceptance in therapy. *American Journal of Psychotherapy* 39:175–186.

Oremland, J. D., and Windholz, E. (1971). Some specific transference, countertransference and supervisory problems in the analysis of a narcissistic personality. *International Journal of Psycho-Analysis* 52:267–275.

Ostow, M. (1987). Comments on the pathogenesis of the borderline disorder. In *The Borderline Patient: Emerging Concepts in Diagnosis, Psychodynamics, and Treatment*, vol. 2, ed. J. S. Grotstein, M. F. Solomon, and J. A. Lang, pp. 289–315. Hillsdale, NJ: Analytic Press.

Pack, A. (1987). The role of psychopharmacology in the treatment of borderline patients. In *The Borderline Patient: Emerging Concepts in Diagnosis, Psychodynamics, and Treatment*, vol. 2, ed. J. S. Grotstein, M. F. Solomon, and J. A. Lang, pp. 177–186. Hillsdale, NJ: Analytic Press.

Perlmutter, R. A. (1982). The borderline patient in the emergency department: an approach to evaluation and management. *Psychiatric Quarterly* 54:190–197.

Perry, J. C., and Cooper, S. H. (1986). A preliminary report on defenses and conflicts associated with borderline personality disorder. *Journal of the American Psychoanalytic Association* 34:863–893.

Peto, A. (1963). The fragmentizing function of the ego in the analytic situation. *International Journal of Psycho-Analysis* 44:334–338.

——— (1967). Dedifferentiations and fragmentations during analysis. *Journal of the American Psychoanalytic Situation* 15:534–550.

Piers, G., and Singer, M. B. (1953). *Shame and Guilt: A Psychoanalytic and a Cultural Study.* Springfield, IL: Charles C Thomas.

Pildis, M. J., Soverow, G. J., Salzman, C., and Wolf, J. G. (1978). Day hospital treatment of borderline patients: a clinical perspective. *American Journal of Psychiatry* 135:594–596.

Pine, F. (1974). On the concept of "borderline" in children: a clinical essay. *Psychoanalytic Study of the Child* 29:341–368.

Pitts, W. M., Gustin, Q. L., Mitchell, C., and Snyder, S. (1985). MMPI critical item characteristic of the DSM-III borderline personality disorder. *Journal of Nervous and Mental Disease* 173:628–631.

Plakun, E. M., Burkhardt, P. E., and Muller, J. P. (1985). Fourteen-year follow-up of borderline and schizotypal personality disorder. *Comprehensive Psychiatry* 26:448–455.

Plakun, E. M., Muller, J. P., and Burkhardt, P. E. (1987). The significance of borderline and schizotypal overlap. *Hillside Journal of Clinical Psychiatry* 9(1):47–54.

Pope, H. G., Jonas, J. M., Hudson, J. I., et al. (1983). The validity of DSM-III borderline personality disorder. *Archives of General Psychiatry* 40:23–30.

Racker, H. (1953). A contribution to the problem of countertransference. *International Journal of Psycho-Analysis* 43:313–324.

——— (1957). The meaning and uses of countertransference. *Psychoanalytic Quarterly* 26:303–357.

——— (1958). Psychoanalytic technique and the analyst's unconscious masochism. *Psychoanalytic Quarterly* 27:555–562.

——— (1968). *Transference and Countertransference.* London: Hogarth.

Rangell, L. (1955). The borderline case (panel report). *Journal of the American Psychoanalytic Association* 3:285–298.

Rapaport, D., Gill, M. M., and Schafer, R. (1945-1946). *Diagnostic Psychological Testing.* 2 vols. Chicago: Year Book.

Razin, A. M. (1971). A–B variable in psychotherapy: a critical review. *Psychological Bulletin* 75(1):1–21.

Reich, A. (1953). Narcissistic object choice in women. *Journal of the American Psychoanalytic Association* 1:22–44.

——— (1960). Pathologic forms of self-esteem regulation. In *Annie Reich: Psychoanalytic Contributions*, pp. 288–311. New York: International Universities Press.

Reider, N. (1957). Transference psychosis. *Journal of the Hillside Hospital* 6:131–149.

Rifkin, A., Leviton, S., and Galewski, J. (1972a). Emotionally unstable character disorder: a follow-up study. I. Description of patients and outcome. *Journal of Biological Psychiatry* 4:65–79.

Rifkin, A., Quitkin, F., Carillo, C., Blumberg, A. G., and Klein, D. F. (1972b).

Lithium carbonate in emotionally unstable character disorder. *Archives of General Psychiatry* 27:519–523.

Rinsley, D. B. (1977). An object relations view of borderline personality. In *Borderline Personality Disorders: The Concept, the Syndrome, the Patient*, ed. P. Hartocollis, pp. 47–70. New York: International Universities Press.

—— (1980). Diagnosis and treatment of borderline and narcissistic children and adolescents. *Bulletin of the Menninger Clinic* 44:147–170.

—— (1985). Notes on the pathogenesis and nosology of borderline and narcissistic personality disorders. *Journal of the American Academy of Psychoanalysis* 13:317–328.

—— (1987). A reconsideration of Fairbairn's "original object" and "original ego" in relation to borderline and other self disorders. In *The Borderline Patient: Emerging Concepts in Diagnosis, Psychodynamics, and Treatment*, vol. 2, ed. J. S. Grotstein, M. F. Solomon, and J. A. Lang, pp. 219–231. Hillsdale, NJ: Analytic Press.

Robbins, M. D. (1976). Borderline personality organization: the need for a new theory. *Journal of the American Psychoanalytic Association* 24:831–853.

—— (1981a). The symbiosis concept and the commencement of normal and pathological ego functioning and object relations: II. Developments subsequent to infancy and pathological processes. *International Review of Psycho-Analysis* 8:379–391.

—— (1981b). The symbiosis concept and the commencement of normal and pathological ego functioning and object relations: I. Infancy. *International Review of Psycho-Analysis* 8:365–377.

Rochlin, G. (1961). The dread of abandonment: a contribution to the etiology of the loss complex and to depression. *Psychoanalytic Study of the Child* 16:451–470.

—— (1973). *Man's Aggression: The Defense of the Self*. Boston: Gambit Press.

Romm, M. E. (1957). Transient psychotic episodes during psychoanalysis. *Journal of the American Psychoanalytic Association* 5:325–341.

—— (1959). Influences determining types of regression. *Psychoanalytic Quarterly* 28:170–182.

Rosenfeld, H. (1978). Notes on the psychopathology and psychoanalytic treatment of some borderline patients. *International Journal of Psycho-Analysis* 59:215–221.

—— (1979). Difficulties in the psychoanalytic treatment of borderline patients. In *Advances in Psychotherapy of the Borderline Patient*, ed. J. LeBoit and A. Capponi, pp. 187–206. New York: Jason Aronson.

Rosenfeld, S. K., and Sprince, M. P. (1963). An attempt to formulate the meaning of the concept "borderline." *Psychoanalytic Study of the Child* 18:603–635.

——— (1965). Some thoughts on the technical handling of borderline children. *Psychoanalytic Study of the Child* 20:495–517.

Ross, N. (1967). The "as-if" personality. *Journal of the American Psychoanalytic Association* 15:59–82.

Roth, B. E. (1982). Six types of borderline and narcissistic patients: an initial typology. *International Journal of Group Psychotherapy* 32:9–27.

Rothstein, A. (1982). The implications of early psychopathology for the analyzability of narcissistic personality disorders. *International Journal of Psycho-Analysis* 63:177–188.

——— (1984). Fear of humiliation. *Journal of the American Psychoanalytic Association* 32:99–116.

Rule, J. (1973). The actor's identity crises (postanalytic reflections of an actress). *International Journal of Psychoanalytic Psychotherapy* 2:51–76.

Sadavoy, J., Silver, D., and Book, H. E. (1979). Negative responses of the borderline to inpatient treatment. *American Journal of Psychotherapy* 33(3):404–417.

——— (1981). The resident and the borderline inpatient: a supervisor's perspective. *Canadian Journal of Psychiatry* 26:155–158.

Sarwer-Foner, G. J. (1977). An approach to the global treatment of the borderline patient: psychoanalytic, psychiatric, and psychopharmacological considerations. In *Borderline Personality Disorders: The Concept, the Syndrome, the Patient*, ed. P. Hartocollis, pp. 345–364. New York: International Universities Press.

Saul, L. J., and Warner, S. L. (1977). The psychotic character. *International Journal of Psychoanalytic Psychotherapy* 6:243–252.

Schafer, R. (1983). *The Analytic Attitude*. New York: Basic Books.

Schaffer, N. D. (1986). The borderline patient and affirmative interpretation. *Bulletin of the Menninger Clinic* 50:148–162.

Scheidlinger, S. (1984). Psychoanalytic group psychotherapy today—an overview. *Journal of the American Academy of Psychoanalysis* 12:269–284.

Scheidlinger, S., and Holden, M. A. (1966). Group therapy of women with severe character disorders: the middle and final phases. *International Journal of Group Psychotherapy* 16:174–189.

Scheidlinger, S., and Pyrke, M. (1961). Group therapy of women with severe dependency problems. *American Journal of Orthopsychiatry* 31:776–785.

Schulz, C. G. (1980). All-or-none phenomena in the therapy of severe disorders. In *The Psychotherapy of Schizophrenia*, ed. J. S. Strauss et al., pp. 181–190. New York: Plenum.

——— (1984). The struggle toward ambivalence. *Psychiatry* 47:28–36.

Schwartz, H. J. (1987). Illness in the doctor: implications for the psychoanalytic process. *Journal of the American Psychoanalytic Association* 35:657–692.

Searles, H. F. (1960). *The Nonhuman Environment in Normal Development and in Schizophrenia*. New York: International Universities Press.

———— (1965). *Collected Papers on Schizophrenia and Related Subjects.* New York: International Universities Press.

———— (1973a). Concerning therapeutic symbiosis: the patient as symbiotic therapist, the phase of ambivalent symbiosis, and the role of jealousy in the fragmented ego. *Annual of Psychoanalysis* 1:247–262.

———— (1973b). Some aspects of unconscious fantasy. *International Journal of Psychoanalytic Psychotherapy* 2(1):37–50.

———— (1976). Transitional phenomena and therapeutic symbiosis. *International Journal of Psychoanalytic Psychotherapy* 5:145–204.

———— (1977). Dual- and multiple-identity processes in borderline ego functioning. In *Borderline Personality Disorders: The Concept, the Syndrome, the Patient*, ed. P. Hartocollis, pp. 441–455. New York: International Universities Press.

———— (1978). Psychoanalytic therapy with the borderline adult: some principles concerning technique. In *New Perspectives on Psychotherapy of the Borderline Adult*, ed. J. F. Masterson, pp. 43–65. New York: Brunner/Mazel.

———— (1978–1979). Concerning transference and countertransference. *International Journal of Psychoanalytic Psychotherapy* 7:165–188.

———— (1984). Transference responses in borderline patients. *Psychiatry* 47:37–49.

———— (1985). Separation and loss in psychoanalytic therapy with borderline patients: further remarks. *American Journal of Psychoanalysis* 45:9–27.

Segal, H. (1957). Notes on symbol formation. *International Journal of Psycho-Analysis* 38:391–397.

———— (1977). Countertransference. *International Journal of Psychoanalytic Psychotherapy* 6:31–37.

Selzer, M. A., Koenigsberg, H. W., and Kernberg, O. F. (1987). The initial contact in the treatment of borderline patients. *American Journal of Psychiatry* 144:927–930.

Serban, G., and Siegel, S. (1984). Response of borderline and schizotypal patients to small doses of thiothixene and haloperidol. *American Journal of Psychiatry* 141:1455–1458.

Shapiro, E. R. (1978). Research on family dynamics: clinical implications for the family of the borderline adolescent. *Adolescent Psychiatry* 6:360–376.

———— (1982). The holding environment and family therapy with acting-out adolescents. *International Journal of Psychoanalytic Psychotherapy* 9:209–226.

Shapiro, E. R., Shapiro, R. L., Zinner, J., and Berkowitz, D. (1977). The borderline ego and the working alliance: indications for individual and family treatment in adolescence. *International Journal of Psycho-Analysis* 58:77–87.

Shapiro, E. R., Zinner, J., Shapiro, R. L., and Berkowitz, D. A. (1975). The influence of family experience on borderline personality development. *International Review of Psycho-Analysis* 2:399–411.

Shapiro, L. N. (1973). Confrontation with the "real" analyst. In *Confrontation in Psychotherapy*, ed. G. Adler and P. G. Myerson, pp. 207–223. New York: Science House.

Shapiro, R. L. (1979). Family dynamics and object-relations theory: an analytic group-interpretive approach to family therapy. *Adolescent Psychiatry* 7:118–135.

——— (1987). The family in the psychoanalysis of the young adult. *Psychoanalytic Inquiry* 7:59–75.

Shapiro, R. L., and Zinner, J. (1975). Family organization and adolescent development. In *Task and Organization*, ed. E. Miller. London: John Wiley.

Siegman, A. J. (1967). Denial and screening of object images. *Journal of the American Psychoanalytic Association* 15:261–280.

Sifneos, P. (1972). *Short-term Psychotherapy and Emotional Crisis*. Cambridge: Harvard University Press.

Simon, J. I. (1984). The borderline syndrome in adolescents. *Adolescence* 19:505–520.

Singer, M. (1987). Inpatient hospitalization for borderline patients: process and dynamics of change in long- and short-term treatment. In *The Borderline Patient: Emerging Concepts in Diagnosis, Psychodynamics, and Treatment*, vol. 2, ed. J. S. Grotstein, M. F. Solomon, and J. A. Lang, pp. 227–242. Hillsdale, NJ: Analytic Press.

Singer, M. T. (1977). The borderline diagnosis and psychological tests: review and research. In *Borderline Personality Disorders: The Concept, the Syndrome, the Patient*, ed. P. Hartocollis, pp. 193–212. New York: International Universities Press.

Skodol, A. E., Buckley, P., and Charles, E. (1983). Is there a characteristic pattern to the treatment history of clinic outpatients with borderline personality? *Journal of Nervous and Mental Disease* 171:405–410.

Slavinska–Holy, N. (1980). Treatment of the borderline in homogeneous groups and the use of the "body transference technique." In *Group and Family Therapy*, ed. L. Wolberg and M. Aronson, pp. 121–133. New York: Brunner/Mazel.

——— (1983). Combining individual and homogeneous group psychotherapies for borderline conditions. *International Journal of Group Psychotherapy* 33:297–312.

Slavson, S. R. (1964). *A Textbook in Analytic Group Psychotherapy*. New York: International Universities Press.

Slipp, S. (1973). The symbiotic survival pattern: a relational theory of schizophrenia. *Family Process* 12:377–398.

Smith, R. J., and Steindler, E. M. (1983). The impact of difficult patients on treaters: consequences and remedies. *Bulletin of the Menninger Clinic* 47:107–116.

Snyder, S., and Pitts, W. M. (1985). Characterizing anger in the DSM-III borderline personality disorder. *Acta Psychiatrica Scandinavica* 72:464–469.

———— (1986). Characterizing paranoia in the DSM-III borderline personality disorder. *Acta Psychiatrica Scandinavica* 73:500–505.

Socarides, C. W. (1968). *The Overt Homosexual*. New York: Jason Aronson.

———— (1980). Homosexuality and the rapprochement subphase. In *Rapprochement: The Critical Subphase of Separation-Individuation*, ed. R. F. Lax, S. Bach, and J. A. Burland, pp. 331–352. New York: Jason Aronson.

Soloff, P. H. (1987). Neuroleptic treatment in the borderline patient: advantages and techniques. *Journal of Clinical Psychiatry* 48 (Suppl.)8:26–30.

Soloff, P. H., George, A., Nathan, R. S., and Schulz, P. M. (1987). Characterizing depression in borderline patients. *Journal of Clinical Psychiatry* 48:155–157.

Soloff, P. H., George, A., Nathan, R. S., Schulz, P. M., and Perel, J. M. (1986a). Paradoxical effects of amitriptyline on borderline patients. *American Journal of Psychiatry* 143:1603–1605.

Soloff, P. H., George, A., Nathan, R. S., Schulz, P. M., Ulrich, R. F., and Perel, J. M. (1986b). Progress in pharmacotherapy of borderline disorders: a double-blind study of amitriptyline, haloperidol, and placebo. *Archives of General Psychiatry* 43:691–697.

Solomon, L., and Grunebaum, H. (1982). Stages in social development: friendship and peer relations. *Hillside Journal of Clinical Psychiatry* 4:95–126.

Spence, D. P. (1982). *Narrative Truth and Historical Truth*. New York: Norton.

Spiegel, L. A. (1966). Affects in relation to self and object: a model for the derivation of desire, longing, pain, anxiety, humiliation, and shame. *Psychoanalytic Study of the Child* 21:69–92.

Spotnitz, H. (1969). *Modern Psychoanalysis of the Schizophrenic Patient*. New York: Grune & Stratton.

Sterba, R. (1934). The fate of the ego in psychoanalytic therapy. *International Journal of Psycho-Analysis* 15:117–126.

Stocking, M. (1973). Confrontation in psychotherapy: considerations arising from the psychoanalytic treatment of a child. In *Confrontation in Psychotherapy*, ed. G. Adler and P. G. Myerson, pp. 319–345. New York: Science House.

Stolorow, R. D., Atwood, G. E., and Lachman, F. M. (1981). Transference and countertransference in the analysis of developmental arrests. *Bulletin of the Menninger Clinic* 45:20–28.

Stolorow, R. D., Brandschaft, B., and Atwood, G. E. (1983). Intersubjectivity in psychoanalytic treatment: with special reference to archaic states. *Bulletin of the Menninger Clinic* 47:117–128.

Stone, L. (1954). The widening scope of indications for psychoanalysis. *Journal of the American Psychoanalytic Association* 2:567–594.

Stone, M. H. (1979). Psychodiagnosis and psychoanalytic psychotherapy. *Journal of the American Academy of Psychoanalysis* 7:79–100.

—— (1980). *The Borderline Syndromes: Constitution, Personality, and Adaptation.* New York: McGraw-Hill.

—— (1983a). Conflict resolution in schizotypal versus affective borderlines. *Journal of the American Academy of Psychoanalysis* 11:377–389.

—— (1983b). Psychotherapy with schizotypal borderline patients. *Journal of the American Academy of Psychoanalysis* 11:87–111.

—— (1985). Schizotypal personality: psychotherapeutic aspects. *Schizophrenia Bulletin* 11:576–589.

—— (1986). Exploratory psychotherapy in schizophrenia-spectrum patients: a re-evaluation in the light of long-term follow-up of schizophrenic and borderline patients. *Bulletin of the Menninger Clinic* 50:287–306.

—— (1987a). Psychotherapy of borderline patients in light of long-term follow-up. *Bulletin of the Menninger Clinic* 51(3):231–247.

—— (1987b). Systems for defining a borderline case. In *The Borderline Patient: Emerging Concepts in Diagnosis, Psychodynamics, and Treatment,* vol. 1, ed. J. S. Grotstein, M. F. Solomon, and J. A. Lang, pp. 13–35. Hillsdale, NJ: Analytic Press.

Story, I. (1982). Anorexia nervosa and the psychiatric hospital. *International Journal of Psychoanalytic Psychotherapy* 9:267–302.

Strupp, H. (1960). *Psychotherapists in Action.* New York: Grune & Stratton.

Sugarman, A. (1979). The infant personality: orality in the hysteric revisited. *International Journal of Psycho-Analysis* 60:501–513.

Tashjian, L. D. (1979). Failure in treatment of a borderline patient. Case report 85. *Psychiatric Opinion* July/August:43–47.

Tonkin, M., and Fine, H. J. (1985). Narcissism and borderline states: Kernberg, Kohut, and psychotherapy. *Psychoanalytic Psychology* 2:221–239.

Tucker, L., Bauer, S. F., Wagner, S., Harlam, D., and Sher, I. (1987). Long-term hospital treatment of borderline patients: a descriptive outcome study. *American Journal of Psychiatry* 144:1443–1448.

Uchill, A. B. (1978). Deviation from confidentiality and the therapeutic holding environment. *International Journal of Psychoanalytic Psychotherapy* 7:208–219.

van Dam, H. (1987). Countertransference during an analyst's brief illness. *Journal of the American Psychoanalytic Association* 35:647–655.

Waldhorn, H. F. (1960). Assessment of analyzability: technical and theoretical observations. *Psychoanalytic Quarterly* 39:478–506.

Waldinger, R. J. (1987). Intensive psychodynamic therapy with borderline patients: an overview. *American Journal of Psychiatry* 144:267–274.

Waldinger, R. J., and Gunderson, J. G. (1984). Completed psychotherapies with borderline patients. *American Journal of Psychotherapy* 38:190–202.

—— (1987). *Effective Psychotherapy with Borderline Patients: Case Studies.* New York: Macmillan.

Wallerstein, R. S. (1967). Reconstruction and mastery in the transference psychosis. *Journal of the American Psychoanalytic Association* 15:551–583.

—— (1986). *42 Lives in Treatment: A Study of Psychoanalysis and Psychotherapy.* New York: Guilford.

Weingarten, L. L., and Korn, S. (1967). Pseudoneurotic schizophrenia: psychological test findings. *Archives of General Psychiatry* 17:448–453.

Weinshel, E. M. (1966). Severe regressive states during analysis (panel report). *Journal of the American Psychoanalytic Association* 14:538–568.

Weisman, A. D. (1972). Confrontation, countertransference and context. *International Journal of Psychoanalytic Psychotherapy* 1(4):7–25.

Wender, P. H., Reimherr, F. W., and Wood, D. R. (1981). Attention deficit disorder ("minimal brain dysfunction") in adults: a replication study of diagnosis and drug treatment. *Archives of General Psychiatry* 38:449–456.

Werman, D. (1984). *The Practice of Supportive Psychotherapy.* New York: Brunner/Mazel.

Whitehorn, J. C., and Betz, B. (1954). A study of psychotherapeutic relationships between physicians and schizophrenic patients. *American Journal of Psychiatry* 111:321–331.

—— (1957). A comparison of psychotherapeutic relationships between physicians and schizophrenic patients when insulin is combined with psychotherapy and when insulin is used alone. *American Journal of Psychiatry* 113: 901–910.

—— (1960). Further studies of the doctor as a crucial variable in the outcome of treatment of schizophrenic patients. *American Journal of Psychiatry* 117:215–223.

Widiger, T. A., Frances, A., Warner, L., and Bluhm, C. (1986). Diagnostic criteria for the borderline and schizotypal personality disorders. *Journal of Abnormal Psychology* 95:43–51.

Wile, D. B. (1972). Negative countertransference and therapist discouragement. *International Journal of Psychoanalytic Psychotherapy* 1(3):36–67.

Wilson, A. (1985). Boundary disturbance in borderline and psychotic states. *Journal of Personality Assessment* 49:346–355.

Wilson, M. R., and Soth, N. (1985). Approaching the crisis in adolescent long-term psychiatric hospitalization: current problems and treatment innovations. *Psychiatric Annals* 15(10):586–595.

Winnicott, D. W. (1955). Metapsychological and clinical aspects of regression within the psychoanalytic set-up. *International Journal of Psycho-Analysis* 36:16–26.

—— (1958). *Collected Papers.* New York: Basic Books.

—— (1960). Ego distortion in terms of true and false self. In *The Maturational Processes and the Facilitating Environment*, pp. 140–152. New York: International Universities Press.

—— (1965). *The Maturational Processes and the Facilitating Environment.* New York: International Universities Press.

—— (1969). The use of an object. *International Journal of Psycho-Analysis* 50:711–716.

————— (1971). *Playing and Reality.* New York: Basic Books.

Wishnie, H. A. (1975). Inpatient therapy with borderline patients. In *Borderline States in Psychiatry*, ed. J. E. Mack, pp. 41–62. New York: Grune & Stratton.

Wong, N. (1980a). Combined group and individual treatment of borderline and narcissistic patients: heterogeneous versus homogeneous groups. *International Journal of Group Psychotherapy* 30:389–404.

————— (1980b). Focal issues in group psychotherapy of borderline and narcissistic patients. In *Group and Family Therapy 1980*, ed. L. Wolberg and M. Aronson, pp. 134–147. New York: Brunner/Mazel.

Woollcott, P. (1985). Prognostic indicators in the psychotherapy of borderline patients. *American Journal of Psychotherapy* 39:17–29.

Wurmser, L. (1978). *The Hidden Dimension.* New York: Jason Aronson.

Yalom, I. D. (1985). *The Theory and Practice of Group Psychotherapy.* 3rd ed. New York: Basic Books.

Zetzel, E. R. (1970). *The Capacity for Emotional Growth.* New York: International Universities Press.

————— (1971). A developmental approach to the borderline patient. *American Journal of Psychiatry* 127:867–871.

Zinner, J. (1978). Combined individual and family therapy of borderline adolescents: rationale and management of the early phase. *Adolescent Psychiatry* 6:420–427.

Zinner, J., and Shapiro, E. R. (1975). Splitting in families of borderline adolescents. In *Borderline States in Psychiatry*, ed. J. E. Mack, pp. 103–122. New York: Grune & Stratton.

Zinner, J., and Shapiro, R. (1972). Projective identification as a mode of perception and behavior in families of adolescents. *International Journal of Psycho-Analysis* 53:523–530.

————— (1974). The family group as a single psychic entity: implications for acting out in adolescence. *International Review of Psycho-Analysis* 1:179–186.

INDEX

Aarkrog, T., 55
Abend, S. M., 4, 10, 13, 15, 19, 20, 22, 62, 71, 74, 79, 88, 99, 116, 127, 177, 178, 179, 180, 182, 183, 200, 219, 227, 255, 262, 306
Acting-out
  and countertransference, 244
  self-destructive, 321–322
Activity, versus regression, 347–348
Adelman, S. A., 410
Adler, D. A., 409, 411, 412, 413, 414
Adler, G., 14, 17, 18, 19, 22, 31, 34, 41, 72, 74, 81, 107–110, 125, 128, 137, 151–153, 154, 161, 186, 187, 189–190, 192, 224, 226, 228, 229, 230, 241, 254, 300, 303, 304, 305, 306, 308, 312, 316, 318, 325, 327–328, 329, 333, 334, 335, 340, 349, 354, 355, 391, 393, 394, 396, 398, 399, 400, 401
Adolescence, borderline syndromes in, 53–61
  developmental conclusions of, 60–61

diagnostic difficulties in, 54
  pathological features of, 54–60
Affects, 77–78
Aggressive aspects, of interactions, 224–228
Aggressive transferences, 183–185, 290–292
Alexander, F., 302
Alter-ego transference, 187–188
Ambivalent symbiosis, 181
Analyst, transference of, to patient, 210
Analyzability, of borderline syndromes, 70–83
Andrulonis, P. A., 414
Antisocial behavior
  confrontation and, 310–311
  in diagnosis, 57
Appel, G., 46, 71, 214, 236, 254, 265, 267
Applebaum, S. A., 151, 155
Approaches, 84–129
  dimensions of, 115
Arkema, P. H., 11
Arlow, J. A., 34

"As-if" personality
  case studies of, 557–570
  description of, 557
  diagnosis of, 48–50
Assessment, of borderline patients for
    psychoanalysis, 71–83
Atkin, S., 19
Atkins, N. B., 144, 240, 241, 266, 336,
    354, 355
Atwood, G., 88
Authority, of therapist, 168
Autonomy
  in borderline families, 371–372
  and therapeutic alliance, 169

Balint, M., 126, 240–241, 333, 334, 382,
    384, 385, 386, 387–388
Barley, W. D., 391
Basic fault, 334
Beatson, J. A., 18
Beresin, E., 116
Berg, M., 24, 26–27, 195, 213
Berger, P. A., 411, 412, 413
Berkowitz, D. A., 372
Berry, S. L., 366, 368
Betz, B., 131
Bion, W. R., 112, 119, 125, 153, 180
Blanck, G., 90–92, 123, 137, 138, 179,
    259, 266, 269
Blanck, R., 90–92, 123, 137, 138, 179,
    259, 266, 269
Blatt, S., 29
Blos, P., 371
Blum, H. P., 13, 17, 18, 19, 22, 36, 62,
    118, 183, 230–231, 340
Book, H. E., 120, 403
Borderline, use of term, 8–9
Boris, H. N., 254, 301, 308
Boschan, P. J., 577
Boyer, L. B., 95–97, 99, 101, 119,
    124, 137, 138, 148, 149, 181,
    216, 220, 221, 226, 228, 254,
    256, 258, 259, 265, 267,
    269–270, 308, 354
Brenner, C., 139
Brinkley, J., 411

Brody, E. B., 9, 178, 179
Bromberg, P. M., 45
Brown, L. J., 112, 396, 399, 402
Buie, D. H., 14, 18, 19, 22, 74,
    81, 107–110, 125, 128, 162,
    220, 224, 225, 226, 228, 243,
    300, 303, 304, 306, 308, 312,
    328, 331, 345, 372, 392–393,
    410
Burke, W. F., 216
Burnham, D. L., 13, 108

Campbell, K., 123
Caretaking, by therapist, 168–169
Carr, A. C., 24, 26
Carsky, M., 391, 403
Cassimatis, E. G., 47
Cattell, J. P., 32
Chediak, C., 209–210
Chessick, R. D., 36, 97–99, 101, 124,
    127–128, 137, 138, 141, 144, 145,
    148, 149, 150, 162, 169, 186, 226,
    231, 255, 266, 299, 303, 307, 325,
    410
Chestnut Lodge, 67
Chethik, M., 55
Chopra, H. D., 18
Chwast, J., 57, 58
Clifton, A. R., 170, 214, 268, 346, 347,
    348, 354
Clinical resources, limited, 378
Closed group, open versus, 362
Cole, J. O., 408, 411, 412, 413,
    414
Collum, J. M., 36
Colson, D. B., 27, 64, 138, 401,
    402, 406
Combinatory thinking, 26
Combined therapy
  individual and family as, 374–376
  individual and group as, 361–362
Communication, between hospital staff
    and therapist, 398–399
Compliance, with therapist, 168
Confabulated thinking, 26
Confidentiality, 150–151, 156–157

Confrontation(s), 299–315
  in borderline spectrum, 307–308
  guidelines for, 314–315
  heroic, 302
  versus interpretation, 301
  meaning of, 300–302
  role of, in therapy, 299–300
  therapeutic alliance and, 308–309
Containment-separateness, 217
Cooper, S. H., 10, 18, 20
Coppolillo, H. P., 11, 192
Corwin, H. A., 165, 273, 301, 302, 311,
  346
Countertransference, 209–249
  aspects of borderline, 220
  definition of, 209–212
  difficulties of, therapeutic response
    to, 232–233, 236–248
  model of, 212–220
  monitoring of, 239–241
  regression and, 354–355
  transference versus, in approach,
    127–129
  variation of, 220–231
Countertransference contamination,
  303–305
Countertransference enactments,
  232–233
Cowdry, R. W., 408, 411, 412, 413
Crabtree, L. H., 400, 405, 406
Crisis intervention, 377–378
Cullander, C. C. H., 74

Davanloo, H., 380
Day, M., 359, 361, 363
Defensive organization, 79
Denial, confrontation and,
  309–310
Deniker, P., 33
DeSaussure, J., 12, 15
Deutsch, H., 49, 558, 560
Devereux, G., 301
Diagnosis, 3–61
  differential, 31–53
  levels of differentiation in, 8–23
  problem of, 3–8

Diagnostic indicators, of regression,
  340
Diagnostic Interview for Borderlines, 5
Diatkine, R., 73
Dickes, R., 138, 140, 162, 345
Differentiation, 154–155
Displacement, 194
Disruptions, in therapeutic alliance,
  162–163
  management of, 170–172
Distrust, of therapist, 167
Dora case, 237
Dreams, 338–339
Drive organization, 78–79
Drugs, 407–415
  diagnoses and selection of,
    413–414
  dynamics of taking, 410
  limited application of, 414–415
  problems in prescribing, 408–409
  target symptoms and selection of,
    411–413
  use of, 407–408
DSM III, 6, 24, 25, 31, 32,
  35, 63–64, 408, 413, 419,
  420
Dysphoric personality
  case studies of, 452–479
  diagnosis of, 36–41

Easser, R., 42
Ego defects, 19–22
Ego flexibility, 75–76
Ego functions, autonomous, 76
Ego intactness, 74–75
Eigen, M., 47
Ekstein, R., 18, 19, 39
Ellison, J. M., 409, 411, 412, 413, 414
Emotional reactivity, of therapist, 237–
  239
Empathic connection, 218
Empathic identification, with patient,
  210
Envy, 283–285
Erikson, E. H., 51, 371
Erotic aspects, of interactions, 230–231

Evans, R. W., 24, 25
Expressive psychotherapy,
118–119
supportive versus, 115–118,
363–364
Extra sessions, 157–158

Fabulizing, 26
Fairbairn, W. R. D., 102–103, 269
False-self personality
case studies of, 529–556
diagnosis of, 47–48
Family emotional system, 372–374
Family interaction, 370–371
Family patterns, 368–376
Family therapy, 366–376
therapeutic alliance in, 368–370
Fast, I., 21, 51
Feighner, J. P., 412
Feinsilver, D. B., 88, 147, 153–154,
192, 214, 215, 221, 307, 400
Feinstein, S. C., 392
Fine, H. J., 187
Finell, J. S., 212, 225, 227, 229
Fintzy, R. T., 13, 18
Fisher, S. F., 16
Freud, S., 153, 186, 203, 204, 230,
280, 283, 284, 293, 385, 457
Friedman, H. J., 10, 17, 22, 116,
117, 120, 178, 225, 242, 316,
394, 400
Friedman, L., 165
Friedman, R. C., 10, 63
Frieswyk, S., 64
Frijling-Schreuder, E. C. M., 9, 13, 18,
19, 39, 40
Frosch, J., 16, 17, 19, 33, 34, 123, 193,
194, 333, 335, 339, 340, 346

Galatzer-Levy, R. M., 55
Gardner, C. S., 49
Gardner, D. L., 413
Gediman, H. K., 49–50
George, A., 35
Gill, M. M., 24, 120

Giovacchini, P. L., 13, 17, 18, 19, 34,
36, 46, 95–97, 99, 101, 112, 119,
123–124, 141, 144, 160, 162, 167,
181, 183, 186, 193, 195, 196, 197,
214, 215, 225, 226, 228, 229, 238,
240, 256, 269–270, 336, 339, 354
Gitelson, M., 256
Global Assessment Scale, 64
Glover, E., 71
Goldberg, A. I., 72, 78
Goldman, R., 380
Goldstein, E. G., 24
Goldstein, M. J., 59
Goldstein, W., 123
Good-enough mother, 124, 151
Gordon, C., 116
Green, A., 225
Greenacre, P., 179, 229
Greenberg, R., 11
Greenson, R. R., 73, 139, 211, 301, 302
Greenspan, S. I., 74, 199
Grinberg, L., 59, 212, 214, 215,
338–339
Grinberg, R., 59
Grinker, R. R., 7, 59, 118
Grotstein, J. S., 113, 199
Group therapy, 359–365
selection for, 359–361
structure of, 361–365
Grunebaum, H., 360
Gudeman, J. E., 349, 354
Guilt, shame and, 281–283
Gunderson, J. G., 4–5, 6, 7, 8, 11,
18, 19, 24, 36, 37, 39, 60, 67–68,
92–95, 116, 118, 127, 128, 131,
209, 211, 332, 368, 373, 391,
392, 393, 394, 395, 396, 398,
399, 400, 401, 405, 406, 408,
411, 413, 420
Guntrip, H., 45, 46, 102–103, 333, 505
Gutheil, T. G., 138, 139, 328, 406
Guttman, S. A., 71, 72

Hartocollis, P., 394, 396, 400,
402
Havens, L. L., 138, 139, 409

Hedberg, D. L., 412
Heimann, P., 119
Herschman, P. L., 402
Hoch, P. H., 32, 412
Holden, M. A., 363
Holding environment, 151–154
Homogeneous group, versus
    heterogeneous, 362–363
Hooberman, D., 414
Horner, A. J., 14, 111, 181
Horton, P. C., 11
Horwitz, L., 359, 360, 361, 363
Hospital
    admission to, 396–398
    discharge from, 404–405
Hospitalization, 390–406
    in borderline spectrum, 390–391
    case study of, 403–404
    difficulties in, 405–406
    as limit setting, 323–324, 400–401
    long-term, 395–396
    and prognosis, 63
    purposes of, 393–394
    reasons for, 391–393
    short-term, 394–395
    therapeutic/administrative splits in,
        399–400
    transference/countertransference
        problems in, 401–403
Humiliation, 285
Hunt, H. F., 24
Hymowitz, P., 413
Hysterical continuum
    case studies of, 419–504
    diagnosis of, 31–44

Idealization, 243–244
Idealizing interaction, 229
Identification, of interaction, 217
Identity stasis
    case study of, 571–583
    diagnosis of, 51–53
Imhof, J., 226, 393
Individual therapy
    combined with family, 374–376
    combined with group, 361–362

Integrated approach, 119–122
Intellectual understanding, and dyadic
    interaction, 210
Internal processing, of interaction,
    217–218
Internalization(s)
    as component of interaction,
        246–248
    pathological, 385
Interpretation(s), 253–298
    affirmative, 260–262
    within borderline spectrum,
        263–264
    confrontation versus, 301
    definition of, 253–254
    interaction versus, 233,
        236–237
    nature of, 254–255
    process of, 264–270
    schema of, 270–298
    strategy of, 255–263
    and therapeutic alliance, 258–259
    versus therapeutic relationship,
        122–123
Introjective basis, of
    countertransference, 212–214
Introjective configuration, delineating
    of, 275–292
Introjects
    derivation of, 292–295
    surrendering of, 295

Jacobs, T. J., 232–233
Jacobsberg, L. B., 32
Jacobson, E., 16, 283, 371
Jealousy, pathological, case of,
    382–388
Jenike, M. S., 65
Johansen, K. H., 11
Jones, J. E., 59
Jones, S. A., 367
Joseph B., 220

Kaplan, L., 87
Keiser, S., 12

Kernberg, O. F., 4, 6–7, 8, 9, 10, 13, 14, 15, 16, 17, 18, 19–20, 21, 22, 23, 24, 37–38, 39, 40, 52, 53, 54, 55, 58, 60, 62, 63, 66, 68–70, 71, 72, 73, 74, 75, 77, 79, 85–88, 90, 91, 92, 93, 98, 100, 103, 118–119, 120, 122–123, 124, 127–128, 138, 144, 145, 146, 162, 170, 172, 177, 178, 179, 181, 182, 183, 184, 186, 193, 194–196, 197, 199–200, 209, 211, 215, 219, 221, 224, 225, 227, 240–242, 244, 253, 254, 255, 256–258, 259, 260–262, 263–264, 268–269, 275, 276, 279, 287, 306, 310, 317, 321–322, 325, 327, 330, 335, 336, 341, 342, 343–344, 349, 350, 361, 362, 369, 370, 393, 396, 399, 400

Khan, M. M. R., 334, 335

Kinston, W., 287

Kirman, W. J., 210

Klein, D. F., 19, 43, 411, 412, 413, 414

Klein, M., 87, 112–115, 119, 125, 126, 127, 128, 198–199, 214, 285

Knapp, P. H., 71

Knight, R. P., 84, 116–117, 118, 340

Kohut, H. S., 14, 70, 71, 73, 88, 99, 107, 108, 109, 124, 151, 164, 165, 185–186, 187–188, 189–191, 197, 211, 219, 277, 280, 283, 286, 505

Kolb, J. E., 5, 411

Korn, S., 32, 33

Kramer, P., 22

Kris, A. O., 120

Kris Study Group, 73, 99–101, 102, 116, 127, 182, 200, 262–263, 306, 307

Krohn, A., 12, 40, 181, 183, 221, 240

Kwawer, J. S., 24, 28, 29

Lachar, D., 25

Lachman, F. M., 505

Laing, R. D., 539

Lane, R. D., 338

Langs, R. J., 112, 142, 147, 148, 149, 150, 165–166, 167, 170, 173, 174, 196, 212, 213, 214, 219, 221, 223, 225, 226, 238, 244

Lehmann, A. E., 412

Leibovich, M. A., 381

Lerner, H., 29, 391, 401

Lerner, H. D., 24, 28

Lesser, S., 42

Levin, S., 280, 312–313

Levine, H. B., 151

Libidinal transferences, 182–183

Liebowitz, M. R., 43, 414

Limit setting, 316–331
  forms of, 318–321
  in hospitalization, 323–324, 400–401
  nature of, 317–318
  need for, 316–317
  regression and, 349–350
  specific contexts of, 321–331
  in therapeutic alliance, 145
  beyond therapy, 329–331
  within therapy, 324–328

Lionells, M., 43

Little, M., 41, 113, 119, 125, 162, 193, 233, 240, 255, 333, 335, 339

Loewald, H. W., 212–213

Long-term outcome
  in outpatient treatment, 67–68
  prognosis for, 63–64

Luborsky, L. L., 120

Mahler, M. S., 14, 87, 90–91

Malan, D. H., 380

Malin, A., 199

Maltsberger, J. T., 162, 215, 220, 224, 225, 228, 243, 322, 328, 331, 341, 344, 345, 392–393, 410

Mandelbaum, A., 367, 371, 373

Mann, J., 380

Mannino, F. V., 199

Marcus, E., 391, 393, 400

Martin, J., 49

Masterson, J. F., 13, 39, 63, 88–90, 91, 94, 119, 123, 128, 137, 138, 196, 245, 325, 373
May, P. R. A., 131
McDevitt, J. B., 14
McDougall, J., 220
McGlashan, T. H., 63–64, 67, 181, 183, 186, 193, 200, 214, 215, 225
McLean Group, 368
McWilliams, N., 171, 225
Meissner, W. W., S. J., 7, 13, 14, 15, 16, 18, 20, 22, 24, 27, 31, 33, 37, 38, 40, 45, 46, 49, 50, 52, 55, 60, 69, 72, 73, 74, 79, 87, 94, 101, 108, 109, 114, 129, 137, 141, 148, 150, 157, 164, 169, 174, 178, 180, 184, 186, 188, 191, 195, 196–197, 198, 200, 203, 212, 214, 230, 237, 243, 244, 248, 249, 270, 272, 273, 278, 287, 292, 293, 297, 298, 312, 313, 340, 341, 344, 348, 355, 365, 366, 371, 372, 373, 374, 409, 410, 413, 414, 420, 457, 502, 569
Menninger Study, 71, 79, 93, 118, 138
Mental set, of therapist, 217
Merger through extension of grandiose self, 187–188
Meyer, J. K., 60
Miller, A., 278
Milman, D. H., 414
Mirror transference, 187–188
Mitchell, S. A., 88, 211
MMPI, 24
Modell, A. H., 9, 10, 47, 103–107, 109, 125, 139, 177, 192, 194, 221, 266, 284–285, 292, 334, 505
Money, limited resources of, 378–379
Money-Kyrle, R. E., 213
Monroe, R. R., 320, 321, 331
Morgenstern, A., 177, 180
Morris, H., 11
Morrison, A. P., 287, 313
Motivation, 80
Mourning, of transference object, 295–298
Munschauer, C. A., 336

Murray, J. M., 302
Myerson, P. G., 43, 186, 229, 244, 254, 305, 308, 337

Nadelson, T., 226, 227, 240
Narcissism
  confrontation and, 311–313
  in diagnosis, 16
Narcissistic alliance, 164–165
Narcissistic aspects, of interactions, 228–230
Narcissistic configurations, 277–280
Narcissistic transferences, 185–189, 288–290
National Institutes of Health, 369
Need–fear dilemma, 13
Negotiation, 156
Not-good-enough mother, 47

Object constancy, 12–13
Object needs, 13–14
Object relations, 9–11
Object countertransference, 210
Objects, experience of, 11–12
Olinick, S. L., 254, 269
Omer, H., 167
Open group, versus closed, 362
Oremland, J. D., 227
Outpatient treatment, 65–70

Pack, A., 408, 412
Paranoid dynamics, 384–385
Paranoid spikes, 184, 222–223
Pathology, levels of, 9–23
Patient, as person, general response to, 210
Patient-induced countertransference, 210
Perlmutter, R. A., 20, 394–395
Perry, J. C., 18, 20
Peto, A., 335, 337, 346
Piers, G., 282
Pildis, M. J., 395

Pine, F., 36, 46
Pitts, W. M., 6, 25, 78
Plakun, E. M., 35, 64
Polatin, P., 32, 412
Power, in therapeutic misalliance, 167–168
Pressure, of interaction, 217
Primitive affective personality disorder(s)
    case studies of, 435–451
    diagnosis of, 33–35
Primitive (oral) hysteric(s)
    case studies of, 480–504
    diagnosis of, 42–44
Prognosis, 62–83
Prognostic indicators, 68–70
Projection
    in diagnosis, 18–19
    and transference, 195–198
Projective basis, of countertransference, 212–214
Projective counteridentification, 215
Projective identification, 198–200
Projective system
    exploring of, 271–273
    testing of, 273–275
Pseudoschizophrenia
    case studies of, 420–434
    description of, 420–421
    diagnosis of, 32–33
Psychiatric emergency department (PED), 395
Psychosis, 339–340
Pyrke, M., 363

Quintart, J. C., 33

Racker, H., 212, 215–216, 227
Rangell, L., 8, 256, 268
Rapaport, D., 24
Razin, A. M., 131
Reality testing
    confrontation as, 302–303
    regression and, 348–349

Reception, by therapist, 216–217
Reciprocal countertransference, 215
Regression, 332–355
    borderline, 335–340
    confrontation and, 305–307
    countertransference issues in, 354–355
    diagnostic indicators of, 340
    forms of, 332–335
    limit setting and, 328–329
    recurrent, 350–354
    technical modifications of, 345–350
    therapeutic aspects of, 345–350
Regressive potential
    in borderline regression, 335–338
    in diagnosis, 17–18
Reich, A., 40, 278, 565
Reider, N., 335, 339, 340
Relational emphasis, 123–126
Relationship potential, 79–80
Representational conjunction or disjunction, 216
Resonant countertransference, 215
Responsibility, in therapeutic misalliance, 168
Rewarding object-relations part-unit (RORU), 89–90
Rifkin, A., 413–414
Rinsley, D. B., 31, 61, 88–90, 94, 196, 373
Roath, M., 366, 368
Robbins, M. D., 18, 87, 111, 181
Rochlin, G., 280
Romm, M. E., 335
Rorschach, 10, 11, 25, 26, 27, 28, 29, 33, 64, 385, 386
Rosenfeld, H., 113–114, 119, 125–126, 361
Rosenfeld, S. K., 18, 19, 38, 39, 40, 56
Ross, N., 49
Roth, B. E., 361
Rothstein, A., 16, 72, 73, 165, 285, 337
Rule, J., 557

Sadavoy, J., 396, 403
St. Peter, S., 24, 28

Sarwer-Foner, G. J., 407, 411, 412
Saul, L. J., 35
Schaefer, R., 24
Schafer, R., 260, 270
Schaffer, N. D., 123, 124, 260–262,
    266, 270
Scheidlinger, S., 359, 360, 361, 363
Schizoid continuum
  case studies of, 505–583
  diagnosis of, 44–53
Schizoid personality
  case studies of, 506–528
  diagnosis of, 45–46
Schreber case, 385, 386
Schulz, C. G., 148, 400
Schwartz, G. B., 338
Schwartz, H. J., 227
Searles, H. F., 110–112, 125, 128, 181,
    184, 186, 193, 195, 196, 212, 213,
    214, 221, 225, 333
Segal, H., 119, 199
Self, cohesive, 14–16
"Selfobject" transferences, 151–152,
    165, 181, 182, 189–192, 193, 197,
    202–203, 204, 219
Self-organization, 80–82
Selzer, M. A., 144, 145
Semrad, E., 359, 361, 363
Serban, G., 413
Shame, 280–281
  and guilt, 281–283
Shapiro, E. R., 366, 367, 368, 369, 370,
    372, 373
Shapiro, L. N., 303
Shapiro, R. L., 199, 366, 367, 369, 371,
    372
Short-term therapy, 377–389
  contexts for, 377–379
  implementation of, 381–388
  selection for, 380–381
  termination of, 389
Siegel, S., 413
Siegman, A. J., 180
Sifneos, P., 380
Signal affect, 217
Simon, J. I., 54, 57, 59, 63, 138, 391,
    395, 398

Singer, M., 394–396
Singer, M. B., 282
Singer, M. J., 4–5, 8, 18, 19, 24, 36, 37,
    39, 60, 411
Singer, M. T., 24–25, 26, 33
Skodol, A. E., 65
Slavinska-Holy, N., 361, 363, 365
Slavson, S. R., 360, 363
Slipp, S., 199
Smith, R. J., 215, 225
Snyder, S., 6, 78
Socarides, C. W., 60
Soloff, P. H., 6, 35, 411, 413
Solomon, L., 360
Soth, N., 398
Spence, D. P., 290
Spiegel, L. A., 280
Spotnitz, H., 210
Sprince, M. P., 18, 19, 38, 39, 40, 56
Steindler, E. M., 215, 225
Sterba, R., 139
Stern, T. A., 414
Stocking, M., 148, 254, 264, 301, 308
Stolorow, R. D., 81, 88, 215, 216, 243,
    505
Stone, L., 73, 133, 241
Stone, M. H., 3, 27, 32, 33, 62, 64, 65–
    66, 69, 70, 82, 420, 481
Story, I., 392
Stress, patient's inability to tolerate,
    379
Strupp, H., 210
Subjective countertransference, 210
Sugarman, A., 42, 43
Suicide
  limit setting and, 322–323
  regression and, 340–345
Superego defects, 22–23
Superego functioning, 76–77
Supportive therapy, versus expressive,
    115–118, 363–364
Sustaining object, 151

Tansey, M. J., 216
Tarasoff ruling, 325
Tashjian, L. D., 406

TAT, 26, 27, 28–29
Telephone calls, 159–160
Termination
  and countertransference, 245–246
  of short-term therapy, 389
Testing, psychological
  classic view of, 24–25
  and diagnosis, 24–30
  process of, 29–30
  and prognosis, 64
  of projective system, through
    interpretation, 273–275
  role of, 30
Tests
  projective, 26–29
  structured, 25
Therapeutic alliance, 137–175
  and borderline spectrum, 141–142
  components of, 140–141
  confrontation and, 308–309
  definition of, 138–139
  deviations in, 162–169
  difficulties of, 137–138
  early distortions in, 146–147
  establishment of, 144–161
  failure of, 346–347
  in family therapy, 368–370
  first contact in, 155
  interpretation and, 258–259
  limit setting in, 145
  maintenance of, 169–175
  nature of, 138–144
  need for, 144–145
  structuring in, 147–150, 241–242
  and transference, 201–203
Therapeutic framework, 160–161
Therapeutic misalliance(s), 142–144,
    163–169
  issues of, 167–169
  management of, 173–175
  relation of transference to, 203–204
Therapeutic relationship, 122–126
Therapeutic response
  to countertransference difficulties,
    232–233, 236–248
  to narcissistic introjects, 285–288
Therapeutic symbiosis, 181

Therapist-related countertransference,
    210
Therapist(s), 130–134
  same versus different, in group
    therapy, 364–365
Time, limited resources of, 378–379
Tonkin, M., 187
Transference, 176–208
  characteristics of, 176–182
  versus countertransference, in
    approach, 127–129
  interpretation of, 204–208
  management of, 200–208
  mechanisms of, 194–200
  negative, 242–243
  variants of, 182–194, 288–292
Transference/countertransference
    interactions
  in borderline spectrum, 218–220
  differential aspects of, 234–235
  versus interpretation, 233,
    236–237
  process of, 216–218
Transference/countertransference
    problems, in hospitalization,
    401–403
Transference object, mourning of,
    295–298
Transference psychosis, 193–194
Transitional object relations, 10–11
Transitional relatedness, 192–193
True self, 47–48
Tucker, L., 396
Twinship, 187–188

Uchill, A. B., 150
UCLA Family Project, 59
Uribe, V., 392

van Dam, H., 227
Verbal feeding, 256

Wagner, S., 49
WAIS, 25